Helen Clarke

The
INTERNATIONAL CRITICAL COMMENTARY
on the Holy Scriptures of the Old and New Testaments

GENERAL EDITORS

G. I. DAVIES, F.B.A.

Professor of Old Testament Studies in the University of Cambridge
Fellow of Fitzwilliam College

AND

G. N. STANTON, HON. D.D.

Lady Margaret's Professor of Divinity in the University of Cambridge
Fellow of Fitzwilliam College

CONSULTING EDITORS

J. A. EMERTON, F.B.A.

Emeritus Regius Professor of Hebrew in the University of Cambridge
Fellow of St John's College, Cambridge
Honorary Canon of St George's Cathedral, Jerusalem

AND

C. E. B. CRANFIELD, F.B.A.

Emeritus Professor of Theology in the University of Durham

FORMERLY UNDER THE EDITORSHIP OF

S. R. DRIVER
A. PLUMMER
C. A. BRIGGS

ISAIAH 1–27

A CRITICAL AND EXEGETICAL COMMENTARY

ON

ISAIAH 1–27

BY

H. G. M. WILLIAMSON, F.B.A.

Regius Professor of Hebrew in the University of Oxford
Student of Christ Church

IN THREE VOLUMES

VOLUME 1

Commentary on Isaiah 1–5

t&t clark

T&T Clark International
A Continuum Imprint

The Tower Building
11 York Road
London SE1 7NX

80 Maiden Lane,
New York, NY 10038
USA

© *H. G. M. Williamson, 2006*

First published 2006
Reprinted 2007

www.tandtclark.com

British Library Cataloguing-in-publication Data
A catalogue record for this book is available at the British Library

ISBN 10: 0 567 04451 3
ISBN 13: 978 0 567 04451 8

The NewJerusalem and GraecaII fonts used to print this work are available
from Linguist's Software, Inc., PO Box 580, Edmonds, WA 98020-0580 USA.
Tel (425) 775-1130. www.linguistsoftware.com

Typeset and copy-edited by Forthcoming Publications Ltd
www.forthcomingpublications.com

Printed and bound in Great Britain by Biddles Ltd, King's Lynn, Norfolk

For Keith and Marcus

a belated welcome

CONTENTS OF VOLUME I

GENERAL EDITORS' PREFACE

Much scholarly work has been done on the Bible since the publication of the first volumes of the International Critical Commentary in the 1890s. New linguistic, textual, historical and archaeological evidence has become available, and there have been changes and developments in methods of study. In the twenty-first century there will be as great a need as ever, and perhaps a greater need, for the kind of commentary that the International Critical Commentary seeks to supply. The series has long had a special place among works in English on the Bible, because it has sought to bring together all the relevant aids to exegesis, linguistic and textual no less than archaeological, historical, literary and theological, to help the reader to understand the meaning of the books of the Old and New Testaments. In the confidence that such a series meets a need, the publishers and the editors are commissioning new commentaries on all the books of the Bible. The work of preparing a commentary on such a scale cannot but be slow, and developments in the past half-century have made the commentator's task yet more difficult than before, but it is hoped that the remaining volumes will appear without too great intervals between them. No attempt has been made to secure a uniform theological or critical approach to the problems of the various books, and scholars have been selected for their scholarship and not for their adherence to any school of thought. It is hoped that the new volumes will attain the high standards set in the past, and that they will make a significant contribution to the understanding of the books of the Bible.

G. I. D.
G. N. S.

PREFACE

During the many years that this commentary has been in preparation I have received encouragement, help and support from many friends and colleagues. While I am grateful to them all, a few deserve particular mention.

The original invitation to write came from Professor John Emerton, and I appreciate the confidence that he thus placed in me; his support in this as in many other ways means a great deal to me. His successor as general Old Testament editor of the series, Professor Graham Davies, quickly but carefully read the whole; he made numerous corrections, and also advanced many valuable suggestions which I have nearly always accepted. For guidance on the use of the Peshitta I am indebted to Dr Gillian Greenberg and most especially to Dr Alison Salvesen. The publisher of the series changed during the course of writing; to the staff of the old T&T Clark, and particularly to their successors at T&T Clark International, I am grateful for patience and understanding.

It is now nearly a hundred years since G.B. Gray published his ICC volume on Isaiah 1–27. His work retains its importance, and it has constantly been at my side in the preparation of this volume. While no one can replace Gray, I nevertheless hope that the inclusion of new evidence of which he could not possibly have known (such as the Dead Sea Scrolls) as well as the use of methods of analysis which have been developed since he wrote will be found to justify the publication of this new commentary in the same series.

In recent years it has been a joy to welcome two sons-in-law into our family. They must often wonder what I do. Now they know.

H.G.M.W.
Christ Church, Oxford

BIBLIOGRAPHY

Commentaries on Isaiah (marked **) and other frequently cited monographs (marked *) are referred to in the body of the commentary by author's name alone. Other works listed in this bibliography are cited by short title.

Ackroyd, P. R., 'A Note on Isaiah 2_1', *ZAW* 75 (1963), 320–21.
—'Isaiah i–xii: Presentation of a Prophet', in *Congress Volume: Göttingen, 1977* (VTSup 29; Leiden, 1978), 16–48 (repr. *Studies in the Religious Tradition of the Old Testament* [London, 1987], 79–104).
Aitken, K. T., 'Hearing and Seeing: Metamorphoses of a Motif in Isaiah 1–39', in P. R. Davies and D. J. A. Clines (eds), *Among the Prophets: Language, Image and Structure in the Prophetic Writings* (JSOTSup 144; Sheffield, 1993), 12–41.
**Alexander, J. A., *Commentary on the Prophecies of Isaiah* (repr., Grand Rapids, 1978; original publication in 2 vols: 1846–47).
Allegro, J. M., *Qumrân Cave 4: I (4Q158–4Q186)* (DJD 5; Oxford, 1968).
Anderson, B. W., '"God with Us"—In Judgment and in Mercy: The Editorial Structure of Isaiah 5–10(11)', in G. M. Tucker, D. L. Petersen and R. R. Wilson (eds), *Canon, Theology, and Old Testament Interpretation: Essays in Honor of Brevard S. Childs* (Philadelphia, 1988), 230–45.
Anderson, R. T., 'Was Isaiah a Scribe?', *JBL* 79 (1960), 57–58.
**Auvray, P., *Isaïe 1–39* (SB; Paris, 1972).
Baer, D. A., 'It's All About Us! Nationalistic Exegesis in the Greek Isaiah (Chapters 1–12)', *SBLSP* 40 (2001), 197–219.
Bardtke, H., 'Die Latifundien in Juda während der zweiten Hälfte des achten Jahrhunderts v. Chr (Zum Verständnis von Jes 5, 8-10)', in A. Caquot and M. Philonenko (eds), *Hommages à André Dupont-Sommer* (Paris, 1971), 235–54.
**Barnes, W. E., *Isaiah* (The Churchman's Bible; 2 vols; London, 1901).
Barr, J., *Comparative Philology and the Text of the Old Testament* (Oxford, 1968).
Barré, M. L., 'A Rhetorical-Critical Study of Isaiah 2:12-17', *CBQ* 65 (2003), 522–34.
Barstad, H. M., *The Religious Polemics of Amos: Studies in the Preaching of Am 2,7B-8; 4,1-13; 5,1-27; 6,4-7; 8,14* (VTSup 34; Leiden, 1984).

Bartelmus, R., 'Beobachtungen zur literarischen Struktur des sog. Wein-berglieds (Jes 5,1-7)', *ZAW* 110 (1998), 50–66.

Bartelt, A. H., 'Isaiah 5 and 9: In- or Interdependence?', in A. B. Beck *et al.* (eds), *Fortunate the Eyes that See: Essays in Honor of David Noel Freedman in Celebration of his Seventieth Birthday* (Grand Rapids, 1995), 157–74.

—The Book Around Immanuel: Style and Structure in Isaiah 2–12 (BJS 4; Winona Lake, Ind., 1996).

*Barth, H., *Die Jesaja-Worte in der Josiazeit: Israel und Assur als Thema einer produktiven Neuinterpretation der Jesajaüberlieferung* (WMANT 48; Neukirchen–Vluyn, 1977).

Barth, J., *Beiträge zu Erklärung des Jes* (Karlsruhe and Leipzig, 1885).

Barthel, J., *Prophetenwort und Geschichte: Die Jesajaüberlieferung in Jes 6–8 und 28–31* (FAT 19; Tübingen, 1997).

*Barthélemy, D., *Critique textuelle de l'Ancien Testament. II. Isaïe, Jérémie, Lamentations* (OBO 50/2; Freiburg and Göttingen, 1986).

Barton, J., 'Natural Law and Poetic Justice in the Old Testament', *JTS* NS 30 (1979), 1–14.

—'Ethics in Isaiah of Jerusalem', *JTS* NS 32 (1981), 1–18.

—*Isaiah 1–39* (Old Testament Guides; Sheffield, 1995).

Becker, J., *Isaias—der Prophet und sein Buch* (SBS 30; Stuttgart, 1968).

*Becker, U., *Jesaja—von der Botschaft zum Buch* (FRLANT 178; Göttingen, 1997).

Beentjes, P. C., *The Book of Ben Sira in Hebrew* (VTSup 68; Leiden, 1997).

Ben Zvi, E., 'Isaiah 1,4-9, Isaiah and the Events of 701 BCE in Judah', *SJOT* 5 (1991), 95–111.

Bentzen, A., 'Zur Erläuterung von Jesaja 5, 1-7', *AfO* 4 (1927), 209–10.

**—*Jesaja I: Jes. 1–39* (Copenhagen, 1944).

Berger, P.-R., 'Ein unerklärtes Wort in dem Weinberglied Jesajas (Jes 5₆)', *ZAW* 82 (1970), 116–17.

*Berges, U., *Das Buch Jesaja: Komposition und Endgestalt* (HBS 16; Freiburg, 1998).

Berlin, A., *The Dynamics of Biblical Parallelism* (Bloomington, 1985).

Beuken, W. A. M., 'Isaiah Chapters lxv–lxvi: Trito-Isaiah and the Closure of the Book of Isaiah', in J. A. Emerton (ed.), *Congress Volume: Leuven, 1989* (VTSup 43; Leiden, 1991), 204–21.

**—*Jesaja 1–12* (HThKAT; Freiburg, 2003).

Biton, S., 'A New Outlook on Isaiah 5,17', *BethM* 168 (2001), 84–91 (Hebrew).

Bjørndalen, A. J., 'Zur Frage der Echtheit von Jesaja 1,2-3; 1,4-7 und 5,1-7', *NTT* 83 (1982), 89–100.

—*Untersuchungen zur allegorischen Rede der Propheten Amos und Jesaja* (BZAW 165; Berlin, 1986).

Blenkinsopp, J., 'Fragments of Ancient Exegesis in an Isaian Poem (Jes 2₆-₂₂)', *ZAW* 93 (1981), 51–62.

**—*Isaiah 1–39: A New Translation with Introduction and Commentary* (AB 19; New York, 2000).

*Blum, E., 'Jesajas prophetisches Testament: Beobachtungen zu Jes
    1–11', *ZAW* 108 (1996), 547–68, and 109 (1997), 12–29.
Boecker, H. J., *Redeformen des Rechtslebens im Alten Testament*
    (WMANT 14; Neukirchen–Vluyn, 1964).
Borowski, O., *Agriculture in Iron Age Israel* (Winona Lake, Ind., 1987).
*Bosshard-Nepustil, E., *Rezeptionen von Jesaia 1–39 im Zwölfpropheten-
    buch: Untersuchungen zur literarischen Verbindung von Propheten-
    büchern in babylonischer und persischer Zeit* (OBO 154; Freiburg
    and Göttingen, 1997).
Bovati, P., *Re-Establishing Justice: Legal Terms, Concepts and
    Procedures in the Hebrew Bible* (JSOTSup 105; Sheffield, 1994).
—'Le langage juridique du prophète Isaïe', in Vermeylen (ed.), *The Book
    of Isaiah*, 177–96.
**Box, G. H., *The Book of Isaiah* (London, 1908).
Branden, A. van den, 'I gioielli delle donne di Gerusalemme secundo
    Isaia 3,18-21', *BeO* 5 (1963), 87–94.
Brekelmans, C., 'Deuteronomistic Influence in Isaiah 1–12', in Vermeylen
    (ed.), *The Book of Isaiah*, 167–76.
Brenner, A., *Colour Terms in the Old Testament* (JSOTSup 21; Sheffield,
    1982).
Brettler, M., *God is King: Understanding an Israelite Metaphor* (JSOTSup
    76; Sheffield, 1989).
Brockington, L. H., 'The Greek Translator of Isaiah and his Interest in
    ΔΟΞΑ', *VT* 1 (1951), 23–32.
*—The Hebrew Text of the Old Testament: The Readings Adopted by the
    Translators of the New English Bible* (Oxford and Cambridge, 1973).
Brooke, G. J., '4Q500 1 and the Use of Scripture in the Parable of the
    Vineyard', *DSD* 2 (1995), 268–94.
—'The Qumran Pesharim and the Text of Isaiah in the Cave 4 Manu-
    scripts', in A. Rapoport-Albert and G. Greenberg (eds), *Biblical
    Hebrew, Biblical Texts: Essays in Memory of Michael P. Weitzman*
    (JSOTSup 333; London, 2001), 304–20.
Brown, W. P., 'The So-Called Refrain in Isaiah 5:25-30 and 9:7–10:4',
    CBQ 52 (1990), 432–43.
Broyles, C. C., and C. A. Evans (eds), *Writing and Reading the Scroll of
    Isaiah: Studies of an Interpretive Tradition* (VTSup 70/1-2; 2 vols;
    Leiden, 1997).
**Brueggemann, W., *Isaiah 1–39* (Westminster Bible Companion; Louis-
    ville, Ky., 1998).
**Budde, K., 'Zu Jesaja 1–5', *ZAW* 49 (1931), 16–40, 182–211; 50 (1932),
    38–72.
Buhl, F., 'Zu Jes 1₅', *ZAW* 36 (1916), 117.
Burney, C. F., 'The Interpretation of Isaiah i 18', *JTS* 11 (1909–10),
    433–38.
**Calvin, J., *Calvin's Commentaries. III. Isaiah* (Grand Rapids, n.d.).
Carr, D., 'Reaching for Unity in Isaiah', *JSOT* 57 (1993), 61–80.

—'Reading Isaiah from Beginning (Isaiah 1) to End (Isaiah 65–66): Multiple Modern Possibilities', in Melugin and Sweeney (eds), *New Visions*, 188–218.

Caspari, W., 'Hebräisch בין temporal. (Zur Jes. 5, 12)', *OLZ* 16 (1913), 337–41.

Cassuto, U., *Biblical and Oriental Studies*. II. *Bible and Ancient Oriental Texts* (Jerusalem, 1975).

Cazelles, H., 'Qui aurait visé, à l'origine, Isaïe ii 2-5?', *VT* 30 (1980), 409–20.

—'Quelques questions de critiques textuelle, historique et littéraire en Is. 4, 2-6', *EI* 16 (1982), 17*–25*.

Cersoy, P., 'L'apologue de la vigne au chapitre v^e d'Isaïe (versets 1-7)', *RB* 8 (1899), 40–49.

Chamberlain, J. V., 'The Functions of God as Messianic Titles in the Complete Qumran Isaiah Scroll', *VT* 5 (1955), 366–72.

Chaney, M. L., 'Whose Sour Grapes? The Addressees of Isaiah 5:1-7 in the Light of Political Economy', *Semeia* 87 (1999), 105–22.

**Cheyne, T. K., *The Prophecies of Isaiah* (2 vols; London, 1880–81).

—*The Book of the Prophet Isaiah: Critical Edition of the Hebrew Text* (SBOT 10; Leipzig, 1899).

Childs, B. S., *Isaiah and the Assyrian Crisis* (SBT, 2nd series 3; London, 1967).

**—*Isaiah* (OTL; Louisville, 2001).

—*The Struggle to Understand Isaiah as Christian Scripture* (Grand Rapids, 2004).

Chilton, B., 'Two in One: Renderings of the Book of Isaiah in Targum Jonathan', in Broyles and Evans (eds), *Writing and Reading*, 547–62.

Chisholm, R. B., 'Structure, Style, and the Prophetic Message: An Analysis of Isaiah 5:8-30', *BibSac* 143 (1986), 46–60.

Claassen, W. T., 'Linguistic Arguments and the Dating of Isaiah 1:4-9', *JNSL* 3 (1974), 1–18.

Clark, D. J., 'The Song of the Vineyard: Love Lyric or Comic Ode? A Study of the Oral and Discourse Features of Isaiah 5.1-7', in E. R. Wendland (ed.), *Discourse Perspectives on Hebrew Poetry in the Scriptures* (UBS Monograph Series 7; Reading, 1994), 131–46.

**Clements, R. E., *Isaiah 1–39* (NCB; Grand Rapids and London, 1980).

—'The Prophecies of Isaiah and the Fall of Jerusalem in 587 B.C.', *VT* 30 (1980), 421–36.

—'Beyond Tradition-History: Deutero-Isaianic Development of First Isaiah's Themes', *JSOT* 31 (1985), 95–113 (repr. *Old Testament Prophecy: From Oracles to Canon* [Louisville, Ky., 1996], 78–92).

—'A Light to the Nations: A Central Theme of the Book of Isaiah', in J. W. Watts and P. R. House (eds), *Forming Prophetic Literature: Essays on Isaiah and the Twelve in Honor of John D.W. Watts* (JSOTSup 235; Sheffield, 1996), 57–69.

—'"Arise, Shine; for your Light has Come": A Basic Theme of the Isaianic Tradition', in Broyles and Evans (eds), *Writing and Reading*, 441–54.

Clifford, R. J., *The Cosmic Mountain in Canaan and the Old Testament* (HSM 4; Cambridge, Mass., 1972).
Cohen, A., 'Studies in Hebrew Lexicography', *AJSL* 40 (1923–24), 153–85.
Cohen, C., 'A Philological Reevaluation of Some Significant DSS Variants of the MT in Isa 1–5', in T. Muraoka and J. F. Elwolde (eds), *Diggers at the Well: Proceedings of a Third International Symposium on the Hebrew of the Dead Sea Scrolls and Ben Sira* (STDJ 36; Leiden, 2000), 40–55.
—'The Enclitic-*mem* in Biblical Hebrew: Its Existence and Initial Discovery', in C. Cohen, A. Hurvitz and S. M. Paul (eds), *Sefer Moshe: The Moshe Weinfeld Jubilee Volume* (Winona Lake, Ind., 2004), 231–60.
Cohen, H. R., *Biblical Hapax Legomena in the Light of Akkadian and Ugaritic* (SBLDS 37; Missoula, Mont., 1978).
**Condamin, A., *Le livre d'Isaïe* (EB; Paris, 1905).
Conrad, E. W., *Reading Isaiah* (Minneapolis, 1991).
Dahood, M. J., 'Ugaritic *ṭat* and Isaia 5,18', *CBQ* 22 (1960), 73–75.
—' "Weaker than Water": Comparative *beth* in Isaiah 1,22', *Biblica* 59 (1978), 91–92.
Daiches, S., 'Der Schmuck der Töchter Zions und die Tracht Ištars', *OLZ* 14 (1911), 390–91.
Dalman, G., *Arbeit und Sitte in Palästina* (7 vols; Gütersloh, 1928–42).
Darr, K. P., *Isaiah's Vision and the Family of God* (Louisville, Ky., 1994).
Davidson, R., 'The Interpretation of Isaiah ii 6ff.', *VT* 16 (1966), 1–7.
Davies, A., *Double Standards in Isaiah: Re-evaluating Prophetic Ethics and Divine Justice* (BibIntS 46; Leiden, 2000).
*Davies, E. W., *Prophecy and Ethics: Isaiah and the Ethical Tradition of Israel* (JSOTSup 16; Sheffield, 1981).
Davies, G. I., 'The Destiny of the Nations in the Book of Isaiah', in Vermeylen (ed.), *The Book of Isaiah*, 93–120.
Dearman, J. A., *Property Rights in the Eighth-Century Prophets: The Conflict and its Background* (SBLDS 106; Atlanta, 1988).
*Deck, S., *Die Gerichtsbotschaft Jesajas: Charakter und Begründung* (FzB 67; Würzburg, 1991).
—'Kein Exodus bei Jesaja?', in F. Diedrich and B. Willmes (eds), *Ich bewirke das Heil und erschaffe das Unheil (Jesaja 45,7): Studien zur Botschaft der Propheten. Festschrift für Lothar Ruppert zum 65. Geburtstag* (FzB 88; Würzburg, 1998), 31–47.
Delekat, L., 'Ein Septuagintatargum', *VT* 8 (1958), 225–52.
**Delitzsch, F., *Commentar über das Buch Jesaia* (4th edn; Leipzig, 1889); ET, *Biblical Commentary on the Prophecies of Isaiah* (Edinburgh, 1890).
DeVries, S. J., *From Old Revelation to New: A Tradition-Historical and Redaction-Critical Study of Temporal Transitions in Prophetic Prediction* (Grand Rapids, 1995).

Diedrich, F., and B. Willmes (eds), *Ich bewirke das Heil und erschaffe das Unheil (Jesaja 45,7): Studien zur Botschaft der Propheten. Festschrift für Lothar Ruppert zum 65. Geburtstag* (FzB 88; Würzburg, 1998).

*Dietrich, W., *Jesaja und die Politik* (BEvTh 74; Munich, 1976).

Dijkstra, M., 'Is Balaam also among the Prophets?', *JBL* 114 (1995), 43–64.

**Dillmann, A., *Der Prophet Jesaia* (KeHAT; 5th edn; Leipzig, 1890).

Dobberahn, F. E., 'Jesaja verklagt die Mörder an der menschlichen Gemeinschaft', *EvTh* 54 (1994), 400–12.

Dobbs-Allsopp, F. W., *Weep, O Daughter of Zion: A Study of the City-Lament Genre in the Hebrew Bible* (BibOr 44; Rome, 1993).

*Donner, H., *Israel unter den Völkern* (VTSup 11; Leiden, 1964).

Driver, G. R., 'Linguistic and Textual Problems: Isaiah i–xxxix', *JTS* 38 (1937), 36–49.

—'Difficult Words in the Hebrew Prophets', in Rowley (ed.), *Studies in Old Testament Prophecy*, 52–72.

—'Hebrew Notes', *VT* 1 (1951), 241–50.

—'Notes on Isaiah', in J. Hempel and L. Rost (eds), *Von Ugarit nach Qumran: Beiträge zur alttestamentlichen und altorientalischen Forschung, Otto Eissfeldt zum 1. September 1957 dargebracht von Freunden und Schülern* (BZAW 77; Berlin, 1958), 42–48.

—'Isaiah i–xxxix: Textual and Linguistic Problems', *JSS* 13 (1968), 36–57.

Driver, S. R., *A Treatise on the Use of the Tenses in Hebrew and Some Other Syntactical Questions* (3rd edn; Oxford, 1892).

**Duhm, B., *Das Buch Jesaia* (HKAT 3/1; Göttingen, 1892; 4th edn, 1922).

*Ehrlich, A. B., *Randglossen zur hebräischen Bibel. IV. Jesaia, Jeremia* (Leipzig, 1912).

**Eichrodt, W., *Der Heilige in Israel: Jesaja 1–12* (BAT 17/1; Stuttgart, 1960).

Eitan, I., 'A Contribution to Isaiah Exegesis', *HUCA* 12-13 (1937–38), 55–88.

Emerton, J. A., 'The Textual Problems of Isaiah v 14', *VT* 17 (1967), 135–42.

—'The Translation of Isaiah 5,1', in F. García Martínez, A. Hilhorst and C. J. Labuschagne (eds), *The Scriptures and the Scrolls: Studies in Honour of A.S. van der Woude on the Occasion of his 65th Birthday* (VTSup 49; Leiden, 1992), 18–30.

—'The Historical Background of Isaiah 1:4-9', in S. Ahituv and B. A. Levine (eds), *Avraham Malamat Volume* (*EI* 24; Jerusalem, 1993), 34–40.

—'Are there Examples of Enclitic *mem* in the Hebrew Bible?', in M. V. Fox *et al.* (eds), *Texts, Temples, and Traditions: A Tribute to Menahem Haran* (Winona Lake, Ind., 1996), 321–38.

—'A Phrase in a Phoenician Papyrus and a Problem in Isaiah 5.14', in J. C. Exum and H. G. M. Williamson (eds), *Reading from Right to Left: Essays on the Hebrew Bible in Honour of David J. A. Clines* (JSOTSup 373; London, 2003), 121–27.

*Ernst, A. B., *Weisheitliche Kultkritik: Zu Theologie und Ethik des Sprüchebuchs und der Prophetie des 8. Jahrhunderts* (BTS 23; Neukirchen–Vluyn, 1994).

Evans, C. A., 'On the Vineyard Parables of Isaiah 5 and Mark 12', *BZ* NF 28 (1984), 82–86.

Fechter, F., 'Enttäuschte Erwartungen: Die Sprache der Bilder in Jesaja 5,1-7', *BN* 104 (2000), 69–82.

**Feldmann, F., *Das Buch Isaias* (EHAT 14; 2 vols; Münster, 1925–26).

*Fey, R., *Amos und Jesaja: Abhängigkeit und Eigenständigkeit des Jesaja* (WMANT 12; Neukirchen–Vluyn, 1963).

Fichtner, J., 'Jesaja unter den Weisen', *TLZ* 74 (1949), 75–80; ET, 'Isaiah Among the Wise', in J. L. Crenshaw (ed.), *Studies in Ancient Israelite Wisdom* (New York, 1976), 429–38.

—'Jahwes Plan in der Botschaft des Jesaja', *ZAW* 63 (1951), 16–33 (repr. *Gottes Weisheit: Gesammelte Schriften zum Alten Testament* [Stuttgart, 1965], 27–43).

Fischer, I., *Tora für Israel—Tora für die Völker: Das Konzept des Jesajabuches* (SBS 164; Stuttgart, 1995).

*Fischer, J., *In welcher Schrift lag das Buch Isaias den LXX vor? Eine Textkritische Studie* (BZAW 56; Giessen, 1930).

**Fohrer, G., *Das Buch Jesaja* (Zürcher Bibelkommentare; 2nd edn; 3 vols; Zurich and Stuttgart, 1964–67).

—'Jesaja 1 als Zusammenfassung der Verkündigung Jesajas', *ZAW* 74 (1962), 251–68 (repr. *Studien zur alttestamentlichen Prophetie [1949–65]* [BZAW 99; Berlin, 1967], 148–66).

—'Entstehung, Komposition und Überlieferung von Jesaja 1–39', in *Studien zur alttestamentlichen Prophetie (1949–1965)* (BZAW 99; Berlin, 1967), 113–47.

Folmer, M. L., 'A Literary Analysis of the "Song of the Vineyard" (Is. 5:1-7)', *Jaarbericht Ex Oriente Lux* 29 (1985–86), 106–23.

Freedman, D. N., 'Headings in the Books of the Eighth-Century Prophets', *AUSS* 25 (1987), 9–26.

Fuhs, H. F., *Sehen und Schauen. Die Wurzel ḥzh im Alten Orient und im Alten Testament: ein Beitrag zum prophetischen Offenbarungsempfang* (FzB 32; Würzburg, 1978).

Fullerton, K., 'The Rhythmical Analysis of Is. 1:10-20', *JBL* 38 (1919), 53–63.

—'The Original Form of the Refrains in Is. 2:6-21', *JBL* 38 (1919), 64–76.

Gates, O. H., 'Notes on Isaiah 1:18b and 7:14b-16', *AJSL* 17 (1900–1901), 16–21.

**Gesenius, W., *Philologisch-kritischer und historischer Commentar über den Jesaia* (2 vols; Leipzig, 1821).

*Gibson, J. C. L., *Davidson's Introductory Hebrew Grammar—Syntax* (Edinburgh, 1994).

Ginsberg, H. L., 'Some Emendations in Isaiah', *JBL* 69 (1950), 51–60.

Gitay, Y., 'The Effectiveness of Isaiah's Speech', *JQR* NS 75 (1984–85), 162–72.

—Isaiah and his Audience: The Structure and Meaning of Isaiah 1–12 (SSN 30; Assen, 1991).

Goldingay, J., 'If your Sins are like Scarlet...(Isaiah 1:18)', *StTh* 35 (1981), 137–44.

—'Isaiah i 1 and ii 1', *VT* 48 (1998), 326–32.

**—*Isaiah* (New International Biblical Commentary; Peabody and Carlisle, 2001).

*Gonçalves, F. J., *L'Expédition de Sennachérib en Palestine dans la littérature hébraïque ancienne* (EB NS 7; Paris, 1986).

Gordon, R. P., *Holy Land, Holy City: Sacred Geography and the Interpretation of the Bible* (Carlisle, 2004).

Goshen-Gottstein, M. H., 'Theory and Practice of Textual Criticism: The Text-Critical Use of the Septuagint', *Textus* 3 (1963), 130–58.

Gossai, H., *Justice, Righteousness and the Social Critique of the Eighth-Century Prophets* (New York, 1993).

Gosse, B., 'Isaïe 1 dans la rédaction du livre d'Isaïe', *ZAW* 104 (1992), 52–66.

—'Isaïe 4,2-6 dans la rédaction du livre d'Isaïe', *Revue d'histoire et de philosophie religieuses* 73 (1993), 131–35.

Grabbe, L. L. (ed.), *'Like a Bird in a Cage': The Invasion of Sennacherib in 701 BCE* (JSOTSup 363; London, 2003).

Graffy, A., 'The Literary Genre of Isaiah 5,1-7', *Biblica* 60 (1979), 400–9.

Graham, W. C., 'Notes on the Interpretation of Isaiah 5:1-14', *AJSL* 45 (1928–29), 167–78.

Gray, G. B., 'Critical Discussions. Isaiah 2_6; 25_{1-5}; 34_{12-14}', *ZAW* 31 (1911), 111–27.

**—*A Critical and Exegetical Commentary on the Book of Isaiah I–XXVII* (ICC; Edinburgh, 1912).

Grol, H. W. M. van, 'Paired Tricola in the Psalms, Isaiah and Jeremiah', *JSOT* 25 (1983), 55–73.

Haag, E., 'Sündenvergebung und neuer Anfang: Zur Übersetzung und Auslegung von Jes 1,18', in J. J. Degenhardt (ed.), *Die Freude an Gott—unsere Kraft: Festschrift für Otto Bernhard Knoch zum 65. Geburtstag* (Stuttgart, 1991), 68–80.

Haelewyck, J.-C., 'La cantique de la vigne. Histoire du texte vieux latin d'Is 5,1-7(9a)', *ETL* 65 (1989), 257–79.

Halpern, B., 'Jerusalem and the Lineages in the Seventh Century BCE: Kinship and the Rise of Individual Moral Liability', in B. Halpern and D. W. Hobson (eds), *Law and Ideology in Monarchic Israel* (JSOTSup 124; Sheffield, 1991), 11–107.

Hardmeier, C., *Texttheorie und biblische Exegese: zur rhetorischen Funktion der Trauermetaphorik in der Prophetie* (BEvTh 79; Munich, 1978).

—'Jesajaforschung im Umbruch', *VF* 31 (1986), 3–31.

Hartenstein, F., *Die Unzugänglichkeit Gottes im Heiligtum: Jesaja 6 und der Wohnort JHWH's in der Jerusalemer Kulttradition* (WMANT 75; Neukirchen–Vluyn, 1997).

Hasel, G. F., *The Remnant: The History and the Theology of the Remnant Idea from Genesis to Isaiah* (2nd edn; Berrien Springs, 1974).

Haupt, P., 'Isaiah's Parable of the Vineyard', *AJSL* 19 (1902–1905), 193–202.

Hausmann, J., *Israels Rest: Studien zum Selbstverständnis der nachexilischen Gemeinde* (BWANT 124; Stuttgart, 1987).

**Hayes, J. H., and S. A. Irvine, *Isaiah, the Eighth-Century Prophet: His Times and his Preaching* (Nashville, 1987).

Hayman, L., 'A Note on Isa. 1:25', *JNES* 9 (1950), 217.

Hentschke, R., *Die Stellung der vorexilischen Schriftpropheten zum Kultus* (BZAW 75; Berlin, 1957).

Hermisson, H.-J., 'Zukunftserwartung und Gegenwartskritik in der Verkündigung Jesajas', *EvTh* 33 (1973), 54–77 (repr. in *Studien zu Prophetie und Weisheit: Gesammelte Aufsätze* [FAT 23; Tübingen, 1998], 81–104).

Herrmann, S., *Die prophetischen Heilserwartungen im Alten Testament: Ursprung und Gestaltwandel* (BWANT 85; Stuttgart, 1965).

Hillers, D. R., '*Hôy* and *Hôy*-Oracles: A Neglected Syntactic Aspect', in C. L. Meyers and M. O'Connor (eds), *The Word of the Lord Shall Go Forth: Essays in Honor of David Noel Freedman in Celebration of his Sixtieth Birthday* (Winona Lake, Ind., 1983), 185–88.

**Hitzig, F., *Der Prophet Jesaja* (Heidelberg, 1833).

Höffken, P., 'Probleme in Jesaja 5,1-7', *ZTK* 79 (1982), 392–410.

**—*Das Buch Jesaja: Kapitel 1–39* (NSK-AT 18/1; Stuttgart, 1993).

—*Jesaja: Der Stand der theologischen Discussion* (Darmstadt, 2004).

*Hoffmann, H. W., *Die Intention der Verkündigung Jesajas* (BZAW 136; Berlin, 1974).

Høgenhaven, J., 'The First Isaiah Scroll from Qumran (1QIa^a) and the Massoretic Text: Some Reflections with Special Regard to Isaiah 1–12', *JSOT* 28 (1984), 17–35.

*—*Gott und Volk bei Jesaja: eine Untersuchung zur biblischen Theologie* (AThDan 24; Leiden, 1988).

Holladay, W. L., 'Isa. iii 10-11: An Archaic Wisdom Passage', *VT* 18 (1968), 481–87.

**—*Isaiah: Scroll of a Prophetic Heritage* (Grand Rapids, 1978).

—'A New Suggestion for the Crux in Isaiah i 4b', *VT* 33 (1983), 235–37.

Honeyman, A. M., 'Isaiah i 16 הִזַּכּוּ', *VT* 1 (1951), 63–65.

Horgan, M. P., *Pesharim: Qumran Interpretations of Biblical Books* (CBQMS 8; Washington, 1979).

Horst, P. W. van der, 'A Classical Parallel to Isaiah 5^8', *ExpT* 89 (1977–78), 119–20.

**Houbigant, C.-F., *Biblia Hebraica cum Notis Criticis. IV. Prophetae Posteriores* (Paris, 1753).

Houston, W., 'Was there a Social Crisis in the Eighth Century?', in J. Day (ed.), *In Search of Pre-Exilic Israel: Proceedings of the Oxford Old Testament Seminar* (JSOTSup 406; London, 2004), 130–49.

Houtman, A., 'Doom and Promise in the Targum of Isaiah', *JJS* 49 (1998), 17–23.

Houtman, C., *Der Himmel im Alten Testament: Israels Weltbild und Weltanschauung* (OTS 30; Leiden, 1993).

Huesman, J., 'Finite Uses of the Infinitive Absolute', *Biblica* 37 (1956), 271–95.

Hummel, H. D., 'Enclitic *Mem* in Early Northwest Semitic, Especially Hebrew', *JBL* 76 (1957), 85–107.

Hunter, A. V., *Seek the Lord! A Study of the Meaning and Function of the Exhortations in Amos, Hosea, Isaiah, Micah and Zephaniah* (Baltimore, 1982).

Irsigler, H., 'Speech Acts and Intention in the "Song of the Vineyard" Isaiah 5:1-7', *OTE* 10 (1997), 39–68.

Irvine, S. A., 'The Isaianic *Denkschrift*: Reconsidering an Old Hypothesis', *ZAW* 104 (1992), 216–31.

**Jacob, E., *Esaïe 1–12* (CAT 8a; Geneva, 1987).

Janzen, W., *Mourning Cry and Woe Oracle* (BZAW 125; Berlin and New York, 1972).

Jeffers, A., *Magic and Divination in Ancient Palestine and Syria* (SHCANE 8; Leiden, 1996).

Jensen, J., *The Use of* tôrâ *by Isaiah: His Debate with the Wisdom Tradition* (CBQMS 3; Washington, 1973).

—'Weal and Woe in Isaiah: Consistency and Continuity', *CBQ* 43 (1981), 167–87.

—'Yahweh's Plan in Isaiah and in the Rest of the Old Testament', *CBQ* 48 (1986), 443–55.

Jeremias, J., *Theophanie: Die Geschichte einer alttestamentlichen Gattung* (WMANT 10; 2nd edn; Neukirchen–Vluyn, 1977).

Jirku, A., 'Weitere Fälle von afformativem *–ma* im Hebräischen', *VT* 7 (1957), 391–92.

Jones, D. R., 'The Traditio of the Oracles of Isaiah of Jerusalem', *ZAW* 67 (1955), 226–46.

—'Exposition of Isaiah Chapter One Verses One to Nine', *SJT* 17 (1964), 463–70.

—'Exposition of Isaiah Chapter One Verses Eighteen to Twenty', *SJT* 19 (1966), 319–27.

—'Exposition of Isaiah Chapter One Verses Twenty One to the End', *SJT* 21 (1968), 320–29.

Junker, H., 'Die literarische Art von Is 5,1-7', *Biblica* 40 (1959), 259–66.

Kaddari, M. Z., 'Concessive Connectors in the Language of Isaiah', *OTWSA* 22-23 (1979–80), 103–12.

**Kaiser, O., *Das Buch des Propheten Jesaja, Kapitel 1–12* (ATD 17; 5th edn; Göttingen, 1981;ET, *Isaiah 1–12: A Commentary* [OTL; London, 1983]).

Kedar-Kopfstein, B., 'Divergent Hebrew Readings in Jerome's Isaiah', *Textus* 4 (1964), 176–210.

Keel, O., *Goddesses and Trees, New Moon and Yahweh: Ancient Near East and the Hebrew Bible* (JSOTSup 261; Sheffield, 1998).

Kellermann, D., 'Frevelstricke und Wagenseil: Bemerkungen zu Jesaja v 18', *VT* 37 (1987), 90–97.

Kessler, R., *Staat und Gesellschaft im vorexilischen Juda vom 8. Jahrhundert bis zum Exil* (VTSup 47; Leiden, 1992).

—'"Söhne habe ich grossgezogen und emporgebracht…": Gott als Mutter in Jes 1,2', in R. Kessler *et al.* (eds), *"Ihr Völker, klatscht in die Hände!" Festschrift für Erhard S. Gerstenberger zum 65. Geburtstag* (Munich, 1997), 134–47.

**Kilian, R., *Jesaja 1–12* (Die Neue Echter Bibel 17; Würzburg, 1986).

**Kissane, E. J., *The Book of Isaiah, Translated from a Critically Revised Hebrew Text with Commentary*. I. *i–xxxix* (Dublin, 1941).

**Knobel, A., *Der Prophet Jesaia* (KeHAT 5; 3rd edn; Leipzig, 1861).

Koenen, K., *Heil den Gerechten—Unheil den Sündern! Ein Beitrag zur Theologie der Prophetenbücher* (BZAW 229; Berlin, 1994).

*Koenig, J., *L'Herméneutique analogique du judaïsme antique d'après les témoins textuels d'Isaïe* (VTSup 33; Leiden, 1982).

Kohler, K., 'Emendations of the Hebrew Text of Isaiah', *Hebraica* 2 (1885–86), 39–48.

Köhler, L., 'Ein verkannter hebräischer irrealer Bedingungssatz (Jes 1:19)', *ZS* 4 (1926), 196–97.

König, E., *Historisch-kritisches Lehrgebäude der hebräischen Sprache* (Leipzig, 1881).

—*Historisch-Comparative Syntax der Hebräischen Sprache* (Leipzig, 1897).

**—*Das Buch Jesaja* (Gütersloh, 1926).

*Kooij, A. van der, *Die alten Textzeugen des Jesajabuches: Ein Beitrag zur Textgeschichte des Alten Testaments* (OBO 35; Freiburg and Göttingen, 1981).

—'Accident or Method? On "Analogical" Interpretation in the Old Greek of Isaiah and in 1QIsa[a]', *BiOr* 43 (1986), 366–76.

—'Interpretation of the Book of Isaiah in the Septuagint and Other Ancient Versions', *SBLSP* 40 (2001), 220–39.

Korpel, M. C. A., 'The Literary Genre of the Song of the Vineyard (Isa. 5:1-7)', in W. van der Meer and J. C. de Moor (eds), *The Structural Analysis of Biblical and Canaanite Poetry* (JSOTSup 74; Sheffield, 1988), 119–55.

—'Structural Analysis as a Tool for Redaction Criticism: The Example of Isaiah 5 and 10.1-6', *JSOT* 69 (1996), 53–71.

Kselman, J. S., 'A Note on Isaiah ii 2', *VT* 25 (1975), 225–27.

*Kustár, Z., *"Durch seine Wunden sind wir geheilt": Eine Untersuchung zur Metaphorik von Israels Krankheit und Heilung im Jesajabuch* (BWANT 154; Stuttgart, 2002).

Kutsch, E., '"Wir wollen miteinander rechten": Zu Form und Aussage von Jes 1,18-20', in L. Ruppert *et al.* (eds), *Künder des Wortes: Festschrift für Josef Schreiner* (Würzburg, 1982), 23–33 (repr. in *Kleine Schriften zum Alten Testament* [BZAW 168; Berlin and New York, 1986], 146–56).

*Kutscher, E. Y., *The Language and Linguistic Background of the Isaiah Scroll (1QIsaᵃ)* (STDJ 6; Leiden, 1974).

Laato, A., *'About Zion I Will Not be Silent': The Book of Isaiah as an Ideological Unity* (ConB, Old Testament Series 44; Stockholm, 1998).

Lack, R., *La symbolique du livre d'Isaïe* (AnBib 59; Rome, 1973).

*Lagarde, P. de, *Semitica*. Vol. I (Göttingen, 1878).

Landy, F., 'Vision and Voice in Isaiah', *JSOT* 88 (2000), 19–36.

—'Torah and Anti-Torah: Isaiah 2:2-4 and 1:10-26', *BibInt* 11 (2003), 317–34.

*Leclerc, T. L., *Yahweh is Exalted in Justice: Solidarity and Conflict in Isaiah* (Minneapolis, 2001).

Ley, J., 'Metrische Analyse von Jesaia K. 1', *ZAW* 22 (1902), 229–37.

L'Heureux, C. E., 'The Redactional History of Isaiah 5.1–10.4', in W. B. Barrick and J. R. Spencer (eds), *In the Shelter of Elyon: Essays on Ancient Palestinian Life and Literature in Honor of G. W. Ahlström* (JSOTSup 31; Sheffield, 1984), 99–119.

Liebreich, L. J., 'The Compilation of the Book of Isaiah', *JQR* NS 46 (1955–56), 259–77; 47 (1956–57), 114–38.

Limburg, J., 'Swords to Plowshares: Text and Contexts', in Broyles and Evans (eds), *Writing and Reading*, 279–93.

Lipiński, E., 'De la réforme d'Esdras au règne eschatologique de Dieu (Is 4,3-5a)', *Biblica* 51 (1970), 533–37.

Loewenclau, I. von, 'Zur Auslegung von Jesaja 1, 2-3', *EvTh* 26 (1966), 294–308.

Loewenstamm, S. E., 'Isaiah i 31', *VT* 22 (1972), 246–48.

Lohfink, N., and E. Zenger, *The God of Israel and the Nations: Studies in Isaiah and the Psalms* (Collegeville, Minn., 2000).

Loretz, O., 'Weinberglied und prophetische Deutung im Protest-Song Jes 5,1-7', *UF* 7 (1975), 573–36.

—'*Kj* "Brandmal" in Jes 3,24?', *UF* 8 (1976), 448.

*—*Der Prolog des Jesaja-Buches (1,1–2,5)* (UBL 1; Altenberge, 1984).

—'Zitat der ersten Hälfte einer Weinberg-Parabel in Jes 5,1-7', *UF* 29 (1997), 489–510.

**Lowth, R., *Isaiah: A New Translation; with a Preliminary Dissertation, and Notes* (2 vols; London, 1778).

Luc, A., 'Isaiah 1 as Structural Introduction', *ZAW* 101 (1989), 115.

**Luther, M., *Luther's Works*. XVI. *Lectures on Isaiah Chapters 1–39* (St Louis, 1969).

Lys, D., 'La vigne et le double je: exercice de style sur Esaïe v 1-7', in *Studies on Prophecy* (VTSup 26; Leiden, 1974), 1–16.

Ma, W., *Until the Spirit Comes: The Spirit of God in the Book of Isaiah* (JSOTSup 271; Sheffield, 1999).

Machinist, P., 'Assyria and its Image in the First Isaiah', *JAOS* 103 (1983), 719–37.

McKane, W., *Prophets and Wise Men* (SBT 44; London, 1965).

—*The Book of Micah: Introduction and Commentary* (Edinburgh, 1998).

McLaughlin, J. L., *The marzēaḥ in the Prophetic Literature: References and Allusions in Light of the Extra-Biblical Evidence* (VTSup 86; Leiden, 2001).

Magonet, J., 'Isaiah 2:1–4:6: Some Poetic Structures and Tactics', *ACEBT* 3 (1982), 71–85.

—'Isaiah's Mountain or The Shape of Things to Come', *Prooftexts* 11 (1991), 175–81.

Mankowski, P. V., *Akkadian Loanwords in Biblical Hebrew* (HSS 47; Winona Lake, Ind., 2000).

**Marti, K., *Das Buch Jesaja* (KHAT 10; Tübingen, 1900).

Marx, A., 'Esaïe ii 20, une signature karaïte?', *VT* 40 (1990), 232–37.

Matthews, V. H., 'Treading the Winepress: Actual and Metaphorical Viticulture in the Ancient Near East', *Semeia* 86 (1999), 19–32.

Mattioli, A., 'Due Schemi letterari negli Oracoli d'Introduzione al Libro d'Isaia: Is 1:1-31', *RivB* 14 (1966), 345–64.

**Mauchline, J., *Isaiah 1–39: Introduction and Commentary* (Torch Bible Commentaries; London, 1962).

Meier, S. A., *Speaking of Speaking: Marking Direct Discourse in the Hebrew Bible* (VTSup 46; Leiden, 1992).

Melugin, R. F., 'Figurative Speech and the Reading of Isaiah 1 as Scripture', in Melugin and Sweeney (eds), *New Visions*, 282–305.

Melugin, R. F., and M. A. Sweeney (eds), *New Visions of Isaiah* (JSOTSup 214; Sheffield, 1996).

Milgrom, J., 'Did Isaiah Prophesy during the Reign of Uzziah?', *VT* 14 (1964), 164–82.

Moberly, R. W. L., 'Whose Justice? Which Righteousness? The Interpretation of Isaiah v 16', *VT* 51 (2001), 55–68.

Moor, J. C. de, 'The Targumic Background of Mark 12:1-12: The Parable of the Wicked Tenants', *JSJ* 29 (1998), 63–80.

**Motyer, J. A., *The Prophecy of Isaiah* (Leicester, 1993).

Mowinckel, S., 'Die Komposition des Jesajabuches 1–39', *ActOr* 11 (1932–33), 267–92.

—*Prophecy and Tradition: The Prophetic Books in the Light of the Study of the Growth and History of the Tradition* (Oslo, 1946).

Muchiki, Y., *Egyptian Proper Names and Loanwords in North-West Semitic* (SBLDS 173; Atlanta, 1999).

Muntingh, L. M., 'The Name "Israel" and Related Terms in the Book of Isaiah', *OTWSA* 22-23 (1979–80), 159–82.

Napier, B. D., 'Isaiah and the Isaian', in *Volume du Congrès: Genève, 1965* (VTSup 15; Leiden, 1966), 240–51.

Neveu, L., 'Isaïe 2,6-22: le Jour de YHWH', in *La vie de la Parole: de l'Ancien au Nouveau Testament. Études d'exégèse et d'herméneutique bibliques offerts à Pierre Grelot* (Paris, 1987), 129–38.

Niditch, S., 'The Composition of Isaiah 1', *Biblica* 61 (1980), 509–29.

Niehr, H., 'Bedeutung und Funktion kanaanäischer Traditionselemente in der Sozialkritik Jesajas', *BZ* NF 28 (1984), 69–81.

—'Zur Gattung von Jes 5,1-7', *BZ* NF 30 (1986), 99–104.

Nielsen, K., *Yahweh as Prosecutor and Judge: An Investigation of the Prophetic Lawsuit (Rîb-Pattern)* (JSOTSup 9; Sheffield, 1978).

—'Das Bild des Gerichts (*rib*-pattern) in Jes. i–xii', *VT* 29 (1979), 309–24.

—There is Hope for a Tree: The Tree as Metaphor in Isaiah (JSOTSup 65; Sheffield, 1989).

Nötscher, F., 'Entbehrliche Hapaxlegomena in Jesaia', *VT* 1 (1951), 299–302.

O'Connell, R. H., *Concentricity and Continuity: The Literary Structure of Isaiah* (JSOTSup 188; Sheffield, 1994).

Oesch, J. M., 'Jes 1,8f und das Problem der "Wir-Reden" im Jesajabuch', *ZKTh* 116 (1994), 440–46.

Olivier, J. O. J., 'Rendering ידיד as Benevolent Patron in Isaiah 5:1', *JNSL* 22/2 (1996), 59–65.

Ollenburger, B. C., *Zion the City of the Great King: A Theological Symbol of the Jerusalem Cult* (JSOTSup 41; Sheffield, 1987).

Olley, J. W., *'Righteousness' in the Septuagint of Isaiah: A Contextual Study* (Missoula, Mont., 1979).

—'"Hear the Word of YHWH": The Structure of the Book of Isaiah in 1QIsaᵃ', *VT* 43 (1993), 19–49.

**Orelli, C. von, *Der Prophet Jesaja* (Munich, 1887); ET, *The Prophecies of Isaiah* (Edinburgh, 1889).

**Oswalt, J. N., *The Book of Isaiah Chapters 1–39* (NICOT; Grand Rapids, 1986).

*Ottley, R. R., *The Book of Isaiah According to the Septuagint (Codex Alexandrinus)* (2 vols; Cambridge, 1906).

Paas, S., *Creation and Judgement: Creation Texts in Some Eighth Century Prophets* (OTS 47; Leiden, 2003).

**Penna, A., *Isaia* (Torino, 1964).

Perlitt, L., 'Jesaja und die Deuteronomisten', in V. Fritz *et al.* (eds), *Prophet und Prophetenbuch: Festschrift für Otto Kaiser zum 65. Geburtstag* (BZAW 185; Berlin and New York, 1989), 133–49.

Peters, J. P., 'Two Fragments of Hebrew Popular Melodies', *JBL* 5 (1885), 88–90.

Peursen, W. Th. van, 'Guarded, Besieged or Devastated? Some Remarks on Isaiah 1:7-8, with Special Reference to 1QIsaᵃ', *Dutch Studies in Near Eastern Languages and Literature* 2 (1996), 101–10.

Pfaff, H.-M., *Die Entwicklung des Restgedankens in Jesaja 1–39* (Europäische Hochschulschriften xxiii/561; Frankfurt am Main, 1996).

Platt, E. E., 'Jewelry of Bible Times and the Catalog of Isa 3:18-23', *AUSS* 17 (1979), 71–84, 189–201.

Popper, W., 'Parallelism in Isaiah, Chapters 1–10', in L. I. Newman and W. Popper, *Studies in Biblical Parallelism* (Berkeley, 1918).

—*Parallelism in Isaiah: Chapters 1–35 and 37.22-35* (Berkeley, 1923).

*Porath, R., *Die Sozialkritik im Jesajabuch: Redaktionsgeschichtliche Analyse* (Europäische Hochschulschriften 23/503; Frankfurt, 1994).
Premnath, D. M., 'Latifundialization and Isaiah 5.8-10', *JSOT* 40 (1988), 49–60.
Prinsloo, W. S., 'Isaiah 5:1-7: A Synchronic Approach', *OTWSA* 22-23 (1979–80), 183–97.
**Procksch, O., *Jesaia I* (KAT 9/1; Leipzig, 1930).
*Pulikottil, P., *Transmission of Biblical Texts in Qumran: The Case of the Large Isaiah Scroll 1QIsaᵃ* (JSPSup 34; Sheffield, 2001).
Rehm, M., *Der königliche Messias im Licht der Immanuel-Weissagungen des Buches Jesaja* (Kevelaer, 1968).
Renaud, B., *La formation du livre de Michée: Tradition et actualisation* (EB; Paris, 1977).
Rendtorff, R., 'Zur Komposition des Buches Jesaja', *VT* 34 (1984), 295–320; ET, 'The Composition of the Book of Isaiah', *Canon and Theology* (Edinburgh, 1994), 146–69.
Rignell, L. G., 'Isaiah Chapter 1: Some Exegetical Remarks with Special Reference to the Relationship between the Text and the Book of Deuteronomy', *StTh* 11 (1957), 140–58.
Roberts, J. J. M., 'Form, Syntax, and Redaction in Isaiah 1:2-20', *PSB* NS 3 (1982), 293–306.
—'Isaiah 2 and the Prophet's Message to the North', *JQR* NS 75 (1984–85), 290–308.
—'Double Entendre in First Isaiah', *CBQ* 54 (1992), 39–48.
—'The Meaning of "צמח ה'" in Isaiah 4:2', *Jewish Bible Quarterly* 28 (2000), 20–27.
Robertson, E., 'Isaiah Chapter 1', *ZAW* 52 (1934), 231–36.
Rogers, J. S., 'An Allusion to Coronation in Isaiah 2:6', *CBQ* 51 (1989), 232–36.
Rowley, H. H. (ed.), *Studies in Old Testament Prophecy Presented to Professor Theodore H. Robinson* (Edinburgh, 1950).
Rubinstein, A., 'The Theological Aspect of Some Variant Readings in the Isaiah Scroll', *JJS* 6 (1955), 187–200.
Rudman, D., 'Zechariah 8:20-22 & Isaiah 2:2-4/Micah 4:2-3: A Study in Intertextuality', *BN* 107/108 (2001), 50–54.
Ruffenach, F., 'Malitia et Remissio Peccati: Is.1,1-20', *VD* 7 (1927), 145–49, 165–68.
Ruiten, J. van, and M. Vervenne (eds), *Studies in the Book of Isaiah: Festschrift Willem A. M. Beuken* (BETL 132; Leuven, 1997).
Ruppert, L., 'Die Kritik an den Göttern im Jesajabuch', *BN* 82 (1996), 76–96.
Sauer, G., 'Die Umkehrforderung in der Verkündigung Jesajas', in H. J. Stoebe (ed.), *Wort—Gebot—Glaube: Walther Eichrodt zum 80. Geburtstag* (AThANT 59; Zurich, 1970), 277–95.
Sawyer, J. F. A., *The Fifth Gospel: Isaiah in the History of Christianity* (Cambridge, 1996).
Schmitt, J. J., 'The City as Woman in Isaiah 1–39', in Broyles and Evans (eds), *Writing and Reading*, 95–119.

Schmitt, R., *Magie im Alten Testament* (AOAT 313; Münster, 2004).

Schoneveld, J., 'Jesaia i 18-20', *VT* 13 (1963), 342–44.

**Schoors, A., *Jesaja* (De Boeken van het Oude Testament 9A; Roermond, 1972).

Schottroff, W., 'Das Weinberglied Jesajas (Jes 5₁₋₇): Ein Beitrag zur Geschichte der Parabel', *ZAW* 82 (1970), 68–91.

Schreiber, A., 'Zwei Bemerkungen zu Jesaja', *VT* 11 (1961), 455–56.

Schwally, F., 'Miscellen', *ZAW* 11 (1891), 253–60.

Schwartz, B. J., 'Torah from Zion: Isaiah's Temple Vision (Isaiah 2:1-4)', in A. Houtman, M. J. H. M. Poorthuis and J. Schwartz (eds), *Sanctity of Time and Space in Tradition and Modernity* (Jewish and Christian Perspectives Series 1; Leiden, 1998), 11–26.

Scott, R. B. Y., 'The Literary Structure of Isaiah's Oracles', in Rowley (ed.), *Studies in Old Testament Prophecy*, 175–86 .

**—'The Book of Isaiah, Chapters 1–39', in G. A. Buttrick (ed.), *The Interpreter's Bible* (New York and Nashville, 1956), V, 149–381.

*Seeligmann, I. L., *The Septuagint Version of Isaiah: A Discussion of its Problems* (Leiden, 1948).

Selms, A. van, 'Isaiah 2:4: Parallels and Contrasts', *OTWSA* 22-23 (1979–80), 230–39.

Seybold, K., 'Die anthropologischen Beiträge aus Jesaja 2', *ZTK* 74 (1977), 401–15.

—'Das Weinberglied des Propheten Jesaja (5,1-7)', in *idem*, *Die Sprache der Propheten: Studien zur Literaturgeschichte der Prophetie* (Zürich, 1999), 111–22.

Sheppard, G. T., 'More on Isaiah 5:1-7 as a Juridical Parable', *CBQ* 44 (1982), 45–47.

—'The Anti-Assyrian Redaction and the Canonical Context of Isaiah 1–39', *JBL* 104 (1985), 193–216.

Skehan, P. W., 'Some Textual Problems in Isaia', *CBQ* 22 (1960), 47–55.

**Skinner, J., *The Book of the Prophet Isaiah, Chapters i–xxxix* (CBSC; Cambridge, 1897).

**Slotki, I. W., *Isaiah* (Soncino Bible; London, 1949).

Smith, L. P., 'The Use of the Word תורה in Isaiah, Chapters 1–39', *AJSL* 46 (1929), 1–21.

**Snijders, L. A., *Jesaja*. Vol. I (De Prediking van het Oude Testament; Nijkerk, 1969).

Speier, S., 'Zu drei Jesajastellen: Jes. 1,7; 5,24; 10,7', *TZ* 21 (1965), 310–13.

Spreafico, A., 'Nahum i 10 and Isaiah i 12-13: Double-Duty Modifier', *VT* 48 (1998), 104–10.

**Stacey, D., *Isaiah 1–39* (Epworth Commentaries; London, 1993).

*Stansell, G., *Micah and Isaiah: A Form and Tradition Historical Comparison* (SBLDS 85; Atlanta, 1988).

Steck, O. H., *Friedensvorstellungen im alten Jerusalem* (ThSt 111; Zurich, 1972).

—*Die erste Jesajarolle von Qumran (1QIs^a)* (SBS 173/1-2; Stuttgart, 1998).

—'Zur konzentrischen Anlage von Jes 1,21-26', in I. Fischer, U Rapp and J. Schiller (eds), *Auf den Spuren der schriftgelehrten Weisen: Festschrift für Johannes Marböck* (BZAW 331; Berlin, 2003), 97–103.

**Steinmann, J., *Le prophète Isaïe: sa vie, son oeuvre et son temps* (Lectio Divina 5; Paris, 1950).

Stiebert, J., *The Construction of Shame in the Hebrew Bible: The Prophetic Contribution* (JSOTSup 346; Sheffield, 2002).

Sweeney, M. A., 'Structure and Redaction in Isaiah 2–4', *HAR* 11 (1987), 407–22.

—*Isaiah 1–4 and the Post-Exilic Understanding of the Isaianic Tradition* (BZAW 171; Berlin, 1988).

**—*Isaiah 1–39 with an Introduction to Prophetic Literature* (FOTL 16; Grand Rapids, 1996).

—'The Book of Isaiah as Prophetic Torah', in Melugin and Sweeney (eds), *New Visions*, 50–67.

—'Micah's Debate with Isaiah', *JSOT* 93 (2001), 111–24.

Thomas, D. W., 'A Lost Hebrew Word in Isaiah ii 6', *JTS* NS 13 (1962), 323–24.

—'The Text of Jesaia ii 6 and the Word שׂפק', *ZAW* 75 (1963), 88–90.

Toloni, G., ''Αγαπάω come rilettura dei LXX di šaʿašûʿîm (Is 5,7) e šaʿaʿ (Sal 94[93],19)', *RivB* 44 (1986), 128–56.

Tomasino, A. J., 'Isaiah 1.1–2.4 and 63–66, and the Composition of the Isaianic Corpus', *JSOT* 57 (1993), 81–98.

Tromp, N. J., 'Un démasquage graduel: lecture immanente d'Is 5,1-7', in Vermeylen (ed.), *Book*, 197–202.

Troxel, R. L., 'Exegesis and Theology in the LXX: Isaiah v 26-30', *VT* 43 (1993), 102–11.

—'Economic Plunder as a Leitmotif in LXX-Isaiah', *Biblica* 83 (2002), 375–91.

Tsevat, M., 'Isaiah i 31', *VT* 19 (1969), 261–63.

Tucker, G. M., 'Prophetic Superscriptions and the Growth of a Canon', in G. W. Coats and B. O. Long (eds), *Canon and Authority: Essays in Old Testament Religion and Theology* (Philadelphia, 1977), 56–70.

**—'The Book of Isaiah 1–39: Introduction, Commentary, and Reflections', in L. E. Keck *et al.* (eds), *The New Interpreter's Bible* (Nashville, 2001), VI, 25–305.

*Tur-Sinai, N. H., 'A Contribution to the Understanding of Isaiah i–xii', in C. Rabin (ed.), *Studies in the Bible* (ScrH 8; Jerusalem, 1961), 154–88.

Uchelen, N. A. van, 'Isaiah i 9—Text and Context', in A. S. van der Woude (ed.), *Remembering all the Way...: A Collection of Old Testament Studies Published on the Occasion of the Fortieth Anniversary of the Oudtestamentisch Werkgezelschap in Nederland* (OTS 21; Leiden, 1981), 155–63.

Ulrich, E., 'The Developmental Composition of the Book of Isaiah: Light from 1QIsaᵃ on Additions in the MT', *DSD* 8 (2001), 288–305.

Vargon, S., 'The Description of the Coming of the Enemy in Isaiah 5:26-30', *BethM* 44 (1999), 289–305 (Hebrew).

—'The Historical Background and Significance of Isa 1,10-17', in
   G. Galil and M. Weinfeld (eds), *Studies in Historical Geography
   and Biblical Historiography Presented to Zecharia Kallai* (VTSup
   81; Leiden, 2000), 177–94.
Vaux, R. de, *Ancient Israel: Its Life and Institutions* (2nd edn; London,
   1965).
*Vermeylen, J., *Du prophète Isaïe à l'apocalyptique: Isaïe, I–XXXV,
   miroir d'un demi-millénaire d'expérience religieuse en Israël* (EB; 2
   vols; Paris, 1977–78).
—(ed.), *The Book of Isaiah* (BETL 81; Leuven, 1989).
**Vitringa, C., *Commentarius in Librum Prophetiarum Jesaiae* (2 vols;
   Leeuwarden, 1714–20).
*Vollmer, J., *Geschichtliche Rückblicke und Motive in der Prophetie des
   Amos, Hosea und Jesaja* (BZAW 119; Berlin, 1971).
**Wade, G. W., *The Book of the Prophet Isaiah* (Westminster Com-
   mentaries; 2nd edn; London, 1929).
Walsh, C. E., *The Fruit of the Vine: Viticulture in Ancient Israel* (HSM
   60; Winona Lake, Ind., 2000).
Watson, W. G. E., 'The Pivot Pattern in Hebrew, Ugaritic and Akkadian
   Poetry', *ZAW* 88 (1976), 239–53.
—*Classical Hebrew Poetry: A Guide to its Techniques* (JSOTSup 26;
   Sheffield, 1984).
Watts, J. D. W., 'The Formation of Isaiah Ch. 1: Its Context in Chs. 1–4',
   SBLSP 1 (Missoula, Mont., 1978), 109–19,
**—*Isaiah 1–33* (WBC 24; Waco, Tex., 1985).
—*Isaiah* (Dallas, 1989).
—'Jerusalem: An Example of War in a Walled City (Isaiah 3–4)', in L. L.
   Grabbe and R. D. Haak (eds), *'Every City Shall be Forsaken': Urban-
   ism and Prophecy in Ancient Israel and the Near East* (JSOTSup
   330; Sheffield, 2001), 210–15.
Webb, B. G., 'Zion in Transformation: A Literary Approach to Isaiah', in
   D. J. A. Clines, S. E. Fowl and S. E. Porter (eds), *The Bible in Three
   Dimensions: Essays in Celebration of Forty Years of Biblical Studies
   in the University of Sheffield* (JSOTSup 87; Sheffield, 1990), 65–84.
Weil, H.-M., 'Exégèse d'Isaïe, III, 1-15', *RB* 49 (1940), 76–85.
Weinfeld, M., 'Zion and Jerusalem as Religious and Political Capital:
   Ideology and Utopia', in R. E. Friedman (ed.), *The Poet and the
   Historian: Essays in Literary and Historical Biblical Criticism* (HSS
   26; Chico, Calif., 1983), 75–115.
—*Social Justice in Ancient Israel and in the Ancient Near East* (Jerusalem
   and Minneapolis, 1995).
*Wendel, U., *Jesaja und Jeremia: Worte, Motive und Einsichten Jesajas
   in der Verkündigung Jeremias* (BTS 25; Neukirchen–Vluyn, 1995).
Weren, W. J. C., 'The Use of Isaiah 5,1-7 in the Parable of the Tenants',
   Biblica 79 (1998), 1–26.
Wernberg-Møller, P., 'Studies in the Defective Spellings in the Isaiah-
   Scroll of St Mark's Monastery', *JSS* 3 (1958), 244–64.

Werner, W., 'Israel in der Entscheidung: Überlegungen zur Datierung und zu theologischen Aussage von Jes 1,4-9', in R. Kilian (ed.), *Eschatologie: Festschrift für Engelbert Neuhäusler* (St Ottilien, 1981), 59–72.

—*Eschatologische Texte in Jesaja 1–39: Messias, Heiliger Rest, Völker* (FzB 46; Würzburg, 1982).

—*Studien zur alttestamentlichen Vorstellung vom Plan Jahwes* (BZAW 173; Berlin, 1988).

Westermann, C., *Grundformen prophetischer Rede* (Munich, 1960); ET, *Basic Forms of Prophetic Speech* (Cambridge and Louisville, Ky., 1991).

*Whedbee, J. W., *Isaiah and Wisdom* (Nashville and New York, 1971).

**Whitehouse, O. C., *Isaiah i–xxix* (CB; Edinburgh, 1905).

Wieringen, A. L. H. M. van, 'The Day Beyond the Days: Isaiah 2:2 within the Framework of the Book of Isaiah', in F. Postma *et al.* (eds), *The New Things: Eschatology in Old Testament Prophecy. Festschrift for Hank Leene* (ACEBT, SS 3; Maastricht, 2002), 253–59.

*Wiklander, B., *Prophecy as Literature: A Text-Linguistic and Rhetorical Approach to Isaiah 2–4* (ConB, Old Testament Series 22; Malmö, 1984).

Wildberger, H., 'Die Völkerwallfahrt zum Zion: Jes. ii 1-5', *VT* 7 (1957), 62–81.

**—*Jesaja* (BKAT 10/1-3; 3 vols; Neukirchen–Vluyn, 1972–82; 2nd edn of vol. I, 1980); ET, *Isaiah 1–12, 13–27, 28–39* (3 vols; Minneapolis, 1991–2002).

Williams, G. R., 'Frustrated Expectations in Isaiah v 1-7: A Literary Interpretation', *VT* 35 (1985), 459–65.

Williamson, H. G. M., 'Isaiah 1.11 and the Septuagint of Isaiah', in A. G. Auld (ed.), *Understanding Poets and Prophets: Essays in Honour of George Wishart Anderson* (JSOTSup 152; Sheffield, 1993), 401–12.

—*The Book Called Isaiah: Deutero-Isaiah's Role in Composition and Redaction* (Oxford, 1994).

—'Synchronic and Diachronic in Isaian Perspective', in J. C. de Moor (ed.), *Synchronic or Diachronic? A Debate on Method in Old Testament Exegesis* (OTS 34; Leiden, 1995), 211–26.

—'Isaiah and the Wise', in J. Day, R. P. Gordon and H. G. M. Williamson (eds), *Wisdom in Ancient Israel: Studies in Honour of J. A. Emerton* (Cambridge, 1995), 133–41.

—'Isaiah xi 11-16 and the Redaction of Isaiah i–xii', in J. A. Emerton (ed.), *Congress Volume: Paris, 1992* (VTSup 61; Leiden, 1995), 343–57.

—'Relocating Isaiah 1:2-9', in Broyles and Evans (eds), *Writing and Reading*, 263–77.

—'Isaiah 6,13 and 1,29-31', in van Ruiten and Vervenne (eds), *Studies in the Book of Isaiah*, 119–28.

—*Variations on a Theme: King, Messiah and Servant in the Book of Isaiah* (Carlisle, 1998).

—'"From One Degree of Glory to Another": Themes and Theology in Isaiah', in E. Ball (ed.), *In Search of True Wisdom: Essays in Old Testament Interpretation in Honour of Ronald E. Clements* (JSOTSup 300; Sheffield, 1999), 174–95.

—'Isaiah and the Holy One of Israel', in A. Rapoport-Albert and G. Greenberg (eds), *Biblical Hebrew, Biblical Texts: Essays in Memory of Michael P. Weitzman* (JSOTSup 333; London, 2001), 22–38.

—'Biblical Criticism and Hermeneutics in Isaiah 1.10-17', in C. Bultmann, W. Dietrich and C. Levin (eds), *Vergegenwärtigung des Alten Testaments: Beiträge zur biblischen Hermeneutik. Festschrift für Rudolf Smend zum 70. Geburtstag* (Göttingen, 2002), 82–96.

—'Isaiah 1 and the Covenant Lawsuit', in A. D. H. Mayes and R. B. Salters (eds), *Covenant as Context: Essays in Honour of E. W. Nicholson* (Oxford, 2003), 393–406.

—'Judgment and Hope in Isaiah 1.21-26', in J. C. Exum and H. G. M. Williamson (eds), *Reading from Right to Left: Essays on the Hebrew Bible in Honour of David J.A. Clines* (JSOTSup 373; London, 2003), 423–34.

—'The Formation of Isaiah 2.6-22', in C. McCarthy and J. F. Healey (eds), *Biblical and Near Eastern Studies: Studies in Honour of Kevin J. Cathcart* (JSOTSup 375; London, 2004), 57–67.

—'Isaiah, Micah and Qumran', in G. A. Khan (ed.), *Semitic Studies in Honour of Edward Ullendorff* (Studies in Semitic Languages and Literatures 47; Leiden, 2005), 203–11.

—'A Productive Textual Error in Isaiah 2.18-19', in the *Festschrift* for N. Na'aman (forthcoming).

Willis, J. T., 'The Genre of Isaiah 5:1-7', *JBL* 96 (1977), 337–62.

—'On the Interpretation of Isaiah 1:18', *JSOT* 25 (1983), 35–54.

—'The First Pericope in the Book of Isaiah', *VT* 34 (1984), 63–77.

—'An Important Passage for Determining the Historical Setting of a Prophetic Oracle—Isaiah 1.7-8', *StTh* 39 (1985), 151–69.

—'Lament Reversed—Isaiah 1,21 ff.', *ZAW* 98 (1986), 236–48.

—'Isaiah 2:2-5 and the Psalms of Zion', in Broyles and Evans (eds), *Writing and Reading*, 295–316.

Wolff, H. W., *Dodekapropheton 4: Micha* (BKAT 14/4; Neukirchen–Vluyn, 1982); ET, *Micah: A Commentary* (Minneapolis, 1990).

Würthwein, E., 'Kultpolemik oder Kultbescheid? Beobachtungen zu dem Thema "Prophetie und Kult"', in E. Würthwein and O. Kaiser (eds), *Tradition und Situation: Studien zur alttestamentlichen Prophetie Artur Weiser zum 70. Geburtstag am 18.11.1963 dargebracht von Kollegen, Freunden und Schülern* (Göttingen, 1963), 115–31 (repr. *Wort und Existenz*, 144–60).

—*Wort und Existenz: Studien zum Alten Testament* (Göttingen, 1970).

Yee, G. A., 'A Form-Critical Study of Isaiah 5:1-7 as a Song and a Juridical Parable', *CBQ* 43 (1981), 30–40.

Yeo Khiok-Khng, 'Isaiah 5:2-7 and 27:2-6: Let's Hear the Whole Song of Rejection and Restoration', *Jian Dao* 3 (1995), 77–94.

**Young, E. J., *The Book of Isaiah: The English Text, with Introduction, Exposition, and Notes* (NICOT; 3 vols; Grand Rapids, 1965).

Zapff, B. M., *Redaktionsgeschichtliche Studien zum Michabuch im Kontext des Dodekapropheton* (BZAW 256; Berlin and New York, 1997).

Zeron, A., 'Das Wort *niqpā*, zum Sturz der Zionstöchter (Is. iii 24)', *VT* 31 (1981), 95–97.

*Ziegler, J., *Untersuchungen zur Septuaginta des Buches Isaias* (Alttestamentliche Abhandlungen 12/3; Münster, 1934).

Zohary, M., *Plants of the Bible* (Cambridge, 1982).

Zolli, E., 'Jesaja 5, 30', *TZ* 6 (1950), 231–32.

Zorrell, F., 'Isaiae cohortatio ad poenitentiam (caput 1)', *VD* 6 (1926), 65–79.

EDITIONS CITED

HEBREW TEXT
K. Elliger and W. Rudolph (eds), *Biblia Hebraica Stuttgartensia* (Stuttgart, 1977). In this edition, Isaiah was edited by D. W. Thomas.
M. H. Goshen-Gottstein (ed.), *The Book of Isaiah* (HUBP; Jerusalem, 1995).
D. W. Parry and E. Qimron (eds), *The Great Isaiah Scroll (1QIsaᵃ): A New Edition* (Leiden, 1998).
E. Ulrich *et al.* (eds), *Qumran Cave 4. X. The Prophets* (DJD 15; Oxford, 1997).

GREEK VERSIONS
J. Ziegler (ed.), *Isaias* (5th edn; Göttingen, 1983).

LATIN VERSION (VULGATE)
R. Weber (ed.), *Biblia Sacra iuxta Vulgatam Versionem*, II (2nd edn; Stuttgart, 1975).

SYRIAC VERSION (PESHITTA)
S. P. Brock (ed.), *The Old Testament in Syriac According to the Peshiṭta Version*, III/1: *Isaiah* (Leiden, 1987).

ARAMAIC VERSION (TARGUM)
J. F. Stenning, *The Targum of Isaiah* (Oxford, 1949).
A. Sperber (ed.), *The Bible in Aramaic. III. The Latter Prophets According to Targum Jonathan* (Leiden, 1962).
B. D. Chilton, *The Isaiah Targum: Introduction, Translation, Apparatus and Notes* (The Aramaic Bible 11; Edinburgh, 1987).

EARLY COMMENTARIES
Jerome, *S. Hieronymi Presbyteri Opera. 1/2. Commentariorum in Esaiam Libri i-xi* (Corpus Christianorum, Series Latina; Turnhout, 1963).
Rabbinic commentators: M. Cohen (ed.), *Mikra'ot Gedolot 'Haketer': Isaiah* (Ramat Gan, 1996).
M. Friedländer, *The Commentary of Ibn Ezra on Isaiah* (3 vols; London, 1873–77).

ABBREVIATIONS

α	Aquila
AB	Anchor Bible
ABD	D. N. Freedman (ed.), *The Anchor Bible Dictionary* (6 vols; New York, 1992)
ACEBT	*Amsterdamse Cahiers voor Exegese van de Bijbel en zijn Traditie*
ActOr	*Acta Orientalia*
AfO	*Archiv für Orientforschung*
AHI	G. I. Davies, *Ancient Hebrew Inscriptions: Corpus and Concordance* (2 vols; Cambridge, 1991 and 2004)
AJSL	*American Journal of Semitic Languages and Literature*
AnBib	Analecta Biblica
ANET	J.B. Pritchard (ed.), *Ancient Near Eastern Texts Relating to the Old Testament* (3rd edn; Princeton, 1969)
AOAT	Alter Orient und Altes Testament
ArOr	*Archiv Orientální*
ASTI	*Annual of the Swedish Theological Institute*
ATD	Das Alte Testament Deutsch
AThANT	Abhandlungen zur Theologie des Alten und Neuen Testaments
AThDan	Acta Theologica Danica
AUSS	*Andrews University Seminary Studies*
AV	Authorized Version
BAram	Biblical Aramaic
BASOR	*Bulletin of the American Schools of Oriental Research*
BAT	Die Botschaft des Alten Testaments
BBB	Bonner biblische Beiträge
BDB	F. Brown, S. R. Driver and C. A. Briggs, *A Hebrew and English Lexicon of the Old Testament* (Oxford, 1907)
BeO	*Bibbia e Oriente*
BETL	Bibliotheca Ephemeridum Theologicarum Lovaniensium
BethM	*Beth Miqra*

BEvTh	Beiträge zur evangelischen Theologie
BH	Biblical Hebrew
BHK	R. Kittel (ed.), *Biblia Hebraica* (3rd edn; Stuttgart, 1937)
BHS	W. Rudolph and H. P. Rüger (eds), *Biblia Hebraica Stuttgartensia* (Stuttgart, 1967–77)
BibInt	*Biblical Interpretation*
BibIntS	Biblical Interpretation Series
BibOr	Biblica et Orientalia
BibSac	*Bibliotheca Sacra*
BiOr	*Bibliotheca Orientalis*
BJRL	*Bulletin of the John Rylands University Library of Manchester*
BKAT	Biblischer Kommentar: Altes Testament
BL	H. Bauer and P. Leander, *Historische Grammatik der hebräischen Sprache* (Halle, 1922)
B. Meg.	Babylonian Talmud, *Megillah*
BN	*Biblische Notizen*
BSOAS	*Bulletin of the School of Oriental and African Studies*
B. Sota	Babylonian Talmud, *Sota*
BSt	Biblische Studien
BTB	*Biblical Theology Bulletin*
BTS	Biblisch-Theologische Studien
BWANT	Beiträge zur Wissenschaft vom Alten und Neuen Testament
BZ	*Biblische Zeitschrift*
BZAW	Beihefte zur *Zeitschrift für die alttestamentliche Wissenschaft*
CAD	I. J. Gelb *et al.* (eds), *The Assyrian Dictionary of the Oriental Institute of the University of Chicago* (Chicago, 1956–)
CAT	Commentaire de l'ancien testament
CB	Century Bible
CBQ	*Catholic Biblical Quarterly*
CBQMS	*Catholic Biblical Quarterly*, Monograph Series
CBSC	Cambridge Bible for Schools and Colleges
CD	Damascus Document
CDA	J. Black, A. George and N. Postgate, *A Concise Dictionary of Akkadian* (Wiesbaden, 1999)
ch./chs	chapter/s
ConB	Coniectanea Biblica
CoS	W. W. Hallo and K.L. Younger (eds), *The Context of Scripture* (3 vols; Leiden, 1997–2002)
CR:BS	*Currents in Research: Biblical Studies*
DBS	L. Pirot and A. Robert (eds), *Dictionnaire de la Bible, Supplément* (Paris, 1928–)

DCH	D. J. A. Clines (ed.), *The Dictionary of Classical Hebrew* (Sheffield, 1993–)
DDD	K. van der Toorn, B. Becking and P. W. van der Horst (eds), *Dictionary of Deities and Demons in the Bible* (2nd edn; Leiden and Grand Rapids, 1999)
DJD	Discoveries in the Judean Desert
DNWSI	J. Hoftijzer and K. Jongeling, *Dictionary of the North-West Semitic Inscriptions* (Leiden, 1995)
DSD	*Dead Sea Discoveries*
DUL	G. del Olmo Lete and J. Sanmartín, *A Dictionary of the Ugaritic Language in the Alphabetic Tradition* (2 vols, 2nd edn; Leiden, 2004)
EB	Études bibliques
EHAT	Exegetisches Handbuch zum Alten Testament
EI	*Eretz-Israel*
ET	English translation
ETL	*Ephemerides Theologicae Lovanienses*
EvTh	*Evangelische Theologie*
ExpT	*Expository Times*
FAT	Forschungen zum Alten Testament
FOTL	The Forms of Old Testament Literature
FRLANT	Forschungen zur Religion und Literatur des Alten und Neuen Testaments
FzB	Forschung zur Bibel
GK	*Gesenius' Hebrew Grammar* as edited and enlarged by the late E. Kautzsch, ET, A. E. Cowley (2nd edn; Oxford, 1910 = 28th German edn, 1909)
GN	Geographical name
GNB	Good News Bible
HAL	W. Baumgartner *et al.*, *Hebräisches und Aramäisches Lexikon zum Alten Testament* (5 vols; Leiden, 1967–95)
HAR	*Hebrew Annual Review*
HAT	Handbuch zum Alten Testament
HBS	Herders biblische Studien
HKAT	Handkommentar zum Alten Testament
HR	E. Hatch and H. A. Redpath, *A Concordance to the Septuagint and the Other Greek Versions of the Old Testament (Including the Apocryphal Books)* (3 vols; Oxford, 1897–1906)
HS	*Hebrew Studies*
HSM	Harvard Semitic Monographs
HSS	Harvard Semitic Studies
HThKAT	Herders Theologischer Kommentar zum Alten Testament
HTR	*Harvard Theological Review*

HUBP	The Hebrew University Bible Project
HUCA	*Hebrew Union College Annual*
IB	*Interpreter's Bible*
ICC	International Critical Commentary
IEJ	*Israel Exploration Journal*
IOS	*Israel Oriental Studies*
ISBE	G. W. Bromiley *et al.* (eds), *The International Standard Bible Encyclopedia* (rev. edn; Grand Rapids, 1979)
JANES	*Journal of the Ancient Near Eastern Society*
JAOS	*Journal of the American Oriental Society*
JBL	*Journal of Biblical Literature*
JCS	*Journal of Cuneiform Studies*
JJS	*Journal of Jewish Studies*
JM	P. Joüon and T. Muraoka, *A Grammar of Biblical Hebrew* (Subsidia biblica 14; 2 vols; Rome, 1993)
JNES	*Journal of Near Eastern Studies*
JNSL	*Journal of Northwest Semitic Languages*
JQR	*Jewish Quarterly Review*
JSJ	*Journal for the Study of Judaism*
JSOT	*Journal for the Study of the Old Testament*
JSOTSup	*Journal for the Study of the Old Testament, Supplement Series*
JSPSup	*Journal for the Study of the Pseudepigrapha, Supplement Series*
JSS	*Journal of Semitic Studies*
JTS	*Journal of Theological Studies*
K	Kethibh
KAI	H. Donner and W. Röllig, *Kanaanäische und aramäische Inschriften* (3 vols; 2nd edn; Wiesbaden, 1966–69)
KAT	Kommentar zum Alten Testament
KeHAT	Kurzgefasstes exegetisches Handbuch zum Alten Testament
KHAT	Kurzer Hand-Commentar zum Alten Testament
KTU	M. Dietrich, O Loretz and J. Sanmartín, *Die keilalphabetischen Texte aus Ugarit* (Neukirchen–Vluyn, 1976)
Leš	*Lešonénu*
lit.	literally
LXX	Septuagint
MGWJ	*Monatschrift für Geschichte und Wissenschaft des Judentums*
ms(s)	manuscript(s)
MT	The Masoretic Text
NCB	New Century Bible
NEB	New English Bible
NF	neue Folge

NICOT	New International Commentary on the Old Testament
NIDOTTE	W.A. VanGemeren (ed.), *New International Dictionary of Old Testament Theology & Exegesis* (Carlisle, 1996)
NIV	New International Version
NJPS	New Jewish Publication Society Translation
NRSV	New Revised Standard Version
NS	new series
NSK-AT	Neuer Stuttgarter Kommentar – Altes Testament
NTT	*Norsk Teologisk Tidsskrift*
OBO	Orbis Biblicus et Orientalis
OLZ	*Orientalistische Literaturzeitung*
OTE	*Old Testament Essays*
OTL	Old Testament Library
OTS	*Oudtestamentische Studiën*
OTWSA	*Die Ou-Testamentiese Werkgemeenskap in Suider Afrika*
P	Peshitta
p(p).	page(s)
PEQ	*Palestine Exploration Quarterly*
Pes. de Rab. Kah.	*Pesiqta de Rab Kahana*
PSB	*Princeton Seminary Bulletin*
Q	Qere
1QH	Hymn Scroll from Qumran Cave 1
1QIsa^a	Scroll of Isaiah from Qumran Cave 1
1QS	Manual of Discipline from Qumran Cave 1
3QpIsa	(fragmentary) Commentary on Isaiah from Qumran Cave 3
4QpIsa^{a-e}	Fragments of commentaries on Isaiah from Qumran Cave 4
4QIsa^{a-r}	Fragments of Isaiah manuscripts from Qumran Cave 4
RB	*Revue biblique*
REB	Revised English Bible
RHR	*Revue de l'histoire des religions*
RivB	*Rivista Biblica*
RSV	Revised Standard Version
RV	Revised Version
σ	Symmachus
SB	Sources bibliques
SBLDS	Society of Biblical Literature Dissertation Series
SBLSP	Society of Biblical Literature Seminar Papers
SBOT	Sacred Books of the Old Testament
SBS	Stuttgarter Bibelstudien
SBT	Studies in Biblical Theology
ScrH	*Scripta Hierosolymitana*

SHCANE	Studies in the History and Culture of the Ancient Near East
SJOT	*Scandinavian Journal of the Old Testament*
SJT	*Scottish Journal of Theology*
SOTSMS	Society for Old Testament Study Monograph Series
SSI	J.C.L. Gibson, *Textbook of Syrian Semitic Inscriptions* (3 vols; Oxford, 1971–82)
SSN	Studia Semitica Neerlandica
STDJ	Studies on the Texts of the Desert of Judah
StTh	*Studia theologica*
θ	Theodotion
T	Targum
TA	*Tel Aviv*
TBü	Theologische Bücherei
TDOT	G. J. Botterweck and H. Ringgren (eds), *Theological Dictionary of the Old Testament* (Grand Rapids, 1974–)
THAT	E. Jenni and C. Westermann (eds), *Theologisches Handwörterbuch zum Alten Testament* (2 vols; Munich, 1971–76)
ThSt	Theologische Studien
ThWAT	G. J. Botterweck and H. Ringgren (eds), *Theologisches Wörterbuch zum Alten Testament* (Stuttgart, 1970–)
TLOT	E. Jenni and C. Westermann (eds), *Theological Lexicon of the Old Testament* (3 vols; Peabody, 1997)
TLZ	*Theologische Literaturzeitung*
TQ	*Theologische Quartalschrift*
TTZ	*Trierer Theologische Zeitschrift*
TynB	*Tyndale Bulletin*
TZ	*Theologische Zeitschrift*
UBL	Ugaritisch-biblische Literatur
UBS	United Bible Societies
UCOP	University of Cambridge Oriental Publications
UF	*Ugarit Forschungen*
V	Vulgate
v(v).	verse(s)
VD	*Verbum domini*
VF	*Verkündigung und Forschung*
VT	*Vetus Testamentum*
VTSup	Supplements to *Vetus Testamentum*
WBC	Word Biblical Commentary
WMANT	Wissenschaftliche Monographien zum Alten und Neuen Testament

WO	B.K. Waltke and M. O'Connor, *An Introduction to Biblical Hebrew Syntax* (Winona Lake, Ind., 1990)
ZA	*Zeitschrift für Assyriologie*
ZABR	*Zeitschrift für Altorientalische und Biblische Rechtsgeschichte*
ZAH	*Zeitschrift für Althebräistik*
ZAW	*Zeitschrift für die alttestamentliche Wissenschaft*
ZDMG	*Zeitschrift der deutschen morgenländischen Gesellschaft*
ZDPV	*Zeitschrift des deutschen Palästina-Vereins*
ZKTh	*Zeitschrift für katholische Theologie*
ZS	*Zeitschrift für Semitistik und verwandte Gebiete*
ZTK	*Zeitschrift für Theologie und Kirche*

INTRODUCTION

As this is only the first of a projected three volumes of commentary on Isaiah 1–27, it is obvious that the time has not yet come for an introduction to this part of the book of Isaiah in its entirety. Pending that, however, it may be helpful briefly to introduce the commentary itself. I am aware that it is long for so few chapters, so that some guidance is in order to help readers to consult it profitably.

Each section of the commentary is in four parts. First, I have provided a translation which incorporates the results of my text-critical, philological and poetic analysis. In this, I have aimed for clarity rather than literary finesse. Readers who do not have a facility in Hebrew should find it useful if they want to turn straight to the exegetical part of the commentary and need to compare my rendering on which the commentary is based with a standard English translation.

Second, set in small print, there is a verse-by-verse text-critical and philological commentary, something for which the ICC has always been particularly valued. Here my aim has been first to explain the received Hebrew (Masoretic) text and why it may have been found problematic, second to set out alternative witnesses to the text, whether directly in Hebrew (the Dead Sea Scrolls) or indirectly in the ancient versions, and thirdly to evaluate this evidence with the aims of explaining the diversity of witnesses and of reaching as nearly as possible the form of text that might have existed when the book of Isaiah was completed. On occasions, this involves unattested textual conjecture, and so I have tried to include references to many of those which have been proposed in the past, even if they are now outmoded. The commentary may thus be useful as a work of reference, since it may well be that future evidence will require revision of current decisions on these matters. I am aware of many conjectures that I have not included (mainly because they have had no impact on continuing work), but I hope that I have been reasonably comprehensive with regard to those proposals which have been influential in the past or continue to be favoured by at least some scholars.

Many commentators see the work of the textual critic reaching back further—perhaps even as far as the original writing of the eighth-century prophet—but that seems to me usually to be the task of literary and redaction criticism and so is attended to later in the commentary. I realize that these distinctions are sometimes rather artificial, and I have tried to point out where I have occasionally broken my own rule, but I still think it best to have a clear default position. To relegate that to the time when the received text was stabilized seems to me to be too late for a work of historical-critical scholarship, since we have a considerable body of evidence that reaches behind that time which should not be ignored. Equally, to push back earlier is not only unduly speculative, but, as I have just indicated, it tends to denigrate the work of later editors on the still developing book in an unjustified manner.

In this section of the commentary I have also included some linguistic and philological discussion of words whose meaning is uncertain. There have been many times when I have been uncertain whether to include such material here or in the fourth section, and when in doubt I have included a cross-reference. Generally speaking I have been guided by the consideration whether the discussion is accessible to a non-Hebraist or not and whether the points at issue are strictly linguistic or exegetical (discussion of the latter being reserved for the fourth section).

The third section of the commentary on each passage deals with issues relevant to the passage as a whole. I have sought always to describe its place in the book (or at least its wider context in that part of the book), its poetic shape, its form or genre (where relevant), and the history of its composition (including a discussion of its date). The work of source and redaction criticism inevitably includes informed speculation and hypothesis (more so than is recognized in many commentaries), so that I have tried to indicate clearly which parts of the analysis are more or less certain. In framing my own suggestions on these matters, I have been generous in including discussion of the work of others, but no one familiar with the literature on Isaiah will expect to find full and comprehensive coverage; the days when that was possible have long since passed.

The final section is exegetical in the traditional manner, based of course on the decisions reached in the earlier sections but accessible to those who may not be able to grapple with the complexities of the Hebrew text itself. Again, it is easy to get carried away in this work and to write extended treatments of subjects that are only suggested by the text. My rule of thumb all along has been to include only such material as will contribute directly to an understanding of the text of Isaiah.

The scheme of references to secondary literature is explained at the start of the bibliography. The bibliography itself does not include every work cited, but it does include all those cited that are directly concerned with Isaiah as well as some others which are mentioned repeatedly; the remainder are cited in full where they appear in the text. I have not extended the bibliography to other works on Isaiah which I have not cited, so that it should not be regarded as in any way comprehensive.

For those who require the sort of introduction to Isaiah or to the first part of it which is not provided here, I cannot do better than refer to the introductory guide by my colleague John Barton, *Isaiah 1–39*. A recent survey of current research is provided by Höffken, *Jesaja*, while for the history of interpretation one may consult Sawyer, *Fifth Gospel*, and Childs, *Struggle*.

My own approach to some of the major issues of composition and interpretation relating to the book as a whole may be found respectively in

Book and *Variations*. Some further reflections on the wider book are also inevitably included in the discussion of certain key passages in the commentary, such as 1.1, 2.1, 4.2-6, 5.1-7, 5.8 and 5.25-30. Briefly, my understanding is as follows.

Chapter 1 functions now as an introduction to the book as a whole. Though it includes material of different dates, including a good deal from Isaiah himself, it has been assembled and edited as a unity at a late stage in the development of the book.

In an earlier and significant form of the book, most of chs 2–5 comprised the first major section (hence the justification for including chs 1–5 in this volume). It was followed by chs 6–12 as a second major panel; before the final hymn of praise in ch. 12, the second half of ch. 11 has close points of comparison with 5.25-30. The atmosphere in this second panel is generally positive (or else previous statements of judgment are set in a salvific context). The first section, chs 2–5, on the other hand, is largely concerned with announcing and justifying judgment, though not before a vision is presented in 2.2-4 which governs much of the remainder of the book; from that, 2.5-6 effects the transition to judgment on those of the people of God who ought to implement the vision but are in no position to do so. This lengthy section concludes with a passage, 5.25-29/30, which was moved to its present position and adapted to bring the announcement of judgment to a climax.

Isaiah 4.2-6 clearly interrupts this section. It is a late expression of future hope which in the final form of the book makes a separate section of chs 2–4. This is one of those cases where the results of synchronic and diachronic analysis do not easily mesh. Nevertheless, it is the earlier redaction which seems to have had the greater impact on the overall shape of the book, and the present volume reflects that by the way that it treats the whole of chs 1–5.

COMMENTARY ON ISAIAH 1–5

EXHORTATION TO REPENT
(Chapter 1)

The first chapter of Isaiah raises most of the introductory questions which a critical commentary on many parts of the book must face. These include: determination of the extent of the passage; the relationship between and the arrangement of the shortest units in the passage; the literary genre of each unit in isolation and in possible combination with other units; the authenticity (i.e. Isaianic authorship) of each unit; the identification of the historical background of the authentic units; the date and setting of later units; the redactional stages in the development of the passage, their purpose, date and association with redactional activity elsewhere in the book; and the purpose of the passage in the book as a whole.

In many commentaries, the approach has been to start from what is historically earliest, that is to say the material relating to Isaiah himself, and then to treat the later material as merely a series of 'additions' of lesser importance. On this view, a fundamental premise is that material is authentic unless it can be proved otherwise, and further that the basic shape of the work, or at least that which one should strive to recover, was determined in early times, either by the prophet or by his immediate successors. Consequently, a major role of commentary writing is historical reconstruction.

More recent scholarship has pointed to difficulties with this approach. In the first place, the text of the finished work is what is presented to us, so that it ought to claim our primary attention. Secondly, and contrary to the impression which has often been given, the further back through the history of the text's evolution we press, the more hypothetical our conclusions become. This is particularly the case with Isaiah, where it is agreed that material from a period spanning at least two centuries has been collected. We must therefore be clear about the fact that reconstruction of the eighth-century prophet's ministry is fraught with uncertainty. Thirdly, and in development of this point, attention has come increasingly to be paid to the work of the later redactors of the work, and it has become apparent that they did far more than just add material at various places. There is evidence, for instance, that they also rearranged some of the material which they inherited, so that it is often difficult to be sure of the 'original' setting and context even of 'authentic' material. Finally, they used and re-used older material to serve new and contemporary ends, so that the commentator often has to work on two levels—that of the 'original' words in their historical setting and that of the later context in which they have now been placed ('*relecture*').[1]

---

[1] See especially Becker, *Isaias*; Sweeney, *Isaiah 1–4*; Melugin, 'Figurative Speech'; Berges.

These points, which the exegetical sections of this commentary will endeavour to keep in mind and to illuminate, are well exemplified in this opening chapter. Some of the critical problems listed above are best treated in the commentary on the chapter's individual units, but others need to be addressed globally by way of introduction.

The most important such question concerns the extent of the first passage for analysis. Working principally on the basis of what may be ascribed to Isaiah himself and then how far the first unit extends, commentators have arrived at an astonishing variety of conclusions. In his 1984 survey of proposals,[2] Willis lists the following: 1.1–4.6;[3] 1.2–2.5;[4] 1.2-31;[5] 1.2-3 + 21-31;[6] 1.2-17;[7] 1.2-9;[8] 1.2-7;[9] 1.2-6;[10] 1.2-4;[11] 1.2-3.[12] Willis himself favours 1.2-20, a view he shares with Budde and Roberts,[13] among others.

This listing is misleading to the extent that some who isolate only a few verses as the first unit also agree that they may have been incorporated into a larger literary section (note, for instance, how Penna is said to favour both 1.2-9 and 1.2-31). This fact alone is sufficient to show that Willis is operating with two criteria simultaneously—historical and literary—and indeed his own proposal (that 1.2-20 is a single oracle delivered near the end of Isaiah's career) is based on arguments which seem to confuse the two. Even without this reservation, however, it is clear that little certainty can be gained about even the starting point for a commentary along exclusively historical lines.

In the case of Isaiah 1, the results of a redaction-critical and a final-form reading coincide in a manner which inspires greater confidence that this is the better way to start, and to leave more narrowly historical speculations to the comments on the individual units. The presence of a

---

[2] Willis, 'First Pericope'. Some more recent suggestions are surveyed in Deck, 95–99.

[3] Watts, 'Formation'.

[4] Ackroyd, 'Isaiah i–xii'; more recently, see Berges, 50–56.

[5] Alexander; Barnes; Ley, 'Metrische Analyse'; Feldmann; Zorrell, 'Isaiae cohortatio'; B. Gemser, 'The Rîb-* or Controversy-Pattern in Hebrew Mentality', in M. Noth and D. W. Thomas (eds), *Wisdom in Israel and the Ancient Near East, Presented to Professor Harold Henry Rowley* (VTSup 3; Leiden, 1955), 120–37; Rignell, 'Isaiah Chapter 1'; Penna; Mattioli, 'Due Schemi'; R. North, 'Angel-Prophet or Satan-Prophet?', *ZAW* 82 (1970), 31-67.

[6] Niditch, 'The Composition of Isaiah 1'.

[7] Marti; Whitehouse; Box; Wade; Gray; Duhm.

[8] Cheyne; Dillmann; Ruffenach, 'Malitia et Remissio Peccati'; König; Procksch; Fischer; Penna; Eichrodt; Jones, 'Exposition... One to Nine'; Young; Auvray.

[9] Robertson, 'Isaiah Chapter 1'.

[10] P. A. Vaccari, *I Profeti–1 Isaia–Geremia* (Florence, 1952), not available to me.

[11] F. Brown, 'The Measurements of Hebrew Poetry as an Aid to Literary Analysis', *JBL* 9 (1890), 71–106 (82–85).

[12] Bentzen; Slotki; Steinmann; Scott; Fohrer; Wildberger; von Loewenclau, 'Auslegung'; Childs, *Assyrian Crisis*, 21; E. Osswald, 'Zur Abgrenzung alttestamentlicher Predigtperikopen', in M. Weise (ed.), *Wort und Welt: Festschrift für Prof. D. Erich Hertzsch* (Berlin, 1968), 243–50; Claassen, 'Linguistic Arguments'; Holladay; Nielsen, *Yahweh as Prosecutor*; Clements.

[13] Roberts, 'Form, Syntax, and Redaction'.

new heading at 2.1 clearly marks out the whole of ch. 1 as a major section in the book as we now have it. (Against attempts to downplay the importance of 2.1, see the comments *ad loc*.) At the same time, a rigorous redaction-historical analysis of the growth of the book suggests that 2.1 marks the start of the exilic edition of Isaiah, and that ch. 1 was added later.[14] The presence of probably late material in the chapter is thus no argument against its overall unity, nor does this view preclude the conclusion that some, perhaps much, of the chapter may originally have been written by Isaiah himself. The important point for the commentator is that units of different origin have been assembled here for the first time as a redactional unity, and that they must therefore be interpreted in the light of one another and the whole, not in part or in isolation. There never was a part of ch. 1 less than the whole which preceded ch. 2 as an opening of the book in its supposed 'original' form. If, as will be maintained below, there is authentic Isaianic material here, then it will be necessary to speculate from where else in the book it may have been extracted if we wish to recover its possible historical context.[15]

It will be helpful to relate this conclusion to the results of some other more recent studies of the chapter, as this will provide further guidelines for interpretation. First, it shares some points in common with Vermeylen's analysis but finds (paradoxically) that he is not sufficiently rigorous from a redaction-critical viewpoint. Vermeylen (pp. 42–71), agrees that shorter units of varying origin have been assembled here, but he limits this conclusion to vv. 2-20, which he thinks was united into a so-called *rîb*-pattern (see on vv. 2-3 below) by the Deuteronomists of the exilic period. Verses 21-26, 27 and 28-31 are then regarded as a series of subsequent additions (pp. 71–111). In the end, therefore, Vermeylen returns to an historical reading (the difference from the usual being that his history starts in the exile rather than with Isaiah), and it is subject to the same objections as they. Nevertheless, his analysis (if correct) reminds us that some of the smallest units may theoretically already have been joined before they were moved to their new, present position in the book. This possibility will therefore have to be considered below, and if justified it will, of course, add yet a further complication to the task of reconstructing Isaiah's own ministry.

Secondly, the view has sometimes been advanced that Isaiah 1 was consciously assembled to serve as an introduction to the book. The most celebrated example of this approach is that of Fohrer, 'Jesaja 1 als Zusammenfassung', who argued for the chapter as a summary of Isaiah 1–39. Verses 2-26 were an orderly arrangement of Isaianic materials to summarize the prophet's message, and 1.27-31 + 2.2-4 demonstrated a similar process of expansion to that attested elsewhere in the book in order to bring the section to a close on a note of promise. Others, however, have

---

[14] See the summary at 1.1 below; in more detail, Williamson, 'Synchronic and Diachronic', and *Book, passim*.

[15] Barth, 220; Williamson, 'Relocating Isaiah 1:2-9'.

gone further by noting connections between this chapter and 65–66 in order to suggest that it serves as an introduction to the book as a whole.[16]

It is clear that 'introduction' is being used in different ways in these works, and further that there is little agreement about the form of the book that is being introduced. The thoughtful discussion of Carr on the matter is thus to be welcomed.[17] Among other things, he reasonably observes that the chapter fails to introduce a number of themes which are central to the remainder of the book (whether chs 2–39 or the whole of the book) and that its rhetorical standpoint differs sharply from that of chs 65–66: in ch. 1 the reader is confronted with a real choice (e.g. vv. 18-20) which will make a material difference to his or her destiny (vv. 21-31), and it seeks to influence that choice, whereas chs 65–66 present the consequences of a choice which has already been made. On the basis of these observations, Carr concludes that ch. 1 cannot function as an introduction in the sense of a summary, nor can it have been written to serve as a paired *inclusio* with the conclusion of the book. He then further points out that 'though at early stages some redactors seem to have systematically rearranged earlier materials, later redactors did not completely integrate their materials into their overall macrostructural conception... Instead, later editors merely added their texts to the margins of earlier units... No editor intervened deeply enough into the book to make it all conform to an overall conception' (pp. 77–78). These are important observations, which fit well with the redaction-critical conclusions made about the nature of the chapter above. It was added at a late stage in the history of the growth of the book, by which time much of the remainder was already in an authoritative, and hence fixed, form. It thus serves as an introduction to the book in the sense of an appeal to the reader to repent in the light and on the basis of all that is to follow; it prepares the reader's frame of mind at the start of the book rather than anticipating what is to come.

Thirdly, it is just such an interpretation which Sweeney, *Isaiah 1–4*, has advanced in the context of his redaction-critical analysis (see especially pp. 101–33). He argues that elements of varying ages have been welded together here into a coherent structure, which he summarizes as 'an exhortation to the people to choose righteousness'. He sets out the structure as follows:

Exhortation to Repent	1.1-31
I. Superscription	1
II. Exhortation Proper: Trial Genre	2-31
A. Speech of the accuser	2-20
1. Announcement of YHWH's accusation against Israel	2-3
2. Admonition concerning continued wrongdoing	4-9
3. Prophetic Torah on proper service of YHWH	10-17
4. Appeal to begin legal proceeding	18-20

[16] Liebreich, 'Compilation'; Lack, *La symbolique*, 139–41; Sweeney, *Isaiah 1–4*, 21-24. A more complex proposal along similar lines is presented by Tomasino, 'Isaiah 1.1–2.4 and 63–66'.

[17] Carr, 'Reaching for Unity', esp. 71–75. He has developed his argument, with particular attention to the differences between the two passages, in 'Reading Isaiah'.

It is not necessary to agree with Sweeney on every detail to appreciate that his approach, at any rate, is the one towards which our previous discussion has been leading. In the commentary following, questions will be raised about some of the details, including especially the extent to which it is appropriate to speak of a trial genre. In addition, it must be appreciated as an important further principle for interpretation that not every detail in each small unit may be best suited to serve the main purpose for which the redactor has selected it for inclusion. If some of the units were originally written to serve another purpose, we must not expect that the result will be as free flowing a text as if it had all been composed for the present context from scratch.[18] The contribution of the unit to the chapter as a whole, and thus its connections with adjacent units, must be the primary focus for exegesis. If there remain unevennesses, then they may help in the more uncertain attempt to reconstruct the possible earlier use of the material.

Two further preliminary observations about this chapter are in order here. First, as regards the connections which have been observed between this chapter and 65–66, it will emerge that they are not all of equal weight and significance. As will be seen, the most impressive, and hence the only ones which might be thought to rise to the level of significance for a history of composition, are confined to vv. 29-31 and possibly 2-3. For the rest of the chapter, there is nothing which could not be explained as part of the general influence of earlier Isaianic material on the later parts of the Isaianic tradition in general, and to the extent that these are shared or even heightened by 65–66, these may be due to the author(s) of the latter rounding off the work as a whole with a sense of closure.[19] Verses 29-31 (and to some extent 2-3) give a markedly different impression, however, and in this case it may well be that our redactor's hand is itself in evidence, framing his assemblage with conscious reference to the ending of the book which he was thus introducing.

Secondly, the use of catchwords between some of the units which make up the chapter is noteworthy.[20] Here we shall find that sometimes this was part of the basis on which the redactor arranged his material, and sometimes that he has himself intervened more sharply than we might otherwise have supposed in the material which he collected. Naturally, the same conclusion will hold for what commentators concerned only with the work of the eighth-century prophet have called glosses, for they too may have been added as part of the text which has been consciously given to us. The term gloss, then, is appropriate only in the case of additions made after this stage in the arrangement of the chapter had been reached.

---

[18] This may help explain, for instance, the various ways in which speaker and addressee are identified; see the chart in Deck, 93–94, and the commentary below; see too Watts, 'Formation'.

[19] Cf. Beuken, 'Isaiah Chapters lxv–lxvi'.

[20] See especially Fohrer; Sweeney, *Isaiah 1–4*, 120.

TITLE
(1.1)

[1.1]The vision which Isaiah the son of Amoz saw concerning Judah and Jerusalem, in the days of Uzziah, Jotham, Ahaz, (and) Hezekiah, the kings of Judah.

ישעיהו (1QIsaᵃ's erroneous [or Aramaizing?] ישיהו] ישעיהו has been corrected supralinearly; for extra-biblical attestations of the name, see Fowler;[1] *AHI* i. 381–82; *AHI* ii. 169–70): it is uncertain whether this name should be analysed as a nominal or a verbal sentence—'Yahweh is (my?) salvation' (BDB, 'Salvation of Yah', is unlikely) or 'Yahweh has saved'. Arguments from word order are inconclusive, since parallels for both suggestions are attested in sufficient numbers to discount the argument from probability.[2] The verbal root ישע is attested only in the niph'al and hiph'il in Biblical Hebrew, but there are other examples of personal names which use the qal of roots elsewhere attested only in derived forms.[3] The hiph'il is certainly used in some comparable names (e.g. הושע, הושעיה), but other related names are also ambiguous (e.g. ישעי). The vocalization of the name suggests that our uncertainties may be of ancient origin. MT's יְשַׁעְיָהוּ (T יְשַׁעְיָה) indicates a verbal interpretation, but 3QpIsa ישעיה[4] (depending on how this should be vocalized) and LXX Ησαίας may, and such alternative Greek spellings as Ιεσσειά, Ιεσσίας, Ιοίας etc. (cf. HR *Supplement*, 83, 87), and V *Isaias*, seem certainly to, suggest a possible nominal form יֵשַׁעְיָהוּ or more probably יִשְׁעִיָהוּ (for the use of the noun as a divine appellative, cf. Ps. 27.1).

אמוץ (for extra-biblical attestation of the name, cf. *AHI* i. 286; *AHI* ii. 134): this name is usually and reasonably explained as a shortened form of אמציהו, 'Yahweh is strong/mighty' (note also אמצי), with secondary, hypocoristic vocalization (cf. Noth, *Personennamen*, 38 and 190). Since adjectives are regularly formed by *qātôl* vocalization, however, it could also be simply an adjectival name, with reference either to the deity or (in hope) to the child.

על: 1. Theoretically, either 'concerning' or 'against'. At first sight, the same ambiguity is inherent in LXX κατά. In the comparable heading at 2.1, however, LXX renders with the unambiguous περί. It is thus clear that the translator was influenced by the positive nature of 2.2-4 to render 'concerning', and thus that he intended κατά in 1.1 to mean 'against', because of the negative nature of 1.2ff. If the heading is to the whole book (or even to the whole of ch. 1 alone), as argued above, then the more general 'concerning' is clearly the appropriate rendering (cf. Jerome, *super*; he too regards LXX and θ as meaning *contra*, and commends the more neutral *de* [?= περί] of σ). 2. In prose, it is usual (though not invariable) for the preposition to be repeated before each noun (cf. JM §132g). In this case, lack of repetition may be due to 'Judah and Jerusalem', as a stereotyped phrase, being regarded as a single entity.

יהודה: uncertain etymology; for discussion, see Millard and Zobel.[5]

[1] J. D. Fowler, *Theophoric Personal Names in Ancient Hebrew: A Comparative Study* (JSOTSup 49; Sheffield, 1988), 348.

[2] Fowler, 71–72, 84, *contra* M. Noth, *Die israelitischen Personennamen im Rahmen der gemeinsemitischen Namengebung* (BWANT III/10; Stuttgart, 1928), 15–21.

[3] Cf. Delitzsch; Noth, 36.

[4] The ending of the word is lost in 4QIsaᵇ, but the editors argue that it would also have been spelt ישעיה on the basis of the scroll's spelling elsewhere.

[5] A. R. Millard, 'The Meaning of the Name Judah', *ZAW* 86 (1974), 216–18; H.-J. Zobel, *ThWAT* iii. 512–16 = *TDOT* v. 482–84.

ירושלם: since the name is certainly attested in the Amarna Letters as *urusalim* (later Akkadian *ursalimmu*) and is usually thought to occur in the even earlier Egyptian execration texts (where the precise reading is unclear),[6] it is obvious that it is of pre-Israelite origin[7] and that its etymology is therefore not important for our purposes ('foundation of [the god] Shalem' is now the most widely accepted suggestion, displacing the previously proposed 'city of peace'[8]). The Masoretic vocalization is noteworthy, however, in view of the regular 'defective' orthography and the consistent evidence from antiquity that the final syllable was pronounced -*em*; cf. Gk Ιερουσαλημ *vel sim.*, Lat *Hierusalem*, BAram יְרוּשְׁלֶם, and probably the abbreviated BH form שָׁלֵם.[9] The persistence of this tradition makes it unlikely that the dual form arose as a consequence of the spread of the city on to the western hill (already pre-exilic) or that it reflects the upper and lower city. It is more probably a late and artificial backformation by analogy with בֵּית/בַּיִת etc.; cf. (perhaps) שָׁמַיִם*/שָׁמֶם.

בִּימֵי: not repeated before each of the following names for stylistic reasons; cf. JM §129*b*. LXX correctly, but unnecessarily, specifies with ἐν βασιλείᾳ. The addition of a supralinear י in 1QIsaᵃ to read בְּיוֹמֵי reflects Aramaic influence; cf. Kutscher, 24 and 204. The same correction was probably also intended at 38.10, though the additional letter was incorrectly placed.

עֻזִּיָּהוּ: 'Yahweh is my strength' (for extra-biblical attestation of the name, see *AHI* i. 457). 1QIsaᵃ spells עזיה (and at 6.1; 7.1). Although the use of the shorter ending יה became more frequent in names in later times, its pre-exilic use is also well attested in epigraphic sources, so that variations of this sort should be ascribed primarily to scribal preference or inconsistency and not be used to draw chronological conclusions.[10] For this particular king in the Old Testament, the long form occurs eighteen times and the short form five times. He was also known as עֲזַרְיָהוּ. This name, though not this king (as was once thought), is attested in Akkadian as Azri-Iāu.[11]

יוֹתָם: 'Yahweh is perfect' or 'Yahweh has shown himself upright'; cf. יהותם at *AHI* ii. 166. It is disputed whether extra-biblical יתם (*AHI* i. 382; *AHI* ii. 170) is the same name.[12]

אָחָז (for extra-biblical attestation of the name, see *AHI* i. 273; ii. 128–29; it would appear that seal 100.141 refers to this very king): an abbreviated form of יהואחז, 'Yahweh has grasped (by the hand)'; in Akkadian, he appears as *Iaū-ḫazi*[13] (which incidentally confirms that his full name was not the alternative אחזיהו[14]).

[6] This is denied, however, by N. Na'aman, 'Canaanite Jerusalem and its Central Hill Country Neighbours in the Second Millennium B.C.E.', *UF* 24 (1972), 275–91.

[7] Cf. J. J. Schmitt, 'Pre-Israelite Jerusalem', in C. D. Evans *et al.*, *Scripture in Context: Essays on the Comparative Method* (Pittsburgh, 1980), 101–21.

[8] See the discussion by W. S. LaSor, *ISBE* II (rev. edn), 999–1000, who shows that the issue remains uncertain; F. Stolz, *Strukturen und Figuren im Kult von Jerusalem: Studien zur altorientalischen, vor- und frühisraelitischen Religion* (BZAW 118; Berlin, 1970), 181–218.

[9] Cf. J. A. Emerton, 'The Site of Salem', in J. A. Emerton (ed.), *Studies in the Pentateuch* (VTSup 41; Leiden, 1990), 45–71.

[10] See also Deck, 90–92, *contra* Freedman, 'Headings'.

[11] Cf. K. Radner (ed.), *The Prosopography of the Neo-Assyrian Empire*, 1/1.*A* (Helsinki, 1998), 240, and for discussion, see S. Dalley, 'Yahweh in Hamath in the 8th Century BC: Cuneiform Material and Historical Deductions', *VT* 40 (1990), 21–32.

[12] In the case of one seal, at least, it has been suggested that the script is Edomite and that ליתם might therefore mean 'Belonging to the orphan'; cf. J. Naveh and S. Shaked, 'A Recently Published Aramaic Papyrus', *JAOS* 91 (1971), 379–82 (381 n. 3); P. Bordreuil and A. Lemaire, *Semitica* 29 (1979), 75 (no. 7); M. Cogan and H. Tadmor, *II Kings: A New Translation with Introduction and Commentary* (AB 11; New York, 1988), 181.

[13] Cf. H. D. Baker (ed.), *The Prosopography of the Neo-Assyrian Empire*, 2/1: Ḫ-K (Helsinki, 2000), 497.

[14] For the latter, see G. Barkay and A. G. Vaughn, 'New Readings of Hezekian Official Seal Impressions', *BASOR* 304 (1996), 29–54 (nos. 15–17).

יְחִזְקִיָהוּ: 1. This name also occurs frequently with the spellings חִזְקִיָּה, חִזְקִיָּהוּ, and יְחִזְקִיָּה.[15] For the long and short endings, see under עֻזִּיָּהוּ above. The initial *yôd* usually being considered secondary, the vocalization of the first syllable with *ḥîreq* has often led to the name being analysed as a nominal sentence, 'Yahweh is my strength' (the *qitl* form of חֹזֶק is attested at Ps. 18.2; it is otherwise *qotl*). Akkadian transcriptions of the name, however, consistently 'agree in vocalizing the first part of the name *ḥa-za-qi*'.[16] This points firmly to an analysis of the first element as a qal perfect with *ḥireq compaginis*. Kutscher, 104–6, followed by Layton, 124, has explained the development of the Masoretic vocalization on the basis of the recognized processes of Hebrew phonology as *ḥazaqîyāh(û)>*ḥazqîyāh(û)>ḥizqîyāh(û)*. This analysis may also help explain the secondary development of the spelling with prefixed *yôd*, as though from an imperfect. 2. It is noteworthy that there is no conjunction before this last name in the list, a feature shared by Hos. 1.1 and Mic. 1.1, 'as though they were copied directly from an official list or docket' (Freedman, 'Headings', 12). Clearly, therefore, the initial *yôd* should not be emended to *wāw*. 1QIsaᵃ has חִזְקִיָּה, and this has subsequently been corrected by the addition of a *yôd*. Since this scroll distinguishes *wāw* and *yôd* rather clearly, this should not be adduced as evidence for an emendation. 3QpIsa has a conjunction before Jotham and Hezekiah,[17] and in LXX and P we find three conjunctions; Brooke, 'Qumran Pesharim', 312, concludes that this shows the tendency for texts to be expanded over time, and that MT should therefore be preferred.

To what is this verse a heading? The answers of the commentators depend upon the prior positions they take regarding the composition of the book of Isaiah in part or in whole. For many in the past, it has been a given starting point that Isaiah 1–39 is a work completely separate from 40–66, and they thus assume that this verse introduces only 1–39, a conclusion bolstered by the fact that none of the kings mentioned is referred to after ch. 39 (e.g. Orelli; cf. Wildberger). Still working within this same framework, others note that there is a comparable form of heading at 13.1, introducing a discrete literary section, the oracles against the nations, and so conclude that this verse introduces chs 1–12 (e.g. Marti; Gray; Skinner) or even (for the first half of the verse only), in view of 2.1, ch. 1 alone (e.g. Vitringa; Lowth; Condamin; Mowinckel, 'Komposition', 273–75).

More recently, much attention has been focussed upon the connections between the various parts of the book as a whole and upon the fact that parts of 1–39 were almost certainly added later than the time of composition of parts, at least, of 40–66. In addition, a considerable number of correspondences has been observed between chs 1 and 65–66, as was mentioned above. Taken together, these points have reintroduced the possibility that the verse introduces the whole of Isaiah (e.g. Blenkinsopp; Berges; Childs), a conclusion welcome, of course, both to conservative

---

[15] For extra-biblical occurrences, see *AHI* i. 348 and 372; ii. 157 and 166; add F. M. Cross, 'A Bulla of Hezekiah, King of Judah', in P. H. Williams and T. Hiebert (eds), *Realia Dei: Essays in Archaeology and Biblical Interpretation in Honor of Edward F. Campbell, Jr. at his Retirement* (Atlanta, 1999), 62–66.

[16] S. C. Layton, *Archaic Features of Canaanite Personal Names in the Hebrew Bible* (HSM 47; Atlanta, 1990), 123, with references, to which add K. L. Younger, 'Yahweh at Ashkelon and Calaḥ? Yahwistic Names in Neo-Assyrian', *VT* 52 (2002), 207–18, and Baker, *Prosopography*, 2/1, 469.

[17] 4QIsaᵃ, ᵇ, ʲ all include parts of v. 1, but unfortunately not the precise material relevant to this point.

commentators and to those who operate within a non-historical and exclusively literary framework.[18]

The understanding of the development of the book adopted here—one which affirms the necessity of tracing the literary history of the work, but which sees the inclusion of the second half of the work as an integral part of this process—supports this second position. Inevitably in the case of a work which has had such a long and complex literary history, the earliest stages, associated with the historical prophet Isaiah of Jerusalem, will be the most hypothetical; all the evidence at our disposal indicates not only that later material has been added to his own, but also that subsequent editors have sometimes rearranged parts of his work, so detaching the sayings from their original contexts in order to enable them to serve the fresh purposes of these later tradents. Only tentatively, therefore, can it be suggested that the form of heading used in the earliest form of the book was that now found at 6.1 and 14.28, where it will be proposed that these headings introduced the two major historical periods of Isaiah's ministry, under Ahaz and Hezekiah respectively. The closely related forms of heading at 2.1 and 13.1 introduce major sections in the work as it was developed (with the inclusion of the basic material in 40–55) at the end of the exilic period, possibly even by Deutero-Isaiah himself (cf. Williamson, *Book*, 162–64). Chapter 1, with its heading, must, therefore, have been assembled after this time, and so be close, if not identical, in date to the emergence of the book in its final form. With this conclusion its connections with chs 65–66 and its function as an invitation to the book in the sense described in the introduction to this chapter above coheres well. The heading is therefore to be regarded as serving a dual function, introducing both ch. 1 and the book as a whole.[19] The consequences for interpretation are outlined below.

Though not decisive in themselves, the form and wording of the verse tend to support this conclusion. The first half is most closely comparable with 2.1 and 13.1. There, however, the first word in each case (דבר, 'word' and משא, 'oracle') is selected as an appropriate summary description of the material which each heading introduces in the following chapters. In imitating that form of heading, our editor needed to find a more general word in view of the fact that he was introducing the whole. He therefore took his cue from the verb חזה, 'saw', in both other cases and so entitled the work חזון, 'vision', a word which was appropriate on other grounds as well (see the commentary below).

Secondly, although the wording of the whole of the rest of the first half of the verse is identical with 2.1, he has changed the order slightly in order

---

[18] See especially Webb, 'Zion in Transformation'; contrast, however, Conrad, *Reading Isaiah*, 117–19.

[19] Cf. Sweeney, *Isaiah 1–4*, 28–32. Goldingay, 'Isaiah i 1 and ii 1', has argued that the use of חזון means that the heading cannot cover more than ch. 1 alone. From this, he develops the suggestion that 2.1 is a colophon to ch. 1, not an introduction to the following section. For discussion, see the comments on חזון below and the discussion in the commentary at 2.1.

to bring the name of the prophet forward into a slightly more prominent position.

Thirdly, by adding the list of kings in the second half of the verse, he has conformed his heading to the form adopted in the headings to a number of the other prophetic books (on which see, for instance, Wildberger). Once the view is accepted that this heading is a part of the latest redaction of the book of Isaiah, the evidence for the suggestion that this list is itself a later addition disappears. That suggestion depends upon the notion that this heading was once attached to only a part of the book at a much earlier stage of its development (e.g. Scott), or even that it goes back to Isaiah himself (Feldmann; Procksch). Apart from the inherent probability that, as in the case of the other prophets, these third person headings are the work of later editors, there is further evidence in this particular case that the verse must have been composed considerably later than the eighth century; see on 'vision' and 'Judah and Jerusalem' below.

The inclusion of Jotham's name, despite the fact that no saying of Isaiah is explicitly dated to his reign (he is mentioned only in connection with Ahaz in 7.1), suggests that this part of the verse has been influenced by factors external to the book itself. In the case of the headings to the prophetic books in general, several possible such influences have been suggested.[20] The proposal that they are to be compared with Akkadian colophons[21] is to be rejected in all but the most general terms, for colophons 'most frequently provide data concerning the scribe who copied [the text] and its sponsor or owner, less frequently facts concerning the date, contents, or title of the work, and almost never present the name of an author'.[22] In addition, they stand at the end, not the beginning, of the work. The closest formal extra-biblical parallels come from the superscriptions of Egyptian wisdom texts, such as Amenemhet (*CoS* i. 36), Any (*CoS* i. 46) and Ptah-Hotep;[23] cf. Tucker, 'Prophetic Superscriptions'; Wildberger. Although direct influence is improbable, these superscriptions may point legitimately to an element of scribal concern in the framing of the headings.

For more precise insights into the identity and concerns of these 'scribes', however, it is necessary to look within the biblical corpus. The most widely canvassed opinion is that in several cases, at least, these headings have been framed as part of a wider 'Deuteronomistic' editing of the prophetic books concerned.[24] It is noteworthy, for instance, that in the

[20] See the survey in Tucker, 'Prophetic Superscriptions'.

[21] So H. M. I. Gevaryahu, 'Biblical Colophons: A Source for the "Biography" of Authors, Texts and Books', in *Congress Volume: Edinburgh, 1974* (VTSup 28; Leiden, 1975), 42–59.

[22] Tucker, 'Prophetic Superscriptions', 66; he refers further to W. G. Lambert, 'Ancestors, Authors and Canonicity', *JCS* 11 (1957), 1–14.

[23] Cf. M. Lichtheim, *Ancient Egyptian Literature*. I. *The Old and Middle Kingdoms* (Berkeley, 1973), 62.

[24] See, for instance, the ground-breaking study of W. H. Schmidt, 'Die deuteronomistische Redaktion des Amosbuches', *ZAW* 77 (1965), 168–93; also Tucker, 'Prophetic Superscriptions', 69. There is much debate at present about the extent of Deuteronomistic editing in the prophets generally which cannot be discussed here; for some representative

cases of Hos. 1.1 and Amos 1.1 the kings are listed in a synchronic manner and with Judah placed first in a style reminiscent of the books of Kings. It has been claimed, furthermore, that the phrase 'The word of Lord which came to...' (e.g. Hos. 1.1; Joel 1.1; Mic. 1.1; Zeph. 1.1; a similar phrase is frequent in Jeremiah and Ezekiel, though not in the headings) is Deuteronomistic.[25] The suggestion that some of the prophetic books (including their headings) have undergone Deuteronomistic redaction is plausible, but this is not the case with Isaiah (despite suggestions to the contrary), as will be seen repeatedly below.[26] Thus, if Isa. 1.1 shows affinities with the headings to these other books (in addition to the general similarities in phrasing, note the absence of the conjunction between the names of any of the kings), the explanation must be that it shows direct literary influence from them rather than from a common traditio-historical circle (*contra* Vermeylen, 41).

Freedman, 'Headings', has advanced the alternative suggestion that the similarities between the headings of Hosea, Amos, Isaiah, and Micah are such that they can be best explained as due to a common eighth-century editing of these works in distinction from the editing of the later seventh- and sixth-century prophets. This is unlikely, however (cf. Deck, 88–92). We have already noted that the dominant influence on the first half of our verse is Isa. 2.1 and 13.1. Freedman's linguistic arguments are weak (see above), and he takes no account of elements in Isa. 1.1 which are suggestive of a much later date (see below). Furthermore, he fails to point out that the wording of the headings in Hos. 1.1 and Mic. 1.1 is of the distinctive Deuteronomistic style shared especially by Jeremiah, but not by Amos or Isaiah. The various elements in the headings to the prophetic books are shared to varying degrees by the several books in ways which defy any such neat chronological scheme.[27]

Our conclusion must, therefore, be that the editor responsible for Isa. 1.1 has been influenced from a literary point of view by other headings within the book, but also by the forms of heading of other prophetic books. This seems a reasonable conclusion to reach in view of the relatively late date which must be assigned him on other, independent grounds already noted. This suggests awareness of a developing corpus of prophetic literature with which, not unnaturally, he wished Isaiah to be associated. As Tucker reasonably concludes, 'While the superscriptions to the prophetic books do not represent the stage of canonization, they do reveal the decisive turning point when—at least for certain circles in Israel—the spoken prophetic words had become scripture' ('Prophetic Superscriptions', 70).

---

examples of the arguments, see L. S. Schearing and S. L. McKenzie (eds), *Those Elusive Deuteronomists: The Phenomenon of Pan-Deuteronomism* (JSOTSup 268; Sheffield, 1999).

[25] Cf. T. Lescow, 'Redaktionsgeschichtliche Analyse von Micha 1–5', *ZAW* 84 (1972), 46–85 (61–64).

[26] See provisionally Brekelmans, 'Deuteronomistic Influence'.

[27] Diversity within similarity in this regard is stressed by H.-M. Wahl, 'Die Überschriften der Prophetenbücher', *ETL* 70 (1994), 91–104.

The vision: חזון also appears as part of a title to a prophetic book in Obadiah 1 and Nah. 1.1, and its predominant usage, as of other words derived from the same root, relates to prophecy.[28] According to Petersen,[29] חזה, 'seer', is not to be distinguished from נביא, 'prophet', in terms of role, since both functioned as 'central morality prophets'. Rather, during the period of the divided monarchy the former title was the preferred Judean term, and reflects the prophet's legitimation as a herald of the divine council, while the latter term was Israelite, where the prophet was regarded predominantly as a covenant spokesman. In a general sense, therefore, חזון seems to be appropriate in association with Isaiah, and in the only textually clear passage which can with confidence be ascribed to Isaiah where חזים, 'seers', is used, he refers to them in a positive sense (30.10); it is not impossible that he would have allowed himself to be described as a חזה (cf. Fuhs, *Sehen und Schauen*, 211–18).

It is noteworthy that this verb is not used of Isaiah's presence in the divine council of ch. 6 (v. 1 uses rather ראה), and that in 2.1 and 13.1 'word' and 'oracle' stand as object. Elsewhere too, both verb and noun are most closely associated with a word from God (e.g. Gen. 15.1; 1 Sam. 3.1; 2 Sam. 7.17; Jer. 23.16; Hos. 12.11; Ps. 89.20), so that the word is used predominantly with the content of the revelation, not its mode, in mind.[30] Not surprisingly, this was later extended to cover the written record of the prophetic word (so explicitly at Hab. 2.2, and by clear implication at Obad. 1 and Nah. 1.1; note too the related חזות הכל at 29.11, with reference to an apparently extended corpus of written material, presumably the book of Isaiah—הספר החתום—in the form in which it existed at a relatively late stage in its development). Given the use of the verb at 2.1 and 13.1, the cognate noun thus suggested itself to our editor as an appropriately general word to entitle the very varied material which follows both in ch. 1 and in the book as a whole. (T already interprets the word as 'prophecy'.)

Goldingay, 'Isaiah i 1 and ii 1', has objected to this line of interpretation by arguing that there is no clear evidence elsewhere to justify stretching the sense of חזון 'to mean anything other than a single vision' (p. 329). He is probably right to maintain against Wildberger[31] that 1 Sam. 3.1 and Hos. 12.11 do not justify the suggestion that חזון is a collective, but it does not follow from this, conversely, that it could not be used to cover

[28] Cf. A. Jepsen, *ThWAT* ii. 822–35 = *TDOT* iv. 280–90; Fuhs, *Sehen und Schauen*, 227–37; E. Ben Zvi, *A Historical-Critical Study of the Book of Obadiah* (BZAW 242; Berlin, 1996), 11–13. For some broader reflections, triggered by the juxtaposition of the imagery of 'seeing' here and of 'hearing' in the next verse, see Landy, 'Vision and Voice'.

[29] D. L. Petersen, *The Roles of Israel's Prophets* (JSOTSup 17; Sheffield, 1981).

[30] On the basis of passages where the latter is described, Jepsen concludes that it was received 'usually at night during a (deep) sleep and sometimes associated with emotional agitation'; this should not, however, necessarily be extended to occurrences of the root where no attendant description is included.

[31] Much earlier, Ehrlich had also proposed that חזון represents a collective term, whereas חזיון refers to only a single vision.

more than the content of a single revelatory experience. Indeed, Goldingay
effectively concedes this point when he agrees that ch. 1 'summarizes
much of Isaiah's message as a whole and covers the whole time-frame of
his ministry'. On the other hand, neither Judah nor Jerusalem nor any of
the kings listed in the rest of the verse are explicitly mentioned anywhere
else in ch. 1, so that it is difficult to see how the verse could serve as an
introduction to ch. 1 without there being at the least some allusion to the
remainder of the book where these words and phrases come to explicit
expression. More than this, however, it is clear that even within ch. 1 there
is a collection of material of diverse origin, so that although it has been
carefully welded together as a literary unity it nevertheless itself represents more than 'a single purported revelation issuing from the experience
of seeing something with the mind's eye which could not be seen by the
physical eye' (p. 326). There seems to be no difference in principle, only
in scale, of extending this to cover a whole book. Goldingay himself
allows that 'in the case of Nahum, the entire book could also be read as
one vision' (p. 327; note that in fact the title in Nahum refers explicitly to
what follows as a ספר חזון). It is difficult to understand why, over the
course of time, this could not equally have been extended to cover a much
longer book, such as Isaiah, conceived *qua* book as a single revelation
from God. (There are parallels for this in the use elsewhere of דבר and
תורה.) Goldingay's observations thus tell us something valuable about how
the book was perceived by one of its latest editors, and it seems more
profitable to follow that insight than to disallow the steady development in
the use of the term to which the textual evidence seems to point. Finally, it
should be repeated that the choice of word here, when compared with 2.1
and 13.1, was as much determined by the presence of the verb חזה (which
Goldingay agrees 'is used more broadly') than by the consideration that in
earlier times it was more restricted. The use of the English word 'vision'
has itself undergone a not dissimilar semantic extension, especially in
recent times.

Although the concluding phrase of 2 Chron. 32.32 shows that 'the
vision of Isaiah' there cannot refer directly to our book of Isaiah, it is
likely that the Chronicler's wording has been influenced by knowledge of
Isa. 1.1, so making it the earliest external testimony to this title.[32] The
word only ever occurs in the singular, but the Chronicler's usage demonstrates that it may be used to cover more than a single event, as other
passages also most naturally suggest. The use of the singular cannot,
therefore, be used to argue that this title once stood as a heading to ch. 6
and that it was moved to its present position only secondarily, *contra*
Budde, 18–19; Schoors. Nor does the Chronicler's usage support Marti's
suggestion that חזון was coined for prophecy taken together as instruction
for the end time, parallel with תורה as instruction for the present.

Of Isaiah: this need no more be construed narrowly as a 'genitive of
authorship' (to use WO's terminology, p. 143) than 'the gospel of Jesus

---

[32] It was later probably used also at Sir. 48.22, but the Hebrew text for the relevant
part of this verse has not survived.

Christ' in Mark 1.1. It is probable that the editor was aware that not every word which follows was penned by Isaiah of Jerusalem (not least because he himself may have been responsible for some parts), and equally that he was unconcerned by this fact in framing his title. If the emphasis of חזון is on content rather than mode of reception, it is entirely proper for it to include interpretation and amplification of the original prophet's words. Had Isaiah 40–66 ever been completely separate from 1–39, it would indeed have been difficult to see how this title could legitimately refer to it; but if the Isaianic corpus as a whole has developed with the work of Isaiah of Jerusalem always prominent within it as a source and inspiration, then the title חזון ישעיהו, 'the vision of Isaiah', may be regarded as wholly appropriate.

Nearly everything that we know about the person of the prophet has to be gleaned from the book itself, and this inevitably involves many individual judgments of a literary, historical and exegetical nature. A summary is therefore best reserved until after a reading of the text.

Amoz: only ever referred to as the father of the prophet. There is therefore simply no evidence either to prove or disprove such theories as that he was the brother of King Amaziah (probably due to no more than the fact that both names derive from the same root; cf. *B. Meg.* 10*b*; *B. Sota* 10*b*; *Pes. de Rab. Kah.* 14.3), that he was a prophet (this would be the logic of the argument at *B. Meg.* 15*a*; LXX uses Ἀμώς for both אמוץ and the prophet עמוס, which may have misled some early Christian writers whom Jerome corrects), or that he is Amoz the scribe mentioned on a seal of unknown provenance.[33]

Judah and Jerusalem: again, taken over in this form from 2.1, but obviously appropriate as a heading both to this chapter and to the book, even though, as already noted, neither term is directly mentioned in the remainder of the first chapter. Naturally, it does not exclude the presence of material relating to other nations, since it concentrates on the main emphasis of the work only (Calvin; Auvray); nevertheless, it is likely that these other oracles were read principally in terms of their political relationships with Judah and also, by the time of our editor, as exemplifying theological principles which were applicable to his immediate readership.

Isaiah himself seems always to have preferred the word order 'Jerusalem and Judah' (cf. 3.1, 8; 5.3; 22.21), usually with the inclusion of qualifying terms such as 'men of' or 'inhabitants of'. As has been demonstrated by Jones, 'Traditio', 239–40, the order found in our verse, together with its shortened, stereotyped phraseology, came into use only in the exilic and later periods as virtually a technical term for the exilic/post-exilic community. Its use in the headings at 1.1 and 2.1 is thus a further small pointer to the fact that they derive from the exilic edition of Isaiah at the earliest.

The list of various *kings of Judah* seems accurately to supply the chronological framework for Isaiah's ministry. 6.1 refers to the death of

---

[33] So Anderson, 'Was Isaiah a Scribe?' The seal in question (*AHI* i. 100.074, p. 130) reads אמץ הספר.

Uzziah, but, since it will be seen there that the chapter need not necessarily describe the prophet's initial call, the possibility must be left open that his ministry began earlier in that king's reign. (It is simply not possible specifically to date much of the Isaianic material in the early chapters of the book.) At the other end, *Hezekiah* is not mentioned in what are generally taken to be authentically Isaianic passages, though chs 36–39 are explicitly set in his reign and it is universally agreed that some of Isaiah's oracles are to be dated then. No later Judaean king is mentioned in the book. The editor will thus have derived his information primarily from the book itself, though as already noted he was probably influenced in his precise phrasing of it by comparison with such passages as Hos. 1.1 (where the same four kings are listed in the same form).

The absolute dates of these kings are a matter of unresolved debate. The issue is hardly relevant for the interpretation of Isaiah, so that reference must be made to the many standard discussions of Israelite and Judaean chronology.[34] Hughes's proposed dates for these kings are: Uzziah, 772–?747; Jotham, ?747–737; Ahaz, 737–722; Hezekiah, 722–694.

---

[34] For a survey with full discussion and analysis, see J. Hughes, *Secrets of the Times: Myth and History in Biblical Chronology* (JSOTSup 66; Sheffield, 1990).

FUNDAMENTAL INDICTMENT
(1.2-3)

[2]Hear, O heavens,
   and give ear, O earth,
      for the Lord has spoken:
'I have raised children and brought (them) up,
   but they have rebelled against me.
[3]The ox knows its owner
   and (even) the ass its master's feeding trough,
(but) Israel does not know,
   my people have no understanding (at all).

2. ארץ...שמים: although the vocative is usually definite, this is not an invariable rule, especially in poetry; cf. GK §126*e*. The suggestion that this is due to the fact that 'the heavens' are not present (JM §137*g*) is unimaginative and does not account for the parallel ארץ; besides, the otherwise similar Deut. 32.1 has השמים. 1QIsaᵃ in fact has הארץ (and a few LXX mss add the article here); this is usually dismissed as secondary. It is perhaps worth noting, however, that in several places in MT (including Isa. 13.13; 40.12; 51.6*b*), שמים without the article stands in parallel with הארץ with it (Houtman, *Himmel*, 59), and that at a time when ארץ was pronounced as a monosyllable the article could have been added to retain rhythmic symmetry. In the present passage it would also further the word-initial alliteration. Either reading is therefore possible.

כי יהוה דבר: a stereotypical phrase, especially in Isaiah, so that the perfect should not be emended to the participle דֹּבֵר, *contra* Lowth, Budde, 20; see Meier, *Speaking*, 156–58, though he admits that 'Isa 1:2 is the only occurrence of the phrase marking the introduction of speech'.

גדלתי ורוממתי: copulative *wāw* with two perfects, 'representing different aspects of the same event, not different actions in a sequence of events'; WO, 540; cf. Driver, *Tenses*, §§131–32; Gibson, 103.[1] Note too that the po'lel of ע"ו verbs is a regular substitute for the pi'el of the strong verb; GK §72*m*. The two verbs appear in parallel with the same meaning as here in 23.4 (and note, in view of the next comment, that they follow a separate statement about birth); Gesenius additionally compares Ezek. 31.4.

גדלתי: LXX: ἐγέννησα (contrast σ and θ, ἐξέθρεψα; Jerome and V, *enutrivi*). This equivalence appears not to be attested anywhere else in the Old Testament, where γεννάω most commonly renders a form of ילד. (The pi'el of גדל is rendered very variously in the LXX, including by ἐξέθρεψα at Isa. 23.4; 49.21.) Although God is rarely the subject of ילד (cf. Deut. 32.18; Ps. 2.7), he does so appear (albeit in a somewhat oblique sense) at Isa. 66.9. In view of the frequently noted vocabulary links between Isaiah 1 and 66, this may be significant, especially as the LXX misunderstood 66.9, so that any connection would have to have been at the level of the underlying Hebrew text. It is thus likely that the LXX *Vorlage* read ילדתי or הולדתי, either of which make superficial sense in the context and both of which are orthographically close to MT. A few commentators have preferred this reading to MT (e.g. Lowth, though his further appeal to T is unjustified),[2] but this is improbable. If it were the case, we should expect it to be followed by a *wāw*-consecutive.

---

[1] See too E. J. Revell, 'The Conditioning of Stress Position in *waw* Consecutive Perfect Forms in Biblical Hebrew', *HAR* 9 (1985), 277–300 (279).

[2] See too Paas, *Creation and Judgement*, 363–71.

The LXX (or its *Vorlage*) may have been influenced by 49.21 and 51.18 (where ילד and גדל occur in parallel), whereas 23.4 strongly supports MT.

רוממתי: LXX (ὕψωσα), P and V (*exaltavi*), followed by such as Dillmann, Cheyne, Duhm, Marti, and Feldmann, see here a reference to Israel's exaltation among the nations. (Kimhi and Procksch further took גדלתי this way, but the verb is never used in this sense in Isaiah and certainly could not do so here without the support of רוממתי.) 23.4 again tells against this interpretation, as does the syntax of our verse which, as noted, indicates that the two verbs should be related, if not necessarily synonymous, in sense. Nothing in the context points beyond the analogy of parental care; cf. Gray; Bjørndalen, *Untersuchungen*, 179–83.

Budde, 20, followed by Loretz, 34, conjecturally proposes that בנות ילדים or ילדים should be restored between the conjunction and רוממתי for metrical reasons, because of the 'impossibility' of the copulative *wāw*, and in order to balance the construction in 23.4. The first argument is unnecessary (see below); for the second, see above; the third overlooks the difference in context, for בנים here stands as a collective image for Israel (v. 3). The consequential need to postulate the loss of half a line at the end of the verse (Loretz) is then eliminated. None of these conjectures has any textual support.

3. אבוס: *qᵉṭûl* and *qᵉṭôl* forms with initial א are regularly vocalized with *ṣere* (GK §84ᵃq); they are not modified in the construct singular; see, for instance, 1 Sam. 2.18 (אפוד), 2 Kgs 1.8 (אזור), and Prov. 7.16 (אטון) (*contra* Ehrlich). (Against the possibility of a direct loan from Akkadian, see Mankowski, *Akkadian Loanwords*, 15–16.)

בעליו: the so-called *pluralis excellentiae* or *maiestatis* (GK §124i; JM §136d; WO, 123), used with בעל + suffix to indicate ownership, mastery, as opposed to the singular form which is used for 'husband'. It is not clear whether the supralinear correction of קונהו to קוניהו in 1QIsaᵃ is intended as an extension of this principle or is merely orthographic; cf. GK §93ss.

ידע...התבונן: LXX and some mss of V add the direct object 'me', and T paraphrases to a similar end: דחלתי...למתב לאוריתי. While such interpretations may appear obvious in the immediate context, they are probably too restrictive in the light of the use of these verbs in Isaiah generally (see below), and are certainly not to be followed (*contra* Lowth). In fact, LXX consequentially fails to translate the suffix on עמי; α and θ thus correct the second με to μου.

עמי (so too 4QIsaᵃ): similarly, the addition of the conjunction before this word in 1QIsaᵃ, a number of other Hebrew mss, LXX, P and some mss of V is not only unnecessary but stylistically inferior.

Although some commentators regard these verses as an integral part of a larger section (whether 2-9 or 2-20), it is best to treat them as an independent unit in terms of their present function in the chapter (so, for instance, Wildberger; Childs, *Assyrian Crisis*, 21; Sweeney, *Isaiah 1–4*, 102; Deck, 99–106). Verse 4 begins with הוי, 'Woe!', which is usually, if not invariably, used to start a new section. The addressee changes from heaven and earth (with Israel referred to in the third person) in 2-3 to the people in 4-9; they are mentioned in the third person in v. 4 as objects of הוי, but this quickly shifts to second person address in v. 5. Furthermore, whereas 2-3 is the prophetic citation of a divine speech, 4-9 records the prophet's own address. Finally, there is a shift in tone between the sections from sharp accusation to reproachful rebuke.[3] Metrical considerations have sometimes been adduced to bolster this conclusion, but they should be used with caution, both because of uncertainties about the

---

[3] Cf. Fohrer, 'Jesaja 1 als Zusammenfassung', 254–55 = *Studien*, 151.

subject in general and because of variation within these two sections themselves (see the provisional analyses below) which preclude the drawing of
a sharp line of demarcation.

Even within its brief compass, the passage exhibits many of the best
features of biblical poetry. As Kugel and especially Berlin,[4] among others,
have pointed out, the parallelism in v. 3 is far more subtle than simply the
restatement of the same idea in different words.[5] In the first line, there is a
conscious decline from the ox to the ass which is matched by the movement from the owner as the object of the ox's knowledge/recognition to
the master's crib or feeding trough of the ass's; hence the '(even)' added
in translation—even the dullest of creatures is aware of the source of its
sustenance. This, then, sets the context for the introduction of the people,
who are contrasted with this unflattering comparison, indicated by the
addition of '(but)' in the translation. The contrast is made explicit by the
use of the same verb as governed the first line, ידע, now negated. The second half of the second line, however, also takes the issue further: 'Israel'
is now called 'my people', to indicate a closer relationship, making their
behaviour the more unnatural, startling and so reprehensible. It is thus fully
justified to see the last word of the verse as marking some kind of nadir in
the downward cycle—my people do not even have as much understanding
as the ass, who at least knows which side his bread is buttered; in fact,
they have no understanding 'at all'.

This same emphasis is reinforced at a more formal level by the rhythm
or metre of the passage.

[Even among those who accept that there is some kind of rhythm or
metre in Hebrew poetry, there is little agreement as to how it should be
described or analysed formally. Proposals vary from the counting of major
stresses through syllables to individual letters.[6] Syllable and letter counting are purely heuristic devices to give an indication of line length (no one
supposes that the poets themselves counted them), though a problem with
the former is our uncertainty about various aspects of pronunciation in
biblical times, and both methods are more susceptible to the distortions of
even small textual changes, such as the addition of the definite article, than
the counting of stresses. As will be seen, the latter allows for considerable
flexibility, since small words, for instance, may or need not be counted as
stress bearing. Since it is agreed that Hebrew poetry was not governed by
the strict metrical rules of Greek and Latin,[7] but since at the same time it is
difficult to expunge all impression of rhythm (despite a number of recently
expressed opinions to the contrary), the counting of stresses will be used
in this commentary as the means of conveying the least emphasis on any

---

[4] J. L. Kugel, *The Idea of Biblical Poetry: Parallelism and its History* (New Haven
and London, 1981), 9; Berlin, *Dynamics*, 96–99 and 137.

[5] Contrast the otherwise superficially comparable Jer. 8.7.

[6] For a survey, see Watson, *Classical Hebrew Poetry*, 87–113.

[7] Isaiah 1 was sometimes used in the past as an example to justify stricter metrical
systems than would generally now be accepted; see, for instance, F. Brown, 'The Measurements of Hebrew Poetry as an Aid to Literary Analysis', *JBL* 9 (1890), 71–106; Ley,
'Metrische Analyse'.

formalized metrical pattern. Gerard Manley Hopkins' 'sprung rhythm' suggests itself as a distant analogy (and we know from his own writing that this was a very conscious style). It is important to add that rhythm did not operate in isolation in biblical poetry. It is one element to be considered along with parallelism and various syntactical features which in combination contribute to the nature of poetry. As is well known, many lines do not display parallelism at all, but may yet be rhythmically balanced. Similarly, irregularity of metre may be compensated for by stricter parallelism or tighter poetic syntax. All these features must be considered together, so that emendation on the basis of metre alone will rarely be convincing.[8]]

Verse 2*b* has three full stresses in its first half, which straightforwardly sets out God's care for his people. The second half too may be analysed as three stresses (cf. König), but two of the three words are short, so that reading is slowed down. The result is that a certain emphasis falls on the second half and space is created to consider its startling announcement. This in turn is syntactically reinforced by the emphatic והם with which it starts (cf. Driver, *Tenses*, 201). Similarly, in v. 3*b* the presence of the repeated short negative particle makes a 3 + 3 stress reading of this line more ponderous than in the case of 3*a* with its complement of words of fuller length. Thus in both verses the external form is well used to serve the total effect the poet wished to convey.

Verse 2*a* is set off in content from what follows as being the introductory summons to attend to the divine speech. Appropriately, it takes a slightly different and more staccato rhythm of 2 + 2 + 2. Furthermore, although there is an obvious parallelism between the first two phrases, they achieve their effect principally by the use of repeated sound patterns (emphatic in שמעו שמים, somewhat less so in האזיני ארץ, though it is not impossible that הארץ should be read, as noted above; ארץ may, of course, have been pronounced *ars* at that time). An attempt to reflect this accounts for the choice of words in the translation.[9] More speculatively, it is also possible that the poet has tied 2*b*-3 together by his choice of the less common verbal form התבוננן, which Alter, *Art*, 144–45, has suggested may flaunt 'a false but poetically apt etymology of *banim*, "sons," so that [the line] contains a shadow meaning of "My people did not act as sons"', thus picking up on the first word of 2*b*, which itself is emphasized as being an object preceding its verb.

The opening of the passage also plays an important introductory role to the longer 'poem' which the redactor has constructed out of the various units which make up the present chapter. כי יהוה דבר is echoed in the slightly fuller speech formula at the end of v. 20, the opening two imperatives recur at v. 10 (where significantly the vocatives are replaced by the people of Sodom and Gomorrah, in clear association with v. 9), and בנים and עם help in particular to link this section with the one immediately

[8] See further R. Alter, *The Art of Biblical Poetry* (New York, 1985), 8–9.
[9] Cf. J. Stampfer, 'On Translating Biblical Poetry: Isaiah, Chapters 1 and 2:1-4', *Judaism* 14 (1965), 501–10.

following. It is, of course, difficult to be sure to what extent these echoes are deliberate, but they suggest that within the chapter as a whole vv. 2-20 are some kind of a major unit, and this is supported by considerations of content too (as we shall see). Whether this also points to the hand of the final redactor of the chapter in this introductory line remains to be considered.

The interpretation of this passage has been complicated by the inability of commentators to agree upon its social and conceptual background. Both form-criticism and the overtones of specific items of vocabulary have been used to help solve this issue. Some of the latter will be referred to in the detailed commentary below, but the broader issues need to be addressed here. Two specific proposals have been advanced in this regard, of which the first is the most widely proposed but also the most complex.

(i) Many scholars have suggested that these verses either are or are a part of a 'prophetic lawsuit' (alternatively 'covenant lawsuit' or 'prophetic/covenant *rîb*'). It is agreed that this is a genre which represents God as formally accusing his people and finding them guilty, but there is lack of agreement over whether a more specific background should be sought in the imagery of the lawcourt, or in the cult, or in the particular indictment of covenant infringement (itself often associated with secular ancient Near Eastern treaties).[10]

This theory has become so pervasive in recent interpretations of the chapter that I have devoted a separate study to it: 'Isaiah 1 and the Covenant Lawsuit'. I have sought there to show first that form-critically there is no justification for finding a lawsuit in this chapter[11] and secondly that none of the phraseology or vocabulary to which appeal has sometimes been made is exclusively covenantal.[12] Indeed, in my opinion the preoccupation of several commentators with this idea has distorted the exegesis of the chapter to such an extent that some of its background and major contributions to a theology of the book have been overlooked.[13]

---

[10] For surveys of opinions, see Nielsen, *Yahweh as Prosecutor*, 5–26; Houtman, *Himmel*, 117–22; O'Connell, *Concentricity*, 38–42.

[11] This is apparent not least from the significantly different analyses of the chapter or parts of it in such studies as Mattioli, 'Due Schemi'; J. Harvey, *Le plaidoyer prophétique contre Israël après la rupture de l'alliance: étude d'une formule littéraire de l'Ancien Testament* (Bruges, Paris and Montreal, 1967); Vermeylen, 42–49; Nielsen, *Yahweh as Prosecutor*, 27–29 (developed further in 'Das Bild des Gerichts'); Wildberger; Niditch, 'Composition'; Roberts, 'Form, Syntax, and Redaction'; and Willis, 'First Pericope'.

[12] The theory has also been sharply rejected by Bovati, *Re-Establishing Justice*, 77–79, and 'Le langage juridique'. Some have gone further and questioned whether there ever was such a genre as a 'prophetic lawsuit' at all; see M. de Roche, 'Yahweh's *rîb* against Israel: A Reassessment of the So-Called "Prophetic Lawsuit" in the Preexilic Prophets', *JBL* 102 (1983), 563–74; D. R. Daniels, 'Is there a "Prophetic Lawsuit" Genre?', *ZAW* 99 (1987), 339–60.

[13] See too the forceful comments of L. Perlitt, *Bundestheologie im Alten Testament* (WMANT 36; Neukirchen–Vluyn, 1969), 139; see also the more nuanced discussion in U. Rüterswörden, 'Bundestheologie ohne ברית', *ZABR* 4 (1998), 85–99, who takes strong issue with Becker's attempt (p. 185) to find a thoroughgoing (and later) covenantal background to 1.2-20.

In several of these studies, it is clear that the call to heaven and earth is the basis for the whole theory of a prophetic lawsuit. It is either the only element to which reference is made (as in Wildberger), or it is the sole basis for selecting texts for analysis and comparison in the first place.[14] This is unsatisfactory,[15] however, for both elsewhere in the ancient Near East and in the Old Testament appeal is made to them in a wide variety of contexts, such as exorcisms, prayers and hymns.[16] As Houtman, *Himmel*, 117–37, has rightly stressed, each passage must be studied in its own context first to see whether there are other features which can help determine whether we are dealing with a lawsuit or not. In Jer. 2.12, for instance, the heavens are summoned to register revulsion at Israel's behaviour, not to act as judges or witnesses. Similarly in our passage, it is not God as plaintiff who summons the heavens and the earth (which appears to have been the invariable practice in Israelite trials; cf. Davies, 53–55), but rather the prophet. He would therefore have to be functioning as some kind of court official, but there is no evidence for such a role. There is thus much to be said for seeking to interpret this passage without trying to press every element into the form of either a secular or a covenantal lawsuit. That does not, of course, rule out the possibility that individual elements may be drawn by way of metaphor from that background.

(ii) The second suggested background for this passage is wisdom. Whedbee, in particular, has drawn attention to several features which he thinks show special affinity with the wisdom tradition of ancient Israel.[17] These are: (a) The father–son relationship (see also Wildberger). In many places in Proverbs, the teacher addresses his pupils as his sons and refers to himself as their father, while in the wisdom text Ahiqar the writer several times complains that though he has bestowed great care on his adopted son, Nadan has turned into a seditious rebel against him. (b) The use of an animal parable. Both in Proverbs and elsewhere, 'the sages often had recourse to the animal kingdom to draw analogies for their lessons'. (c) The use of the verbs ידע and התבונן are best understood 'within a wisdom context'.

It must be questioned how far these observations can take us (cf. Davies, 61–62). The father–son metaphor for God's relationship with Israel seems clearly to be that of the natural family, as the verbs which govern 'sons' suggest. Although the wisdom writers made use of analogies drawn from the animal kingdom, there is no evidence to suggest that

---

[14] So explicitly Harvey, *Le plaidoyer*, 31 (see too 85–90 and 106–7), and M. Delcor, 'Les attaches littéraires, l'origine et la signification de l'expression biblique "Prendre à témoin le ciel et la terre"', *VT* 16 (1966), 8–25.

[15] Contrast the more satisfactory approach of Bovati, *Re-Establishing Justice*, who logically begins from passages in which there is an explicit reference to *rîb* (see p. 36). Not surprisingly, he therefore makes little use of Isa. 1 in his detailed reconstruction of the procedure.

[16] See Davies, 43–45, and Whedbee, 31–35, for details; see too the cautionary remarks of J. R. Boston, 'The Wisdom Influence upon the Song of Moses', *JBL* 87 (1968), 198–202.

[17] Whedbee, 26–43; see too Wendel, 44–46.

such use was restricted to them, and as for the verbs in v. 3*b*, they are both far too common for any such conclusion to be drawn from them. As will be seen, their use in the book of Isaiah is of more importance for the interpretation of this passage.

Part of the problem behind this proposal is the rigid distinction which it was once fashionable to draw between wisdom and prophecy as completely separate tradition circles. If that distinction is no longer so clearly drawn, then it becomes possible rather to propose that both the wisdom writers and this passage were drawing, each in their own way, upon a common epistemological basis, thus illuminating some of the fundamental beliefs which were taken for granted in ancient Israel (cf. my essay 'Isaiah and the Wise').

We must now turn from these questions of background to a discussion of the origin and date of the passage. It has been assumed by most commentators that it comes from Isaiah himself on the ground that nothing specifically tells against such a conclusion. The introduction to this chapter above, however, has argued that in view of what can be discerned about the nature of the composition of Isaiah 1 this line of reasoning is not persuasive. If the chapter was assembled as one of the last stages in the growth of the book of Isaiah as a whole, there can be no presupposition that material within it is Isaianic unless proved otherwise.

Positive arguments for Isaianic authorship, when they are advanced, include what is considered to be his characteristic use of parabolic imagery and his comparison of the people to children (29.23, regarded as inauthentic by many, however; 30.1, 9; cf. Sweeney, *Isaiah 1–4*, 125). Neither point is exclusively Isaianic, however.

Sweeney, *Isaiah 1–4*, 126, makes the further point that since the nature of Israel's rebellion is not specified it is likely always to have stood in relation to another text which made the accusation clear, and this he finds in vv. 4-9.[18] He notes, for instance, the catchwords 'sons' and 'people' (not 'offspring') in 2 and 4, the theme of ignorance in 3 and 5, and the rebellion as the cause of the people's suffering in v. 5. Since 4-9 is Isaianic, 2-3 must be so as well. This is an interesting line of argument, but not finally compelling. On the one hand, 2-3 could equally well have been written as a redactional heading precisely to fit in as an introduction to the following verses (cf. Kaiser), while on the other hand if 2-3 were Isaianic, it would have had to be drawn from elsewhere in Isaiah, where its meaning would have been clear (see further below). 'Sons' and 'people' are the only words the two passages have in common, and they could have influenced a later editor to juxtapose two originally separate oracles on the catchword principle.

More recently, the argument from vocabulary has been used to suggest a much later date for these verses.[19] This is equally inconclusive, however, for none of the words or constructions are necessarily late. The fact that

---

[18] Contrast, however, Deck, 106–14.

[19] So, for instance, Vermeylen, and Gosse, 'Isaïe 1'. Vermeylen's arguments in this regard have been examined critically by Bjørndalen, 'Zur Frage der Echtheit', 89–90.

Isaiah does not elsewhere certainly use אבוס or ב פשע, for instance, tells us nothing, for he may have had no need to use them, while to argue that so common a word as שמים 'confirme qu'il s'agit d'un passage tardif' (Gosse, 'Isaïe 1') is clearly absurd. Equally, the use of words in later passages of the book of Isaiah is generally inconclusive. Since there are many examples of the later imitation of earlier parts of the Isaianic corpus, it needs to be established which passage is dependent on which. The present passage does not, however, seem to provide any certain data on which to base a decision whether it was already part of the written deposit of Isaiah of Jerusalem on which other passages may have drawn or *vice versa*.

Comparison of the passage with material outside the book of Isaiah has also led to suggestions of a later date.[20] Vermeylen, for instance, compares Jer. 8.7, which certainly shares several striking features in common with v. 3, but which can tell us nothing about relative dating.[21] More boldly, Kaiser sees broader Deuteronomic influence in this passage.[22] To the extent that Kaiser is generally indebted to Vermeylen's suggestion that 2-20 has been assembled as a *rîb* based on the covenant as known from Deuteronomy, the force of his argument has already been blunted by our previous remarks, and the same applies to his separate reference to the appeal to heaven and earth. More generally, although Israel is sometimes depicted as God's son in Deuteronomy (8.5; 14.1; 32.5-6), there is no evidence in Isa. 1.2-3 for the specifically covenantal nature of the relationship which is so distinctively characteristic of Deuteronomy, and in addition it is widely agreed that Deuteronomy 32 has a separate origin from Deuteronomy as a whole.[23]

Our conclusion so far is that we simply cannot say for certain when or by whom this passage was composed. From both a thematic and a linguistic point of view it fits perfectly as an introduction to Isaiah 1, so that it would be hazardous in the extreme to seek a basis for interpretation either in the proposal of an alternative literary or historical setting or in some overriding traditio-historical context. With that firmly stated, some concluding speculations of a more literary-historical nature which seem to do justice to all the evidence so far noted may be permitted.

We have seen that v. 2a is unusual in that it is the only place where 'for the Lord has spoken' precedes the words to which it refers, so that it is more likely to have been borrowed from v. 20 to form an *inclusio* than *vice versa*, and in that both major parts of the line are clearly used as structuring devices later in the chapter (vv. 10 and 20). As there is no inherent connection between this line and those immediately following, it is thus attractive to ascribe this line to the final redactor of the chapter. The summons to hear is obviously suitable for the opening to such a work,

---

[20] The precarious nature of such arguments, however, is clear from the fact that Paas, *Creation and Judgement*, 368, uses similar comparisons with passages in Hosea (esp. 11.1-4) to argue for probable Isaianic authorship.

[21] On the contrary, Wendel, 57–60, argues for dependence on Isaiah by Jeremiah.

[22] See previously Rignell, 'Isaiah Chapter 1', who used the argument to favour an earlier date for Deuteronomy, however.

[23] Cf. P. Sanders, *The Provenance of Deuteronomy 32* (OTS 37; Leiden, 1996).

and it also makes clear the identity of the speaker of the following lines once they were no longer in their original context.[24] If this is correct, then it may further help account for the echo, by way of the heavens and the earth, of this chapter in 65.17; 66.1 and 22. Even though the pair is used in different ways in the two passages, it is one of the connections between the opening and close of the book by which scholars have been most impressed;[25] if its presence in 1.2 is due to the final redactor, then its occurrence in both places is easier to explain.

While we have seen that vv. 2b-3 cannot be proved to come from Isaiah, they equally do not share the features of 2a which are suggestive of the redactor of the chapter as a whole. A decision would certainly be made easier if a suitable location for them could be found within an authentically Isaianic context. I suggest that this might possibly have been between 30.8 and 9. In v. 8 Isaiah is commanded to write something down to serve as a witness in a coming day, but what he is commanded to write has never been agreed upon by the commentators. 1.2b-3 would fit admirably at this point as the start of what was to be written. It encapsulates God's grievance against his people, which 30.9 then goes on immediately to explain. That verse begins with כִּי, 'because', and then describes the nation as 'a rebellious people (עַם), lying sons (בָנִים)', picking up precisely on the words used for the nation in 1.2-3 and amplifying the nature of their rebellion ('sons that will not listen to the law of the Lord'). The passage beginning at 30.9 thus supplies what scholars such as Sweeney and Deck have felt to be lacking after 1.3 while 1.2-3 supplies what many have puzzled over with regard to the connection of 30.8 with its context. 1.2-3 are, of course, first person address by God, an epigrammatic statement of his case against Israel, which Isaiah then goes on to explain (כִּי) with appropriate third person reference to God. A comparable shift occurs, for instance, in the Song of the Vineyard in 5.1-6 + 7.[26] If, because of its position following 30.8, the redactor of ch. 1 considered 1.2b-3 to be a concise summary of Isaiah's mature message, we can readily understand why he should have extracted it to stand at the head of the present form of the book.

We conclude, therefore, that v. 2a may be a redactional introduction to the passage and that 2b-3 may be an Isaianic fragment, possibly originally located between 30.8 and 9. Whether or not these literary-critical speculations are accepted, however, it remains the case that the passage functions now, and effectively, as a forceful introduction to ch. 1, which itself introduces the post-exilic edition of Isaiah. It states God's grievance against his people in an arresting manner, something which will then have to be explained and a way of escaping its consequences be outlined in the remainder of the chapter.

[24] See further Williamson, 'Relocating Isaiah 1.2-9'. A similar conclusion is reached (partly on other, and, in my opinion, unacceptable grounds) by von Loewenclau, 'Zur Auslegung von Jesaja 1, 2-3'; Vermeylen, 63–64; and Kustár, 62–65.

[25] See especially Tomasino, 'Isaiah 1.1–2.4 and 63–66'.

[26] In fact, such switches are not uncommon in prophetic speech; cf. Westermann, *Grundformen* = *Basic Forms*.

2a. In the book of Isaiah, there is repeatedly mentioned the close relationship between hearing/seeing and knowing/understanding (together with their negative counterparts); indeed, it has been recognized as one of the most powerful themes to unite the main divisions of the canonical work.[27] It is not inappropriate, therefore, that a summons to hear God's word should stand as an introduction to the book. However, we are about to be told that Israel does not 'know' or 'have understanding'; it is evident, therefore, that they are incapable of hearing, even though we should have expected them to be the first recipients of a prophetic work. Instead, the summons must be addressed to the heavens and the earth.[28] Since Israel's failure to hear is depicted in terms which show it to be contrary to nature, this appeal makes good sense; heaven and earth have seen the unfolding of history since the time of creation, and can therefore confirm that such behaviour is unheard of and unnatural.[29] As at Jer. 2.12, the expected response is an expression of astonishment and horror. A further possible motivation for this choice of addressee comes from a consideration of the frequently observed recurrence in 66.1, 'The heaven is my throne, and the earth is my footstool'. The consequence of that fact is that God looks for the one who is 'poor and of a contrite spirit and who trembles at my word' (66.2). The contrast with Israel in the following lines is obvious.

In the light of our conclusion that this line is the work of the final (and late) redactor of the chapter, it is noteworthy that comparable appeals are also used redactionally at the start of some other prophetic books or major sections of books. However, as we have seen to be the case here in Isaiah, they are fitted to the particular rhetorical concerns of each book, and are adapted accordingly.[30] Micah 1.2, for instance, addresses 'ye peoples, all of you' and 'the earth, and all that is in it', as part of that book's device for using the judgment of Israel as a warning to the nations generally (see especially the reprise at 5.15).[31] Sometimes (unlike in Isaiah), this is stated explicitly to be part of a *rîb* (cf. Hos. 4.1; Mic. 6.2), but it would clearly be mistaken to draw the conclusion that this is the only setting for such a summons. The closest verbal parallel to our line occurs at Deut. 32.1, though the verbs there occur in the reverse order. The improved alliteration in Isaiah suggests that, if there is dependence, it is probable that it is Isaiah which is later, a conclusion which fits our proposed redactional

---

[27] For 1–39 alone, see the detailed analysis of Aitken, 'Hearing and Seeing'. For the extension of the theme into Deutero-Isaiah, see Clements, 'Beyond Tradition-History', and Williamson, *Book*, 46–51.

[28] Approaching the same problem from the other direction, Bovati, *Re-Establishing Justice*, 81, states, 'Reference to a third party is an *artifice* which means in the first place that the opposed party is not listening' (original emphasis).

[29] Cf. Houtman, *Himmel*, 125.

[30] The verbs themselves (and their synonyms) occur too frequently—even in parallel —and in too wide a variety of contexts to be pressed into a single form-critical straight-jacket; cf. Hardmeier, *Texttheorie*, 311–12.

[31] See J. L. Mays, *Micah: A Commentary* (London, 1976), 40–41; H. W Wolff, *Dodekapropheton 4*, 14, 20, 23–24 = *Micah: A Commentary*, 45–46, 51, 54–55.

setting.[32] There may thus have been several possible sources of influence, both from within the book of Isaiah and beyond, which contributed to our redactor's formulation, but he has not drawn upon them mechanically.

Heavens...earth: 'heaven and earth' occurs commonly in the Old Testament as a merismus for 'the cosmos', but the words occur even more frequently in poetry (as here) as the components of a stereotyped phrase distributed over parallel lines.[33] It would therefore be a mistake to seek to identify individual roles for each element (such as two witnesses in a legal case).[34]

For the Lord has spoken: this and closely related phrases are characteristic of the Isaianic corpus; cf. 1.20; 21.17; 22.25; 25.8; 40.5; 58.14.[35] As already noted, its unique use in this verse to introduce rather than conclude divine speech supports the view that it has been borrowed by the redactor under influence from v. 20. It is noteworthy that it there rounds off a saying about the advantages of 'hearing' (v. 19) and the disadvantages of 'rebelling' (v. 20) in the context of a choice which is set before the people. It seems, therefore, that part of the redactor's purpose is to show that, although Israel is at present incapable of hearing, and hence knowing and understanding, this can be reversed in the future.[36] The response to God's word (see too v. 10, with its use of the same verbs as in 2*a*) is the decisive factor.

2b. *I have raised children and brought (them) up*: as established in the textual notes above, God here speaks of his relationship with Israel (v. 3) under the simple and natural image of parenthood.[37] Isaiah has very little

---

[32] It is not clear to me why such a conclusion should be incompatible with the canonical observation that the intertextuality here displayed points to the uniting of the law and the prophets (Childs).

[33] For statistics and full analysis, see Houtman, *Himmel*, 26–49. For the stylistic device in question, see E. Z. Melamed, 'Break-up of Stereotype Phrases as an Artistic Device in Biblical Poetry', *ScrH* 8 (1961), 115–53 (and see too S. Talmon's essay in the same volume; subsequent studies of the device are listed in Watson, *Classical Hebrew Poetry*, 332). Melamed discusses our pair on pp. 140–42.

[34] See already Hitzig, in dispute with Gesenius, and more recently the cautionary remarks in Boecker, *Redeformen des Rechtslebens*, 83–84.

[35] The form כי פי יהוה דבר (1.20; 40.5; 58.14) occurs elsewhere only at Mic. 4.4, where there is probably Isaianic influence (see on 2.2-4); כי יהוה דבר occurs four times outside Isaiah.

[36] Cf. Aitken, 'Hearing and Seeing', 14.

[37] Kessler, 'Söhne habe ich grossgezogen', has shown that these verbs are usually used in contexts where it is clearly the mother who is responsible; see, for instance, 23.4 and 49.21, as well as the maternal imagery which dominates the central part of ch. 66, with which this passage has some connection. Recent studies in social history have also emphasized the important role of mothers in the upbringing of children in ancient Israel, while the use of maternal imagery for God is not uncommon, especially in the book of Isaiah. To set alongside this is the observation that in Deut. 32, which has several points of contact with this passage, similar activity (though not specifically with these verbs) is ascribed to God as father, and that in the law of the rebellious son (Deut. 21.18-21) both parents jointly take responsibility (though that passage is not directly referred to here; see below). The usual assumption of the commentators that God here speaks exclusively in the guise of a father is probably unjustified.

to say about what elsewhere in the Old Testament is presented as the establishment and early history of the nation, such as the Exodus, so that it is unlikely that he had any such specific events in mind here. (At most, he might, if pressed, have pointed to the founding of the Davidic dynasty, the assurance of God's presence in the Jerusalem temple and the consequent sense of stability as tokens of God's fatherly concern.) Rather, he will have started from the present sense of nationhood and experience of divine goodness in many spheres (agricultural, economic and social, as well as political and more narrowly religious), and have extrapolated from there in a metaphor which was universally understood and applicable. Exegetically, nothing is gained (and perhaps even something of the image's impact is lost) by attempts to read in particular covenantal or wisdom traditions in their narrow, technical sense. While such matters may have suggested themselves to the later editor who selected this paragraph to introduce his work and to subsequent readers in the post-exilic period, he has wisely refrained from writing them in explicitly. By leaving the metaphor untouched, he has retained its broad appeal, and, as with the introduction of the notions of hearing and understanding, he has highlighted a theme that recurs under a variety of guises throughout the remainder of the book (cf. Darr, *Isaiah's Vision*, esp. 46–84).

But they have rebelled against me: in the present context, 'rebelled' is clearly to be understood as rejection of parental authority with all that that entails of family breakdown, something of great social significance in a society where the family unit was the chief means of support, not least in old age. It is both an ungrateful and a socially disruptive attitude. The verb used (פשע ב)[38] seems best to be understood as 'revolt, rebel, cast off allegiance to authority'.[39] It is well attested in political contexts (e.g. 1 Kgs 12.19; 2 Kgs 1.1; 3.5, 7), though not surprisingly it occurs most frequently in the Old Testament with reference to rebellion against God, when its content can, of course, include cultic or idolatrous sin. Alongside these uses, the closely related noun also refers occasionally to transgression against the accepted norms of family life (e.g. Gen. 31.36; 50.17; Prov. 28.24) as well as other inter-personal relationships (e.g. 1 Sam. 24.12; 25.28). Once again, therefore, it would be a mistake to seek to limit the nature of the rebellion in this verse either to idolatry or to Judah's

---

[38] Neither the verb nor the noun occurs elsewhere in authentic sayings of Isaiah (on 1.28, see below), though they are common in Deutero-Isaiah (on which see H. W. Hertzberg, 'Die "Abtrünnigen" und die "Vielen". Ein Beitrag zu Jesaja 53', in A. Kuschke [ed.], *Verbannung und Heimkehr: Beiträge zur Geschichte und Theologie Israels im 6. und 5. Jahrhundert v. Chr. Wilhelm Rudolph zum 70. Geburtstag* [Tübingen, 1961], 97–108) and other later parts of the book. However, the unusual use of the word in 1.2, deriving as it does from the imagery of father and children, together with the fact that the word is generally common and certainly attested by the eighth century if not before, means that it cannot be used to cast doubt on the authenticity of these verses; contrast Gosse, 'Isaïe 1'.

[39] See S. M. Paul, *Amos* (Minneapolis, 1991), 45. For full analysis with literature, see H. Seebass, *ThWAT* vi. 791–810 = *TDOT* xii. 133–51.

misguided political alliances, though both may be included. Rather, the choice of vocabulary arises out of the line's initial imagery.

Since neither the verb nor the noun ever occurs in Deuteronomy (and hardly ever in other Deuteronomic literature either), it is most unlikely that we have here a specific reference to the law of the rebellious son (Deut. 21.18-21; the verbs used there are סרר, מרה and לא שמע). Admittedly, 30.9 (which was suggested above as the possible original location of this saying) comes closer, for there the *people* (not the children) are called מרי, and the children are those who 'are not willing to listen (שמוע) to the law of the Lord'. But שמע is far too common a word to build a case upon it, and the children are there first described as כחשים, 'lying', which again is not Deuteronomic, while Deut. 21.18's initial סורר occurs only once elsewhere in Isaiah (30.1).[40] Rather, the Deuteronomic law should be seen as just one strand in the evidence for the (unremarkable) case that Israel, in common with its neighbours in the ancient Near East, expected children to be respectful and obedient to their parents.[41] This expectation finds expression also in the decalogue (Exod. 20.12; Deut. 5.16), other legal codes (e.g. Exod. 21.15, 17) and frequently in wisdom literature, narrative texts and elsewhere. In other words, it was part of the accepted social norm, requiring no special revelation. That is what makes it so effective in Isaiah's indictment.

The use of the same verb in the very last verse of the book (66.24), again followed by בי, has been frequently observed. While it contributes strikingly to the sense of closure for the book as a whole, it should be emphasized that there is an important difference to be considered. In the first chapter, the possibility of restoration is still held out, as the continuation will show. By the end of the book, however, those who persist in their rebellion, without heeding the calls and incentive to repent, will be finally and gruesomely destroyed. The sense of appeal in this introductory chapter is thus heightened by this verbal echo. See further on v. 28 below.

3. The analysis of this verse's use of poetic parallelism offered above has necessarily included more or less all that needs to be said in terms of exegesis.

Feeding trough (אבוס): although the text of Prov. 14.4 has been questioned by some, and Job 39.9 would allow the alternative rendering 'stall' (these are the only other occurrences in the Old Testament), 'feeding trough' is clearly to be preferred (cf. Kimhi and Gesenius). The related verb (pass. pt., 'fattened') is more likely to refer to feeding than keeping animals penned up; the noun מאבוס (Jer. 50.26) seems clearly to mean some sort of storehouse (probably 'granary'), and Akkadian *(bīt) abūsu(m)* means 'storehouse, stable' (*CDA*, 3). In our verse too, the imagery in the context of the movement of thought as analysed above is better served by 'feeding trough'.

---

[40] Against Vermeylen's contrary view, see further Williamson, *Book*, 87–91.
[41] Cf. O. Eissfeldt, 'Sohnespflichten im Alten Orient', *Syria* 43 (1966), 39–47 = *Kleine Schriften* IV (Tübingen, 1968), 264–70.

Know...have understanding: it has already been noted that these verbs introduce a significant theme in the book of Isaiah as a whole.[42] In Deutero-Isaiah, failure to know and understand is associated particularly with idolatry (44.18, 19). Conversely, the purpose of God's new work of salvation is that his people may come to a true knowledge of who he is and be witnesses to it (41.20; 43.10; cf. 52.15, and contrast 40.21). Comparable ideas surface elsewhere in the Isaiah tradition, for example 29.23-4; 32.3-4; 56.10-11. Furthermore, Beale[43] has argued precisely on these and other grounds (such as the use of comparable language at Ps. 135.15-17 and elsewhere) that the sin of idolatry lies behind the hardening saying in ch. 6, which also includes our vocabulary. Is there, then, a case for seeing a particular reference to idolatry here? Probably not. For one thing, the necessarily associated language of having eyes but not seeing, having ears but not hearing, is absent, and the inferred connection between vv. 2*a* and 3*b* accepted above is not strong enough to contradict this. More importantly, however, it seems likely that Deutero-Isaiah is introducing an interpretation of the earlier texts suitable for his specific situation rather than merely reproducing them. Everything we have seen about 1.2-3 points to the widest possible application of these words, appropriate to an introductory text. Thereafter, the book will take up and explain the words in a variety of more particular contexts. Finally, if I am right in my speculation that these verses originally stood between 30.8 and 9, then the context there would point to wider concerns than just idolatry, including political alliances and rejection of the prophetic word.

[42] See Watts, *Isaiah*, 3–10. Indeed, this is more or less elevated to the goal of prophecy as a whole by W. H. Schmidt, 'Einsicht als Ziel prophetischer Verkündigung', in Diedrich and Willmes (eds), *Ich bewirke das Heil*, 377–96.

[43] G. K. Beale, 'Isaiah vi 9-13: A Retributive Taunt against Idolatry', *VT* 41 (1991), 257–78.

INITIAL WOE PRONOUNCEMENT
(1.4)

[4]Woe to the sinful nation, the guilt-laden people,
    a generation of evil-doers, children who act corruptly;
  they have abandoned the Lord, they have spurned the Holy One of Israel,
    they have become estranged (and gone) backwards.

חמא: 1QIsaᵃ, חוטה; for the use of ה in participles of ל"א verbs here and elsewhere, see Kutscher, 164.

כבד עון: for the segholate construct form of כבד (instead of the expected כְּבַד), see GK §93hh; Dillmann speculates that the form is preferred here for rhythmic effect. The noun following the construct of the adjective gives the latter greater definition (cf. GK §128x; Gibson, 33), hence 'heavy because of their iniquity, guilt'; emendation to מכביד (Ehrlich) is unnecessary.

זרע מרעים: similarly, this does not mean 'descendants of evil-doers', as though the ancestors were necessarily evil, but a 'seed' (= generation; cf. BDB, 283 [5]) consisting of evil-doers; see GK §128l, and cf. בית מרעים at 31.2.

נזרו אחור: so too 1QIsaᵃ, but not rendered in the LXX; see below. θ and some later Greek texts clearly follow MT with ἀπηλλοτριώθησαν εἰς τὰ ὀπίσω (see the rendering of נזרו at Ezek. 14.5), as probably do V (abalienati sunt retrorsum), T (slightly paraphrastic: אסתחרו והוו לאחרא...) and P (somewhat simplified, with second person throughout), unless they presuppose סוג or סג; they sometimes use comparable translation equivalents elsewhere with אחור נסוג, but it is by no means certain that they must therefore have done so here (contra Donner, 120)—they may either have assimilated their rendering to that of the more familiar phrase, or simply have thought (not unreasonably) that it meant more or less the same. נזרו is the perfect niphʻal of זור I, attested otherwise only at Ezek. 14.5 in a not dissimilar context, meaning 'they have become estranged'.[1] אחור, a noun meaning 'the back part', is used adverbially, as frequently, here with the pregnant sense of 'to go backwards', a common enough construction; cf. GK §119ee-gg. The phrase therefore means that they have abandoned following Yahweh in favour of some older form of apostasy. Although many have found this difficult and proposed alternatives, none seems preferable: Marti, for instance, proposes emending to נסגו אחור, 'they have turned backward', i.e. backslidden, which occurs several times elsewhere, and which would be attractive because of the contrast at 50.5 (where the preceding clause seems similarly to contrast with 30.9), but for that very reason it is difficult to see how the error could have occurred. Ehrlich suggests reading a qal, זָרוּ, with God as the implied object: 'sie haben ihn hinter sich geschoben', while Budde, 21, in partial dependence on Cheyne, Book, 110, suggests נָזְרוּ מאחריו (niphʻal of נזר, 'to dedicate, separate oneself'), but this is both further from the MT and unsupported; the use at Ezek. 14.7 suggests the possibility of confusion between זור and נזר. Kohler, 'Emendations', 39, goes so far as to propose נְזִירֵי (חֵרֶב) אַשּׁוּר, 'Ye single parts left by Assur...', which he joins to the following verse. Driver's proposal ('Linguistic and Textual Problems', 36–37) to find a verb זרר by comparison with Arabic zarra, 'to press, squeeze, drive back' (so, presumably, 'they have been driven back') is unsuitable in a context which is stressing the people's wilful rebellion, and it is not clear

---

[1] A. Guillaume, 'Hebrew Notes', PEQ 79 (1947), 40–44, postulates a different root זור, cognate with Arabic zawira, Akkadian zâru and Aramaic zwr, meaning 'turn, incline' (cf. Hebrew סור); but we should not then expect the niphʻal.

why he thinks that T supports it. Tur-Sinai, 155–56, suggests emending אחור to either יחד or כאחד, while Holladay, 'New Suggestion', conjectures נָזְרוּ אָחֵר, 'they have dedicated themselves (to) another'. For the verb, see above; he then notes parallels for the idea of forsaking God being followed by references to going after other gods. However, since this is already inherent in the MT as interpreted above, his main argument is hardly conclusive. In addition, unless לאחר is read (which moves further from the MT), the expression is unacceptably compressed. The further, and separate, question of whether the phrase is a gloss is discussed below.

Although the use of 'people' and 'children' in this verse makes for a close association with the preceding verses, the introductory 'woe' indicates clearly that, from a purely formal point of view, this is the start of a new literary unit. Woe-oracles occur frequently in the book of Isaiah, and in every case הוי stands at the head of its paragraph. The apparent exception at 1.24*b* (and see 17.12) is not relevant, because the woe there is used as an independent interjection, not as the introduction to an invective as here and elsewhere. The link with the preceding two verses is therefore to be ascribed to the skill of the redactor in assembling appropriate material from elsewhere in the book for his new compilation here.

Most commentators assume that v. 4 is part of a longer unit comprising vv. 4-9. This seems unlikely, however. There is a marked change of mood between vv. 4 and 5.[2] The woe-oracle is a sharp word of judgment against the people, whereas v. 5 starts a passage which is more personal, involved and intense. Appropriately, this is reflected in the change from third to second person plural.[3] It is true that woe-oracles are sometimes developed in the second person (e.g. 5.8),[4] but elsewhere this is always to amplify the ground for the woe, not to indicate the means for its mitigation, as would be the case here. No other woe-oracle in Isaiah continues in the way pre-supposed here, whereas there are several examples of brief, self-contained woe-oracles that would parallel v. 4 taken on its own, for example 5.18-19, 20, 21. Since the woe form contains the threat of judgment within itself, no development is necessarily required. We may confidently con-clude that, whereas v. 4 has been well integrated into its new context in ch. 1, it was brought in as an independent piece by the redactor and was not previously joined with either what now precedes or follows it.

There is no regularity to the length of poetic line which follows the use of 'woe'; contrast, for instance, 5.11 and 18. In the present case it is fol-lowed by four terse phrases in apposition. The harsh tone which this sets is suitably matched by a semantic progression through the four parallel nouns, moving from גוי, the broadest term for a nation[5] (and used most commonly for non-Israelite nations) to עם, which implies a broad

---

[2] This is noted too in a quite separate manner by Carr, 'Reading Isaiah', 200.

[3] Cf. L. J. de Regt, 'A Genre Feature in Biblical Prophecy and the Translator', *OTS* 44 (2000), 230–50 (231), and 'Person Shift in Prophetic Texts', *OTS* 45 (2001), 214–31 (225).

[4] Cf. Hillers, '*Hôy* and *Hôy*-Oracles'; Roberts, 'Form, Syntax, and Redaction', 296–301.

[5] Cf. R. E. Clements, *ThWAT* i. 965–73 = *TDOT* ii. 426–33, who stresses its stronger political colouring by comparison with עם.

relationship among the people at the widest level,[6] to זרע, 'seed, generation', which implies a familial relationship between contemporaries, to
בנים, 'children', the closest of family ties (cf. Sweeney, *Isaiah 1–4*, 104).
The judgment implied in the use of woe is thus progressively narrowed
and hence sharpened.

The last three clauses of the verse, by contrast, are more matter-of-fact
in tone, and this is reflected in the repeated use of the prose particle את.
They supply a general reason for the judgment pronounced. The question
of whether these clauses, either in whole or in part, are an integral part of
the oracle or whether they have been added secondarily, can be answered
only in the light of the longer compositional history of the verse.

Deck, 106–9 (see too Mauchline, and more hesitantly Auvray and
Höffken), is one of the few scholars to have recognized the independent
nature of 1.4. Mainly because of its generalized expression, she argues
that it is a redactional addition which reflects in retrospect on the fall of
Jerusalem. While clearly this suggestion cannot be categorically ruled out,
it is noteworthy that the verse does not seem to fit with the nature of the
redactor's activity as we have been able to observe it elsewhere in the
chapter (see on vv. 2-3 above). It therefore seems preferable first to inquire
whether it is possible to suggest how this verse might fit in with his
procedure of compiling material from elsewhere in the book of Isaiah into
a new redactional unity.

With the same reservations about the hypothetical nature of the exercise as were voiced above with regard to vv. 2*b*-3, the proposal may be
advanced that this verse was taken by the redactor from an earlier setting
between 5.7 and 8—that is to say, between the Song of the Vineyard in
5.1-7 and the woe series in 5.8-24. Apart from the obvious point that woe
sayings seem generally to have been grouped in series at first (though
sometimes later material has subsequently intervened to break up these
series), the single most important clue which leads to this conclusion is the
close similarity between 1.4*b* and 5.24*c* which concludes the series: 'for
they have rejected the instruction of the Lord of Hosts and spurned the
word of the Holy One of Israel'. Not only are the two lines similar in the
way that they give a general explanation for the woe pronounced in terms
of turning away from God, but there are also striking similarities in
vocabulary: the use in both cases of the verb נאץ, the divine title 'the Holy
One of Israel' and the repeated use of the prose particle את. If, as is widely
believed, 5.8-24 represents an early collection of Isaianic woe-oracles, it
would be attractive to suppose that this early redactor added a parallel
introduction and conclusion to the material which he thus assembled. This
would clearly be part of the pre-exilic composition of Isaiah, and would
perhaps help explain the presence of vocabulary which scholars such as
Vermeylen, 55–57, 174–75, and Kaiser consider Deuteronomic[7] (although

---

[6] Cf. R. M. Good, *The Sheep of his Pasture: A Study of the Hebrew Noun 'Am(m) and
its Semitic Cognates* (HSM 29; Chico, Calif., 1983); E. Lipiński, *ThWAT* vi. 177–94 =
TDOT xi. 163–77.

[7] Cf. Bjørndalen, 'Zur Frage der Echtheit', 92.

this is not the same as an argument for a Deuteronomic redaction as generally understood), as well as the use of prose particles. Next, we may observe that the woes in Isaiah 5 are all directed at particular sections of the population, whereas 1.4 refers to the people as a whole. This in itself is not a problem, as 30.1 (which has some other similarities with 1.4) demonstrates. But it may be suggested that 1.4 would thus have functioned very effectively following 5.1-7, for it would have helped bridge the shift from national condemnation in 5.7 to specific in 5.8-24. It is also worth noting that on this view there would have been seven woes in the series, which is pleasing (on the separate issue of 10.1-4, see the introduction to 5.8-24 below). Finally, a position at the start of the woe series would have lent the verse the kind of prominence which might have brought it particularly to the attention of the compiler of ch. 1; a similar consideration was seen to be a factor in his selection of 1.2b-3.

If, regardless of particular details, this proposal is generally along the right lines, it follows as a consequence that 1.4c must always have been a part of ch. 1. The issue whether or not it represents a very early redactional addition in the process of the first ordering of the sayings of Isaiah of Jerusalem does not affect this conclusion, since all such activity must have preceded the time when ch. 1 was assembled. In other words, there was never a version of ch. 1 which did not include 1.4c.

That leaves open only the question about the status of the last two words in the verse, נזרו אחור. As has been noted, these words have no equivalent in the LXX, and they are thought to disrupt the poetic structure of the passage. Thus most commentators conclude that they are a later gloss, either to explain or to expand upon v. 4c (e.g. Feldmann; Wildberger; Watts) or as a variant on תוסיפו סרה in v. 5 (Duhm). (Gray's alternative suggestion that it is the second clause which is a gloss seems improbable in view of the close parallel in 5.24.) None of these arguments is ultimately conclusive, however. The textual evidence is ambiguous: the attestation of the clause by 1QIsaᵃ should not be underestimated (and note that it is partially attested in the fragmentary 4QIsaᵇ and that space calculations indicate that it also stood in 4QIsaʲ), and it is possible that the LXX translator had difficulty with it (as have many commentators since), and so simply left it out. Moreover, he may have been encouraged in this direction by his habit, as seen frequently elsewhere, of dealing in an imprecise manner with lists in particular; note that the clause in question is the third of three that are broadly similar.[8] Secondly, it is curious that an explanatory gloss should itself have proved far more difficult to understand than the clauses it is supposed to be explicating. Furthermore, Wildberger's suggestion that it 'seeks to bring out the fact that Israel had at one time stood in a loyal relationship with its Lord' overlooks the obvious point that this is already inherent in the clauses which precede it. Finally, once it is realized that this verse was not continued by vv. 5-9 when it was originally composed, the force of the argument from metre is blunted. On the one hand, we should note that the 'redactional parallel' in 5.24c is also

---

[8] For discussion of this translation characteristic, see Williamson, 'Isaiah 1.11'.

far longer than its prevailing context. On the other hand, three-stich lines are by no means unparalleled, and we have seen reason to believe that 1.4 marks the end of the small unit 2-4 in the compilation of the present form of ch. 1. Lengthening of a line to produce a slight rallentando is not uncommon at the end of poetic units, so that its occurrence here is not surprising. One possibility that might be considered, therefore, is that the phrase was added by the redactor at the time of the compilation of the chapter in order to effect a catchword connection with the following verses (cf. זר in v. 6 and זרים in v. 7).[9] The situation is thus uncertain, but there do not appear to be sufficient grounds for regarding the clause as a wholly secondary and later gloss; it seems to have entered the text no later than the time of the composition of ch. 1 in its present form.

We may thus conclude that this verse was drawn from elsewhere in the book of Isaiah in order to introduce and further ground a note of judgment following the condemnation of vv. 2-3. It connects well with those verses by catchword and theme, and brings the first small section of the chapter to its conclusion. The core of the verse, at least, derives ultimately from Isaiah of Jerusalem, though it seems already to have passed through one stage of early redaction (when it was incorporated in ch. 5) before it was brought into its present setting. Beyond that it is difficult to go. Its similarities with 30.1 might suggest a date late in Isaiah's ministry, and this would bring it into line with the preferred date for most, if not all, of the woes in ch. 5 below. But its content is sufficiently general to be suitable for any date.

4. *Woe*: the background and form of the 'woe' oracles in the prophets and elsewhere have been frequently discussed in the past, and there seems little need to rehearse the history of the debate again here. Zobel[10] provides a clear and concise summary, which reflects the resolution of past disagreements. We need note here only that the sayings are an adaptation of the laments for the dead (cf. 1 Kgs 13.30; Jer. 22.18; 34.5), that there is no need to postulate an intermediate phase of use in early (clan) wisdom on which the prophets drew (see especially Davies, 83–86) and that though they may be followed by associated threats, this is by no means always the case. Even where they stand alone, as here, they amount by their very form 'to a prediction of death, a proclamation of the judgment of Yahweh'.

In the preaching of the prophets, the use of 'woe' will have functioned rhetorically as a strong device for attracting the hearers' attention.[11] Its

---

[9] The frequency of the use of words on the base *zr* in this passage is noted by R. B. Chisholm, 'Wordplay in the Eighth-Century Prophets', *BibSac* 144 (1987), 44–52.

[10] H.-J. Zobel, *ThWAT* ii. 382–88 = *TDOT* iii. 359–64, with literature, to which add Vermeylen, 603–52; Hardmeier, *Texttheorie*; McLaughlin, *The* marzēaḥ, 89–94 (a very useful summary).

[11] Hardmeier, *Texttheorie*. For this reason, I have retained the traditional rendering 'woe'. Because of the element of direct address, it is becoming more common nowadays to render 'Alas!', followed by second person (see recently McLaughlin, *The* marzēaḥ, 94). While this can be justified syntactically, despite the use sometimes of third person references (see Hillers, '*Hôy* and *Hôy*-Oracles'), it sounds a little feeble in English.

re-use in the present decidedly literary context, however, suggests that the focus for exegesis must be on content. In juxtaposition with vv. 2-3 it expresses the inevitable judgment that must follow from Israel's culpable failure to understand the required response to God's paternal care for his people, a failure which the second half of v. 4 will spell out in more prosaic terms.

It was shown above that the four terms used to designate the people (*nation...people...generation [seed]...children*) manifest a conscious semantic development in the direction of narrowing. The use of עַם, 'people', and בנים, 'children', shows that the same group is intended as in vv. 2-3, whence we also learn that they are named 'Israel'. There is thus an implication that both the nation corporately and the individuals who comprise it are alike guilty. It is less certain, by contrast, whether there is any such point to be made out of the choice of vocabulary which describes their sin: חטא, 'sinning, sinful', עון, 'iniquity, guilt', מרעים, 'evil-doers', and משחיתים, 'those who act corruptly' (*contra* Stacey). The first two words are extremely common, and occur frequently in parallel.[12] It is true that a distinction is often popularly made between the 'basic' ideas of 'missing the road' and 'erring from the road', and there is no doubt that such subtleties can be made to fit many passages.[13] Furthermore, Wildberger has argued with regard to this verse that 'עון is much more developed in the direction of pointing toward guilt, so that it is only when one puts the two words next to each other that the sin–guilt connection can be fully understood... At this point it is intimated, once again according to the understanding of the synthetic view of life with its action–consequences sequence, that when the עון (offense) takes place, the punishment has already been set in motion.' Nevertheless, it is unlikely that Isaiah (or his later editor) was influenced by such considerations in his choice here. עון occurs probably five times in the words of Isaiah (1.4; 5.18; 6.7; 22.14; 30.13).[14] In the first three of these cases it occurs in the closest possible parallelism with חטא or its derivatives, while in the fourth (22.14) it is especially striking that it is the subject of the passive verb יְכֻפַּר, exactly as חטאת is at 6.7. Finally, the context at 30.13 suggests that the iniquity consists of rejecting the prophetic word in favour of political alliances as part of the anti-Assyrian rebellion, and for this חטאת is similarly used (twice) in 30.1. These occurrences[15] suggest that, whatever may be said about other Old Testament writers, Isaiah himself drew little distinction between the

---

[12] For a full analysis, see R. Knierim, *Die Hauptbegriffe für Sünde im Alten Testament* (Gütersloh, 1965).

[13] See, for instance, R. Youngblood, 'A New Look at Three Old Testament Roots for "Sin"', in G. A. Tuttle (ed.), *Biblical and Near Eastern Studies: Essays in Honor of William Sanford LaSor* (Grand Rapids, 1978), 201–5.

[14] Elsewhere in 1–39 at 13.11; 14.21; 26.21; 27.9; 33.24. For a broader discussion of the root, see K. Koch, *ThWAT* v. 1160–77 = *TDOT* x. 546–62.

[15] For חטא and its derivatives, one may add at least 1.18 as Isaianic. At 3.9 the word is apparently used with reference to social injustice, but it will be suggested below that this may be part of an exilic addition. For the root in general, see K. Koch, *ThWAT* ii. 857–70 = *TDOT* iv. 309–19.

two words but used them (as פשע in v. 2 above) for various types of sin
and iniquity (social and political as well as cultic) generally. It goes without saying that he believed that such behaviour would be judged unless
there was repentance and forgiveness or atonement (1.18; 6.7; 22.14).

The second descriptive pair, both participles, seems equally resistant to
over-subtle exegesis. An additional difficulty is that, while both verbs are
reasonably common, we cannot be sure to what extent, if at all, Isaiah or
other writers would have made a mental link between the participle used
nominally and the use and range of meaning of the verb proper. בית מרעים
in 31.2 (if authentic) gives us the nearest analogy for 'a generation of evil-
doers' without defining it particularly closely (the context again is political
alliances, and the parallel is 'workers of wickedness [אָוֶן]') (and see too
9.6; 14.20), while Isaiah does not elsewhere use משחית. It is *possible* that
the word is used here under influence from Deut. 32.5;[16] if so, there is even
less chance of recovering any particular nuance in meaning that Isaiah
might have had in mind. We may conclude, therefore, that the development
which is often a part of even synonymous parallelism through the first half
of the verse resides in the nouns describing the people, and that the
various terms to indicate their sin and evil are used in a general way, with
no other concern than to show that the nation was corrupt in every part.

Abandoned...spurned...become estranged (and gone) backwards: here
too there is probably a slight crescendo through the line, reflected also in
the choice of divine names, from *the Lord* (the commonest name for the
God of Israel) to *the Holy One of Israel* (the distinctively Isaianic title; see
below). That נאץ, pi'el,[17] is a strong term in First Isaiah is confirmed by its
use, again in the second position, at 5.24, where it follows מאס, 'reject'
(see too Jer. 33.24). Israel has not just drifted away from God, but wilfully
turned its back on him. In 5.24 the objects of the first two verbs are 'the
instruction (תורה) of the Lord of Hosts' and 'the word of the Holy One of
Israel', whereas here they are personal. As we have already seen, however, there is little distinction between the two in Isaiah's thinking: it is
impossible to remain loyal to God without hearing/obeying his word.

No doubt influenced by his understanding of vv. 2-3, Wildberger
makes the further claim here that Isaiah uses two verbs 'which are rooted
in the covenant tradition'. He notes in particular the occurrences at Deut.
31.16 and 20, where the verbs are separately parallel with an expression
referring to the breaking of a covenant (הפר ברית), and so thinks that this
line gives a more precise meaning to the non-specific first half of the verse.
This, however, displays muddled semantic method.[18] There is nothing

---

[16] Unfortunately, Deut. 32.5 is thought by most scholars to be seriously corrupt, or if
not then at least to display highly unusual syntax; see most recently P. Sanders, *The
Provenance of Deuteronomy 32* (OTS 37; Leiden, 1996), 145–48. It is thus a precarious
starting point for particular semantic theories.

[17] In relations between God and people, the qal is generally used with God as subject
and the pi'el with people as subject; cf. L. Ruppert, *ThWAT* v. 129–37 = *TDOT* ix. 118–
25.

[18] Cf. J. Barr, *The Semantics of Biblical Language* (Oxford, 1961), 218: 'illegitimate
totality transfer'.

inherently 'covenantal' about either verb, and since we have found no specific allusions to 'the covenant' elsewhere in the passage, we cannot conclude that 'an accusation is leveled concerning the breaking of the covenant'. To this point, God's relationship with Israel has been pictured only under the natural image of parent and child; it is the break in that relationship, accordingly, which this line describes.[19]

While the first two verbs already lead us to expect that Israel has turned away from the Lord in favour of some other god or gods (cf. Jer. 5.7), this is made clearer in the last clause of the verse (see the textual notes above and Ezek. 14.5). Although no further detail is supplied, it is noteworthy that idolatry is a concern of the whole of the book of Isaiah in all its major divisions. This clause would therefore be an appropriate comment at any time of the book's history, and if early could well have been applied differently by successive redactors and readers. If, as so many have assumed, the clause was added only late in the history of composition (on this, see above), the previous clauses might have been intended originally to refer to social injustice alone (see the wider context in ch. 5); that, however, is historical speculation; as the chapter now stands, the injury of turning to other gods is added to the insult of abandoning the Lord; see too on vv. 29-31 below.

The Holy One of Israel: as is well known, this divine title is especially characteristic of the book of Isaiah in most of its major divisions. It occurs as such twenty-five times, and there are a further four virtually identical uses.[20] Taking these altogether, the distribution is fourteen times in chs 1–39, thirteen times in 40–55, and twice in 56–66. This is misleading, however, for only a minority of the occurrences in 1–39 are in passages which can be securely ascribed to Isaiah himself, while not a few seem to derive from either late pre-exilic or exilic redactions.[21] When to this it is added that the title comes only twice (and then in a single passage) in Trito-Isaiah[22] and not at all in either 24–27 (the Isaiah Apocalypse) or 34–35, it looks as though a limited use by Isaiah himself was seized upon by his

---

[19] See too E. Gerstenberger, *ThWAT* v. 1200–8 (esp. 1202–3) = *TDOT* x. 584–92 (586–87).

[20] 1.4; 5.19, 24; 10.20; 12.6; 17.7; 29.19; 30.11, 12, 15; 31.1; 37.23; 41.14, 16, 20; 43.3, 14; 45.11; 47.4; 48.17; 49.7; 54.5; 55.5; 60.9, 14; note too קדוש, 'his Holy One' (with Israel as antecedent in both cases), 10.17; 49.7; קדוש יעקב, 'the Holy One of Jacob' (parallel with 'the God of Israel'), 29.23; and קדושכם, 'your Holy One' (followed by appositional 'the creator of Israel'), 43.15.

[21] This is deliberately expressed somewhat vaguely, because each case requires separate analysis, which cannot be undertaken here; see the discussion of each reference in the commentary *ad loc*. As an indication, Wildberger (who is generally rather conservative on such matters) allows only seven of the occurrences to be Isaianic (1.4; 5.19, 24; 30.11, 12, 15; 31.1), but we have already seen that there is some reason to ascribe two of these (1.4; 5.24) to an early redactional phase in the book's compilation. I cannot go so far as Loretz, 97–110, however, who denies that Isaiah himself ever used the term. I have discussed Loretz's treatment of 31.1, for instance, in 'Isaiah and the Holy One of Israel', and see too more generally G. C. I. Wong, 'Isaiah's Opposition to Egypt in Isaiah xxxi 1-3', *VT* 46 (1996), 392–401.

[22] Note further that both occur in what is generally considered to be the earliest part of Trito-Isaiah and that one of these (60.9) is a clear citation of 55.5.

later redactors, reached its high point in the work of Deutero-Isaiah and the redaction(s) of 1–39 most closely associated with him, and then dropped away rather quickly in the subsequent compositional history. It would thus be a mistake to speak of the title as characteristically Isaianic, if by that is meant characteristic of the eighth-century prophet; rather, it was a title which he used occasionally and which exerted a particular influence on the subsequent Isaianic tradition up to and including the time of Deutero-Isaiah.

Three of the six Old Testament occurrences of the title[23] outside the book of Isaiah serve to reinforce this conclusion. 2 Kings 19.22 occurs in a speech attributed to Isaiah which has a parallel in Isaiah itself (37.23). Although it is probable that 2 Kings 18–20 was the source for Isaiah 36–39, there is nevertheless a considerable weight of evidence to suggest that these chapters were originally drafted in Isaianic circles (however that should be defined in detail) and that they were incorporated from there as a separate source by the Deuteronomic Historian.[24] This reference therefore fits precisely the picture we have already established. Initially less obviously, the same may be true for Jer. 50.29 and 51.5. The wording of the oracles against Babylon in Jeremiah 50–51 as a whole displays a number of striking affinities with phrases which are otherwise peculiarly characteristic of the book of Isaiah, of which this is but one example. So far as I am aware, this feature of these chapters has not been the object of particular study, so that it is not possible at present to give an adequate explanation for this feature. It seems beyond doubt, however, that there is some connection with the Isaianic tradition, so that these occurrences of our title fit in with the pattern of distribution already noted.[25]

The other three references in the Old Testament outside the book of Isaiah to 'the Holy One of Israel' come in the Psalms: 71.22; 78.41; 89.19. Their significance for our purposes is more difficult to evaluate, not least because of the problems of dating. Those who believe that Isaiah himself coined the title (probably on the basis of his vision recounted in ch. 6) must naturally believe that the Psalms are later and dependent upon him.[26] This is far from certain, however,[27] and even if the Psalms in question

---

[23] In addition, Ezek. 39.7 is very similar, though the variation in wording suggests that it is independent of the Isaiah tradition.

[24] See Williamson, *Book*, 189–211. For a response to the objections raised by J. Vermeylen, 'Hypothèses sur l'origine d'Isaïe 36–39', in van Ruiten and Vervenne (eds), *Studies in the Book of Isaiah*, 95–118, see F. Gonçalvès, '2 Rois 18,13—20,19 par. Isaïe 36–39: encore une fois, lequel des deux livres fut le premier?', in J.-M. Auwers and A. Wénin (eds), *Lectures et relectures de la Bible: Festschrift P.-M. Bogaert* (BETL 144; Leuven, 1999), 27–55.

[25] For the dating of Jer. 50–51, see D. J. Reimer, *The Oracles Against Babylon in Jeremiah 50–51: A Horror Among the Nations* (San Francisco, 1993).

[26] E.g. Procksch; G. Bettenzoli, *Geist der Heiligkeit: Traditionsgeschichtliche Untersuchungen des QDS-Begriffes im Buch Ezechiel* (Florence, 1979), 25–49; K. Elliger, *Deuterojesaja* (BKAT 11/1; Neukirchen–Vluyn, 1978), 151.

[27] For a strong defence of the early date of Ps. 78, for instance, see J. Day, 'Pre-Deuteronomic Allusions to the Covenant in Hosea and Psalm lxxviii', *VT* 36 (1986), 1–12, and P. Stern, 'The Eighth Century Dating of Psalm 78 Re-argued', *HUCA* 66 (1995), 41–65.

were of a later date there would still be a strong possibility that they were drawing on more ancient cult tradition (see below). On balance, it is more probable that the use in the Psalms is independent of Isaiah and that he did not himself, therefore, coin the phrase.[28]

In the light of these data, we may suggest, not that (as has sometimes been held) Isaiah coined the title because of his overwhelming experience of the 'thrice-holy' God recounted in Isaiah 6 (where significantly the title does not occur), but rather that it was precisely reflection on this account by later tradents (and there is abundant evidence that it strongly influenced all parts of the Isaianic literary tradition; see in part *Book*, 37–56) that led them to fasten on this title which Isaiah had certainly used on occasion and to give it especial prominence.

It follows from this, not only that the still highly disputed etymology of קדוש,[29] but also the putative religio-historical background of the phrase 'the Holy One of Israel' will have only marginal significance for the use in Isaiah. There need be little doubt that the ascription of holiness to Yahweh has as its background the comparable ascription to El in the Ugaritic texts,[30] and that this was also therefore probably predicated of El Elyon in the pre-Israelite Jerusalem cult (note the proximity of holiness to Elyon in Ps. 46.5), whence it would have been transferred to Yahweh sometime after Jerusalem became part of Israel. From there, it would have been but a short step to the development of the fuller title, though the textual evidence already surveyed suggests that its use was confined to a relatively restricted circle within the Jerusalem cult.[31] Since Isaiah probably drew his use of the title from that already long-established circle, it is doubtful whether he was aware of any of this, however. He may have seized on the title under the influence of his experience recounted in ch. 6, but it is odd that the title itself does not occur in that chapter. (Conversely, as already

---

[28] See too M. Gilbert, 'Le Saint d'Israël', in *Il a parlé par les prophètes: thèmes et figures bibliques* (Namur, 1998), 191–204.

[29] See the summary of views in W. Kornfeld, *ThWAT* vi. 1181–85 = *TDOT* xii. 521–26, with further bibliography. For a cautionary tale on the dangers of etymologizing from the English word 'holy', see Barr, *Semantics*, 111–14.

[30] See especially W. H. Schmidt, 'Wo hat die Aussage: Jahwe "der Heilige" ihren Ursprung?', *ZAW* 74 (1962), 62–66; Niehr, 'Bedeutung und Funktion'; C.-B. Costecalde, *DBS* x. 1372–82; more generally, M. S. Smith, *The Origins of Biblical Monotheism: Israel's Polytheistic Background and the Ugaritic Texts* (Oxford, 2001), 93–97; somewhat differently, A. van Selms, 'The Expression "The Holy One of Israel"', in W. C. Delsman *et al.* (eds), *Von Kanaan bis Kerala: Festschrift für Prof. Mag. Dr. Dr. J.P.M. van der Ploeg O.P. zur Vollendung des siebzigsten Lebensjahres am 4. Juli 1979* (AOAT 211; Kevelaer and Neukirchen–Vluyn, 1982), 257–69.

[31] So correctly Wildberger. Wildberger goes on to claim that the addition of the name 'Israel' points to a synthesizing of Jerusalem and old Israelite traditions, so that he finds here an allusion to the covenant with its review of the history of the relationship between God and his people in which the face of God is revealed. He thinks that this is suitable for the present context in Isaiah. See too M. Garcia Cordero, 'El Santo de Israel', in *Mélanges Bibliques rédigés en l'honneur de André Robert* (Paris, 1957), 165–73. This is more than questionable, however. As Høgenhaven, 197, rightly points out, it is a mistake to draw implications from the separate elements of the title; rather, the meaning of the title is determined precisely from the combination of the constituent elements.

suggested, ch. 6 probably accounts for the fact that later Isaianic tradents made more frequent use of the title.) More likely, for reasons unknown to us, he reflected on the title (so that ch. 6 may be in part the fruit of this reflection rather than its source) and so vested it with a creative significance of his own. In that case, it is the use attested in his prophecies that alone can tell us the meaning of the title in his writing.[32]

In this connection, it is noteworthy that the most securely Isaianic uses of the term are those which come in chs 30 and 31. The context here suggests that the primary point of reference is the exclusive loyalty which Israel (or strictly Judah) should show to Yahweh particularly with regard to political alliances with other nations. It would not be difficult to relate 5.19 (the next most secure reference, and probably the only other one) to this general realm of ideas (see too the use of קדשׁ in 8.11-15). This can certainly be derived from the use of 'holy' in ch. 6, where the point at issue is the absolute sovereignty of the Lord of Hosts, the divine king.

Isaiah's reaction to that vision is a heightened consciousness of his own lostness in the presence of the divine majesty. This includes an initial element of cultic unworthiness (6.5), but it is certainly not limited to that: Wildberger points to the fact that already in the entrance liturgies (Pss. 15 and 24) uncleanness includes what we would think of as ethical demand. More immediately, however, Isaiah's purification involves the purging of iniquity and sin (עון, חטאת; 6.7), which we saw above have a broad application in Isaiah. The uses of 'the Holy One of Israel' here in 1.4 and in 5.24, which are among the earliest redactional workings of Isaiah's sayings, fit well with this, and suggest an alternative legitimate development (cf. 5.16) from ch. 6 to the application to the political realm in Isaiah's own thought.

Against this should be set the majority of the later uses of the term, including those in Deutero-Isaiah, where it is used in association with the redemption and salvation of his people. This is doubtless due primarily to the changed circumstances at the time when such prophecies were uttered, but may also have drawn out the reverse side of such verses as 30.15 and 31.1. It is not impossible that this links back to some extent to the pre-Isaianic use in the Jerusalem cult, though it will have reached these later tradents through the prism of Isaiah's own use rather than reflecting an immediate appeal to an independently transmitted use in the cult.[33]

---

[32] For a more broad-ranging and synthetic analysis than that which follows, see J. G. Gammie, *Holiness in Israel* (Minneapolis, 1989), 74–101. It is interesting, however, that Gammie too puts the political implications first in his list (pp. 80–83). For wider, canonical reflections on the title and the theme of holiness in Isaiah as a whole, see J. B. Wells, *God's Holy People: A Theme in Biblical Theology* (JSOTSup 305; Sheffield, 2000), 130–59.

[33] For a fuller discussion of all the above, see Williamson, 'Isaiah and the Holy One of Israel'; see most recently J. L'Hour, 'L'Impur et le Saint dans le Premier Testament à partir du livre du Lévitique, II', *ZAW* 116 (2004), 30–54.

ONLY ZION IS LEFT
(1.5-9)

[5]Why will you go on being beaten (and) persist in your defection?
  The whole head has become sick, and the whole heart is faint.
[6]From the sole of the foot to the head there is no soundness in it,
  Only bruises and weals and wounds still bleeding;
They have not been pressed out, nor bandaged, nor softened with oil.
[7]Your country is a wasteland, your cities burned with fire;
  In your very presence foreigners are devouring your land.
  [It is a wasteland like the overthrow of Sodom.]
[8]And the daughter of Zion is left like a hut in a vineyard,
  Like a shelter for the night in a cucumber field, like a guard-city.
[9]Had the Lord of Hosts not left us some survivors,
  We should soon have become like Sodom (and) resembled Gomorrah.

5. על מה: as usually, 'upon what ground? wherefore?' hence, 'why?' (BDB 554A [f];
Gibson, 184); so LXX, P and (probably) T. An alternative understanding is suggested by V
super quo; Jerome *in quo* (but linked with a rather different construal of the rest of the line
from MT), as at Job 38.6; 2 Chron. 32.10. This has been preferred by many,[1] though not
always with a plausible understanding of the second half of the line. The commoner
meaning seems more likely;[2] as Gray puts it, 'the person who chastises does not take pains
to discover a spot on which no stroke has yet fallen'. Wade also observes in support that
at this point the people are still addressed in the plural; the move to the image of the
people as a single body does not come until the second half of the verse at the earliest. It
is therefore a mistake to adduce v. 6 in favour of the rendering 'where?', as many have
done. Kissane adds that the word also governs the second half of the line, and so must
mean 'why?', but this is not certain (see below). On the vocalization of מה, see GK §37e
(distance from the principal tone of the sentence).

  תוסיפו סרה: the syntactical relation of this clause to the preceding has been explained in
three ways: (i) a relative clause without אשר, 'you who persist…' (e.g. Duhm; so probably
the versions, which generally render with a participle); (ii) a circumstantial clause, and so
subordinate to the first: 'seeing that you persist/by persisting…' (e.g. Kimhi; Houbigant;
GK §156d; Delitzsch, and, of course, those who take על מה as 'where?'); (iii) a second
independent clause, governed by על מה, as above (e.g. Hitzig and Gray). In meaning, there
is little difference except that (i) and (ii) lay slightly greater emphasis on the people's
defection as the cause of their punishment. (This is nevertheless clearly implied by [iii]
also.) Since parallels can be adduced for all three possibilities (so that the conjectural
addition of כי is unnecessary, *contra* Budde), certainty is not attainable. Two points marginally favour (iii), however. First, other circumstantial clauses of this sort normally
adduced elsewhere in Isaiah 1–39 do not generally put the verb first (cf. 5.11; 10.24;
30.31; note that in the second two passages this is not just a case of the subject of the verb
coming first, as regularly in circumstantial clauses). It is true that outside Isaiah there are

---

[1] E.g. Lowth; Gesenius; Knobel; Dillmann; Duhm; Marti; Buhl, 'Zu Jes 1₅'; Feldmann; Procksch; Jacob.
[2] Cf. Calvin; Vitringa; Delitzsch; Orelli; Condamin; Skinner; Gray; Slotki; Young.
Ehrlich's emendation to כל מה = 'The more you are beaten the further you go in your
defection', seems to miss the point of the line entirely.

some closer analogies for the construction appealed to here, but the context is then clearer. The importance of word order for syntax is now more appreciated than it once was, so that this point may carry some weight. Secondly, there is a measure of parallelism between the two clauses 'עוד being parallel in thought to תוסיפו, and סרה, *defection*, which necessarily implies punishment, to תכו' (Gray). Furthermore, while the metre is 3 + 2, the length of the second half is the equivalent of the first (five syllables each). The form of the line thus fits every requirement of the inverted *abc//b'c'* type couplet,[3] something which does not apply to the examples of circumstantial clauses adduced as analogies. On balance, therefore, it is preferable to take על מה as governing both halves of the line.

כל־ראש...כל־לבב: again, there is slight ambiguity (retained in several of the versions): either 'every head...', so continuing the individualized image of the first half of the line (so P), or 'the whole head...', indicating a shift to the image of the people as a single body, as certainly in the next verse. The latter is generally favoured as contextually more appropriate. On the omission of the article in poetry, cf. GK §127c; JM §139e. According to Gibson, 29, 'The nouns *heart, soul, eyes* etc., when following a constr. adj., usually want the Art. in poetry... Particularly when, as essentially coll., they follow כל'. Delitzsch objects that this is never the sense when כל occurs several times in succession. The examples he gives, however, are not the same as the present passage (at least in MT): in 15.2 and Ezek. 7.17, the first כל is followed by a definite and plural noun (ראשיו/הידים).

לחלי: ל may designate a condition or state into which something or some one has come (so BDB, 516B [k]); cf. especially 2 Chron. 21.18 with this same noun. Driver, 'Isaiah i–xxxix', 36 (followed by Watts), postulates a Hebrew חֲלָא* = 'pustules' on the basis of 2 Chron. 16.12 and Arabic cognates, and further maintains that לבב/לב can mean not just 'heart' but also 'intestines'. He thus arrives at a translation: 'every head is for (i.e. soon to be covered with) pustules and every stomach disordered'. But quite apart from a questionable interpretation of 2 Chron. 16.12,[4] (i) his starting point (that we expect a reference to physical suffering, for which חלי is unsuitable) is mistaken, since √חלה can refer to the results of physical wounds (e.g. 2 Kgs 8.29; Jer. 6.7), (ii) דוי only ever occurs with 'heart' elsewhere (Jer. 8.18; Lam. 1.22), so that the phrase must have the same meaning here, and (iii) since the whole passage is clearly metaphorical, it is doubtful whether we should look for strict consistency in the description (after all, 'pustules' are not the result of beating either). If the main aim is to denote the serious nature of the condition, it would seem appropriate to begin with a reference to the head and the heart.

דוי: 1QIsaᵃ דוה is simply a rather more common form of the same adjective; see further the detailed comments below.

6. מכף־רגל ועד־ראש: anarthrous; cf. English, 'from top to toe'. Elsewhere, קדקד always stands in the position of ראש here (cf. Deut. 28.35; 2 Sam. 14.25; Job 2.7), so that Budde suggests that it should be read here too, ראש having come in mistakenly under the influence of v. 5. It is true that sometimes in Isaiah a scribe seems to have assimilated to a similar word shortly before (see, for instance, 1.7; 6.11; 11.4), but in each case the two words in question are orthographically very similar, which would not be the case here. In addition, our phrase is distinguished from the comparisons cited in that they all have possessive suffixes.

אין־בו מתם: for the nominal form, cf. GK §85k; BL §61dη (p. 493); JM §88Lj. We should not revocalize or emend on the basis of the commoner derivative from תמם, namely תם (either מתֹם [so Haupt in Cheyne, *Book*, 110; Gray; Procksch], or תמים, or תם אין במו תם [so Hummel, 'Enclitic *Mem*', 105, and Kaiser]): the same form occurs at Ps. 38.4, 8, again with אין, and again in a context of physical sickness. It thus appears to have a particular 'medical' sense, whereas the meaning of תם ranges far more widely. Although strictly speaking there is no antecedent for בו, the sense is quite clear in context (*contra* Ehrlich). The clause as a whole appears not to be represented in the LXX (contrast α, σ and a

---

³ Cf. Watson, *Classical Hebrew Poetry*, 174–77.

⁴ Cf. H. G. M. Williamson, *1 and 2 Chronicles* (NCB; Grand Rapids and London, 1982), 276–77, for discussion.

considerable number of mss [see the apparatus in Ziegler's edition], as well as the other primary versions), and so Marti suggested that it was a gloss, based on Ps. 38.4, 8. Gray correctly observes, however, that LXX has a negative before the following nouns (οὔτε... οὔτε), so that it must at least have read אין, but that since the resulting text ('there is no wound nor…') is impossible in context, LXX must represent a defective text (i.e. with אין, but מתם בו accidentally lost).[5] Even this last conclusion may not be necessary, however. It could equally well be that the translator did not recognize the rare word מתם, guessed from the (narrower) context that it was another in the list of wounds which follows, and then in his regular manner treated the list loosely (see on the last clause of v. 4 above).[6] As most more recent commentators observe, omission of the clause would be rhythmically impossible.

זרו: with the accent on the penult., this is probably a passive of the qal of זרר, cognate with Arabic *zarra*, 'to press, squeeze'; cf. GK §67*m* with 52*e*; JM §82*l*. Alternatively, BDB, 266–67 (and cf. WO, 374 n. 30), suggests the passive of זור, with similar meaning, while Hitzig construes as a pu'al of זרה, a postulated by-form of זור. Less plausibly, Marti suggested that זרר was a by-form of צרר, 'bind up', used here in a developed technical sense of 'pressed out' (Duhm; otherwise it would be synonymous with חבשו; but this seems unnecessarily complicated).

רככה: this switch to an apparently fem. sg. form following two plurals is difficult. It has traditionally been explained as a feminine for impersonal (cf. GK §144*b*; Knobel; Delitzsch; Duhm; König): 'and no softening has been effected with oil', but, as Gray objects, 'the change of cstr. is extraordinary'. Delitzsch seeks to ease this by proposing that the three verbs form a sort of chiastic structure with the nouns of the previous line, but since this verb corresponds with חבורה (the second noun) the scheme does not work (as Delitzsch concedes), and anyway it still does not explain why the relation between this verb and its subject is different from that of the other two; similarly Procksch (and cf. Hitzig), who relates the first two verbs to the first two nouns, and the third to the third (מכה). Dillmann suggests alternatively that the form is individualizing, 'and none of the wounds has been softened', since this treatment was not needed for every wound; but then nor was זרו. Others emend, most obviously to רככו (e.g. Budde, but with no adequate explanation as to how the anomalous MT could have arisen), or by rearrangement of clauses (e.g. moving ומכה טריה to follow חבשו [Gray]; poetically very attractive and achieving excellent line balance, but unfortunately wholly conjectural and somewhat radical). It might just be worth considering whether we have here a relic of the old third person feminine plural perfect form (as in Aramaic). There are a few places where this may occur in the Old Testament (e.g. 1 Sam. 4.15; Neh. 13.10, rejected by GK §44*m*; JM §42*f*), and it is noteworthy that V renders all the verbs in this line as singular (P avoids the problem by using infinitives throughout). Did they once all have plural ה- endings (preferred for euphonic reasons, to avoid too many 'u' vowels), of which the first two were scribally assimilated to the familiar form in the course of time (cf. Houbigant, though construing as singular)? This suggestion is no less conjectural than the others which have been noted above. Fortunately, the meaning is not seriously in doubt.

The LXX rearranges the three verbs in this last line into what might be thought to be their 'logical' order (as well as changing the construction, so that the verbs are represented as nouns): 'there is no means to apply a balm, or oil, or bandages'. This again, however, is characteristic of the way the translator handled lists (see above). Poetic balance clearly favours the order in MT: the longer phrase ולא רככה בשמן nicely balances the two short phrases of the first half of the line, and could hardly come comfortably between them, as 'logic' might seem to dictate (note too the order in Luke 10.34). Marti's conjecture, on the basis of all the problems in this line, that the first two verbs should be deleted as a

---

[5] See most recently Kustár, 46.

[6] Less plausibly, because the syntax would be extremely harsh, if not impossible (an awkward *casus pendens*?), Ottley suggests that LXX may have taken the phrase with what follows: 'neither (to) wound nor…is there any means to apply…'.

marginal gloss on פצע וחבורה, is not helpful. It appears not to have been taken up by any subsequent commentator.

7. שממה: although theoretically this could equally be vocalized as an adjective (שְׁמֵמָה), it was understood as a noun at least as early as the time of the glossator responsible for the last line in the verse (see below), and so should be retained. The staccato rhythm of the two-member nominal sentence is maintained by the lack of conjunction before עריכם.

שרפות אש: a parade example of a passive ptcp. used in the construct before a genitive of the cause or instrument; cf. GK §116*l*; JM §121*p*; WO, 144, 617; Gibson, 31, 134.

אדמתכם...אתה: *casus pendens* with resumptive pronoun; cf. GK §143*a*; JM §156*aa* (who note that this construction is frequently dictated by the demands of poetic parallelism); Gibson, 180–81.

ושממה: 1QIsa³ reads ושממו עליה, 'and they will be appalled at it'. In the light of other similarities between this passage and Lev. 26.31-33, this appears to be an assimilation to Lev. 26.32, emphasizing exegetically that the fate of Jerusalem is an outworking of the covenant curses in the law.[7] LXX (ἠρήμωται) and V (*desolabitur*) also render as a verb, but probably merely by reading וְשָׁמְמָה.

זרים (second occurrence): MT, 'as overthrown by foreigners', is inappropriate, since according to the earlier part of the verse it is in fact foreigners who are doing the overthrowing. Elsewhere, מהפכה always refers to the overthrow of Sodom and Gomorrah (Deut. 29.22; Isa. 13.19; Jer. 49.18; 50.40; Amos 4.11),[8] so that most commentators (since Houbigant, at least) conjecturally emend זרים to סדם here. Most likely a scribe was unconsciously influenced by the earlier occurrence of the similar looking זרים. (Alternatively, a marginal correction of that occurrence may have mistakenly replaced סדם on the 'cuckoo' principle.[9]) The invariable use of מהפכה makes other proposed emendations[10] less likely, for example זרם, 'an inundation' (Lowth, seeking to improve on Ibn Ezra, who supposed that זרם = זרים), זדים, 'insolent ones' (Tur-Sinai, 156); גלים, 'piles of stones' (Ziegler, 16); note too V *hostili* = צרים. The alternative proposal to emend ושממה to וְשָׁמוּהָ (Ehrlich) does not solve the main problem, while to adopt this as well as סדם (Kissane) is unnecessary. Recent attempts to defend MT are unconvincing (Willis, 'Important Passage'; Watts; Motyer; Beuken). For the secondary status of the line as a whole, see below.

8. ונותרה: although it would be possible to vocalize as a participle, ונותרה (so Budde), this is not necessary, and the word order is somewhat against it. For the participle (v. 7) + *waw* with the perfect to express 'an event as going on at roughly the same time as a previous event', see Gibson, 103; to his examples, one might add especially Amos 8.14 (הנשבעים...ואמרו, 'those who swear…and say'), and Mic. 3.5 (הנשכים...וקראו, 'who bite…

---

[7] Cf. Kutscher, 319–20; Speier, 'Zu drei Jesajastellen', 310–11; Koenig, 218–21; van Peursen, 'Guarded', 103; Pulikottil, 69–70; differently Cohen, 'Philological Reevaluation', 46–47, but he does not take account of the likelihood that the word introduces a gloss.

[8] Delitzsch uses this observation to argue that MT should be construed as an objective genitive, 'an overthrow such as comes upon foreigners'; see previously Kimhi, and most recently van Peursen, 'Guarded', 104. This would be difficult after the sense of the previous line, however; see Dillmann; Young.

[9] Cf. L. C. Allen, 'Cuckoos in the Textual Nest', *JTS* NS 22 (1971), 143–50, and 'More Cuckoos in the Textual Nest', *JTS* NS 24 (1973), 69–73.

[10] Procksch offers two suggestions: (i) סדם ועמרה, but to add 'and Gomorrah' on the basis that the two towns are usually mentioned together is unnecessary, especially if, as maintained below, the whole line is a brief exegetical gloss (note that סדם occurs on its own at 3.9, though not there following מהפכה; for the separate proposal that ועמרה was corrupted into ונותרה, see on v. 8); (ii) אלהים את־הערים (כמהפכת), with reference to Jer. 20.16. This is Procksch's favoured solution, because he thinks it supplies the length of line he expects. But if the line is a gloss, such an argument is irrelevant. In any case, metrical considerations alone cannot justify so wild a conjecture.

and cry'), cited by WO, 631; see too Isa. 6.2-3.[11] (See below, however, for the further possibility that in fact a future reference was intended originally, before the text came into its present setting in ch. 1.) This supposed difficulty with the MT was one of the principal reasons why Robertson, 'Isaiah Chapter 1', 233–34, proposed emending to וְעָמְרָה, which would then be joined to the gloss at the end of the previous verse.[12] Robertson also found unnecessary difficulties with the meaning of the word in context (see below), and claimed that the reference to Sodom in v. 7 more or less demands a reference to Gomorrah as well; but see my comments in n. 10 above on Procksch. There is thus no compelling reason to emend MT. The interpretation of 1QIsaᵃ ונתרת is disputed: either defective spelling with Aramaizing ending (Kutscher, 191), or Hebrew נתר with the same meaning as the niphʻal of יתר,[13] or Aramaic נתר = 'fall, sink, collapse'.[14] All of these are rightly regarded as textually inferior to MT, however.

בת־ציון: for discussion, see below.

כמלונה: 1QIsaᵃ וכ'; LXX, V and P also have a conjunction here, and the fact that, with the exception of P, they do not have it before their renderings of כעיר suggests that it stood in their *Vorlagen* and was not simply added *ad sensum*. It is not necessarily to be preferred, however; see vv. 4 and 7 for similarly terse style.

כעיר נצורה: apparently, 'like a guarded city', but since that is precisely what 'the daughter of Zion' was, there is no point of comparison.[15] This conclusion cannot be circumvented by appeal to the so-called כ *veritatis* (so, for instance, Gesenius, who had already appealed to the same usage in v. 7), even if such a use were permissible elsewhere (a possibility rejected by GK §118x; even when it is accepted, it is only on the basis of an exact comparison, not actual identity; cf. JM §133g; WO, 203). Following two previous points of comparison, our phrase must fall into the same category as well (*pace* Claassen, 'Linguistic Arguments', 15–16). Nor can one argue that this is written in the aftermath of the siege,[16] and that therefore Jerusalem is no longer actually under siege (or better, blockade[17]); the standpoint of the description, whenever it was written, clearly reflects the Assyrian campaign, so that even in its aftermath there would be little force to the comparison. It is possible that נצור may also mean 'preserved' (cf. Isa. 49.6; Ezek. 6.12[18]), but neither text is certain, and in any case it does not give good sense here (*contra* Barnes and Kissane). Alternatively, some have used Ezek. 6.12 as well as Jer. 4.16 to find a hostile sense in נצר, which could give a passive 'besieged', but again the textual support is

[11] So P and T (LXX and V translate with future tenses). This explanation of the verbal sequence seems unfortunately to have been overlooked by Oesch, 'Jes 1,8f', with whose general approach to Isa. 1 I am otherwise in broad agreement.

[12] See too B. Stade, 'Emendationen', *ZAW* 22 (1902), 328; Budde; Vermeylen, 51; Loretz, 28, 36, 86–87. For critical discussion of some of Loretz's more idiosyncratic arguments, I refer to Emerton, 'Historical Background'.

[13] Wernberg-Møller, 'Defective Spellings', 250.

[14] Koenig, 295–97; van Peursen, 'Guarded', 105–6.

[15] It is surprising that in this connection no one has suggested emendation to בצורה, which regularly qualifies עיר, 'a fortified city'; the confusion of *beth* and *nun* is easily supposed, and at 27.10 especially the image is associated with being solitary and abandoned, which at first blush fits the present context exactly. However, there it is because the city has been deserted following a defeat, which would not fit so well. The possibility may be considered that בצורה stood in the form of the present text known to the author of 27.10 (and 25.2 as well, in all probability) and that it influenced him in his writing without that necessarily suggesting that it is a superior reading for the text here itself.

[16] *Contra* F. Jarratt, 'The Cottage in the Vineyard', *ExpT* 3 (1891–92), 464, who arbitrarily maintains that the reference is to a 'city that has been besieged'.

[17] Cf. W. Mayer in Grabbe, *'Like a Bird'*, 179–81, though he accepts that the effects 'were similar to the effects of full-scale siege but without the costs'.

[18] Cf. W. Zimmerli, *Ezechiel 1–24* (BKAT 13/1; Neukirchen–Vluyn, 1969), 141 = *Ezekiel*, i (Philadelphia, 1979), 181.

questionable, and the meaning poor, since Jerusalem was in fact besieged/blockaded. The same problem confronts the alternative vocalization נְצוּרָה, niph'al participle of צור II, 'besiege', hence 'besieged' (T; Rashi;[19] Dillmann; Condamin; Feldmann; Procksch; Donner, 119–21; Gonçalves, 246). An additional difficulty for this suggestion is that the niph'al is not attested elsewhere. Of the primary versions, LXX, P and T all have 'besieged', so that they clearly attest the consonantal text, though whether it is fair to cite them in favour of the revocalization (*BHS*) is less certain in view of what we have seen. V *quae vastatur* (which *BHS* thinks we should 'compare' to the same end) furnishes even less impressive support in this regard, though it is probably also based on MT. (Unfortunately, and uncharacteristically, Jerome offers no comment on the phrase.) 1QIsa[a] *seems* to have נצודה (see the plate, *contra* the printed text). Since it is difficult to make sense of this,[20] it may be no more than a ר/ד confusion, in which case it too effectively supports the MT. There is thus no textual evidence, *sensu stricto*, for emendation, though suggestions have been made, for example Ehrlich, כְּעָבֹר בָּצִיר, 'when the vintage harvest is over'; Wutz, כעיר בצירה, 'like a tent-peg in a pen' (cf. Arabic *ṣir* = 'tent-peg', and *ṣîra* = 'pen', as almost certainly at Mic. 2.12),[21] on which Wildberger has sought to improve by vocalizing the first word as עַיִר to give 'like an ass's foal in a pen'; Kaiser, כמעצר בצירה, 'like a refuge in a pen'. These suggestions are hardly convincing in themselves, and in addition they involve an awkward shift following two references to buildings or constructions of some kind. An older approach to MT (e.g. Hitzig; Duhm; Marti) perhaps deserves modified consideration in the light of more recent discovery. It is postulated that נצורה is an infinitive noun, formed from √נצר by analogy with such nouns as שמועה, קבוצה and גבורה, meaning 'watch, guard'. Then, with appeal to 2 Kgs 17.9 (מגדל נוצרים; further comparison with Isa. 65.4 does not seem to be helpful) and the fact that עיר need not mean only 'city' in our modern sense, they therefore proposed 'watchtower'. This would certainly give good sense, but seems to press the flexibility of עיר too far[22] (note that in 2 Kgs 17.9 the watchtower is *contrasted* with the city in terms of small to great). Since those scholars were working, however, and since Dillmann rejected this approach on the ground that 'es keine Wacht*städte* (Castelle!) gibt', many such border fortresses have in fact been excavated,[23] while there is also evidence that cities near the borders could be specially fortified to serve the same purpose (e.g. 2 Chron. 11.5-12[24]). They served as both watch- and guard-centres. Almost by definition they will have been in isolated locations, which is the point at issue in the comparison being drawn (cf. Knobel, though without the need to follow his etymological speculations regarding עיר; Wade; Watts).

---

[19] Kimhi and Ibn Ezra both compare נצורים, 'secret places(?)', at Isa. 65.4, and so interpret as 'ruined'. However, apart from the fact that some have questioned the text at 65.4, the semantic shift involved is considerable. Kimhi perhaps realized this, as in he end he reverts to citing T.

[20] In Biblical Hebrew, it would mean 'hunted', which clearly makes no sense. Van Peursen, 'Guarded', 106, thinks in terms of Mishnaic Hebrew, 'captured', which might reflect actualizing interpretation; alternatively, did they somehow link it with מצודה, 'stronghold'?

[21] F. Wutz, 'Abweichende Vokalisationsüberlieferung im hebr. Text', *BZ* 21 (1933), 9–21 (11–12).

[22] Though not as far as König's 'ein schon aufs Korn genommener Alarmplatz'! For a thorough survey of the use of עיר, including fortified settlements, see F. S. Frick, *The City in Ancient Israel* (SBLDS 36; Missoula, Mont., 1977), 25–75.

[23] See, e.g., Z. Meshel, 'The Architecture of the Israelite Fortresses in the Negev', in A. Kempinski and R. Reich (eds), *The Architecture of Ancient Israel* (Jerusalem, 1992), 294–301; Z. Yeivin, 'Two Watchtowers in the Jordan Valley', *EI* 23 (1992), 155–73 (Hebrew).

[24] It is of interest to note here that N. Na'aman has dated the source for this list precisely to the reign of Hezekiah; see 'Hezekiah's Fortified Cities and the *LMLK* Stamps', *BASOR* 261 (1986), 5–21.

9. יהוה צבאות: the syntax of this familiar title has long been a puzzle, because the usual interpretation seems to fly in the face of the general rule that personal names cannot be used in the construct state. The inscriptions discovered at Kuntillet 'Ajrud, however, have added important new evidence for this discussion, since we there find the divine name used in a comparable construction: 'Yhwh of Samaria' and 'Yhwh of Teman'. The whole debate has been thoroughly surveyed by Emerton,[25] so that there is no need to rehearse it again here. Whether or not we should assume an ellipse of אלהי, 'the Lord (God) of Hosts', the practical outcome is the same: 'there can thus no longer be any syntactical objection to understanding *jhwh ṣᵉbaʾôt* as "Yahweh of *ṣᵉbaʾôt*"' (p. 9). There is no longer any need to suggest either that צבאות is in apposition or that the tetragrammaton has ceased to be regarded as a proper name and come simply to be an equivalent for 'God'. For further discussion, see below.

שריד: LXX σπέρμα, V *semen*. As this is the only occurrence of this word in Isaiah, the Greek translator may have imitated Deut. 3.3 (note that in both verses the same verb is also used); cf. Ziegler, 106.

כמעט: the Masoretic punctuation joins this word with the first half of the verse, 'a very few survivors'; so too, probably, the paraphrase of T, ברחמוהי (Wildberger), and Ibn Ezra. LXX, P and V certainly do not include it in the first half of the verse, but it is less certain that they did not read it at all (*BHS*). While it is true that the word is not rendered at all in P, the construction in the LXX, at least (ὡς...ἄν, twice), is thought by some to indicate a measure of emphasis ('we would *nearly* have become...'), in which case it could indicate that כמעט is construed with the second half,[26] and van Uchelen, 'Isaiah i 9', 158, draws a similar conclusion from the use of the pluperfect in V; see too Rashi and Kimhi. If כמעט goes with the first half, it qualifies a noun, שריד. In such cases, however, we should expect it to precede the noun (Isa. 26.20; Ezra 9.8; 2 Chron. 12.7[27]). In the passages to which Gesenius appeals to circumvent this difficulty, special syntactical conditions apply: at Prov. 10.20 it is used as a predicate, and at Ps. 105.12 (parallel 1 Chron. 16.19) it stands in apposition, as the line division and Masoretic punctuation show. More importantly, however, van Uchelen is right to point to the only other passage where it occurs with לולי, Ps. 94.17, for there too it introduces the apodosis. Since on a number of other occasions the apodosis after לולי is introduced with an intensifying conjunction with a temporal element (כי אז, כי עתה; cf. Gibson, 155; van Uchelen, 158), it is reasonable to suppose that the same applies here: 'If the Lord had not been my help, my soul would soon have dwelt in silence'.[28] To this I should add as further strong support the use of כמעט in Ps. 81.15, where it introduces the apodosis after לו (the positive counterpart of לולי) in the previous verse: 'If my people would hearken..., then I would soon subdue...'. The nuance 'almost' = 'soon' also fits Ps. 2.12; Job 32.22 (where some would additionally vocalize the preceding לא as לְא); perhaps too Gen. 26.10.[29] Recognition of this construction should be decisive, therefore, for Isa. 1.9, and it further removes the standard objection that 'if Yahweh had not allowed some to escape, Judah would have been clean wiped out, and,

---

[25] J. A. Emerton, 'New Light on Israelite Religion: The Implications of the Inscriptions from Kuntillet 'Ajrud', *ZAW* 94 (1982), 2–20 (3–9); see too Paas, *Creation and Judgement*, 231–33. It is of interest to note that the title יהוה צבאות has now been found in an inscription (sixth century BCE?) of unknown provenance published by J. Naveh, 'Hebrew Graffiti from the First Temple Period', *IEJ* 51 (2001), 194–207.

[26] Baer, 'It's All About Us!', 198–200, argues that the translator purposely left כמעט untranslated as a later nationalistic expression of his appreciation of the size and importance of the diaspora community.

[27] Perhaps too Ezek. 16.47, but the text there is uncertain.

[28] *Contra* J. Wehrle, 'Die PV kᵊ=maʿt als Indikator für den Satzmodus in Sprechakten', in W. Gross *et al.* (eds), *Text, Methode und Grammatik: Wolfgang Richter zum 65. Geburtstag* (St. Ottilien, 1991), 577–94.

[29] See too W. W. Fields, *Sodom and Gomorrah: History and Motif in Biblical Narrative* (JSOTSup 231; Sheffield, 1997), 173.

therefore, not almost, but quite like Sodom' (Gray; see too Marti; Wildberger). Precisely the same objection could be levelled against Ps. 94.17 if כמעט = 'almost', but 'soon' fits both passages admirably (so too Wade, and Lowth's translation). A welcome result of moving כמעט to the second half of the line is that the two halves are rhythmically far better balanced. It also becomes unnecessary to delete the word as an inappropriate gloss (Marti; Condamin; Procksch).

כסדם...לעמרה: 1QIsaᵃ, כסדם...לעומרה לעומרה. For these spellings, with which the Greek Σοδομα and Γομορρα should be compared, see D. M. Beegle, 'Proper Names in the New Isaiah Scroll', *BASOR* 123 (1951), 26–30, and cf. J. Ziegler, 'Die Vorlage der Isaias-Septuaginta (LXX) und die erste Isaias-Rolle von Qumran (IQIsᵃ)', *JBL* 78 (1959), 34–59 (51).

The basic delimitation of the extent of this unit is clear, once the independence of v. 4 is accepted, as argued above. Within the larger passage comprising the whole of ch. 1, a new section obviously begins at v. 10.

Within vv. 5-9, various parts have been regarded as secondary. Most commentators agree that the last three words of v. 7 are a later gloss, not a few maintain that v. 9 is a later redactional addition, and some have further argued that this also includes v. 8.

In evaluating these proposals, it is necessary once again to make more clear than has usually been the case at what level these proposals operate. In discussing the structure of vv. 2-20 above, it was suggested that v. 10 is part of the carefully constructed framework to be attributed to the final redactor of the chapter as a whole. This emerges in particular from the combination of the imperatives in v. 2*a* with the reference to Sodom and Gomorrah in v. 9. If that is so, then it follows that v. 9 must have been part of the material which he inherited and which he was seeking to forge together into a wider unity. In other words, as we have seen with some other proposed additions, there never was a version of ch. 1 which did not include v. 9, and by extension, therefore, v. 8. That does not, of course, rule out the possibility that they might have been added secondarily within their original context in Isaiah (wherever that may have been). That, however, is a separate issue, and one which should not be allowed to intrude into an exegesis of ch. 1 itself.

These considerations do not apply to the final clause in v. 7. In addition to its clearly intrusive nature within the poetic rhythm of the passage (contrast van Grol, 'Paired Tricola'), it links the description of the country as a wasteland with the destruction of Sodom (v. 9) in an explanatory manner (note the typical introductory *waw*-explicative). It is not entirely appropriate, however, for v. 9 in fact maintains that the country has *not* suffered the same degree of destruction as Sodom. While the clause is thus certainly secondary in some sense, it is less easy to know whether it too was already in place when ch. 1 was compiled or whether it was added only subsequently. It would be possible, for instance, to see the gloss as part of a re-reading of the passage in the light of the fall of Jerusalem to the Babylonians (note that שממה, 'wasteland', is used particularly frequently in Jer. and Ezek.), but equally, as a learned scribal note, this point could have been made at any later time, not only under the immediate impact of the events in question. Because its 'exegesis' of 'wasteland' does not fit comfortably with the thought of the chapter as a whole at this point, I am tentatively inclined to regard it as wholly secondary.

The function of this unit within the developing thought of the chapter is relatively clear and straightforward. Following the severe indictment and grounding of judgment in the opening verses, this passage goes on to observe that the country has already suffered heavily, though in God's goodness the destruction has not been complete. The condition is perilous, however, and becomes the source of the opening question, which effectively serves as an impassioned plea for a change of direction, which alone might save them. This final ray of hope will then be taken up again later in the chapter.[30]

There can be little doubt that, working sometime in the post-exilic period, the chapter's compiler will have had the thought of the fall of Jerusalem to the Babylonians uppermost in his mind. Whereas at the time this appeared to be a final destruction, it inevitably came to be viewed less drastically once restoration took place. Part of the mechanism by which this reinterpretation was effected was, of course, the development of the idea of a remnant, explicit so frequently, for instance, in Ezra and Nehemiah, but undergirding much post-exilic preaching so far as it can be reconstructed from the available literature.[31] Although it is most unlikely that this thought was present in the eighth-century formulation of this passage, it will inevitably have been the way in which v. 9 especially came to be understood. Furthermore, since post-exilic Judah was very much reduced in size by comparison with the pre-exilic kingdom and its inhabitants conscious of a perceived threat from the surrounding nations, the description of Jerusalem in vv. 7-8 will have struck an immediate chord at that time.[32] As examples of specific points of contact, we may note the sense of frustration in Neh. 9.36-37 that the fruit of the land which 'we' were given to eat (אכל) now goes to foreign kings (cf. Isa. 1.7) and the sense of an isolated community in Jerusalem as a remnant which escaped only through the grace of God in Ezra 9.6-15 (cf. Isa. 1.8-9). The use of the first person plural (v. 9) in such post-exilic penitential prayers is also widespread.[33] Thus, while נותרה, הותיר and שריד can (and should) all be understood neutrally in terms of their original pre-exilic usage, they lent themselves equally naturally to reinterpretation at the time of their post-exilic re-use here.

---

[30] In 'Biblical Criticism', I have sought to show in greater detail how important this element of double punishment (one already experienced and one that is still only potential at this point) is for the redactional unity of the chapter as a whole.

[31] See Hausmann, *Israels Rest*; R. Mason, *Preaching the Tradition: Homily and Hermeneutics after the Exile* (Cambridge, 1990).

[32] Cf. Oesch, 'Jes 1,8f'; Pfaff, *Restgedankens*, 35–39.

[33] For orientation on this type of material, see H.-P. Mathys, *Dichter und Beter: Theologen aus spätalttestamentlicher Zeit* (OBO 132; Freiburg and Göttingen, 1994); R. A. Werline, *Penitential Prayer in Second Temple Judaism: The Development of a Religious Institution* (Atlanta, 1998); M. J. Boda, *Praying the Tradition: The Origin and Use of Tradition in Nehemiah 9* (BZAW 277; Berlin and New York, 1999).

Finally at this level, we should note that this paragraph introduces for
the first time the idea of a drastic narrowing within the people of God.
Although that is not the main point here, it assumes considerable importance later in the chapter (see on vv. 27-28), and this section helps to lay
the groundwork for that development.

Analysis of the rhythmic structure of the passage is complicated by the
large number of short words and construct forms, leaving doubt as to the
number of stresses in several lines (note the generous use of *maqqeph* by
the Masoretes). While there is clearly no overall regularity, certain features nevertheless stand out.[34] The first four lines in vv. 5 and 6 may be
construed as $3 + 2, 2 + 2$ repeated, suggestive of the lament form, suitable
to the content, while the last line of v. 6 is longer (the Masoretes want
$3 + 3$, though $2 + 2 + 2$ would also be possible), a device which we have
already noted sometimes marks the end of a (sub-)section. Verses 7-8
(without the gloss at the end of v. 7) are clearly a repeated $2 + 2$, a more
staccato rhythm which underlines the dramatic nature of the content, and
which we have seen is reinforced by the general absence of the conjunction. Finally, v. 9 differs again ($3 + 2$ [or 3], $3 + 2$), coinciding with the
change of speaker.

We may now move on to the (exegetically secondary) task of considering the context of this passage in the work of the eighth-century prophet
Isaiah. On the assumption which is shared with almost all commentators
that part, at least, goes back to him, this has to be associated once again
with the inevitably speculative quest for its original literary location elsewhere in the book. The unit is clearly not complete in itself; it certainly
lacks its opening, and since, as we have seen, v. 9 must have belonged
with it already at this earlier stage, the ending too is less than satisfactory
because of the unannounced switch in person which does not appear to
lead anywhere or be given any satisfactory explanation. It would therefore
be a mistake first to strip away possibly secondary material; an adequate
decision about the original shape of the unit can be decided only when it is
viewed in its original wider context.

The only previous suggestion to have been made in this regard is that
of Barth (220 n. 48), who thinks that this passage originally stood at the
end of ch. 31. It is clear, however, that he is only able to do this because
he includes v. 4 in the paragraph. Its introductory הוי enables him to suggest that 1.4-8 (he takes v. 9 as secondary) was another in the woe series
in chs 28–31. (His additional reference to 'den sachlichen und historischen
Zusammenhang' with 32.9-14 does not seem to get us very far.) Without
v. 4, however, this cannot be right, because there would be too abrupt a
change of person in ch. 31, and no connection of content.

Taking the content of the passage generally and its second person
plural address specifically as guides, only two possibilities come in for
serious consideration. Isaiah 22.1-14, though it starts out by addressing
Jerusalem in the second person feminine singular, shifts to second person

---

[34] Contrast E. Sachsse, 'Untersuchungen zur hebräischen Metrik', *ZAW* 43 (1925),
173–92 (177–79).

masculine plural by the end of the passage. Furthermore, a case might be made for a contextual connection with vv. 12-14: the people's response of joyful celebration (v. 13) to God's call for weeping and mourning (v. 12) could lead on to the question in 1.5. Finally, the use by the people of the first person plural proverb in 22.13*b* might help account for the same in 1.9. Despite all this, however, the suggestion is to be rejected. The passage ends in v. 14 with a categorical and unmitigated statement of complete judgment (עַד־תְּמֻתוּן), which picks up on the use of נמות in the proverb cited in v. 13. After such an emphatic and, from a literary point of view, conclusive statement, there seems to be no room to insert material which (as 1.5-8 or 9 suggests) implies that there is still some possible future for those who survived the disaster. Furthermore, it is difficult to see what might have triggered the addition (if that is what it is) of 1.9 in such a context. Nothing in what precedes suggests it, and it would not lead anywhere without some sort of continuation.

Isaiah 30.15-17, by contrast, provides an eminently suitable setting for 1.5-9 (and it is not necessary for our present purposes to delay over the much disputed issue whether 30.15-17 always belonged with the preceding passage or whether it owes its present location to the work of a subsequent redactor). We have here a sort of dialogue between the prophet and the people; he addresses them in the second person plural, and their responses are couched in the first person plural. The possibility of salvation on certain conditions is extended to them (v. 15), but they reject this. It seems that it is the leaders and the warriors who are initially referred to, and the passage moves towards its conclusion with the statement that many of them will flee, leaving 'you' (who by definition must now be a slightly different group) 'as a beacon on the top of a mountain, and as an ensign on a hill'. Not surprisingly, this is taken by whoever added the passage beginning in v. 19 as a reference to Jerusalem and its inhabitants.

Following the decimation in v. 17, the question in 1.5 would seem to follow naturally enough. It implies that there has already been a serious disaster, and the prophet pleads with his listeners not to make matters worse by continuing in their defection (סרה, a possible echo of 30.1, סוררים). The result of their doing so is that 'the daughter of Zion' will be left[35] isolated just as the people are in 30.17. ונותרה in 1.8 obviously picks up on נותרתם in 30.17, and in both cases vivid images are adduced to illustrate the consequent isolation, introduced in each case by a repeated כ.

The troublesome v. 9 also seems to fit well on this hypothesis. In 30.16-17 there is a lively little dialogue between the prophet and his audience. Following the prophet's presentation of God's conditional promise in v. 15 which the people reject (ולא אביתם), the response of the people is clearly marked by ותאמרו, followed by speech in the first person plural.

---

[35] This raises the possibility, at least, that ונותרה in 1.8 was indeed meant to have a future, rather than a present, reference when originally penned (cf. Oesch, 'Jes 1,8f'). As seen in the textual notes, a present rendering is grammatically legitimate, but it would be pleasing if our proposal sidestepped what some have regarded as an impossibility and which they have used as an excuse for emendation.

This dialogue goes to and fro twice in v. 16, and, following the initial
ויאמרו, the changes in person are sufficient to indicate the change of
speaker, so that there is no further explicit marker. The people continue in
their misguided trust in military might, which the prophet sarcastically
rejects by the use of word-play, and he continues with an amplification of
this in v. 17. If 1.5-9 was originally located at this point, the first person
plural in v. 9 could again be understood as the people's response. The
wider context set by 30.16 would be sufficient for this to be the obvious
understanding of the change of person. In this round of dialogue, however,
the use of word-play is the reverse of that in the first. Whereas in 30.16 the
prophet picked up the people's statements in order to reverse their
expectations, this time the people pick up on the prophet's warning that
the daughter of Zion will be left isolated (ונותרה, 1.8) and in 1.9 use the
same verb (הותיר) now with the positive sense of having been preserved by
God.

The possibility that 1.9 might be part of a dialogue has been raised in
the past by van Uchelen, 'Isaiah i 9', but rejected in large part (see
Gonçalves, 251) because of the lack of contextual evidence within ch. 1
that a dialogue is in process. The proposal advanced here removes this
difficulty, and furthermore integrates this dialogue with its context by the
comparable use of word-play. It is noteworthy too (and by no means
unparalleled) that a passage which was meant to be read dismissively in its
original context has been taken positively and seriously by a later reader,
namely the compiler of ch. 1.

If 1.5-9 be read in this position, 30.18 would then represent the
prophet's response to the people's attempt to reverse the force of his warning in 1.8. He concedes that some have indeed survived (or will survive),
but reaffirms (cf. 30.15) that their only lasting hope is in patient waiting
upon the Lord. There are, of course, some who doubt the authenticity to
Isaiah himself of 30.18, but this is not serious for our purposes, since it
will certainly have been in place before the compilation of ch. 1. Either
1.9 + 30.18 will be Isaianic, or both verses will be part of a later addition,
developing redactionally the dialogue initiated in 30.15-17. The important
point is that 30.18 provides a natural conclusion to the section beginning
with v. 15 as reconstructed here. On balance, it seems that the case for the
authenticity of both verses is considerably strengthened by this reconstruction.

A final point to be made has no probative force, but is very satisfying if
the case is in fact correct. Isaiah 30 continues in vv. 19-26 with a passage
which is universally regarded as late. In the manner of many such additions in Isaiah, however, it draws on the preceding passage for some of its
ideas and vocabulary. Thus v. 19 clearly amplifies v. 18, for its חנון יחנך is
based on v. 18's לרחמכם, and we have already noted a further connection
by way of the identification of the prophet's dialogue partners as the
inhabitants of Zion. It is thus noteworthy that the passage ends (v. 26b)
with a reference to 'the day when the Lord binds up (חבש) the hurt of his
people, and heals the stroke of their wound (מכתו)'. This seems to offer a
satisfying reversal of the general situation presupposed in 1.5-6, verses

which additionally include the use of חבש and מכה (as well as the related verb in וחכ).[36] The opening and close of the addition in 30.19-26 thus neatly build on our reconstruction of the material which once preceded it.

This proposal strengthens the case both for the literary integrity of the greater part of 1.5-9 and for associating it with the events of 701 BCE, both conclusions which are still maintained by most recent commentators.[37] Hayes and Irvine, it is true, have sought to argue that the verses refer rather to the aftermath of the earthquake which struck the country during Uzziah's reign (cf. Amos 1.1; Zech. 14.5), but that is only a consequence of their dogmatic assumption that the whole of the first part of the book of Isaiah is arranged in strict chronological order. They do not explain how it comes about that Jerusalem alone should have escaped completely unscathed from what they regard as an otherwise universally destructive cataclysm, nor is their explanation of v. 8 as a reference to looters convincing. Indeed, it is striking that Milgrom, 'Did Isaiah Prophesy?', who anticipates Hayes and Irvine in ascribing 1.10–6.13 to Uzziah's reign, explicitly excludes 1.2-9 from this setting and includes them amongst the latest sayings of Isaiah's ministry.

There is less agreement as to the precise point during the events of that year at which these words were spoken, whether during the course of the Assyrian campaign itself[38] or in its immediate aftermath.[39] It seems that this passage should at least be dated earlier than ch. 22. There, the people of Jerusalem are depicted in celebration following the Assyrian withdrawal, and Isaiah turns away in despair and with a final categorical word of total judgment. Here, by contrast, it seems that the people are still

---

[36] More remotely, it may be asked whether the promise of fertility in 30.23-4 is a reversal of 1.7.

[37] Against the possibility that this could relate to earlier times, such as the Syro-Ephraimite invasion, or the period just before or after the fall of Samaria (e.g. Gesenius; Skinner; Robertson, 'Isaiah Chapter 1'; H. G. Mitchell, 'Isaiah on the Fate of his People and their Capital', *JBL* 37 [1918], 149–62; Snijders), see Claassen, 'Linguistic Arguments', 9–10, and Halpern, 'Jerusalem and the Lineages', 43. König dates the passage to the reign of Jotham, but only because he mistakenly takes vv. 2-9 as a single paragraph, and so concludes that both northern and southern kingdoms must be involved. Equally, an exilic dating or thereabouts (Vermeylen, 54–57; Kaiser) is unnecessary (see Emerton, 'Historical Background', and Kustár, 51–53, for a refutation of the arguments, and specifically on Vermeylen, see Bjørndalen, 'Zur Frage der Echtheit', 90–93) and fails to provide so exact an historical fit as the events of 701 BCE as recorded in the Assyrian annals (see the commentary below). Berges, 62–63, has more recently argued again for a late date, but several of the six arguments he advances repeat older positions (e.g. the supposed late date of the phrase בת ציון and the fact that some of the vocabulary is frequently attested in exilic writings; while others are very weak (e.g. he wonders why a saying from late in Isaiah's ministry should come near the start of the book—but we have seen that the redactor responsible for ch. 1 drew from several different places in order to construct his new introduction to the book). Ben Zvi, 'Isaiah 1,4-9', correctly stresses that an Isaianic date cannot be proved, but his linguistic arguments for finding a later date more probable are extremely weak (see, for instance, the comments on בת ציון in v. 8 below). It is precisely the balance of probability which favours 701 so strongly.

[38] E.g. Dietrich, 191–93; Claassen, 'Linguistic Arguments'.

[39] E.g. Donner, 120–21; Gonçalves, 253–54.

suffering, and he implies that there is still a last chance of escape from the worst of the consequences. On the other hand, v. 9 implies that (in the people's view, at least) they have already been spared from final disaster. The simplest solution is to suppose that the events of the campaign were more complex than many recent scholars believe, with more than one 'false dawn' for the inhabitants of Jerusalem during its course.[40] Alternatively, if the 'simple' view of the campaign is adopted (currently the most favoured view), we must suppose that Isaiah was writing immediately after the withdrawal but with its effects still vividly in mind, and before it was even certain that the affair was at an end. (Of course, if v. 9 is not Isaianic, a setting during the campaign becomes unproblematic.) Since in any case there may well have been some time lapse between oral proclamation and commitment to writing, conflation of more than one closely related setting in the text is not unlikely, so that overly elaborate attempts to pinpoint precise timings may be mistaken in principle.

We return finally, then, to the question of literary unity, and in particular the authenticity of vv. 8 and 9. The case against v. 9 alone is the stronger and more widely adopted,[41] based principally on the change of person, the apparent softening of the impact of the previous verses and the introduction of Sodom and Gomorrah on the basis, it is maintained, of their presence in the next verse. As we have seen, however, this last argument should be reversed, since it is v. 10 which is more readily to be explained as redactional, while the first two arguments are both naturally answered by our understanding of the original placement of this oracle in ch. 30.[42] The case for also including v. 8 as secondary (e.g. Robertson, 'Isaiah Chapter 1'; Vermeylen, 51–53; Kaiser;[43] Loretz; Höffken; Pfaff,

---

[40] This is by no means impossible, but a resolution of the issue would take us into highly contentious and well-nigh intractable problems of historical reconstruction. It may be noted here that some of the arguments for the two-campaign theory (which is itself now largely discredited) have also been used sometimes to argue that the course of events in 701 BCE was indeed complex, with Hezekiah first 'paying off' Sennacherib and so expecting that to be the end of the matter, and then Sennacherib changing his mind (perhaps because of news of the Egyptian advance) and so returning to subdue Jerusalem; see, for instance, H. H. Rowley, 'Hezekiah's Reform and Rebellion', *BJRL* 44 (1961–62), 395–461 = *Men of God: Studies in Old Testament History and Prophecy* (London, 1963), 98–132; Willis, 'An Important Passage'. In that case, Isa. 1.5-9 could fit neatly between these two phases of the campaign. A decision involves, of course, giving considerable, though still critical, credence to the narratives in 2 Kgs 18–19 (Isa. 36–37), discussion of which would take us far beyond what can sensibly be undertaken here; for recent significant studies with further bibliographical orientation, see W. R. Gallagher, *Sennacherib's Campaign to Judah* (SHCANE 18; Leiden, 1999), and Grabbe, *'Like a Bird'*.

[41] E.g. Marti; F. Crüsemann, *Studien zur Formgeschichte von Hymnus und Danklied in Israel* (WMANT 32; Neukirchen–Vluyn, 1969), 163–64; Barth, 190–91; Clements, 'The Prophecies of Isaiah'; Gonçalves, 249–51; Hausmann, *Israels Rest*, 139–41; Bosshard-Nepustil, 222; these scholars do not, however, agree among themselves about the date of the addition.

[42] Even without that, not all scholars are convinced that the difficulties are insuperable; see most recently Emerton, 'Historical Background'; Sweeney, *Isaiah 1–4*, 127–28.

[43] Kaiser also thinks that v. 7 is an exilic redaction, but unnecessarily; see Emerton.

Restgedankens, 35–39[44]) relates primarily to the distribution and meaning of certain items of vocabulary, and must for the most part be judged weak, if not completely implausible. The strongest argument concerns the phrase בת־ציון, and this will be discussed in the comments on v. 8 below. The other examples are trivial and have been dealt with decisively by Emerton, 'Historical Background', and Kustár, 42–45, so that we need not delay further here. Objections on the basis of metre are equally invalid, as our analysis above has shown, and finally suggestions that the passage refers to late ideas of the remnant fail to distinguish between the eighth-century use and meaning of נותר and שריד (both in evidence here) and the probability, discussed above, that these may have been *understood* differently in the later period; see the recent commentaries of Beuken and Blenkinsopp for a more satisfactory appreciation of this point. (It is noteworthy that the root שאר is not used here.) It may be concluded that the last clause in v. 7 is the only late addition to vv. 5-9.

5. It is clear that the rebellion of the people has already been severely punished, that they have still not learnt their lesson, and that the prophet is pleading with them to change course before the final and fatal blow falls. The language of *being beaten* is sufficiently broad to encompass both imagery and that to which it relates in this context, so that we should be cautious about limiting its application here. It can encompass beating as punishment (so the surface sense following the description of the rebellious child), being attacked and defeated of either an individual, an army, a country or a city (so the historical reference here), and struck more generally with some disease (so in part the continuation of the imagery in the following line; as Kaiser points out, however, there is nothing in what follows which may not be the direct result of severe flogging).[45] The picture of punishment will thus naturally have been understood of God's use of the Assyrian as the 'rod of my anger' (10.5), and could equally be reapplied to the later Babylonian invader.

Persist in your defection: yet another word to describe turning away from God ('treason, rebellion'; e.g. Deut. 13.6 [5]; Jer. 28.16; 29.32);[46] following so quickly after the already extensive list in v. 4, it is likely that we should again not specify its content too quickly, though in the original historical context, false political alliances may have been uppermost in Isaiah's mind; cf. 30.1 ('cessation of hostilities against the Assyrians is the one action that the people can take to put an end to the suffering described in this passage', Sweeney). As 31.6 specifies, it is the very opposite of 'return, repent (שוב)', the response which the prophet is here vainly urging.

---

[44] In addition, Werner has argued on similar grounds that the whole of 1.4-9 is a post-exilic composition; see 'Israel in der Entscheidung', and *Eschatologische Texte*, 118–26.

[45] See, for instance, BDB, 645–46, and J. Conrad, *ThWAT* v. 445–54 = *TDOT* ix. 415–23, for examples.

[46] Cf. E. Jenni, 'Dtn 19,16: *sarā* "Falschheit"', in A. Caquot and M. Delcor (eds), *Mélanges bibliques et orientaux en l'honneur de M. Henri Cazelles* (AOAT 212; Kevelaer and Neukirchen–Vluyn, 1981), 201–11.

From a second person plural address, the passage moves on to picture the people as a whole under the image of a single body (*The whole head... the whole heart*; see the textual notes). The transition is natural and unforced, but important in the wider context, where this same duality has already occurred in both vv. 2-3 and 4 and will reappear in vv. 7-8. Together with the repeated כל ('the whole'), the reference to *head* and *heart* is clearly intended to demonstrate that the 'sickness' is both all-encompassing and deep-rooted. The body politic is rotten to the core, so that we are close to a fulfilment of the time when the chance of 'healing' following repentance referred to in 6.10 (again in connection with the heart) will be past; cf. Hos. 6.1.

Has become sick: while the word used here (חלי) can, as already noted, refer to physical wounds (e.g. 2 Kgs 8.29; Jer 6.7), it is unlikely in the present context that we should so limit it, as though the figure had been beaten on the head as well as the rest of the body. The parallelism (*the whole heart is faint*) indicates that more is at stake. If we must force consistency on to the whole image, then we may follow Kaiser, who states that 'even if his wounds do not produce fever, his circulation is likely to be severely impaired'; but more probably the prophet is simply piling up pictures of a severely beaten and sick man.

Faint: the root דוה has cognates in most Semitic languages,[47] for example, Akk. *dawû*, 'jerk, convulse' (*CDA*, 58) and Ug. *dwy*, 'fall ill, become sick' (*DUL*, 284, with further cognates). In Biblical Hebrew and its derivatives, it is also associated with menstruation, though there is no evidence to suggest that faintness was associated with loss of blood. The form used here occurs exclusively with 'the heart' in contexts which imply grief or despair rather than purely physical illness,[48] suggesting 'faint' as the best English equivalent. There is nothing of semantic significance to be derived from Wildberger's observation that the grammatical form used here is 'intensive'.

6. The metaphor of the nation as a beaten and untended person continues before it is 'explained' in the following two verses. After the looser description of the immediately preceding line, the whole verse can be naturally understood in terms of one who is suffering from a severe beating.[49]

From the sole of the foot to the head there is no soundness in it reinforces the emphasis of the previous verse on the devastating extent of the blows that have fallen. In the light of vv. 7-8, Kustár, 50, suggests that there is a metaphorical allusion here to the Judean countryside and the capital (head) Jerusalem. *No soundness* is expanded and explained by the

---

[47] Cf. R. E. Averbeck, *NIDOTTE* i. 925–28.

[48] Jer. 8.18; Lam. 1.22; Lachish Letter 3.7 ('For your servant has been sick at heart ever since you sent (that letter) to your servant'); this may tell against introducing it by emendation into Job 6.7.

[49] This approach seems preferable in context to that which finds in the verse a list of 'injuries received in battle' (Oswalt), though as in v. 5 that thought is not far removed. חבורה is never used of wounds sustained in battle. Had that been the intention, we might rather have expected the use of חלל.

following three words for different types of wound.[50] The point of the list, of course, lies in its cumulative effect rather than in the precise definition of each of its parts. The three words also occur together in Prov. 20.30 in a context which states that corporal punishment can lead to reform of character. This is just what Isaiah looked for, but failed to find.

Bruises: פצע can refer either to open wounds (e.g. 1 Kgs 20.73) or to contusions (Deut. 23.2 [1]). The latter is marginally preferable here, since the former is covered by the third term in the list, which seems to aim at being as comprehensive as possible.

Weals (חבורה) usually occurs in association (if not parallel) with פצע, as here (cf. Gen. 4.23; Exod. 21.25; Prov. 20.30), so that it is difficult to arrive at a distinction. Psalms 38.6 (5) ('My wounds grow foul and fester') suggests an open wound (though a number of commentators think of leprosy). Perhaps the best clue comes from the remaining occurrence, Isa. 53.5, where it appears to be the consequence of מוסר, 'physical "discipline"', that is, beating with a rod', as in a number of passages in Proverbs.[51] 'Stripe' or 'weal' therefore seems the most appropriate equivalent.

Wounds (מכה) must, in context,[52] be the result of 'being beaten' (תכו), v. 5 (and see explicitly Deut. 25.3), but distinguished here in that they are טריה, literally 'fresh, moist, raw' (cf. Judg. 15.15), hence probably *still bleeding*; these stripes were so severe that they cut deep into the flesh.

The necessary treatment for such wounds, here neglected, is straightforward: *pressed out*, to remove dirt, which might cause infection, and any 'purulent matter' (Gray), *bandaged* (cf. Ezek. 34.4, 16; Hos. 6.1), and *softened with oil*, both to soothe pain (cf. Jer. 8.22) and perhaps also to soften scabs.

7-8. From metaphor, the passage turns to reality. The countryside and its townships have been devastated, and Jerusalem is left isolated. The only known historical circumstance to which this could refer is the Assyrian invasion of 701 BCE.[53] While there are well-known difficulties in reconstructing some aspects of the detail of the campaign, these main points—and they are the only ones to concern the present passage—are agreed, being attested with a striking degree of coherence by the Assyrian annals,[54] the biblical account (especially 2 Kgs 18.13-16[55]) and the

---

[50] The nouns in the Hebrew text are in each case singular, but English style prefers the plural in such cases; cf. JM §135c.

[51] R. N. Whybray, *Thanksgiving for a Liberated Prophet: An Interpretation of Isaiah Chapter 53* (JSOTSup 4; Sheffield, 1978), 97.

[52] Elsewhere, of course, the word can refer to a wide variety of wounds and diseases. The more restricted use of the word in our verse suggests that we should not associate it directly with the 'covenant curses' of Lev. 26.21 or Deut. 28.61.

[53] A further small pointer to this conclusion is argued by Machinist, 'Assyria and its Image', 724–25, followed by Hartenstein, *Unzugänglichkeit*, 174, who observes that the order which the elements of the destruction in these verses follows exactly replicates the common phraseology in Assyrian royal inscriptions but is found nowhere else in the Hebrew Bible.

[54] For the text of the main source, the Rassam cylinder, see E. Frahm, *Einleitung in die Sanherib-Inschriften* (AfO Beiheft 26; Vienna, 1997), 51–55, and for an accessible translation see *CoS* ii. 302–3. For older analyses, see, for instance, L. L. Honor, *Sennacherib's*

archaeological record.[56] For Isaiah himself, the same 'last chance' appeal as attested already in vv. 5-6 still stands, although the people's response in v. 9 shows them distorting this into a message of God's deliverance already experienced. In the light of this misrepresentation, it is not difficult to imagine Isaiah's despair, as recorded in ch. 22, following soon after.

While the passage cannot have been composed, therefore, as a direct reflection of the later Babylonian invasion, when Jerusalem was in fact captured and destroyed, it is nevertheless likely that, at the much later time of the compiler of ch. 1, it was so reinterpreted.[57] By then, the exile was over, Jerusalem and the temple had been restored, and the community was repositioning itself in continuity with the pre-exilic nation. In that setting, v. 9 could reasonably be seen in a new and more positive light. Confusion over this recontextualization by the chapter's compiler, when he moved this passage from its original setting (suggested above to have been following 30.17), accounts for many of the features to which some commentators have mistakenly appealed to argue for an originally later composition; see further the general introduction to this paragraph above.

7. *Your country is a wasteland*: with *cities* and *land* (אדמה) following, it is likely that *country* here refers to the political entity of Judah rather than the countryside as such. This seems appropriate at the start of the description. *Wasteland* (שממה) is a common word, especially in the prophets, with several equally common synonyms deriving from the same root. It can be applied to a wide range of entities and circumstances, so that it would be unwise to attempt any specific definition here.[58] The state of the country

Invasion of Palestine: A Critical Source Study (New York, 1926); C. van Leeuwen, 'Sanchérib devant Jérusalem', *OTS* 14 (1965), 245–72; E. Vogt, 'Sennacherib und die letzte Tätigkeit Jesajas', *Biblica* 47 (1966), 427–37, though these need to be read in the light of the more recent studies mentioned at the end of n. 40 above, esp. Gallagher, and Mayer in Grabbe, *'Like a Bird'*, 168–200. Gonçalves, 102–4, also helpfully locates this account among the other relevant Akkadian sources.

[55] This is not to deny, of course, that both the biblical texts and the Assyrian annals have ideological points of their own to make; in addition to the studies mentioned already, cf. respectively C. R. Seitz, 'Account A and the Annals of Sennacherib: A Reassessment', *JSOT* 58 (1993), 47–57, and A. R. Millard, 'Sennacherib's Attack on Hezekiah', *TynB* 36 (1985), 61–77; see also J. B. Geyer, '2 Kings xviii 14-16 and the Annals of Sennacherib', *VT* 21 (1971), 604–6.

[56] Grabbe, *'Like a Bird'*, 3–20, gives a helpful up-to-date survey of the data with abundant bibliography. Halpern, 'Jerusalem and the Lineages', provides a wealth of further detail on a number of aspects both of the course and the aftermath of this campaign. The value of his collection of data stands regardless of one's appraisal of the wider conclusions he draws from it.

[57] Indeed, according to van Peursen, 'Guarded', this process of reinterpretation extends in different textual witnesses to much later defeats and destructions at the hands of the Greeks and Romans.

[58] Once again, it would therefore be hazardous to ascribe its occurrence here specifically to a reflection of the 'covenant curses' in Deut. 28 and Lev. 26 (see above, n. 52, and further Høgenhaven, 223–26; Emerton, 'Historical Background'), *contra* Kaiser, Oswalt, and Berges, 63.

ravaged by war, and with many of its population killed, exiled[59] or escaped as refugees, can be imagined. It is worthy of note that the same word is used as part of the description of the complete judgment which is envisaged in 6.11,[60] especially in view of the fact that we saw a possible allusion to 6.10 in v. 5 above. If ch. 22 is anything to go by, Isaiah probably saw in the Judeans' response to the Assyrian invasion a loss of their final chance for salvation, so that an allusion to the outcome of his 'hardening' ministry here is not surprising (see too 5.9). Equally, this will have been seen to have come to an even more cataclysmic fulfilment in the later Babylonian invasion (to which the addition of 6.12-13a may testify), so that it would be only natural for the later compiler of this chapter to re-read the saying in its light. Ultimately, those responsible for the later parts of the book of Isaiah may also have consciously taken up the theme by way of reversal, pointing now to God's restoration of that which had been devastated in the judgment (see, for instance, 49.8, 19; 54.1-3; 61.4; 62.4; for fuller details, see Williamson, *Book*, 51–55). Such a use, re-use, and ultimate reversal of a theme in the Isaianic corpus is by no means unusual.

The destruction of many Judean *cities* (which is retained as a conventional translation; it can refer to 'a wide range of settlements without regard to relative size'[61]), sometimes *with fire*, at the end of the eighth century BCE is well attested archaeologically. There are, of course, uncertainties about dating in some cases, especially in the case of earlier excavations,[62] and equally not every destruction from this period need necessarily have been due specifically to Sennacherib, but some examples are clear beyond any doubt, most notably Lachish.[63] As he himself boasted, 'I besieged forty-six of his fortified walled cities, and surrounding smaller towns, which were without number. …I conquered (them)' (*CoS* ii. 303). In view of the fact that historical reality underlies the present description, we should be cautious about following Wildberger in his suggestion that there is a conscious echo here of the destruction of many of the Canaanite cities in the time of Joshua (cf. Josh. 6.24; 8.28; 11.11, 13), so that 'what had once happened to their enemies when Israel was still under the blessing of Yahweh was now happening to them, as part of the curse' (see further n. 52 above).

---

[59] Sennacherib claims to have taken just over 200,000 of the population as booty; see *CoS* ii. 303. Quite how many of these may have been deported (exiled, from their point of view) is disputed; cf. S. Stohlmann, 'The Judaean Exile After 701 B.C.E.', in W. W. Hallo, J. C. Moyer and L. G. Perdue (eds), *Scripture in Context. II: More Essays on the Comparative Method* (Winona Lake, Ind., 1983), 147–75.

[60] See R. Rendtorff, 'Jesaja 6 im Rahmen der Komposition des Jesajabuches', in Vermeylen (ed.), *The Book of Isaiah*, 73–82 = 'Isaiah 6 in the Framework of the Composition of the Book', in his *Canon and Theology* (Edinburgh, 1994), 170–80; Hartenstein, *Unzugänglichkeit*, 169–75.

[61] J. D. Price, *NIDOTTE* iii. 396–99; see too Frick, *City* (above, n. 22), 25–75.

[62] See the survey in Halpern, 'Jerusalem and the Lineages', 34–41.

[63] See D. Ussishkin, *The Renewed Archaeological Excavations at Lachish (1973–1994)*, II (Tel Aviv, 2004).

The main point of dispute in the second line of the verse concerns the identity of the *foreigners*: are they the Assyrian forces, who will have lived off the local produce of the land during their campaign, or are they the peoples of neighbouring countries to whom Sennacherib handed over part of the Judean territory after he had conquered it? The word itself, זרים, offers no help in resolving this difficulty.[64] It is used some seventy times in the Old Testament in a wide variety of contexts to refer to any who are strange or alien in a given situation. It can certainly be used in an ethnic or political sense, as here,[65] as is made clear by context and/or parallelism in such passages as Isa. 61.5; Ezek. 28.7, 10; 30.12; 31.12; Lam. 5.2, and it is not surprising that there are often threatening overtones in these and other comparable passages. Similarly, the description that they are *devouring* (lit. 'eating') *your land* (אדמתכם...אכלים אתה) is also ambiguous. It has been suggested (e.g. by Donner, 120) that this must refer to the full agricultural exploitation of the land, so that it could not refer to the Assyrians. The identical verb and object occur together only once elsewhere (Gen. 3.17), however, which is hardly an adequate basis on which to base so fine a distinction, and while it is true that there are many examples of less verbally exact, but nevertheless closely comparable, expressions of the same idea (e.g. Isa. 1.19; 5.17; 36.16 and many others; cf. *DCH* i. 243), so too are there of the opposite idea, namely of enemy forces either destroying[66] or living off the land.[67]

Sennacherib claims in his early accounts of this campaign to have handed over Hezekiah's towns which he captured to the kings of Ashdod, Ekron and Gaza, while the Nineveh Bull inscription adds Ashkelon to this list.[68] Quite how much Judean territory was involved is unstated, and opinions differ.[69] Despite this element of uncertainty, and bearing in mind

---

[64] It may, however, eliminate the relating of this passage to the Syro-Ephraimite invasion of Judah, since '*zār* is never used for a fellow Yahwist, even though it be an inhabitant of the Northern Kingdom' (Claassen, 'Linguistic Arguments', 9; cf. Ben Zvi, 'Isaiah 1,4-9', 104–5).

[65] It seems unnecessary to outline the many other uses of the word; for a survey, see L. A. Snidjers, *ThWAT* ii. 556–64 = *TDOT* iv. 52–58.

[66] So Claassen, 'Linguistic Arguments', 11–13, with reference to passages such as Jer. 8.16; 10.25; Ps. 79.7.

[67] E.g. Marti and Gray, with reference to Jer. 8.16.

[68] For introductory surveys of the various Assyrian records, see Gonçalves, 102–4, Millard, 'Sennacherib's Attack', and Mayer in Grabbe, *'Like a Bird'*, 168–200, all with extensive further bibliography.

[69] A 'maximalist' view is adopted by A. Alt, 'Die territorialgeschichtliche Bedeutung von Sanheribs Eingriff in Palästina', in his *Kleine Schriften zur Geschichte des Volkes Israel*, ii (Munich, 1953), 242–49, broadly supported by G. W. Ahlström, *The History of Ancient Palestine* (Minneapolis, 1993), 714–33. Ahlström makes much (pp. 715, 717, 732) of the fact that in the Esarhaddon annals Hezekiah's successor Manasseh is given the title *šar^uru Ia^udi*, 'the king of the city of Judah', arguing that this indicates that Judah had been reduced to little more than a city state, comprising Jerusalem and its surroundings. This needs to be balanced, however, by the title *šar māt Ia^udi*, 'King of the land of Judah', elsewhere; cf. M. Cogan and H. Tadmor, *II Kings: A New Translation with Introduction and Commentary* (AB 11; New York, 1988), 265 and 339; F. Stavrakopoulou, *King Manasseh and Child Sacrifice: Biblical Distortions of Historical Realities* (BZAW

the likelihood that this paragraph would have been written in the wake, rather than during the actual course, of the campaign, it is probable on balance that this situation of some part of former Judean territory being now under the control of *foreigners* best explains our passage (cf. Gonçalves, 254). That its sentiments would have resonated also with the post-exilic compiler of the chapter as a whole (e.g. Neh. 9.36-37) goes without saying.

If all this is correct, *in your very presence* (לנגדכם) has strong rhetorical force. It refers here less to physical proximity (though of course that is not excluded) as to the ignominy of the audience's powerlessness to reverse the effects of their foolish rebellion.

For the gloss which comprises the final line of the verse, see the general introduction to this section above.

8. Before an attempt is made to explain the verse as a whole, comment is required on the phrase *the daughter of Zion* (retained here as a familiar translation). (i) It must be clearly distinguished from the plural 'daughters (בנות) of Zion', which is used four times elsewhere for the female inhabitants of the city (3.16, 17; 4.4; Ct. 3.11).[70] Also, the plural 'daughters of GN' can refer to the cities of a named country (e.g. Pss. 48.12 [11]; 97.8; and probably Jer. 49.3) and frequently to the dependent towns and villages of a major city. None of this is relevant to our phrase in the singular, however.

(ii) While 'daughter of GN' is commonest with Zion, as in our phrase, it also occurs a number of times with other towns or countries, such as Babylon (Ps. 137.8), Judah (Lam. 2.2, 5), and even Jerusalem itself (Zeph. 3.14; Zech. 9.9, both parallel with 'daughter of Zion'). A number of discussions of 'daughter of Zion' proceed without paying adequate attention to these comparable uses; any explanation should aim to cover the phenomenon as a whole.

(iii) The phrase sometimes follows some other feature of the city in the construct state, for example 'the mountain of the daughter of Zion' (Isa. 10.32 [Q], parallel with 'the hill of Jerusalem'; 16.1), 'the Ophel of the daughter of Zion' (Mic. 4.8), 'the gates of the daughter of Zion' (Ps. 9.15 [14]), and 'the wall of the daughter of Zion' (Lam. 2.8, 18).

(iv) While from these last two points it seems clear that the phrase is a metaphor for the city itself (and so by extension for its inhabitants, of course), the nature of the relationship between the two constituent words

338; Berlin, 2004), 102–4. Support from material remains for at least a substantial shift of territorial control is adduced by Halpern, 'Jerusalem and the Lineages', 45–49. Others maintain that the redistribution of land was less extensive, e.g. Y. Aharoni, *The Land of the Bible: A Historical Geography* (London, 1967), 340; N. Na'aman, 'Sennacherib's Campaign to Judah and the Date of the *lmlk* Stamps', *VT* 29 (1989), 61–86. Kaiser's assertion that Sennacherib's claims are 'no more than a figment of the imagination' seems to be unwarranted, however.

[70] 'Daughters of GN' is, of course, common in relation to many other towns and countries as well; cf. H. Haag, *ThWAT* i. 870 = *TDOT* ii. 335 for references. Its male counterpart, 'sons (בני) of GN', is even commoner, including 'sons of Zion' (Joel 2.23; [Zech. 9.13;] Ps. 149.2; Lam. 4.2); cf. *ibid.*, 673–74 = 151.

is disputed. It is commonest by far to construe 'daughter of' as an appositional genitive, as is, in fact, not uncommon with place names (e.g. 'the
land of Egypt', 'the city of Shechem' [Gen. 33.18], etc.).[71] In this case,
Zion is personified as a 'daughter'; see further below. This approach has
been challenged in two ways, however. First, Cazelles[72] has proposed that
the phrase refers to only a part of the city as a whole, namely the newly
settled quarter on the western hill. This seems to fall foul of the data in
point (ii) above and to be unlikely in the case of some of those in point
(iii), and it has not been taken up subsequently. Secondly, Dobbs-Allsopp[73]
has argued that the phrase is the equivalent of divine epithets in Akkadian
in which a goddess is termed *mārat* GN, 'daughter of GN': 'The goddess
was evidently understood as a citizen of the city in which her shrine was
located. Note that the operative species of the genitive in this construction
[i.e. "genitive of location"] is made unambiguous by its use in a divine
epithet: the genitive signifies the location of the goddess's shrine'. In support of this view, Dobbs-Allsopp draws attention to five points of comparison between Mesopotamian city laments, in which the 'weeping
goddess' features prominently, and those occurrences of the comparable
Hebrew idiom which he adjudges to come from similar genres in the
biblical prophets and Lamentations (about three-quarters of the total, in
his estimation). He recognizes, of course, that in view of the monotheistic
tendencies of the biblical writers, *bat* GN will not refer to an actual
goddess; it is, rather, a 'purely literary phenomenon', a metaphor for the
personified city. Nevertheless, it should be determinative in our understanding of the grammatical structure. Despite the impressive learning
displayed by Dobbs-Allsopp, however, it must be questioned whether he
has, in fact, correctly identified the background for our phrase. In particular, it does not seem suitable for those several cases where the GN is the
name of a country, and while it is true that the phrase is often used in
passages of lament over a fallen city, this is by no means always the
case.[74] It may also be questioned whether the use is suitable to those
passages where 'daughter of Jerusalem' stands in parallel with 'daughter
of Zion'. Finally, as Schmitt has pointed out,[75] 'none of the goddesses who
appear in the Hebrew Bible is ever called *bat*'. The grammatical analysis
of the phrase as an appositional genitive seems preferable.

[71] See JM §129*f*(7); WO, 153; Gibson, 32; W. F. Stinespring, 'No Daughter of Zion: A
Study of the Appositional Genitive in Hebrew Grammar', *Encounter* 26 (1965), 133–41;
D. R. Hillers, *Lamentations: A New Translation with Introduction and Commentary* (AB
7A; 2nd edn; New York, 1992), 30–31.
    [72] H. Cazelles, 'Histoire et géographie en Michée iv, 6-13', in *Fourth World Congress
of Jewish Studies*, I (Jerusalem, 1967), 87–89.
    [73] F. W. Dobbs-Allsopp, 'The Syntagma of *bat* Followed by a Geographical Name in
the Hebrew Bible: A Reconsideration of its Meaning and Grammar', *CBQ* 57 (1995),
451–70.
    [74] E. R. Follis, *ABD* vi. 1103, estimates that as many as half the occurrences of
'daughter of Zion' 'reflect dignity, joy, favor, and exaltation'.
    [75] J. J. Schmitt, 'The City as Woman in Isaiah 1–39', in Broyles and Evans (eds),
Writing and Reading the Scroll of Isaiah, 95–119 (97–98).

(v) Why should Zion (as well as some other cities, and sometimes even countries) be personified as a daughter? The question has to be answered on two levels. First, there is the matter of background—where the idea originally came from (as with Dobbs-Allsopp above). Fitzgerald has influentially proposed that the idea goes back to the ancient notion of the capital city as the consort of the patron god of the city,[76] though this is by no means universally agreed;[77] the evidence is lacking for anything more than hypotheses. But even if Fitzgerald's view were correct, it is interesting to note that the image would have already developed to the extent that (a) the city is now personified as a woman in her own right ('daughter' as a term of endearment rather than, say, 'woman' or even 'wife'), and (b) it is questionable whether all uses of the phrase can be sensibly referred to capital cities alone. In other words, it is more likely that we are dealing with a 'dead' or 'conceptual' metaphor, i.e. 'a metaphor so deeply imbedded in the culture as to be virtually invisible, but nonetheless the source of everyday assumptions and speech'.[78] If that is right (and the lack of firm evidence with the consequent multiplication of possible theories suggests strongly that it is), then the origins and history of the term can tell us nothing about its use in our texts. Secondly, then, when we look more synchronically at the biblical data we find that this is but one of a number of female images for cities: daughter, wife, widow, mother, childless woman, queen, and so on. And in this context, a 'dead' metaphor can come to life again, suggesting new lines of imaginative thought in all sorts of directions. There have been many studies of this aspect of our topic in the more recent past,[79] and from the point of view of a sequential

[76] See A. Fitzgerald, 'The Mythological Background for the Presentation of Jerusalem as a Queen and False Worship as Adultery in the Old Testament', *CBQ* 34 (1972), 403–16, and '*BTWLT* and *BT* as Titles for Capital Cities', *CBQ* 37 (1975), 167–83; cf. L. Lucci, 'La figlia di Sion sullo sfondo delle culture extra-bibliche', *RivB* 45 (1997), 257–87.

[77] It is rejected, for instance, by T. Frymer-Kensky, *In the Wake of the Goddesses: Women, Culture, and the Biblical Transformation of Pagan Myth* (New York, 1992), 168–78. She favours a more psychological explanation in terms of the city nurturing and defending its inhabitants (pp. 171–72, though again this may not explain the specific use of 'daughter'); somewhat similarly E. R. Follis (daughters associated with stability and nurturing, in contrast with the more adventurous 'sons', and drawing comparisons with the Greek world), 'The Holy City as Daughter', in E. R. Follis (ed.), *Directions in Biblical Hebrew Poetry* (JSOTSup 40; Sheffield, 1987), 173–84. See also M. Biddle, 'The Figure of Lady Jerusalem: Identification, Deification and Personification of Cities in the Ancient Near East', in K. Lawson Younger, W. W. Hallo and B. F. Batto (eds), *The Biblical Canon in Comparative Perspective* (Lewiston, N.Y., 1991), 173–94.

[78] So J. Galambush, *Jerusalem in the Book of Ezekiel: The City as Yahweh's Wife* (SBLDS 130; Atlanta, 1992), 20 and 36. In this connection it is interesting to note the almost complete absence of references to 'the God of Jerusalem/Zion' in the Hebrew Bible, a title that might have been more prevalent had this whole complex of metaphorical thought been 'live'; cf. Gordon, *Holy Land*, 27–29.

[79] To give only a few prominent examples relating especially to Isaiah, in addition to the studies of Schmitt and Galambush already cited: U. Berges, 'Personifications and Prophetic Voices of Zion in Isaiah and Beyond', in J. C. de Moor (ed.), *The Elusive Prophet: The Prophet as a Historical Person, Literary Character and Anonymous Artist*

commentary, the lesson to be drawn is that the force of the image in the immediate context is both a legitimate, and indeed the necessary, subject of exposition.[80]

(vi) Finally, Vermeylen, 51 (followed by Ben Zvi, 'Isaiah 1,4-9', 99, and Berges, 63), has claimed that the use of this phrase points to a date later than the time of Isaiah for the composition of this passage. Maintaining that it occurs nowhere else in authentically Isaian material, he states that in texts before the end of the eighth century BCE it refers to a town which is dependent on a major city, whereas here it clearly refers to Jerusalem itself. In that sense, the phrase is not attested before the exilic period. This reasoning is open to challenge, however. First, Vermeylen is dependent on Cazelles for his view that the phrase originally referred to the daughter-city of a major centre. We have seen, however, that there is no evidence for this view: the usage appealed to is only ever and exclusively plural, 'daughters'. Secondly, 'daughter of Zion' is agreed by all to be a poetic metaphor, used chiefly by the prophets and the author of Lamentations. The only prophetic writings earlier than Isaiah, however, are Amos and Hosea, both of whom preached to the northern kingdom of Israel, and in whose authentic sayings we should therefore not expect to find a reference to 'the daughter of Zion'.[81] It is therefore a misleading argument from silence to claim that the phrase could not have been current in Isaiah's time.[82] Thirdly, the evidence—or rather, lack of evidence— about the phrase's origins has suggested that it was probably already a 'dead' metaphor by the time it surfaces in our extant literature. This implies that it had long been current in Judah, and as we have seen there are reasons why it may be in Isaiah's writing that it is first attested. It is therefore questionable method to deny that Isaiah could have used the phrase merely because it is not certainly attested before his time.

We may now return to the thought of the verse as a whole. The *daughter of Zion* is compared to various features which seem to be intended to stress her complete solitariness and isolation. This suggests that in this context the phrase is used to heighten the appeal to the reader's compassion; that which should speak of intimate familial relationships is contrasted with the lonely reality. (This seems contextually to be the dominant

---

(OTS 45; Leiden, 2001), 54–82; K. P. Darr, *Isaiah's Vision and the Family of God* (Louisville, Ky., 1994), Chapters 4–5; H.-J. Hermisson, 'Die Frau Zion', in van Ruiten and Vervenne (eds), *Studies in the Book of Isaiah*, 19–39; J. F. A. Sawyer, 'Daughter of Zion and Servant of the Lord in Isaiah: A Comparison', *JSOT* 44 (1989), 89–107; O. H. Steck, 'Zion als Gelände und Gestalt: Überlegungen zur Wahrnehmung Jerusalems als Stadt und Frau im Alten Testament', *ZTK* 86 (1989), 261–81 = *Gottesknecht und Zion: Gesammelte Aufsätze zu Deuterojesaja* (FAT 4; Tübingen, 1992), 126–45.

[80] See too A. Labahn, 'Metaphor and Intertextuality: "Daughter of Zion" as a Test Case', *SJOT* 17 (2003), 49–67.

[81] Even so, some would hold that 'virgin Israel' in Amos 5.2 reflects the same kind of idiom; see, for instance, J. J. Schmitt, 'The Virgin of Israel: Referent and Use of the Phrase in Amos and Jeremiah', *CBQ* 53 (1991), 365–87.

[82] Though the phrase occurs three times in the book of Isaiah's contemporary Micah (1.13; 4.10, 13), most commentators consider all these occurrences to be parts of later additions to the work.

thought, rather than that there is a covert appeal to the whole range of the so-called Zion tradition.[83]) This is a telling use of imagery, and one in which the phrase is also commonly (though not exclusively) used by later writers (see above). It thus adds its voice to the sense of appeal which permeates this whole passage.

The first two points of comparison, the *hut in a vineyard* and the *shelter for the night in a cucumber*[84] *field*, derive, of course, from agricultural practice. Such structures were used for guarding the crops as harvest approached[85] (as well, perhaps, as to accommodate labourers during the harvest itself), so that there is a link in thought also with the third point of comparison, *a guard-city* (for discussion of which, see the textual notes above; it is conceded there that there is an element of uncertainty about the precise identification of this element). There does not seem, therefore, to be any point drawn from their probably temporary nature, however much this might suggest itself to English-speaking readers,[86] and, indeed, is attested elsewhere in the Old Testament (see Gray). Whether there is a sense of play on Zion's sanctuary as a 'booth' (סכה) (here *hut*; Wildberger refers to Pss. 27.5; 31.21 [20] and 76.3 [2]; he might also have added especially Isa. 4.5-6) may be left open.

9. It is speculated above that, in its original context (1.5-9 following 30.17), this verse represents the people's somewhat dismissive response to Isaiah's plea: against his view that the way the daughter of Zion was 'left' isolated (v. 8) constitutes an urgent, and perhaps final, ground for repentance, they respond that they have been 'left' as survivors, suggestive to them of God's favour; they can therefore ignore the prophet's warning, secure in their mistaken belief that Zion was inviolable. Their reference to Sodom and Gomorrah is somewhat sarcastic.

In the present form of the chapter, however, the verse is taken far more positively by the compiler. He associates himself with his readers ('we') in recognizing that the post-exilic community has indeed been spared by God's grace, and he will move on to outline a proper response in the following part of the chapter. In this context, *left* and *survivors* were no doubt understood in a far more developed theological sense than in Isaiah's time (see below).

The divine title *Lord of Hosts* is found frequently in the first part of the book of Isaiah. In other books of which this is true, such as Jeremiah, it occurs overwhelmingly in stereotypical formulae, such as 'thus says the Lord of Hosts' or 'oracle of the Lord of Hosts'. By contrast, whereas there are isolated examples of this same usage also in Isaiah 1–39, the majority

---

[83] So Wildberger; for a survey of the biblical use of 'Zion', with abundant bibliography, see E. Otto, *ThWAT* vi. 994–1028 = *TDOT* xii. 333–65. Naturally, other aspects of thought related to Zion will be considered in their appropriate contexts below.

[84] For closer identification, see Borowski, *Agriculture*, 137.

[85] Cf. Job 27.18, and Dalman, *Arbeit*, ii. 54–63; Walsh, *Fruit*, 128–42; see also A. Stuiber, 'Die Wachhütte im Weingarten', *Jahrbuch für Antike und Christentum*, II (1959), 86–89.

[86] *Contra* Kaiser, and J. L. Rubenstein, 'The Symbolism of the Sukka (Part 2)', *Judaism* 45 (1996), 387–98.

of occurrences (as in the present verse) are what might be called free-standing.[87] This suggests that Isaiah used the title more consciously, so that (as with 'daughter of Zion' in v. 8 above) it is legitimate to inquire after the reason for the choice of the title in each passage in which it occurs. It does not follow, however, as has occasionally been suggested, that Isaiah was the first to coin the term.

It is generally agreed, in view of the distribution of occurrences of the title, that it derives from the Jerusalem cult tradition, and in particular that it was associated with the notion of God as king, dwelling enthroned in his royal palace. Because its earliest attestations are linked with the sanctuary at Shiloh (1 Sam. 1.3, 11) and then with the ark on its journey from Shiloh (1 Sam. 4.4) and ultimately to Jerusalem (2 Sam. 6.2, 18), it has further been suggested that it was from there (rather than, for instance, from earlier Jebusite tradition) and through that means that the title entered the Jerusalem tradition.[88] Such a view is certainly consistent with the important evidence of Isa. 6.1-5, while passages such as 8.18; 18.7; 24.23; and 25.6 further show the extent to which usage in the Isaiah tradition parallels that in the so-called Psalms of Zion (e.g. Pss. 46.8, 12 [7, 11]; 48.9 [8]).

Various suggestions have been advanced about the precise significance of *Hosts* in this connection, such as that it refers to members of the divine council, the divine army, the armies of Israel, the powers (generally) in heaven or on earth or both together, and so on. It is not clear whether all of these would necessarily have been so neatly distinguished, and it is further perfectly possible that the word may have been understood differently over the course of time, under the impact of developing religious ideas. It seems most likely, in view of its use elsewhere in his writings, that Isaiah would have had primarily in mind the members of the divine king's court (cf. especially Isa. 6.1-5 in the light of 1 Kgs 22.19-23) and that these could well have included military 'personnel' (e.g. 31.4-5; cf. Josh. 5.14-15).[89] This latter aspect seems early to have been fused, however, with the idea of God as commander also of the army of his earthly representative Israel (cf. 1 Sam. 17.45), an association no doubt encouraged by the early representation of the ark as a war palladium (e.g. Num. 10.35-36; 1 Sam. 4). It could well be, therefore, that on the assumption that our verse

---

[87] For a full presentation of statistics, see H.-J. Zobel, *ThWAT* vi, 876–92 = *TDOT* xii. 215–32; A. S. van der Woude, *TLOT* ii. 1039–46, and (with a convenient table) T. N. D. Mettinger, *The Dethronement of Sabaoth: Studies in the Shem and Kabod Theologies* (ConB, Old Testament Series 18; Lund, 1982), 12–15.

[88] See the summaries of many variations on this particular theory (with full bibliography) in Zobel and van der Woude (see previous note), and T. N. D. Mettinger, 'YHWH SABAOTH—The Heavenly King on the Cherubim Throne', in T. Ishida (ed.), *Studies in the Period of David and Solomon and Other Essays* (Tokyo, 1982), 109–38; Ollenburger, *Zion*, esp. 37–38; Paas, *Creation and Judgement*, 231–42. Ollenburger refers to Eissfeldt's study of 1950 as 'still definitive'; cf. O. Eissfeldt, 'Jahwe Zebaoth', in *Kleine Schriften* 3 (Tübingen, 1966), 103–23.

[89] J. H. Choi, 'Resheph and YHWH Ṣĕbāʾôt', *VT* 54 (2004), 17–28, argues by analogy with uses of the divine name Resheph in similar constructions that it is 'used to point out and highlight a specific aspect of the deity's nature, in this case, *yhwh*'s nature as a warrior and supreme commander of armies'.

originally represented the Jerusalemites' mistaken interpretation of the Assyrian withdrawal as a sign of God's unconditional commitment to their defence it was this which determined their choice of divine title here. Although the title was common parlance both for them and for Isaiah, they focussed on that aspect which was most conducive to their theology whereas Isaiah himself exercised greater creativity in that he could also use it (as we will see later, e.g. at v. 24) to emphasize God's sovereignty in judging as well as saving his people.

Neither the verb *left* nor its object *survivors* has any necessarily loaded theological force,[90] so that attempts to date the passage late on this basis should be rejected.[91] As already suggested, the choice of verb was prompted primarily by its use in the previous verse, where again its common simple sense is clear.[92] שָׂרִיד, 'survivors', occurs only here in Isaiah. Its most frequent use by far elsewhere (usually with the verb הִשְׁאִיר, 'leave') is for those who survive some military disaster (e.g. Num. 21.35; Josh. 8.22), and that, of course, is precisely what is meant in the present context. There is no doubt, however, that in time the verb certainly (e.g. Isa. 4.3), and the noun possibly (cf. Jer. 31.2; 42.17; 44.14), came also to be used in association with the more technical sense of 'the remnant', and this will have facilitated the more positive re-reading of the verse by the chapter's later compiler (Kilian, for instance, points to similarities with Ezra 9.6-15).

The complete destruction of *Sodom* and *Gomorrah*, as recorded now in Genesis 18–19, was evidently more or less proverbial in ancient Israel, as the number of allusions in other books makes clear.[93] It is therefore beside the point for our purposes to discuss the date and development of the Genesis passage itself. Similarly, Wildberger's comment that Isaiah could not have known the Genesis account because 'these cities were not actually destroyed in a war' is adequately met by the observation that the *tertium comparationis* is the complete nature of the destruction, not the means by which this came about.

---

[90] Cf. Hasel, *The Remnant*, 313–18; Hausmann, *Israel's Rest*, 139–41; differently, W. E. Müller, *Die Vorstellung von Rest im Alten Testament* (Neukirchen–Vluyn, 1973), 62–69.

[91] E.g. Werner, *Eschatologische Texte*, 118–33; Vermeylen, 52 n. 3 (for שָׂרִיד).

[92] See T. Kronholm, *ThWAT* iii. 1079–90 = *TDOT* vi. 482–91.

[93] See J. A. Loader, *A Tale of Two Cities: Sodom and Gomorrah in the Old Testament, Early Jewish and Early Christian Traditions* (Kampen, 1990). He discusses our verse on pp. 58–59.

RIGHTEOUSNESS, NOT RELIGION
(1.10-17)

[10]Hear the word of the Lord, O leaders of Sodom,
  Give ear to the instruction of our God, O people of Gomorrah!
[11]Of what use to me is the multitude of your sacrifices? says the Lord;
  I am fed up with burnt offerings of rams and the fat of well-fed
    animals;
  I take no delight in the blood of bulls and lambs and goats.
[12]When you come to see my face, who has required this of you?
  Trample my courts [13]no more, (nor) bring a worthless offering;
  Incense is an abomination to me.
New moon and sabbath, the summoning of an assembly—I cannot endure
  iniquity and sacred gathering.
[14]Your pilgrim-feasts and festal occasions I hate with my whole being,
  They have become a burden on me, I am weary of bearing it.
[15]And when you spread out your hands, I will hide my eyes from you;
  Even if you multiply prayer, I will not listen;
  Your hands are full of blood.
[16]Wash yourselves, purify yourselves,
  Remove the evil of your doings from my sight.
  Cease to do evil, [17]learn to do good;
  Seek justice, put the oppressor right,
  take up the orphan's case, plead on behalf of the widow.

10. For the spelling of *Sodom* and *Gomorrah* in 1QIsaᵃ, see on v. 9 above. הַאֲזִינוּ: 1QIsaᵃ,
ואזינו (4QIsaᶠ appears to have ה, as in MT, but there is no way of telling whether this was
also preceded by a ו). The scroll appears to have read the first letter of the word as the
conjunction (perhaps under the influence of v. 2; some later mss of the MT also add the
conjunction here), following which the laryngeal was dropped by syncopation. This was
frequent in the case of ל + inf. constr. hiph. (cf. Kutscher, 345), but need not have been
restricted to that form. At 8.9, for instance, the scribe again originally wrote ואזינו for MT
והאזינו, though on this occasion the text was subsequently 'corrected' by the addition of a
supralinear ה. Curiously, the clear parallel with v. 2 is missed by the translator of the LXX
in his rendering of this word; contrast the other versions.
  11. למה־לי: cf. BDB, 554A, '*to what purpose* (sq. ל pers.)'; for an especially close
parallel, see Jer. 6.20, and cf. Gen. 27.46; Amos 5.18; Job 30.2.
  יאמר יהוה: the usual formula in the prophets is אמר יהוה (כה). The use of the imperfect,
as here, is far less common, and seems to be a distinctive stylistic feature of the Isaianic
tradition; cf. 1.18; 33.10; 40.1, 25; 41.21; 66.9.[1] It is hard to detect any difference in
meaning; cf. Driver, *Tenses* §33(*a*); König, 43 and 330. This feature is not as well known
as it might be; it passes without comment, for instance, in the otherwise full and careful
analysis of Meier, *Speaking*.

---

[1] The only other place in MT where this use occurs is at Ps. 12.6 (and even there *Seb*
has אמר); contamination from Isa. 33.10 is not unlikely; see further Williamson, *Book*,
79–81. It is interesting to note תאמר ישבת ציון at Jer. 51.35 in the light of the peculiar
density of parallels between Jer. 50–51 and the Isaianic tradition.

שבעתי and חפצתי: stative verbs, for which the English present tense corresponds to the perfect; cf. GK §106g; JM §112a; Gibson, 63.

וכבשים: at first blush, this word is not rendered in the LXX (though MT is supported by 1QIsaᵃ, 4QIsaᶠ and the other versions). Many commentators have therefore proposed that it should be deleted, citing metrical considerations as a subsidiary supporting argument, for example Marti, Ehrlich, Condamin, Fullerton, 'Rhythmical Analysis', Gray, Feldmann, Begrich,[2] Eichrodt, Fey, 69, Fohrer, Wildberger, Kaiser, Deck, 137, and Ernst, 153. These arguments are weak, however. The Greek translator of Isaiah was especially prone to free renderings of lists in his *Vorlage*, sometimes abbreviating, sometimes expanding, sometimes altering the order and sometimes giving comparable rather than exact equivalents (for a full presentation of the evidence, see Williamson, 'Isaiah 1.11'). That this is so in the present case is supported by two further considerations. (i) He used ἀρνός for מריא in the previous line. It would thus not be surprising if he did not bother to reproduce it when he then came to וכבשים (so already Budde). (ii) Even though in the Hebrew text the lists of sacrificial animals in 1.11 and 34.6-7 differ to some extent, they overlap completely in the LXX (involving several alterations at 34.6-7 in particular). It thus looks as though the five animals in the Greek in the two passages are those which the translator took to be standard sacrificial animals and that he merely listed them accordingly when his *Vorlage* seemed to call for it. Nor is the argument from 'metre' any stronger, especially in view of our uncertainty about the mechanics (if any) of this aspect of Hebrew poetry. Against those who think that this line is too long, it can be replied that in terms of balance of phrases there is general symmetry between this line and the preceding one (verbal element together with two nominal phrases comprising two words each). The slight rallentando caused by the fact that the last of the nominal phrases is made up of two independent nouns rather than the construct relationship of the preceding three phrases is appropriate, as we have already noted earlier, at the end of a minor poetic unit.

12. לראות פני: MT vocalizes as a niph'al with syncopated ה (לֵרָאוֹת for לְהֵרָאוֹת), hence 'to appear in my presence', as already implied by LXX (ὀφθῆναί μοι, *contra* Watts); cf. GK §51l; JM §51b (though both express doubt whether any of the suggested examples of this form are genuine, since all could be vocalized as qal). The niph. of ראה is used a number of times elsewhere in MT for appearing in God's presence, and particular note should be taken of 1 Sam. 1.22, where this is true of the consonantal text (נראה), not just the vocalization (as in the imperfect). את־פני is certainly attested with the meaning 'in the presence of' (e.g. 1 Sam. 2.11; 1 Kgs 12.6; with יהוה at Gen. 19.13, 27; 1 Sam. 2.17; את, of course, is here the preposition, not the object marker), and it would have to be assumed that the same is true here despite the absence of the preposition (see too Exod. 23.15; 34.20; Ps. 42.3). The suspicion thus raised may be strengthened by the observation that whereas the niph. inf. constr. of ראה occurs eight times with its expected spelling, the other two places where it is attested with syncopated ה (Exod. 34.24; Deut. 31.11) both involve appearance in the presence of God, as here. (Note that they also both have את, so that the difficulty is not as acute as in the present passage; nevertheless, it seems clear that we should treat all three together.) Although a case can be made on the basis of these data for the vocalization of MT (see Delitzsch), it is thus extremely attractive to suppose with most commentators that it represents both here and elsewhere a reverential correction of an original qal, לִרְאוֹת,[3] as presupposed by P. (On the date of this correction, with possible implications for correct translation, see the commentary below.)

זאת: according to the present verse division, *this* must refer forward: 'who has required this at your hand—to trample my courts?'. This is possible grammatically: BDB, 260B

---

[2] J. Begrich, 'Der Satzstil im Fünfer', *ZS* 9 (1933–34), 169–209.

[3] See Barthélemy, 3–5, for the history of this proposal. There is a judicious note on the subject in S. R. Driver, *Deuteronomy* (ICC; 3rd edn; Edinburgh, 1902), 198–99, and see A. Geiger, *Urschrift und Übersetzungen der Bibel* (Breslau, 1857), 337–38; C. McCarthy, *The Tiqqune Sopherim and Other Theological Corrections in the Masoretic Text of the Old Testament* (OBO 36; Freiburg and Göttingen, 1981), 197–202.

(middle), refers to a number of examples where זאת refers to a following clause (and these seem more apt than the three suggested by Gray, each of which involves בזאת, which is different), though none, in fact, precisely parallels our example with its unmodified infinitive (Exod. 9.16 and 1 Sam. 25.31 come closest). Equally, however, זאת can refer back in an abstract sense to what precedes (namely the bringing of offerings in v. 11; there is no evidence whatever for the suggestion that a line has dropped out after 12a, specifying the referent of *this*, as proposed by Wildberger, Kaiser, and Ernst, 154 and 157, nor is the proposal necessary. The same applies to Procksch, who postulates a lacuna after מידכם). A decision depends largely on what is considered to be the best way to construe רמס חצרי; see below.

מידכם: to argue that this word (lit. 'from your hand') rules out the possibility that זאת refers forward to the trampling of the courts (so Duhm and Marti) is, of course, absurd. יד is often used non-literally (e.g. דבר ביד!), including to express agency or responsibility (e.g. Gen. 9.5; 1 Sam. 20.16; Job 8.4, etc.). Nor is emendation required (e.g. Ehrlich, מאתכם). The decision about how to construe this line must rest on other considerations.

חצרי: LXX renders as singular, possibly under the influence of the beginning of the verse, where the impression is given of coming into an audience with the divine king (see comments below). From all that we know of the pre-exilic temple, the plural of MT is to be preferred (e.g. 2 Kgs 21.5; 23.12; Ezek. 8.16; 10.5; cf. Wildberger).

12-13. רמס חצרי: apart from proposals to rearrange some of the clauses of this passage, there are three different ways of construing the consonantal text or something very close to it.

(i) MT includes the phrase with the second line of v. 12 as a permutative of זאת: 'Who has required this at your hand—to trample my courts?' As noted above, this is grammatically possible, though it is most unusual for בקש to govern an inf. constr. without ל (for which reason, Houbigant long ago conjectured emending to לרמס); however, see Exod. 4.24 and Jer. 26.21 (Ps. 27.4 is uncertain). 1QIsaᵃ in fact adds a ל at this point (4QIsaᶠ agrees with MT), and since it does the same with הביא in the next verse as well, it looks as though it is in agreement with the Masoretic division of clauses against LXX (= ii below). However, it does not rule out option (iii). The scroll regularly avoids the use of the inf. constr. without ל (cf. Kutscher, 346–47), so that it is likely that it is secondary from a purely textual point of view. Either way, this approach is certainly attested as early as V and P, and it has become the traditional one (so Rashi and many English versions). Naturally enough, it is still favoured by many commentators. T (followed in this respect by Kimhi) is slightly different, but still belongs here: it adds למיתי, 'to come', as the complement of 'this', suggesting that זאת refers to the first part of the the verse ('When you come') and then turns our phrase into an independent sentence, 'Do not trample my courts'.

(ii) LXX takes the phrase with לא תוסיפו following (the absence of ל in this construction is common, of course). It then treats the next clause (הביא מנחת־שוא) as an independent sentence, 'if you bring fine flour, (it is) vain'. This can be aligned with the consonantal text on the assumption that the inf. constr. is construed as the subject of the sentence. It is then usually thought that LXX read מנחה for MT מנחת, though Gray retains the consonants by suggesting a defectively spelt plural, מְנָחֹת (1QIsaᵃ here agrees with MT, and in view of the scroll's tendency towards fuller orthography it is virtually certain that the construct is understood). This approach has been advocated by some of the major commentators on Isaiah, including Duhm (as regards the first part of the proposal), Marti (who then deletes שוא קמרת, however), Gray (especially) and Wildberger, and it has been adopted by NRSV: 'Trample my courts no more; bringing offerings is futile'.

(iii) To these two older approaches, a third one has recently been added by Spreafico, 'Nahum i 10'. Noting especially the parallel between the two infinitives רמס and הביא, he suggests that לא תוסיפו governs them both as a 'double-duty modifier'. This is a poetic device (called 'pivot pattern' or 'two-way middle' by some other scholars) attested in Ugaritic and Akkadian as well as in Hebrew in which a word or phrase at the end of one line is not repeated at the end of a second where it might otherwise have been expected;

rather, the word or phrase in question governs both lines separately. The consequence for metrical analysis is that the second line has a silent stress ('gapping').[4] Not all examples of this device are such as to demand that the element in question be, so to speak, silently repeated in order to gain sense from the line (as in the case of vocatives, for instance), but some are (see Watson, 'Pivot Pattern'), and this would be one such. It is of interest to note that, although he was obviously unaware of recent developments in the study of Classical Hebrew poetry, Duhm already anticipated the substance of this proposal with his explanation of הביא as 'ein weiterer erläuternder Infinitiv'.

It is not easy to choose between these three possibilities, but the third seems to have much to commend itself. It retains the MT with the sole exception of concluding v. 12 at מידכם, thus accounting for the coincidence of two unmodified infs. and avoiding the awkwardness of בקש governing an inf. without ל. As seen, this has the support of 1QIsa[a] (whose addition of ל to both infs., while textually secondary, is compatible with it). The LXX can also be explained on this basis: the translator correctly knew that רמס חצרי goes with what follows, but because he did not recognize the poetic device, he was obliged then to render the following clause independently; in this respect, his translation cannot be used for emendation.[5] (In the light of the passage as a whole, Gray's principal argument in favour of the LXX, namely, that the MT demonstrates a 'less severe utterance', seems hardly justified.) The proposal also seems to give good line balance. Not too much weight should be put upon this point, for reasons already explained, but it is noteworthy that many commentators have proposed all manner of deletions and rearrangements in order to satisfy what they regard as requirements in this regard (there is a helpful listing of some of the proposals in Loretz, 138–48). On this proposal, vv. 12-13 (to go no further for the moment) comprise a string of equal-length half-lines, once the element of 'gapping' is taken into account:

כי תבאו לראות פני
מי בקש זאת מידכם
רמס חצרי לא תוסיפו
הביא מנחת שוא (silent stress)
קטרת תועבה היא לי
חדש ושבת קרא מקרא
לא אוכל און ועצרה

13. קטרת תועבה היא לי: again, there are several ways in which this may theoretically be construed. Least likely (despite the Masoretic accents and T; cf. Dillmann and Delitzsch) is to take קטרת as a construct: 'it is an incense of abomination to me'. This both identifies קטרת and מנחה (so Rashi and Kimhi), which is possible but in my opinion unlikely in this context (see comments below), and blunts the force of what may be the formulaic תועבה היא לי. Secondly, קטרת could be a second object to הביא, with the following words as a relative clause without אשר: 'incense, which is an abomination to me'. This is favoured by Wildberger on the ground that the relative clause functions syntactically as a parallel to שוא in the previous line, and the somewhat terse construction is certainly acceptable in poetry. Alternatively and thirdly, however, the line may be taken as an independent sentence, as translated above (so LXX, V, P, Ibn Ezra and many others since). While there can be no certainty, this may marginally be preferred on the basis of the understanding of the clauses set out above. We seem in this passage to start with two sets of two half-lines which belong closely together and to have a further pair at the end which again belong together but are distinguished from the preceding by a small change of content. The present line is therefore set apart structurally from the remainder. This is further

---

[4] There is a full discussion, with examples, in Watson, *Classical Hebrew Poetry*, 214–21. To his bibliography there, add D. Sivan and S. Yona, 'Style and Syntax: Pivotal Use of Extrapositional Syntagms in Biblical Hebrew', *UF* 26 (1994), 443–54.

[5] See also the note on the second line of v. 14.

supported by the slight break occasioned by the 'silent stress' at the end of the preceding clause.[6]

חדש ושבת: for the syntax (*casus pendens* resumed not by a pronoun or suffix but by a fresh object [און ועצרה]), see Driver, *Tenses* §197, Obs. 2; Gibson, 180–81; cf. Jer. 6.2; 13.27.[7]

קרא מקרא: LXX and V unnecessarily (though understandably) supply the conjunction. Was its lack the initial trigger which led to T's paraphrase from here to the end of the verse? On LXX's rendering ἡμέραν μεγάλην, with reference to the Day of Atonement, see Ziegler, 106, and especially Seeligmann, 102–3.

לא־אוכל: יכל is here used absolutely (or with ellipse of something like לשאת). This is admittedly rare (cf. Ps. 101.5[8]) but seems to be acceptable in poetry; there is no need to emend to אכיל (Schwally, 'Miscellen', 257; Budde). To add an infinitive (e.g. Duhm; Marti) would disturb the rhythmic balance of the passage. LXX construes the verb with the previous words, which in itself is correct (see above), but then starts a new sentence with און etc. as objects of שׂאנה (its treatment of the connection between vv. 12 and 13 is similar, as discussed earlier). In terms of line length, this could only be justified if קרא מקרא and חדשיכם ומועדיכם were to be omitted as later additions (cf. Gray), but this is not the case in the LXX. It is methodologically unsound to pick and choose between the evidence which it supplies. Since LXX was clearly working with a text close to (if not identical with) MT, its construal must be judged a misunderstanding of the syntax of the line; see further the next note.

און: LXX νηστεία, which many have proposed argues for an original צום, 'fast' (so already Houbigant and Lowth). Obviously, in a list of sacred occasions, און seems out of place, whereas 'a fast' fits naturally. Since there is no apparent cause for mechanical scribal error here, the change in MT is usually ascribed to a desire to soften what is otherwise considered an overly categorical statement of rejection of a religious practice which was highly valued in the post-exilic period. It looks like a case of the harder reading being preferable. The force of these arguments should not be denied, and the emendation is certainly possible. Yet the case is not as strong, in my opinion, as some of its protagonists assume. The fact that we are here dealing with a list gives initial pause (see on וכבשׂים at v. 11), and there are further factors which add to the suspicion: we have already noted that LXX provides at best a highly interpretive rendering of קרא מקרא, and also that it was either confused or free in its treatment of the syntax in this line. The allusion to the Day of Atonement earlier in the line may have naturally led the translator to the thought of fasting. In addition, he gives for עצרה following an equivalent (ἀργία = 'idleness, rest, leisure') which is not attested anywhere else either for this word or the closely related עצרה. Then again, it may be questioned whether an adequate explanation for the change in MT has been proposed; the very next line, to go no further, would have been equally offensive, and yet it has apparently been left unchanged. (Koenig's attempt, 414–24, to explain the change on the basis that there was a homonymous root צם which meant 'injustice' [cf. Arabic *ḍwm*], for which און was then substituted, is desperate, not to say fanciful. There is no direct evidence for the existence of this root in Classical Hebrew.) And finally the very fact that we do not have here what so many commentators consider more appropriate (namely, another religious practice) is sufficient to show that the argument from the harder reading is at least two-edged. In the light of the LXX's treatment of this line as a whole, there seems to be a case, therefore, for concluding that the translator may have followed his regular practice of giving general rather than word-for-word equivalents (the combination of צום and עצרה in Joel 1.14 and 2.15 may also have

---

[6] These considerations also tell against Ehrlich's proposal to delete היא לי and Hitzig's suggestion that the same words should be construed as the predicate of the following line with the sense 'are the same to me'.

[7] Cf. G. Khan, *Studies in Semitic Syntax* (London Oriental Series 38; Oxford, 1988), 74.

[8] Cf. L. C. Allen, *Psalms 101–150* (WBC 21; Waco, Tex., 1983), 3 and 5.

exerted some influence). In view of the otherwise united textual witness in support of MT, and the fact that fasting was probably not a significant element of cultic observance in the pre-exilic period (Hentschke, *Stellung*, 97), it should perhaps be retained (see further Ernst, 170–71). There is sufficient doubt, however, to suggest that we should not use it as the basis for a discussion of the prophet's attitude to the cult (*contra* Wildberger). Prudence demands that that issue be settled on more secure grounds (which, as the comments below will show, are not lacking).

עצרה: 1QIsaᵃ, עצרתה, an Aramaic form with emphatic ending. Thus was the Feast of Weeks known in post-biblical times (cf. ἀσαρθα in Josephus and עצרת in Rabbinical Hebrew; Kutscher, 206).

14. חדשיכם, 'your new moons', is unanimously supported by the ancient textual witnesses, so that one should certainly be cautious about emending it (cf. Ernst, 155). Nevertheless, it has long aroused suspicion because it repeats the first word of the previous line without any apparent reason. Marti, followed by Gray, therefore proposed that, together with the following word, it should be deleted as a mitigating gloss, designed to explain that not all new moon festivals are rejected, but only 'yours'. This proposal, however, is part of the more extensive reworking of these verses discussed above, and for reasons of line length cannot be accepted in isolation from other conjectures already rejected. Alternatively, many other commentators[9] have suggested emending to חַגֵּיכֶם, 'your pilgrim feasts'. Wildberger, for instance, observes that חג and מועד often occur together elsewhere, sometimes on their own (Hos. 9.5; Ezek. 46.11), and sometimes in association also with חדש and שבת (Hos. 2.13; Ezek. 45.17). In addition, חג is parallel with עצרת in Amos 5.21. Its occurrence here is therefore wholly appropriate, if not, indeed, expected. Marti's objection that it is synonymous with מועד is not correct (see the commentary). The possibility was already noted at 1.7 that a scribe may have been unconsciously influenced by the occurrence shortly before of a similar looking word.

לְטֹרַח: pre-tonic *qameṣ* before a major pause; cf. GK §102h; JM §103c.

נְשֹׂא: an alternative form of the inf. constr. (more usually, שֵׂאת); cf. GK §66b; 76b. It serves here as a direct object; cf. GK §114c; JM §124c; Gibson, 128.

It is difficult to account fully for the LXX's rendering of the second line: 'You have become a surfeit (πλησμονή) to me, I will no longer forgive your sins'. (i) Are we to suppose a *Vorlage* which began היתם לי (instead of היו עלי)? It seems unlikely. Influence from the second person plural suffixes in the previous line is more probable. (ii) πλησμονή usually renders words from the שבע group, and although טרח does not seem to have caused difficulty at its other occurrence (Deut. 1.12), the translator may have been reduced to guesswork for a rare word. (iii) οὐκέτι ('no longer') is not a satisfactory equivalent for נלאיתי. Unless the translator's *Vorlage* read לא אשא (which is just conceivable as a corruption), it looks as though he started with the elliptical sense of נשא = 'forgive', and worked loosely from there (cf. 55.7, and Ziegler, 60). In the absence of any other evidence for a variant text for this line, it is likely that the translation is unusually free, a conclusion which should be included in weighing its value in the preceding lines as well.

15. ובפרשכם: for the vocalization with *hireq* (against the expected *segol*); see GK §60f; 61e; JM §61d (3)(4). T inserts 'the priests' as the subject, which Kimhi explains with reference to *Berakot* 32b, which links this specifically to the priestly blessing. Kaddari, 'Concessive Connectors', 106, suggests that the preposition here should be taken as a concessive ('in spite of your spreading forth your hands'), not least because it stands in parallel with כי גם. While this is just possible, it seems unlikely simply because of what a reader would expect on the basis of the commonest meaning (note that כי גם follows, and so cannot control the initial reading). The parallelism can be accounted for on the usual rendering in terms of the slight crescendo that often occurs between parallel lines.

---

[9] First, apparently, by Schwally, 'Miscellen', 257. After noting the repetition of חדש, R. Joseph Kaspi comments, והטעם ראש חדש חדש כלומר עשותם חג ורבוי זבחים בראשי חדשים.

At the end of the verse, 1QIsa[a] adds אצבעותיכם בעאון, 'your fingers with iniquity'. Though suitable in terms of sense, this is clearly added secondarily under the influence of 59.3 (whose first part reads 'your hands are defiled with blood'), as demonstrated by the retention of the preposition ב, which is appropriate in 59.3 (following נגאלו בדם) but not in 1.15 (following דמים מלאו).[10] The addition is not supported by 4QIsa[f] or any of the versions.

16. הזכו: by placing the accent on the last syllable, the Masoretes evidently took this as a hithpaʻel of זכה, with assimilation of the ת to the ז; so Ibn Ezra, and cf. GK §54d. The form is not attested elsewhere, however, so that many prefer to construe the word as a niphʻal of זכך, with the accent on the penultimate syllable, even though the niphʻal of זכך is equally unattested.[11] The difference in meaning, if any, is slight. In the nature of the case, it is difficult to be sure which way the versions took it (V *mundi estote*, T אדכו מחוביכון, P ʾtdkw), but the use of καθαρός elsewhere slightly favours זכך in the case of the LXX. Tur Sinai's suggestion, 156, to revocalize as a hiphʻil, הַזַכּוּ (cf. Job 9.30), does not seem so probable in the absence of an otherwise expected object.

הרע: in view of the parallel היטב, this must be an inf. abs. rather than construct (so correctly WO, 597, *contra* JM §124c). For its use as an object, see GK §113d; JM §123b.

17. אשרו חמוץ: the meaning of this phrase is uncertain, and it is not clear that the frequently proposed emendation of the Masoretic vocalization (חָמוּץ for חָמוֹץ) really gets round the difficulty. The piʻel of אשר I (assuming that recent lexicographers are right in distinguishing it from אשר II = 'be happy') occurs rarely—either with the intransitive sense of 'go straight on, advance' (Prov. 4.14; cf. the only occurrence of the qal in Prov. 9.6) or with the transitive meaning of 'lead (on), direct'; the latter occurs twice elsewhere in Isaiah: in both 3.12 and 9.15 (where the puʻal also occurs), those who should lead the people (pl. ptcp.) are accused of in fact leading them astray (התעה). A slight semantic development of this latter sense is attested at Prov. 23.19, '*direct* your mind in the way'. On this basis, it has traditionally been suggested that the present passage attests a further slight development to give either 'keep within bounds' or 'correct, put right'. In line with this approach, most of the rabbinic commentators additionally suggest that the verb is the equivalent of ישׁר, piʻel (in support of which Ibn Ezra compares the possible use of תחימרו for תתאמרו at Isa. 61.6; cf. 1QIsa[a], תתיאמרו, though that verb is now generally explained differently). More recently, Niehr has speculated that there may in fact be some overlap between the two verbs since in his opinion both derive from Akkadian *ešēru*, each preserving separate aspects of its semantic range.[12] It would be unwise to base an explanation on this, however, since in this case it is clearly necessary first to establish the meaning of the verb in Hebrew as a control on etymology rather than allowing a speculative etymological argument to control contextual exegesis.

חמוץ is a *hapax legomenon*. Though there is doubt about whether it is related to חמץ I, 'be sour', or to חמס, 'treat violently', or to neither,[13] its general sense is clear and not in

---

[10] This point is completely overlooked by Cohen, 'Philological Reevaluation', 47, in his attempt to justify the superiority of the scroll reading. None of his positive arguments is strong (for the absence of a parallel, see the poetic analysis below). See further Koenig, 221–28, and van der Kooij, 'Accident or Method?', 372.

[11] This might perhaps be marginally preferred, if indeed זכך were more closely associated with the cult (which suits the immediate context best) than זכה, which appears to have more forensic overtones, as maintained by Honeyman, 'Isaiah i 16', who is followed by Wildberger. But this line of semantic argument is highly questionable, as shown by Jensen, *Use*, 78. Hunter, *Seek*, 183, agrees, stating that neither verb is really a cultic word and that both are used more often in wisdom contexts. A. Negoiță and H. Ringgren, *ThWAT* ii. 569–71 = *TDOT* iv. 62–64, likewise see the one as merely a by-form of the other, with no difference in meaning.

[12] H. Niehr, 'Zur Etymologie und Bedeutung von ʾšr', *UF* 17 (1986), 231–35. Niehr himself favours revocalization of חמוץ in view of the following line, but this is not certain; see below.

[13] See D. Kellermann, *ThWAT* ii. 1061–67 = *TDOT* iv. 488–89.

dispute. The participle of the same root occurs at Ps. 71.4, where it is parallel with רשע, 'the wicked one', and synonymous with מעול, 'the unjust one'. Akkadian *ḥamaṣu*, 'to tear off, away' (*CDA*, 103), and Imp. Aram. חמץ, 'steal, rob' (*DNWSI*, 382),[14] support this. *Qātôl* nouns are generally either abstract or active, and the latter is clearly appropriate here.[15] Though it has usually been rendered 'the oppressor', the more specific '(violent) thief' may be justified on the basis of the cognates now known; thus, for the clause as a whole, cf. Kimhi: הדריכו גזל.

The ancient versions, however, all render the word as a passive (LXX and θ ἀδικούμενον; α βλαπτόμενον; σ πεπλεονεκτήμενον; V *oppresso*; T דאניס; P *tlymy*; see too Rashi, החזיקו את הגזול), presumably assuming a vocalization חָמוּץ.[16] Since the following line refers to two specific classes of oppressed people, many commentators have adopted this (e.g. Procksch; Kaiser; Wildberger; Hunter, *Seek*, 178–79); cf. already AV, 'relieve the oppressed', and now NRSV, 'rescue the oppressed'. This initially strong-looking evidence is questionable, however. (i) The clause as rendered is not parallel with the next two, since they both enjoin taking up the legal cases of the orphan or widow (שפט and ריב), something which cannot be said for אשר, whatever its precise significance. (ii) It is not a problem that both oppressor and oppressed are treated in the same context, as 11.4 (and cf. Ps. 72.4) shows. (iii) It is likely that the versions were themselves influenced in their rendering of a *hapax legomenon* by what follows, and that they then had to struggle with אשר. As Gray suggests, they no doubt connected it with the familiar אשרי 'and then rendered freely',[17] but 'rescue', 'help', or 'acquit' are clearly illegitimate translations. (iv) Modern scholars too have had difficulty with the verb.[18] Bewer compared Akkadian *ašāru*, 'to take care of',[19] while Driver, 'Linguistic and Textual Problems', 37, appealed to (much later) Aramaic אשר, 'be strong', and in the pa'el, 'strengthen'. However, apart from the fact that it is precarious from the point of view of method to appeal to otherwise unknown words (or meanings of words) in support of a textual emendation, it is far from clear that 'strengthen the oppressed' provides a suitable meaning. Wildberger is thus right to attempt to stay within the confines of the usage of the word elsewhere in Isaiah, but his paraphrase 'führt den Unterdrückten wohl' is as speculative as the traditional interpretation, and suffers from the additional disadvantage of curiosity. On balance, therefore, it seems best to retain the MT, which gives good sense in the context (see the commentary below).

From a formal point of view, it is clear that a new unit of text begins at v. 10 with its call to listen. Similarly, v. 18 has a separate speech formula of its own, and the subject matter shifts perceptibly. Conversely, the two main parts of 10-17 (11-15, 16-17) are related rhetorically (see the commentary on v. 11) and there is a clear connection between them in that v. 15 concludes with hands full of blood, while the first imperative in v. 16,

---

[14] Kellermann also suggests some remoter cognates.

[15] Gesenius compares רָזוֹן beside רָזֹן and עָשׁוֹק beside עֹשֶׁק; see too P. Wernberg-Møller, 'Observations on the Hebrew Participle', *ZAW* 71 (1959), 54–67 (58).

[16] Barthélemy, 6–7, maintains that it could be an intransitive adjective equivalent to a passive (though this is not his favoured solution), in which case there can be no certainty about which vocalization the versions assumed. This seems improbable. The argument derives more from medieval attempts to justify the passive on the basis of MT than from what we should expect the ancient translators to have assumed, judged by the renderings they came up with.

[17] Rignell, 'Isaiah Chapter 1', 151, does the same with his support of the rendering of P. On the LXX here, see further Olley, *'Righteousness'*, 59.

[18] Cheyne's proposed emendation to יסרו, 'chastise' (*Book*, 111), won the support of Marti, but has otherwise not found favour. Clearly emendation should only be adopted if all else fails.

[19] J. A. Bewer, 'Lexical Notes', *AJSL* 17 (1900–1901), 167–70.

'wash yourselves', follows directly on from this. In common with most commentators, therefore, 10-17 may be regarded as a unit in the text which we now have.[20] Its literary integrity has been generally accepted, and with good reason (*pace* Höffken). The few suggestions of isolated glosses are examined and rejected in the commentary or textual notes (e.g. on vv. 11 and 16), and once the text of 12-13 is correctly understood, there is no need to postulate that material has been lost or that the order of clauses has become confused.

This is not to say, however, that those who define the unit as 10-20, or even 2-20, are wholly mistaken, for as we have seen there is justification for both possibilities in terms of the structure which the final redactor has given to this first chapter of the book. In the commentary on vv. 2-3, it was observed that 2*a* was carefully formulated to indicate the structure in two parts of 2-20. Verse 10 is clearly the turning point in this, as its introductory imperatives to 'hear' and 'give ear' pick up those in 2*a*, while its reference to Sodom and Gomorrah provides a link with v. 9.[21] Similarly, the speech formula at the end of v. 20 echoes that in 2*a*. Our passage is therefore a building block in a larger edifice.

Within the overall redactional unit of ch. 1, the passage follows the initial statements of condemnation and threat in vv. 2-9. There remains a possibility, however, that those who have survived may yet have a future (v. 9), and the terms for this are developed next. Whereas it is implied that the people think that the proper response is frantic and plentiful cultic activity (11-15), the passage shows that this is useless in God's sight, since what he requires rather is a complete change of moral attitude and behaviour (16-17). On this basis, he will go on to plead for just such a change (18-20) before spelling out the consequences of the choice to be made (21-31).[22] That such a lesson was needed in the post-exilic period is clear from passages like ch. 58 within the book of Isaiah and Joel 2.12-14 beyond it.

The unit may be divided into smaller sub-sections. The introductory nature of v. 10 has already been noted, and it is confirmed by the inclusion of a separate speech formula in v. 11 as well, perhaps, as by the shift from first to second person plural address (as things now stand, v. 10 continues the first person plural address, 'our God', from v. 9). Next, vv. 16-17 are clearly marked off by their content, as the prophet moves from critique to remedy. This is supported by the change in rhythm at this point (see below). Within the criticism of the cult proper in vv. 11-15, there is a move following 13*a* from offerings to sacral occasions. While vv. 11-13*a*

---

[20] In the commentary on vv. 18-20, it will be suggested that v. 18 was originally part of 11-17 before it was all included in ch. 1. The addition of vv. 19-20, however, has taken v. 18 with it, and as we shall see, v. 10 has been added to the start, so that from a synchronic point of view 10-17 must now be treated as a unit.

[21] It will be suggested in the introduction to 2.2-5 below that the paralleling of 'Torah' and 'the word of the Lord' may have been drawn from knowledge of that passage; these are the only two places where this particular pair occurs in the book. If so, then the wording of every element in v. 10 can be seen to have been drawn from elsewhere.

[22] See further Williamson, 'Biblical Criticism and Hermeneutics'.

might be considered to be held together by the occurrence of two rhetorical questions, the same consideration can also support the view that they form two sub-sections, the first indicating that God has no need of offerings, and the second pointing rather to the wrong attitude of the offerers.

Analysis of the poetic structure of the passage should follow this outline. This has been confused in the past in particular by the proposal of Begrich that the whole of the first part of the passage can be reconstructed to fit a 3 + 2 rhythm.[23] This involved several otherwise unsupported textual changes, and while few have followed him all the way in this, his proposals have nevertheless left a mark on subsequent textual and poetic discussions. It seems better from the point of view of method to decide the textual issues on their own merits, and then to seek to offer a descriptive appreciation of the results. As Wildberger rightly comments, 'a uniform metrical pattern can hardly ever be expected'. The following outline therefore presupposes the text-critical decisions reached in the notes.

The introductory v. 10 is clearly in 3 + 2. The redactor may simply have imitated the rhythm of the first line he was introducing (11a), or he may have felt that this struck an appropriately solemn note for what was to follow. The first two lines of v. 11 are similarly 3 + 2, but the third line is longer (2 + 2 + 2). However, since there is phraseological symmetry between it and 11b (see the notes), this may be regarded as an intentional slight rallentando at the close of a sub-section. Verses 12-13a comprise equal half-lines of four words each (once the element of gapping is recognized in the middle of 13a), probably to be read as 3 + 3. This section is therefore well tied together with regular rhythm. The next sub-section, 13b-15, also starts with half-lines of four words each, so following on from the preceding, but in the case of the first half-line there is a difference in that it cannot be read as three stresses; it has to be four. The same could apply to its partner (depending on how לֹא is to be treated); either way, the slight shift within the same general framework is apparent, appropriate to the content. Thereafter, however (14-15), we revert to the 3 + 2 (or 2 + 3 in the case of 15a) with which the passage started. Once again, however, there is a most effective conclusion. The last line of 15, which contains the severest element of the indictment ('your hands are full of blood'), is not followed by its expected two-beat partner.[24] We have here no rounding off by a lengthening rallentando, but a gap which leaves the reader startled and gives pause for reflection on the shocking nature of what has just been said. Finally, in vv. 16-17, the divine injunction follows with rapid fire—two staccato imperatives to begin with, and six with accompanying noun (hence 2 + 2) to conclude. This leaves only the middle line of v. 16 unaccounted for. The proposal to delete it seems initially attractive from this point of view, but it is argued in the commentary that there is no good reason for doing so. On the assumption that it is an integral part of the text, it is preferable to explain it (as a 3 + 2) as a regular

[23] See. J. Begrich, 'Der Satzstil im Fünfer', *ZS* 9 (1933–34), 169–209 (203–8) = *Gesammelte Studien zum Alten Testament* (TBü 21; Munich, 1964), 132–67 (163–67).
[24] It is surely misleading that *BHS* prints the first two words of v. 16 as though they made up this anticipated half-line.

line serving to introduce the following series of imperatives. As a statement of the general principle involved (and note too the introduction of the first person by God), its longer length, which draws attention to the line, may not be inappropriate.

As has been noted previously, we cannot be sure about how Hebrew poetry was read and so construed. Descriptively, however, the analysis presented above (which would not be materially affected were we to count syllables rather than stresses) suggests an intelligible fit between form and content.

Discussion of the form, or genre, of the passage has been confused to some extent by the failure to take seriously the nature of v. 10 as a redactional introduction. Most form-critical analyses start out from this verse, and so conclude that it is either wisdom instruction, priestly Torah, or prophetic word (see the commentary below). If the view is correct which sees this verse as the passage's latest component, however, then it is likely that some such generalized designation as 'prophetic Torah'[25] best suits what the redactor has made of the whole. This, however, is not a form-critical designation, *sensu stricto*, and adds little to the task of interpretation (Childs). Nor does it help with the categorization of the material which was so introduced.

Verses 11-17 seem to draw on a variety of forms, without fitting any of them in its totality.[26] Good arguments have been advanced to support the view that it has elements in common with priestly pronouncements about the acceptability or otherwise of offerings, with the instructions of the sages about the right way to live, and so on (see the survey in Wildberger). While this may be readily accepted, problems arise when the attempt is made to force the whole into one or other of these moulds or when terminological parallels are confused with form-critical analysis.

A similar point may be made with regard to the much debated parallel with the words of Amos, especially in Amos 5.21-27.[27] That the general theme and a good deal of vocabulary are common to the two passages cannot be denied. Equally, however, these do not at any point take the form of citation, so that direct literary dependence is hard to establish.[28] Alongside this, there are also striking parallels with other prophetic, wisdom and psalmic texts to be considered (some examples are cited in the commentary). It seems that justice can be done to the full extent of the evidence only on the assumption that Isaiah shared with a number of other authors and tradition circles a common epistemological outlook. That he was perhaps particularly influenced in this as in some other matters by

[25] So, for instance, Westermann, *Grundformen*, 146 = *Basic Forms*, 203; Sweeney.

[26] Against Würthwein's proposal ('Kultpolemik oder Kultbescheid?') to associate this passage with a number of others under the genre label 'prophetischer Kultbescheid', see Høgenhaven, 210–11.

[27] The fundamental study remains that of Fey, 68–77. For a more recent careful discussion, see Ernst, 161–68, who seeks to do justice to both the similarities and differences between the passages.

[28] For what it is worth, this tells against the suggestion that the passage in Isaiah is a late, literary text based on Amos (so, for instance, Becker, 183–84). The tendency in such late prophecy was to give actual citations of earlier works.

Amos, a Judean who worked shortly before him, need not be denied, but it is unnecessary to postulate literary dependence in order to account for this. Indeed, to do so runs the risk of distorting the particular nature of his contribution to this topic.

The date and possible original setting of vv. 11-17 within the ministry of Isaiah are more difficult to decide than was the case with regard to the previous sections of this chapter because, unlike them, the passage seems to be a complete whole (note the speech formula in 11*a*). We cannot expect, therefore, to find a passage within the body of the work where its removal to its present location may have left traces of possible disturbance.

Sweeney has proposed a date during Hezekiah's reign, following his reform of the cult but prior to the invasion by Sennacherib (see too Vargon, 'Historical Background'). He suggests that the criticism of cultic activity is due to the fact that Hezekiah's reform was linked with his preparation for the revolt against Assyria. While obviously this cannot be ruled out categorically, it seems to read more into the text than is there, and there remain other reasons for preferring an earlier date, as is generally supposed. There are not many references to the cult in Isaiah's oracles, but those that there are indicate a development in his thinking, parallel with the development in his thought generally (see Williamson, *Book*, 95–106). During Hezekiah's reign, three passages are relevant. Two of them come from the period before Sennacherib's invasion, 29.1-2 and 13-14, and in both the noteworthy feature is that cultic observance is now clearly stated to be unable to stave off the coming judgment: 'let the festivals run their round. Yet I will distress Ariel', and 'Because this people draw near...so I will again do amazing things with this people, shocking and amazing'. Similarly, in one of the few passages to come in the aftermath of the invasion, the message is similar: while God looked for repentance, the people instead were offering all manner of sacrifices, but to no avail—'Surely this iniquity will not be forgiven you until you die' (22.12-14). Such an attitude seems foreign to the thought of 1.11-17, however, which does not yet indicate the inevitability of judgment. There remains a possibility for reform, based upon right moral conduct. This attitude may be held to reflect better the first phase of Isaiah's ministry, when he himself had experienced forgiveness and cleansing in a cultic setting (6.5-7), and when he still held fast to the possibility of an improvement within his own lifetime, even if he came gradually to appreciate that it would not be immediate (8.16-18). Barth, 220, suggests a possible original setting for the passage following 3.9*a*, or 3.12, or 3.15. The last is perhaps most likely; more than that can hardly be said.

10. Appropriately to this point where the chapter's compiler turns to introduce a direct appeal to his readers to amend their way of life (see above), he uses the broadest possible terms to define the statement of God's will for his people, *the word of the Lord*, and *the instruction of our God*.[29] By

---

[29] For a comparable example, with references to other passages in the prophets where the same device occurs, see G. I. Davies, *Hosea* (NCB; London and Grand Rapids, 1992), 113–14.

way of example, what follows is more specific, although in fact it encompasses some of the major distinctives of the prophetic understanding of the
divine imperative. Those who believe that this verse derives from the
eighth-century prophet himself seek to define *instruction* (*tôrâ*) more narrowly, restricting it, for instance, to wisdom instruction,[30] priestly *tôrâ*[31] or
the prophetic word.[32] Needless to say, all three possibilities have good
evidence to which they can appeal: the form of this verse, for instance, is
that of the *Lehreröffnungformel*, which seems to originate in wisdom
circles,[33] the clear association with the cult in the following verses draws
the verse to some extent into the priestly realm, and the very fact that a
prophet is speaking here, adapting familiar forms to his own purposes, is
held to justify the label 'prophetic torah'. It is doubtful, however, whether
any of these or other comparable arguments should be pressed once it is
appreciated that it is not the eighth-century Isaiah, but the late chapter's
compiler who has penned these words.[34] By his time, Torah will have
come to be used more widely and generally for all types of divine revelation relevant to the proper way to conduct one's life, including all those
which have been specified above.[35] The word need not yet have come to
be used as a technical term for the Pentateuch (although it was certainly
already used for this in some passages of late historiography). The usage
here has a close parallel in the similarly editorial and summarizing 5.24*c*,
where it stands (this time as the leading term) in parallel with the equally
general אמרה ('word'). Fischer notes that the only other passage in Isaiah
where Torah is parallel with *the word of the Lord* is 2.3, where the nations
are addressed, rather than the people of Israel as here.[36] She sees in this a
trajectory which stretches through much of the book, reaching its climax

[30] See especially Jensen, 68–84. He finds partial support in the comments of Gray and
Kissane.

[31] E.g. Duhm; Procksch; J. Begrich, 'Die priesterliche Tora', in P. Volz, F. Stummer
and J. Hempel (eds), *Werden und Wesen des Alten Testaments* (BZAW 66; Berlin, 1936),
63–88 = *Gesammelte Studien zum Alten Testament* (TBü 21; Munich, 1964), 232–60.

[32] E.g. Smith, 'The Use of the Word תורה'; J. Lindblom, *Prophecy in Ancient Israel*
(Oxford, 1962), 156; Westermann, *Grundformen*, 146 = *Basic Forms*, 203. Wildberger
finds strong links with both wisdom and the cult (especially the latter here), but finally
concludes that the modifications to the priestly *tôrâ* by the prophet are sufficient here to
justify the label 'prophetische[r] Thora'; similarly Sweeney.

[33] See H. W. Wolff, *Dodekapropheton 1: Hosea* (BKAT 14/1; Neukirchen–Vluyn,
1961), 121–23 = *Hosea* (Philadelphia, 1974), 96–97.

[34] Berges, 65, points out that שמעו דבר יהוה occurs elsewhere in Isaiah only at 66.5.

[35] See Kaiser: 'such a mixture of tradition forces us to put the question…whether what
we have here is…a piece of writing from a later period which was written specifically for
its present literary context'. It is not necessary, however, to extend this conclusion to the
whole of the paragraph. Needless to say, there have been many discussions of תורה in the
Old Testament; for initial orientation and bibliography, see F. García López, *ThWAT* viii.
597–637.

[36] Fischer, *Tora*, 23. Other studies of Torah in the book of Isaiah as a whole include
Sweeney, 'Prophetic Torah', and A. Labahn, *Wort Gottes und Schuld Israels: Unter-
suchungen zu Motiven deuteronomistischer Theologie im Deuterojesajabuch mit einem
Ausblick auf das Verhältnis von Jes 40–55 zum Deuteronomismus* (BWANT 143;
Stuttgart, 1999), 110–17.

in 51.1-8, where the two sets of addressee are brought together; only as Israel takes the Torah to heart can she fulfil her wider mediatorial and revelatory role.

By addressing *leaders* and *people*, the author naturally refers to the whole population, but regarded in the hierarchical manner which is so characteristic both of Isaiah and of those who wrote under his influence. קָצִין, 'leader', occurs twelve times in the Old Testament.[37] Whereas Arabic *qāḍîn* means specifically 'judge', the Hebrew use of this word is far more general, leadership in a specific sphere having to be supplied on the basis of the context. Thus in 3.6-7 it seems to refer to civic rule in general, whereas in 22.3 there is a hint that military leadership may be foremost.[38] Similarly, it occurs in parallel with רֹאשׁ, 'head', at Mic. 3.1 and 9, again for civil leaders, though this time with particular responsibility for the administration of justice, and in close association with it in Judg. 11.6 and 11 (cf. 8, 9), where military leadership is in view. Joshua 10.24 and Dan. 11.18 similarly refer to a leader in war, but Prov. 6.7 (see the parallel) and 25.15 bring us back to the general, civil realm. A similarly general sense is most appropriate in the present verse, though it is not clear why this particular word should have been chosen; perhaps, in view of the word's use elsewhere, it was regarded as appropriate in this link passage between the military focus of the previous paragraph and the more general, civic one which this verse now introduces.

Reference to the leaders and people of Jerusalem as of *Sodom* and *Gomorrah* (cf. Jer. 23.14) is indeed 'caustic' (Gray), but the point goes deeper than that. The people have just been represented as referring to Sodom and Gomorrah to indicate by dissimilarity their privileged status in God's sight (v. 9). In picking up on their wording, however, the compiler reverses that misapprehension, and shows that in fact they stand under imminent threat of the same fate. This has the effect of making of the following verses a most urgent call to repentance.[39] If in addition to that there is also a suggestion that Jerusalem's sin is comparable to that of Sodom and Gomorrah, then it is unlikely to be on the basis of the tradition in Genesis 19. The following paragraph may, however, be thought to sit comfortably with the 'alternative' catalogue of Sodom's sins in Ezek.

[37] Cf. K. Nielsen, *ThWAT* vii. 93–95 = *TDOT* xiii. 86–88; K. T. Aitken, *NIDOTTE* iii. 960–61.

[38] For likely military use outside the Bible, see *AHI* ii. 37.004.3 and 37.005.2-3.

[39] Cf. Vollmer, 161–62; Hoffmann, 95. K. A. Tångberg, *Die prophetische Mahnrede: Form- und traditionsgeschichtliche Studien zum prophetischen Umkehrruf* (FRLANT 143; Göttingen, 1987), 61–64, argues that the close of the section (vv. 16-17) has the same effect. The position adopted above seems uncontroversial so far as the present form of the text is concerned, though it has been blunted by the long-running dispute over whether Isaiah himself preached repentance or only announced judgment, his apparent warnings being no more than an indirect means to reinforce his condemnation. That particular issue is better addressed in vv. 16-17 below, where (unlike here) we probably have some words from Isaiah himself. I have discussed the issue at some length in my essay 'Biblical Criticism', with reference to previous literature; see too especially the surveys in Hunter, *Seek*, and Ernst, 173–78.

16.49-50,[40] so that as a secondary motive for his choice of designation for his readers this may also have been in the compiler's mind.

11. The first part of the prophet's condemnation (vv. 11-15) comprises a sharp criticism of the attitude which attended the people's cultic practices, and it is introduced here with a rhetorical question which clearly expects a negative answer. There has been a long history of debate as to whether Isaiah (and the other pre-exilic prophets) rejected the cult out of hand or whether it is only current practice and attitude which is criticized. It is not, perhaps, necessary now to rehearse this in full,[41] because there is general agreement that the former view was too one-sided; were it true, it would imply that Isaiah also rejected prayer out of hand (see v. 15), which seems improbable. Wildberger also urges that the repeated emphasis in this section on second person plural suffixes (*your*) echoes the role of a priest in declaring whether a particular sacrifice was acceptable; in stating that it was not, the prophet (any more than a priest) did not thereby reject sacrifice in and of itself. Perhaps the most important point to note, however, is that the force of the very negative attitude presented in vv. 11-15 is designed rhetorically to highlight the positive instruction (primarily ethical) of vv. 16-17. By saying 'not this, but that', the prophet does not say that 'this' is wrong in itself, but rather that it is of lesser importance than 'that' and indeed offensive without it.[42] The same rhetorical structure is found in Isaiah's immediate predecessor Amos, especially at 5.21-24 (4.4-5 and 5.4-6, 14 are comparable), as noted by Fey, 68–77 (who in fact argues for direct influence). Similar sentiments may also be found in the wisdom literature, where the force of both negative and positive are made explicit by parallelism, for example 'The sacrifice of the wicked is an abomination to the Lord, but the prayer of the upright is his delight' (Prov. 15.8).[43] The argument that the cult is not rejected as such, therefore, should

[40] So too J. F. A. Sawyer, 'The Ethics of Comparative Interpretation', *CR:BS* 3 (1995), 153–68 (154–55).

[41] For introductory surveys and bibliography, see, for instance, H. H. Rowley, *From Moses to Qumran: Studies in the Old Testament* (London, 1963), 67–138; R. E. Clements, *Prophecy and Covenant* (SBT 43; London, 1965), Chapter 5; E. Haag, 'Opfer und Hingabe im Alten Testament', in J. Schreiner (ed.), *Freude am Gottesdienst: Aspekte ursprünglicher Liturgie* (Stuttgart, 1983), 333–46; Wildberger, *ad loc.*; for a strong statement of the first opinion, see Hentschke, *Stellung*, 94–103, on which see, however, H.-J. Hermisson, *Sprache und Ritus im altisraelitischen Kult: Zur "Spiritualisierung" der Kultbegriffe im Alten Testament* (WMANT 19; Neukirchen–Vluyn, 1965), 132–43; and of the second, Würthwein, 'Kultpolemik oder Kultbescheid?'.

[42] Cf. C. Lattey, 'The Prophets and Sacrifice: A Study in Biblical Relativity', *JTS* 42 (1941), 155–65, and H. Kruse, 'Die "dialektische Negation" als semitisches Idiom', *VT* 4 (1954), 385–400.

[43] See the analysis of L. G. Perdue, *Wisdom and Cult: A Critical Analysis of the Views of the Cult in the Wisdom Literatures of Israel and the Ancient Near East* (SBLDS 30; Missoula, Mont., 1977), 155–58. He demonstrates that here too there is no question of the rejection of sacrifice *per se*. See also H. J. Boecker, 'Überlegungen zur Kultpolemik der vorexilischen Propheten', in J. Jeremias and L. Perlitt (eds), *Die Botschaft und die Boten: Festschrift für Hans Walter Wolff zum 70. Geburtstag* (Neukirchen–Vluyn, 1981), 169–80; Ernst, 170–73 (he also notes that Hentschke completely overlooked this material in adopting his extreme position on prophecy and the cult).

not lead us to underestimate the force of what is here being said. It was clearly a necessary word in the eighth century, but was equally relevant to the post-exilic period (e.g. Isa. 58 on fasting and Sabbath observance and 66.3-4 on sacrifice).

Of what use to me: there is an element of purpose in this expression. Whatever the worshippers hoped to achieve by piling up great quantities (*the multitude*) of sacrifice, it will get nowhere with God—and by implication it will not profit them either.

Sacrifice (זבח): this is the most general term for sacrifice in Hebrew, and indeed there are cognates in most other Semitic languages as well.[44] It 'designates all blood sacrifices which involve a ritual meal',[45] and further definition is governed by context on each occurrence. Here it stands appropriately as the leading term in parallel (as at Hos. 6.6; Ps. 51.18 [16]) with the more specific whole *burnt offerings* (עולה), so that one most naturally thinks mainly (though not necessarily exclusively) of the שלמים (זבח), 'peace offerings' or 'communion sacrifices' (NRSV, 'sacrifice of well-being), a private or public sacrifice in which both the deity (symbolically) and the participants (including the priests) consumed the animal. The principal priestly legislation for such sacrifices is found in Leviticus 3 and 7.11-38. In the *burnt offerings*, by contrast, the whole of the animal was consumed on the altar as a gift to God (cf. Lev. 1). It is not relevant to consider here the many theories and histories of such sacrifices; it is sufficient in the present context to appreciate that together these terms cover the leading regular sacrificial ceremonies in the temple (this being the context clearly indicated in the following verses), and that those involved evidently considered that they would be automatically effective in securing and retaining God's favour across the board.

The progressively nearer definition continues with the references to *fat* (or 'suet') and *blood*, for in all sacrifices these elements were to be strictly reserved for the deity (cf. Lev. 3.17;[46] 1 Sam. 2.15-17 and 14.34 suggest the antiquity of this legislation). *Rams*, *bulls* and *lambs* all appear in the primary legislation about sacrifice in Leviticus 1–7. (He-)*goats* (עתודים) do not, but their female counterparts (עזים) do, and they themselves occur frequently in the descriptive passage Num. 7.10-88. Thus *well-fed animals* (מריאים), which are found nowhere in those passages, seem to be an odd one out in this context. With the exception of 11.6, the word always occurs elsewhere in connection with sacrificial animals (cf. 2 Sam. 6.13; 1 Kgs 1.9, 19, 25; Ezek. 39.18; Amos 5.22), though none is sufficiently precise to settle the issue whether it refers descriptively to any species or only specifically to cattle of some kind (cf. Akk. *mīru(m)*, 'breeding bull'; *mīrtum*, 'breeding cow'). As is etymologically obvious, the main point of reference is that these animals were specially fattened for sacrifice (and

---

[44] For details and very full bibliography, see J. Bergman, H. Ringgren and B. Lang, *ThWAT* ii. 509–31 = *TDOT* iv. 8–29.

[45] R. de Vaux, *Studies in Old Testament Sacrifice* (Cardiff, 1964), 37.

[46] There are exceptionally full discussions of these and related matters in the relevant sections of J. Milgrom, *Leviticus 1–16* (AB 3; New York, 1991).

hence for consumption), and so it is not by chance that it is they which qualify *fat*. This, together with the absence of the word from legislative texts and the apparently random order of the present list (suggesting that the prophet is simply piling up examples for rhetorical effect) all support the view that the word could stand for or qualify any ritually acceptable animal. Wildberger's comment is apt: 'it must have been particularly objectionable to the prophet that fattening up the sacrificial animals was thought to result in a greater effect upon Yahweh'.

The verbs stand at the beginning (*I am fed up with*) and at the end (*I take no delight in*) of their respective lines, a chiastic structure which by its unusual placement perhaps gives especial emphasis to the second. The first is heavily ironic: if the worshippers had at the back of their minds the idea that somehow they were meeting God's needs (שבע can often be used neutrally to mean 'to satisfy'), he clearly throws the whole notion back in their faces (cf. Ps. 50.7-15). The second, however, may be associated with the technical language of cultic acceptability (see too 1 Sam. 15.22; Hos. 6.6; Mal. 1.10; Pss. 40.7 [6]; 51.8, 18 [6, 16]), elsewhere often in close association with רצה, 'be pleased with'. Normally, an offerer who 'followed the rules' could anticipate an assurance from the priest that his offering had been accepted. If so, God's word here reverses normal expectations by the addition of the negative, and so becomes one of formal rejection. The following verses include other possible examples of such negative declarative formulae.[47]

12. *To see my face* means to come to the sanctuary to worship.[48] While the expression is used in particular for attendance at the great pilgrimage feasts (e.g. Exod. 23.17; Deut. 16.16),[49] there is no reason to limit it to these times alone; the following verses refer to many other regular occasions. The phrase is an anthropomorphism. In such passages as Gen. 43.3, Exod. 10.28 and 2 Kgs 25.19 it is used for people appearing before those of greatly superior status, such as Pharaoh or the king, so that its transfer to the sphere of human encounter with the divine is entirely natural and in line with a host of other similar metaphorical usages.[50] In contrast with what has sometimes been claimed, therefore, it offers no evidence that

---

[47] See G. J. Botterweck, *ThWAT* iii. 110–12 = *TDOT* v. 101–3, for a discussion of this technical usage; see too E. Würthwein, 'Amos 5, 21–27', *TLZ* 72 (1947), 143–52 = *Wort und Existenz*, 55–67, and R. Rendtorff, 'Priesterliche Kulttheologie und prophetische Kultpolemik', *TLZ* 81 (1956), 339–42.

[48] The same is even clearer in the case of the Akkadian parallel (of which the Hebrew expression might even be just a calque), as argued by V. Sasson, 'The Eyes of Eli: An Essay in Motif Accretion', in J. Kaltner and L. Stulman (eds), *Inspired Speech: Prophecy in the Ancient Near East: Essays in Honor of Herbert B. Huffmon* (JSOTSup 378; London, 2004), 171–90 (186); the further development of this by Wilson is fiercely disputed by Veenhof, however; cf. E. J. Wilson, 'The Biblical Term *lir'ot 'et penei yhwh* in the Light of Akkadian Cultic Material', *Akkadica* 93 (1995), 21–25, and K. R. Veenhof, '"Seeing the Face of God": The Use of Akkadian Parallels', *Akkadica* 94–95 (1995), 33–37.

[49] J. Reindl, *Das Angesicht Gottes im Sprachgebrauch des Alten Testaments* (Erfurter Theologische Studien 25; Leipzig, 1970), and M. S. Smith, *The Pilgrimage Pattern in Exodus* (JSOTSup 239; Sheffield, 1997), 100–9.

[50] See Brettler, *God is King*, 94.

there must have been an image of God in the temple,[51] any more than does
Isaiah's own exclamation 'my eyes have seen the king, the Lord of Hosts'
in 6.5. It does, however, raise the question whether lay worshippers had
greater access to the heart of the sanctuary, where the ark was stationed, in
the first, pre-exilic temple than was permitted in the second. From many
passages in the Psalms and elsewhere (not least Isa. 6), it seems very
likely. If so, then it should be considered (especially in view of the early
evidence of the LXX[52]) that the reinterpretation represented by the revocalization—'to appear before me' (see the textual notes above)—in fact goes
right back to the compiler of this chapter himself, for by his time the sanctuary proper would certainly have been off limits for the laity. It would
represent a change on a par with, for instance, the similar considerations
which may have governed the Chronicler's rereading of parts of his Kings
Vorlage, such as the account of Joash's coronation in 2 Chron. 23.1-21; cf.
2 Kgs 11.4-20.[53] (This seems to be a more plausible explanation for the
change than that usually suggested by the commentators, namely that
according to later orthodoxy no one could see God and live.) If that is the
case, then, of course, the translation 'appear before me' should, for reasons already emphasized, be retained, with *to see my face* relegated to the
stage of the pre-history of the final form of the text.

Who has required this?: on the argument above that *this* refers especially to the offerings of v. 11, the people might well have reasonably
responded that God himself required it, since the law repeatedly demands
that they should not appear before him empty-handed (Exod. 23.15; 34.20;
Deut. 16.16). Yet this again need not be a case of complete rejection of the
cult by the prophet (see on v. 11 above). Even without what some regard
as the softening of the MT verse division, making *trample my courts* the
referent of *this*, the passage as a whole clearly mixes apparently categorical rejection of the cult with indications that it is the people's attitude in
coming to the temple that is the real target of his invective. Individual
clauses, such as the present one, need to be read in the light of the whole.
When this is done, we can easily see that that this is another case of powerful rhetoric which is not to be elevated into the status of an absolute
principle.

Trample my courts: it is unnecessary to debate whether this refers principally to the worshippers or their sacrificial animals. The underlying lack
of a proper regard for the sanctity of God's house is the prophet's
principal target.

[51] Cf. N. Na'aman, 'No Anthropomorphic Graven Image: Notes on the Assumed
Anthropomorphic Cult Statues in the Temples of YHWH in the Pre-Exilic Period', *UF* 31
(1999), 391–416, with full references to those who take the opposite point of view;
O. Keel, 'Warum in Jerusalemer Tempel kein anthropomorphes Kultbild gestanden haben
dürfen', in G. Boehm (ed.), *Homo Pictor* (Munich and Leipzig, 2001), 244–82.
[52] Cf. C. T. Fritsch, 'A Study of the Greek Translation of the Hebrew Verbs "to See",
with Deity as Subject or Object', *EI* 16 (1982), 51*–56*.
[53] See my *1 and 2 Chronicles* (NCB; Grand Rapids and London, 1982), 315–18.

13. *Offering*: although מנחה came later to be used specifically of the cereal-offering (see especially Lev. 2),[54] and was so rendered here by the LXX (σεμίδαλις, 'fine flour'), it also and early frequently has the sense of a gift which an inferior makes to a superior when seeking his favour: 'in every instance it is more or less obvious that the presentation of this gift is directed toward attaining a specific goal'.[55] Rejection of the notion that God can be manipulated by bribes is universal in the Old Testament, however, and the point is made here by the qualification *worthless* (שוא). Gifts offered in this spirit are 'empty' or 'vain', and hence *worthless* in the sense that they will not attain that which the worshippers intend.

Incense: there is doubt about the correct translation of קטרת here. The word is of frequent occurrence in the Priestly portions of the Pentateuch and writings strongly associated with them (Ezekiel and Chronicles), and in these cases it certainly refers to incense and incense offerings. The difficulty arises from its very sparse attestation elsewhere, and even more so in pre-exilic texts. Gray has argued, principally on etymological grounds, that it originally referred to the savour (from the smoke) of sacrifices in general which was thought to be agreeable to the deity. He thus renders 'sacrificial savours' (cf. Kaiser: 'Opferrauch'), and finds here a thought very close to Amos 5.21 (where קטרת itself does not occur, however). While the etymological considerations need not be questioned, this sense of the word is secure only at Ps. 66.15 (1 Sam. 2.28 is possible, but by no means certain[56]). Without the strong contextual steer provided by the Psalmist, the commoner meaning is perhaps to be preferred; the chapter's later compiler would certainly have taken it so.

Incense was widely used in the cults of the ancient Near East, but in view of accumulating evidence for its early use in orthodox Israelite religion as well, it is not necessary to conclude that it is here condemned as a 'heathen abomination'.[57] Rather, this is another example of a practice like all the others in this passage where wrong motivation rendered otherwise proper rituals totally unacceptable. Like the others considered already (and some other matters still to come), we have noted that it too came to be more tightly regulated after the exile. It is thus likely that the later compiler will have interpreted the word in closer association with the other offerings mentioned here than Isaiah himself probably intended.

An abomination: a word widely used in both priestly and wisdom circles to characterize ritual and ethical acts which were abhorrent and

---

[54] Cf. A. Marx, *Les offrandes végétales dans l'ancien testament: du tribut d'hommage au repas eschatologique* (VTSup 67; Leiden, 1994). Marx carefully distinguishes profane and sacred uses of the word, and further, under the second category, generic and specific usages. For the present verse, see especially pp. 10–11.

[55] H.-J. Fabry, *ThWAT* iv. 995 = *TDOT* viii. 416. (Fabry lists many examples, such as Gen. 32.14 [13]ff.; 43.11ff.; 2 Kgs 8.8-9.)

[56] Cf. M. Haran, *Temples and Temple-Service in Ancient Israel* (Oxford, 1978), 233–39; K. Nielsen, *Incense in Ancient Israel* (VTSup 38; Leiden, 1986), 54.

[57] Wildberger. P. Heger remains cautious about whether incense was used in the Jerusalem cult as early as the time of Isaiah, but allows that it probably was; cf. *The Development of Incense Cult in Israel* (BZAW 245; Berlin, 1997), 192 n. 3.

categorically to be rejected. The use in the present passage and its background have been carefully analysed by Jensen, *Use*, 74–77. He points out that in Proverbs, where the word is used frequently and mostly in connection with Yahweh, it comes twice in passages which condemn the sacrifice of the wicked (15.8; 21.27), and that the use of the term generally is to be compared with several passages in Egyptian instruction literature. He finds little, by contrast, to connect the term specifically with the Jerusalem priesthood, for while it occurs six times in H in connection with sexual perversion, it is never found in P (narrowly defined). Use in Deuteronomy for cultic malpractice may therefore also reflect wisdom influence. Finally, he criticizes Wildberger's suggestion that '(it) *is an abomination* (תועבה היא)' is a cultic declaratory formula. The words occur in five other texts,[58] dealing with a wide range of issues, of which only Deut. 17.1 is related to the cult (the others are Gen. 43.32; Lev. 18.22; Deut. 7.25; 24.4).

While all this is well said, there appears to be something rather artificial about such attempts to impose rigid categories on the circles which could or could not use a word or phrase of such widespread occurrence.[59] Even if it is true that there was no formula in the strict sense by which a priest declared of some cultic act that 'it is an abomination', we have seen in v. 11 that Isaiah probably did take up the kind of language which was so used, and it is difficult to avoid the impression here that he was aping such declarations, even if he coined, so to speak, his own formula to do so. Perhaps the whole force of his declaration is that he has applied to a ritual act the kind of saying which would have been universally recognized as being commonly used for the condemnation of social or ethical misconduct. The result is far stronger rhetorically than the use of a familiar cultic formula would have been. We have already noted the apt comparison with Prov. 15.8 ('The sacrifice of the wicked is an abomination to the Lord, but the prayer of the upright is his delight'); we may now also add Prov. 21.27 ('The sacrifice of the wicked is an abomination; how much more when brought with evil intent'), 28.9 ('When one will not listen to the law, even one's prayers are an abomination') and as the best commentary on the whole passage, as Jensen, *Use*, 83, rightly says, 21.3 ('To do righteousness and justice is more acceptable to the Lord than sacrifice').

At this point there is a slight shift from sacrificial offerings to sacral occasions of various kinds. The monthly feast to celebrate the *new moon* is mentioned in a number of texts which reflect pre-exilic practice: 1 Samuel 20 is particularly instructive, indicating that the feast was religious in character (v. 26), that attendance was expected without question by those in Saul's entourage (vv. 5, 18, 24-29) and that it was also a likely occasion for the annual family sacrifice (vv. 6, 29); Amos 8.5 further shows that it was a day of rest from work; see too 2 Kgs 4.23; Hos. 2.13

[58] None of the other passages cited by Wildberger includes the vital היא or הוא element.
[59] Note, by contrast, the balanced treatment of R. E. Clements, 'The Concept of Abomination in the Book of Proverbs', in M. V. Fox *et al.* (eds), *Texts, Temples, and Traditions: A Tribute to Menahem Haran* (Winona Lake, 1996), 211–25.

(11). Like the other practices already noted in this passage, it was later the subject of more precise priestly regulation at the central sanctuary (Num. 28.11-15) and it continued to be celebrated in the post-exilic period (e.g. Ezra 3.5; Neh. 10.34 [33]).[60]

The *sabbath* is closely joined with the new moon, as here, in several of the early texts just mentioned (2 Kgs 4.23; Hos. 2.13 [11]; Amos 8.5). While the antiquity of the observance is thus not in doubt, there has been a long and unresolved debate[61] as to whether it was already the weekly sabbath of later times, or whether it too was originally observed on a monthly basis, at the time of the full moon. While our verse can hardly help settle the issue (*pace* Hasel), the following points are suggestive of a weekly sabbath from early times: Ps. 81.4 (3) uses a different word (כסא) for the full moon festival (and cf. Prov. 7.20); the regulations for a weekly day of rest are embedded in what are usually regarded as the earliest law codes (Exod. 23.12; 34.21) as well as the decalogue in both of its recensions, and it is more plausible to assume that these reflect ancient custom than that they are later innovations or revisions in every case; and the same collocation of new moon and sabbath occurs in many certainly post-exilic texts (such as Isa. 66.23) without the possibility being drawn from them that the sabbath was observed only monthly.

The word for *assembly* in a religious context usually occurs in the Priestly writing in the fuller form מקרא קדש, 'holy assembly',[62] and it is not attested in any other pre-exilic text (4.5 is post-exilic; see the commentary *ad loc.*). For this reason, it has sometimes been maintained that it must have been added here later.[63] It would be surprising in that case, however, had the fuller 'technical' form not been used, and the structure of the passage as set out above also tells against deletion. Despite the lack of other early attestation, it may therefore be suggested that we again have here an example of an early usage, this time to refer to any religious gathering which (unlike the new moon and sabbath, of course) had to be specially

---

[60] See further H.-J. Kraus, *Worship in Israel: A Cultic History of the Old Testament* (Oxford, 1966), 76–78; A. Caquot, 'Remarques sur la fête de la "néoménie" dans l'ancien Israël', *RHR* 158 (1960), 1–18; de Vaux, *Ancient Israel*, 469–70; R. North, *ThWAT* ii. 759–80 = *TDOT* iv. 225–44; Keel, *Goddesses and Trees*, 60–109 (104–9).

[61] This cannot be traced here in full. For discussions which take differing views and which give access to fuller bibliography, see de Vaux, *Ancient Israel*, 475–83; A. Lemaire, 'Le sabat à l'époque royale israélite', *RB* 80 (1973), 161–85; G. F. Hasel, ' "New Moon and Sabbath" in Eighth Century Israelite Prophetic Writings (Isa. 1.13; Hos. 2.13; Amos 8.5)', in M. Augustin and K.-D. Schunck (eds), *"Wünschet Jerusalem Frieden": Collected Communications to the XIIth Congress of the International Organization for the Study of the Old Testament, Jerusalem 1986* (Frankfurt am Main, 1988), 37–64; E. Kutsch, 'Der Sabbat—ursprünglich Vollmondtag?', in *Kleine Schriften zum Alten Testament* (BZAW 168; Berlin, 1986), 71–77; I. Willi-Plein, 'Anmerkungen zu Wortform und Semantik des Sabbat', *ZAH* 10 (1997), 201–6. The discussion is further complicated by a dispute over the connection with the Babylonian *šab/pattu*, though it is clear either way that the institution developed in its own way in Israel; see especially W. W. Hallo, 'New Moons and Sabbaths: A Case-study in the Contrastive Approach', *HUCA* 48 (1977), 1–18.

[62] Cf. E. Kutsch, 'מקרא', *ZAW* 65 (1953), 247–53.

[63] E.g. Schwally, 'Miscellen', 257; Marti; Gray equivocates.

summoned; Wildberger suggests penitential days during a national emergency as an example. (The regular annual festivals follow in the next verse.) Only later was the word taken over into the more formal system of priestly regulation, and the chapter's later compiler again no doubt read the passage in that light.

The rendering *sacred gathering* is deliberately vague because of the considerable difficulties in determining the precise significance of this word (this is not helped by the problems surrounding other forms of the root in Hebrew as well[64]). It is used variously for an assembly involving a great sacrifice in honour of Baal (2 Kgs 10.20), an assembly involving fasting in the face of a disaster (Joel 1.14; 2.15), and some sort of general religious festival (parallel with חג in Amos 5.21); the closely related עצרה occurs in the religious calendars for (the ceremonies on?) the eighth day of Tabernacles (Lev. 23.36; Num. 29.35; cf. Neh. 8.18; see too the concluding day of the dedication of the temple in 2 Chron. 7.9) and the seventh day of Unleavened Bread (Deut. 16.8). The one secular use is at Jer 9.1 (2), 'group, company'. There seems, therefore, to be something of a distinction between those passages where the idea of assembly for a variety of religious purposes is foremost (עצרה) and those in the calendars where cessation of work for a day of religious ceremony is stressed (עצרת).[65] Once again, our verse seems to fit earlier usage, though the chapter's final compiler may have had the later, more technical sense in mind. On this occasion it will not have seemed quite so appropriate, however, given that the word is not there used for a particular occasion, but rather for a single aspect of several different ones. This process seems to have been continued to its logical outcome in 1QIsaᵃ; see notes above.

According to MT, what God *cannot endure* is the mixing of religious observance with *iniquity*, 'the criminal way of thinking' (Wildberger). This adds another word (primarily at home in the wisdom literature) to those many which described Israel's sins in vv. 2-5; see 1 Sam. 15.23 for its use in a comparable context. Even if the text is unsound here (see notes above), this expresses well what we have seen to be the force of Isaiah's rhetoric throughout this passage. The very fact that it comes unexpectedly adds to its impact on the reader.

14. It is likely that *pilgrim-feasts* (assuming that this emendation is correct) once referred to a variety of religious ceremonies which involved pilgrimage to a sanctuary,[66] and practice may have varied from one region and period to another. In due course, however, the term came to be reserved for the three major annual feasts (cf. Exod. 23.14-17),[67] and it seems likely that this was already the case by Isaiah's time, while *festal occasions* is a more general word for any calendrically determined

---

[64] See the summary of proposals in D. P. Wright and J. Milgrom, *ThWAT* vi. 333–38 = *TDOT* xi. 310–15.

[65] Cf. E. Kutsch, 'Die Wurzel עצר im Hebräischen', *VT* 2 (1952), 57–69.

[66] Cf. B. Kedar-Kopfstein, *ThWAT* ii. 730–44 = *TDOT* iv. 201–13. He also notes that the word's etymology is uncertain.

[67] See de Vaux, *Ancient Israel*, 470–73. Haran, *Temples and Temple-Service*, 289–316 (above, n. 56), insists further that the pilgrimage had to be explicitly to a temple.

ceremony.[68] Not surprisingly, the two terms came to overlap almost completely in the course of time (cf. Lev. 23), and they may have been taken as more or less synonymous by the chapter's later compiler. Either way, they stand appropriately at the climax of this list of festivals which began in 13*b*.

Like Amos shortly before him (Amos 5.21), Isaiah declares that God *hates*[69] such ceremonies. This usage certainly implies rejection (cf. Mal. 1.3), but its force should not be softened by restricting its application to the technical language of acceptance or rejection of offerings in the official cult (Wildberger). Slightly more apt is reference to its use in connection with God's rejection of Canaanite cultic practices in Deuteronomy (e.g. 12.31): the Jerusalem cult is on a par with that which the Israelites were commanded utterly to destroy. However, *hate* is a common word, and its use with the intensifying 'my soul' here shows that God's response is one of emotional revulsion, not a deliberative act which coldly weighs up whether the sacrifice has been offered in accordance with particular rules.

The anthropomorphism is continued into the second line with its talk of a *burden* too heavy to be borne any longer. LXX (see above) and T (followed, e.g., by Kimhi[70]) seek to get round such bold language by assuming an elliptical use of *bear* (נשא) in the sense of 'forgive'. But the object of *bear* is clearly the *burden*,[71] the image being sustained to the end of the line, as made clear by the use of the verb to be *weary*.

15. Following denunciation of the current practice of offerings (11-13*a*) and festivals (13*b*-14), the section reaches its climax with this declaration that even prayer will be ineffective because of the supplicants' self-evident guilt in the moral realm (hands full of blood). The position and transparency of the verse thus provide an important exegetical clue to the underlying thought of the more controversial preceding sections. The context also suggests that prayer at the sanctuary, accompanying the preceding rituals, is primarily in view.

The first two lines furnish an example of what Willis calls 'alternating parallelism'.[72] This confirms (if confirmation were needed) that the gesture to *spread out...hands* is one of *prayer*. Various postures in public prayer are mentioned, whether standing, kneeling, bowing down or prostrate,[73]

---

[68] Cf. de Vaux, *Ancient Israel*, 470; K. Koch, *ThWAT* iv. 744–50 = *TDOT* viii. 167–73.

[69] Literally 'my soul hates', with נפש used, as frequently, to express intensity of emotion; C. A. Briggs, 'The Use of נפש in the Old Testament', *JBL* 16 (1897), 17–30; C. Westermann, *TLOT*, 743–59.

[70] Ibn Ezra's דרך משל is better.

[71] This in response to Wildberger, whose puzzlement is itself puzzling. Indeed, the concern to make this clear may explain the choice here of the rare alternative form of the infinitive construct, נשא instead of the much commoner שְׂאֵת, as suggested in my contribution to the forthcoming *Festschrift* for S. Japhet.

[72] J. T. Willis, 'Alternating (ABA'B') Parallelism in the Old Testament Psalms and Prophetic Literature', in E. R. Follis (ed.), *Directions in Biblical Hebrew Poetry* (JSOTSup 40; Sheffield, 1987), 49–76.

[73] For references, see de Vaux, *Ancient Israel*, 458–59; D. R. Ap-Thomas, 'Notes on Some Terms Relating to Prayer', *VT* 6 (1956), 225–41, and especially M. I. Gruber,

and there are passages which indicate that, as might be expected, these
varied during the course of the liturgy (e.g. Neh. 9.3-5; cf. Ps. 95.6). Each
position no doubt expressed symbolically the predominant mood and
nature of the prayer. To spread the hands (i.e. to raise one's hands close
together to face height with the palms [כפים] turned outwards) is usually
thought to have indicated a sense of need, as in Ezra 9.5, where Ezra is
said also to have knelt and where the prayer following makes no petition
as such, but simply presents the community to God as in need of forgiveness and restoration (see especially v. 15). Naturally enough, an expression of need may also be accompanied by petition (e.g. Exod. 9.29, 33;
1 Kgs 8.22, 38, 54; Ps. 28.2; Lam. 2.19; 2 Chron. 6.12-13, 29), though not
inevitably (Isa. 25.11[?]; Jer. 4.31; Pss. 44.21; 143.6; Job 11.13; Lam.
1.17). There has been some discussion about the origins of this gesture.
Keel, for instance, suggests that it may have begun as an indication of
aversion, an 'attempt to restrain a superior, numinous opposite by means
of conjuring, thus rendering it serviceable or averting it'.[74] Alternatively,
and perhaps more plausibly, it has been interpreted as an act of surren-
der.[75] That the original significance of the gesture, whatever it was, had
been forgotten when it was used in prayer is rendered probable by the
striking reversal of the image in Isa. 65.2, where God is said to spread out
his hands all day long to a rebellious people.

No matter whether the prayer is offered in a 'correct' manner from a
formal point of view or repeated frequently, God *will not listen*. Indeed, he
will *hide* his *eyes*, an unusual expression, not used elsewhere with God as
subject (though cf. Lam. 3.56 with ears rather than eyes as object). When
used of people, the expression signifies a deliberate decision to disregard
something (Lev. 20.4; Ezek. 22.26; Prov. 28.27)—to turn a blind eye, as
we might say. Although there is a degree of semantic overlap with the
common expression (not least in Isaiah) 'to hide the face' (הסתיר פנים),
they are not synonymous, and this verse should not be drawn into the discussion of that theme in the book as a whole without qualification.[76] The
point here is simply that, although God is aware that the people are praying, he deliberately refuses to pay attention because of their ethical guilt.

Aspects of Nonverbal Communication in the Ancient Near East (Studia Pohl 12; Rome,
1980), 22–181. Gruber argues on p. 43 that פרש כפים (as here) is the pre-exilic equivalent
of post-exilic פרש ידים.

[74] O. Keel, *The Symbolism of the Biblical World: Ancient Near Eastern Iconography
and the Book of Psalms* (London, 1978), 313. On pp. 308–21 Keel includes line drawings
of a number of iconographical remains to illustrate the position of the hands in supplica-
tion. These demonstrate an element of variety with regard to both the precise form of the
gesture and to its significance. This suggests that we should be cautious about over-
precision on these matters with regard to our particular text.

[75] D. J. A. Clines, *Job 1–20* (WBC 17; Dallas, 1989), 267–68, with reference to R. A.
Barakat, 'Arabic Gestures', *Journal of Popular Culture* 6 (1973), 749–87, for contemporary Middle Eastern examples. Clines also helpfully distinguishes this gesture (using פרש,
as here, or occasionally נשא) from the quite different 'stretching out' (נטה) of the hands as a
gesture of appeal (as at Prov. 1.24).

[76] See S. E. Ballentine, *The Hidden God: The Hiding of the Face of God in the Old
Testament* (Oxford, 1983).

This latter point is illustrated by the tersely added statement that *your hands are full of blood*, though the following imperatives in vv. 16-17 indicate that their guilt is even more widespread. Although the statement thus forms an appropriate transition to what follows (and note especially the opening of v. 16), it should not be separated from its inclusion in the present verse; it is with the introduction of the sustained series of imperatives that the transition occurs (*contra* Marti; Procksch).

The word for *blood* is here plural (דמים), a form which nearly always refers to blood which has been violently shed (e.g. Gen. 4.10; Exod. 22.1; cf. GK §124*n*). This is not the blood of the sacrifices in v. 11 (singular), but of murder. There is heavy irony in the fact that the very hands which are stretched out in prayer proclaim openly the supplicant's guilt—and this may explain the slightly unusual word order, whereby *blood* precedes the verb on which it is dependent.[77] In addition, of course, such people should never have been allowed into the sanctuary in the first place, according to Ps. 24.4 (so rightly Kaiser), so that even those who may not literally have blood on their hands become guilty by association.

16-17. Although this whole passage bears close comparison with Jer. 7.3-15, a crucial distinction now emerges. Unlike the later prophet, the divine response to the abuse which has been described is not to threaten the destruction of the temple, but rather to call urgently and insistently for deeds which betoken repentance.[78]

This rather obvious point has been obscured, especially in German scholarship, by a curious debate as to whether this passage is a call to repentance with the intention of averting God's judgment or whether it is simply a rhetorical device to underline the inevitability of judgment.[79] To couch the discussion in these terms leads to a distortion of the text, and this applies equally to the present form of the text in its current redactional setting and to its likely setting within the ministry of the eighth-century prophet.

So far as the present text is concerned, the shape of the chapter as a whole (see the introduction above), together with the close association of 1.10-17 with 18-20 in particular, makes clear that these words are intended as a call to make a life-or-death decision about proper conduct. In the post-exilic setting which has to be presupposed for this redactional assemblage, the call to right conduct is urgent and insistent, and the destiny of each individual is dependent upon it (vv. 19-20 and 27-31).

With regard to the original eighth-century context, several points should be remembered. First, v. 10, upon which some of the debate has

[77] Cf. Driver, *Tenses* §208 (3).

[78] The echoes of 1.16-17 in Jer. 2.33; 4.22, and 13.23, as discussed by Wendel, 98–123, reinforce this distinction, inasmuch as they indicate that the people have not been willing or able to meet these demands.

[79] Some of the major proponents of this latter view include Sauer, 'Umkehrforderung'; W. H. Schmidt, *Zukunftsgewißheit und Gegenwartskritik: Grundzüge prophetischer Verkündigung* (BSt 64; Neukirchen–Vluyn, 1973); G. Warmuth, *Das Mahnwort: Seine Bedeutung für die Verkündigung der vorexilischen Propheten Amos, Hosea, Micha, Jesaja und Jeremia* (BEvTh 1; Frankfurt, 1976); less extremely Hunter, *Seek*.

turned (see above), is almost certainly to be discounted for this purpose, being part of the final redactional framework for the chapter as a whole. Secondly, it will be suggested below that v. 18 may have been an integral part of 11-17 in the earliest form of the text, before it was included in the present chapter and joined with 19-20. If so, it suggests that vv. 16-17 were more open to the future than has sometimes been claimed. Thirdly, we are hampered by the fact that we cannot be sure when to date the passage within Isaiah's ministry, and in addition we lack any wider literary context within which it may originally have been set. If it was early, as suggested above, then it is not unreasonable to think that Isaiah at that time still looked for repentance and forgiveness, just as he himself had experienced, according to ch. 6. Finally, the issue of whether or not Isaiah expected his audience to respond to his words is not strictly relevant for exegesis, and the probability that in fact his perception about this changed over the course of time should not be overlooked.[80]

In the light of this, exegesis should not be deflected by wider dogmatic concerns. Taken as a whole, vv. 11-17 clearly expose and explain God's rejection of the people's current cultic practice and then move on to give instruction about what should be done about it. This has nothing *directly* to do with ultimate judgment, and to bring that notion into play at this point deflects the reader from attending to the urgent word of vv. 16-17. Similarly, 'repentance' is only implied, not immediately demanded. The passage calls for a radical change of conduct, no more and no less. It is a divine imperative which should not be avoided by such side issues as motivation or consequence.

16. The opening imperatives function effectively to join the following ethical demands with what precedes. We have already noted the transitional nature of 'your hands are full of blood' (v. 15), and *wash yourselves* follows on naturally from this. While the word is certainly familiar from cultic contexts elsewhere, as many commentators observe, that it not its primary significance here; after all, Isaiah would hardly call for reform of ritualistic abuse by merely advocating additional ritual.[81] Rather, he has cleverly chosen a word which moves the reader on from one sphere of discourse to another. The situation is similar with the closely related *purify yourselves*, since, as already noted (see textual notes), this word too (whatever its precise derivation) clearly moves imperceptibly between the cultic and ethical spheres. There is no conjunction between these two imperatives; they function more or less as a hendiadys.

Remove the evil of your doings from my sight (lit., 'from before my eyes') provides the final point of transition, in that it gives a general

---

[80] I have discussed this whole topic at greater length in 'Biblical Criticism'. This debate naturally touches on much wider hermeneutical issues about the interpretation of prophetic judgment sayings than can be addressed here; for some recent orientation, see K. Möller, 'Words of (In-)evitable Certitude? Reflections on the Interpretation of Prophetic Oracles of Judgement', in C. Bartholomew, C. Greene and K. Möller (eds), *After Pentecost: Language and Biblical Interpretation* (Carlisle and Grand Rapids, 2001), 352–86.

[81] So correctly in this respect V. Sasson, '*šmn rḥṣ* in the Samaria Ostraca', *JSS* 26 (1981), 1–5 (4).

statement which will be amplified by the following series of specific (and
no doubt illustrative) demands. While it thus functions effectively in
context, doubts have been raised as to whether it is an original part of the
text.[82] From a formal point of view, it is said to interrupt the extended
sequence of double imperatives and lacks parallelism, while the phrase
'the evil of your doings' is most familiar from Deuteronomic passages in
Jeremiah. Moreover, it is the only line in 16-17 to introduce God in the
first person, and finally, its content is more or less repeated in the following 'cease to do evil', a feature not found elsewhere in this passage. While
these considerations give pause, they are not fully convincing: the form of
the two unqualified imperatives preceding is not the same as the pairs of
imperatives with object in the following, for instance, and the terminology
is not necessarily later than Isaiah; see Hos. 9.15, and note that Hos. 7.2
('now their [evil] deeds surround them, they are before [נגד] my face') is
also similar. The other objections too can be countered by the observation
that the line stands intentionally isolated by virtue of its position as an
introduction to the following series of demands: significantly, it is precisely the first of the series, 'cease to do evil', which links up most closely
with it in terms of content, while the introduction of God in the first person is effective at this point, since it reinforces the connections between
11-15 and 16-17. Finally, no good reason has been advanced as to why a
later glossator should have made what is, *ex hypothesi*, a redundant addition. On balance, the line should be retained.

The combination of *evil* and *good* (v. 17), whether in nominal, adjectival or, as here, verbal forms, is extremely common (usually in the opposite order), and does not always have legal or ethical significance. For
Isaiah, however, it clearly did: a child may be too young to have acquired
moral discernment (7.15-16), but for adults the confusion of these fundamental categories is blameworthy in the highest degree (5.20). Like children, therefore, Isaiah's audience need to *learn* to do good and exercise
their wills to *cease* doing evil. Like Amos before (see Amos 5.14-15), the
following lines suggest that the primary focus is on the administration of
justice (see too 1 Kgs 3.9), but the exhortation need not be limited to that;
by Jeremiah's time (perhaps with a reflection on this passage) the language is used in the broadest sense (Jer. 4.22; 13.23; see too Ps. 34.15).

17. *Justice* (משפט) is a major concern of Isaiah, as it was of Amos. Used
on its own, as here,[83] it can have a wide range of meanings in the first part
of Isaiah, including punitive judgment (4.4; 34.5), the place of judgment
(28.6), the legal process in a narrow forensic sense (3.14), legal rights
(10.2), and even simply what is correct (28.26) and right (32.7). Clearly,
common sense has to determine what is most appropriate in each context.

---

[82] See, for instance, Dietrich, 21, followed by Ernst, 157–58. The older suggestion of
Duhm and Marti that the next line ('cease to do evil, learn to do good') is secondary has
rightly been abandoned in view of the line's close integration with the pattern of the
following clauses (*pace* Loretz, 147).

[83] For its distinctive combination with צדקה, see on 1.21 below. For introductory
bibliography on this much discussed word, see B. Johnson, *ThWAT* v. 93–94 = *TDOT* ix.
86. There is a survey of previous studies in Gossai, *Justice, Righteousness*.

In the present passage, the administration of justice in both its negative and positive aspects seems to be in view, so that in that sense this is close to the concerns of Amos and some other prophets. However, as Wildberger points out, the distinctive feature here is that unlike Amos, who was concerned that justice should be 'established' (Amos 5.15), Isaiah urges that it be sought out (see too Isa. 16.5)—a positive exhortation to set right what is wrong in society[84] rather than a passive role of waiting for particular cases to be brought to trial and then judged fairly. As in the previous line, therefore, the *good* has to be learned and pursued. It is more than avoidance of wrong by the learning and keeping of rules. The following clauses give specific examples of this principle.

The first example is somewhat uncertain (see the textual notes above). Adopting a slight change to the vocalization, many commentators align it with the two following ones, but on the view adopted above it has a different and, it may be claimed, a greater force. The *oppressor* (adopted here as the rendering of an uncertain word—it might refer more narrowly to a thief; either way, a wicked person is in view) is not just to be punished, which would be the minimum which could be expected of the courts. Rather, there should be an active attempt to *put* him *right*, to direct him in such a way that he reforms his conduct.

The *orphan* (strictly, 'fatherless'[85]) and *widow*,[86] as a pair or in combination with other groups, such as the oppressed or the resident alien, are a standard example of the neediest group in society throughout the ancient Near East.[87] Already Hammurabi, for instance, towards the end of his law code, explained that part of his aim in having the stela inscribed and set up was 'in order that the mighty might not wrong the weak, to provide just ways for the waif and the widow' (*CoS* ii. 351B), while the Ugaritic king Danel is said to have 'judged the widow's case, made decisions regarding the orphan' (*CoS* i. 346A). The same obtained in Israel, as attested frequently in legal, wisdom and other poetic texts.[88] Lacking an adult male to

---

[84] For this figurative sense of דרש, see S. Wagner, *ThWAT* ii. 315–16 = *TDOT* iii. 295–96.

[85] There is no instance where it can be clearly demonstrated that an 'orphan' had lost both parents, but there is some to show that a child who had lost his or her father alone could be so termed; see, for instance, the self-description of King Eshmun'azar of Sidon: יתם בן אלמה, 'orphan, son of a widow'; *KAI* 14.3; J. C. L. Gibson, *Textbook of Syrian Semitic Inscriptions*, 3: *Phoenician Inscriptions* (Oxford, 1982), 106–7, and Lam. 5.3, 'We have become orphans without a father; our mothers are like widows'; for a different interpretation, see J. Renkema, 'Does Hebrew *YTWM* Really Mean "Fatherless"?', *VT* 45 (1995), 119–22.

[86] Cf. P. S. Hiebert, '"Whence Shall Help Come to Me?" The Biblical Widow', in P. L. Day (ed.), *Gender and Difference in Ancient Israel* (Minneapolis, 1989), 125–41; C. S. Leeb, 'The Widow: Homeless and Post-Menopausal', *BTB* 32 (2002), 160–62.

[87] See F. C. Fensham, 'Widow, Orphan, and the Poor in Ancient Near Eastern Legal and Wisdom Literature', *JNES* 21 (1962), 129–39, Davies, 102–6, and Leclerc, 34–39, for a survey of the evidence.

[88] In view of the fact that most of the ancient Near Eastern evidence refers to the role of kings in this regard, it is possible that the biblical material attests an element of 'democratization'. For a suggestion that the appearance of this class of society in biblical

protect their interests, they needed someone else to perform this role, all the more so in that they were clearly more open than most to exploitation. Thus God himself is sometimes described as their protector (e.g. Deut. 10.18; Pss. 10.14, 18; 68.6 [5]), and it follows that kings and other well-placed members of society should do the same, as Job exemplifies (Job 29.12; 31.16-18, 21). Frequently in these passages, as in the verse under discussion, it is the need to uphold their rights in court which is empha-sized.[89] *Take up the...case* and *plead on behalf of* are virtually synony-mous and imply the need for charitable altruism in the wider interests of a humane society.

Strictly speaking, such injunctions are relevant to only a part of society (orphans and widows, at least, being excluded), and it is certainly the case that Isaiah addressed himself most frequently to the leaders of the people. It would be foolish, however, to argue on the basis of such casuistry that therefore others were meant to be exempt. Apart from the fact that the nature of ancient society meant that inevitably its leadership was most often the primary addressee (see on 'leaders' and 'people' in v. 10 above), it should be remembered that in this passage these imperatives are illustra-tive of the principles for conduct given in more general terms in the previous lines.

---

literature owes more to elitist ideology than is generally supposed, see M. Sneed, 'Israelite Concern for the Alien, Orphan, and Widow: Altruism or Ideology?', *ZAW* 111 (1999), 498–507.

[89] Davies, 97–100, draws attention to cases where the demands for justice may have extended beyond the strict application of law.

AN INVITATION TO FORGIVENESS
(1.18-20)

[18]Come, now, and let us settle our differences, says the Lord:
Though your sins be like scarlet, they could become white like snow;
Though they be red like crimson, they could become like wool.
[19]If you are willing and obedient, you will feed on the best of the land,
[20]but if you refuse and rebel, you will be devoured by the sword;
for the mouth of the Lord has spoken.

18. לכו־נא ונוכחה: against both MT and 1QIsa[a], 4QIsa[f] lacks the final ה (surely inferior). Although a simple *waw* with the cohortative often expresses purpose or consequence (cf. JM §116; Gibson, 106; WO, 575), this is not the case when, as frequently, it follows an introductory imperative of a verb of motion (הלך, בא or קום). In this construction, where the initial verb serves almost as an auxiliary, there is no difference in sense whether or not the following cohortative is introduced by *waw*; cf. Gibson, 82 (who finds in this construction a particular example of the use of the plural cohortative to introduce a note of mutual encouragement), and WO, 574. The use of the particle נא is unusual in such a setting. Despite some doubts which have been expressed, the commonest use of this particle seems to be to introduce an element of politeness into an address,[1] and that is not unsuitable here, where an effort is being being made to engage the other party in dialogue, even though the unequal relationship between them does not require this. The alternative, which sees in the particle an expression of some sort of logical consequence (here, presumably 'then'),[2] is not impossible, of course, but neither is it demanded.

יאמר יהוה: see on v. 11 above.

כשנים: traditionally, it has been explained that the definite article appears here (as also with the following three nouns) because it is a comparison; see GK §126o; JM §137i; Gibson, 28. Barr, however, has shown that this explanation is inadequate, not least because the same vocalization is commonly found with each of the inseparable prepositions when followed by a single word in poetry.[3] Whether this is the result of the influence of the later reading tradition (as Barr suggests for some, though by no means all, cases) or reflects the maintenance of the presumed primitive vowel of these prepositions (so JM §137i, n. 2, with reference to §103b), or, indeed, is due to quite other causes, remains uncertain.

The plural form, שנים, is unexpected. The only other occurrence of the plural in MT (for a word which occurs more than forty times) is at Prov. 31.21, לְבֻשׁ שנים, 'clothed in scarlet'.[4] At 2 Sam. 1.24 and Jer. 4.30 the singular also refers to clothing. For this reason

---

[1] T. Wilt, 'A Sociolinguistic Analysis of *nā*', *VT* 46 (1996), 237–55; apparently independently A. Shulman, 'The Particle נא in Biblical Hebrew Prose', *HS* 40 (1999), 57–82. They both mainly discuss narrative sources, but there is no reason to argue for a distinctive use in poetry.

[2] WO, 684, citing T. O. Lambdin, *Introduction to Biblical Hebrew* (New York, 1971), 170.

[3] J. Barr, '"Determination" and the Definite Article in Biblical Hebrew', *JSS* 34 (1989), 307–35 (325–33).

[4] The text is not above suspicion, however, and many commentators revocalize or emend; MT is defended, however, by W. McKane, *Proverbs: A Commentary* (OTL; London, 1970), 668–69. At the least it should be noted that the final ם could be due to dittography.

T (כתימין כצבעין) interprets here as dyed garments, and this has been followed by, for instance, Gesenius, Delitzsch, Marti, Gray (who also compares בדים, 'linen clothes'), and Kaiser. The difficulties for this understanding, however, are that (i) there is no contextual steer towards a reference to clothing (as there plainly is in the other passages), and that (ii) the close parallel in the next line, תולע, tells against it. To set against the evidence of T, it should be noted that all the other versions render by a colour term alone (though of course it is impossible to know whether this represents the singular form or an interpretation of the plural). It has therefore long been proposed that the final ם should be deleted (as in a few Masoretic manuscripts), and this now has the weighty support of 1QIsa[a], כשני.[5] While this should be preferred, it is less clear how the error arose in MT. Driver's suggestion[6] that it arose as a conflation of two readings of the following word, namely כשלג and משלג (for which he compares Ps. 51.9, ומשלג אלבין, in a not dissimilar context), is possible.[7]

יהיו...ילבינו: there is no particular textual or grammatical difficulty with these verbs. The major dispute about translation has to be decided exegetically, and so is treated in the commentary below.

אם (second occurrence): there are certainly many manuscripts which add the conjunction ו, so conforming the pattern in this verse to that in vv. 19-20. The versions cannot, of course, help decide an issue like this. The fact that the previous word ends with a ו (noted by Gray) is two-edged: it could as well lead to dittography in the manuscripts cited as to haplography in the alternative tradition. While certainty is unattainable, it should be noted that there are differences between 18 and 19-20, not only in the person of the verb following the conjunctions, but especially in that 19-20 are antithetical (so that 'but if' is wholly appropriate), whereas 18 is strictly parallel, 'though...though', so that no conjunction is required; indeed, it seems stylistically inferior.

19. ושמעתם: this is not best taken as an example of the second of two co-ordinated verbs being the equivalent of an object clause (i.e. 'willing to obey'); apart from the fact that this would clearly not fit the precisely parallel construction in the next line (where 'refuse to rebel' would be the exact opposite of the intended sense), the emphasis here is not just on the willingness to obey, but on actual obedience, *contra* GK §120e; JM §177e; Gibson, 120.[8] Curiously, Wildberger cites Joüon with approval in his notes, but (correctly) does not follow him in his translation.

טוב: the context suggests that this is a case where an abstract noun in the construct state may be used to express the superlative; cf. Gibson, 46.

20. חרב תאכלו: the verb has traditionally been construed as a pu'al, and the construction is then explained by GK §121c as follows: 'Verbs which in the active take two accusatives retain in the passive construction at least *one* accusative, namely that of the second or remoter object, whilst the nearer object now becomes the subject'. However, a problem immediately arises, which has to be explained in a footnote: 'In the active, the sentence would be *I will cause the sword to devour you*; by the rule stated above, ...this would become in the passive, *the sword* (nom.) *shall be made to devour you* (acc.). Instead of this, the remoter object is here made the subject, and the nearer object is retained in the

---

[5] 4QIsa[f] is very fragmentary here, and unfortunately our word is not preserved.

[6] Driver, 'Linguistic and Textual Problems', 37, supported with some possible examples of similar double readings by Seeligmann, 64.

[7] It is probably preferable to A. Jirku's proposal that it is an example of an 'afformative -*ma*' ('Weitere Fälle', 392); see too M. Dahood, 'Hebrew–Ugaritic Lexicography IV', *Biblica* 47 (1966), 403–19 (412), and Hunter, *Seek*, 191–92. The existence of enclitic *mem* in Biblical Hebrew is strongly questioned by Emerton, 'Enclitic *mem*'. Cohen, 'Enclitic-*mem*', 245–48, has responded robustly, but it nevertheless seems better to me not to appeal to this (hypothetical) phenomenon if alternative, equally plausible explanations are to hand.

[8] Köhler, 'Ein verkannter hebräischer irrealer Bedingungssatz', suggests that the line should be construed as an unfulfilled conditional: 'Wenn ihr wolltet und gehorchtet, würdet ihr das Gute des Landes essen'.

accusative.' Despite strong support from Barthélemy, 8, therefore, it is not clear that this verse really fits the construction, and to this a further difficulty should be added, namely that it is now considered very doubtful whether אכל had a pu'al in classical times (note the absence of a pi'el). Instead, most grammarians now agree that such forms should be construed as a passive of the qal,[9] in which case an explanation of the syntax based on a verbal theme which takes two accusatives collapses. If this is right, then חרב must be construed as an 'accusative of instrument' (WO, 175), even though doubts have been expressed as to whether this is ever used for an instrument of a passive:[10] 'you will be devoured by the sword'.

This is clearly how the clause was taken by 1QIsaᵃ, since the scroll in fact reads בחרב, and it is by no means certain that Kutscher, 410, is right to argue that this demonstrates a misunderstanding of the construction discussed above; the scribe could equally well have understood an unusual grammatical usage and clarified it correctly. The same approach is also adopted by T and P, though of course it is impossible to tell whether or not they read a ב before חרב. Rashi offers no comment on the phrase, but Kimhi and Ibn Ezra also follow this interpretation, and give other examples for the omission of a ב.

LXX and V render 'the sword shall devour you'. Clearly, therefore, they did not have a preposition before חרב, but it is difficult to speculate further. It might initially be supposed that they were rendering loosely in order to draw out the parallelism between this line and v. 19, and this seems to gain particular support in the case of LXX from the fact that against the Hebrew the first clause in each case is translated with precisely the same verbs (cf. Ziegler, 15). It is then puzzling, however, that (like V) it uses different verbs for אכל. It is also possible that LXX had a text which read תאכלכם in place of תאכלו (Lowth, Budde).[11] In the absence of stronger textual attestation, however, it seems better just to assume that they were rendering our consonantal text a little freely, with the verb construed as a qal.

A previous generation of scholars was troubled by the lack of an exact contrast with v. 19, and so revocalized the verb as a qal: תֹּאכְלוּ, 'you will feed on'. Most then naturally thought that חרב also needed to be changed, for instance to חֳרָבוֹת, 'ruins', giving a clause which has an exact parallel at 5.17 (Marti), or (חָרֻב(ים, 'carob-pod(s)', 'husks' (NEB: 'locust-beans'), a word not attested in the Hebrew Bible, but frequent later and characteristic of times of hardship (Gray), and this latter proposal has continued to attract support.[12] Alternatively, Driver ('Notes', 42) cited various idioms in Arabic (and English) to support the translation 'you shall eat the sword', rather like English 'have a taste of the sword', which had been previously suggested by Hitzig and Duhm. The starting point for these proposals is questionable, however; not only might an exact repetition of תֹּאכְלוּ be

---

[9] See already GK §52e; also JM §58; WO, 373–76, with a full bibliography of other discussions, to which add now J. Hughes, 'Post-Biblical Features of Biblical Hebrew Vocalization', in S. E. Balentine and J. Barton (eds), *Language, Theology, and The Bible: Essays in Honour of James Barr* (Oxford, 1994), 67–80 (71–76).

[10] It is accepted, for instance, by König, *Syntax* § 332v, and Driver, 'Notes', 42, but queried by JM §126l.

[11] One might be tempted to think that this came about by a running together of תאכלו with the following כי, since against the rendering of the identical clause in the last line at 40.5, which represents כי by ὅτι, here we have only γάρ. Against this, however, 58.14 renders as here, so that the argument is precarious.

[12] M. Held, 'Studies in Comparative Semitic Lexicography', in H. G. Güterbock and T. Jacobsen (eds), *Studies in Honor of Benno Landsberger on his Seventy-Fifth Birthday, April 21, 1965* (Chicago, 1965), 395–406 (395–98), adds Akkadian parallels for this. See more recently R. Borger, 'Johannisbrot in der Bibel und im Midrasch: Über Fortschritt, Rückschritt und Stillstand in der biblischen Philologie', *ZAH* 14 (2001), 1–19, and A. van der Kooij, 'Textual Criticism of the Hebrew Bible: Its Aim and Method', in S.M. Paul *et al.* (eds), *Emanuel: Studies in Hebrew Bible, Septuagint and Dead Sea Scrolls in Honor of Emanuel Tov* (VTSup 94; Leiden, 2003), 729–39 (733–34).

thought inelegant, but the pairing of different verbal themes in parallel lines is well attested (cf. Berlin, *Dynamics*, 36–40). In addition, 5.17 refers to animals and is 'less obviously applicable' to people (Gray), 'carob-pods' or 'locust-beans' has rightly been dropped by REB (cf. Barthélemy, 8), and while it is a common-place in the Hebrew Bible to speak of the sword devouring someone (*DCH* i. 245B, lists a dozen passages, including Isa. 31.8), there is no example of the idiom 'to eat the sword'. In view of the fact that 1QIsaᵃ already attests a passive understanding of the verb, it seems best not to emend the vocalization. Whether the preposition ב has been lost (so Blenkinsopp, but conjectured already by Houbigant) or is to be understood is immaterial.

This passage is the rhetorical climax of the chapter as a whole.[13] It confronts the reader with a stark choice. Past experience should have taught the people that rejection of God leads to severe punishment in the political arena; only God's grace has given some of them a second chance (vv. 2-9). Their response, by way of increased cultic activity, has been shown up as empty because of its separation from an ethical lifestyle (10-17). Based on the imperatives in 16-17, therefore, they must now choose whether to follow the possibility (18) of obedience, which can lead to blessing (19), or of refusing this last appeal, which will lead to final disaster (20). The remainder of the chapter will develop the appeal by pointing out the consequences either way, and indicating that even at the individual level the choice will have irreversible consequences. This sense of climax is reinforced by the closing statement that 'the mouth of the Lord has spoken', both as a significant statement in its own right, and as rounding out the section started in v. 2.

The central part of the passage is marked by a high degree of parallelism between the adjacent lines rather than within each line, though 18*b* and *c* effectively use chiasm to create an internal contrast. This similarity between the two pairs of lines seems at first to be further supported by the fact that each begins with אם, though, as the translation shows, there is a slight difference in sense between the first pair and the second; this is supported by the use of the conjunction at the start of v. 20, which has no analogue in v. 18. The metre of these central lines is also reasonably well balanced, 3 + 2 throughout, if טוב הארץ may be taken closely together; even if not, the slightly longer stich is hardly significant.

This main section is framed by two shorter lines (18*a* and 20*b*) which lack parallelism within themselves, but which balance each other by virtue of their both referring to the fact that the Lord speaks or has spoken. They thus receive a certain emphasis in reading. The effect of this is to draw particular attention to the very first words of the passage, since they are the only element which is not part of the speech formulae: 'Come, now, and let us settle our differences'. The length of this phrase joins it to the imperatives which precede: this last and climactic imperative is in fact an urgent appeal to the people to act for their own benefit.

While the central role of the passage within the chapter as a whole is thus abundantly clear, the questions of its origin and original unity are not,

---

[13] The fact that Carr, 'Reading Isaiah', is able (controversially) to argue that these verses should be linked more with what follows than with what precedes indicates at the least that they serve as the pivot on which the chapter turns.

so that it is necessary to preface the following discussion with a reminder that this is the less important (and more speculative) exercise for exegesis. Nevertheless, it raises important questions, not least about redaction, which should not be shirked.

Several possibilities have been canvassed by previous scholars. (i) The whole passage might be a direct continuation of (10)11-17 and ascribed to Isaiah himself. (ii) Verse 18 might be the same, with vv. 19-20 as a later, redactional addition. (iii) The passage might be an independent fragment by Isaiah, joined only redactionally to 10-17. (iv) It might be a later addition in its entirety. (v) It might be an original continuation of 10-17, but the whole now viewed as much later in date than Isaiah. (vi) Within most of these possibilities, the separate question of whether the closing words of v. 20 have been added later has also sometimes been raised.

In trying to steer a course through this minefield, we must first tackle the question whether vv. 19-20 or, indeed, the paragraph as a whole, show evidence of Deuteronomic style. In the wake of Kaiser's commentary and Vermeylen's monograph, the possibility of Deuteronomic editing has become a major point of controversy with regard to the first part of Isaiah as a whole. This passage is the first instance so far encountered where the discussion rises above the general, so making it an important test case.[14]

Needless to say, commentators have always drawn attention to similarities, whether general or specific, between Isaiah 1 and Deuteronomy, and as late as 1958, for instance, Rignell, 'Isaiah Chapter 1', could use them as an argument that parts, at least, of Deuteronomy must have been presupposed by the historical Isaiah. In the decades since, however, the topic of Deuteronomic editing of other parts of the prophetic corpus has persuaded most that if there is a direct connection to be made, the conclusions to be drawn are quite other. Although the possibility that individual elements of Isaiah's preaching might have influenced the Deuteronomists remains open, the more usual path has been to ascribe such connections to the work of later redactors. Vermeylen's work is the most detailed attempt to track this down (and in fact he argues for two separate Deuteronomic redactions of Isa. 1–39), while Kaiser has outstripped him in suggesting that virtually the whole of this first part of the book is post-exilic, though an important element within it includes Deuteronomic reflection on the fall of Jerusalem and the exile. The series for which he was writing, however, did not allow him to lay out the technical evidence in full, so that it is with Vermeylen's presentation that we may most usefully engage.

This reappraisal of Isaiah went hand-in-hand with work on other prophetic books, and, as might have been anticipated, it has provoked a mixed

---

[14] The prose material in chs 7, 20, 22 and 36–39 should be considered separately. More recently, this has been argued with particular reference to Deut. 32 by R. Bergey, 'The Song of Moses (Deuteronomy 32.1–43) and Isaianic Prophecies: A Case of Early Intertextuality?', *JSOT* 28.1 (2003), 33–54. It is noteworthy, however, that so far as Isa. 1 is concerned the most striking echoes that he lists come in lines which it is here maintained are later than Isaiah of Jerusalem (e.g. vv. 2*a*, 4, 10 and 20). These results were reached independently, long before the publication of Bergey's article.

response.[15] The arguments are conducted in two spheres in particular: is the thought of the passage so close to that of Deuteronomy that some association must be postulated; and, is the language too close to the distinctive style of Deuteronomy to be mere coincidence?

I take as a starting point the observation that there is such a clear and obvious difference between the bulk of Isaiah 1–35 and the book of Jeremiah that the literary process which lies behind each cannot simply be equated. If any prophetic book comes close to being a product of the Deuteronomists, then it is Jeremiah. For Isaiah, the case at best can be presented in terms of redactional insertions and modifications rather than wholesale composition. In that sense, it stands closer to what many would believe with regard to the editing of Amos. In principle, the addition of vv. 18-20 or 19-20 would be a reasonable, and even plausible, example, and each such passage would have to be treated on its own merits.

As regards ideology, the choice between obedience or rejection of God's direction is certainly a prominent one in Deuteronomy, but it is not restricted to that book, or even to those which come most closely under its influence. Indeed, it is rather a widespread notion, from which no consequences should be drawn without further support.[16] For this passage, therefore, the whole weight of the argument has to be borne by the language.

Vermeylen, 57–63, gives as positive a presentation of the case for Deuteronomic language as he can. On the one hand, he is concerned to demonstrate that the language is not characteristic of Isaiah, and on the other, that some of it is typical of Deuteronomic style. Not all his arguments are convincing, however.

(i) Five of the thirteen words or phrases he discusses tell us nothing either way. It is not surprising in the least that they do not occur elsewhere in Isaiah, nor do they have any 'Deuteronomic' overtones. Equally, the fact that some occur only in texts later than Isaiah is immaterial: שׁלג, 'snow'; לבן as a verb 'to become white'; אדם, 'to be red' (the preponderance of occurrences in P is, of course, subject determined); תולע, 'crimson'; צמר, 'wool'.

(ii) טוב, 'good things/best of', might have been expected to occur elsewhere in the authentic words of Isaiah, but it happens not to. That is no argument against authenticity, however, and it is certainly not distinctive of Deuteronomic style.

---

[15] See the useful surveys of the whole debate, together with bibliography and discussion of particular examples, in L. S. Schearing and S. L. McKenzie (eds), *Those Elusive Deuteronomists: The Phenomenon of Pan-Deuteronomism* (JSOTSup 268; Sheffield, 1999). With regard specifically to Isaiah, see the critical appraisals of Hardmeier, 'Jesajaforschung im Umbruch'; Brekelmans, 'Deuteronomistic Influence'; Perlitt, 'Jesaja und die Deuteronomisten'; Deck, 139–45; A. Laato, *History and Ideology in the Old Testament Prophetic Literature: A Semiotic Approach to the Reconstruction of the Proclamation of the Historical Prophets* (ConB, Old Testament Series 41; Stockholm, 1996).

[16] See, for instance, M. Weinfeld, *Deuteronomy and the Deuteronomic School* (Oxford, 1972), esp. 307–13, *contra* the claims which are sometimes made for an exclusive link between such teaching and the Deuteronomic school, for example by Kutsch, 'Wir wollen miteinander rechten', esp. 31 = *Kleine Schriften*, 154, and Kustár, 63–64.

(iii) יכח is similar (it occurs primarily in wisdom literature), though I should differ from Vermeylen in attributing its use in 11.3 and 4 to Isaiah.

Vermeylen's remaining examples require slightly more discussion:

(iv) He observes that חטא is characteristic of Deuteronomy, whereas elsewhere Isaiah prefers חטאה (5.18) and חטאת (3.9; 6.7; 30.1). Brekelmans, 'Deuteronomistic Influence ', 172–73, however, points out that Deuteronomic literature always uses חטאות for the plural, in contrast with חטאיכם of our passage.

(v) שמע and אבה are, of course, common, and their occurrences together have been thoroughly examined by Perlitt.[17] Among his conclusions, the following should be noted. This is the only passage apart from Job 39.9 (out of a total of 55) where אבה occurs in a positive sense. In Deuteronomic literature, the subject of the phrase 'not willing to hear' is always God (unlike here), and where Israel is 'not willing', the following verb is different. He argues that the combination—both paratactic and hypotactic—is attested in pre-Isaianic (and so also, of course, pre-Deuteronomic) secular contexts (2 Sam. 13.14, 16; 1 Kgs 20.8), and since outside of Isaiah it emerges only in Ezekiel (3.7; 20.8), and then later in Lev. 26.21 etc., he suggests that the shift from secular to religious usage must have already been established by the exilic period. This is best accounted for if the shift had happened in the meantime, for which the genius of Isaiah is the easiest explanation (cf. 28.12; 30.9, 15[18]). Rather than uphold direct influence from one body of literature on the other in this particular regard, he suggests that there was a parallel development in Isaianic and Deuteronomic circles, and that in some particular respects Deuteronomy was, in fact, influenced by Isaiah. It is not necessary to go all the way with Perlitt in order to conclude that the usage in our verse has features which set it apart from normal Deuteronomic style and align it rather with other passages in Isaiah. But equally, there are at least two features of the phrase which distinguish it from virtually all other attested usages.

(vi) מאן and מרה. These two verbs do not occur together elsewhere. Vermeylen is right to point out that this is the only passage in Isaiah where מאן occurs, but its widespread use elsewhere (including in 'theological' contexts) shows equally that it is not distinctively—or even characteristically—Deuteronomic; it is particularly frequent in Jeremiah's poetry. מרה too is unattested in this sense elsewhere in Isaiah, though the hiph'il occurs at 3.8 and the noun מרי at 30.9. In this case, the word features prominently in Deuteronomic literature (and note especially the frequent phrase מרה את־פי יהוה), though again it is by no means limited to it.

(vii) Although פי יהוה occurs frequently elsewhere (especially in D and P), the full speech formula used here is characteristic of Isaiah (and cf.

---

[17] Perlitt, 'Jesaja und die Deuteronomisten'. It should be noted that Perlitt interacts primarily with Kaiser, who goes further than Vermeylen in arguing that 28.7ff. and 30.8ff. are also late, but this means that his arguments are even stronger on Vermeylen's presuppositions.

[18] I studied this material independently in *Book*, 89–91, and arrived by a different route at fully compatible conclusions.

Mic. 4.4).[19] It is difficult to say whether it is wholly independent, or whether it reflects a development of Deuteronomic language. The fact that it follows closely after מרה suggests that it might.

The results of this analysis may be summarized as follows. There is nothing even remotely Deuteronomic about v. 18, and no good reason, purely from the point of view of language, to deny it to Isaiah. Verses 19-20 are different, however. Not only are they not Deuteronomic, but they manifest some linguistic uses which are rare, and indeed in some respects unique. Although there are connections with other Isaianic passages (especially 30.9), there are also features which set them apart from him. While it would be foolish to suggest that Isaiah could not have expressed himself in a unique manner, the combination of special features in this one short passage, together with its links with material of exilic origin (especially Jeremiah and Ezekiel), are suggestive, at least, of the work of a later redactor. One could well understand it as a reflection on the Babylonian conquest: if Isaiah had left open the possibility of change (vv. 16-18), the stark alternatives of 19-20, culminating in the threat of complete military disaster, gave theological justification for what had occurred. He did this, however (as Perlitt has stressed on the basis of 28.12; 30.9, 15) from within the Isaianic tradition; not surprisingly, it moves in the same direction as Deuteronomy while remaining independent of it.

Other commentators have used different arguments to reach a similar conclusion. Marti, for instance, observes that according to the speech formula in v. 18, God is the speaker, whereas according to that in v. 20 it is the prophet. Less convincingly, Sweeney maintains that the second person plural address form of 19-20 disrupts the third person plural verb pattern of 18; against this, it is clear from the suffix on חטאיכם that 18 is also addressed to a second person plural audience. He has a slightly stronger argument, however, in observing that while v. 18 connects smoothly with 10-17, 19-20 have no direct connection in content with those verses but hark back rather to the situation presupposed in 4-9. This too would fit well with the work of a redactor rounding off a major section within the chapter. Earlier (*Isaiah 1–4*, 128–29), Sweeney had further noted that the two pairs of אם clauses differ both formally (only the second pair uses the conjunction) and in sense. None of these arguments is particularly strong.[20] They are fully compatible with the view that a redactor is responsible for 19-20, but they cannot establish it.

While Deck, 145, is right to conclude that there can be no certainty in a case like this, the most likely explanation, in my opinion, is that v. 18 was the original Isaianic conclusion of 11-17, serving to encourage a response to the imperatives of 16-17[21] (it was therefore made conditional by its

[19] Sweeney, *Isaiah 1–4*, 129 n. 78, mistakenly claims on the basis of Vermeylen's analysis that the complete phrase is 'frequently used in the Deuteronomistic literature'. In fact, Vermeylen does not claim this, and his presentation of the data is correct.

[20] See, for instance, the response of Hoffmann, 99–101, and Willis, 'Interpretation'.

[21] An additional argument in support of this conclusion has been advanced by Leclerc, 30, who observes that שפט (v. 17) and יכח (v. 18) occur together elsewhere in Isaiah as a regular word-pair; cf. 2.4; 11.3 and 4.

context, as has been more widely recognized than is sometimes stated; see below). Its speech formula therefore balanced that at the beginning of the passage (v. 11). At a later stage, while 11-18 were still in their original setting, 19-20 were added by an Isaianic redactor in order to sharpen up this conditional element in the light of later experience, and to do so in ways which drew on the language of the master but used it in the expression of ideas which were closer to those of the by then dominant Deuteronomic school (e.g. blessing as the enjoyment of the best of the land).[22] The final speech formula may be ascribed to this same redactor. Thus the late compiler of ch. 1 will have been able to draw on 11-20 as a whole for his new assemblage. He will have prefaced v. 10 as a connection (see above), and also drawn on the already present 20*b* in his formulation of 2*a*. The original setting of 11-18, and then of 11-20 will thus be the same as 11-17 (see above).

18. Appropriate to its role of introducing the concluding section of the whole of vv. 2-20, the initial *come, now* injects a note of concerned urgency. 'The phrase commonly introduces a proposal for the mutual benefit of the parties, or, at least, for that of the party addressed' (Gray).

The precise translation equivalent for נוכחה, *let us settle our differences*, is not easily decided in view of both the slightly unusual form of the word and the variety of uses for the root elsewhere. It should therefore be emphasized as a matter of method that the context should be used to help determine the meaning rather than this word being used to settle wider considerations of form or setting.[23]

The niph'al of יכח occurs in only two other passages of the Hebrew Bible. At Gen. 20.16 it means 'you are justified/vindicated/exonerated'. Unfortunately, because of textual difficulties, it is not clear whether the את preceding is to be taken closely with the verb as a preposition. At Job 23.7 it means 'argue/dispute/reason with', and there it is followed by the preposition עם, 'with'. While the latter implies a (metaphorical) court setting, the former does not. The passive meaning of Gen. 20.16 is clearly unsuitable to our present context, and while that of Job 23.7 could fit (cf. the traditional rendering, 'let us reason together'), there is a difference: the lack of a preposition in our passage and the use of the first person plural mean that the niph'al has here to be understood reciprocally.[24] The niph'al of דין, 'be disputing with one another', at 2 Sam. 19.10, and of שפט, 'go to trial together (יחד)' at Isa. 43.26, may be compared.

---

[22] Sweeney draws attention especially to parallels in two of the framework speeches in the Deuteronomistic History, namely Deut. 1.26 and 1 Sam. 12.14-15. Vermeylen adds several other generally comparable passages, such as Deut. 11.13-17, 26-28; 28; 30.15-18; see also Lev. 26.3-8.

[23] Contrast, for instance, Boecker, *Redeformen des Rechtslebens*, 68–70.

[24] While it might be thought that the hithpa'el would be more suitable for this, the only occurrence (Mic. 6.2) shows that this theme was used with an active sense, 'contend with (עם)'. That the niph'al can be used to express reciprocity is, of course, well established; cf. GK §51*d*; JM §51*c*.

More broadly, יכח, especially in the hiph'il, occurs frequently with such meanings as 'judge', 'arbitrate', 'reprimand' and 'correct'.[25] There are thus disagreements over whether it was originally a 'wisdom' term which has been transferred secondarily to a judicial setting, or *vice versa*, and whether (to use now questionable terminology) its 'basic meaning' is 'to determine what is right (in the court)' or 'to reprimand'. Although commentators on Isaiah often go into such usages at length, it is not clear that they help understand the present passage by doing so. There is nothing in the immediate context to suggest even a metaphorical court-room setting,[26] and if the niph'al is indeed reciprocal, with no third party introduced before whom arbitration might be sought, it is difficult to see how such a setting could fit the context. Further afield, such a case might be made on the basis that these verses bring to a climax the section which began with v. 2, and that in the opening of this section there is also legal language. This claim was examined and rejected above, however, so that it seems best simply to drop this whole line of approach (and still more so Wildberger's attempt to smuggle in a reference to the covenant relationship between God and Israel). Rather, as in the opening verses, the language can be well understood as continuing the portrayal of the relationship as a natural, family one, where all sorts of dispute occur from time to time. The use of the root יכח is quite as at home in such a setting as in that of the law court (e.g. Prov. 3.12; 2 Sam. 7.14).[27] Of course, the meaning of the hiph'il cannot be directly transferred to our passage, for reasons already noted. The context, however, indicates God's desire to bring this whole dispute to a conclusion (just as, by analogy, the legal process can do), so that *settle our differences* is slightly to be preferred to the traditional 'reason together' (cf. Willis, 'Interpretation', 38–40). It is also important to note, as a context for what follows, that the use of the niph'al elsewhere looks for a positive outcome to the discussion.[28]

The major interpretative issue in the second and third lines of the verse concerns the rendering of the main verbs. The many proposals which have been made may be broadly classified and evaluated as follows.[29]

[25] For surveys, in addition to the commentaries and particular discussions mentioned below, see G. Mayer, *ThWAT* iii. 620–28 = *TDOT* vi. 65–71; G. Liedke, *THAT* i. 730–32 = *TLOT*, 542–44; Boecker, *Redeformen des Rechtslebens*, 45–47; Bovati, *Re-Establishing Justice*, 44–48.

[26] So rightly, for instance, Burney, 'Interpretation'; Gray; D. R. Daniels, 'Is there a "Prophetic Lawsuit" Genre?', *ZAW* 99 (1987), 339–60 (348–49); Kutsch, 'Wir wollen miteinander rechten'.

[27] In addition, Bovati, *Re-Establishing Justice*, 44–45, notes that the word is often parallel with יסר and that it occurs most frequently in wisdom and wisdom-related literature.

[28] This point is stressed especially by Schoneveld, 'Jesaia i 18-20'. He goes on to argue that this points away from any separation of 19-20 from 18, since אבה may have the overtone of 'agree, accept' (Deut. 3.19; 1 Kgs 20.9; Prov. 1.10). This latter point is helpful in terms of exegesis of the text as it now stands, but it cannot, of course, be used as a decisive argument against the view that 18 once stood alone without 19-20; on the one hand, a later redactor may have drawn out the implications of the force of נוכחה as gracious invitation, and on the other, the verb itself does not *demand* such a continuation.

[29] For a fuller summary of opinions, see especially the helpful survey by Willis, 'Interpretation'. Only major representatives of each position are mentioned here.

(i) The oldest attested approach takes the verbs as a simple imperfect indicative, and thus sees the lines as offering an unconditional promise of forgiveness. Indeed, the LXX takes this even further than the Hebrew text by casting the lines as a statement of divine intent: 'though your sins be as purple, I will make them white as snow; though they be like scarlet, I will make them white as wool'. V and P are similarly categorical, though without the use of the first person (but on Jerome's commentary, see [ii] below). In fact, in spite of the uncontextualized use of the verse in popular piety and what might be assumed from reading the commentators who take a different approach, this interpretation has not been widely adopted either in antiquity or in modern times; most of those said to hold it in fact adhere rather to what I have categorized as the second approach. It does, however, appear to be the view of Delitzsch, Ehrlich and Eichrodt; they then explain the following conditionals (vv. 19-20) as referring to what is required to maintain oneself in a state of grace after this first divine act of unconditional restoration.

It is often said that this interpretation is incompatible with what we know from elsewhere of Isaiah's position. While that is true of the eighth-century prophet, the possibility should be borne in mind that this section might be of later origin (see above),[30] and in this connection the parallel between 1.10-20 and 43.22-28[31] deserves mention. In the latter passage too we find a prophetic indictment of the people's cultic practices (43.22-24), just as in 1.11-15. Then also, towards the close of the passage, there is an invitation to enter into (legal) dialogue with God, again cast as a plural cohortative, הזכירני נשפטה יחד, 'accuse me, let us go to trial together' (43.26), not unlike the first line of 1.18. And most striking of all, there is between these two an apparently unconditional statement of God's intention to wipe the past slate clean: 'I, I am He who blots out your transgressions for my own sake, and I will not remember your sins' (43.25; cf. 44.22). While it is true that the three elements mentioned do not occur in the same order in the two passages, they do at least attest the likelihood that 1.18 could have been read in this unconditional manner from early times, and that the order of indictment followed by forgiveness followed by a call to choose the right path thereafter reflects the basic shape of the book of Isaiah as a whole in its three main parts.

Despite this, an interpretation of 1.18 along these lines runs into insuperable contextual difficulties (and this without regard to whether or not they reflect Isaiah's own preaching).[32] As the text now stands, vv. 19-20 clearly inject a conditional note, and there is nothing to suggest that this refers to what follows forgiveness rather than the terms which accompany

---

[30] See too Haag, 'Sündenvergebung und neuer Anfang', who defends this interpretation by seeing vv. 18-20 as composed by the post-exilic redactor of 1.2-20 in the light of Jer. 31.31-34.

[31] On this latter passage, see the full discussion by J. Goldingay, 'Isaiah 43,22-28', ZAW 110 (1998), 173–91.

[32] Kutsch's objection to this view ('Wir wollen miteinander rechten')—that sins cannot be made white, only people; sin remains sin—may be true, but it is a somewhat pedantic point to make in what is, after all, a highly charged passage of poetical rhetoric.

it. Similarly, if 19-20 are a redactional addition and v. 18 is taken as the original conclusion of 11-17, then it would be difficult not to believe that the promise presupposes a response to the imperatives of 16-17. And finally, this reading of the second half of v. 18 seems to empty the first line of any force (this is precisely the point at which the parallel order with 43.22-28 breaks down).

Before we leave this approach, however, there is one point of major theological importance to be derived from it, and that is the impossibility of human effort alone overcoming the stain of sin. The critique of vv. 11-15 clearly leads to this conclusion with regard to ceremonial efforts, and without the presence of v. 18 it might have been inferred that to fulfil the commands of vv. 16-17 would itself be sufficient. Much else in the book of Isaiah shows that this cannot be so, however, and although most of the interpretations of v. 18 have this point in common, it is this first one which perhaps makes the point most emphatically. For that reason if for no other, it therefore deserves to be recalled in exegesis.

(ii) In his commentary on this passage, Jerome, while retaining an indicative translation of the verbs, as in (i) above, makes clear that the offer to cancel sin is conditional upon obeying the imperatives of vv. 16-17.[33] T's paraphrase is similar, as is clear from its rendering of the opening of the verse: 'Then, when ye return to the law, ye shall entreat from before me, and I will carry out your entreaty, saith the Lord; though your transgressions…' (Stenning). The medieval Jewish commentators take a similar line, as do the Christian reformers.[34] It is an approach which might be thought closely to reflect Isaiah's own experience as recorded in 6.5-7, and if v. 18 (alone) was the original continuation of 11-17, then there would seem to be much to be said in favour of it.

(iii) The third approach is essentially the same as the second, but looks forward, primarily, to the following two verses rather than back to the preceding ones. Verses 19-20 spell out clearly the alternatives of obedience leading to blessing and refusal to obey leading to judgment. Since, therefore, the conditional element in the speech is more strongly emphasized, it is clear that the offer to cancel sin is still only potential. In order to make this clear, the verbs are rendered as 'hypotheticals', as in the translation given above: *they could become white…they could become like wool*. Driver, *Tenses* §143, iv, implies that this is the natural translation in view of the imperfect in both halves of the sentences introduced by אִם ('if' or 'though'), 'corresponding to the double optative in Greek', and he cites many examples of the same construction (e.g. Gen. 13.16; Num. 22.18; Amos 5.22, etc.). It must be remembered, however, that the same con-

---

[33] After quoting them, he continues, *et si hoc fecerit, tunc peccata…dimittentur* etc.; see too Ruffenach, 'Malitia et Remissio Peccati'.

[34] See, for instance, Luther in his comments on the first line of the verse, and Calvin *ad loc.*: 'For if we sincerely turn to him, he will immediately return to favour with us', and this following a lengthy exposition of the first line of the verse which concentrates on explaining why Isaiah has just (vv. 16-17) spoken 'chiefly about the second table of the law'. More recently, see W. R. Betteridge, '"Obedience and not Sacrifice": An Exposition of Isa. 1.18-20', *The Biblical World* 38 (1911), 41–49; Clements and Sweeney.

struction also applies to non-hypothetical conditional sentences, as Driver himself, of course, knew well (cf. *Tenses* §136 [β]), and as vv. 19-20 themselves illustrate. Once again it is clear that the issue has to be decided exegetically, since syntax allows more than one possibility. This approach has been followed by many commentators, including Gray, Young, Oswalt, Watts, and Childs, as well as Willis, 'Interpretation'.[35] While the eventual sense is close to that in (ii), it is to be preferred over it in terms of the text as we now have it, and indeed it does not add anything which is not implied by (ii).

(iv) The remaining proposals do not appear to have any representation in antiquity (not in itself a conclusive factor, of course), but arise from more recent perceptions of what Isaiah (or a later author) could or could not have meant. It is frequently asserted as a starting point that he could not have offered forgiveness unconditionally (even though, as we have seen, this has rarely been maintained), that the portrayal of divine activity is incompatible with that in vv. 21-26 following, and further that he could not have suggested that the 'colour' of sin could be changed; it is people that must change (so especially Kutsch, 'Wir wollen miteinander rechten'). In addition, those who take the view that Isaiah was not really urging repentance as a way of averting judgment but rather preaching in order to justify the inevitability of judgment are obliged to seek some other interpretation for this verse if it is indeed from Isaiah. Curiously, the possibility that it might be a later addition is not usually followed by those who find its apparent meaning to be at odds with their understanding of the historical Isaiah.

The oldest attempt to get round these perceived difficulties (at least since J. D. Michaelis in the eighteenth century) is to render the lines as questions: 'if your sins are like scarlet, how can they become white like snow? etc.'. Kaiser, Kutsch, 'Wir wollen miteinander rechten', and Wildberger are among those who have adopted this approach in recent times.[36] It has the advantages that it shows the true seriousness of sin and heightens the force of the following two verses. There is no cheap forgiveness on offer; the only escape for the people is a radical change in their whole way of life.

While the importance of these latter points should not be denied, it is uncertain whether this approach can be upheld. It is true that in general

---

[35] See too Jones, 'Exposition...Eighteen to Twenty', who arrives essentially at this position by the alternative route of stressing the sovereign freedom of the judge.

[36] An alternative approach to the same solution is advanced by Fohrer, 'Jesaja 1 als Zusammenfassung', 159–63, followed by Hoffmann, 96–105, and J. Harvey, *Le plaidoyer prophétique contre Israël après la rupture de l'alliance: étude d'une formule littéraire de l'ancien testament* (Paris and Montreal, 1967), 41–42. Taking his cue from the initial invitation of v. 18, he thinks that a dialogue is to be expected, in which Isaiah's audience would have first replied with words such as 'even if our sins are red like crimson, they can become white as snow, etc.'. The present form of the rest of v. 18 is then Isaiah's rejection of this confidence, in which the pronominal suffixes are changed (from 'our' to 'your') and the position taken is rejected by throwing the statement back as a question, 'can they become white as snow?'. The expected answer, of course, is 'no!', and vv. 19-20 then give the real solution.

terms it is possible in Classical Hebrew (as in many languages) for questions to be asked merely by tone of voice without the presence of an
interrogative word or particle.[37] The very fact that this is well recognized,
however, demonstrates that it is usually clear from the context; the
decision not to employ the interrogative ה implies that there is no doubt
about the intention. In the present case, however, there is much stronger
ground for doubt than just unclarity, partly because it does not seem to fit
with the positive expectations aroused by the use of נוכחה, and more especially because, as Burney showed long ago, this would apparently be the
only example of the apodosis of a conditional or concessive sentence
being turned into a question without the use of the interrogative.[38] The
argument of those who have in a general way stated that the interrogative
would be expected (e.g. Dillmann, Budde, Procksch and Sweeney) is thus
stronger than they realize, while conversely, not a single proponent of this
view has to my knowledge even tried to respond to the linguistic difficulties which it raises.[39]

(v) Duhm (followed in particular by Marti, and more recently by, for
instance, Scott and Høgenhaven, 207) used similar arguments to those in
(iv) against the more traditional renderings, but proposed that the apodosis
of the two conditional statements was intended to be heavily ironic or
sarcastic: 'of course you can turn your scarlet sins white!' Isaiah mocks
his audience's efforts to remove the stain of their sin, and Marti compares
Jer. 2.22 as an unambiguous statement of what is here indicated by irony.
Duhm prefers this approach to (iv) because he thinks that the references to
like snow and *like wool* are an obvious exaggeration. Psalm 51.9 (where
the use of the comparative מן is if anything even stronger) adequately
refutes this suggestion, however.

(vi) Finally, there are those who effectively see in these lines a continuation of the summons in vv. 16-17, and so translate the verbs as jus-
sives: 'they must become white, etc.'.[40] This approach is clearly possible,
but one may doubt whether it is to be preferred. First, it does not seem to
suit the continuation in vv. 19-20 so well, where from a formal point of
view the apodosis of the conditionals is certainly not jussive and from the

[37] Those who maintain that this is the case here refer to such authorities as GK §150*a*;
JM §161*a*; it should be noted, however, that this construction is not as frequent as is
sometimes implied; cf. H. G. Mitchell, 'The Omission of the Interrogative Particle', in
R. F. Harper, F. Brown and G. F. Moore (eds), *Old Testament and Semitic Studies in
Memory of William Rainey Harper*, I (Chicago, 1908), 115–29.

[38] Burney, 'Interpretation', who discusses and dismisses the other possible examples
to which appeal has been made. Gesenius had already objected more vaguely that he
would have expected כי in place of אם.

[39] The word order in the two lines is, of course, determined by their chiastic structure,
the point being to highlight the contrast between red and white. Such a word order is not
infrequently found in conditional sentences where there is no possibility of a question
(e.g. Amos 5.22; Ps. 27.3*b*), and it has nothing to do with indicating an interrogative, as it
can sometimes in English.

[40] E.g. Gates, 'Notes', Procksch, and especially Goldingay, 'If your Sins'. There is a
difference, however, in that whereas Goldingay sees this as a realistic demand, Procksch
regards it as impossible, so that judgment will inevitably follow.

point of view of content there is a promise attached to a condition of obedience. Secondly, if (as is possible) v. 18 once stood as the conclusion of 11-17 without 19-20, so avoiding the first difficulty, then the fact still remains that this would imply that the people could remove the stain of sin by their own efforts, something which Isaiah's own experience (cf. ch. 6) seems to tell against.

In conclusion, then, option (iii) seems to offer the most satisfactory explanation of the text as we now have it, though (ii), from which it differs little, would be possible in an earlier form of the text, if 19-20 were added later. The principal objections which have been raised against it are not cogent. It mirrors Isaiah's own early experience, and has parallels elsewhere in the book as a whole. If v. 18 was the original conclusion of 11-17, then, on the arguments advanced for 11-17 above, it will come from the earlier part of his ministry; contrasts with 22.1-14, for instance, are not relevant. And if it is not Isaianic, then, of course, the historical argument is in any case invalid. Furthermore, those who reject this line do so on the too quick assumption that what they are objecting to is an unconditional offer of forgiveness, whereas this has only ever been maintained by a few; arguments levelled at a straw man are self-defeating. As to the perceived contradiction with vv. 21-26, it may be held that the situations presupposed are not analogous, since those who there are purged out are explicitly those who have failed to implement the imperatives of vv. 16-17 (see the commentary below), and so fall foul of the condition in v. 20. Account must also be taken of the different rhetorical thrust of each passage.

Although the discussion above has spoken in terms of forgiveness, it is true that this is not explicitly mentioned. Rather, what we have is a rare image of God's removal of the stain of sin under the guise of a change in colour, something which fits well after the previous verses with their attention to the blood not only of the sacrifices but also of violence and to the command to 'wash yourselves, purify yourselves' (see especially Sweeney). There are, of course, many images in the Hebrew Bible for the removal of sin, and it would be pedantic to argue that, in a poetic saying, the present one should be understood as fundamentally different. Imagery for such a mystery is never likely to be wholly consistent, so that it would be as pointless to argue that the sins are not removed, only changed into white sins, as to hold that sin which is covered or hidden or which God promises to 'remember no more' nevertheless remains present. The point, of course, is that if the people choose to change their way of life, then God is willing to ensure that the past failings need not be held irrevocably against them.

Scarlet...crimson: strictly speaking, the second of these words refers to a worm, and then specifically to the kermes worm (*coccus ilicis*) from the female of which the *scarlet* dye was extracted. The two words occur frequently in the priestly section of the Pentateuch in a tautologous construct relationship to refer to dyed material (with the words in either order, e.g. Lev. 14.4, 6, 49 on the one hand and Exod. 25.4; 26.1 on the other). 'It is clearly understood in narrative and prophetic sources that the two distinct terms relate to the same extra-linguistic entity',[41] so that the appearance of them both here is to be attributed to no more than the demands of parallelism.

White like snow: Psalm 51.9 has already been referred to as expressing a similar point of view. At Dan. 7.9 (Aramaic), the clothing of the Ancient of Days is also *white as snow*, while his hair is said to be 'like lamb's *wool*'.[42] This may be reflected in T's rendering of our verse (taking *nq'* as 'pure'), though of course the addition only spells out what is implicit in the text.[43]

19. The conditions already implicit in v. 18 are now spelt out in two closely parallel lines which may be broadly categorized as an example of the 'two ways'. While such a pattern is familiar within covenantal contexts (e.g. Deut. 30.15-18), based ultimately on the 'blessings and curses' element, it is by no means limited to this. It is a well-known characteristic of wisdom literature as well, for instance, to go no further. Indeed, it is so natural an element of all human educational language, in whatever social sphere, that it scarcely seems necessary to seek any specific background for it at all. The question whether the particular language of the passage points us more narrowly in the direction of the Deuteronomistic literature has been discussed above.

It is extremely rare to find the verb to be *willing* used without the negative (Job 39.9 is the only other example, out of a total of some 55 occurrences),[44] so that this positive part of the conditional pair draws attention to itself. What the people are invited to 'hear/obey' is not expressly mentioned. While in a Deuteronomic context it would be natural to think of the Torah, here, so far as the present redactional setting of the saying is concerned, we must inevitably think rather of the imperatives of vv. 16-17.

To *feed on the best of the land* again leads some to think (perhaps by familiarity) of passages in the covenantal blessings and curses, where some individual items in this phrase occur; Wildberger, for example, compares Lev. 26.5, 10, 16, 26; Deut. 28.31, 33, and then refers to Deut. 6.11 to show that טוב ('good', hence *best*) is used in the same circle of ideas. He also notes that references to the 'sword' (see v. 20) occur in some of the same contexts as the instrument of punishment. Once again, however, it must be questioned whether this is sufficient to cause us to think that the present passage is specifically rooted in 'the covenant tradition'. Contextually, it is preferable to see in this promise a reversal of the threat of v. 7, and this points us to the fact that enjoying the good things of the land is a widespread aspiration (cf. Gen. 45.18, 20; Jer. 2.7). Several of

---

[41] Brenner, *Colour Terms*, 144.

[42] For this rendering, rather than the familiar 'like pure wool', see M. Sokoloff, "*ʿămar nĕqēʾ*, "Lamb's Wool" (Dan 7:9)', *JBL* 95 (1976), 277–79.

[43] These references, to go no further, are sufficient to rule out the curious interpretation that what is here suggested is that the people's situation is going to go from bad to worse, *white like snow* being sometimes a description of leprosy; R. C. Bailey, '"They Shall Become as White as Snow": When Bad is Turned into Good', *Semeia* 76 (1996), 99–113.

[44] E. Jenni, '"Wollen" und "Nicht-Wollen" im Hebräischen', in *Hommages à André Dupont-Sommer* (Paris, 1971), 201–7.

the passages which Wildberger cites have parallels in political treaties between states elsewhere in the ancient Near East, and all this for the simple reason that they give expression to a very obvious and basic human hope. It is more likely that such language entered Isaiah and the 'covenant' passages along parallel lines rather than that he can only have derived them under influence from the latter.

At a strictly verbal level, the only exact parallel for our phrase in its entirety is Ezra 9.12. This occurs in a passage which cites and alludes to a variety of earlier legal and prophetic texts, so that it is likely that Ezra is here directly quoting our passage. It is of interest that this demonstrates how over the course of time one passage came to be read in the light of others during the period of increasing canonical awareness. It is not surprising that at this later stage obedience and its consequent blessing should have come to be associated closely with the Pentateuchal law; see too Neh. 9.25, 36.

20. *Refuse and rebel* expresses the exact converse of the first part of v. 19. Isaiah nowhere else uses the verb *refuse*, and *rebel* occurs only once elswhere (3.8) in an unusual form. He does, however, describe the people as 'rebellious' at 30.9, where he elaborates with the words 'children who are not willing to hear/obey the law of the Lord', thus presenting a similar portrayal to that of 1.19-20 taken together.

Be devoured by the sword: the original has a closer verbal contrast with 19*b* than can be idiomatically expressed in English ('be fed to the sword' perhaps comes closest).[45] Within the chapter, it implies that disobedience will lead to the completion of the work of judgment by the hand of foreigners only partially executed in v. 7, while further afield the idiom is common for complete annihilation (see textual notes). Not surprisingly, it occurs both in 'covenantal' and in general secular contexts.

For the mouth of the Lord has spoken: see on v. 2 above. The phrase joins somewhat loosely to the foregoing, and yet serves to round out the whole of vv. 2-20 in an emphatic manner. The choice now set before the people reflects what may be called the rhetorical present for the reader. In this sense, vv. 18-20 are the climax of the passage. The remainder looks more to the future and to the consequences of each of the choices now set before them by way of an incentive to obey.

---

[45] For the use of wordplay by repetition of a word with a different sense, see R. B. Chisholm, 'Wordplay in the Eighth-Century Prophets', *BibSac* 144 (1987), 44–52.

PURIFYING FAITHLESS ZION
(1.21-26)

[21]How she has become a whore,
    the once faithful city;
full of justice,
    righteousness used to lodge in her—but now murderers.
[22]Your silver has become dross,
    Your fine liquor adulterated with water.
[23]Your rulers are rebels and partners with thieves;
    each one loves a bribe and chases after gifts;
they do not take up the orphan's case, nor does the widow's cause come
    before them.
[24]Therefore—saying of the Sovereign, the Lord of Hosts, the Strong One
    of Israel—
Ah! I will relieve myself of my foes,
    and avenge myself on my enemies,
      [25]and turn my hand against you.
I will smelt away your dross as with alkali,
    and remove all your tin impurities.
[26]And I will restore your judges as at the first,
    and your counsellors as at the beginning;
afterwards you will be called 'the city of righteousness',
    'faithful city'.

21. איכה: 1QIsaᵃ היכה; cf. 14.12, where it reads similarly for MT איך. This seems to reflect Late Biblical Hebrew usage; cf. היך at 1 Chron. 13.12 for איך in the parallel 2 Sam. 6.9; otherwise only at Dan. 10.17. Kutscher, 390, hesitantly suggests that it is a 'blend' of איכה + היך.

היתה: 1QIsaᵃ frequently spells the perfect of היה with a double י, as here; the difference seems to be purely orthographic (cf. Kutscher, 159).

LXX includes Σιων at the end of the first line, in apposition with 'faithful city'. While that cannot be right as it stands (since MT's 3 + 2 rhythm is clearly superior in a lament), the possibility has sometimes been favoured that it reflects a text in which ציון stood at the start of the second line. On the widely held assumption that the last two words of the verse are a later gloss (and with בה ילין treated as a single stress), the second half of the verse could then be construed comfortably as 3 + 2 as well (see, for instance, Duhm, Marti, Condamin, Gray, Budde, Procksch and Kissane). In his consideration of this, Wildberger also suggests that the unusual form of the next word might then be pointed מִלֵּאתִי to give 'I filled Zion with justice', but he then dismisses the whole proposal on the ground that a first person speech by God would not be expected at the start of a lament. While this argument is valid against the proposed repointing (for which there is no textual support), it does not answer the case for including a reference to Zion with the Masoretic pointing of the remainder retained. The case for that is in many ways attractive, but it faces the problem that it is much easier to explain how the LXX reading (or its Hebrew *Vorlage*) might have arisen secondarily than to see how the word could have been lost from all other textual traditions: (i) Zion appears at the start of v. 27 in the MT, but in the LXX it has been construed incorrectly at the end of v. 26 to give a nearly identical phrase with what LXX has in v. 21 ('the faithful mother-city Zion'). It would then not be in the least surprising if this reading of v. 26 had influenced v. 21. (ii) At 33.5 we have מלא ציון משפט וצדקה. In view of the close similarity with 1.21, influence from here may also be suspected. Sound method dictates, therefore, that, for all its admitted attractions, the LXX tradition should be regarded as secondary at this point. Such exegetical cross-references in the LXX of Isaiah are by no means rare (cf. Ziegler, 56–80), so that the addition may have been made by the translator himself, without any Hebrew *Vorlage*; a clear case of this procedure occurs in the second line of v. 31 below.[1]

מְלֵאֲתִי: revocalization to a first person singular perfect verb being ruled out on form-critical grounds, this must be a construct feminine adjective, מְלֵאֲת, with a so-called *ḥireq compaginis*, perhaps as a relic of the old genitive, or better, construct case-ending.[2] For other examples, see GK §90*l*, 95*h*; JM §93*m* (interestingly, a comparable example comes again following איכה in Lam. 1.1). Was this form chosen here precisely to lengthen slightly the otherwise rather short first half of the line?

יָלִין: a clear example of the use of the imperfect to express the past frequentative or continuous (appreciated already by Jerome in dispute with α and θ; cf. GK §107*b*; JM §113*f*; Driver, *Tenses* § 30).

22. היה לסיגים: 1QIsaᵃ has היו לסוגים. These two differences (which in the case of the verb cannot be justified grammatically) suggest influence from the similar Ezek. 22.18, היו לי בית ישראל לסוג (K; Q proposes לסיג). Though Koenig does not appear to discuss this verse, it would be a further small example of what he calls 'l'herméneutique analogique'.

סָבְאֵךְ: there is doubt about the precise meaning of this rare noun.[3] The context shows clearly that some kind of highly valued drink is intended, and the oldest interpretations suggest wine (so the versions and Kimhi; Rashi is less specific: 'drinks'). However, while this may find support from the Arabic *sibāʾ*, 'wine' (though if this is a loan-word, as has been suggested, its evidence is of less value), the Akkadian *sību* means 'beer' of some kind.[4] The related verb indicates that hard drinking is involved (e.g. Deut. 21.20; Prov. 23.20), which fits, but since it can govern either יין (Prov. 23.20) or שכר (Isa. 56.12), it does not help us decide whether it is a drink based on grain or the grape. The translation *fine liquor* attempts to avoid the problem by retaining the ambiguity; Walsh, *Fruit*, 204, prefers simply 'drink'.

מהול is a *hapax legomenon*, but on the basis of Post-Biblical Hebrew and Aramaic, there seems no reason to doubt the usual explanation that it is a variant form of מול;[5] see further the commentary below. This possibility can stand whether or not במים is deleted as a later explanatory gloss. An older alternative, which is not now generally followed

[1] Suggestions to delete other parts of the line, such as ילין בה (Feldmann), or to regard one or other of the first two phrases as a variant on the other, and so to delete one (Janzen, *Mourning Cry*, 58) have no textual support and seem even less plausible; against the latter, in particular, the parallelism of צדק and משפט is stereotypical in Isaiah and elsewhere, and exegetically must not be disturbed; see the commentary below.

[2] This is the usual explanation; cf. G. R. Driver, 'The Origin of "Ḥireq Compaginis" in Hebrew', *JTS* 26 (1924–25), 76–77. For a different opinion, however, see W. L. Moran, 'The Hebrew Language in its Northwest Semitic Background', in G. E. Wright (ed.), *The Bible and the Ancient Near East: Essays in Honor of William Foxwell Albright* (Garden City, 1961), 54–72 (60); he points out that the presence of an *i* ending on three participles in the Amarna Letters cannot be explained as a remnant of the genitive since case endings were still in use at the time, and on this basis he rejects the usual explanation in those cases where *ḥireq compaginis* occurs on a participle in Hebrew; he also disposes of some other examples by revocalizing them as infinitives absolute (again with parallels from Amarna). While obviously there can be no certainty about the matter, it is a weakness that Moran adopts a 'divide and rule' line of argument and that even then he has to concede that his explanations do not cover all the examples in Hebrew.

[3] Ehrlich's attempt to avoid the problem by emending to זהבך מהול בדילים is no solution.

[4] *CDA*, 321. J.-J. Hess, 'Was bedeutet סבא Jesaias 1₂₂?', *MGWJ* 78 (1934), 6–9, also cites widespread, though later, Arabic evidence to the same effect.

[5] For other examples of ע"ו verbs which also have an ע"ה form, see GK §77*f*.

(though cf. *BHS*), is to emend to מוֹהַל, which in Post-Biblical Hebrew (and cf. Arabic *muhla*) is said to mean some kind of fruit or olive juice.[6] It is unwise, however, to introduce another *hapax legomenon* by way of emendation while at the same time relying on the deletion of במים. It might also have been expected that the word would be preceded by the preposition ל.

במים: on the use of the definite article, see GK §126*n*, but see too on כשנים in v. 18 above. Dahood, 'Weaker than Water', suggests that the ב here is equivalent to מן, used as a comparative: 'your choice wine is weaker than water'. This is doubtful, however. His starting point is mistaken, because he thinks that the reference is to drinking habits, where he claims that the addition of water to wine was considered good practice, so that the traditional rendering cannot be correct. Regardless of whether such mixing was good practice in those times,[7] it is far more likely that the reference here is to the practice of the merchants, not the consumers (LXX already took this line explicitly by paraphrase: 'your dealers mix the wine with water', and similarly P, 'your tavern-keepers'; see too Gesenius); see the commentary below. In addition, while it is likely that in certain constructions involving 'movement away from' ב may be the equivalent of the English 'from' (as in Ugaritic; Ps. 18.9 is the standard example), that is a far cry from establishing that ב and מן are interchangeable across the whole of their semantic range. Finally, the rendering of מהול by 'weak' (through an association with אמל) is at best speculative.

23. סוררים: it is probable that the renderings of α, θ and σ already represent (as Jerome seems to have suspected) an association of סרר with סור, 'to turn aside', as is sometimes found also in the medieval commentators (e.g. Rashi on this verse; Ibn Ezra on Hos. 4.16, etc.). However, whether or not they are etymologically related, the two words are clearly to be distinguished in the language of the Hebrew Bible. Jenni[8] maintains that there are two separate nouns סרה related to each of these roots, and he associates סרה at 1.5 with סרר; it is not at all certain, however, that Isaiah's readers would have made the same connection, and Wildberger is probably mistaken in conflating them in his comments on 1.5.

כלו: for the singular suffix, see JM §146*j*. 1QIsaᵃ has the plural suffix, כלם, 'all of them', and follows this, of course, with construct plural forms of the two following participles: אוהבי and רודפי. The versions may have known the text in this form, since they too render with plurals, though in the case of the LXX without any equivalent of כלו or כלם itself. The difficulty of knowing whether the versions read a different text or were simply interpreting the MT *ad sensum* in such cases, however, is highlighted by the fact that in its interpretive expansion following, T uses the familiar idiom in the singular for reciprocity, 'a man to his neighbour'. While the difference in sense is slight, and either text form is possible, MT is slightly to be preferred as the harder reading. In addition, the scroll reading may well have been influenced by Jer. 6.28 (כלם ש/סרי סוררים).

שלמנים: this *hapax legomenon* is the precise equivalent of Akkadian *šulmānu*, 'gift, bribe'. Since this is a primary noun in Akkadian, and since in that language there is no word which is etymologically and semantically equivalent to Hebrew שלם, it is clear that our word cannot be connected with the latter, as was assumed in antiquity (the versions tend to render 'repayment', while the medieval commentators follow T's paraphrase based on this[9]) and almost universally since.[10]

---

[6] Slightly differently Barth, *Beiträge*, 3–4, who compares this word in order to defend MT as meaning 'verbrüht, verwässert', followed by Th. Nöldeke, in a review of F. Delitzsch's *Prolegomena* in *ZDMG* 40 (1896), 741. Note too how Kimhi cites his father's comparison with Arabic אלמהל.

[7] Lowth already argued strongly to the contrary, whereas Walsh, *Fruit*, 203, argues that it was good practice in the classical world but not in Israel.

[8] E. Jenni, 'Dtn 19,16: *sarā* "Falschheit"', in A. Caquot and M. Delcor (eds), *Mélanges bibliques et orientaux en l'honneur de M. Henri Cazelles* (AOAT 212; Kevelaer and Neukirchen–Vluyn, 1981), 201–11.

[9] אמרין גבר לחבריה עביד לי בדיני דאשלים לך בדינך, 'they say one to another, Assist me in my case, so that I may *repay* you in your case'.

24. נאם: though much discussed, the uncertain etymology of this word is unlikely to illuminate its use and meaning in Biblical Hebrew generally or in Isaiah in particular. It is probably an example of cases where 'stereotyped archaisms are commonly used to describe speaking in all languages'.[11] This suggestion is reinforced by the unusual invariability in spelling and vocalization by the Masoretes, suggesting that it functions in the current form of the language more as a particle than a noun. Later (see 1QIsaᵃ נאום; elsewhere נאם also occurs; cf. Kutscher, 174 and 498–99), this uniform pronunciation was dropped, and the word could be treated as a monosyllable (cf. Origen's transcription *noum*). Meier argues forcefully that 'the congruence between the phonetic contours—both consonantal and vocalic—of [the Akkadian particles] *umma/anumma* and Hebrew נאם is impressive', and he demonstrates further that there is 'equally impressive semantic and syntactic overlap between these particles'.[12] Although it most usually occurs in the Hebrew Bible at the close of a divine speech, this is by no means invariably so; the present passage is only one of a number where it stands in an introductory position, as it can also for human speech (e.g. Num. 24.3-4; 2 Sam. 23.1; Ps. 110.1; Prov. 30.1, etc.). It is difficult to see any distinction in usage between it and the common verb אמר (see especially the parallel between Jer. 49.18 and 50.40), and indeed, it is often translated as though it were a verb (e.g. 'says the Lord'). It is likely that the related verb, which occurs only once in Biblical Hebrew (Jer. 23.31) but becomes more common in the post-biblical period, is a denominative, coined long after the etymological origins of the word were forgotten.

האדון: because, out of respect for tradition, I have used 'the Lord' as a rendering throughout this commentary for the tetragrammaton (the divine name 'Yahweh'), it is necessary to use an alternative equivalent for this word (lit., 'the lord' as a title rather than a name), in view of the divine name which follows immediately (perhaps for the same reason it is not separately translated by V). 'Sovereign' is again conventional.

יהוה צבאות: see on v. 9.

אביר ישראל: the LXX does not construe this as another divine title, but refers it to the leaders (plural) of Israel, following the 'woe': Οὐαὶ οἱ ἰσχύοντες Ισραηλ. This is scarcely evidence that the phrase is a later addition to the text (Marti, Gray, Budde). Rather, Seeligmann, 104, finds here an example (among others) of a passage where the translator has been influenced by the ideas preached generally by the prophets; 5.22, where the first three words are identical in the Greek, might be especially compared.

הוי: 1QIsaᵃ usually agrees with MT in its representation of this word, but here it has הוה. The explanation is far from certain. Kutscher, 229, suggests that it may be an equivalent of הוא, with which he compares הו at Amos 5.16.

אנחם: although the niph'al of נחם is common enough, the sense demanded by the context is highly unusual; at the only other place where it is followed by מן (Judg. 2.18) the meaning is clearly different ('be moved to pity by'), and the sense at Isa. 57.6 (+ על), which is often compared, is disputed: if 'be appeased' is right there, then it would offer some support for the required sense here. The hithpa'el, which overlaps considerably with the niph'al in the case of this verb, occurs at Gen. 27.42 (+ ל) and (with assimilated ה) at Ezek. 5.13 (though some question the text in this instance). In both these cases, a meaning similar to that required in our passage seems to be present. It needs to be stressed that part of the reason for the choice of word here is to achieve an alliterative effect with ואנקמה following. The occurrence of an unusual meaning for a familiar word is thus not too surprising, and it should not be made the excuse for over-reliance on dubious etymologizing.[13]

---

[10] See Cohen, *Biblical Hapax Legomena*, 40–41 and 68–69. Cohen also rejects on similar grounds some more recent attempts to link the word with the sacrificial שלמים. See also Mankowski, *Akkadian Loanwords*, 144–46.

[11] G. R. Driver, *Problems of the Hebrew Verbal System* (Edinburgh, 1936), 145.

[12] Meier, *Speaking of Speaking*, 308, summarizing his discussion on 298–314. He also refers to alternative etymological proposals; see also H. Eising, *ThWAT* v. 119–23 = *TDOT* ix. 109–13.

[13] Cf. J. Barr, *The Semantics of Biblical Language* (Oxford, 1961), 116–17. Barr here criticizes N. H. Snaith, 'The Language of the Old Testament', *IB* i. 220–32 (225–26) (and

Nor do the versions offer much help. LXX (οὐ παύσεται γάρ μου ὁ θυμὸς ἐν τοῖς ὑπεναντίοις) has linked the word with נוח, and then had to render freely to get the required sense (there is no evidence for a text with לא). T has rendered by way of a double translation, introducing before the 'woe' the notion of comfort for Jerusalem (see especially the use of נחם at 40.1-2), and then paraphrasing with the use of stereotypical targumic vocabulary (למעבד פורעוות¹⁴דין) for the second, more in line with the obvious demands of the context. P is similar to T's second rendering. V is the most satisfactory with *heu consolabor super hostibus meis*. Neither here nor elsewhere is it necessary to impart the sense of vengeance into the verb;[15] that point is adequately made in the second half of the line (just as it is by להרגך at Gen. 27.42, while at Ezek. 5.13 והנחמי follows the outpouring of God's anger). Rather, the thought is of God gaining comfort/relief for himself after the wrath provoked by the people's misdeeds (cf. Rashi and Ibn Ezra) through the act of vengeance which follows. Thus, at Ezek. 16.42, which starts off with a similarly strong expression of the venting of God's wrath as we find in 5.13, והנחמתי of the latter verse is replaced, so to speak, by ושקמתי, 'and I will be calm, relaxed'.

אנחם מצרי ואנקמה מאויבי: the first hand of 1QIsaᵃ reads אנקם ואקם מצריו אאובו, while a suspended ה has later been added above the line between the מ and א of מאובו. This can scarcely be the definite article. More likely a scribe misplaced the letter, so that it follows the 'wrong' מ, intending it to be an assimilation of the previous word towards the ואנקמה of the Masoretic tradition; some other examples of misplaced suspended letters in this scroll are listed by Kutscher, 531.[16] The reading of the first hand is to be preferred in this respect, since it brings the two alliteratively related words אנקם and אנחם closer together (for the use of conjunctive *waw* in such a position, see on v. 2 above); partial and hence inconsistent expansion in the Masoretic tradition would not be surprising (see further on the next verse); while there is admittedly balance between 24*b* and 25*b* in this respect (short form in the first half, and long form in the second), the occurrence of ואשיבה in 25*a* and 26*a* suggests that this may not have been deliberate. The use of third person masculine singular suffixes on the two nouns is less easily explained. Most of the versions support MT's first person here, and this must be correct. In its paraphrase, however, T renders צרי as 'the enemies of the people (סנאי עמא)', while for the second noun it has a singular (as in the scroll?) without any suffix, 'the adversary (בעיל דבבא)'. Although the nature of T's rendering throughout this verse precludes certainty, it is possible that it was working with a text similar to that in the scroll and, understanding the suffixes which then have no antecedent to refer to the people, turned the line into an expression of God's vengeance on behalf of Israel against external enemies, while judgment of the corrupt internal leaders is left to the next verse. Since the verbs cannot be other than first person singular (so that there is no possibility of the scroll meaning 'he will relieve himself of his foes, etc.'), I can assume only that the scroll already anticipated this same reinterpretation.[17] It represents an understandable softening of Isaiah's shocking pronouncement.

see his earlier article, 'The Meaning of "The Paraclete" ', *ExpT* 57 [1945/46], 47–50), but behind this stands the work of D. Winton Thomas, to whom Barr does not refer; cf. 'A Note on the Hebrew Root נחם', *ExpT* 44 (1932/33), 191–92; other studies include H. Van Dyke Parunak, 'A Semantic Survey of *NHM*', *Biblica* 56 (1975), 512–32 ('a cessation of wrath through its execution'); J. Scharbert, *Der Schmerz im Alten Testament* (BBB 8; Bonn, 1955), 62–65; and J. Jeremias, *Die Reue Gottes: Aspekte alttestamentlicher Gottesvorstellung* (2nd edn; Neukirchen–Vluyn, 1997).

[14] The manuscript evidence for the presence of this word is mixed, however, and opinions differ; contrast, for instance, the editions of Stenning (who includes it) and Sperber (who omits it).

[15] So rightly H. Simian-Yofre, *ThWAT* v. 366–84 (375–76) = *TDOT* ix. 340–55 (348).

[16] The only other possibility which suggests itself is that somehow there was an intended contrast between 'his enemies' and 'those who love him (אוהבו)', but it is difficult to see how they would then have understood אנקם.

[17] Alternatively, van der Kooij, 97, developing a suggestion by Chamberlain, 'Messianic Titles', 370–72, suggests that the suffixes refer back to צדק in v. 21. Since it is the

The LXX's free rendering of this verse is continued into the last clause: nowhere else is κρίσιν ποιεῖν ever used to render the verb נקם:.

25. 1QIsaᵃ reads והשיב instead of MT ואשיבה. For the shorter form, see on the previous verse and on ואסירה below. Chamberlain and van der Kooij (cf. n. 17) make a virtue of the apparent shift from first to third person to suggest that the Messiah/Teacher of Righteousness has intercessory power with God: 'and he will turn my hand against...'. Their solution has the attraction of seeking to explain the differences here and in the previous verse in a consistent manner. As already seen, however, there are problems with their treatment of v. 24, and here no parallel is offered for the idea of a human being 'turning' God's hand. There are sufficient examples of ה/א confusion (among others) to suggest that 'the laryngeals and pharyngeals were indistinguishable in the dialect of the scribe of the Scr[oll]' (Kutscher, 508) and that this may be no more than an interchange of the same sort. On p. 505 Kutscher lists other passages where the scroll has ה in place of MT א (see already on איכה in v. 21).

כבר: on the use of the preposition, see GK §118*w*. Despite this, many commentators (e.g. Lowth, Marti, Ehrlich, Gray, Wade, Procksch, Kaiser, Loretz, 111–14, Blenkinsopp) object either that a comparison is out of place here, since the whole line is already metaphorical, or that there is doubt about the process involved, and so emend to כְּבֹר, 'in a furnace'. Admittedly, metathesis of two similar-looking consonants could easily have occurred, and the proposed sense is appropriate (see especially 48.10; Ezek. 22.18; Prov. 17.3; 27.21). However, all the ancient evidence available[18] supports the present consonantal text, even though sometimes understood differently; LXX εἰς καθαρόν, V *ad purum*, P *ldkyw* (all, therefore, associating the word with the noun and adjective בר, 'purity, pure'), and T כמא דמנקן בבוריתא. בר as an alternative form of ברית (Jer. 2.22; Mal. 3.2) is attested at Job 9.30. The objections raised against MT seem to be either hypercritical or misplaced; see the comments below. Nor is it necessary, therefore, to repoint as an infinitive absolute pi'el of כבר, with the postulated meaning 'thoroughly' (so Hayman, 'Note'), or, with Duhm, partially to follow the LXX in redividing as ואצרפך בר, with the consequence that סיניך has to be joined to the second half of the line, followed awkwardly by a *waw*-apodosis (see Marti's criticisms).

ואסירה: 1QIsaᵃ again has the shorter form, as consistently through vv. 24-25. Though the other examples are not attested in the very fragmentary 4QIsaᶠ, on this occasion it too lacks the final ה. This reinforces the suggestion made above that there was a somewhat random tendency towards expansion in this regard in the textual tradition which lies behind the MT.

In place of the second two clauses of this verse, LXX has three. This has sometimes been used to help fill out what initially looks like the lack of a clause to balance the first one in the verse, while alternatively part of the additional material in LXX has been thought to be a later addition to the Greek (cf. Gray; Ziegler, 61, 81). The whole matter has been thoroughly examined afresh by Koenig, 83–86, who not only points to some interpretive renderings of the text by the translator (partially in line with T's later approach to this verse, so that this may represent a common exegetical tradition; see too Baer, 'It's All About Us!', 202–3), but also and more significantly observes that the rendering of the line has worked in a reference to the text of 13.11 which accounts for the additional material. This technique of the translator has already been observed above (e.g. at v. 21), and the present verse is only one of a number of examples which Koenig discusses at length. While not all his examples are convincing, the case here is strong. It follows that the LXX should not be used here for major textual reconstruction.

---

subject of ילין, it was understood as a person, namely the 'Teacher of Righteousness', whose 'enemy' then becomes the wicked priest, of course. However, it is not at all certain that textual variations in the scroll should be attributed to specifically Qumran ideology (see too Pulikottil, 26–27, with reference to this verse), and צדק seems very remote to serve as an antecedent here.

[18] Unfortunately, because of physical damage, the word is not preserved in any Qumran manuscript.

26. ואשיבה: so too 1QIsaᵃ (against its usual spelling in these verses), but 4QIsaᶠ has
[וא]שיב; see on ואסירה in the previous verse. LXX renders ἐπιστήσω, an almost unparalleled equivalence (though cf. 2 Sam. 8.3, if MT is sound); unless this is simply a stylistic
variation, in view of the same word at the start of v. 25, I suspect that the *Vorlage* may
have (erroneously) read ואציבה (rather than ואקימה, which has been suggested). T ואמני ביך
may also possibly be compared.

שפטיך: GK §135*m* suggests that the suffix here is objective, 'judges for you'. Though
technically correct, since clearly the same individuals are not involved, it puts the emphasis in the wrong place; the focus is on the office, not the actual people.

כבראשנה...כבתחלה: for the use of two inseparable prepositions together, see GK §118*s*,
n. 2; JM §133*h*; contrast כבר in the previous verse.

יקרא: 1QIsaᵃ יקראו, an impersonal plural qal for MT's niph'al. This construction occurs
frequently in Isaiah, and in most of these cases the scroll makes the same change; for
details, see Kutscher, 402.[19] Either is grammatically possible, but MT is to be preferred;
the scroll conforms the idiom to the form which became common later.

For the rendering of the close of this verse in the LXX, see on v. 21 above, and
Seeligmann, 113–14.

There can be no doubt that, within the major unit which has been assembled by the compiler of ch. 1, v. 21 begins a new section. The concluding
nature of the end of v. 20 was noted above, and v. 21 starts with its own
introductory איכה, 'how!' (cf. Lam. 1.1; 2.1, etc.).[20]

There is less agreement, however, over whether the unit closes at v. 23,
26, 28 or 31.[21] As we have seen before, part of this disagreement stems
from a failure to appreciate the nature of the composition of ch. 1 as a
whole. In the light of our previous analysis, it may readily be agreed that
v. 21 introduces a section which extends to the end of the chapter (and
indeed, that in the final form of the text the chapter as a whole should be
treated as a single compositional unit), but as in the earlier sections, so here
too there are grounds for affirming that this is made up of smaller paragraphs. Once this fact is grasped, it emerges clearly that the majority view
is correct which sees 21-26 as such a paragraph. Internally, it is held
together form-critically (see below) as also by the reprise of some of the
themes of 21-23 in 24-26 (see the attention to the image of refining silver,
and especially the obvious *inclusio* between vv. 21 ('faithful city' and

[19] Kutscher does not mention 54.5 and 56.7 as additional passages where the change
might have been made but was not.

[20] Blum even goes so far as to suggest that this paragraph was the start of an early
collection of Isaiah's writing, assembled by the prophet in advance of the 701 BCE crisis.
He thinks that this was concentrically arranged as a 'ring-composition', with 7.9 at its
heart, thus: (A) 1.21-26; (B)(a) 2.7, 10, 12-17; (b) 3.1-7, *12-15, 16-24; (C)(a) 5.1-24*a*;
(b) 5.24*b*-29; (D) 6.1-11 + *7 + 8.1-18; (C′)(b) 9.7-20; (a) 10.1-4; (B′)(b) 10.5-15; (a)
10.27*b**-34; (A′) 11.1-5. In the course of defending this hypothesis, Blum makes many
valuable observations (for instance, the connections of our present paragraph with 11.1-5
are well taken), and his defence of Isaianic authorship of the material listed is frequently
helpful. It is clear, however, that the suggested history of composition differs radically
from that adopted in this commentary (e.g. on the growth of the so-called *Denkschrift* in
chs 6–8, which is at the heart of the proposal, and on the nature of ch. 1, so far as the
present discussion is concerned), so that a detailed interaction at this point would be
unnecessarily distracting.

[21] For a full survey of opinions, see Willis, 'Lament Reversed'. He refers to a much
wider selection of secondary literature than is possible here.

'righteousness') and 26. Thus, to break the paragraph at v. 23 is unjustified.[22]

Similarly, although there is a clear connection in thought with the verses which immediately follow,[23] that need not preclude us from seeing them as a separate paragraph. There is no conjunction or other connection between vv. 26 and 27, there is a shift from second to third person address, and the emphasis changes rather markedly (see the commentary there). On the other hand, v. 29 is linked closely to 28 by its initial כִּי, so that to introduce a major break at that point in justification for linking 27-28 with 21-26 is itself unwarranted.

The form of the passage is that of the classic prophetic judgment speech: an indictment (21-23) followed by 'therefore' with an extended messenger formula (24a), and then the announcement of judgment (24b-25; on 26, see below). As often, the two main elements are verbally and conceptually associated.[24] Within this overarching form, the indictment takes the form of a funerary dirge (21), which is appropriately echoed in the exclamatory הוֹי at the start of the announcement of judgment. This should not be regarded as a separate element, however; it is well within the range of variations which the prophets, as creative speakers or writers, could use within a single genre.[25]

The paragraph as it now stands takes its appropriate place in the unfolding of the chapter as a whole. The previous section ended with the presentation of a stark choice to the people: obey and find blessing or rebel and be devoured by the sword. That division among the people is now developed. Because corruption has permeated the city as a whole, the whole will have to go through the fire of judgment, and in this process the wicked will be removed. Something will remain, however, as the basis for the restored city of v. 26, and in the context of the chapter we must assume that this is made up of those who fulfil the conditions of vv. 18-19. That same thought will then be underlined in the following verses (see on 27-28 below).

---

[22] *Contra*, for instance, Robertson, 'Isaiah Chapter 1', 235, Scott, Kaiser and Watts; their error is mainly to ascribe form-critical independence to the funeral dirge, without recognizing that this has been used, as sometimes elsewhere, as an element of a larger judgment speech.

[23] So especially Willis, who cites Procksch, Eichrodt and Auvray among those who are of the same opinion. A major consideration for Willis is his conviction that 21-28 can be ascribed in its entirety to Isaiah, a view not shared here.

[24] See especially Westermann, *Grundformen = Basic Forms*, C and D, Wildberger, and Sweeney.

[25] For this and many similar examples, see again Westermann, D (esp. V. 4), and further Hardmeier, *Texttheorie*, 348–54 (Hardmeier categorizes the opening verses as the parody of an *Untergangslied* rather than a funerary dirge; he is closely followed by Stansell, *Micah and Isaiah*, 57–60). Dobbs-Allsopp, *Weep, O Daughter of Zion*, 148–52, draws attention to parallels with the city-lament genre, including the restoration theme of v. 26. However, while the parallels need not be denied, the invective + לָכֵן + announcement structure clearly shows that the dominant genre is that of the judgment speech, and this must be taken into account in consideration of v. 26 as well. It is a pity that Dobbs-Allsopp appears to have been unaware of Hardmeier's work.

It has sometimes been objected that there is an inconsistency between 18-20 and 21-26. The former (as indeed most of the chapter) lays emphasis on the people's own responsibility for their predicament whereas here God speaks of his personal intervention for a saving purpose. So far as this relates to the question of the authenticity to Isaiah himself of this paragraph, the issue again turns on v. 26, on which see below; vv. 21-25 can certainly be accommodated to his thought elsewhere without difficulty. In terms of the chapter as a complete unit, however, the distinction made seems to be a false one. The compiler will inevitably have thought that divine intervention would be necessary if the conditions of 18-20 were to be realized; how else could the promise of blessing or the threat of judgment be made effective? They are hardly a law of nature. As it stands, our paragraph does no more than spell out how God will work out the threat and promise of 19-20. The emphasis in each case may be different, but without the present paragraph the words of 19-20 would be empty. Reticence about detailing the human instruments he may use for this purpose is a characteristic we have noted throughout the chapter (though 7-9 and 20 have indicated that it is likely to take a military form); it is not a distinguishing feature of this particular passage.

In moving back now to the inevitably more speculative task of seeking to identify the shape of the original material which the chapter's compiler may have inherited and adapted,[26] we find that many small proposals for the deletion or addition of words and phrases have been driven by the desire to make the whole passage conform to the 3 + 2 rhythm of the lament. Budde's proposals have been particularly influential in this regard. In some cases, there are additional supporting arguments, but in others not. On the basis of the method adopted in this commentary, the latter proposals should not be accepted (though in some cases their attractiveness is readily admitted). A more promising approach is to investigate whether we can detect the hand of the chapter's compiler (with whose methods we are to some extent familiar) in integrating the passage into his wider composition.

The most convincing candidate for the compiler's hand is the last line of v. 23.[27] The words are drawn almost entirely from the last line of v. 17 and must be dependent upon it. The point being made is an obvious one, namely that the wayward 'rulers' are precisely those who do not fulfil the demands on which escape from the threatened judgment depends. The line therefore functions very well to help integrate one part of the chapter with another, and it cannot have stood here before the chapter as a whole was assembled. In support of this conclusion, we may note that the line as it stands is rhythmically hopeless (even Budde gives up the attempt to improve it, and simply deletes!) and that it fits with the compiler's procedure elsewhere of using catch-words and phrases to link one passage to another (see, for instance, on vv. 10 above and 28 below).

[26] For the following, see too my essay 'Judgment and Hope'.

[27] So, for instance, Vermeylen, 73, who cites Budde, Fey and Vollmer in support; see further Kaiser, and Deck, 146–47.

It is probable that the last two words of v. 21, 'but now murderers', fit into the same category. To the rhythmical argument that they overload the line may be added the observation that, just as the last line of 23 draws on the climax of 16-17, so these two words draw on the climax of the indictment in 11-15 ('your hands are full of blood'). They also introduce a 'personal' element which might not be expected before v. 23. The case is not as strong here, because the vocabulary is different (though the use of מלא at the start of the line in 21 may have drawn attention to a parallel with the end of 15), but since it fits conceptually with the strong case based on 23, it seems plausible.[28] Most commentators just delete the words, but if they are to be attributed to the chapter's compiler, then clearly they should be retained in terms of the text which he intended and which we have inherited from him.

'With water' (במים) is often deleted from the end of v. 22 for metrical reasons. Although this would restore a further 3 + 2 line, it should be noted that the following line is rhythmically different again, so that it is not clear how strong this argument is, even taken on its own terms. The line can certainly be construed without it, but that is not evidence. In this case there are no supporting arguments of the sort noted earlier, so that (slightly reluctantly!) the temptation to delete should be resisted.[29]

Wildberger follows Fohrer in deleting the first three words of v. 25 as a later gloss, intended to 'nail down' the identity of the 'enemies' of v. 24. He thinks this also gets round the problem of the repetition of ואשיבה (v. 26). The latter point should be differently handled, in my opinion, however (see below). The words fit their present context perfectly, and introduce a characteristically Isaianic picture into the description of the judgment. If the words are taken as the third element of a tristich, then there would seem to be much to be said for retaining them.

Verse 26 is usually taken as an integral part of the original paragraph, and as such has often been used as the basis for reconstructing the nature of Isaiah's hopes for the future.[30] There are several reasons, however, which have not been previously noted, for ascribing this verse to the compiler of the chapter in its final form rather than to the original material

---

[28] The argument that, on form-critical grounds, the phrase should be retained because of the need to contrast 'Zion's glorious past with her woeful present' (Dobbs-Allsopp, *Weep, O Daughter of Zion*, 149; cf. Janzen, *Mourning Cry*, 58) is not compelling since this element in any case follows immediately in vv. 22-23. On p. 151, Dobbs-Allsopp himself categorizes these two verses as an example of the 'reversal motif'. Nor does emendation (to either ועדת or וחבר; so Popper, 'Parallelism', 307) address the problems directly.

[29] Budde's other proposals are even more conjectural and will not be discussed further: add ציון to v. 21 (but see the textual notes above); add היו to the first phrase of 23; delete אביר ישראל from 24a; add ואצתך באש to 25a; delete כל from 25b; replace אחרי־כן by ו and add עוד before עיר in 26b.

[30] In addition to many of the standard commentaries and monographs on Isaiah, see, for instance, K. Budde, 'Über die Schranken, die Jesajas prophetischer Botschaft zu setzen sind', *ZAW* 41 (1923), 154–203 (158–60); Herrmann, *Die prophetischen Heilserwartungen*, 127–29; Jensen, 'Weal and Woe'; Hermisson, 'Zukunftserwartung und Gegenwartskritik'; see too Jones, 'Exposition…Twenty One to the End'.

which he inherited. (i) Form-critically, the verse does not sit well with what precedes. As we have seen, 21-25 take the form of a standard prophetic judgment speech, and a sudden switch to a climactic expression of hope for the future is not to be expected.[31] In fact, the effect of including v. 26 is to turn the whole passage into what Hanson has termed a 'salvation-judgment oracle', a form which he finds in several passages in Trito-Isaiah and which, he argues, is a development of the classic judgment oracle not attested prior to the sixth century.[32] It is comparable with what Westermann calls the 'fate of the godly, fate of the ungodly' group of texts, which he also maintains are the result of later additions to early texts.[33] The effect of dividing the fate of the nation into two groups is, of course, the result of the increasing individualization which characterizes the post-exilic material in the book of Isaiah, even if its origins in general terms may be traced as early as the late pre-exilic period (cf. Koenen, *Heil den Gerechten*). (ii) Nothing in 21-25 prepares us for what comes in this verse. Although from the imagery of refining it may legitimately be inferred that something pure will emerge at the end, this is not the use to which the previous verses put the image. Verses 24b-25 focus univocally on the removal of the impurity, not the emergence of the good.[34] (iii) The renaming of the city (and the form of words which that takes here) is a distinctively late notion, and like some other elements in this last part of the chapter (26-31) it has close parallels in Isaiah 56–66 in particular (see the comments below for details). It must be judged very probable that this verse reflects comparable influence. In addition, the somewhat prosaic אחרי־כן does not occur elsewhere in Isaiah (or in any other pre-exilic prophet). Although DeVries, *From Old Revelation to New*, 116–17, assumes that it is Isaianic here, the manner of its use as he describes it in fact suggests a contrary conclusion: 'In any case, this contrasting of epochs does not prove to be typical for Isaiah's preaching'. (iv) The reason why the verse is usually held together with 21-25 is, of course, the *inclusio* with v. 21. In fact, however, this is not a device which can be found elsewhere in Isaiah's own writing, but it is exactly what we have seen to mark the work of our chapter's compiler when introducing or, as here, rounding off a section (see especially vv. 10 and 20). This device, therefore, points away from v. 26 as part of the original composition and in the direction of the compiler. (v) The repetition of ואשיבה at the start of the verse is again something which is characteristic of redactional additions in general (see, for instance, 5.30), and it is not foreign to our compiler's style (e.g. the

[31] H. G. L. Peels, *The Vengeance of God: The Meaning of the Root NQM and the Function of the NQM-Texts in the Context of Divine Revelation in the Old Testament* (OTS 31; Leiden, 1995), 110, for instance, finds the usual combination of *Scheltwort* and *Drohwort* in 21-25, but then concludes that because of the inclusion of 26 the passage is 'a prophetic word sui generis'.

[32] P. D. Hanson, *The Dawn of Apocalyptic* (Philadelphia, 1975), 106–8, 119–20, 143–45, 162–63.

[33] C. Westermann, *Prophetische Heilsworte im Alten Testament* (Göttingen, 1983), Chapter 10 = *Prophetic Oracles of Salvation in the Old Testament* (Louisville, Ky., 1991).

[34] The force of this point is recognized by Deck, 147.

references to Sodom and Gomorrah in v. 10).[35] For these reasons, I conclude that v. 26 was added by the redactor in order to draw out the positive implications of what was only latent in the earlier material (see the end of ch. 6 for another possible example of this kind of development).

A possible objection that may be raised against this conclusion is the supposed concentric structure which some have found in 21-26. This is presented slightly differently by different commentators, but may typically be summarized as 24b corresponding to 23, 25 to 22, 26a to 21b and 26b to 21a.[36] On closer inspection, however, this argument is not as strong as it initially appears. While the echo of 21 in 26 is readily accepted, it is not as intricate as the structure suggests, since the most obvious connection with 21b is 'righteousness', which comes in 26b, not 26a as proposed. In fact, there is no clear echo of 21b in 26a at all. If 26a refers to anything specific in the previous verses it is 23, part of which we have seen to be the work of the final editor. Once this is recognized, then the proposed structure does little more than draw attention to a commonplace, attested frequently elsewhere, namely that an announcement of judgment often echoes the indictment with which it is related. In this case, the most obvious connection is, of course, the 'dross' image (22 and 25, though note that the latter does not make any reference to the liquor image of 22b), while 24b may certainly be said to announce judgment against those condemned in 23a, though without the use of a single word in common. Thus, on the understanding of the original shape of this passage outlined above, it may be suggested that 21 formed a generalized introduction, followed by a two-part indictment (22 and 23a), which, following the speech formula (24a), was answered by the announcement of judgment in reverse order (or chiastically, if that terminology be preferred) in 24b and 25 (an ABCC'B' pattern). This seems as satisfying as the proposed concentric pattern, but the important point to make is that such patterns can rarely be used to predetermine literary-critical judgments; rather, they should follow the results of such an analysis in a descriptive manner. Finally, when 26 was added by the compiler, he based its conclusion (26b) on the whole of 21 in line with his practice elsewhere. 26a is not concentrically integrated, but rather furnishes a reversal of the whole of the indictment.

I thus conclude that the form of saying which the compiler inherited comprised 21 (without ועתה מרצחים)-23a + 24-25. If this is right, then it is clear that we cannot detect a regular rhythm without indulging in completely reckless textual reconstruction.[37] The opening 3 + 2, of course, is to

---

[35] Kaiser, who is one of the very few commentators to recognize that v. 26 is a separate addition, bases almost his entire case on this point.

[36] So, for instance, Fey, 64, Lack, *Symbolique*, 164–67, Wildberger, Hardmeier, *Text-theorie*, 350, Becker, 193, Berges, 69, and Beuken; differently Vermeylen, 71, Deck, 146. Steck, 'Zur konzentrischen Anlage', is aware of some of the problems outlined above, but still seeks to uphold the structure on a modified basis.

[37] For an alternative approach to the poetic analysis of this passage, see M. C. A. Korpel and J. C. de Moor, 'Fundamentals of Ugaritic and Hebrew Poetry', *UF* 18 (1986), 173–212 (202–4). In addition, Lack, *Symbolique*, 167–70, and Gitay, 'Effectiveness', draw attention to several examples of the use of assonance in this passage.

be expected following איכה, as it is in 24*b* following הוי. 23*a*, interestingly, reverts to the terse 2 + 2 which we have seen sometimes elsewhere as indicative of agitated speech, and the tricolon of 24*b*-25*a* is noteworthy, giving a certain appropriate emphasis to 25*a*. It is likely that the extended speech formula of 24*a* deliberately stands outside the rhythmic structure. It appears that the chapter's compiler paid no heed to the poetic context when he added 23*b*. At 26, he first composed a line of 3 + 2, echoing the start of the passage which he was deliberately referring back to, but then added a longer second line to round out the unit (this practice too has already been noted elsewhere). Interestingly, he seems to have followed the same procedure in adding vv. 27-28 as well. The combination of textual uncertainties and our ignorance of all the factors which influenced the writing of ancient Hebrew poetry suggest that reticence is the best policy in the analysis of a passage such as this one.[38]

The Isaianic authorship of the core of this passage has been almost universally accepted: its theme (especially once v. 26 is regarded as later), language and use of imagery all fit his work as known from elsewhere extremely well. The few voices which have more recently been raised against this consensus have not found favour. In particular, Vermeylen's extended analysis of the vocabulary (80–93) fails in its claim to establish Deuteronomic overtones: the words to which he appeals are far too general for such a conclusion, and there is no example of stereotypical Deuteronom(ist)ic phraseology.[39] Moreover, against Robertson, 'Isaiah Chapter 1', 235, and Kaiser, we have seen that there are strong reasons for maintaining the essential unity of the passage, and the fact that certain parts of the passage could fit later periods well (see, for instance, the parallels with parts of Lamentations and the theme of refining, which recurs in Jeremiah and Ezekiel[40]) is no argument that they must therefore have been composed then. The fact that it has been possible to distinguish rather clearly the additions made by the chapter's compiler indicates that he was working with inherited material here, in marked contrast with the following verses.

It is usually argued that the fact that life in the city seems to be proceeding as normal, together with the lack of reference to any specific crisis, such as the Assyrian invasion of 701 BCE, points to a date within the first

[38] Analysis of Lam. 1–3 has demonstrated the extent to which there is variety of line length and division even within extended passages which predominantly follow the 3 + 2 pattern; cf. D. N. Freedman and J. C. Geoghegan, 'Quantitative Measurement in Biblical Hebrew Poetry', in R. Chazan, W. W. Hallo and L. H. Schiffman (eds), *Ki Baruch Hu: Ancient Near Eastern, Biblical, and Judaic Studies in Honor of Baruch A. Levine* (Winona Lake, Ind., 1999), 229–49.

[39] See, for instance, the terse critique by Blum, 564 n. 75, and more fully Høgenhaven, 56–57.

[40] These latter points of comparison are pressed by Becker, 194. We may note further that an exilic date for the passage is favoured by M. Wischnowsky, *Tochter Zion: Aufnahme und Überwindung der Stadtklage in den Prophetenschriften des Alten Testaments* (WMANT 89; Neukirchen–Vluyn, 2001), 146–54, and that Pfaff, *Restgedanken*, 40–43, argues for a post-exilic *Aktualisierung* under Deuteronomic influence. Höffken equivocates between exilic and post-exilic.

part of Isaiah's ministry (e.g. Wildberger, Clements and Sweeney).[41] Even if the Assyrian practice of deportation lies behind the imagery of refining, there is no need to doubt that this would have been known about in Jerusalem long before the Judeans came to have first-hand experience of it for themselves.

On the assumption that this is right, then a final speculation may be allowed as to the place at which this material originally stood in the earlier book of Isaiah and from which the chapter's compiler will have moved it. There are only three other passages in the first half of the book of Isaiah where Zion is addressed in the second person singular, and of these 3.25 gives us the obvious points of connection we are looking for.[42] 3.16 is the clear start to a new section, where 'the daughters of Zion' are the subject of invective in the third person feminine plural. After the later addition of the list of finery in 18–23, this main theme is resumed in 24. Verse 25, which follows, does not seem to fit, however: it is addressed to a second person feminine singular, 'Thy men shall fall by the sword, and thy warriors in battle'. Verse 26 is again awkward, since it moves to a third person feminine singular reference, apparently Jerusalem: 'And her gates shall lament and mourn; ravaged, she shall sit upon the ground'. Finally, 4.1 (4.2 starts a new section) reverts to the women, and so could be either an original continuation of 3.24 or yet another fragment. Its theme looks like a close 'female' counterpart to the 'male' 3.6. Older commentators were inclined to change some of the suffixes in order to smooth out the difficulties in these verses, but this is by no means certain; there are other passages in Isaiah where similar phenomena are more likely to be explained as the result of redactional activity.

In the present case, it may be claimed that 3.25 would fit very comfortably as the original continuation of 1.21-25. Just as the imagery of debased silver in 1.22 is explained in 23a as a reference to rebellious rulers, so the refining image of 1.25 would be explained by the defeat in battle of 3.25. This too could make for an attractive literary pattern of a different sort from that discussed earlier: an introductory cry (21) followed by the image of corruption (22) and explanation (23a); then, in close parallel, an introductory divine cry of vengeance in 24, followed by the image of refining (25) and explanation (3.25). This would make for a satisfying complete unit on its own. One could well see how 1.21-25 + 3.25 could have stood after 3.16-24 in an earlier version of the collection of Isaiah's sayings. There is a tidy move from the women of Jerusalem to the city

---

[41] For a review of the very few who have favoured a late-Isaianic date, see Willis, 'Lament Reversed', 243–45.

[42] This was suggested previously by Barth, 220 n. 48. The other two passages are 12.6, which can obviously be discounted for these purposes, and 29.1-5. If 1.21-25 were from the latter part of Isaiah's ministry, a setting before 29.1 might be considered (note, for instance, the unusual use of קריה in 1.21 and 29.1, and the use of הוי in both 1.24 and 29.1; indeed, Høgenhaven, 57, uses these and other points of comparison to uphold a late date for 1.21-26. His argument depends on 1.26, however, which we have seen should not be attributed to Isaiah himself). However, 29.1 seems to be fully satisfactory as the start of a section, and it does not demand that anything once stood before it.

itself under the image of a זונה. The compiler of ch. 1 will have broken off his use of the original passage, of course, because he wanted to be able to develop the positive implications of 1.25 rather than end on the note of defeat in battle, which was Isaiah's own original intention in using the image.

21. The passage is introduced with an exclamatory *how!* (איכה, elsewhere also איך), which is characteristic of the funerary dirge (e.g. 2 Sam. 1.19-27; Jer. 48.17).[43] While it is not difficult to see how such a form may have been adapted metaphorically to the lament over a destroyed city (as notably in the book of Lamentations, which begins in 1.1 with this same exclamation; see too 2.1; 4.1, 2; Jer. 9.19), it should not be supposed that this was a peculiarly inner-Hebrew development. There are many parallels in Mesopotamian literature which reach back to much earlier times.[44] The prophet should be envisaged as the speaker (divine involvement is explicitly introduced only at v. 24), similar to the (sometimes professionally hired) leader of the mourning at a funeral. Whereas in Lamentations the city has in fact already been destroyed (so that it is easy to imagine how our passage might have been understood by the chapter's later redactor and subsequent readers), Isaiah himself uses it as a forceful means of announcing the coming fate of the city (see the comparable use of 'woe!' in 1.4). Fully in line with this, the lament does not bewail the destruction of the city by the enemy, but rather its loss of moral rectitude. Only later (vv. 24-25) is the threat of enemy action envisaged, and then strikingly by God himself. Once again, therefore, Isaiah demonstrates that he is not bound by traditional forms, but rather uses them creatively to achieve maximum rhetorical impact.

Rather than the common word for *city* (עיר), Isaiah here uses קריה, a word mostly (though not quite exclusively) confined to poetic usage. At 29.1 it is explicitly associated with David, and that is likely the period to which he refers here too. It is tempting to think that there is a veiled allusion to the so-called Zion tradition, and the descriptive terms which follow add something to the case. However, frequency of usage in other contexts means that this cannot be certain.[45]

In order to understand the significance of the city's degeneration to the status of a *whore*, it is necessary first to consider the other terms which characterize the city's former status: *faithful*(ness), *justice* and *righteousness*. Each of these words can, of course, be analysed individually,[46] but it

---

[43] See the classic study of H. Jahnow, *Das hebräische Leichenlied im Rahmen der Völkerdichtung* (BZAW 36; Giessen, 1923), who characterizes the present passage as a parody of the genre (pp. 253–55).

[44] Cf. Dobbs-Allsopp, *Weep, O Daughter of Zion*, esp. 90–92. The major thesis of his book is that we should in fact recognize the city lament as a genre in its own right.

[45] Wildberger's further speculations along this line are refuted by Vollmer, 158–60. For a possible background to the language of this verse in Canaanite mythology, see Niehr, 'Traditionselemente', 70–71.

[46] Thus, for instance, within the first part of Isaiah, to go no further, משפט, 'justice', can refer to punitive judgment (4.4; 34.5), to the place of judgment (28.6), to the legal

is their use in close association with one another which needs to be appreciated in the present context.

'Justice and righteousness', here occurring in parallel but elsewhere in the Old Testament frequently as a hendiadys, has been the subject of a magisterial analysis by Weinfeld.[47] He demonstrates convincingly that throughout the ancient Near East this phrase (or its equivalents) is by no means limited to the sphere of the law courts alone, but that it refers more broadly, both positively and negatively, to social justice throughout society, often entailing notions of equality and freedom. Its introduction and maintenance are particularly the responsibility of the king, but it extends too to the other leaders of society and, indeed, to individual citizens.

Building on Weinfeld's analysis, it may be said that in adopting such language here, Isaiah evidently considered these qualities to be those of the ideal society, and, in line with his thought elsewhere, the following verses demonstrate that they were in particular the responsibility of the leading members of society; Isaiah's ideal was clearly hierarchical, a derivative of his fundamental appreciation of the absolute supremacy of God himself, from whom all authority derives.

This combination of words occurs frequently in the first half of Isaiah—indeed, the combination is more frequent than the use of either term on its own. Thus, of the 22 occurrences of משפט, 'justice', half fall into this category,[48] and, with only one exception (32.1), it is always the leading term of the pair. Conversely, the proportion of linked uses of צדק/ צדקה, 'righteousness', is even higher, 13 out of 20.[49] Finally, strengthening the conclusion that this usage in Isaiah goes further than just the sharing of a common ancient Near Eastern idiom, we should note that, as in the present verse, so elsewhere too the word pair is associated several times with *faithful* נאמנה, and other derivatives of the same root; cf. 1.26-27; 11.4-5; 16.5; 28.16-17; 33.5-6. It seems clear that our verse is giving expression to something close to the heart of Isaiah's concerns. Just as the present verse describes the ideal of the past with this language, so he will later condemn the present generation for its lack (see especially 5.7), and return to it again as a characterization for the restoration of the ideal society of the future (28.16-17). Furthermore, this phraseology features

process (3.14), to legal rights (10.2), and even simply to what is correct (28.26) and right (32.7). Similarly, צדק/צדקה, 'righteousness', with the related verb and adjective, can refer to the opposite of those who are wicked and guilty (5.23; 26.10), and hence are innocent (3.10; 29.21), as well as to justified punishment (10.22). For a helpful survey of other studies, see Gossai, *Justice, Righteousness*, as well as the articles in the main theological dictionaries.

[47] Weinfeld, *Social Justice*; see too H. Cazelles, 'De l'idéologie royale', *JANES* 5 (1973), 59–73; H. Niehr, *Herrschen und Richten: Die Wurzel špṭ im Alten Orient und im Alten Testament* (FzB 54; Würzburg, 1986); Gossai, *Justice, Righteousness*; Leclerc, *Yahweh is Exalted*.

[48] In parallel: 1.21, 27; 5.7, 16; 16.5; 28.17; 32.1, 16; as a hendiadys: 9.6; 33.5; in close association: 26.9.

[49] This initially curious fact is to be explained by the facts that the two occurrences of the word at 32.17 amplify its use in v. 16, where it is in parallel with משפט, and that at 11.4 it is used in association with the related verb שפט.

prominently in his depiction of the ideal king (9.6; 11.4-5) and in his approving citation of a proverb about the quality of rule of kings in general (32.1).[50]

The golden age to which Isaiah looks back is almost certainly that of David (so Jerome). In addition to the suggestive association of words at 29.1 already noted, there are other passages where he refers approvingly to that period (e.g. 9.6; 11.1); he is familiar with the alternative name of Jerusalem as 'the city of David' (22.9), he refers to the dynasty as 'the house of David' (7.2; 22.22; whether these passages can be ascribed to Isaiah is uncertain, however), and he appears to know of some of David's military successes (28.21; cf. Vollmer, 163–65). Furthermore, it should be noted that he never refers by name to any king between David and those of his own time. The suggestion that he had, for instance, the reign of Jehoshaphat especially in mind (Delitzsch; cf. Kimhi) is thus entirely without support.

In the light of this rather broad analysis of Isaiah's depiction of the golden age, it now becomes clear that we should not define its converse, the city's characterization in the present as a *whore*, too narrowly.[51] Because of the depiction of Israel's religious unfaithfulness in Hosea under this image, commentators often suppose that idolatry is in mind here as well, especially as this is explicitly condemned by Isaiah elsewhere (e.g. in ch. 2). Similarly, we might be tempted to see it as an image for political unfaithfulness—the development of alliances with Egypt, for instance, instead of trusting in God, as in chs 30–31. On the other hand, v. 23 points us more immediately in the direction of the perversion of justice, even if the use of 'rulers' (rather than judges) suggests that the whole administration, rather than just the judicial system, is in view. In fact, however, in this programmatic opening line of the passage, there is no need to seek to choose between these options. Faithfulness to God, in Isaiah's view, encompasses every department of life, religious, social and political, so that it may reasonably be deduced that the opposite of the ideal society will include all of these.

Righteousness used to lodge in her: although it has frequently been observed that there are a number of links by way of personal names between Jerusalem and צדק (perhaps originally a divine title for the god of the city),[52] it is most unlikely that Isaiah would have been influenced by this in the least, even if he was aware of it. His choice of language here has been shown to be adequately explained by quite other considerations.

But now murderers: a forceful addition by the chapter's compiler, to stress the link between the city's present inhabitants and those condemned earlier on (especially v. 15); see further on v. 23.

---

[50] For a study of these passages with this point particularly in mind, see my *Variations on a Theme*, Chapter 2.

[51] For the theme in general in the prophets, see G. Baumann, *Liebe und Gewalt: Die Ehe als Metapher für das Verhältnis JHWH in Israel in den Prophetenbüchern* (SBS 185; Stuttgart, 2000). For a 'heterological' reading, see Landy, 'Torah and Anti-Torah'.

[52] E.g. R. A. Rosenberg, 'The God Ṣedeq', *HUCA* 36 (1965), 161–77, Wildberger, Clements, N. W. Porteous, *Living the Mystery: Collected Essays* (Oxford, 1967), 97–99, and Høgenhaven, 54–55.

22. It is perfectly natural for a lament to slip from third to second person with reference to the one who is being mourned; see, for example. 2 Sam. 1.25-26; 3.33-34; Lam. 2.13. Here, the address moves to second person feminine singular,[53] with reference to the city.

To the metaphor of the faithful city's becoming a whore, two more are added (note the repetition of היה ל, 'become') in this verse before the reality is spelt out more directly in the next verse. While some uncertainty attends the details of each because of the use of rare and technical vocabulary to describe processes about which we do not have direct knowledge, the general sense in each case is clear.

The first metaphor envisages a reversal of the usual procedure in the preparation of silver. *Dross* (or 'slag') refers to the impurities which are removed during this process. סיג occurs some half a dozen times in the Hebrew Bible, and is (probably) always plural;[54] it derives from the verb סוג, 'move away' (cf. 1QIsa^a סוגים), hence the 'removed pieces'.[55]

The uncertainty in this case arises from the fact that the process involved three separate stages, so that we cannot be sure whether one in particular is in mind or the second two in a more general way. In the first stage, the ore was heated in order to allow the sulphur to escape. Secondly. using a greater heat, a lead-silver alloy was separated from other metallic substances (cf. Ezek. 22.18), and finally, by 'refining', the silver was separated from the lead by cupellation: 'by sending a stream of air across the surface of the molten mass, the lead and other impurities were preferentially oxidized, producing a dross on the surface of the liquid ore. This dross, which contained most of the lead, was then skimmed off. The remaining lead was absorbed by the porous cupel [a shallow clay receptacle], and the silver, still in solution, was drained away'.[56]

Because this final stage of the process was technically difficult, it could easily go wrong and the refiner be left, not with pure silver, but with a silver-like dross. Some commentators (e.g. Wildberger, following Köhler) have therefore suggested that the point of our verse is that the process had gone awry: instead of silver, only dross has been produced. This is mistaken, however. The starting point of the metaphor is *your silver*, something good and pure to represent Jerusalem's former golden age (to this

[53] LXX curiously moves initially to second person plural, but already by the second half of the verse reverts to following the Hebrew more closely.

[54] In addition to the present verse, 1.25; Ezek. 22.18 (×2), 19; Ps. 119.119; Prov. 25.4; 26.23. The Q of the first occurrence in Ezek. 22.18 has the singular, but on the basis of the versions many commentators read as a plural here as well.

[55] For further discussions of the word, see L. Köhler, 'Alttestamentliche Wortforschung. Sīg, sīgîm = Bleiglätte', *TZ* 3 (1947), 232–34; S. Abramski, '"Slag" and "Tin" in the First Chapter of Isaiah', *EI* 5 (1958), 105–7 (Hebrew); see too for some related matters H. H. P. Dressler, 'The Lesson of Proverbs 26.23', in L. Eslinger and G. Taylor (eds), *Ascribe to the Lord: Biblical and Other Studies in Memory of Peter C. Craigie* (JSOTSup 67; Sheffield, 1988), 117–25.

[56] D. I. Block, *The Book of Ezekiel, Chapters 1–24* (NICOT; Grand Rapids and Cambridge, 1997), 717, based upon R. J. Forbes, *Studies in Ancient Technology*, VIII (Leiden, 1964), esp. 226–39; see too P. R. S. Moorey, *Ancient Mesopotamian Materials and Industries: The Archaeological Evidence* (Oxford, 1974), 232–33.

extent, cf. Lam. 4.1-2). What is envisaged is a reversal of the process by which that silver was produced—it has now unnaturally turned to dross. But is it a reversal of the second or the third stage of the process? Ezekiel 22.18 (which seems to allude to our passage) suggests the second, since it refers to the dross as consisting of a number of metals (copper, tin, iron and lead),[57] and this would be supported by v. 25, if the reference there is indeed to tin rather than lead. Alternatively, it may be that Isaiah himself was not aware of such fine distinctions and that he simply refers to the process in general, including both the second and third stages. All he needed to know was that in the production of silver, waste material, dross, was removed and discarded; his point is that silver Jerusalem has become something debased and worthless.

The second metaphor concerns *fine liquor*, whose precise nature cannot be defined (see the textual notes), but which was evidently highly valued. The translation is often offered that it was 'mixed' with water (so the versions and many since), which is correct in one sense, but slightly misleading. In biblical language, to mix (מסך) drinks is to add various ingredients which make them stronger and more intoxicating (e.g. Isa. 5.22; Ps. 75.9; Prov. 9.2, 5; 23.30; Ct. 8.2; cf. Lowth). Here, however, as Marti suggests, the language (related to circumcision) may be compared with Arabic ʿudah maqṭūʿah, 'cut aloes-oil', Latin *vinum castrare*, French *couper du vin*, Spanish *trasegar*, and, as the best which can be done to approach this in English idiom, to *adulterate* (i.e. to dilute).[58] As the LXX clearly saw, this is most probably a reference to the underhand activities of unscrupulous merchants, seeking to maximize their profits: the fine drink is therefore no longer available. Naturally, *water* will have been the obvious ingredient to use for this purpose. Whether the word was added in order to explain an unusual term or was part of the text from the start is difficult to decide (see above); exegetically, either is possible.

23. From imagery, Isaiah turns to explicit description. As often elsewhere, it is the leaders in society who are singled out for particular condemnation.

The word for *rulers* (שרים) is frequently, but in modern English misleadingly, translated 'princes'. Although members of the royal household may have been included among them, it is clear from the widespread usage of the word in the Old Testament and beyond (cf. *AHI* i. 505–6) that it encompasses many from the upper levels of society who were in positions of leadership (and so, no doubt, ultimately answerable to the king). This variety may already be seen from the fifteen occurrences of the word within Isaiah 1–39, to go no further. Military leadership is clear at 3.3, 21.5 and 31.9, and probable also at 10.8 (with reference to the Assyrians), while this meaning may also lie behind the unique title 'prince of peace' at 9.5. At 30.4 it refers to ambassadors, at 19.11 (and so presumably the two occurrences in 19.13) to (foreign) royal advisers, and at 3.14 it is closely

---

[57] Cf. W. Zimmerli, *Ezechiel 1–24* (BKAT 13/1; Neukirchen–Vluyn, 1969), 516–17 = *Ezekiel 1* (Philadelphia, 1979), 463.

[58] It may be noted that in modern English parlance, illegally sold drugs which have been tampered with in order to make them go further are also said to have been 'cut'.

associated with the elders of the people. The uses at 3.4, 23.8 and 34.12 are less explicit, and seem to refer to rulers or leaders in a general way. Finally, at 32.1, in what is probably a proverb, 'rulers' are associated with the king in the administration of justice. In the present verse, it is initially attractive to think similarly of officials in the judicial system,[59] particularly because of the contextual steer in the last line of this verse and in v. 26a. As seen above, however, both these lines stem from the chapter's compiler (and so they narrow the use of the word in the final form of the text), so that Isaiah's original meaning may have been broader; the lure of bribes reaches further than the law courts alone, of course. The word *rulers* (and *rebels*) has been chosen here in particular in order to catch an echo of the alliteration in the Hebrew שָׂרַיִךְ סוֹרְרִים; for this same combination, see Hos. 9.15 and Jer. 6.28. Literary dependence and influence respectively are possible, though in view of Isaiah's apparent fondness for alliteration elsewhere (e.g. 1.24; 5.7) it is equally likely that more than one author could have hit upon this combination independently.

Rebels: in the law concerning the incorrigible son, and elsewhere, this word is linked with another of similar meaning (סוֹרֵר וּמוֹרֶה, Deut. 21.18, 20; cf. Jer. 5.23; Ps. 78.8), and it is further explained by the words 'who does not heed his father and his mother'. There is thus an element of intractable wilfulness and stubbornness about it, so that not surprisingly it can also be compared with the recalcitrance of a heifer (Hos. 4.16). Such characteristics are well illustrated in the religious realm by Neh. 9.29: 'They turned a stubborn (סוֹרֶרֶת) shoulder and stiffened their neck and would not obey'; see too Zech. 7.11. Elsewhere, late in his ministry, Isaiah condemns Judah as 'rebellious children' (30.1) because of their entry into foreign alliances rather than remaining loyal to God. There is no indication that that particular failing is in view here; probably the family image, which has been so prominent earlier in the chapter, is continued: Jerusalem's rulers pursue their own selfish agenda in callous disregard of God's standards of behaviour.

Partners with (lit. companions of) *thieves* jarringly earths the previous description by equating the leaders of the community with common criminals; perhaps the thought of bribes is already particularly in view. The effect is not unlike the (redactor's) equally shocking addition of 'but now murderers' in v. 21. Indeed, it is noteworthy that virtually the whole of the second half of the decalogue is alluded to in this passage: murder (21) and theft (23) at the straightforward level, false witness and covetousness (23b) by implication, and adultery (21a) and disobedience to parents (23a) as religious metaphors. This is not to say that the allusion is conscious, or even that Isaiah was necessarily familiar with the decalogue as we know it. As noted elsewhere, such similarities between the wisdom literature, law and Isaiah need not suggest more than that they all shared certain basic assumptions about the qualities of an ethical life.[60]

---

[59] A. Phillips, *Ancient Israel's Criminal Law: A New Approach to the Decalogue* (Oxford, 1970), 18–20, argues that in fact, following Jehoshaphat's judicial reform (2 Chron. 19.4-11), the שָׂרִים combined military and judicial functions.

[60] So correctly Dietrich, 14–24; see too Davies, 106–9.

Bribe and *gifts* are more or less synonymous, both words apparently developing in sense from the neutral meaning of gift to the perverted habit of seeking to gain unjustified influence thereby. This was naturally one means for perverting the course of justice in the courts (e.g. Exod. 23.8; Deut. 16.19; cf. Isa. 5.23),[61] but it can also apply in the political realm (e.g. 1 Kgs 15.19; 2 Kgs 16.8) and in other walks of life (Mic. 3.11). The emphasis in the present verse is less on the sphere of activity within which such bribes were used (so that we may allow a broad range of application) as on the covetous motivation (*loves* and *chases after*) of those in positions of power to exploit their situation for their own ends rather than to seek the good of society at large.[62] There is also, of course, an implication of favouritism towards those of their own class, since they will have been the only ones with sufficient resources to offer bribes in the first place. Thus, the rulers are condemned for colluding together to maintain and further their privileged position.

For the last line of the verse, see on v. 17. The chapter's compiler has apparently added this line in order to make explicit that the rulers are guilty of precisely not obeying the injunctions there listed. They have thus forfeited their one hope of averting the judgment to come.

24. As discussed above, *therefore* marks the regular transition from invective to threat in prophetic oracles, addressed either to individuals or to the community, and it is often, though not invariably, followed by a messenger formula, an equivalent of which also occurs here. In view of the fact that the previous invective has been wholly negative, we expect a word of judgment to follow, and this is likely to have been the case in Isaiah's original wording (vv. 24b-25), before the redactional addition of v. 26 which concentrated on drawing out the more positive implications of his threat (see above).

The solemnity of the announcement is underlined by the unusual piling up of divine titles after the marker that divine speech is to follow. Such speech formulae are in any case less common in Isaiah than in some other prophets. According to Vetter, on 269 out of 376 occurrences in all *saying of* (נאם, on which see the notes above) is followed simply by 'the Lord', while in the remaining cases there is either a variation on or expansion of this name,[63] including quite often the use of *the Sovereign* and/or *the Lord of Hosts* (see especially 19.4). Nowhere else, however, do we find such a lengthy expansion as here.

The Sovereign (הָאָדוֹן, literally, 'lord, master', as in a master–servant relationship,[64] but especially, in human relationships, of the king[65]) is used

---

[61] On the limits of the efficacy of such laws in practice, see Davies, 93–94.

[62] Bovati, *Re-Establishing Justice*, 196, makes the interesting suggestion that there may be an implicit contrast with the frequent use of אהב in terms referring to God's love of justice (e.g. Ps. 37.28) and that the use of רדף contrasts with the equally frequent use of expressions for the 'pursuit' of justice (e.g. Deut. 16.20).

[63] D. Vetter, *THAT* ii. 1 = *TLOT* ii. 693.

[64] Cf. E. Jenni, *THAT* i. 31–38 = *TLOT* i. 23–29; also O. Eissfeldt, *ThWAT* i. 62–78 = *TDOT* i. 59–72. Both include further bibliography and discussion of the (disputed) etymology of the word. See now the major study of M. Rösel, *Adonaj—warum Gott 'Herr' genannt wird* (FAT 29; Tübingen, 2000).

several times in combination with *the Lord of Hosts* in Isaiah (cf. 3.1;
10.16, 33; 19.4), and in the same combination, but with the form אדנ׳, in
3.15; 10.23, 24; 22.5, 12, 14, 15; 28.22. As already noted (see on v. 9
above), it is likely that Isaiah derived the title *Lord of Hosts* from the
Jerusalem cult tradition (even if it did not originate there), and the same is
likely to be true both of the title *the Sovereign* and of this particular combination, which may represent an early fusion of the indigenous Jebusite
cult and of the traditions which reached Jerusalem in early Israelite times
by association with the ark. In addition to its greater than usual frequency
in Isaiah's writing and that of his followers, Wildberger has pointed out
how many personal names associated with this title are linked to Jerusalem, both from pre-Israelite times (e.g. Adonizedek [Josh. 10.1, 3], Adoni-
bezek [Judg. 1.5-7]) and from the period of the early monarchy (e.g.
Adonijah [1 Kgs 1.8 etc.] and Adoniram [1 Kgs 4.6]).[66]

The really striking feature of the present passage, however, is that
whereas God was considered under these titles to be the mighty defender
of his people in the popular piety of Jerusalem (see on v. 9), Isaiah turns
such thoughts on their head by showing that he can equally well use his
power against his people if, by their immorality, they transform themselves into his 'foes' and 'enemies' (see the next line). We have no earlier
evidence than this for such a reversal of one of the central tenets of faith in
the Jerusalem cult. The same point applies too to the final divine title in
this line.

The Strong One of Israel: although this precise title is not attested elsewhere, it must be the equivalent of 'the Strong One of Jacob', which is
mentioned at Gen. 49.24; Isa. 49.26; 60.16; Ps. 132.2, 5. It is generally
held that the vocalization of אֲבִיר is an artificial device to distinguish the
use of the word with reference to God from the commoner form אַבִּיר.[67]
The latter too can mean strong, but also mighty and valiant. By extension,
it was also used to refer to certain animals, such as horses and bulls.[68] It is
therefore often suggested that the divine title originally signified 'the Bull
of Jacob', but that this was theologically unacceptable to later writers,
either because of association with Baal or because of the golden calves set
up at Bethel and Dan after the division of the monarchy. While possible,
this final step in the argument is by no means certain; the golden calf, for
instance, is never called אביר, but always עגל. Be that as it may, this
probably ancient title for God must also have been known in Jerusalem
(perhaps again, remarkably, by way of some association with the ark, if

---

[65] Brettler, *God is King*, 40–44.

[66] In contrast, however, Brettler, 41, associates the title אדון with the ark as well.

[67] Cf. GK §84b*f*. For a different opinion, see N. M. Sarna, 'The Divine Title *'abhîr
ya'ăqôb*', in A. I. Katsch and L. Nemoy (eds), *Essays on the Occasion of the Seventieth
Anniversary of the Dropsie University (1909–1979)* (Philadelphia, 1979), 389–96, who
argues (with a full survey of alternative opinions) that אֲבִיר, 'strong one', existed as part of
the divine title from the earliest times. Peels, *Creation and Judgement*, 386–88, seems to
equivocate, calling it 'a play upon the ancient metaphor'.

[68] The various uses are documented by A. S Kapelrud, *ThWAT* i. 43–46 = *TDOT* i.
42–44, and H. H. Schmid, *THAT* i. 25–27 = *TLOT* i. 19–21.

the evidence of Ps. 132 is to be believed), and it will have suited Isaiah's purpose in the present context well (following on from 'the Lord of Hosts') because of its reference to God's strength, perhaps particularly with overtones of military might.[69] The substitution of *Israel* for 'Jacob' fits well with a number of other divine titles in Isaiah (including, of course, 'the Holy One of Israel'; see on v. 4 above) which similarly use this name.[70] Whatever the significance of the name may have been in earlier times, there can be no doubt that by Isaiah's time *Israel* had acquired more than political overtones, especially in cultic circles. Despite the bitter divisions between the two monarchies, there was an awareness of an overarching sense of identity which finds its most natural explanation in terms of common origin. It is of interest that, in line with the overall shape of the book of Isaiah, the two later occurrences of 'the Strong One of Jacob' both stand in apposition with 'redeemer' and follow a reference to God as saviour (60.16 in fact looks like a citation of 49.26).

As well as introducing the woe-oracle proper (see on v. 4 above), הוי can also stand as an independent interjection, either as a cry of lament (e.g. Isa. 17.12; Jer 47.6) or as a form of summons (e.g. Isa. 55.1; Zech. 2.10-11). The former is clearly appropriate here (hence *Ah!*), since it echoes the sentiment of the איכה which opened the paragraph (v. 21). Although it thus marks the start of the divine speech, it does not justify treating this section separately from the previous verses.

The sense of this second line of the verse is easier to paraphrase than to render into good English. The heart of the matter is that God will *avenge* himself of those who, by their misdeeds, have turned themselves into his *enemies*. The verb indicates an element of loss on God's part,[71] in this case of loyalty in relationship, so that retribution is considered justified; it is not a case of spite or vindictiveness. How he will achieve this is not stated. We might assume, of course, that he will use human agents (such as the Assyrians), though so-called natural disasters are not ruled out, but the lack of any direct statement to this effect, combined with the extended list of divine titles in the introductory line, emphasizes his personal involvement in whatever happens; his control of the historical process is absolute. In this way, he will comfort himself for, or *relieve* himself of, the frustration which the people's disobedience has caused him. This awkward form of wording is dictated more by the desire for alliteration than by linguistic precision. Finally, although his actions are fully justified, the introductory exclamation הוי indicates that they are only undertaken with regret and as a last resort. The kind of activity which hitherto had been undertaken on

[69] Not surprisingly, this is only one of a large number of terms for human might which are also attributed to God; cf. Brettler, *God is King*, 57–68, for a full survey.

[70] Cf. Høgenhaven, 14–16, who further discusses 'the God of Israel' (frequent), 'the Light of Israel' (10.17) and 'the Rock of Israel' (30.29).

[71] For a full study of נקם in the Hebrew Bible, see Peels, *The Vengeance of God* (above, n. 31). He discusses this verse on pp. 109–18. He rightly rejects the view that Isa. 1 is a lawsuit, but maintains nevertheless that the notion of the covenant has a 'latent presence'. He thus introduces the idea of God watching over the keeping of the covenant into the background of his understanding of vengeance—unnecessarily, in my opinion.

behalf of his people against their enemies is now turned back against them (see, for instance, Amos 5.18-20). Although Wildberger goes too far in suggesting that the language is sufficiently technical to conjure up the thought of the Day of the Lord, his point that the hopes which typically came to expression under that title are here reversed is justified. In later strata of the book, this will be reversed yet again in Israel's favour; see especially 34.8; 61.2; 63.4, and cf. 49.8.

Even when full allowance has been made for the fact that Isaiah was influenced by a desire for alliteration in his choice of אנחם, the sentiment which he attributes to God gives legitimate cause for unease to modern readers, who enjoy the benefit of much theological reflection in the intervening millennia. This was already sensed by Ibn Ezra, who (apologetically?) drew attention to the anthropopathic nature of the language, and Lowth's extended comment on the matter retains its value.

25. *Turn my hand against*: יד occurs frequently as the object of השׁיב in a variety of contexts.[72] However, when combined with the preposition על, as here, the sense seems always to be of a single, decisive blow (cf. Ezek. 38.12; Amos 1.8; Zech. 13.7;[73] Ps. 81.15[74]). It would therefore be a mistake to infer that there is a reference to a further punishment, beyond that mentioned in vv. 5-9, for instance (so Dillmann, Feldmann), nor is it necessary to follow Rashi and Kimhi in assuming that the verb is chosen to imply one attack after another. The words spell out with stark precision (*against you*, feminine singular, with reference to the city) that the previous line has indeed been referring to the people of Jerusalem, now characterized as God's 'foes' and 'enemies'; any suggestion that God is there said to be acting against the external enemies of his people (as in popular expectation) is thus ruled out. The verse division is therefore unfortunate, and has led many commentators to assume either that these words are a later addition or that a balancing half line has been lost (most recently Blenkinsopp). Rather, these words may be best interpreted as the third element of a tricolon, an unusual but by no means unparalleled poetic device, which on this occasion gives emphasis to this final, climactic statement.

Elsewhere, and without the preposition על, *against*, the phrase can be used of someone withdrawing ('causing to return') his hand after an act of aggression (e.g. Josh. 8.26; Isa. 14.27; in fact in both these cases the point is negative) or refraining from embarking upon such a course in the first place (e.g. Ezek. 20.22, and negatively at Lam. 2.8). In addition, although

---

[72] There is therefore no need to emend to ואשׁימה, *contra* Kohler, 'Emendations', 40.

[73] The attempt by Delitzsch and Young to use Zech. 13.7 as an indication that the phrase may be used to indicate salvation and blessing cannot be justified; cf. C. L. Meyers and E. M. Meyers, *Zechariah 9–14* (AB 25C; New York, 1993), 388–89. They further point out the interesting fact that the passage in Zechariah continues with a metallurgical metaphor. The thought, though not the technical vocabulary, for the most part, is similar to what follows here, and may provide further evidence of how an originally negative description could legitimately be interpreted later as implying hope.

[74] Jer. 6.9 is only a partial exception. Although an element of repetition may be included, the phrase seems nevertheless to be used for the final act of stripping the vine. The context is in any case rather different from the others listed above.

Isaiah spoke quite frequently of God's *hand* as his instrument of judgment, not least in the so-called refrain poem (cf. Isa. 5.25; 9.11, 16, 20;
10.4), later on this became the focus for a reversal, whereby God's hand
became an instrument for restoration and salvation (e.g. 11.11; 49.22).[75] It
is thus not difficult to see how at a later stage in the development of the
book of Isaiah the phrase here might have been thought to include an element of hope (grammatically, this would be possible if עליך were understood as a relative clause without אשר: 'I will withdraw my hand [which
has been] against you'). This may not be unrelated to the repetition of
ואשיבה at the start of v. 26 (see below), even though it is there used with a
different sense. As shown above, however, the stereotypical language of
the phrase rules out this possibility at the level of primary composition
(*contra* Young, Oswalt).

Appropriately to everything which has come before in this paragraph,
the next line uses the image of refining metal to emphasize the fact of the
removal of all that is worthless. The two objects, *dross* and *tin impurities*
indicate this, as for certain does the second verb, *remove*. Only the first
verb, *smelt*, could have more positive overtones, but the object *dross*, and
the general context indicate that the focus is on the removal of impurity
(hence *smelt away*) rather than the production of precious metal. Within
the context of the original Isaianic saying, therefore, this should be seen as
an expression of judgment; nothing in the preceding verses allows the
possibility that this will include the thought of hope for a remnant. It is
only the chapter's later compiler who has seized upon the possibility which
the metaphor provides for turning this in a more positive direction by the
addition of v. 26. The later handling of the end of ch. 6, and the use of the
imagery of a felled tree which can yet sprout again, may be compared.

For a description of the process involved in the production of precious
metal, see on v. 22 above. As seen there, *dross* refers to all the impurities
which were removed during the refining process. There, in an unnatural
reversal of the normal procedure, Jerusalem had gone from being silver to
being dross. This, then, is the material with which the present verse has to
start. In the course of smelting, *alkali* (a derivative of various plants which,
as potash, could be formed into either a solution or powder; also used as a
cleansing agent in washing;[76] cf. Job 9.30; ברית in Jer. 2.22; Mal. 3.2)
could be added as a reagent to accelerate the process of separation. The
point here, therefore, is that the effects of the smelting will be as quick and
clean as possible. Hence even within an extended metaphor, *as with* is not
inappropriate; smelting could be done without the use of alkali, but on this
occasion it will be undertaken in the most efficient manner possible.

Tin impurities: this is the only passage where בדיל occurs in the plural.
By analogy with the use of the plural of other collective nouns, this will
refer to particles of the relevant substance (cf. GK §124*l* and JM §136*b*),
here paraphrased with an eye to the wider context as *impurities*. The iden-

[75] See my essay 'Isaiah xi 11-16 and the Redaction of Isaiah i–xii'.

[76] The rendering of this verse in *DCH* ii. 258, 'I shall refine your dross (so that it
becomes) like soap' is no doubt based on this more frequent usage, but it does not, *prima
facie*, seem probable.

tification of metals in antiquity is hazardous, and indeed there is considerable evidence that they were frequently confused, not least in the case of *tin* and lead.[77] In terms of usage, we should normally expect בדיל to refer to tin, since it is clearly distinguished from עפרת, which is almost certainly lead, at Num. 31.22; Ezek. 22.18, 20; 27.12. On the other hand, we should expect lead here, in view of the usual process in the extraction of silver, or possibly some kind of alloy.[78] Once again, it must be asked whether Isaiah would have been aware of these fine distinctions. Silver-bearing ores are not found in Israel, and metal-working was a specialized craft, often undertaken by foreigners. I have therefore retained *tin* as the most likely technical equivalent when the word was used in specialized circles, but readily agree that Isaiah himself might have been confused either about the process or about the nature of the metals involved or about the precise definition of the word. Fortunately, the main point of his metaphor is clear, despite all these uncertainties: whatever is not silver is to be removed.

26. Although Isaiah himself concentrated exclusively on the negative, judgmental aspect of the metaphors which he used to describe God's actions in response to the abuses of Jerusalem's leaders in his own day (vv. 21-25), a redactor (most probably the compiler of ch. 1 as a whole; see above) has not illegitimately drawn out the positive implications which were latent within Isaiah's own words: if impurity was to be removed, what remained would be pure.[79]

This is described by picking up the first word of v. 25, but using it in a more positive sense: *I will restore*. This, of course, implies a return to a previously healthy state *as at the first...as at the beginning*, by which, in context (see on v. 21), the Davidic age must be meant. *Judges* and *counsellors* appear together in the list of 3.2-3 (among other officials of varied rank), and they no doubt reflect the same officials as those called more generally 'rulers' in v. 23. Both groups were appointed by the king, the first for the administration of justice, and the second for political services. No consequences should be drawn from the lack of reference to the king here; the wording is driven more by a concern to reverse the previous catalogue of failure than to present a full portrayal of the new age.[80]

---

[77] See my remarks in 'The Prophet and the Plumb-Line: A Redaction-Critical Study of Amos vii', *OTS* 26 (1990), 101–21 (110–11). On בדיל in particular, see also L. Köhler, 'Alttestamentliche Wortforschung. Bᵉdīl und *bᵉdīlīm', *TZ* 3 (1947), 155–56, and Abramski (above, n. 55); see also G. R. Driver, 'Babylonian and Hebrew Notes', *Welt des Orients* 2 (1954–59), 19–26 (21–24); B. Landsberger, 'Tin and Lead: The Adventures of Two Vocables', *JNES* 24 (1965), 285–96; Forbes (above, n. 56), 200–1, and 9 (1964), 155–59; and Moorey (above, n. 56), 295–96.

[78] Cf. D. Levene and B. Rothenberg, 'Tin and Tin-Lead Alloys in Hebrew and Jewish Aramaic', in A. Rapoport-Albert and G. Greenberg (eds), *Biblical Hebrew, Biblical Texts: Essays in Memory of Michael P. Weitzman* (JSOTSup 333; Sheffield, 2001), 100–12.

[79] Baer, 'It's All About Us!', 202–3, argues that the LXX translator also followed this interpretation in his rendering of v. 25; see the textual notes above.

[80] See D. K. Stuart, 'The Prophetic Ideal of Government in the Restoration Era', in A. Gileadi (ed.), *Israel's Apostasy and Restoration: Essays in Honor of Roland K. Harrison* (Grand Rapids, 1988), 283–92.

Afterwards you will be called: the renaming of the city of Jerusalem in the new age as a reversal of her period of judgment is a characteristically Trito-Isaianic theme (see especially 62.4, 12; cf. 60.14, 18). More widely, this general theme is also applied (often with the use of the same idiom as here) to the renaming of the community, a notion already adumbrated to some extent in Deutero-Isaiah and the other exilic prophets.[81] The new names in question usually reverse, of course, the situation described by the old name(s), which may be either explicitly mentioned or merely implied. Here, in a context which is stressing the theme of restoration, the names are indicative of a return to the circumstances which prevailed in the original, ideal age; of the four words translated *'the city of righteousness'*, *'faithful city'*, three come straight from v. 21, while the fourth is the commonest word for *city* (עיר), chosen to supply a parallel for the more colourful קריה.

---

[81] In Trito-Isaiah: 58.12; 61.3, 6; 62.2; in Deutero-Isaiah: 43.7; 48.1, 2 (and cf. 35.8); elsewhere: Jer. 3.17; 33.16; Ezek. 48.35; Zech. 8.3.

RANSOMED OR CRUSHED
(1.27-31)

[27]Zion will be ransomed by justice,
  and those in her who repent by righteousness;
[28]whereas rebels and sinners alike will be crushed,
  and those who abandon the Lord will perish.
[29]For they will be ashamed of the terebinths which you have desired,
  and you will be abashed because of the gardens which you have
  chosen.
[30]For you will be like a terebinth whose foliage withers,
  and like a garden which has no water;
[31]and the strong one will become tow, and his work a spark;
  and both of them will burn together, with none to quench them.

27. Following פדה, we might expect the preposition to be the so-called ב-*pretii* (cf. GK §119*p*; JM §133*c*), while the use of the niph'al also allows the possibility that it might be the ב-*instrumenti* (cf. GK §§119*o* and *q*; 121*f*; JM §§ 132*e*; 133*c*). The context alone can determine this, so that a decision must be reserved for the comments below.[1]

ושביה: the plural participle of שוב with suffix could mean either 'those who return to her' (with objective suffix; see, for instance, כל־באיה in Prov. 2.19) or, with a 'genitive of nearer definition' (cf. GK §116*i*), 'her repenters' = 'those in her who repent'. Contextual parallels may be found for both senses, and either is grammatically possible here; see further below. There is no textual warrant whatsoever for changing the consonantal text (though note that 4QIsa[f] seems to have suffered a clear case of dittography: ושביה וש[ב]יה). The old suggestion of Döderlein, still favoured by *BHS*, to read וישביה, 'and her inhabitants' (see ישב ציון in 10.24 and cf. 30.19 for the idea), though slight as an emendation, is thus not to be entertained (*pace* Eitan, 'Contribution', 56). (The same applies to שׁבָה, suggested by Tur-Sinai, and even more to Ehrlich's וירושלם.) In any case, it gives poor sense, since its inclusiveness is at odds with the contrast which is to follow in v. 28 (so rightly Wildberger). While most of the versions support the consonantal text, some presuppose a different vocalization (all decidedly inferior): LXX and P וְשָׁבֶיהָ;[2] V *reducent eam* seems to presuppose a hiph'il, however (Professor G. I. Davies suggests perhaps וְיֹשֶׁבֻּהָ).

28. For this verse as a contrast with v. 27 (hence 'whereas'), see Gibson, 172.

ושבר: MT vocalizes as a noun, 'and a crushing of…', which GK §147*c* explains as an example of an exclamation 'in which, owing to the excitement of the speaker, some indispensable member of the sentence is suppressed'. Here, it is implied that expression is given to a wish, 'and may there be a crushing of…'. This does not seem to be very appropriate in the context, however, and in any case the saying is far more abrupt than the other examples cited by GK. Though accepted by many older commentators and still, for instance, by Young and Watts, it seems most improbable. The consonantal text is supported

---

[1] J. Kennedy, 'Isaiah i. 27', *ExpT* 27 (1915–16), 523, proposed emending to either חפרה or הפרה (as well as reading the following word as וישביה) in order, as he thought, to harmonize with the preceding verses; but this rests on a misunderstanding of the coherence of the passage as a whole.

[2] For the later addition of a doublet reflecting the MT, see Seeligmann, 32; other aspects of the LXX's rendering of this verse are discussed by Olley, *Righteousness*, 66–68, and Baer, 'It's All About Us!', 212–13.

by 1QIsaᵃ. P follows MT by rendering as a noun, but not surprisingly the other versions render with a finite verb, though whether they presuppose a different consonantal text is hard to say: LXX καὶ συντριβήσονται, and T ויתברון might suggest וְנִשְׁבְּרוּ[3] or וְשֻׁבְּרוּ[4] (though the puʿal of שבר is not attested elsewhere, that is hardly a strong objection [*contra* Wildberger], since the piʿel is); יְשַׁבְּרוּ (*BHS*) is less likely, because we certainly require the conjunction. V *et conteret* perhaps presupposes וְשַׁבַּר or וְשָׁבַר[5], 'and he (*sc.* God, or impersonal) will crush'.[6] These latter have the advantage of retaining the consonantal text whereas the passive mood of the other proposals may be thought contextually more appropriate. MT's vocalization might just be explained by the observation that the piʿel nowhere else has people as its object, whereas they are several times said to be the recipient of the noun. If that is so, then וְשַׁבַּר might be preferred, but it is not a strong argument, and firm evidence for a decision is lacking.[7] Fortunately, the general sense is not affected.

29. כי: there is no particular reason to support the suggestion of WO, 665, that this is an example of the emphatic כי. As will be seen immediately below, the editor has gone to some lengths to indicate that he intends this and the following verses to be an explanatory extension of the previous verse.

יבש: this third person plural form is difficult in view of the second person plural forms which follow, especially ותחפרו, with which in other respects it is closely parallel. Consequently, most commentators adopt the slight emendation to תבשו. Attractive as this may be in certain respects, there are nevertheless grounds for caution: (i) the consonantal text is supported by both 1QIsaᵃ and 4QIsaᶠ. (ii) Although the versions differ, their renderings can be most easily explained if they were working on the basis of the same text as MT and grappling with the same difficulties as observed by modern scholars: LXX and P use third person plural throughout this and the following verse; they therefore clearly read יבש, and probably accommodated the following verbs to it (though see on חמדתם below for an alternative suggestion). V uses third person plural for the whole of the first line of the verse, but then reverts to the second person for the second line; again, יבש must be presupposed, but the process of accommodation has not been seen through so rigorously as in LXX and P. Only T has second person plural throughout the verse, but as Gray (who accepts the emendation) candidly admits, this is to be explained, in the light of the other evidence, as 'a correction rather than a survival from a continuous correct tradition'.[8] In the light of these first two points, it is clear that if there has been a corruption, it must have been very early in the history of the text (in itself not impossible, of course). (iii) As will be argued below, the role of the chapter's redactor at this point should not be overlooked. It would be intelligible if he had introduced a third person here to allow for a smooth transition from v. 28, before switching to the second person for rhetorical effect later in the verse; cf. Ibn Ezra and Sweeney, *Isaiah 1–4*, 130. (iv) Such switches of person are not uncommon in the prophets (cf. GK §144p), as noted already by Kimhi. In this connection, it is particularly interesting to observe that precisely the converse switch (i.e. from second to third person plural) occurs within a single line of poetry at 61.7, again in association with the root בוש; is this pure coincidence? At any rate, the relative frequency of the phenomenon suggests the need for caution before emending all examples on a piecemeal basis if other evidence is lacking; it may be simply that what appears to us to be unacceptably harsh was tolerated by writers in antiquity. (v) Nielsen, 210–11, suggests that in

---

[3] This is favoured by, for instance, Procksch and Wildberger.

[4] Favoured by Houbigant, Gray and Kaiser.

[5] Cf. Tur-Sinai, 157.

[6] Alternatively, Huesman, 'Finite Uses', 286, suggested an original inf. abs., וְשָׁבֹר. While Wildberger is right to object that Huesman's translation 'shall be destroyed' is impossible for the qal, it could presumably still stand as an active verb. But then there seems to be no advantage over conjecturing the simpler finite form.

[7] W. Popper's וְשָׁבְתוּ ('Parallelism', 309) is attractive as a parallel for יכלו, but there is, as we have seen, no evidence for such a departure from the consonantal text.

[8] The same will apply to the three medieval manuscripts of MT which read תבשו. On their textually inferior character, see Barthélemy, 10.

the present case there may be a have been a further motive for using the form יבש, namely a desire to play on the roots בוש and יבש; the latter, of course, would refer forward to the theme of v. 30.[9]

מאילים: despite considerable confusion in antiquity (see below), there can be no doubt about the meaning of this word in context: it is parallel with מהגנות, and these two words are then repeated in the singular in the comparisons drawn in v. 30: כאלה and כגנה. Clearly, therefore, אילים is meant to be a plural of אלה, and for this the translation 'terebinth' is assured. From the evidence we have, however, this seems to have been appreciated in antiquity only by σ (ἀπὸ τῶν δρύμων), and later by the rabbinic commentators. Usually, the word is rendered 'idols'; cf. LXX ἐπὶ τοῖς εἰδώλοις (and probably the slightly more ambiguous α: ἀπὸ τῶν ἰσχύρων), V ab idolis, and P; interestingly, T has a double rendering: מאילני מעותא. The reason for all this is not far to seek. 1QIsaᵃ spells the word אלים (as does the MT at 57.5[10]), and this could easily be understood as the plural of אל.[11] The plene spelling in the MT is certainly later. This raises the question whether the standard lexica are correct to list איל and אלה as separate words for 'terebinth'.[12] According to this division, the former only ever occurs in the plural (apart, perhaps, from the geographical name איל פארן, from which one should be cautious about drawing wider conclusions) and the latter only ever in the singular. The most economical hypothesis would be to assume that the plural of אלה was אלים (cf. שנים/שנה, etc.), and that in the (proto-) Masoretic tradition plene spelling was usually (though not consistently) introduced over the course of time in order to avoid confusion with the plural of אל.

חמדתם: GK §144p, Marti and Budde suggest vocalizing as a noun with suffix, חֶמְדָּתָם. The advantage of this is that it continues the third person reference from the first part of the line. Marti and Budde then proceed to make the following two lines third person as well (בחרו, ויחפרו and יהיו), in line with the LXX; they conjecture that it was the misunderstanding of חמדתם as a verb which led to the need for the further changes. While they thereby neatly overcome the problems noted in connection with יבש, it comes at too high a price. Not only is the consonantal text now supported by the evidence of the Qumran scrolls (which they could not have known about, of course), but their proposal also destroys the tight parallelism between the two lines of the verse, which requires אשר to be followed by a verb. Furthermore, Gray is right to observe that the LXX cannot be invoked in support of a reading of the word as a noun; the conjecture is thus based upon a faulty use of the evidence.

ותחפרו: copulative waw, as in 1.2 above, but this time with the imperfect; cf. Gibson, 104: 'this usage…is particularly characteristic of poetic parallelism, the two clauses neatly balancing one another'.

30. נבלת עלה: for the construction (with a fem. construct of the participle, in agreement with אלה), cf. כבד עון in v. 4 above. The spelling of עלה is directly supported by 1QIsaᵃ and indirectly supported by LXX (and V?) inasmuch as it does not recognize that the final ה is a suffix (something which would have been clear had its Vorlage read עליה). While a spelling with yod (עליה) is possible (cf. GK §93ss), and found in a number of later manuscripts, it is not, therefore, to be preferred (contra Wildberger); cf. GK §91d.

---

[9] Tur-Sinai, 157, in fact suggested reading יָבֵשׁ, but this seems improbable: it involves the further deletion of the מ on מאילים (to give 'for the oaks which you have desired shall dry up'), and it also destroys the obvious parallelism between the two lines of the verse.

[10] This assumes that the parallelism points to this interpretation; the versions, however, followed by some moderns, prefer 'idols' here as well; see the survey in K. Koenen, *Ethik und Eschatologie im Tritojesajabuch: Eine literarkritische und redaktionsgeschichtliche Studie* (WMANT 62; Neukirchen–Vluyn, 1990), 40 n. 182.

[11] The plural of אל is rare, but it is worth noting nonetheless that it never occurs in Isaiah; for 'gods', the book consistently uses אלילים (8 times; the singular also occurs once).

[12] Doubts about the word's etymology are expressed by M. H. Pope, *El in the Ugaritic Texts* (VTSup 2; Leiden, 1955), 16–19.

אשר מים אין לה: cf. GK §152*o*. 1QIsaᵃ has a different word order, namely אשר אין לה (*sic*) מים, while MT is supported by 4QIsaᶠ and, in Kutscher's opinion (563), by LXX (though this cannot be certain, of course), P and T. While either is possible, it is easier to suppose that the scroll's reading originated as a slight easing rather than the reverse.

31. חסן is an adjective, used here as a noun; at its only other occurrence in the Hebrew Bible, Amos 2.9, it is used to describe the Amorite, who was 'as strong as the oaks (כאלונים)', so that it seems to be eminently suitable in the present context. The alternative suggestions, that it refers either to 'stored wealth'[13] or to 'semiprocessed flax',[14] are therefore unnecessary (though for the possibility of word-play, see the comments below) and suffer the added disadvantage of being less appropriate: on the basis of the preceding verses, we expect a reference both to the idolater and his idol which can then be resumed by the שניהם of the following line. Though חָסֹן itself is a rare word, חסין occurs in Ps. 89.9 with the meaning 'strong', and חסן, 'power' comes twice in Biblical Aramaic (Dan. 2.37; 4.27).[15]

At first sight, ופעלו might seem to present a difficulty for this view, since it looks like a participle, 'and his/its maker'. For this reason, many commentators have adopted the proposal of Michaelis to vocalize as ופָעֲלוֹ. This is unnecessary, however, since there are clearly attested instances where *qōtal* nouns retain initial *ḥōlem* in inflected forms. The standard example is וְחָרֹי at Isa. 52.13 (cf. GK §93*q*), though more relevant is ופָעֳלוֹ, exactly as in our verse, at Jer. 22.13 (cf. JM §96A*j*) and the construct plural ופָעֳלֵי at Mic. 2.1,[16] which has apparently been previously overlooked by the grammarians. Indeed, Barthélemy, 12, goes so far as to state that this is the standard form with third masc. sing. suffix when preceded by *waw*. It is noteworthy that all the ancient versions understood the word as the noun פֹּעַל.

The major rabbinic commentators insisted against this that the word must be a participle.[17] Consequently, while Rashi explained חסן as a reference to unjustly gained wealth, Kimhi and Ibn Ezra saw in it a reference to the idols themselves. They thus arrived at an interpretation of the line very similar to that defended above, but with a precisely reverse identification of the two nouns. This has also been favoured by some modern commentators (e.g. Gray in his commentary, though not in his translation). There is no evidence for this understanding of חסן, however, and Kimhi's comparison with Isa. 40.20 is weak. It is more probable that the interpretation arose from a correct understanding of what the line 'ought' to mean, based on the context, combined with a failure to recognize that ופעלו need not necessarily be construed as a participle.

The textual witnesses to this line show a similar variety to that noted already in v. 29. Though badly damaged, 4QIsaᶠ alone fully supports the MT.[18] 1QIsaᵃ has החסנכם and ופעלכם. Talmon explains the occurrence of both the article and the suffix on חסן as the result of a scribal conflation of variant readings.[19] This variant is attested otherwise only

---

[13] So NJPS, by association with the verb חסן, 'to store', in 23.18, and the noun חֹסֶן, 'treasure', in 33.6; Jer. 20.5, etc.

[14] So Tsevat, 'Isaiah i 31', on the basis of Rabbinical Hebrew; but cf. Loewenstamm, 'Isaiah i 31', for a rejoinder, and Nielsen, 207–9, for critical comments on both.

[15] For other cognates, see *HAL* i. 324, and perhaps *DNWSI*, 393.

[16] Cf. W. Rudolph, *Micha–Nahum–Habakuk–Zephanja* (KAT 13/3; Gütersloh, 1975), 51–52.

[17] The rendering defended above is followed with much the same arguments, however, by Isaiah of Trani. For a listing of other medieval and renaissance authorities, see Barthélemy, 12.

[18] Its reading is ל[ן]חסן[ה...]; the editors (P. W. Skehan and E. Ulrich) comment that 'the proximity of *samek* and *lamed* precludes a pronominal suffix' (p. 102).

[19] F. M. Cross and S. Talmon (eds), *Qumran and the History of the Biblical Text* (Cambridge, Mass., and London, 1975), 246–47, *contra* Kutscher, 557, who thinks rather that the scribe merely changed his mind while writing the word. Cohen, 'Philological Reevaluation', 47–48, emends the scroll reading by deleting the initial ה and finds the result superior to MT.

by V (*fortitudo vestra* and *opus vestrum*), and it is not easy to decide whether this represents an alternative textual tradition or whether both readings attest separate attempts to align the verse more closely with v. 30.[20] LXX[21] and P both translate as though the nouns had third person plural suffixes, but this is almost certainly a continuation in translation of their consistent rendering already noted throughout vv. 29-31. Interestingly, they appear to be joined on this occasion by T in its translation of ופעלו, which would be stronger evidence in view of T's use of the second person previously, but this is deceptive. It is merely the result of T's interpretation of חסן as 'the strength of the wicked (pl.)' (hence no suffix), which then formed a third person plural antecedent for its rendering of ופעלו as 'the work of their hands' (ועובד ידיהון); T may well, therefore, presuppose MT. In summary, it is easier to understand that the versions have accommodated their translations to their treatment of this paragraph as a whole than to conclude that they presuppose a superior text to the marginally harder MT. Conjectural emendations are also unnecessary.[22]

ניצוץ occurs only here in the Hebrew Bible. The meaning 'spark' has long been presupposed on the basis of the use of the verb נצץ at Ezek. 1.7, 'gleam, sparkle', Arabic *nâḍa*, 'sparkle, flash', and Post-Biblical Hebrew. Any lingering doubts (cf. Gray) have been removed by the occurrence of the word in a clear context in one of the Hebrew manuscripts of Ben Sira 11.32: מניצוץ ירבה נחלת, 'from a spark there grows a fiery coal'.[23]

שניהם יחדו: LXX expands to οἱ ἄνομοι καὶ οἱ ἁμαρτωλοὶ ἅμα on the basis of v. 28, where the identical phrase occurs. This strengthens the case that LXX's addition of Σιων in v. 21 above is due to a similar case of explanatory assimilation to the wider context.

This paragraph develops the division between the righteous and the wicked which was already introduced at the end of the previous section. Although this theme has been adumbrated earlier in the chapter (especially 1.19-20), it is now brought to a climax. The fate of the wicked is clearly final, with no second chance possible (see especially v. 31), and the language of v. 27 suggests that the salvation of those who repent is also of a final kind. The chapter thus ends on a very similar note to the book of Isaiah as a whole. This division between two groups in the community comes to frequent expression in chs 56–66; there are, as will be seen, some close linguistic similarities; and the final verses of the last chapter in particular include some notable echoes of this passage. There is thus a sense in which ch. 1 reflects the outline of the thought of the book as a whole, and this is appropriate to an introduction (*contra* Luc, 'Isaiah 1'); the purpose seems to be to encourage the audience to read all that follows in an engaged and responsive manner, since their final destiny depends crucially on the response that they will make to its urgent appeal.

Although the poetic rhythm of the passage is unremarkable (though note that the last two lines in v. 31 echo the 3 + 2 of the first line, v. 27, which itself connects with the previous paragraph; 28-30 are less regular), it uses some familiar devices to gain an overall coherence. Verse 27 is joined to the preceding by the use of catchwords (so that there is a clear

---

[20] Contrast Kedar-Kopfstein, 'Divergent Hebrew Readings', 196–97, and van der Kooij, 312.

[21] For other aspects of the LXX rendering of the line, see Ziegler, 92–93.

[22] For example, Lagarde's proposal (p. 5), to read חַמָּן, 'sun-image', in place of חסן, and בְּעֻלּה, 'its Baal', in place of פעלו (on which note Duhm's criticisms), and Tur-Sinai's suggestion (pp. 157–58) that פעלו is a corruption of עָלֵפוּ, 'its dry leaves', with חסן understood as a 'strong trunk'.

[23] For the text, see Beentjes, *Ben Sira in Hebrew*, 38.

sense in which vv. 21-31 are meant to be read as a single whole), and v. 28 is an obviously associated antithetical partner to 27. The fact that it draws heavily on vv. 2-4 is appropriate as we approach the conclusion of the chapter. Verses 29-31 are also closely associated with one another by the use of shared imagery—terebinths and gardens in 29 and 30, and desiccation leading to fire in 30-31.[24] Finally, 27-28 is joined to 29-31 in two ways. First, the repetition of יחדו in 28 and 31 acts as a modest form of *inclusio*, while secondly, and more importantly, the difficult opening of v. 29 functions as a join between the two parts; כי is an obvious connective particle, and in particular the apparently harsh use of the third person plural in יבשׁ (which there is no textual support for changing; see above) serves to link this predominantly second person plural section with the third person vv. 27-28 which precede (cf. Sweeney). Whether this is satisfactory from a modern standpoint or not, it seems clear that there has been a serious attempt to create an overall unity in these verses which must be respected in exegesis.

That said, the very fact that there has been such an artificial attempt to create a unity points to the likelihood that material of separate origins has here been combined; it is impossible to imagine that anyone would have composed a section like this from scratch. The unexpected use of the second person plural in vv. 29-30 against the third person in 27-28 and 31 is the most obvious indication of this. Probably the commonest explanation is that 29-31 represent an original Isaianic fragment, with 27-28 as a later (post-exilic) redactional expansion of 21-26 (e.g. Duhm; Procksch; Wildberger). Other possibilities have been canvassed, however, such as that 31 is an original continuation of 27-28 (so hesitantly Gray), that 28-31 belong together as a unit, separate from 27 (Vermeylen, 105–8), or that 27-28 and 29-31 are both later additions, neither deriving from Isaiah (Marti; Clements; Kaiser).

Those who ascribe 29-31 to Isaiah himself disagree about its original setting, whether it is an early saying directed against the northern kingdom, or against Judah, or a later saying against Judah, perhaps related to Hezekiah's cultic reforms. The most impressive attempt to trace its place of origin (very much in line with the kind of methods used above for some earlier parts of the chapter) has come from Nielsen, *Hope*, 211–14. In her view, it belonged originally with the refrain poem of 9.7-20. She notes, for instance, the use of comparable tree imagery (9.9) and of the forest fire as a description of God's wrath in 9.17-18. Strikingly, this stanza concludes (v. 20) with a reference to Ephraim and Manasseh acting together (יחדו) against Judah. In Nielsen's view, therefore, 1.29-31 may originally have followed this as a reference to the joint invasion of Judah by the northern kingdom and Aram (note the use of tree and fire imagery at 7.2 and 4, which relate to the same period). In support of her view, she further notes that the passage has the right number of lines to create a full stanza of the refrain poem (though she concedes that the rhythm differs), and that its initial כי has a parallel in 9.17.

---

[24] See Nielsen, 204–11, for a detailed analysis of the coherence of vv. 29-31.

In my view, however, this intriguing suggestion (certainly the most compelling to date) faces two serious difficulties.[25] In the first place, as Nielsen agrees, the stanza would have had originally to be in the third person plural, and she sees the retention of this in יבשו as evidence of the original form. But her explanation for the harsh change to second person, 'a degree of adaptation to ch. 1's direct addressing of Jerusalem', is not convincing. The prevailing context (vv. 27-28), and indeed some earlier parts of the chapter, including its opening in vv. 2-3, are in the third person, and there is no reason whatsoever why vv. 29-30 should not have been left in the third person too. Furthermore, the evidence points rather strongly towards their having been in the second person from the start: what causes the modern reader difficulty is not initially encountering the third person יבשו, but rather the sudden switch to second person thereafter. It is far more plausible to envisage that יבשו has been changed to fit the present context than that the following two verses have been changed from a form that would have fitted to one that does not. The probability must be that the redactor was here working under the restraint of some kind of source which was couched in the second person, and that he has done his best to join it smoothly to the preceding. In that case, however, the source cannot have been part of the (third person) refrain poem in ch. 9. Finally on this point, the evidence we have adduced for the nature of the redactor's method earlier in the chapter indicates that he respected the form of his sources in this regard; indeed, that is precisely one of the reasons why it has been possible for us to trace his procedure in the first place. Were Nielsen's conjecture correct, he would here have reversed his usual procedure for no good reason and in a manner which introduces unnecessary difficulties.

The second difficulty which Nielsen's view faces is one which also faces all those who think that these verses preserve an original Isaianic fragment, namely that the evidence points rather to this being an altogether later composition. The close connections with the third part of the book have often been noted before, for instance in Smith's summary: 'Yahweh's saving of the repentant in Zion (cf. שוב [1.27; 59.20]); illicit cults in gardens (cf. אילים [1.29; 57.5] and גנה/גן [1.29-30; 65.3; 66.17]); the people choosing these things (cf. בחר [1.29; 65.12; 66.4]); the forsakers of Yahweh (cf. עזבי יהוה [1.28; 65.11]); and shame for these activities (cf. בוש [1.29; 65.13; 66.5])'.[26] To these more may be added, such as the particular association with the closing verses of ch. 66, noted in the comments on v. 28 below, and the comparison of v. 30 with 64.5*b*. It is true that not all are peculiar to the various passages mentioned, and it is often stated that, for instance, the kind of illicit cultic practices referred to were common throughout the biblical period (though the distinctive language used here

---

[25] Wendel, 133–34, objects further that the refrain poem concentrates on specific past national history, unlike the future-oriented and personal imagery of the present passage.

[26] P. A. Smith, *Rhetoric and Redaction in Trito-Isaiah: The Structure, Growth and Authorship of Isaiah 56–66* (VTSup 62; Leiden, 1995), 186; for similar comments, see, for instance, Vermeylen, 105–8; Barth, 292; Loretz, 59; Gosse, 'Isaïe 1'.

to describe them is repeated in the book only in Trito-Isaiah). While this may well be true, there is a concentration of similarities here which reaches beyond the level where they can be picked off one by one in this manner, and it is striking that they encompass the whole of 27-31 (and, indeed, 26 as well, as we have seen), and so include 27-28, which nearly all commentators recognize to be later. Finally, as was pointed out long ago by Marti, there is particular force to the inclusion of בחר in this list, since Isaiah never uses this word with the kind of technical religious sense which it has here, although it becomes common in later parts of the book (see on v. 29 below). The evidence for the post-exilic composition of these verses in circles very close to those attested in Isaiah 56–66 seems overwhelming.

The conclusion towards which these considerations seem to point is that while the chapter's final redactor was primarily responsible for this passage, he has made use in vv. 29-31 of material from about his own time which he has derived from elsewhere. The purpose of his composition will have been to round off the chapter in a way which showed the contemporary relevance to his readers of the earlier writing of Isaiah which he was introducing. If this is correct, then he obviously cannot have borrowed the substance of 29-31 from the work of Isaiah of Jerusalem, as he did earlier in the chapter, but must have derived it from a much later part of the book, presumably somewhere in Isaiah 56–66 (unless, as is possible, it is of quite separate origin). It is noteworthy, for instance, that the passage in ch. 57 which condemns cultic practices which are similar to those mentioned here starts off in the second person plural (vv. 3-5), and that in 65.11-16, following a passage which refers to similar practices (vv. 3-7), the judgment of the עזבי יהוה is pronounced in the second person (including ואתם תבשו!) in contrast to God's faithful servants, who are referred to in the third person. A passage such as ours would therefore not be out of place in this general context. While further speculation would be hazardous, the concentration of parallels with the last two chapters of Isaiah suggests the likelihood that we should seek an original setting there.[27] Isaiah 66.5 is an isolated saying whose final terse line והם יבשו, 'but they shall be ashamed', looks as though it might once have had a continuation.[28] The verse addresses those who 'tremble at [God's] word', and refers to the taunts of 'your brothers' who hate and reject them. Is it possible that the passage then turned to address these scoffers to pronounce their fate with the words of 1.29-31? Verse 6 following could then be seen as a response to this. If so, when the material was removed, והם יבשו might have been substituted for the original כי [אתם?] תבשו, which in that context would mean 'But you will be ashamed', in order to leave an indication, at least, that the scoffers would eventually be punished. Nothing relevant to the

---

[27] It is striking that, while Carr, 'Reading Isaiah', demonstrates that there are significant differences in emphasis between Isa. 1 and 65–66, he also maintains that 1.29-31 show closer conceptual affinity with 65–66 than they do with the bulk of ch. 1.

[28] For a survey of discussions of the difficulties which commentators have experienced over this line, see Koenen, *Ethik und Eschatologie* (above, n. 10), 201.

interpretation of 1.29-31 in its present context hangs on this speculation, however.

27. *Zion* appears here for the first time as a name in its own right (as opposed to 'the daughter of Zion' in v. 8), and it seems to mark the climax of the gradual narrowing process which has been apparent throughout the chapter. From an address to the whole nation in the opening verses, there is a movement to the remnant of a disaster by v. 9. By word association, this remnant is then explicitly addressed in v. 10, and the possibility of a further division is reached with the conditionals in vv. 18-20. This is then worked out in vv. 21-26, so that those who eventually survive to be referred to here as Zion are, so to speak, the remnant of a remnant.[29] It should thus be clear that so far as this opening chapter and this particular verse are concerned, there can be no question of an immediate reference to the popular so-called Zion tradition, if by that is meant that residence in the city is itself sufficient to guarantee survival and salvation. Rather, Zion here stands as a more or less abstract concept for the ideal people of God—those who have been saved through the judgment of the preceding paragraphs.[30]

A second characteristic of this group is that they *repent*. The word שביה might equally be translated 'those who return to her', and a decision as to which is more likely correct is finely balanced. In favour of the latter is the repeated verse 35.10 and 51.11, 'and the ransomed of the Lord shall return, and come to Zion with singing'. The coincidence in each of the three verses of the verbs פדה and שוב,[31] together with the reference to Zion, is certainly suggestive, and it could well be that the late compiler of ch. 1 is here making a conscious allusion to these other verses. On the other hand, there is no hint of exile in the present passage. In the coming judgment on Jerusalem, the wicked will apparently perish there and then (v. 28), so that the natural assumption must be that the deliverance takes place in the same context. Again, if we limit our inquiry to the use of the plural participle of שוב, we find that it is indeed used twice elsewhere for those who returned from Babylon (Ezra 6.21; Neh. 8.17), but that in both those cases the meaning is made explicit ('from the exile' and 'from the captivity'), which is obviously not the case here. Finally, apart from the two verses already noted, שוב is not used elsewhere in the book of Isaiah with the sense of return from exile, whereas the meaning 'repent' is not infrequent, and commentators have drawn particular attention to 59.20, 'And he will come to Zion as Redeemer, to those in Jacob who turn from transgression (שבי פשע)'. While it must be admitted that the arguments are finely balanced, the immediate context tips the balance in favour of the meaning

---

[29] Comparing this paragraph with similar later material elsewhere in Isaiah, Blenkinsopp even goes so far as to speak of 'a specific, pietistic, even sectarian point of view'.

[30] Indeed, Koenen, *Heil den Gerechten*, 92, finds in these verses a fusion of Zion and Deuteronomic traditions.

[31] There is only one other occurrence of פדה in Isaiah (29.22), but there is no apparent connection there with our verses. It is further possible that the noun פדות in 50.2 should be revocalized as an inf. constr.

'repent' here, and the possibility may even be considered that there is a conscious interpretation of 35.10 and 51.11 in the light of 59.20, making the thought of those verses more suitable for the post-exilic community who were already back in the land. If this is correct, then there is a suggestion here that even at this late hour, and regardless of previous conduct, it is still not too late to respond to the sustained exhortation of the chapter as a whole.

The nature of the deliverance is described as being *ransomed* (niph'al of פדה). It is usually claimed that the meaning of this verb developed from a relatively restricted legal and cultic usage to embrace a much wider religious sense of deliverance and rescue.[32] Whether such an inner-Hebrew semantic development can be maintained, in view of the use of the same word in many cognate Semitic languages, may be questioned, but in either case it is clear that by the time of our author the word could be used with the sense of rescue or liberation from a wide variety of dangerous situations and threatening opponents. In such contexts (notably in the Psalms), God is always the subject of the verb (as he is here by implication, though the verb itself is passive). It is thus most unlikely that any particularly technical sense is intended here.

Rather more difficult to understand is the precise force of the preposition ב, 'in, with, by', which links the verb with *justice* and *righteousness*. Of the 58 occurrences of this verb in the Hebrew Bible, only about ten are accompanied by this preposition,[33] and these may be grouped into four different categories. (i) At Job 5.20 ב introduces the state of danger (famine and war) from which one is delivered. This is clearly not the case here. (ii) In Ps. 55.19 it introduces the state in or into which the Psalmist is redeemed, and this is Vermeylen's preferred option here (p. 107). However, although this is clearly suitable in the Psalm, where the following noun is שלום, 'peace', it is less clear that *justice* and *righteousness* can describe a state. If they could, then this verse would effectively repeat the thought of v. 26. (iii) In the legal texts, the preposition introduces the price paid for the ransom—the so-called ב-*pretii*; cf. Exod. 13.3; 34.20; Lev. 27.27; Num. 18.16. In the latter two cases, the element of cost is particularly stressed, and this is true also of a passage such as Ps. 49.8-9, even though the preposition itself is not used. This is a common understanding of the preposition in our verse as well. It implies that the *justice* and *righteousness* are human qualities, and that they are the 'price' of deliverance.[34] While it may be going rather too far to speak of Zion earning or deserving her salvation, the thought is clearly moving in that direction. (iv) Not surprisingly, all the clear examples in the previous group have a human

---

[32] Cf. J. J. Stamm, *THAT* ii. 389–406 = *TLOT* ii. 964–76; H. Cazelles, *ThWAT* vi. 514–22 = *TDOT* xi. 483–90 (with much additional literature); R. L. Hubbard, *NIDOTTE* iii. 578–82.

[33] Even so, this is double the number of those which Vermeylen, 107, claims. To that extent, his discussion is slightly misleading.

[34] E.g. Luther; Gesenius; Hitzig; Marti; Cheyne; Gray; Budde; Kissane; Wildberger; Leclerc, *Yahweh is Exalted*, 44. Rashi and Kimhi too are explicit in their understanding that the justice and righteousness are deeds performed by the people.

subject. In a final group of examples, however, God is the subject, and the nouns introduced by ב are clearly not a monetary price, but rather a divine attribute which focusses on his effort in the work of redemption.[35] The most explicit translation would therefore be 'by means of' (ב-*instrumenti*). This is clear at Neh. 1.10 ('whom you redeemed by your great power and your strong hand'), and it is probable that Deut. 9.26 should be understood in the same way ('whom you redeemed by your greatness'; cf. the continuation of the verse: 'whom you brought out of Egypt with a mighty hand'). There are other passages where a similar thought is present, even though the preposition is not used. On this view, *justice* and *righteousness* are divine qualities, and the verse develops v. 26 by explaining that the deliverance promised there to the survivors of the purificatory judgment will not be arbitrary, but rather based on his standards.[36]

It is not easy to decide between the third and fourth options. In the first place it is noteworthy that they can be divided precisely according to whether the subject of the verb is God or a human being. At first sight, this might seem decisively to favour the fourth possibility, but the force of this argument is blunted by the fact that the verb is unusually cast as a passive. Though of course God is the implied subject, the situation is not as straightforward as if the author had used an active verb (as he easily could). By making Zion the grammatical subject, the emphasis of the verse is different from the other examples in this group. Secondly, the uses of the two nouns earlier in the chapter refer to human deeds of justice and righteousness, and so we might suppose that the same applies here. This has to be balanced, however, by the fact that the verse is almost certainly to be ascribed to the chapter's compiler, who may have been as much influenced by the use of this vocabulary elsewhere in the book as in the preceding material which he has adopted from elsewhere. In this connection, the uses at 4.4 and especially 5.16 provide significant parallels for the idea of God working in justice and righteousness.[37] Neither argument is therefore decisive.

The only other argument which I can see to help resolve this difficulty is that in the following verse the situation is clear—the wicked will be punished because of their bad deeds and faithlessness. If the two verses are indeed to be taken closely together as a contrasting pair, then it would seem most likely that our verse intends to make the converse point about the deliverance of those who practise justice and righteousness.[38] A small point in further support of this approach is that since v. 28 clearly picks up vocabulary from earlier in the chapter to describe the wicked, we might expect v. 27 to do the same with respect to the righteous. The reference therefore is to human deeds and the third option outlined above is to be

[35] This point was especially stressed by L. Morris, *The Apostolic Preaching of the Cross* (3rd edn; London, 1965), 24.

[36] So, for instance, Calvin; Lowth; Dillmann; Delitzsch; von Orelli; Fischer; Procksch; Young; Kaiser; Childs.

[37] This has been challenged with regard to 5.16 by Moberly, 'Whose Justice?'. See the discussion below, *ad loc.*

[38] So too Koenen, *Heil den Gerechten*, 91–92.

preferred. Nevertheless, this needs to be qualified in two respects. First, as we have seen, the ב-*pretii* is only ever used in this connection when a human being is the redeemer, but that is clearly not the case here. While the grammar is unaffected, 'by' should be understood to mean 'because of' rather than more narrowly 'at the price of'. Secondly, the reference in the second half of the verse to those *who repent* indicates that deliverance is more than simply a matter of desert; even for those who have previously sinned, there is still an alternative way of salvation; God's redemption encompasses more than a simple weighing of human deeds.

It would thus be a mistake, in my view, to try to force a wedge in this verse between God's act of deliverance and the survival of the people based on what they deserve because of their deeds (as has sometimes been done). The fact that *justice* and *righteousness* refer primarily to their character and deeds is not to be separated from the active work of God in deliverance.[39] All the inhabitants of the city, according to vv. 21-26, will be put through the refining fire, and, as the passive *be ransomed* makes clear, God will be seen to be active as the unexpressed subject in ensuring that it is the righteous who survive, not the wicked. If it is still possible by an extreme form of logic-chopping to detect a certain roughness to the thought of the chapter as it emerges overall, then it must be recalled that this will be due in part to the fact that some of it has been borrowed more-or-less unchanged from elsewhere in the book and in part to the fact that we are dealing here with poetry whose primary aim is hortatory and rhetorical, and not with an attempt to construct a work of systematic theology.

28. As Rashi rightly observes, the three classes of those who are to be judged (*rebels, sinners* and *those who abandon the Lord*) come straight from vv. 2-4 above (*q.v.*)—and he might have added that they come in the same order as well. This seems to be another example of the fondness of the chapter's compiler for the use of *inclusio*, already noted several times. There is, of course, a subtle shift in thought, in that at the start of the chapter they seem to apply to the people as a whole, whereas by this late stage we have been made aware that there is in fact to be a division, and that not all will suffer the fate here described. There is no reason, however, why he should not be allowed to introduce such a refining of the initial statement following all that comes in between.

Perish (יכלו) has the sense of coming to a complete end. This is not a further act of segregation, but the ultimate fate of the wicked. This is then spelt out in detail in the following verses, and it parallels the sense of the final verse of the book as a whole.[40] That this is conscious may be suggested by the use there as here of *rebels* (פשעים) as well as by the reprise of ואין מכבה, 'with none to quench' at the end of v. 31, by לא תכבה,

---

[39] The new people of Zion 'will be constituted of those who decide for divine righteousness. They do not redeem themselves, however; rather they are redeemed, an indirect yet clear reference to Yahweh as the one who effects liberation'; J.J. Stamm, *TLOT* ii. 975 = *THAT* ii. 404). See too Oswalt and Motyer. The Targum also manages to include a reference to both.

[40] Cf. Tomasino, 'Isaiah 1.1–2.4', 90–91.

'will not be quenched', in 66.24.[41] The similarities in certain respects with 33.14-15, at the very centre of the book, are also noteworthy.

29. The mention of *terebinths* and *gardens* has been understood by nearly all commentators to indicate a reference to illicit cult practice (and this regardless of whether they ascribe the words to Isaiah or to a later redactor). The conceptual and verbal parallels with Isa. 57.5, 65.3 and 66.17, however they should be understood diachronically (see above), would seem to be conclusive in this regard; indeed, the last two of these passages and 1.29-30 are the only places in the whole Hebrew Bible where *gardens* occur with this connotation. This approach is also supported by the use of choice and shame language in the verse. Against this, Budde, 35–39, maintained that the references implied no more than the pride of the wealthy in their luxurious estates, while Fohrer[42] appealed to 5.8 to support an interpretation of the passage as a polemic against the wealthy. This minority view has been thoroughly examined by Nielsen,[43] however, who shows that a number of the other passages to which Budde appealed for support in fact also refer to the widespread notion of the sacred tree.

Because most biblical references to this type of cult inevitably occur in strongly polemical contexts, it is difficult to reconstruct the precise nature of the cult in question. There are often strongly sexual overtones to the language used in this connection, however (e.g. Hos. 4.12-13; Isa. 57.5; Jer. 2.20; 3.13), so that it is generally assumed that some sort of fertility rites are in view,[44] while Ezek. 6.13 makes clear that sacrifice to idols could also be involved. In addition, however, some have found allusions to various forms of divination (e.g. Gen. 12.6; Judg. 6.19), necromancy (Isa. 57.5; note that 1 Chron. 10.12 refers to burial under a terebinth, and cf. Gen. 35.8) and incubation rites (Isa. 65.3-4). Even less certain is the question whether the terebinth was merely regarded as marking a sacred site or whether the tree itself was identified with a goddess (אלה as the female of אל, though it should be noted that the word is not attested as such in Classical Hebrew; contrast Ugaritic *ʾlt* [*DUL*, 66]), presumably Asherah;[45] at best, this is an inference, since such an identification is never

---

[41] For a survey of analyses of these and related points of similarity, see Carr, 'Reading Isaiah'.

[42] Fohrer has been hesitantly followed by Høgenhaven, 186–87, and by Stiebert, *The Construction of Shame*, 91.

[43] Nielsen, 203–10; see too Wildberger.

[44] See especially S. Ackerman, *Under Every Green Tree: Popular Religion in Sixth-Century Judah* (HSM 46; Atlanta, 1992), 186–92, who further associates this with the cult of Asherah. See too Nielsen, 79–85, for a wide-ranging survey of 'conceptions of the tree as holy'; more generally, cf. *DDD*, 850–51, and K. Jaroš, *Die Stellung des Elohisten zur Kanaanäischen Religion* (OBO 4; Freiburg and Göttingen, 1974), 213–57.

[45] Cf. W. F. Albright, *Yahweh and the Gods of Canaan: A Historical Analysis of Two Contrasting Faiths* (London, 1968), 165, and especially now Keel, *Goddesses and Trees*, 16–57. In an article which includes much useful further bibliography on this whole topic, J. E. Taylor maintains that though Asherah was represented at cultic sites by a living tree, cut and pruned into a particular cultic form, this was not the אלה itself (which 'still stood apart from the asherah and other symbols and seems to have been separated from any necessary association with the cult of Asherah', p. 40), but some other, smaller tree: 'The Asherah, the Menorah and the Sacred Tree', *JSOT* 66 (1995), 29–54.

made in our extant texts. It is not in the nature of polemic to make such fine distinctions, however, so that it would probably be a mistake to assume that our passage refers narrowly to any one particular rite or practice.

There are four species of *terebinth* which are native to Israel, though only two which fit the range of biblical evidence, the *pistacia atlantica* and the *pistacia palaestina*. Because the former achieves greater height and age than the latter, Zohary concludes that it is most likely the species in question here.[46]

The use of *desire* (חמד)[47] and *choose* (בחר)[48] in parallel indicates that those being referred to are fully responsible for their own fate. The latter term is, of course, heavy with theological overtones: just as God had chosen Israel to be his own people, so they were challenged to choose to serve him alone (e.g. Josh. 24.15). It implies an exclusive relationship, which God jealously protects. Isaiah of Jerusalem does not appear ever to use the word in this technical sense, perhaps because his understanding of the relationship between God and Israel is not primarily based on the Exodus tradition, where such vocabulary is mainly at home when applied to the nation as a single entity. Within the book as a whole, it comes to prominence later on, when God repeatedly reaffirms his choice of Israel in Deutero-Isaiah (cf. 41.8, 9; 43.10; 44.1, 2; 49.7; see too the redactional use at 14.1), and then in the last part of the book, where we find the converse of Israel choosing to follow other cults, as here (65.12; 66.3-4). In this latter passage, we then find the ironic response—that God will choose to turn away from them. Despite the implications of the English translation equivalents, we should therefore not limit this language to the spheres of emotion or intellect alone; rather an active and deliberate pursuit of the object is intended.

Similarly, to *be ashamed* (בוש)[49] and *be abashed* (חפר)[50] can have both subjective and objective meanings. The latter seems clearly to be in view here:[51] although the devotees of such cults may have hoped for fertility and blessing, and perhaps further for deliverance from harm, their hopes will not be realized (cf. Gray: they will 'fail to receive expected help'). As we might say colloquially, they will be completely let down. Isaiah 20.5-6

---

[46] Zohary, *Plants*, 110–11.

[47] For fuller discussions, with bibliography, see G. Wallis, *ThWAT* ii. 1020–32 = *TDOT* iv. 452–61, and E. Gerstenberger, *THAT* i. 579–81 = *TLOT* i. 433–35.

[48] Cf. H. Seebass, *ThWAT* i. 592–608 = *TDOT* ii. 73–87, and H. Wildberger, *THAT* i. 275–300 = *TLOT* i. 209–26.

[49] Cf. H. Seebass, *ThWAT* i. 568–80 = *TDOT* ii. 50–60, and F. Stolz, *THAT* i. 269–72 = *TLOT* i. 204–7.

[50] Cf. J. Gamberoni, *ThWAT* iii. 116–21 = *TDOT* v. 107–11. In more than half of its occurrences, it stands in parallel with בוש, as here.

[51] See Stiebert, *The Construction of Shame*, 87–109. She shows convincingly that appeal to analogies with honour/shame societies is wholly inappropriate to the situation in Isaiah (though see on 4.1 below). She also suggests (pp. 92–93) that M. A. Klopfenstein, who is generally closer to the mark, may have gone further than is warranted in limiting the terminology to legal or courtroom contexts; cf. *Scham und Schande nach dem Alten Testament: Eine begriffsgeschichtliche Untersuchung zu den hebräischen Wurzeln bôš, klm und ḥpr* (ATANT 62; Zurich, 1972), esp. 60–61.

and 30.3 are fine and especially clear illustrations of this sense (they also make clear that the meaning is not necessarily restricted to the narrow sphere of cultic infidelity); see too Jer. 12.13; Mic. 3.7 (with the same parallelism as here), etc. This, of course, is the exact opposite of the fate of those who choose to trust in God, as the psalmists often affirm or pray (e.g. Pss. 25.2-3; 31.18; 69.7, etc.). The following two verses then develop a metaphor, based on the language of this verse, to indicate how such a shaming will come about: the idolaters will become like their idols, and both will suffer the same destruction.

30. Far from providing a symbol of prosperity and fertility, the *terebinth* and *garden* are used here as images of fading mortality. The reference to the loss of *foliage* here is not, of course, to part of the annual cycle, but rather to the result of prolonged drought, which will lead eventually to the death of the tree. Furthermore, as the rabbinic commentators observe, the dry ground means that there is no hope that seed will take root as a means of ensuring future growth (in contrast with the glossator's comment at the end of ch. 6). As at Ezek. 19.12-14, all this desiccation is but the prelude for a final, cataclysmic fire (v. 31), which will destroy all that remains.

It may well be that there is a reflection in this passage on the final verse of ch. 6.[52] The judgment on the wicked is described in a similar manner, with three striking points of connection between the two passages, namely the references to a *terebinth* (the singular אלה occurs only in these two verses in Isaiah), the loss of *foliage* (which is attested in antiquity as one possible interpretation of שלכת in 6.13) and the destruction by fire (בער, v. 31). In view of our understanding of the present passage as deriving from a relatively late phase in the development of the Isaianic tradition, it looks as though our redactor took up the climax of the word of judgment from that prominent account in the ministry of Isaiah and reapplied it here at the culmination of his exhortatory introduction to the work as a whole. This conclusion will stand, of course, whether he was himself the first author of these words or whether he derived them from elsewhere; see the discussion above. Either way, he has demonstrated a fine appreciation for the need to reapply the message which Isaiah first gave to the changed circumstances of his later day, and he has done so in a manner which the comparisons with various passages in chs 56–66 show were very much to the point.

31. There is an element of irony in the reference to the idolater as *the strong one*. He will have believed that he was indeed filled with power through his form of worship, but it will not profit when God's judgment is revealed. This would be reinforced if there is, as has been suggested, a word-play on חסן, 'strength', and חוסן, a word for uncombed flax in Mishnaic Hebrew. The supposed strength is as feeble as flax, as will be seen from its processing into *tow*: 'Wie man aus חוסן Werg macht, so wird auch

---

[52] For a fuller analysis of this point, see my article 'Isaiah 6,13 and 1,29-31'; see too H.-P. Müller, 'Sprachliche und religionsgeschichtliche Beobachtungen zu Jesaja 6', *ZAH* 5 (1992), 163–85, and G. K. Beale, 'Isaiah vi 9-13: A Retributive Taunt against Idolatry', *VT* 41 (1991), 257–78.

euer חסון, euer Starker, zu Werg werden'.[53] This attractive suggestion remains speculative, however. חוסן is unattested as early as the biblical period, when פשתה/פשת was the standard word for flax.[54] Furthermore, the particular use of חוסן for a lamp wick in the Mishnah is also paralleled by פשתה in Isa. 42.3; 43.17, so that the possibility that חוסן is a later word altogether remains likely.

Tow is a by-product of the production of linen from flax. Once the flax had been pulled and bundled, it was left to dry initially in the field or on a roof. After that, the seed pods were removed and the stalks soaked ('retted') for several weeks in order to soften the fibres so that they could be easily separated. They were then dried again, pounded, scraped and combed ('hackled') in order to remove the outer covering and pulp, leaving the fibres ready for spinning. It is this discarded material which is known as *tow* (from נער, 'to shake', referring to the process). It was clearly highly flammable and any strands within it were extremely weak (Judg. 16.7, where strikingly it is again referred to in association with fire), unsuitable for spinning into thread. It is a reasonable deduction that it would have been used as tinder for kindling, needing no more than a *spark* to ignite it, though that does not mean that it should be translated so (*contra* NRSV).

Although the discussion so far has glossed *his work* as though it referred only to an idol, more may in fact be intended. As in English, פעל may refer either to what someone makes or to their deeds. Similarly here it may not just be the idol which is in view but other cultic paraphernalia too, as well as perhaps even the illicit worship practices themselves. A precise definition is no more needed here than in v. 29. As something abhorrent to our writer, they are the *spark* which sets ablaze the whole rotten system—worshipper and cult, *both of them together*.

With none to quench: a familiar formula in such circumstances; cf. Jer. 4.4; 21.12; Amos 5.6. In each of these cases, the reference is to God's wrath, and that is implied here also. For the connections with 6.13 and 66.24, see above on vv. 30 and 28 respectively.

[53] H. Ehrentreu, 'Sprachliches und Sachliches aus dem Talmud', *Jahrbuch der Jüdisch-Literarischen Gesellschaft* 8 (1910 [1911]), 1–34 (7); cf. Nielsen, 207–9, who accepts the possibilty of word-play but rejects the later attempts of Tsevat and Loewenstamm to see in חסן itself a reference to flax (see above, n. 14).

[54] Cf. K. A. Tångberg, 'A Note on *pištî* in Hosea ii 7, 11', *VT* 27 (1977), 222–24, for discussion, and *DNWSI*, 947, for extra-biblical evidence.

HEADING
(2.1)

[2.1]The word which Isaiah the son of Amoz saw concerning Judah and Jerusalem.

Most of the textual and linguistic comments relevant to this verse have been treated already at 1.1. Note, however, that, against its readings there, 1QIsaᵃ here uses the shorter form of the prophet's name (ישעיה) and also attests the developed form of spelling for Jerusalem (ירושלים).

הדבר אשר חזה: whether because this form of heading is unparalleled[1] or because he misread חזה as היה, the LXX translator assimilated the phrase to the form which occurs frequently in Jeremiah (e.g. 7.1; 11.1; 18.1, etc.): ὁ λόγος ὁ γενόμενος παρὰ κυρίου πρὸς... (הדבר אשר היה אל-X מאת יהוה).

As at 1.1, there is little agreement as to how much this heading is meant to introduce. Opinions vary between 2-12,[2] 2-10,[3] 2-5,[4] 2-4,[5] and 2.2-4.[6] Procksch even suggests that it is a heading which covered the early part of Isaiah's ministry comprising 6 + 2-5 + 9.7–10.4.

The occurrence of a similar form of heading at 13.1 clearly indicates that 2-12 is the outer limit which may be considered. Since we have already been led by the similar form of 1.1 to take note of this style of heading, it would seem that at the synchronic level this is indeed the stretch of text which is here introduced.

Diachronic considerations fully support this provisional conclusion. Although 13.1 stands at the start of the oracles against the nations, its immediate reference is to chs 13–14 (משא בבל), and since both the final form of that extended section and its positioning at the start of the oracles against the nations are best explained as late-exilic at the earliest (cf. Williamson, *Book*, 157–75), it seems likely that this was also the time at which the heading was added. If, as is most probable, 2.1 reflects the work

---

[1] Other examples of synaesthesia in the Old Testament (though without reference to the present example), are discussed by B. Kedar-Kopfstein, 'Synästhesien im biblischen Althebräisch in Übersetzung und Auslegung', *ZAH* 1 (1988), 47–60, 147–58.

[2] E.g. Gray; Bartelt, 235; Blenkinsopp. Limburg, 'Swords to Plowshares', 280–81, notes several ways in which ch. 12 forms a frame with 2.2-4.

[3] Fohrer, 'Entstehung', 116.

[4] E.g. Delitzsch; Orelli; Mowinckel, *Prophecy*, 54; Auvray; Young; Oswalt.

[5] E.g. Knobel; Duhm; Skinner; König; Vermeylen; Clements (who accepts that 2.2-4 and 4.2-6 may have been added later); Sweeney; Motyer. An older variation on this possibility was to assume that the verse had been displaced from its original position in front of 2.6, where it served to introduce 2.6–4.6 (e.g. Marti); this unsupported conjecture has rightly been dropped from consideration in more recent times.

[6] E.g. Wiklander, 94. His main argument, that the singular דבר leads us to expect a single oracle following, is clearly mistaken in view of the usage at Hos. 1.1, Joel 1.1 and Mic. 1.1, to go no further.

of the same editor, then it follows both that it cannot introduce the shorter section of chs 2–4, as many have maintained, since 4.2-6 is of later date,[7] and also that it is most reasonable to assume that an editor who introduced such distinctive literary markers intended them to delineate the major sections of the work which he was handling. If, as will be argued below, 6.1 and 14.28 represent an earlier, pre-exilic pattern of division in the book as it then existed, then it will be seen that the exilic redactor has overridden both by the inclusion of more material within his compass of 2-12 and 13ff. As will be seen later, other indications of this level of redaction suggest that the broad conception of 2-12 in its exilic form is of judgment in 2-5 and a movement towards eschatological hope in 6-12.

There are two other and quite different approaches which have been adopted towards this heading, but neither seems plausible. First, as was noted at 1.1, Goldingay, 'Isaiah i 1 and ii 1', has suggested that the verse is a colophon which does not look forward to the following but back to 1.1, with which it forms a framework around the substance of ch. 1. Some of the problems with his proposal have already been noted. It is relevant at this point to note that in the light of the clear introductory function of 13.1, which is closely parallel to our verse, it is far more plausible to assume that the same is true here as well. Although, as Goldingay observes, collections of prophetic oracles do sometimes have a concluding comment (e.g. Jer. 51.64), none ever takes a form anything like the present one. Indeed, in every case where we have a comment similar to this one, it always serves to introduce the following text or book. That דבר can be used for a collection of material is accepted by Goldingay, with reference to Hos. 1.1, Joel 1.1 and Mic. 1.1. And finally, as was observed above, colophons typically include details about the scribe who copied the text and its owner, not about authorship and content. Goldingay's proposal is thus without analogy either within the Old Testament or in the wider ancient Near East.

Secondly, Scott,[8] followed (independently?) by Ackroyd,[9] suggested that the verse is not so much a heading to 2.2-4 as a scribal note to claim authorship for Isaiah in view of the fact that the same passage also occurs in Mic. 4.1-3. This argument is part of a wider case to take 2.2-4 as the conclusion of ch. 1, since it is claimed that many of the sections of Isaiah have been brought to a conclusion on a positive note. This latter point is not strong, however, since we have already seen that ch. 1 as it now stands has a logic of its own which mirrors closely the shape of the book of Isaiah as a whole, so that the chapter may be better understood as a late redactional assemblage designed to introduce the book. Secondly, if it is

---

[7] See the introductory comments on 3.1-9*a* for further discussion of the effects of this addition on the final form of the book.

[8] In addition to his commentary, see 'Literary Structure', 177. See too Rignell, 'Isaiah Chapter 1', 141.

[9] Ackroyd, 'Note'. He responded to Wildberger's initial criticisms of his proposal in 'Isaiah i-xii', 32–34 = *Studies*, 92–94. He has been followed (with minor variations) by, among others, Kaiser, Loretz, 43, Rendtorff, 'Komposition', 305–6 = 'Composition', 156, Höffken, Blum, 565–66, Berges, 55, and Beuken.

true that ch. 1 was added at a late stage in the formation of the book, then arguments from the suitability of ch. 2 as its continuation can equally well be explained on the assumption that the redactor was aware that his compilation in ch. 1 would be followed by ch. 2 and so did not feel himself obliged to complete his own collection with an oracle of hope. Finally, it has to be observed that others are equally impressed by the shape of chs 2–4, which begin and end on a positive note, the section as a whole thus forming a tidy concentric structure.[10] This is not necessarily to give credence to such proposals, but merely to observe that it is hazardous to make such analyses the starting point for further theories. It may be further held against this approach to 2.1 in itself that 2.2-4 deals only with Jerusalem, and not Judah, as the verse would lead us to expect, and that no analogy is offered for the use of such a scribal note. Finally, the close parallel with 13.1 needs again to be borne in mind, because it renders unlikely any suggestion that 2.1 functioned differently from it.

In conclusion, 2.1 was probably added at the same time as 13.1 as a structural marker in the exilic version of Isaiah and it was therefore intended to introduce such parts of 2-12 as were included within that form of the book. Although later additions, such as 4.2-6, have somewhat distorted this pattern, it remains the most attractive option to accept that the heading still functions to introduce the expanded and full text of 2-12.

---

[10] E.g. Delitzsch; Magonet, 'Isaiah 2:1–4.6'.

ZION AND THE NATIONS
(2.2-5)

[2]And in a future time
The mountain of the Lord['s house] will be established
    as the head of the mountains, and it will be loftier than the hills.
And all the nations will stream to it,
    [3]and many peoples will go and say,
'Come, let us go up to the mountain of the Lord,
    to the house of the God of Jacob;
so that he may teach us of his ways,
    and that we may walk in his paths';
for instruction will issue from Zion,
    and the word of the Lord from Jerusalem.
[4]And he will judge between the nations,
    and arbitrate between many peoples;
and they will beat their swords into hoes
    and their spears into pruning hooks.
Nation will not lift up sword against nation,
    neither will they learn war any more.
[5]O house of Jacob, come, let us walk in the light of the Lord.

2-4 are paralleled in Mic. 4.1-3. Although there are several slight differences between the texts, as will be noted, and although many judge, perhaps rightly, that in a number of respects, the text in Micah is superior, it would be a mistake to seek to accommodate the two text forms in every respect.[1] In cases where the text in Isaiah is well supported and makes sense as it stands, its integrity should be respected. It goes beyond the evidence at our disposal to decide whether the changes arose in the course of later transmission or at the point of incorporation of the passage into its respective contexts.

The complicated textual history which may lie behind the present forms of the parallel texts seems to be well illustrated by fragment 1 of 4QIsa[e]. In most major respects, this manuscript parallels MT Isaiah, as is to be expected. At three places, however, it agrees with MT Micah against Isaiah (see below for details), and in one significant respect it goes its own way.[2] With such attested variety, it would be foolhardy in matters of detail to claim priority for one reading or the other: the degree of influence of each passage on the other throughout their early transmission puts any putative 'original' text beyond reach.

2. By adding ὅτι to the start of the verse, LXX joins this passage more closely to the heading. This may be associated with the translation of על by περὶ in 2.1 rather than κατὰ in 1.1.

נכון יהיה: LXX ἐμφανὲς (Mic. 4.1, נכון...יהיה: ἐμφανὲς...ἔτοιμον): as a translation of either or both Hebrew words, this is puzzling. Elsewhere, it refers to something becoming known (נודע, Exod. 2.14) and to God becoming manifest (corresponding to נדרשתי, 'I was sought', Isa. 65.1). Gray toys with the possibility that יִדָּרֵשׁ might have stood in the translator's *Vorlage* (cf. Amos 5.5 for 'seeking' a cult centre), but rightly rejects it

---

[1] Note in this regard that Zech. 8.20-22 seems to be aware of the forms of the text currently attested in both Isaiah and Micah; cf. Rudman, 'Zechariah 8:20-22'.

[2] I have collected these points together in my essay 'Isaiah, Micah and Qumran'.

because it anticipates the following and does not fit well with the next line. In addition, it is difficult to see how the present Hebrew text could have arisen from this. The fact that this curious reading occurs in both Isaiah and Micah at the very point where their word order differs (see below) compounds the problem: if, on the basis of Micah, it is concluded that it renders יהיה alone, then נכון was presumably lacking in Isaiah; if, on the other hand, it renders the whole phrase in Isaiah, then the Micah translator must have known LXX Isaiah (it is difficult to see how else he could have hit upon the same rendering independently), but either misunderstood it or sought to correct it, or alternatively, LXX Micah represents a doublet. Indeed, McKane, *Micah*, 122 (who thinks that it represents a translation of נכון in Isaiah; it might be noted in support of his view that יהיה is lacking from 4QIsa^e³) goes so far as to speculate that the Greek translator of Micah was attempting to take account of the differing positions of נכון in the two texts. Clearly, no solution yet proposed can be considered certain. It is attractive to think that the translator's text may have read יֶחֱזֶה (or that he misread it as such),[4] and that in rendering this he was virtually obliged to slide over נכון. The translator of Micah, however, could not be so free, because of the different word order. He therefore followed LXX Isaiah to start with, but then also offered a rendering of נכון at the place where it stood in his *Vorlage* (= MT). Whatever the explanation, there is no case for emending the Hebrew text on the basis of the Greek at this point.

The word order in Isaiah, however, has raised far more suspicion by comparison with Micah, where נכון follows יהיה. It is often said that the form in Micah gives better poetic balance,[5] and is therefore to be preferred. It is doubtful whether this is sufficient to claim that MT Isaiah is therefore simply in error, for the following reasons: (a) Syntactically, while the Micah word order is more common, that in Isaiah is also securely attested (e.g. Deut 9.7; Ps. 122.2); cf. Driver, *Tenses* §135 (5); Gibson, 138. There is sometimes an element of emphasis involved, which would not be out of place here (cf. Cazelles, 'Qui aurait visé?', 417). (b) Textually, all witnesses clearly support the order in MT with the exception of P, which, however, has other examples of a tendency to level out differences between Isaiah and Micah in this passage (cf. McKane, *Micah*, 123–24), so blunting the force of its evidence. (c) In the text as it stands, the second line is itself balanced, and this would be upset by the addition there of נכון. That this is not the case in Micah is because it has an additional word in the second half of the second line as well (הוא). These two differences need to be considered together where discussions of poetic balance are concerned, and it is obviously less likely that they are unrelated and hence accidental. If this is a hint that there has been some slight deliberate alteration in one case or the other, then clearly the integrity of each text should be respected.[6] (d) Although the line length in Micah is preferred by some, it is won only at the cost of a striking instance of enjambment

---

[3] The matter is complicated by what appears to be an erased *yod* at the point where we should expect to find יהיה. The editors' explanation for this (p. 91) is not entirely convincing (for instance, they do not explain the lack of a word space between נכון and this erased letter, and anyway, why should the start of יהיה have been erased in the first place?). It is tantalizing that this puzzle occurs just where Isaiah and Micah differ from each other, though whether the two points are related is not clear.

[4] Cf. T. J. Meek, 'Some Emendations in the Old Testament', *JBL* 48 (1929), 162–68 (162–63); less plausibly, Budde, and T. H. Robinson, *Die Zwölf Kleinen Propheten* (HAT 14; Tübingen, 1938), 141, suggested יֵרָאֶה (as an alternative, Budde also considered יֵדַע [cf. Exod. 2.14]). This is no argument for emendation as such, however. Renaud, *Formation*, 152, thinks that the curious rendering in LXX is due to no more than the translator's concern to avoid repetition (והיה and יהיה), though this does not explain why he came up with this particular rendering.

[5] See, for instance, Budde; Condamin; Feldmann; Procksch; Renaud, *Formation*, 151; Bartelt, 233.

[6] See too Zapff, *Studien*, 71. Against many, Zapff argues that the superior form in Micah indicates its dependence on Isaiah, not *vice versa*.

(נכון and יהיה in separate lines), which would certainly be unexpected in such a short, highly poetic passage.[7] (e) Although the general poetic structure of this verse is generally held to be superior in Micah, it is itself not above some suspicion (cf. Gray), so that there is a possibility that neither text preserves whatever may have been the 'original'. In that case, it would be unwise to prefer Micah as regards one detail on this basis alone. On balance, therefore, it looks as though each text has chosen deliberately to go its own way, in which case we should not emend either in this particular regard.

הר בית־יהוה: so too MT Micah; the phrase occurs elsewhere only at 2 Chron. 33.15. LXX Micah has τὸ ὄρος τοῦ Κυρίου (i.e. without בית), while LXX Isaiah starts the same but then continues with καὶ ὁ οἶκος τοῦ θεοῦ. The latter certainly looks like a later addition in the direction of the MT; at any rate a *separate* reference to the temple would clearly be out of place in the context[8]—one way or the other, הר must be the subject. It is noteworthy that in v. 3 (*q.v.*) we have הר־יהוה and בית אלהי יעקב in parallel. From various points of view, therefore, it looks as though our phrase in MT has arisen as a conflation. We may postulate that the original text in both Isaiah and Micah read הר־יהוה (e.g. Duhm; Marti; Gray; cf. LXX Mic. and Isa. before the later correction), that this was expanded to the present form at a relatively early stage in the textual transmission (cf. 1QIsaᵃ) and that LXX Isaiah represents a (mistaken) later attempt to insert a correction. Renaud's suggestion (*Formation*, 151, followed by Wolff[9]) that LXX Micah arose as a simplification of LXX Isaiah is desperate, and the fact that בית is attested by the later versions is insignificant, given that the expansion took place long before them.

בראש ההרים: 1QIsaᵃ lacks the article, whereas 4QIsaᵉ = MT. There are several possible renderings:[10] (i) 'on the top of the mountains'; so LXX and P; Knobel; Marti; Gray; Budde; Hillers;[11] McKane. It is argued that ראש(־ים) ההר(־ים) regularly has this sense elsewhere (e.g. 42.11), and so should here as well, and that it follows better from נכון than the alternatives. On the other hand, it makes the comparative in the parallel phrase redundant, and it seems curious with the plural 'mountains'. (ii) 'On the chief of the mountains' (Duhm). This rendering is possible only if the subject is the temple (cf. LXX), but that view has already been seen to be highly unlikely (cf. Gray). (iii) 'As the chief of the mountains'; so Rashi; Wildberger;[12] Rudolph;[13] Wiklander, 70; for the ב-*essentiae*; cf. GK §119i; JM §133c. Despite Dillmann's protestations, this seems to differ little in sense from (iv) 'at the head of the mountains' (Delitzsch; König; Feldmann; Procksch). In both cases, see, for instance, Deut. 20.9; 1 Sam. 9.22; Amos 6.7 for ראש used (as frequently) of rank and priority.

---

[7] Cf. Watson, *Classical Hebrew Poetry*, 332–35; G. B. Gray, *The Forms of Hebrew Poetry* (London, 1915), 126–27.

[8] As Wildberger observes in addition, יסד, not כון, is used elsewhere for the reestablishment of the temple. Baer, 'It's All About Us!', 200–2, however, argues that the LXX was nationalistically motivated in separating between the mountain, to which the gentiles might come, and the temple, to which they might not.

[9] Wolff, *Micha*, 83 = *Micah*, 112.

[10] 'Over/above the mountains' (V and Hofmann, as cited by Delitzsch) does not seem possible; it cannot be squared with נכון, and we should certainly have expected the preposition על. The suggestion that the preposition ב here has the same force as the מן in the parallel phrase with the consequential need to emend by the addition of רם before (ו)נשא is implausible, especially as the different word order in Micah means that the emendation does not work there; cf. Kselman, 'Note'.

[11] D. R. Hillers, *Micah* (Philadelphia, 1984), 49; Hillers' actual translation is 'over the mountaintops', which is unacceptable (see previous note), but his comments seem to align him rather with these other commentators.

[12] Wildberger, 'Völkerwallfahrt', 63. He seems to have abandoned this position in his commentary, however, where, without comment, he renders 'auf dem höchsten Gipfel der Berge' = (i).

[13] W. Rudolph, *Micha-Nahum-Habakuk-Zephanja* (KAT 13/3; Gütersloh, 1975), 76.

ונשא: for the lack of הוא following (cf. Micah), see above; strikingly, it looks as though it was present in 4QIsaᵉ, which only underlines how uncertain any decision about such details must be.[14]

ונהרו: the verb is usually understood as a denominative from נהר, 'river', hence 'to flow, stream' (as with Arabic *nahara*), and this is the understanding of most of the versions (certainly so for α, σ, θ and V; probably for LXX ἥξουσιν,[15] which is less colourful, but certainly cannot be related to נהר II); T's paraphrase ויתפנין למפלח עלוהי is ambiguous in this regard, as are P (depending on how the verb is construed[16]) and the rabbinic commentators. It fits well with the parallel והלכו and the use of the preposition אל following. Outside this passage, however, the verb could only occur twice at most (Jer. 31.12; 51.44), and in both passages there are those who think that נהר II ('to shine', and hence 'to rejoice at'; note that both occurrences are also followed by אל) is more probable.[17] Consequently, a strong minority holds that this same form is attested here too (in which case, נהר I should presumably be dropped from the lexicon altogether).[18] The parallel half of the line, however, strongly supports the traditional rendering, and there is no evidence for Budde's suggestion to get round this difficulty that והלכו should be deleted and replaced by ואמרו from the end of the line.[19]

אליו: so too 4QIsaᵉ; Micah has עליו, and cf. 1 QIsaᵃ עלוהי. The form in Isaiah is usually preferred, the use of על being thought to reflect Aramaic influence (something which is clear in the scroll's suffix). Either form is possible, however (especially if the text is exilic or later), and the same variation is often found elsewhere between manuscripts of the same text.

2-3. עמים רבים...כל־הגוים: Micah lacks כל and also has the reverse order for the two nouns. As regards the latter, LXX translates both words with ἔθνη here, but follows MT Micah there. V supports MT respectively in each case, but T follows the Isaianic order both here and at Micah (P had no choice but to render with the same word in each case.) The same variation occurs in v. 4 below (= Mic. 4.3, where this time T, like the other versions, follows MT), and the two are no doubt related. There may be an element of conscious crescendo in Micah (so Zapff, *Studien*, 71), whereby 'peoples' in 4.1 becomes 'many peoples' in 4.3, and similarly 'many nations' in 4.1 becomes 'mighty nations' in 4.3 (note that עצמים, 'mighty', does not feature in the Isaiah passage at all, but cf. Zech. 8.22). This does not necessarily speak for the priority of either text, however. The presence of כל here is universally attested, but is nevertheless often considered secondary:

[14] This is only the most striking of several examples included in the notes above where this particular scroll follows the Micah rather than the Isaiah text form.

[15] Gordon, *Holy Land*, 64, observes that LXX also paraphrased occurrences of נהר elsewhere.

[16] See the discussion in Roberts, 'Double Entendre', 46 n. 14; note, however, that P Micah clearly construes as נהר I, which is significant in view of the tendency in P to equalize the two texts.

[17] For Jer. 31.12, see, for instance, W. L. Holladay, *Jeremiah 2: A Commentary on the Book of the Prophet Jeremiah Chapters 26–52* (Minneapolis, 1989), 185; W. McKane, *A Critical and Exegetical Commentary on Jeremiah 2* (ICC; Edinburgh, 1996), 793–94 (though both scholars retain נהר I at 51.44); Roberts, 'Double Entendre'; for Jer. 51.44, see especially B. Wiklander, 'The Context and Meaning of NHR 'L in Jer. 51.44', *SEÅ* 43 (1978), 40–64. For some other considerations, see B. Gosse, 'Michée 4,1-5, Isaïe 2,1-5 et les rédacteurs du livre d'Isaïe', *ZAW* 105 (1993), 98–102.

[18] Cf. Ehrlich, 10; Budde; Cazelles, 'Qui aurait visé?', 418; Wiklander, 70–71; L. A. Snijders, H. Ringgren and H.-J. Fabry, *ThWAT* v. 281–91 = *TDOT* ix. 261–70; Schwartz, 'Torah from Zion' (who, however, renders 'will see it', which is even less closely related to 'shine'; his arguments against 'stream' are unusually weak).

[19] There seems to be even less to be said for the suggestion of G. R. Driver, 'Notes on the Psalms', *JTS* 44 (1943), 12–23 (14–15), who proceeds from a consideration of a base *hrr* to propose 'come in noisy excitement'.

it is absent from the parallel in v. 4, and it is thought to make רבים in the second half of the line anti-climactic (e.g. Gray). Neither argument seems compelling, however; it could as well be argued that we expect some sort of equivalent for רבים in the parallel half, and any argument to justify its later insertion could as well apply to the original Isaianic redactor. Again, there is nothing in any of these differences to warrant emendation of either form of the text.

3. לכו ונעלה: for this common construction (imperative + simple *waw* + cohortative), see Gibson, 106–7; but cf. WO, 653–54.

אל הר־יהוה: lacking in 1QIsa[a], a simple enough case of scribal parablepsis.[20] The versions and the parallel in Micah all support the MT. Is it possible that a correction of a 1QIsa[a] text type lies somewhere behind the expansion in the LXX of v. 2?

אל־בית: Micah and 4QIsa[e] ואל; LXX, P and V also have the conjunction here, but this may be no more than an *ad sensum* rendering.

וירנו: 1QIsa[a] has the plural, וירונו, and this seems also to be presupposed by LXX Micah: καὶ δείξουσιν. Both the context and in particular the suffixes on the nouns following show that this cannot be correct; it may have been the consequence of misunderstanding where a supralinear *waw* should be added in the course of developing fuller orthography (cf. Isaiah וירנו and Micah and 4QIsa[e] ויורנו) or alternatively it may be due to metathesis in the fuller form. Either way it is likely to have arisen by error from the form of text attested in MT Micah and 4QIsa[e] rather than MT Isaiah.[21]

מדרכיו: partitive מן, see the comments below. LXX does not offer a rendering of it (similarly V), translates 'his ways' in the singular and then merely has a pronoun in place of 'his paths'. It is not legitimate to isolate only one element of this as a basis for reconstructing a hypothetical 'first edition' of the text (*contra* Cazelles, 'Qui aurait visé?', 419).

ונלכה בארחתיו: it appears that the first hand in 1QIsa[a] deliberately omitted these words for some reason, but left a space for them to be supplied. They were then added later (by a different scribe?) in smaller letters and intruding into the margin, in the form ונאלכה באורחתיו (for the spelling, cf. Kutscher, 20 and 162). Sometimes this may have happened where there is reason to suppose that the scribe could not understand the text he was copying (e.g. at 40.20), but that hardly applies in the present instance; presumably, the version he was copying was slightly damaged at this point.

ארחתיו: vocalization with initial *ḥolem* is common (e.g. 3.12; see too 1QIsa[a]'s *plene* spelling); it does not therefore seem necessary to revocalize to the (to us) expected form אֹרְ in order to avoid confusion with אֹרְחָה, 'caravan' (*contra* Budde; Renaud, *Formation*, 152).

4. הגוים...עמים רבים: see on 2-3 above. At the end of this line, MT Micah adds עד־רחוק, and a rendering of this appears also in P Isaiah (another clear example of P's tendency to equalize these two parallel texts). For reasons of line length, it is usually agreed that the addition in Micah is secondary. Hillers, *Micah*, 50, however, conjectures in the light of 5.26; Jer. 5.15; 23.23; 31.10; and Joel 4.8 that MT Micah represents a conflation of the variant readings גוים עצומים and גוים עד־רחוק. This is not convincing, however, in view of the use of עד; the parallels adduced all have מן (as expected) except for Joel, which has no preposition.

---

[20] Pulikottil, 144–45, argues that this and the reading וירונו in the next line are part of a deliberate interpretive change by the scroll's scribe. But he fails to note that וירונו appears also to be presupposed by LXX Micah, and he is also at fault in assuming that חצא has past reference, 'has departed/proceeded', even though the scroll is identical with MT at that point.

[21] J. A. Wagenaar, *Judgement and Salvation: The Composition and Redaction of Micah 2–5* (VTSup 85, Leiden, 2001), 136, suggests as an alternative explanation that the translators of Micah 'probably wanted to avoid an anthropomorphic image of God and, therefore, inserted an impersonal subject: "they (the inhabitants of Zion?) will show us…"'. However, since this seems to be an isolated reading, not carried through even into the next verse ('he will judge…'), an error in the *Vorlage*, with a text such as 1QIsa[a], seems more likely.

להוכיח ל: the scribe of 1QIsaᵃ wrote the initial הה at the end of a line, and then להוכיח בין at the start of the next. בין was subsequently deleted, and ל (= MT) added supralinearly before עמים. It is impossible now to say whether the first hand represents a genuine variant or a simple scribal error under the influence of the first half of the line.

חרבותם: Micah has חרבתיהם (cf. GK §91n), which Renaud, *Formation*, 153, for instance, prefers because of the parallel with חניתתיהם. But it could as easily be argued that the change is secondary in Micah, due precisely to a desire to introduce ever closer parallelism (Zapff, *Studien*, 72); see on ישא below. 1QIsaᵃ's addition of the prose particle את is obviously secondary.

אתים: the identification of this agricultural implement is uncertain. The traditional 'ploughshares' has a long and impressive history: LXX: ἄροτρον, 'plough', α: ἐχέτλη, 'plough-handle'; better still V *vomer*, 'ploughshare', and P *shy pdn᾽*, 'ploughshare'. If the word is cognate with Akkadian *ittû*, 'seed-funnel (on a seeder-plough)',[22] then the case is clearly strong. T's סיכי is less clear, since as well as 'ploughshare' the word can also refer to a spade. This alternative approach, apparently followed by Kimhi, who links the word with the verb חפר, has been favoured by some because it is thought to suit better the other few occasions where the word occurs. Micah 4.3 and Joel 4.10 are, of course, closely related to our passage, and so cannot help us further; equally, the suggested occurrence at 2 Kgs 6.5 (את־הברזל) is uncertain; it may be no more than the object marker, though if it is an example of our noun, it presumably means 'axe'. At 1 Sam. 13.20-21, however, the word occurs twice in a list of implements which the Israelites used to take to be sharpened by the Philistines, and in each case it follows מחרשת, which on the basis of the familiar root חרש clearly has something to do with ploughing (noted already by Gesenius, Dillmann and others). Now, since the context there of sharpening and here of turning swords into this implement indicates that metal is in view, and since most of the plough was made of wood, it is difficult to see how both these words could refer to different parts of the plough (AV's 'share' and 'coulter'[23] an anachronistic attempt to circumvent this difficulty). Thus, if מחרשת refers to the ploughshare (the only metal part of the plough, and certainly the only one which would need sharpening), את must refer to something else. Beyond that conclusion, we are reduced more or less to guesswork. 'Axe' is unlikely (despite 2 Kgs 6.5), since at 1 Samuel 13 the list includes קרדם, and Jer. 46.22 and Ps. 74.5 suggest that this is an axe. 'Mattock' or 'hoe' is therefore often preferred;[24] it may well be what T had in mind, and it forms a suitable parallel to מזמרה (cf. NEB, REB). Since 'mattock' is unfamiliar to most English readers, I have chosen 'hoe' (cf. GNB at 1 Sam., but curiously not here); it is not the same, however, as the modern form of garden hoe.

ישא: Micah has the plural ישאו; grammatically, either is possible; cf. GK §145c. As already seen above, Micah seems to prefer closer parallelism (cf. [ו]ילמדו).

5. LXX's καὶ νῦν at the start of the verse (which may go back to a *Vorlage* which included ועתה) is not strong enough evidence for emendation, but it demonstrates a fine awareness of the function of this verse in the wider context, following the באחרית הימים of v. 2 (Budde); see further below.

A new literary unit clearly begins with v. 2, following the heading (however understood) in v. 1, and the usual view is that it ends at v. 4. Verses 6ff. are a separate unit, and the two have been redactionally joined by v. 5, which has links with both what precedes and what follows. There is a sense, therefore, in which v. 5 could equally well be construed as the introduction to the following unit (as stressed in particular by Sweeney),

---

[22] *CDA*, 137; see further B. Landsberger, 'Corrections to the Article "An Old Babylonian Charm against *merḫu*"' *JNES* 17 (1958), 56–58 (56).

[23] 'A vertical cutting blade fixed in front of a ploughshare' (*Concise Oxford Dictionary*), from Old French; cf. Rashi's קולטרי״ש, which no doubt influenced the translators of AV.

[24] S. T. Byington, 'Plow and Pick', *JBL* 68 (1949), 49–54.

as it apparently is in 1QIsa^a.[25] In view of the process of composition outlined below, however, it should strictly be taken in isolation. Its inclusion here with vv. 2-4 is partly a matter of convenience, but also an indication that it was added at the same time (and probably by the same editor) as 2-4 were put in their present setting.

Roberts, however, has argued that vv. 2-22 (minus some later minor expansions) form a single coherent unit.[26] To the extent that v. 5 should be regarded as a conscious literary join there is an important insight to be gained from this, but it does not follow that the chapter was originally conceived and written as a single whole. If the different dates ascribed below to the main units are broadly correct, then obviously Roberts cannot be right. At this point, let it suffice to observe that his main argument—from the identity of 'the house of Jacob' in vv. 5-6—is not strong. He maintains that Isaiah himself only ever used 'Jacob' to refer to the northern kingdom,[27] and he deduces from this that v. 5 'offers an invitation to the northern kingdom to come and share in this future that Yahweh was creating'. Then v. 6 (where he construes the phrase as a vocative) introduces the lengthy description of the religious defection of the north. All this fits best, he thinks, with a setting in the time of the Syro-Ephraimite war. The difficulties with this view include the facts that in v. 5 the writer seems to include himself in the house of Jacob ('let us walk'), which could not be true of Isaiah if the northern kingdom were in view, and that the name Jacob there seems clearly to depend in part upon the use of the same name in v. 3 ('the house of the God of Jacob'), where it does not refer exclusively to the God of the northern kingdom but to the God whose temple was in Jerusalem, and so to the two kingdoms together at best; see further Sweeney, 'Structure and Redaction', and the comments *ad loc.* below.

Following the introductory ch. 1, vv. 2-4 have clearly been given a prominent setting in the book as a whole, and indeed a case can be made for the suggestion that they once stood at the very start of the book at an earlier point in its growth. This importance is confirmed by the fact that their major themes are echoed later on, especially in the second half of the book. They outline a vision of the ideal Zion as the centre of God's peace-promoting rule of the whole earth, a vision from which present reality falls far short (as the transition of v. 5 to what follows makes clear; see too on vv. 6-22 below for the connections between the two passages by way of contrasts) but which is never withdrawn or denied, and towards the realization of which many of the more hopeful passages in the book are designed to contribute.

Some verbal and thematic links with ch. 1 have also been observed, such as 'Zion' (1.8, 27), 'sword' (1.20), משפט (six occurrences, compared

---

[25] Cf. Olley, 'Hear the Word of Y$_{HWH}$', esp. 45–46; Steck, *Die erste Jesajarolle.*

[26] Roberts, 'Isaiah 2'; see too Kissane; Cazelles, 'Qui aurait visé?', does not explicitly address this issue, but he thinks that both main parts of the chapter originally referred to the time of the Syro-Ephraimite invasion, and that both were subjected to the same process of later redaction by Deutero-Isaiah.

[27] See too Davidson, 'Interpretation'; Høgenhaven, 17.

with שפט in 2.4), למד (1.17), and the link between כבראשנה (1.26) and ראש
in 2.2, as well as its contrast with באחרית הימים.[28] These are trivial, however, and do not allow any conclusions about composition (or hardly even
for exegesis) to be drawn. Somewhat more striking is the paralleling of
'Torah' and 'the word of the Lord' in 1.10 and 2.3, the only two places in
the book where this occurs. Synchronic consequences were noted at 1.10.
At this point, however, it is worth remembering that there is a strong case
for regarding 1.10 as one of the clearest examples of redactional writing in
ch. 1, on the basis of other elements in the verse. If the compiler of ch. 1
already knew of 2.2-4 in its present setting, it would fit extremely well
with the case argued there that he should have drawn these elements of the
verse from 2.3; the evidence does not favour any suggestion that 2.2-4 was
positioned (still less composed) with knowledge of an already existing
ch. 1.

The passage is straightforward from a poetic point of view, and requires
little comment.[29] Once the first three words of v. 2[30] and ואמרו (and לכו?) in
v. 3 are discounted (being, as often, in anacrusis), the remainder is of
regular line length or rhythm, with just a few exceptions. The last line of
v. 4 is slightly longer than the remainder, and we have seen that poetic
units often vary the length or structure of their last line in order to impart a
sense of closure. Similarly, 3b is shorter (2 + 2), which may help to mark
the end of the speech of the nations which began in the previous line.
Finally, the opening of the poem proper is a repeated 2 + 2 (contrast the
parallel in Micah), which Wildberger imaginatively explains as an attempt
to get the reader anxious about what is to follow. It may not be necessary
to follow him in this to recognize that it forms a reasonable framework to
the poem as a whole with the lengthened last line of v. 4. Verse 5, by
contrast, is a prose redactional addition.

The structure of the passage has been analysed in detail by Magonet,
'Isaiah's Mountain'. He seeks to show, primarily on the basis of word
repetition, that it falls into seven 'chiastically' arranged sections, with the
central, fourth element being v. 3b (noted already above as marked out by
virtue of its being shorter). He finds in this pattern a reflection of the
thought of the passage which focuses on upward movement in its first
half, and movement out or down in the second. This is broadly convincing
(even if some points of detail are questionable), and ties in with what
others have observed with less precision, namely that the first half of the
poem is dominated by movement to Zion, while the second half (starting
from 3c) reflects movement out from Zion.

Critical discussion of this passage has concentrated on the closely interrelated questions of its date and its relationship with the parallel passage in
Micah. The question of date, in turn, naturally spills over into a tradition-

[28] Cf. Zapff, *Studien*, 67; Leclerc, 48.
[29] See further Wildberger; Bartelt, 231–37; Willis, 'Isaiah 2:2-5'. In my opinion, it is a
weakness that Bartelt's elaborate analysis includes adopting the variant word order from
Micah in v. 2.
[30] Differently H. W. M. van Grol, 'Paired Tricola in the Psalms, Isaiah and Jeremiah',
JSOT 25 (1983), 55–73.

historical analysis. Any reasonably circumscribed survey of these issues is thus bound to oversimplify some scholars' positions as well as to be selective in the citation of secondary literature.[31]

Broadly speaking, there are five main views which are currently held about the origins of the passage. (i) Isaianic authorship has been most staunchly defended in recent times by Wildberger. Most of those who have followed him have added little to his arguments,[32] but his traditio-historical analysis has been supported with much greater detail by Willis ('Isaiah 2:2-5'). (ii) A smaller group of scholars (most notably Vermeylen, who associates the passage with Josiah's reform) proposes that while the passage is later than Isaiah, it is nevertheless pre-exilic in date.[33] (iii) An early post-exilic date[34] or (iv) a later post-exilic date (without more precise agreement)[35] remains the majority opinion. Finally, (v) as already indicated, Cazelles has advanced a two-stage theory of development: a genuine oracle of Isaiah, originally directed towards the northern kingdom, was reworked into its present form by Deutero-Isaiah. Although his arguments for an early date have had considerable influence on scholars such as Roberts and Høgenhaven, none has followed him in detail. Indeed, it is noteworthy that his literary-critical division proper is based entirely on vv. 6-22; his discussion of 2-4 follows and presupposes this, and is concerned more with *relecture* and the textual variations by comparison with Micah.

There are three main ways in which one may seek to steer a path through this welter of conflicting opinions:[36] traditio-historical analysis, comparison with other passages which express similar ideas and apparent citations of or references to this text in others. None, of course, can be claimed to be conclusive; the direction of citations is sometimes disputed, for instance, and the assumption that tradition history is unilinear is always

---

[31] For surveys of research (including those who have taken the additional views that the oracle was borrowed from Micah by Isaiah, or that it was borrowed by both from some earlier source), see Wildberger; Vermeylen, 114–17. Cazelles, 'Qui aurait visé?', 409, gives a long list of scholars who have held the various possible opinions.

[32] E.g. Jensen, *The Use of* tôrâ, 85–89; Høgenhaven, 109–11; D. Elgavish, 'The Vision of the Temple Mount', *BethM* 38 (1993), 193–205 (Hebrew), though for a somewhat different approach to the same end, see F. Deist, 'Idealistic *Theologiegeschichte*, Ideology Critique and the Dating of Oracles of Salvation: Posing a Question Concerning the Monopoly of an Accepted Method', *OTWSA* 22–23 (1979–80), 53–78. A brief attempt to defend an early date on rhetorical grounds is offered by Gitay, 39–41. Among earlier scholars within the critical period, particular mention may be made of Duhm, Procksch and Fischer.

[33] Cf. Vermeylen, 114–33; Auvray; Wiklander.

[34] E.g. Gray; Wolff, *Micha*, 87–89 = *Micah*, 117–18; Steck, 69–71; Werner, *Eschatologische Texte*, 151–63; Sweeney, *Isaiah 1–4*, 164–74; *idem*, 'Micah's Debate with Isaiah'.

[35] E.g. Kaiser; Clements; Renaud, *Formation*, 160–81; McKane, *Micah*, 126.

[36] See too especially Sweeney, *Isaiah 1–4*, 164–74; much of the following discussion is in agreement with his analysis. The argument from language is unfortunately inconclusive, and so cannot be used in support of any particular position; cf. E. Cannawurf, 'The Authenticity of Micah iv 1-4', *VT* 11 (1961), 26–33. The fullest presentation of the data is Vermeylen, 121–26; see too Wildberger, 'Völkerwallfahrt', 72–75.

open to the charge of evolutionism in its worst sense. Nevertheless, the case gains strength in the present instance by the fact that the three lines of evidence seem to converge independently, so that they may be regarded as cumulative and mutually supporting.

First, there need be no doubt that the passage stands squarely within the Zion tradition complex. Willis, 'Isaiah 2:2-5', details nine themes which the poem has in common with the Psalms of Zion, which for his purposes he defines as Pss. 9–10; 46; 48; 66; 67; 68; 76; 78; 84; 86; 87; 122; 132; 137; some of these comparisons will be referred to in the comments below. Wildberger, in particular, used these sorts of comparison to argue that there need therefore be no objection to Isaianic authorship. However, apart from the obvious difficulties of building an argument on the basis of psalms, many of which are themselves of uncertain date,[37] and of the fact that there is nothing in this positively to establish an eighth-century date, there are some significant differences between the two bodies of material which seem clearly to point to a later date in the development of the tradition for the Isaiah passage (see too Sweeney, 'Structure and Redaction').

(i) In contrast with the Psalms, the nations here come to Zion in peace and of their own accord, not in order to attack Jerusalem. The aggressive stance of the nations is ubiquitous in the relevant psalms, and it is extremely odd that neither Wildberger nor Willis draws attention to this distinction.[38] Indeed, Willis further includes what he sees as parallels in the idea of the nations 'streaming' to Jerusalem (v. 2) with references to river imagery in the songs of Zion and related passages. Some of these are not related to the use of the theme in our passage at all, however, such as 'the river whose streams make glad the city of God' (Ps. 46.5 [4]), or the living waters which will one day flow out from the Jerusalem temple (Ezek. 47.1-12; Joel 4.18; Zech. 14.8). Where a closer relationship is apparent, the contrast already mentioned is further underlined. He mentions Isa. 8.7; 17.12-14 and Ps. 46.3-4 and 7 (2-3 and 6) as places where 'the attack of foreign nations on Zion' is compared with 'a rampaging, violent, flooding river, which only Yahweh is able to repulse by his invincible power'. With that summary there need be no quarrel, but the fact that the theme is used in 2.2 in such a diametrically opposite way should also be underlined. To equate the peaceful pilgrimage of the nations[39] with their military advance on Jerusalem is clearly unjustified.

[37] For the sake of the present discussion, an early date for the psalms of Zion may be assumed; if they are late, then of course Wildberger's argument collapses in any case. For major discussions of this controversial topic, see J. Schreiner, *Sion-Jerusalem Jahwes Königssitz: Theologie der Heiligen Stadt im Alten Testament* (Munich, 1963); G. Wanke, *Die Zionstheologie der Korachiten in ihrem Traditionsgeschichtlichen Zusammenhang* (BZAW 97; Berlin, 1966); H.-M. Lutz, *Jahwe, Jerusalem und die Völker: Zur Vorgeschichte von Sach 12,1-8 und 14,1-5* (WMANT 27; Neukirchen–Vluyn, 1968).

[38] Wildberger's attempt to deflect this criticism by reference to what he regards as a different motif reflected in Ps. 76.11-12 can hardly be sustained in the light of the context presented by the psalm as a whole.

[39] Schwartz, 'Torah from Zion', objects to the label 'pilgrimage' because the vocabulary here is different from the normal vocabulary of pilgrimage and because there is no suggestion of the nations coming to worship or of attendance at a festival. Instead, he

The two may be related, but if so it must be in terms of development from the latter to the former.

(ii) The theme of disarmament is similar. Here, this is undertaken voluntarily by the nations in response to God's instruction and arbitration; there will then be no further need for armed conflict. In the relevant psalms, however, the nations who are attacking Jerusalem are forcibly disarmed by God's superior power (Willis refers for this to Isa. 9.3-4 [4-5]; Pss. 46.10 [9]; 76.3-4, 6-7 [2-3, 5-6]; and 20 2-3, 7-9 [1-2, 6-8]). The difference is again of the sort which allows us to agree that there may be a connection in the long tradition history relating to Zion, but that there must have been development from one to the other. The fact that here again there are parallels within Isaiah itself for the earlier concept helps to reinforce the impression that 2.2-4 must be later.

(iii) Finally, in our passage the nations come willingly in order to be instructed by God, whereas in the psalms of Zion they submit to him in fear (e.g. Pss. 46.9-12 [8-11]; 48.5-11 [4-10], etc.).

It is this total reversal in the overall atmosphere of the Zion Psalms which makes it so difficult to date the passage as early as the time of Isaiah, for although the prophet was undoubtedly capable of making creative use of the traditions which he may have inherited, there is no parallel for these reversals in other passages which may be reasonably ascribed to him (indeed, we have seen that there are examples where he precisely does not introduce such a reversal), nor is there any evidence that such novel ideas were picked up or developed by anyone else within more than a century of his lifetime. The traditio-historical argument requires us to allow time for significant development, and so points towards a date for this passage considerably later than Isaiah.[40]

Secondly, the general theme and outlook of the passage first find their closest parallels in material from the late exilic and early post-exilic periods, such as Isa. 40–55; 56.6-8; 60; 66.18-21; Jer. 3.17;[41] Hag. 2.7-9; Zech. 2.14-16; 8.20-23. (It may also be observed that the raising up of Mount Zion is found in Ezek. 40.2; see further below.) That is why a similar date is frequently sought for our passage as well. It should be noted, however, that there are some slight distinctions within otherwise general agreement which ought also to be taken into account. No reference is made here, for instance, to the idea that the nations are to be joined with Israel, nor is any interest shown in the notion that the nations will bring gifts and sacrifices. (The lack of reference to their assistance in bringing

stresses the judicial purpose of the visit, a universalizing, in effect, of the law of the High Court of Arbitration of Deut. 17.8-11. While his positive points are clearly correct (see on v. 3 below), the temple is nevertheless mentioned first as the goal of the nations' journey. It is also noteworthy that, unlike in Deut. 17, the desire for instruction here precedes the need for arbitration. I retain the language of 'pilgrimage' out of convention and convenience alone.

[40] Cf. Herrmann, *Die prophetischen Heilserwartungen*, 141–44; Steck, *Friedensvorstellungen*, 69–71.

[41] On this, see especially J. G. McConville, *Judgment and Promise: An Interpretation of the Book of Jeremiah* (Leicester, 1993), 47–48, with an interesting sideglance at 2 Kgs 17.27-28 which, he suggests, may be a parody of Isa. 2.2-4.

back the dispersed Israelites may be less significant, given the present literary setting of the passage.) Both these ideas feature prominently in the passages just listed which are of definitely post-exilic date, so that the possibility should be left open that ours stands early, if not as the first, among this collection.[42] It would not be difficult to see how such ideas might have developed from it.

Finally, attention must be paid to the evidence of apparent citations. (i) At Zech. 8.20-23 there seems to be a clear allusion to our passage. As Renaud has pointed out,[43] the expressions עמים רבים and גוים עצומים occur together only in the Micah version of our passage. The peoples' desire to 'entreat the favour of the Lord' and to 'seek' him are like their stated desire to be taught by him in both forms of the oracle, and in addition the word נלכה is prominent in both passages. While all this could, therefore, be the result of knowledge of the passage in Micah alone, the conclusion of Zech 8.23 with the confession that 'God is with you' looks as though account is being taken of Isa. 7.14; 8.8, 10. This suggests that Zechariah 8 was dependent on the Isaiah tradition as well, and it further precludes the possibility that Isaiah/Micah was dependent on Zechariah. It is possible that the slightly curious עוד of Zech. 8.20 is a conscious acknowledgment of this fact.

(ii) It is probable that 2 Kgs 19.31/Isa. 37.32 has been modelled on Isa. 2.3. They share the same syntactical structure, and some vocabulary elements, and since the verse continues with an apparent citation of Isa. 9.6 ('The zeal of the Lord of Hosts will do this'), it looks as though it is the Kings/Isaiah passage which is dependent on 2.3 rather than the reverse (see Sweeney, *Isaiah 1–4*, 170–71). While this conclusion is compatible with the general direction of our discussion, the uncertainties surrounding the date of the Kings/Isaiah passage preclude the drawing of more specific consequences.[44]

(iii) Both Fishbane[45] and Sommer[46] have made a case for the dependence of Isaiah 60 on 2.2-4. To the general similarity of overall theme, already noted, they draw attention to what they regard as a particularly dense cluster of common vocabulary. Indeed, Sommer argues for a somewhat intricate word-play, and is in danger of spoiling his broadly convincing

---

[42] G. von Rad's conclusion points in a similar direction: '*Isa.* lx stands almost exactly half-way between *Isa.* ii and *Hag.* ii'; 'The City on the Hill', in *The Problem of the Hexateuch and Other Essays* (Edinburgh and London, 1966), 232–42 (241) = 'Die Stadt auf dem Berge', *EvTh* 8 (1948–49), 439–47 (447), repr. *Gesammelte Studien zum Alten Testament* (TBü 8; Munich, 1958), 214–24 (223).

[43] B. Renaud, *Structure et attaches littéraires de Miché iv–v* (Paris, 1964), 73; see too W. Rudolph, *Haggai–Sacharja 1–8– Sacharja 9–14–Maleachi* (KAT 13/4; Gütersloh, 1976), 152; D. L. Petersen, *Haggai and Zechariah 1–8: A Commentary* (OTL; London, 1984), 317; Rudman, 'Zechariah 8:20-22'.

[44] It may be observed here that the same is true of the reversal of 2.4 in Joel 4.10, both because of the uncertain date of the book of Joel, and because there is no indication of whether Joel knew the passage from Isaiah or from Micah.

[45] M. Fishbane, *Biblical Interpretation in Ancient Israel* (Oxford, 1985), 498.

[46] B. D. Sommer, *A Prophet Reads Scripture: Allusion in Isaiah 40–66* (Stanford, 1998), 80–82.

case by over-subtlety. Nevertheless, while this passage falls far short of citation proper, it may be considered to be a literary allusion. In such a case, the dependence of Isaiah 60, rather than the reverse, is clear.

(iv) Among the many possible allusions to our passage in Deutero-Isaiah,[47] the most striking is without doubt the virtual citation at 51.4, 'for a law will go forth from me (כי תורה מאתי תצא) and my justice for a light to the peoples'; cf. 2.3, כי מציון תצא תורה. While this has been noted before, it has not generally been observed that there is a further allusion in the continuation of the passage, where we read that 'my arms will rule/judge (שפט) the peoples', which draws on the wording of 2.4. This being so, we may conclude that Deutero-Isaiah was dependent upon our passage at this point.[48]

Having examined the evidence for time of origin for our passage from three different angles (tradition history, other passages which express similar ideas and citations/allusions), it may be concluded that they all point to the late exilic period as the most likely date for its composition. The citation in Isa. 51.4 is probably the nearest *terminus ad quem*.

A final matter requiring introductory discussion is the evidence to be gleaned from a comparative study of the continuation of the parallel passages in Isaiah and Micah.[49] Following the material which both books share in common, Mic. 4.4 includes an additional two lines (on the extension of this in Mic. 4.5, see the comments on v. 5 below):

> but they shall sit every man under his vine
> and under his fig tree, with none to make them afraid;
> for the mouth of the Lord of Hosts has spoken.

The case has been urged in the past on both strophic[50] and thematic[51] grounds for regarding these lines as an integral and original part of the passage. Even more significant, in my opinion, are the generally overlooked indications that these lines show close affinity with the Isaiah tradition in ways which set them apart from the rest of the book of Micah. The

[47] R. J. Clifford, *Fair Spoken and Persuading: An Interpretation of Second Isaiah* (New York, 1984), 46 n. 8, speaks of 2.1-5 as 'a text mined more than once by Second Isaiah'. Gray wrote long ago that 'The standpoint is substantially that of chs. 40–55'. See, for instance, the nations' desire for God's *tôrâ* at 42.4, the 'establishment' (כון) of Zion at 54.14, and her position as the site of God's self-revelation as presupposed at 40.9 and 51.3-4.

[48] Those who date Isa. 2.2-4 later than Deutero-Isaiah do not generally mention this argument. Sweeney, *Isaiah 1–4*, 173, sees its force all too well, and so attempts to argue that the dependence is the other way round. I have examined his arguments in detail in *Book*, 150–52, and argued that they are not convincing; see too Sommer, *A Prophet Reads Scripture*, 79–80 and 242–44.

[49] For an extensive survey of opinions and discussion of various aspects of the parallel passages, see, in addition to some of the literature already cited, R. L. Schultz, *The Search for Quotation: Verbal Parallels in the Prophets* (JSOTSup 180; Sheffield, 1999), 290–307; more recently, Sweeney, 'Micah's Debate with Isaiah'.

[50] See Marti and Gray.

[51] See Wildberger, 'Völkerwallfahrt', 75–76; Rudolph, *Micha*, 80–81 (above, n. 13); Kaiser (hesitantly); J. L. Mays, *Micah: A Commentary* (OTL; London, 1976), 98; L. C. Allen, *The Books of Joel, Obadiah, Jonah and Micah* (NICOT; Grand Rapids, 1976), 244.

last line, כִּי־פִי יְהוָה צְבָאוֹת דִּבֵּר, uses a form of reference to divine speech
which occurs nowhere else in the Hebrew Bible outside the book of
Isaiah; cf. 1.2, 20; 40.5; 58.14 (see the comments on 1.2-3 above). Moreover, whereas the first part of the verse reproduces a stereotypical vision
of peace, it continues with a phrase, וְאֵין מַחֲרִיד, which recurs at Isa. 17.2
(and elsewhere too, admittedly), but never in Micah. Finally, the divine
title יְהוָה צְבָאוֹת also comes nowhere else in Micah, but it is very common
in Isaiah (see on 1.9). It therefore looks as though this passage (including
Mic. 4.4) may have developed within the circles which were responsible
for the preservation and development of the Isaiah tradition,[52] a setting in
which, of course, its focus on Zion was very much at home. The links with
2.6-22 (see below) also find their most natural explanation on this
hypothesis, and it may further help account for the otherwise surprising
initial conjunction (וְהָיָה). From such a setting it could have found its way
both into its present location in Isaiah and into the exilic/post-exilic
edition of Micah.

Why, then, is Mic. 4.4 not also preserved in Isaiah? It may be suggested that it is the result of a procedure which we shall see repeated
elsewhere (e.g. at 5.25-30 and 8.21-23) of the late exilic redactor of Isaiah
moving material which he inherited to a new position for perfectly intelligible reasons of his own, and including a brief addition of his own (2.5)
in order to underline the purpose for which he included the material in its
new position. It was during this process of selection that the material now
found in Mic. 4.4 was dropped.

2. *In a future time* (בְּאַחֲרִית הַיָּמִים): this phrase occurs thirteen times in the
Hebrew Bible.[53] Although it was understood from early times (cf. LXX) to
have technically eschatological force, this is likely to have reflected the
influence of the meaning which it developed in apocalyptic literature (as
in the occurrences in Daniel). It is now generally agreed (against some
earlier interpreters[54]) that this is not the case in the majority of Old Testament occurrences.

On its own, אַחֲרִית is an abstract noun, referring to 'that which comes
after'; from this, contextual analysis shows that it may have derived or
developed nuances of what results from something, such as future, poster-
ity, remnant, end (not chronological, but with reference to an outcome);[55]
in other words, 'after' may be understood either temporally or logically.

---

[52] This is not to deny that there are also close contextual links between the poem
and Micah, as stressed in particular by L. Schwienhorst-Schönberger, 'Zion—Ort der
Tora: Überlegungen zu Mi 4,1-3', in F. Hahn *et al.*, *Zion, Ort der Begegnung: Festschrift
für Laurentius Klein zur Vollendung des 65. Lebensjahres* (BBB 90; Bodenheim, 1993),
107–25, but a consideration of that would take us beyond our current concerns; see, for
instance, Zapff, *Studien*, 64–77.

[53] Gen. 49.1; Num. 24.14; Deut. 4.30; 31.29; Isa. 2.2; Jer. 23.20; 30.24; 48.47; 49.39;
Ezek. 38.16; Hos. 3.5; Mic. 4.1; Dan. 10.14. The Aramaic equivalent occurs at Dan. 2.28.

[54] See especially W. Staerk, 'Der Gebrauch der Wendung בְּאַחֲרִית הַיָּמִים im at. Kanon',
ZAW 11 (1891), 247–53.

[55] Cf. H. Seebass, *ThWAT* i. 224–28 = *TDOT* i. 207–12.

In the combination found in our phrase, as in the close Akkadian parallel *ina/ana aḫ-ri-a-at ūmī*, it may refer simply to the following time, the future. At Deut. 31.29, for instance, it looks forward to the disasters which will overtake Israel because of their apostasy, something which from the standpoint of the writer was certainly already an at least partial reality. DeVries finds that the same applies to quite a number of the occurrences, and calls them a 'sham future, that is, one that is presented as remotely future but is actually present or past in the speaker's experience'.[56] Even if we do not go as far as this, or include so many passages under this heading, it is nevertheless clear that the future of our phrase may be strongly continuous with the present, without strictly eschatological significance.[57]

The use and context of the phrase in our verse (and Mic. 4.1; see too Ezek. 38.16) suggest that it stands midway in the development from the earlier, neutral to the later, apocalyptic sense. Pointing towards the latter is the fact that only here is the phrase elevated into an independent, formulaic heading, that what follows announces 'a permanent new condition, rather than a unitary historical event' (DeVries, 91), that the future will include certain changes which are strongly discontinuous with the present and that no future beyond this new state can be envisaged.[58] On the other hand, it is not eschatological in the narrow sense of referring to 'the end', since there also remains a clear continuity with the present world of Israel, Zion, temple and the nations.

In the light of this, it seems that there is no justification for translating 'in the remote/distant future', since this implies a timescale to which there is no allusion. Similarly, 'in the last days' is in danger of implying that an eschatological end will soon follow. Rather, the emphasis is on the end of the days as they are currently experienced, characterized by enmity and war, and so especially on the transition to a new era or phase of history.[59] I am not aware of a satisfactory way of rendering this into English on the

[56] DeVries, *From Old Revelation to New*, 89. He refers in particular to E. Lipiński, 'באחרית הימים dans les textes préexiliques', *VT* 20 (1970), 445–50; see too G. W. Buchanan, 'Eschatology and the "End of Days"', *JNES* 20 (1961), 188–93; A. S. Kapelrud, 'Eschatology in the Book of Micah', *VT* 11 (1961), 392–405 (395–96); H. Kosmala, 'At the End of the Days', *ASTI* 2 (1963), 27–37; E. Jenni, *THAT* i. 114–18 = *TLOT* i. 86–88; F. Sedlmeier, 'Die Universalisierung der Heilshoffnung nach Micha 4, 1-5', *TTZ* 107 (1998), 62–81.

[57] Cf. S. Talmon, 'The Signification of אחרית and אחרית הימים in the Hebrew Bible', in S. M. Paul *et al.* (eds), *Emanuel: Studies in Hebrew Bible, Septuagint and Dead Sea Scrolls in Honor of Emanuel Tov* (VTSup 94; Leiden, 2003), 795–810; B. Becking, 'Expectations about the End of Time in the Hebrew Bible: Do they Exist?', in C. Rowland and J. Barton (eds), *Apocalyptic in History and Tradition* (JSPSup 43; Sheffield, 2002), 44–59.

[58] Cf. S. R. Driver's frequently cited definition: 'the final period of the future so far as it falls within the range of the speaker's perspective. The sense attaching to it is thus relative, not absolute, varying with the context'; *A Critical and Exegetical Commentary on Deuteronomy* (ICC; 3rd edn; Edinburgh, 1902), 74.

[59] A strictly synchronic path to the same conclusion may be reached by linking 'days' here with the days of 1.1. What is described will take place after or beyond the days envisaged as being covered by the book; cf. van Wieringen, 'Day Beyond the Days'.

basis of a one-to-one equivalence. *In a future time* is an admittedly unsatisfactory attempt at a dynamic equivalent, from which no conclusions should be drawn which extend beyond the preceding comments.

The mountain of the Lord: as is clear from frequent passages in the psalms and elsewhere, this is a reference to the temple mount (see already the interpretative addition in MT), regarded as God's dwelling place, and elsewhere often named Zion;[60] see especially, for instance, Ps. 68.17 (16): 'the mount that God desired for his abode, where the Lord will reside for ever'; cf. Pss. 74.2; 76: 3 (2); 132.13, etc. (for further references, see Willis, 'Isaiah 2:2-5', 296–97). Isaiah too, and those who followed him, shared this belief (e.g. 8.18).

There was a widespread dogma in the ancient world which associated mountains (and where mountains were lacking, height in general) with proximity to, or representation of, the abode of the gods. Some of the elements by which this was celebrated in older mythology (as known to us best from the Ugaritic texts) were undoubtedly taken over by Israel in her temple worship, as may be clearly seen in Psalms 46 and 48.[61] The present reality was always known to be different, however, for the temple mount was (and is) in reality far less prominent than the adjacent ranges (cf. Ps. 125.2), and similarly the forces of chaos which threatened to overthrow the cosmic mountain as a source of divine order and stability were interpreted in the Psalms of Zion as political enemies who came to attack the city and the sanctuary.

The prophet makes creative use of such language, however, in order to assert that the time is coming when the superiority of Zion's God and his truth will be both seen and acknowledged universally (cf. Calvin; Wildberger; Oswalt), and when the appearance of God's earthly abode, which now failed to correspond with what was believed to be its true nature, will be changed to reflect that present hidden reality (Hillers, *Micah*). Zion, as a microcosm of the created world, was already believed to be *established*, as is clear from, for instance, Ps. 48.9 (8) (cf. 78.69; 87.5; 93.2), and consequently it could never be moved (46.6 [5]) in the face of attack. This passage does not just repeat that thought, as though the participle were the predicate, but builds on it to assert that the mountain will be established *as the head of the mountains*. As discussed in the textual notes, the precise force of this phrase is uncertain, but it seems most probable that it plays on the notion of height (which in any case follows in the parallel) and rank,

---

[60] For arguments that Zion did not originally refer to the temple mount but to the Davidic citadel, see P. J. Leithart, 'Where was Ancient Mount Zion?', *TynB* 53 (2002), 161–75.

[61] Cf. H.-J. Kraus, *Psalms 1–59: A Commentary* (Minneapolis, 1988), 89–92 (with further literature) = *Psalmen 1* (BKAT 15/1; Neukirchen–Vluyn, 1960), lxvi–lxviii; Steck, *Friedensvorstellungen*; Clifford, *Cosmic Mountain*; M. Metzger, 'Himmlische und irdische Wohnstatt Jahwes', *UF* 2 (1970), 139–58. Weinfeld, 'Zion and Jerusalem', esp. 104–14, draws careful distinctions between aspects of this and related beliefs concerning capital cities and their sanctuaries which were common in the ideology of the ancient Near East (going back as far as Sumerian times) and the distinctive ways in which they were developed in this and comparable passages in the prophets.

with the emphasis on the latter: the mountain of the Lord will be supreme, brooking no rival. It is more or less a cultic assertion of monotheism, and as such is a necessary presupposition for the universalism which is to follow.

By setting in parallel the notion that Zion will be *loftier than the hills*, there is certainly a side-long glance at the older notion that the abode of the gods was on the highest of the mountains (alluded to in Pss. 48.2-3 [1-2]; 68.16-19 [15-18]); in the future, the physical inferiority of Zion will be reversed, a notion shared, apparently, by Ezek. 40.2; cf. Zech. 14.10. In the context of the book of Isaiah, however, we must again catch an overtone of the God (or his throne) who is 'high and lifted up (נשא)' (6.1), so that any rival which seeks to make itself lofty—including mountains and hills (2.14)—will be abased. Thus the physical changes are expressive of the complete superiority and supremacy of the God of Zion.

2b-3a. Two traditional elements are here combined creatively to forge a strikingly new vision of the future. On the one hand, Jerusalem was the cult centre *par excellence* for Israelite pilgrimage; although many other centres also attracted pilgrims for a variety of festivals in the pre-exilic period, the effects of cult centralization and the loss of most of the territory of the former kingdoms by the time of the exile meant that Jerusalem alone retained this role in the post-exilic period both for Judeans and for the diaspora. Many of the psalms of various dates as well as other passages attest the aspirations of those who came on such pilgrimages.[62] On the other hand, whenever in earlier texts the foreign nations are drawn into the circle of ideas relating to Zion as God's dwelling place on earth, it is invariably the case, as noted above, that they come in enmity, and they are compared with the chaotic waters which threaten to overwhelm the stability of the established order; see, for instance, Pss. 2.1-3; 46.7 (6); 48.5-8 (4-7); 76.13 (12); Isa. 8.9-10; 17.12-14; Jer. 6.23. In a striking development, however, these two ideas are brought together in extension of the belief that God's just rule will be universally acknowledged to portray the *nations* and *peoples* streaming in peaceful pilgrimage to the sanctuary. For other passages which reflect a similar view and build upon it, see above.

Will stream: see the textual notes. Whichever verb is used here and in Jer. 51.44, it is likely that the two passages are related by means of it, so that there is a further reversal: the nations will no longer stream to Bel and Babylon, once dominant through power but now overthrown by God; rather, they will come to the seat of his authority with the positive desire for his instruction (cf. Gordon, *Holy Land*, 65).

3. *Let us go up* (נעלה): for this mutual encouragement by the nations, cf. Zech. 8.21. עלה is, of course, a common verb, and the obvious one to use in the context of movement towards the now elevated Zion. That it is also

---

[62] For a broad selection of references, see Willis, 'Isaiah 2:2-5', 301–3. On the loose use of the language of 'pilgrimage', see above, n. 39. M. Delcor, 'Sion, centre universel', in *Études bibliques et orientales de religions comparées* (Leiden, 1979), 92–97, even suggests a specific setting for this passage at the Feast of Tabernacles.

used, again quite naturally, as the principal verb for pilgrimage (e.g. Ps. 122.4, Wildberger) should not, therefore, be overpressed. The goal of the journey is *the mountain of the Lord* (as in v. 2), now explicitly defined further as *the house of the God of Jacob*. This divine title does not occur elsewhere in the prophets (apart from the parallel in Micah, though see on 1.24 above), but it is frequent in the Psalms of Zion and others from the same milieu (e.g. 24.6 [emended]; 46.8, 12 [7, 11]; 75.10 [9]; 76.7 [6]; 81.2, 5 [1, 4]; 84.9 [8]; 94.7; 146.5). In many of these passages it is used in contexts which speak of divine protection against enemies, so that its appearance here again underlines the reversal of the earlier motif of enemies coming to attack Jerusalem. It is obvious that it cannot have been an early, pre-Israelite title for the God of Jerusalem; rather, its associations elsewhere (together with the associations of the other divine titles with which it is often used in parallelism, such as 'the Lord of Hosts' [see on 1.9 above]) point strongly to its appropriation from pre-monarchic traditions following the transfer of the ark to the Jerusalem temple (cf. Ps. 132).[63] The fact that Jacob first comes into this passage (and cf. vv. 5-6) by way of this divine title which is so firmly rooted in the Jerusalem cult tradition renders questionable any attempt to argue from it that the original recipients of this oracle were the inhabitants of the northern kingdom.

Of the many reasons why one might undertake a pilgrimage to the sanctuary, only one is mentioned here, namely the search for instruction.[64] The last line of this verse and the first of the next indicate that this relates primarily to the arbitration of major disputes, and for this reason Wildberger argues that the same is therefore referred to in the preceding reference to *his ways* and *his paths*. In support of this, he points to a number of passages where דרך occurs with reference to the 'way' which God opens up for salvation for the one who is falsely accused; the reference is not to instruction for life in general, but to the specific course of action which is required in the immediate context of the dispute. Apart from the questionable interpretation of the significance of 'way' in these psalms,[65] a consideration of the order of the lines here (which Wildberger reverses in his exegesis) suggests that this may be too limited an approach. It is certainly the case that the main focus of the passage is on arbitration, but the presentation suggests that this is only the most prominent outcome of the more general desire to be taught by God. Coming before any other limiting factor, this is certainly what we are led to expect of being taught *his ways*, and as Wildberger himself agrees, this broader usage is equally widely attested in the Psalter, from Ps. 1.6 onwards. Moreoever, the use in parallel with *his paths* (for which Wildberger does not cite any passage to support his case) strengthens the view that this is the most natural interpretation; see, for instance, Pss. 25.4; 27.11; Prov. 3.6.

[63] Cf. Ollenburger, *Zion*, 41–42; Willis, 'Isaiah 2:2-5', 300–1.

[64] See especially Schwartz, 'Torah from Zion', who dissociates this coming for instruction and arbitration from the notion of pilgrimage altogether.

[65] See especially Jensen, *The Use of* tôrâ, 93–94. Jensen further provides a helpful survey of the use of the significant words in this passage, including especially where they appear in combination.

A further pointer in the same direction is the use of מן before דרך, *of his ways*. Most commentators who discuss this agree that the preposition here is partitive;[66] as Gray paraphrases, '*out of* (the treasure of), not *concerning*', and he cites Ps. 94.12[67] and Eccl. 7.10 as parallel examples. The implication is that God's ways are like an extensive storehouse of wisdom and guidance, not all of which can be immediately learnt or applied, but from which the nations wish to be instructed in an appropriate measure. This is then further defined in the following lines. The nations, therefore, express a desire to be taught the right way to live by God, and they demonstrate their sincerity by declaring in advance their intention to follow that out in practice.

For instruction will issue from Zion: the significance of תורה, *instruction*, in this passage and its relationship to the Mosaic Torah has been helpfully clarified by Sweeney in terms of analogy.[68] He points out that in the book as a whole there is a well-known parallel drawn between the first Exodus and the return from the exile in Babylon. In the first Exodus, Israel was given the Torah on Mount Sinai for the regulation of its own life in the land, whereas in the new Exodus God's revelation on Mount Zion is for the regulation of the affairs of the nations, and in particular Israel's relationships within this. In a comparable fashion, Fischer observes a similar balance between the uses of Torah in 1.10 and this verse.

This point may, perhaps, be taken a step further by the force of the parallelism drawn here between *instruction* and *the word of the Lord*. As Weinfeld has pointed out,[69] comparable language appears in Deut. 17.8-13 in connection with decisions reached by the high court of appeal at 'the place which the Lord your God will choose'. In cases relating especially to murder and assault which are too difficult for the local courts, those addressed are to 'go up' (עלה) to this supreme court for a decision, and they are to abide carefully by the Torah and the word which are there handed down. If, as seems reasonable, this comparison holds, then it suggests that this line is narrowing slightly the initially broad range of meaning inherent in *ways* and *paths* to judicial and legal instruction in particular. (This is, of course, fully in line with the continuation of the passage.) It further suggests that we should not define *instruction* in an exclusively 'wisdom' sense, as argued by Jensen, though naturally wisdom is required in deciding such cases; as we have seen previously, it is

---

[66] Wolff, *Micha*, 92 = *Micah*, 121, suggests as an alternative that מן indicates the point of departure; God's ways are the 'origin' of his teaching, and so he translates 'auf Grund' ('on the basis of').

[67] Jensen, *The Use of* Tôrâ, 93 n. 128, states that Gray's 'reference to Ps. 94.16 is probably a typographical error for Ps. 94.10'; in fact, Gray's reference is to 94.12, which is correct, so that Jensen is mistaken on both counts.

[68] Sweeney, 'Prophetic Torah'; cf. Fischer, *Tora für Israel*, 24–36; Lohfink and Zenger, *The God of Israel and the Nations*, 42–57; Landy, 'Torah and Anti-Torah'. Clifford, *Cosmic Mountain*, 157–58, emphasizes both that in the Ugaritic texts El issued authoritative decrees from his mountain abode and that 'the theophany and law-giving of Sinai was renewed in the Jerusalem cult'.

[69] Weinfeld, 'Zion and Jerusalem', 113; see too Wildberger, and Schwartz, 'Torah from Zion'.

unlikely that ancient Israel's social life was organized in such watertight compartments as was once thought.

4. With this verse we finally reach the specific goal of the nations' quest, namely that God should *judge between* and *arbitrate for* them. Although it is not explicitly stated, this implies that he is portrayed as the universal king. A significant element of the role of the pre-exilic king was that he should exercise divinely given wisdom in the settling of disputes between his subjects (and 2 Chron. 19.8-11 suggests that it was under royal jurisdiction that the central court of Deut. 17.8-13 was established); the example of Solomon's judgment in the case of the two prostitutes (1 Kgs 3.16-28) is paradigmatic. Now, by extension, cases of international dispute will be decided by the Great King, and whether again there is any thought that he would delegate some of this responsibility to his people Israel, as may be inferred from later passages in the book, is immaterial at this point. Certainly, there is no hint that the messiah is to act as the judge, as Kimhi, Ibn Ezra and others have proposed. What matters is that the nations refer their disputes to him rather than resorting to war as a means of resolving them.

Arbitrate: the usual hiph'il of יכח, the rare niph'al of which was discussed at 1.18. As seen there (with further literature), the hiph'il has a wide range of meanings, but the parallelism (שפט בין) and the comparable juxtaposition at 11.3-4 point away from a primary sense of 'reprimand' here (of course, in cases of arbitration it may follow that one party is also reprimanded, but that is a secondary consideration; cf. 5.3!). Although it is true that in הוכיח ל the preposition can introduce the object (e.g. Prov. 9.7-8), here it more probably occurs under the influence of the familiar בין...ל combination, distributed over the parallel halves of the line (cf. the first hand in 1QIsaᵃ, noted above).

The consequences of the nations' implementation of God's decisions are then spelt out in terms of a utopian vision of peace which scarcely require further comment.[70] Their influence has been considerable, especially in the more recent past.[71] The main point on which sound exegesis must insist, in view of the appropriation of these lines by widely differing groups of thinkers and activists, is that the vision of peace is not to be treated in isolation, either as promise, aspiration or ground for activity. Rather, it is presented as the natural consequence of the nations seeking, receiving and acting upon God's instruction and arbitration; it follows that it is upon these latter concerns that those whom the vision inspires should initially concentrate.[72]

---

[70] The different perspective on disarmament from that attested in the Zion Psalms has already been pointed out above.

[71] Many examples of the reception history of this passage are provided by J. F. A. Sawyer, *The Fifth Gospel: Isaiah in the History of Christianity* (Cambridge, 1996), esp. 231–33, and Limburg, 'Swords to Plowshares'; for the earlier period, see G. Lohfink, '"Schwerter zu Pflugscharen": Die Rezeption von Jes 2,1-5 par Mic 4,1-5 in der Alten Kirche und im Neuen Testament', *TQ* 166 (1986), 184–209.

[72] For a rather different emphasis, which stresses the exhortation of v. 5 (and cf. also Mic. 4.5), see H. W. Wolff, 'Schwerter zu Pflugscharen—Mißbrauch eines Prophetenwortes? Praktische Fragen und exegetische Klärungen zu Joel 4,9-12; Jes 2,2-5 und Mi

A reverse saying to that found here occurs at Joel 4.10 (ET 3.10): 'Beat your hoes into swords, and your pruning hooks into spears'. Van Selms, 'Isaiah 2.4', has drawn attention to the fact which seems to have been overlooked in recent commentary work (though see such older commentators as Vitringa, Lowth, Gesenius and Dillmann) that there are very close parallels for this in Virgil's *Georgics* i.506–8 ('Respect for the plough is gone; our lands, robbed of the tillers, lie waste, and curved pruning hooks are forged into straight blades') and even more remarkably in Ovid, *Fasti* i.697–700 ('Long time did wars engage mankind; the sword was handier than the share; the plough ox was ousted by the charger; hoes were idle, mattocks were turned into javelins, and a helmet was made out of a heavy rake'). Finally, Martial (*Epigr.* xiv.34) uses the trope in the same manner as Isaiah when he has a sickle write: 'Our Leader's assured peace curved me for quiet employments. I am now the farmer's, I used to be the soldier's'.[73] When this is coupled with the implications of 1 Sam. 13.19, where the Philistines prevented the Israelites from having smiths to make weapons but themselves took care of their agricultural implements (for a price), van Selms suggests that the widespread evidence for turning tools into weapons reflects the longstanding demands of the conscript army in times of war. Our saying in Isaiah (and Micah) would then be a reversal of that almost proverbial saying and would no doubt have been all the more striking for that. He does not doubt that Joel is later in date, and since by that time he thinks that wars would have been fought by standing armies he concludes that Joel's formulation is a sarcastic application of the saying.[74]

Hoes...pruning hooks or 'pruning-knives': the use of these rare words elsewhere shows that they are agricultural implements, while the present verse suggests that they were made (at least partly) of metal. For 'mattock', or *hoe*, see the linguistic notes above. זמר and its derivatives occur elsewhere in the context of viticulture (e.g. Isa. 5.6; Lev. 25.3-4). At 18.5, *pruning hooks* are referred to in a context which makes clear that their use is not related to the harvesting of the grapes but to the earlier process of removing excess growth, so as to allow for the maximum swelling of the grapes.[75]

5. See above for the important redactional function of this verse. It draws its language both from what precedes and what follows; 11.10 is similar in this regard, and 5.30 and 8.23*a* (both of which are also related to

---

4,1-5', *EvTh* 44 (1984), 280–92 = *Studien zur Prophetie: Probleme und Erträge* (Munich, 1987), 93–108.

[73] All translations of Latin texts have been taken from the Loeb Classical Library edition.

[74] To that extent, Bach may have a point when he argues that Joel 4.10 is a proverbial saying, used in its original sense; but the specifically ironic contrast with the Isaiah and Micah vision should not thereby be overlooked or downplayed; cf. R. Bach, *Die Aufforderung zum Kampf und zur Flucht im alttestamentlichen Prophetenspruch* (WMANT 9; Neukirchen-Vluyn, 1962), 72.

[75] Cf. G. Dalman, *Arbeit und Sitte in Palästina, 4: Brot, Öl und Wein* (Gütersloh, 1935), 330–32; Borowski, *Agriculture*, 109.

this verse by their use of the imagery of light or darkness) are comparable. The phrase *house of Jacob* occurs in the next line (v. 6). It is also reminiscent of 'the house of the God of Jacob' in v. 3, even though, of course, 'house' is used in different senses in vv. 3 and 5. The link with v. 6 is therefore the stronger. The expression *come, let us walk* (לכו ונלכה) is undoubtedly modelled on the similar 'come, let us go up' (לכו ונעלה) in v. 3, together with the use of ונלכה itself (again with moral overtones) later in the same verse. Budde goes so far as to declare that 'Kaum jemals liegt der Tatbestand eines Flickvers so handgreiflich zutage wie bei v. 5';[76] see too Sweeney, 'Structure and Redaction'. The aim is to encourage the readers of what follows to live as worthy examples of the principles which have been introduced in vv. 2-4 (*let us walk*, even as the nations are presented as saying they will one day do, v. 3), but from which at present they fall far short. The involvement of the redactor with his readers, as at 1.9, is noteworthy.

The only element for which there is not an immediate verbal trigger in the surrounding context is the phrase *light of the Lord*. It seems to be the editor's way of understanding or characterizing the 'ways', 'paths', 'instruction' and 'word' of v. 3.[77] While there have been suggestions that this choice of language has been influenced by word-play (cf. ירנו [Delitzsch], תורה [Dillmann][78] and/or ארחות [Hitzig]), this seems far less significant than the use of such language elsewhere in the book. Light is a prominent image for salvation (broadly conceived) in all parts of the book of Isaiah,[79] though it is most frequently and creatively used in Deutero-Isaiah (e.g. 42.16; 45.7; 49.9). In the earlier material, 9.1 is a particularly significant example,[80] while the uses in Trito-Isaiah no doubt draw on the earlier examples in the book.[81] It is therefore significant that it occurs as the major theme of the redactional joins here, at 5.30 and at 8.23*a*, all of which can be most easily associated with the exilic redaction of the first part of the book (by Deutero-Isaiah himself, in my opinion); the particular use of this imagery in relation to God's self-revelation occurs at 42.6;

---

[76] This is no justification, however, for then arguing that באור represents a misunderstanding of an original abbreviated form of בארחות.

[77] Cf. Lohfink and Zenger, *The God of Israel*, 39–40, with particular reference to the Targumic rendering of this verse and to the discussion of G. Vermes, 'The Torah is Light', *VT* 8 (1958), 436–38.

[78] In addition, Marti follows Cheyne in pointing out that in Jewish Aramaic תורה is generally rendered אוריא.

[79] See, for instance, the somewhat impressionistic study of P. D. Miscall, 'Isaiah: The Labyrinth of Images', *Semeia* 54 (1991), 103–21; his approach, of course, differs sharply from that adopted here.

[80] Indeed, I have suggested in *Book*, 72–73, that it may be one example among several where First Isaiah's thought and diction in this passage influenced Deutero-Isaiah directly; see too R. E. Clements, 'A Light to the Nations: A Central Theme of the Book of Isaiah', in J. W. Watts and P. R. House, *Forming Prophetic Literature: Essays on Isaiah and the Twelve in Honor of John D.W. Watts* (JSOTSup 235; Sheffield, 1996), 57–69.

[81] See, for example, R. E. Clements, '"Arise, Shine; for your Light has Come": A Basic Theme of the Isaianic Tradition', in Broyles and Evans (eds), *Writing and Reading*, 441–54.

49.6; 50.10-11; and 51.4. Other links in our verse with this phase of the book's growth include the use of Jacob to designate the people,[82] the particular links between our verse and 50.10-11,[83] and the general theme of a movement from a universalistic vision to an exhortation to the house of Jacob to set an example of godly living.[84] At the very least it may be claimed that in such a context the application of vv. 2-4 by our verse makes good sense.

There is nothing in this verse, therefore, which cannot be fully explained and understood on the basis of its immediate literary setting and the outlook of the redactor who was probably responsible for it as we know of him from elsewhere in the book. Marti, in particular, suggested that it was somehow directly related to the verse which follows the parallel in Micah (4.5): 'For all the peoples walk each in the name of its god, but we will walk in the name of the Lord our God for ever'. While Gray is correct to say that 'Mic. asserts what Is. exhorts to', it is likely that any similarity between the two verses is to be explained by the fact that they are both added redactionally to the common material, which not unnaturally will have influenced them. The only close points of comparison between the two verses, such as 'walking', derive directly from the shared material;[85] in other respects, they differ noticeably. The appeal to Micah does not, therefore, contribute significantly to the exegesis of this verse in Isaiah.

---

[82] This name occurs some twenty times in Isa. 40–55 to refer to the exiled Israelites, and among these 'the house of Jacob' is used at 46.3 and 48.1.

[83] Observed already by Clifford, *Fair Spoken and Persuading*, 158 (above, n. 47).

[84] In general terms it may be said that throughout his work Deutero-Isaiah holds out an ideal for the future which includes an important position for the nations but that the way to this is frequently frustrated by the faithlessness of Jacob/Israel. Consequently, he has to devote a good deal of attention to the correction of the faults, such as lack of faith, which he finds among his own people; cf. R. E. Watts, 'Consolation or Confrontation? Isaiah 40–55 and the Delay of the New Exodus', *TynB* 41 (1990), 31–59.

[85] See especially Sweeney, 'Micah's Debate with Isaiah'.

THE DAY OF THE LORD
(2.6-22)

[6]For you have abandoned your people, the house of Jacob,
   for they are full of divination,
and soothsayers and sorcerers
   and the children of foreigners abound.
[7]And his land is full of silver and gold,
   and there is no end to his treasures;
and his land is full of horses,
   and there is no end to his chariots;
[8]and his land is full of idols,
   and they worship each one the work of his hands,
      even that which his fingers have made.
[9]So humanity is humbled and mankind is brought low;
   do not forgive them!
[10]Enter into the rock, and hide yourself in the dust,
   from the terror of the Lord and his glorious majesty.
[11]Humanity's haughty eyes will be brought low,
   and men's pride will be humbled,
and the Lord alone will be exalted
   on that day.
[12]For the Lord of Hosts has a day
against all that is proud and high,
   and against all that is lifted up and lofty;
[13]and against all the cedars of Lebanon [high and lifted up],
   and against all the oaks of Bashan;
[14]and against all the high mountains,
   and against all the hills which are lifted up;
[15]and against every lofty tower,
   and against every fortified wall;
[16]and against all the Tarshish-ships,
   and against all the beautiful boats;
[17]and humanity's haughtiness will be humbled,
   and men's pride will be brought low;
and the Lord alone will be exalted
   on that day,
      [18]but the idols will vanish away completely.
[19]And they will enter [Enter!] into the caves of the rocks,
   and into the holes in the ground,
from the terror of the Lord and his glorious majesty,
   when he arises to terrify the earth.
[20]On that day a man will throw away his silver idols and his gold idols—
which they have made, each one for himself, to worship—to the mole-rats
and the bats, [21]so that they enter into holes in the rocks and into clefts in
the cliffs
   from the terror of the Lord and his glorious majesty,
      when he arises to terrify the earth.
[22]Stop relying on humanity, in whose nostril there is breath, for at what
(value) is he to be reckoned?

6. נטשתה: for the spelling, which is not uncommon, cf. GK §44g. It is supported by 1QIsaᵃ, though 4QIsaᵇ has the more usual נטשה. LXX translates as a third person singular, and consequently 'his people' as well; it also reads 'Israel' in place of 'Jacob': ἀνῆκε γὰρ τὸν λαὸν αὐτοῦ τὸν οἶκον τοῦ Ισραηλ. This has been used as a basis for emendation by a number of commentators, on the grounds that the unannounced shift to second person address to God is awkward and that he is not so addressed in the following. Duhm, therefore (partly anticipated by Houbigant), proposed an original נטש יה עמו עמו, and similar suggestions are favoured by, for instance, Marti, Gray, Budde, Feldmann, and Procksch.[1] There are several objections to such an approach, however. (i) LXX does not include the divine name, so that the lack of a subject is as awkward as in the MT; Duhm's addition of יה is a conjecture only suggested, not textually supported, by LXX. (ii) In MT, God is also addressed in the second person in v. 9b. This too has been questioned, but before the two occurrences are eliminated separately, they should first be considered as mutually supporting. (iii) None of the other versions supports LXX. V and P follow MT, while T renders with a second person plural. As Sweeney, *Isaiah 1–4*, 139–40, observes, it is likely that both LXX and T have resolved the ambiguity of MT in different directions: whereas T took בית יעקב as a vocative (see below), LXX understood it as an accusative, in apposition with עמך, and rendered with a third person verb in order to eliminate any alternative interpretation. If that is so, then its rendering is exegetical, not based on an alternative text. Its substitution of 'Israel' for 'Jacob' is a further small pointer in the same direction. (iv) As Gray admits, it is more difficult to explain how MT could arise from the supposed LXX *Vorlage* than the reverse. (v) Those who adopt the emendation generally do so in the context of wider conjectures about the original form of the poem, such as that a form of the refrain in vv. 10 and 19 once stood in front of v. 6. It is hazardous, however, to base an emendation upon such other conjectures. From the point of view of method, it is better, if possible, to use redactional theories to explain oddities in the present text rather than as a basis for still further changes.

בית יעקב: it is not certain whether this should be construed as an apposition to עמך, as in the translation above, or as a vocative (and therefore the equivalent of the subject of נטשתה). If the latter is correct, the passage as a whole may refer to the northern kingdom, so that a good deal hangs on the correct interpretation; consequently, textual and exegetical considerations overlap, so that some of the relevant factors are treated elsewhere in the commentary. Among the ancient versions, as noted above, P and V retain the ambiguity while LXX and T remove it by each favouring an alternative interpretation. Thus only T favours a clearly vocative sense with its second person plural paraphrase, and in view of the importance of this version for later Jewish commentators, it is hardly surprising that some of them do the same. Roberts's listing of them in support of this interpretation is therefore not as significant as he seems to imply.[2] The fact that they go out of their way to register the ambiguity might rather be held to suggest that they were uncomfortable with T's rendering. Initial difficulties for the vocative rendering, suggesting that it should be considered only if the more normal appositional interpretation proves to be untenable, include (i) the awkward nature of the resulting shift from second person here to third person in the immediately following lines (Sweeney, *Isaiah 1–4*, 140), and (ii) the fact that, outside of purely secular contexts, נטש is far more commonly used with God as subject (Gesenius).

כי מלאו...: this whole line is a well-known *crux*, since there are several difficulties in the text which overlap to some extent and which render any proposal uncertain at best. It should be noted that, apart from orthographic variants, the Qumran scrolls (where preserved) agree with MT.

---

[1] A number of very different proposed emendations were suggested by older commentators, and they are listed by Budde, 191. None seems to have gained any further support, however, and so they will not be considered further here.

[2] Cf. Roberts, 'Isaiah 2', 299. Others who have favoured the vocative rendering in more recent times include Hitzig; König; Cazelles, 'Qui aurait visé?', 412; Wiklander, 71.

The major problems in the MT are: (i) מלאו lacks an object. Those who defend the MT (most recently Beuken) assume an ellipsis, and use 'from the East' to help supply what is missing, i.e. eastern manners and customs (cf. RV), or more particularly idolatrous practices. This is unacceptable, however. While it is true that, especially in poetry, there can be an ellipsis of an object if it follows a verb with which it is regularly associated (e.g. of קול after נשא), that is not the case here. Delitzsch's appeal to Jer. 51.34 and Ezek. 32.6 does not help, for neither passage has the qal of מלא, so that the situation is different, and the fact that, as he says, both use מן to denote the source from which one draws and fills oneself does not meet the primary difficulty. Similarly, the East is not so typically associated with idolatry or divination as to suggest it naturally without further ado; that thought clearly comes to mind only because of עננים in the second half of the line. The supposed analogy cited by Barthélemy of Job 22.24, where 'Ophir' stands for 'gold of Ophir', is therefore inapplicable. (ii) Since there is no object expressed in the first half of the line, ועננים cannot be a second, parallel object. It therefore has to be taken as part of an independent clause (cf. RV 'and *are* soothsayers like the Philistines'), but this is harsh; והם would be expected. (iii) The comparison with the Philistines is most peculiar. Although commentators regularly cite 1 Sam. 6.2 and 2 Kgs 1.2 as evidence that the Philistines consulted oracles and practised divination, that is no more than could be said of any of Israel's neighbours. As Gray rightly says, 'we have no other indication that the Philistines were pre-eminent in divination', still less that their practices in this regard were such as to make them proverbial, as seems to be implied here. Some of those who think that Isaiah was here addressing the northern kingdom suggest either that Philistine soothsayers accompanied their troops who were joining the anti-Judean coalition as part of the build-up to the Syro-Ephraimite invasion, or that they were attending as part of a convocation of holy men at the coronation of Pekah.[3] The problem for all such explanations, however, is that 'they' (the house of Jacob?) are said to be *like* the Philistines in this regard; references to the presence of actual Philistine soothsayers in Israel in whatever capacity are irrelevant.

Although the versions are sometimes cherry-picked in support of one aspect or another of various emendations, they offer no consistent support in favour of an older reading, and may all presuppose more or less the same text as MT. This is obviously the case for V and P. LXX has ὅτι ἐνεπλήσθη ὡς τό ἀπ' ἀρχῆς ἡ χώρα αὐτῶν κληδονισμῶν ὡς ἡ τῶν ἀλλοφύλων. This rendering may be compared with T: ארי אתמליאת ארעכון מטען כיד מלקדמין ועננין כפלשתאי. Both add a reference to the land as the subject of the verb 'be filled' (and of course the third or second person references continue the separate interpretations of 'house of Jacob' in each version discussed above), but on the major point of difficulty here (the lack of an object for מלאו) they diverge. T adds 'idols' (cf. v. 8), while LXX ignores the conjunction on ועננים, and so makes that the object. Since they do not agree at this vital point, it is unlikely that any object was expressed in their *Vorlagen*, and their solutions look like alternative sensible attempts to render what was already a corrupt text. It is therefore also difficult to believe that they had a Hebrew text which had 'their/your land'; it is more likely that they simply took their cue from the threefold ותמלא ארצו which opens each of the following three lines. On both counts, therefore, it is unlikely that Gray is on firm ground in using the LXX as the basis for his further emendation to כי מלאה ארצו כנענים, 'for his land is full of traders'.[4]

The conclusion to which these considerations point is that the text is corrupt, and that the error must have arisen early in the course of transmission, prior to the stage for which we have any independent witness. In such a case, conjectural emendation is the only possible resort, with all its attendant uncertainties. Among the most influential, we may note the following. (i) An early proposed reading, מקסם, 'divination' (Ezek. 12.24; 13.7),

---

[3] Cf. Davidson, 'Interpretation'; Roberts, 'Isaiah 2', 301; Rogers, 'Coronation'. Some generally expressed reservations are voiced by C. S. Ehrlich, *The Philistines in Transition: A History from ca. 1000–730 B.C.E.* (Leiden, 1996), 162–65.

[4] In addition to his commentary, see Gray, 'Critical Discussions'. Budde followed Gray, with slight modifications.

in place of מקדם, was given wide currency through its adoption by Houbigant. Alternatively, Lowth retained מקדם, but suggested that מקסם, which originally stood in front of it, had been lost by haplography. This proposal neatly removes the first major problem in the line, and at the same time, by extension, the second, as has been frequently adopted (sometimes with slight variations); for example, by Knobel, Duhm, Marti, Condamin, Feldmann.[5] (ii) A related suggestion, favoured, for instance, by Dillmann, Procksch, Wildberger and Kaiser, is to read קסמים, 'diviners' (either in place of, or together with, מקדם), since this is thought to provide a better parallel with עננים. Apart from the fact that it is slightly further removed from the consonantal text, the main difficulty with this is that מלאו with a personal subject and a personal object is improbable' (Gray). Whether this objection then applies also to עננים, or whether, being further removed from the verb, the difficulty is then not so acute, remains to be investigated. (iii) Thomas[6] argued that the parallelism favours a personal rather than an abstract object, agreed that קסמים would fit, but then proposed that מעקדים, 'enchanters', would be even better, since it is closer to the consonantal text. The verb עקד, 'bind', which is known in Hebrew, has an Arabic cognate which is frequently used in association with magic. Once this error had occurred, it led to the addition of כפלשתים as a 'balancing gloss'. (For his application of this line of thought to the last line of the verse, see below.) Apart from other uncertainties, this proposal also falls foul of Gray's objection to קסמים, noted at (ii) above. (iv) Driver, 'Isaiah i–xxxix', 36–37, took his cue from the following verse to state that what is required here is something to explain how the 'house of Jacob' had become so rich. Without much discussion, he therefore suggested reading מקדים, 'immigrant traders' (cf. Arabic qadâ, 'was compelled by poverty to migrate from the desert', and Syriac qad(d)î, 'traded profitably'), and he distinguished עננים from מעננים, suggesting that the former means 'talking through the nose' and so speaking bad Hebrew (cf. Neh. 13.24); hence NEB: 'for they are crowded with traders and barbarians like the Philistines'. (Again, this line of thought is continued into the next line.) To the objections already raised by Gray to this type of approach may in this case be added the point of method that it is not acceptable to emend the text in order to introduce words which are not otherwise already attested in Hebrew. As Barthélemy comments, 'C'est construire sur du sable'. Driver's interpretation of עננים is also improbable (see below).

The upshot of this survey is that the first proposal is the only one which is free of difficulties as regards the first half of the line, and it should therefore be pursued. It does not, however, solve the third problem (the unexpected reference to the Philistines), and it may still leave a problem with ועננים as a second (personal) object to מלאו. As already noted, the corruption seems to be early and deep-seated, so that if emendation is called for, we might as well seek a solution which answers all the problems, while acknowledging that any suggestion is hypothetical in the extreme. In this spirit, I suggest that when the slight corruption of מקסם to מקדם occurred by a simple scribal error, this misled a copyist to expect a parallel in the second half of the line, namely a reference to the Philistines on the basis of the similarity with 9.11 and 11.14. If that is right, then there must originally have been a word there which was sufficiently close orthographically to כפלשתים to allow for the error; alternatively, כפלשתים might have been added as a marginal comment (on the basis of 9.11; 11.14) and then later misunderstood as a correction of some word in the text which it resembled (for this textual process, see on 1.7). I propose כשפים, 'sorcerers'. This precise form occurs elsewhere only at Jer. 27.9, where it also follows immediately after a reference to עננים. Significantly, the abstract form כשפים, 'sorceries', stands in parallel with מעוננים at Mic. 5.11 in a passage (5.9-13) which has so many verbal similarities with this section of Isaiah that literary association has sometimes been suspected.[7] In a general way, the two words also occur together at Deut. 18.10 (together with

---

[5] Several commentators suggest that Gesenius adopted this reading; in fact, he described it as 'scharfsinnig genug, wenn gleich unnötig'.

[6] Thomas 'Lost Hebrew Word', and 'Jesaia ii 6'.

[7] Cf. Blenkinsopp, 'Fragments of Ancient Exegesis'; Vermeylen, 135–40; Zapff, Studien, 118–22.

מְקַסֵּם) and 2 Chron. 33.6. A reference to it in the present context is thus almost to be expected (cf. Vermeylen, 137–38). See further immediately below.

וְעֹנְנִים: the usual personal form for 'soothsayers' is מְעֹנְנִים (as, for instance, at Mic. 5.11). For that reason, it has sometimes been suggested that עֹנְנִים is an abstract form, 'soothsaying'. Were this the case, it would neatly avoid the apparent problem of מלאו having both a personal subject and object, and it could then have been followed, on our conjecture, by the similarly impersonal יַשְׂפִּיקוּ. However, the only other occurrence of עֹנְנִים is at Jer. 27.9 (and the fem. sg. עֹנְנָה occurs at Isa. 57.3), where it is clearly personal (so rightly Dillmann), so that an alternative approach to the problem needs to be found (see below). Tur-Sinai, 158, suggested on the basis of 57.3 that the word means 'adulterers' (hence the reference to foreign children in the next line), but there is no justification for this rendering of 57.3.

וּבִילְדֵי נָכְרִים יַשְׂפִּיקוּ: all commentators find great difficulty in arriving at a satisfactory understanding of this clause. There are two verbs שפק/ס, I 'to slap, clap' and II 'to suffice, abound', but neither is attested elsewhere in the hiph'il. The reference to children is also obscure, and ילדי נכרים cannot simply mean 'foreigners' (*pace* Gesenius), since that would require בני (see especially 60.10; 61.5).[8] The ancient versions are as varied as their modern counterparts. LXX καὶ τέκνα πολλὰ ἀλλόφυλα ἐγενήθη αὐτοῖς seems to be based on a loose interpretation of שפק II and to ignore the ב on ילדי (influence from Hos. 5.7, where the LXX rendering is similar to here, is also possible[9]). T appears not to have attempted a translation at all, but to add a general paraphrase *ad sensum*: ובנמוסי עממיא אזלין. P is similar to LXX, again not offering a rendering of ב. V *et pueris alienis adheserunt* introduces a reference to pederasty, as Jerome's commentary spells out, and he thinks that σ (καὶ μέτα τέκνων ἀλλοτρίων ἐκροτῆσαν) is a delicate reference to the same. In fact, σ is far more likely to be following the שפק I approach (see below). How Jerome arrived at his own understanding is unclear, despite his full explanation. He first tells us that the Hebrew has *iespicu*, which seems to presuppose MT (despite the vocalization of the first syllable). He then says that this means ἐσφηνώθησαν ('cleave with a wedge'), which Barr[10] ingeniously traces to post-biblical פקפק, 'drive in a wedge' (with the initial ש treated as a preformative, as in a shaph'el). Barr then declares that he cannot understand how Jerome got from this to *adhaeserunt*. The answer is that he probably did not go directly, but misread (or misunderstood) שפק as שפק/ס, 'join, attach to'. It is difficult not to conclude that Jerome had his own prior understanding of what the text 'ought' to mean and that he fitted his philology, as well as his reading of σ, to it. Had he known it, he might better have cited α in his support: καὶ ἐν παιδίοις ξένων χορηγησοῦσιν ('well supplied with'= שפק II), and also θ: καὶ ἐν τέκνοις αλλοτρίοις ἤρκεσαντο.

This tendency to fit one's translation to what may be thought the most suitable meaning is continued in the modern period too. For instance (i) many commentators seek to make sense of the phrase on the basis of שפק I. Usually an ellipsis of כפים is assumed; for the full phrase, cf. Num. 24.10; Lam. 2.15; Job 27.23; the possibility that there is a similar ellipsis at Job 34.37 (Gesenius) is far from certain, however. Alternatively, Hitzig's conjecture has sometimes been followed (e.g. Duhm; Procksch) to emend ובילדי to וביד, even though elsewhere כף rather than יד is always used. To strike hands with or at someone can be used to express a variety of purposes or sentiments,[11] and this is reflected in the

---

[8] A further peculiarity with this phrase, which has not generally been noted, is the use of the plural for both the construct and the *nomen rectum*. This is contrary to the usual classical style (which requires the *nomen rectum* to be in the singular), and it becomes common in Biblical Hebrew only in its latest phases; cf. R. Polzin, *Late Biblical Hebrew: Toward an Historical Typology of Biblical Hebrew Prose* (HSM 12; Missoula, Mont., 1976), 42–43. It does not appear, however, that this principle can be elevated into a sufficiently hard and fast rule as to require that this usage must be late.

[9] Cf. Ziegler, 107; Seeligmann, 72.

[10] Barr, *Comparative Philology*, 233.

[11] See generally N. S. Fox, 'Clapping Hands as a Gesture of Anguish and Anger in Mesopotamia and in Israel', *JANES* 23 (1995), 49–60 (but without reference to our verse).

interpretations offered: following on from the previous line, some have seen here a reference to some kind of magical ceremony (e.g. Dillmann; Marti, with hesitations; Wildberger: a rite to ward off demonic powers); others look forward to the following verse and think of handshaking as a sign of striking a bargain (e.g. Gray, who cites Arabic parallels; König; Procksch; Clements; cf. Prov. 6.1; 17.18; 22.26 for possible analogies, but always with תקע, never שפק/ס; with ellipsis of כף at Prov. 11.15); finally, without immediate contextual warrant, a few have suggested that there is a reference to entering into foreign alliances, which Isaiah elsewhere opposes (e.g. Orelli; Oswalt). While it is, of course, possible that an idiom has been used here which is not attested elsewhere, it should be recognized that we should have expected the verb to be תקע, not שפק/ס, that an ellipsis of כף is unlikely in a rare phrase and that on the basis of similar idioms elsewhere we should have expected it to be followed by either על or ל, not ב (as several of those who adopt this solution concede). Furthermore, the emendation to בידי does not answer these difficulties and is unsupported, so that there seems to be little advantage in pursuing it.

(ii) Many more recent commentators have therefore attempted to make sense of the line on the basis of the verb being שפק II, for which there is equally impressive warrant in antiquity (recently, for instance, Bartelt, 194–95, and Beuken). Although the verb is less common in Biblical Hebrew, it occurs at 1 Kgs 20.10, and the noun שֶׁפֶק at Job 20.22. Various forms of the root are also attested several times in Ben Sira,[12] as well as in Aramaic and later forms of Hebrew. Some of the occurrences in Ben Sira are particularly significant, both because they attest the use of the hiph'il of this verb, and because they show that שׂ and ס could equally be used for the first radical; see especially 42.17, where הספיקו occurs in ms B beside השפיקו in the Masada manuscript.[13] The former point is of obvious relevance to Isa. 2.6 (the more so since שפק I remains unattested in the hiph'il), while the latter may be compared with the spelling in 4QIsaᵇ, יספקו (presumably qal; this is the only significant variant among the preserved Qumran fragments for this line). Those who follow this approach usually think that there lies behind it a reference to the influence of foreign cults because of inter-marriage (e.g Kaiser), though Driver continued his interpretation of the previous line, 'and is overrun with young foreigners', and Thomas, more boldly, simply deleted ובילדי נכרים as another 'balancing gloss' (though he does not explain this further) and so construed ועננים as the subject: 'and soothsayers abound'.

It seems to me that in the present context there is much to be said for seeking a solution on the basis of שפק II. It forms a better parallel with מלאו,[14] and moreover it draws the verse as a whole into line with the regular pattern of the following lines, where והמלא is balanced by ואין קצה ל. Following my proposal for the previous line, I therefore suggest deleting the ב in ובילדי (cf. LXX and P) and taking the ילדי נכרים as a third subject for the verb following ועננים וכשפים: thus 'and soothsayers and sorcerers and the children of foreigners abound'. This overcomes the problem of the personal ועננים being an object of מלאו, and it allows the verb (whether hiph'il or qal) to have a well-attested sense. The addition of the preposition ב will have been a further consequence of the error already discussed in the previous line. Once that had occurred, this line clearly had to be construed independently, with an impersonal 'they' as the subject (parallel with מלאו); hence it was re-read as 'to abound with'.

Is the result acceptable poetry? The question is complicated by the fact that we are clearly dealing here with a transition between the two main units of the chapter. If Sweeney, *Isaiah 1–4*, 174, is right to see the words בית יעקב as an addition made during the course of the redactional process, then the resulting verse, with the proposed emendations, reads as follows:

כי נטשתה עמך כי מלאו מקסם
ועננים וכשפים וילדי נכרים ישפיקו

---

[12] These are conveniently listed by Thomas, 'Isaiah ii 6', 90.

[13] Cf. Beentjes, *Ben Sira in Hebrew*, 169.

[14] So Popper 'Parallelism', 316–18.

This may be analysed as $(3 + 3) + (2 + 3)$, with an enjambment in the second line. Since the following verse, where there are no textual uncertainties, has a longer than expected first half, the second line in our verse may be consciously shorter in compensation. Clearly, no solution to the problems of this verse is free of all difficulties, but it may be submitted that the solution proposed here is at least good Hebrew and that it faces fewer other objections than most.

7. קצה: so too 4QIsaᵃ; 1QIsaᵃ and 4QIsaᵇ have קץ. While both forms are common in Biblical Hebrew, there is a tendency towards favouring the shorter form with the passage of time and this continued into the post-biblical period (cf. Kutscher, 283). The longer spelling of MT is thus probably more original.

8. Becuase of the regular form of the previous two lines, it is widely believed that an equivalent clause has been lost from the first line of this verse,[15] something along the lines of ואין קצה לעצבתיו (Duhm). The loss of such a clause after the repeated קצה ל אין of the previous verse and before the occurrence at the end of the next line of the similar-looking אצבעתיו would be intelligible enough, and naturally those who think that this poem is entirely regular in terms of line-length and structure (e.g. Gray) are attracted to this. To regain such a regular structure, however, requires several more conjectural changes than just this one, and there is not a shred of textual evidence for the proposed restoration. The next line itself serves to develop the first (a feature not paralleled in v. 7). Since this clearly comes at the end of a minor unit in the chapter, it seems equally plausible to suggest that the verse has been purposely designed as a tricolon, so as to create a minor sense of closure.

ישתחוו: because of the singular suffix on ידיו and אצבעתיו, it is often thought that this plural verb should be emended to the singular, ישתחוה. While this is possible, it is not strictly necessary, since such a construction is not uncommonly used to express a distributive sense; cf. GK §117z; Gibson, 23. In support of this, we may note that the same construction is used in a closely comparable context at v. 20 (אשר עשו־לו להשתחות), and that 1QIsaᵃ agrees with MT. The versions make everything plural, including their rendering of the suffixes; not much weight can be put on this, although for what it is worth it favours a plural verb rather than a singular. The meaning of the verb is not in doubt, though there has been some lively debate about its etymology;[16] for its use here in a 'pivot pattern', see Watson, 'Pivot Pattern', 241.

9. וישח...וישפל: in the context, these verbs describe the consequences of v. 8, and as such may be construed as a regular *waw*-consecutive. In the commentary below, it will be seen that this is perfectly intelligible from the point of view of the final redactor. However, since the imperatives of v. 10 look forward to a time which many think precedes the completion of the actions of this verse, it is usually claimed that this is an equivalent of the 'prophetic perfect'; cf. Kimhi; Driver, *Tenses* §82; Gibson, 102. (At v. 17 the same verbs occur as *waw* + perfect with reference to the same time.) This is not necessary; in the present text, it will be suggested that the past experience of vv. 6-9 is used rather as an adumbration of what may follow (10-19) if there is no response to the preaching. To that extent, it may be agreed that the verbs look both backwards and forwards, and the English present tense is the most suitable way of allowing for that.

אדם...איש: collectives; cf. להם following; JM §135c; WO, 114. Rashi's attempt to distinguish on the basis of rank (cf. AV, RV: 'mean man...great man') is fanciful, and was already rightly rejected by Kimhi. At Ps. 49.3, which Gesenius and Delitzsch compare,[17]

---

[15] The attempt by the LXX to overcome this by construing ידיו למעשה with the first line is clearly unacceptable.

[16] For a survey of the debate until the time he was writing, see J. A. Emerton, 'The Etymology of *hištaḥᵃwāh*', *OTS* 20 (1977), 41–55; see more recently G. I. Davies, 'A Note on the Etymology of *hištaḥᵃwāh*', *VT* 29 (1979), 493–95; S. Kreuzer, 'Zur Bedeutung und Etymologie von *hištaḥᵃwāh/yštḥwy*', *VT* 35 (1985), 39–60.

[17] They also compare Isa. 5.15 and Prov. 8.4, but there is nothing there to support their case.

the point is made explicit by the addition of יחד עשיר ואביון עשיר ואביון; that sense is not, however, inherent in the nouns themselves.

ואל־תשא להם: as often, there is an ellipsis of the object of נשא (cf. GK §117g; Gibson, 110). Because of the following ל, this must be עון; the same ellipsis occurs at Gen. 18.24, 26; Num. 14.19; Hos. 1.6; Ps. 99.8. The versions,[18] Rashi and Kimhi[19] also support this interpretation, although LXX renders the verb in the first person as a direct consequence of its clarification in v. 6 (cf. Sweeney, *Isaiah 1–4*, 140).

4QIsa[a] and [b] have ולא instead of ואל.[20] It is probable that this represents an easing of a perceived theological difficulty, namely, the issuing of a blunt, negative command by the prophet to God. T renders similarly, and probably for the same reason rather than being dependent on a variant text. More drastically, 1QIsa[a] lacks the whole phrase as well as the whole of v. 10. Although it might be possible to associate this with theories about the growth of the passage in part by mistaken repetitions of some of the refrain-like elements, it is difficult to believe that any earlier form of the text went straight from 9a to 11, since it would be (and in 1QIsa[a] is) so jarringly repetitive.[21] Similarly, since v. 10 is also lacking in the scroll, its evidence cannot be cited in favour of suggestions that 9b alone is a later addition (see below). Kutscher, 554, implies that the omission is the result of scribal carelessness. This, of course, is always possible, though it should be noted that there is no obvious cause for a mechanical scribal mistake at this point.[22] There is thus something to be said for Sweeney's ingenious argument (*Isaiah 1–4*, 141) that the omission was deliberate: noting the scroll's different text at v. 3 above, in which it is the people of Jacob who will teach the nations, he suggests that the scroll eliminated these lines which imply that the house of Jacob had sinned, so that the whole of 6-22 is directed against the nations, an interpretation which he finds to be in line with the ideology of the Qumran community.

Despite the lack of direct textual support, many commentators nevertheless have difficulty with this clause, partly because the first half of the line has parallels in 2.11 and 17 and especially 5.15 which do not continue as here, and partly because they judge the sentiment expressed to be improbable. Some simply delete it as a gloss (e.g. Schoors; Wildberger), but since there is no particular reason for such an addition, most suggest emendations, such as: ואם שאת להם, later improved to...ואין (Duhm; *BHS*; cf. Gen. 4.7); replace v. 9 with a slightly modified form of 17-18 (Marti); ואלה תשא להם (Budde); delete the first part of the verse and read the second as ואבל יתשו אלליהם (Procksch); ואל שאל תהמה ('and unto Sheol, to the deep'; cf. 5.14-15; Tur-Sinai); ואל שאת להם (Driver, 'Isaiah i-xxxix', 37; cf. NEB 'and how can they raise themselves?'); ואל תשתע להם (Davidson); ואל תשעה להם ('so you should not look to them [for help]'; Roberts); ואל תשא(ו) להם ('do not gaze at them'; Wiklander). Such a wide variety does not inspire confidence, and leads to the suspicion that the starting point for the proposals may be at fault. First, the 'refrain' element is never identical, so that to find difficulty with a variation here is unnecessary.

---

[18] Strictly speaking, P is ambiguous, since *šbq* can mean either 'forgive' or 'abandon'; it is noteworthy that it used the same verb to render נטש, 'abandon', in v. 6.

[19] Ibn Ezra, by contrast, thinks that there may have been an ellipsis of ראש, נפש or even ארץ (citing Gen. 13.6), but none of these is convincing.

[20] There is also the mark of part of a letter following תשא in 4QIsa[a], though it is not legible. The editors propose either ה (presumably just *plene* spelling) or ו, which would make the verb plural. The preserved context is so fragmentary, however, that we should not speculate further.

[21] *Contra* Ulrich, 'Developmental Composition', 291–92, and Cohen, 'Philological Reevaluation', 48. The parallel with 5.15 is sometimes cited in favour of the view that the compiler of that passage was working from a form of ch. 2 in which v. 11 immediately followed 9a. The repetition in the latter is far more problematic than in ch. 5, however.

[22] Cf. Pulikottil, 41–42, who suggests that the scribe deliberately omitted this material (and made certain other consequential changes noted in v. 11 below) in order to 'bring out logical continuity. Since these words disrupt the flow of thought of vv. 9a and 11-12, the scribe tried to read v. 11 as a commentary on v. 9.'

Secondly, the second person verb form is paralleled in v. 6, and we should first attempt to make sense of both. And finally, can we be so confident as is sometimes implied in prescribing what Isaiah (or a later editor) could or could not have said or thought? A well-supported and intelligible text should at least be the starting point for exegesis.

10. בוא...והסמן: in the context of his discussion of v. 19, Barthélemy, 19–20, seeks to revive what has always been only a minority opinion, namely that these are infinitives absolute rather than imperatives (among the versions, only T; Barthélemy is able to muster slightly more support among medieval commentators, who were in any case probably strongly influenced by T, and of the moderns he mentions Hitzig, Dillmann, Ehrlich, König and Procksch). His proposed rendering is 'il s'agit d'entrer...et de se dissimuler' (and cf. GNB, 'They will hide...'). However, despite (or rather in view of) his appeal to GK §113y, it would be most unusual for this to stand in place of a finite form at the start of a section; it would be expected rather to continue a preceding finite form. When it stands at the beginning of a section, it is mostly as the equivalent of an imperative, so that the sense would be the same in any case (cf. WO, 593–97).

On the absence of this verse from 1QIsaᵃ, see above. LXX, which already softens MT's vividness by the addition of καὶ νῦν at the start of the verse (cf. v. 5) and which renders the verbs as plurals (cf. T and P, and v. 19?), adds at the end ὅταν ἀναστῇ θραῦσαι τὴν γῆν = בקומו לערץ הארץ, as at vv. 19 and 21. It is likely that this is another example of the tendency already noted for the LXX to draw together comparable passages. Not surprisingly in view of the similar but not always identical 'refrains', there are several other examples of this tendency in the present chapter; see below, and Ziegler, 61. There is no justification, however, for following this lead and making the verse identical with 19 in this and other respects (*contra* Gray).

הדר גאנו: two synonymous nouns in a genitival relationship have more or less superlative force; cf. JM §1421m; WO, 267.

11. שפל: although there is no doubt about the meaning, the grammar here is awkward. Following עיני we should expect a plural, and the context further suggests that the verb should be imperfect (cf. the parallel ושח). The comparable 5.15 has תשפלנה, and that is in fact the reading of 1QIsaᵃ here as well (followed, however, by וישח). Kimhi and Ibn Ezra seek to defend MT on the grounds that עין is occasionally masculine elsewhere (e.g. Zech. 3.9; 4.10) and that the verb is to be construed distributively; Kimhi also observes that the tense is 'past in place of future, like ישפל' (i.e. a 'prophetic perfect'; cf. Gibson, 68, 93, 102). More usually nowadays the singular is explained in accordance with a number of other passages where 'the predicate sometimes agrees in gender and number not with the nomen regens, but with the genitive' (i.e. אדם); GK §146a; cf. Gibson, 23. It would certainly be attractive to retain the singular here in view of the poetic balance with ושח, and it is worth noting that 5.15 does not have אדם (the subject there is עיני גבהים), so that it was bound to have a plural. The evidence of some of the later versions, which is sometimes adduced in favour of a plural verb, is not strong in a case like this—they had to use a plural no matter what the *Vorlage* (P avoids the problem by rendering as a causative singular, 'he will bring low...'; could its *Vorlage* have read שפל, understood as a defectively spelt hiph'il?; see below). It is, furthermore, misleading of Wildberger to cite LXX ὑψηλοί in this regard. The LXX construed the first four words of the verse as two separate clauses, and in addition took עיני as an abbreviation for עיני יהוה (οἱ γὰρ ὀφθαλμοὶ κυρίου); cf. Seeligmann, 66. ὑψηλοί was thus his rendering of גבהות, and his version of the next two words (ὁ δὲ ἄνθρωπος ταπεινός) clearly shows that his text was the same as MT. Indeed, it may have been precisely the apparent grammatical difficulty in MT which led him to divide the first part of the verse into separate clauses. In the light of this evidence, it is far more likely that the reading of 1QIsaᵃ is a secondary easing of a perceived difficulty than that it preserves a more primitive text (*contra* Wildberger; Kaiser; Wiklander).

That still does not resolve the question, however, of whether the text suffered corruption (perhaps under influence from v. 17) in the period prior to that for which we have direct evidence. Apart from more radical proposals, such as that the verse as a whole should be deleted or substantially rewritten, several possibilities might be considered:

(i) Huesman, 'Finite Uses', 287, suggested that this was an unrecognized example of the infinitive absolute, שָׁפֵל, in which case considerations of 'tense' and concord would not arise. It is not clear, however, why such a form should have been used here but not in any of the comparable passages, such as v. 17 and 5.15. (ii) A corruption of ישפלו, due to haplography, has sometimes been suggested (e.g. Lowth; König; Tur Sinai). Dillmann was inclined to favour this solution on the ground that none of the examples of agreement with the genitive concerns a singular verb after a plural *nomen regens*. It is not clear how much weight should be put on this point, since other kinds of concord with verbs (including both gender and number) certainly are attested (e.g. Exod. 26.12; Isa. 21.17). (iii) An original ישפל might be considered, so dealing with the problem of the tense, and explaining the concord of gender and number as above. In fact, however, the problem of ושפל in the next verse (*q.v.*) will be explained as a mistaken attempt to correct our word to just this form, which implies that MT was already the reading at that stage. On balance, therefore, MT should perhaps be retained as the more difficult reading, though without total confidence.

12. ושפל, 'and it will become low': though attested by 1QIsa[a] (which, however, omits the second על כל[23]), 4QIsa[b] and all the versions, this word is clearly out of place. Following the parallel, which has two adjectives relating to pride, we expect the same here, not a single adjective (נשא) followed by a verb. In addition, the next four verses all continue with a list of proud things, each described by two words, none of which includes a verb to describe the fact that they will be brought low. Finally, the verb lacks a proper subject and so is not properly integrated into the syntactical flow of the passage. Occasional renderings by an adjective ('high and low') are unjustified (cf. Barthélemy, 16–18), since that would require a different vocalization (שָׁפֵל), and in any case it does not overcome the major difficulty. No attempt to explain these difficulties has been offered; they were mostly not appreciated by older commentators, and they are simply passed over by more modern scholars who nevertheless wish to retain MT.

LXX has an additional word in the second half of the line: ἐπὶ πάντα ὑψηλὸν καὶ μετέωρον, καὶ ταπεινωθήσονται. At 5.15 μετέωρος renders גָּבַהּ, which would certainly be suitable here. It is clear, however, that LXX cannot simply be cited in favour of correcting ושפל to וגבה, as is sometimes carelessly implied; it is just as likely that LXX added the word on its own authority by comparison with the next verse and 57.7, in both of which the same combination of adjectives occurs; as we saw in v. 10 above, such a process of levelling between similar passages in the LXX of Isaiah is quite frequent. At least such a process is no more speculative than the alternative that the LXX read נשא וגבה and that καὶ ταπεινωθήσονται was added only later as a correction in the direction of the then established Hebrew tradition.

Even without the evidence of the LXX, נשא וגבה may be confidently conjectured as the original text.[24] How, then, did ושפל enter the text? The question is seldom asked. I suggest that it may originally have been intended as a marginal correction (read as ישפל) to the שפל of v. 11 (see above). It was misunderstood by a later copyist, however, as a gloss on the present verse intended to supply a cross-reference to 40.4 (there are a number of other connections between this chapter and the opening of 40), and so he erroneously included it here instead of in v. 11.

13. הרמים והנשאים: these words disturb the pattern and rhythm of the passage. As already noted, ten items are listed in vv. 12-16, each one being introduced by על כל, and each one consisting of two words (either noun plus adjective or two nouns in a construct relationship). The two words in question intrude into this pattern and break the close

---

[23] Against Wiklander, who follows this shorter reading, it may be noted that our verse is part of a longer sequence in 12-16, each line of which has a repeated על כל followed by two words. There can therefore be no justification for breaking this consistent pattern here.

[24] In the light of vv. 11, 15 and 17, גבה is superior as a conjectural emendation to Popper's נדול (*Parallelism*, 8*) and Tur-Sinai's שקוף.

parallelism between 'all the cedars of Lebanon' and 'all the oaks of Bashan'. Furthermore, like the ships of v. 16, the cedars of Lebanon do not require such a descriptive qualification; if they did, something similar would be expected in the next clause as well. The words are therefore usually, and rightly, regarded as a gloss (*pace* Barré, 'Isaiah 2.12-17'). It is noteworthy that they occur in the singular in the previous verse and in the plural in the following verse; it therefore seems probable that here they represent an early fragment of (perfectly correct) exegetical activity, explaining to the reader that the generalized description of v. 12 is now being illustrated by the specific items which follow. Appropriately, therefore, the gloss qualifies the first of these items to be listed. It cannot be dated with certainty, but in principle it could be extremely early.

14. The *Vorlage* of the LXX seems to have suffered a form of haplography, having merely ὄρος for ההרים הרמים.

15. It is a quirk of the Leningrad codex that (against the majority of manuscripts) the *mappiq* is omitted from גבה in a number of passages (beside the present verse, see 30.25; 40.9; Ezek. 17.22, 24; 21.31; ויגבה at 5.16 is obviously also to be related), but not at all consistently (e.g. 57.7!).

בצורה: LXX ὑψηλὸν, as in the first half of the line, and clearly inferior. HUBP compares Deut. 3.5 (ערים בצרות חומה נבהה = πόλεις ὀχυραὶ τείχη ὑψηλὰ). This may be coincidental, but in view of what has been noted already in this chapter, the possibility of some sort of cross-reference or 'levelling' by the translator is not impossible.

16. תרשיש: LXX θαλάσσης; cf. T ימא. While this equivalent is common in T, it occurs otherwise in LXX only at Dan. 10.5 (6). There is consequently some dispute about how it should be explained. Seeligmann, 30, suggests that it is merely an inner-Greek corruption of θαρσις. Alternatively, it may be regarded as exegetical (as also in the Targum and elsewhere):[25] the phrase 'ships of Tarshish' had already within the biblical period lost its purely geographical sense and become an equivalent of 'ocean-going ships', as is clear from 1 Kgs 10.22, where the cargoes carried indicate that they sailed south down the Red Sea, and even more so from 1 Kgs 22.48, where they are located at Ezion-geber. 'Ships of the sea' would therefore seem to be a reasonable paraphrase.[26] In view of the evidence from the Targum, we should normally suppose that LXX reflects an earlier form of the same tradition; it remains puzzling in that case, however, why this equivalent should be found here but not elsewhere (cf. 23.1, 6, 14; 60.9; 66.19).

שכיות: a *hapax legomenon*, whose meaning has only relatively recently been recovered. In antiquity, it was associated with שכה, which in later Hebrew and Aramaic means 'to look out', and this led to several possible interpretations of the phrase: LXX θέα, 'sight, view, display', hence 'display of fine ships';[27] V *quod visu pulchrum est* ('everything beautiful to look at', which Delitzsch favoured as referring to all kinds of works of art); P ('watchtowers', as look-outs); T בירנית ('palaces'—a guess?); AV 'pleasant pictures'; RV 'pleasant imagery'; Gesenius (in his *Thesaurus Linguae Hebraeae*, though not in his commentary) suggested 'flags, standards' (of ships, as being conspicuous), and so on. The best defence of this approach is that of Duhm, who thought that it furnished a satisfactory summary of the whole of 12-16, and so led naturally into the refrain in v. 17. Subsequently, the tight structure and parallelism of this section (as observed already by LXX) led

[25] See already Ottley; also J. Barr, 'St. Jerome's Appreciation of Hebrew', *BJRL* 49 (1966–67), 281–302 (291–92), and Review of M. H. Goshen-Gottstein, *The Book of Isaiah: Sample Edition with Introduction*, *JSS* 12 (1967), 113–22 (117–18); M. Mishor, 'Tarshish', *Leš* 34 (1969–70), 318–19 (Hebrew).

[26] Note, however, that A. van der Kooij, *The Oracle of Tyre: The Septuagint of Isaiah 23 as Version and Vision* (VTSup 71; Leiden, 1998), 50, thinks rather of a Jewish tradition in which Tarshish could refer to the Mediterranean.

[27] The fact that LXX includes a reference to ships should not be taken to mean that it understood שכיות to mean 'ships'; that is clearly an interpretative addition by the translator, based intelligently on the context, as his repetition of πλοίων from the first half of the line indicates.

scholars to seek another word for ships here and so proposed an emendation to שׂ/ספינות (cf. ספינה at Jon. 1.5; BDB, 967B; Gray; Procksch). In 1931, however, Begrich (*apud* Budde) suggested a connection with Egyptian *śkty*,[28] and this was then independently associated by Ginsberg and Driver with Ugaritic *ṯkt*, both being words for some kind of ship.[29] Not surprisingly, this convincing proposal has now been generally accepted.[30] There can, of course, be no certainty about how exactly it was spelt and vocalized in Hebrew, though possibly the initial letter was שׂ rather than שׁ (which indicates that the Masoretes themselves understood the word in the way that had become common by their time). Driver suggested שְׂכָה* (hence שכתי here), but the possibility that MT has faithfully preserved the consonantal spelling cannot be ruled out. Muchiki, *Loanwords*, 255–56, maintains that Egyptian *ś* could come into Hebrew directly as שׁ (though is this likely in view of the Ugaritic evidence?) and more plausibly that the vocalization may have been influenced by the parallel אניות.

החמדה: Driver further argued that parallelism demands the name of a country here. He therefore proposed vocalizing הַחֲמָדָּה, 'the desirable (land)', seeing in this a reference to Arabia (cf. *Arabia Felix*);[31] hence NEB 'dhows of Arabia'. While this has an obvious attraction in context, there is no evidence that Arabia was so designated at this early time, and the 'demands' of parallelism by no means require it.[32] More recently, Barré, 'Isaiah 2:12-17', has conjectured that there is here a garbled reference to the (harbour) place-name *Maʾḫādu* associated with ships in the Ugaritic texts (*KTU* 4.81.1). Although the Hebrew cognate common noun is מחוז (Ps. 107.30, and perhaps Isa. 23.10), he never-theless thinks that החמדה is a corruption of an original מחזד; once this word was no longer recognized, it was conformed to a known Hebrew word by metathesis (חמד) and then again later the rare masculine form was changed to the commoner feminine חמדה. He accepts that the addition of the article 'is somewhat more difficult to explain'. This sug-gestion is very acute, and the process of corruption not impossible, but it is certainly highly conjectural and unsupported and it falls foul of the principles that one should not normally both emend and introduce a new *hapax* for a text which in itself is possible and that in comparative philology one should keep with attested consonantal equivalents if possible. The reason for making the proposal in the first place is the desire to maintain what Barré finds to be a very tight chiastic structure in this passage as a whole, but not all will think that this is a good enough reason for textual conjecture. In terms of textual criticism, even on Barré's view it will have been MT which was already in place by the time of the text's redaction, so that one can do no more than take note of this just possible earlier form.

17. ושה: on the lack of strict grammatical concord in some cases when the verb precedes the subject, see GK §145*o*; JM §150*j*.

גבהות has no equivalent in the LXX. It is likely that this shows influence from the rendering of v. 11 (*q.v.*), since the way in which the translator there divided the first clause into two meant that he rendered אדם on its own, and he has simply done the same again here. ושפל is rendered by καὶ πεσεῖται, 'will fall'; since this is the only substantial dif-ference in equivalences between this verse and v. 11, it is possible that he had a *Vorlage*

---

[28] Those who state that Begrich was the first to advance this suggestion are apparently unaware of the same proposal by N. Herz, 'The Exaggeration of Errors in the Masoretic', *JTS* 15 (1913–14), 258–64 (261).

[29] Cf. H. L. Ginsberg *apud* W. F. Albright, 'Baal-Zephon', in *Festschrift Alfred Bertholet* (Tübingen, 1950), 1–14 (5); Driver, 'Difficult Words', 52–53.

[30] For further discussion and bibliography, see Cohen, *Biblical Hapax Legomena*, 41–42 and 69–73. He rightly dismisses alternative emendations by Tur-Sinai, 159, and C. G. Howie, *The Date and Composition of Ezekiel* (Philadelphia, 1950), 60–61.

[31] Procksch had already toyed with the same possibility, though without suggesting the need to revocalize.

[32] See the cautionary remarks of Barr, *Comparative Philology*, 277–82, with discus-sion of our verse on 280–81.

which read וּנְפַל. Alternatively, of course, since he rendered both שפל and שח by the same verb there, he may simply have wished to introduce some free variation here, for stylistic reasons.

18. כליל: since this noun is not used adverbially elsewhere in the Hebrew Bible, it was sometimes thought either that it was a resumptive following האלילים as a *casus pendens*, and hence with a singular verb following (e.g. Dillmann; similarly Ibn Ezra; but since the word is indefinite, this seems difficult), or that it needed to be emended (e.g. Lagarde: כָּלִיל; Ehrlich: כְּצֵל; Budde: כְּלִילָם). However, the adverbial usage, which was long suspected because it gives so much more satisfactory a meaning (e.g. T; Kimhi; Gray, with reference to GK §118*m-r*), has been confirmed by its appearance in Sir. 37.18; 45.14.[33]

18-19. יחלף ובאו: a most interesting case of the overlap of so-called lower and higher criticism. At the textual level, we certainly expect יחלף to be plural (יחלפו, favoured already by Houbigant) following האלילים, and the loss of the *waw* can be easily explained as either haplography or the wrong division of words, depending on what is decided about ובאו. The versions inevitably translated as a plural, so that their evidence to this effect counts for little. Similarly, since retention of MT ובאו would then mean that the idols are the subject of this verb (which would be curious, to say the least!),[34] and since there is an imperative בא in a comparable position in v. 10, it has been usual to move the initial *waw* to the previous word and to revocalize as a plural imperative, בֹּאוּ. However, MT cannot be explained away so simply. In vv. 21-22 there is a patently prosaic addition precisely to explain how the idols could come to be entering the caves, and the need for this can only have arisen if ובאו was already in the text. LXX's use of a causative participle here, εἰσενέγκαντες, strongly suggests that it too recognized the absurdity of MT. The other versions all start v. 19 with a conjunction, so that they too must have read ובאו. Furthermore, 1QIsaᵃ in fact reads יחלופו ובאו, which does not fit with the usual reconstruction of the original text. On the assumption (which is not universally shared) that v. 18 was part of the original text, the textual history at this point must thus have run something like as follows. The 'original' reading was יחלפו, followed either by בא, or, perhaps even better in view of v. 10, בא (singular). Then, by dittography, this became ובאו (or, if the singular בא was the original reading, ובא was first read by dittography and then corrected to ובאו in order to achieve grammatical concord). This must have already taken place during the earliest phase of the transmission of the text, and it became the trigger for the addition of vv. 20-21. It survived at least until the time of 1QIsaᵃ (which therefore does not preserve the 'original' text, *contra* Cohen, 'Philological Reevaluation', 48). Only then (presumably by haplography) was the *waw* on יחלפו lost, so giving rise to MT. Which reading one then prefers will depend entirely upon a decision taken as to the period to which reference is being made, both having been extant during the time when the Hebrew text was in process of formation. In terms of the method adopted in this commentary, ובאו should be preferred, since it was the reading presupposed at the time when the present text (i.e. including vv. 20-21) was being written. However, since from a historical point of view it is so clearly secondary, I have also retained the earlier reading as a bracketed alternative.

19. מערות etc.: LXX has a slightly fuller text than MT, another case of 'leveling' between similar lines, this time v. 21.

ובמחלות: both text and meaning are unanimously attested in antiquity, though modern lexicographers are divided as to whether this *hapax legomenon* should be assigned to חלל = 'bore, pierce', or חלל = 'play the pipe', a denominative from חליל, 'flute, pipe' (i.e. with holes in it). The former seems more natural to me, and it would suggest that there is a distinction between natural caves in the first half of the line and man-made caves in the second. *BHS* draws attention to the fact that in the similar v. 10 ב התמן stands in the same position, so that it is easy to see how attractive it would be to read the same here (in the

---

[33] Cf. Beentjes, *Ben Sira in Hebrew*, 64 and 80.

[34] It is usual to try to avoid this absurdity by rendering ובאו with an impersonal subject, 'they', i.e. people in general. This is understandable in a public version, but such a harmonizing rationalization cannot be admitted in a critical commentary.

plural, of course). However, if the text as we have it makes perfect sense (and it does), if the textual witnesses are agreed (and they are) and if there is no possible way in which scribal error could account for the proposed corruption (and there is not), then we must surely keep to the text we have.

לערץ הארץ: the paranomasia cannot be captured in English; commentators regularly cite Latin instead: *ut terreat terram*.

20. האדם: the generic article (cf. GK §126*l-m*; JM §137*i*) which could therefore equally be represented by a plural in English.

אלילי כספ...אלילי זהבו: cf. GK §135*n*; JM §140*b*; Gibson, 4, 32–33, and J. Weingreen, 'The Construct-Genitive Relation in Hebrew Syntax', *VT* 4 (1954), 50–59.

עשו־לו: there are two possible ways of construing MT. (i) The subject could be an impersonal plural, 'they', referring to the craftsmen who make the idols on behalf of the worshipper; hence 'which they have made for him (האדם)' (e.g. Hitzig; Dillmann; Delitzsch). (ii) The subject could be האדם, taken as a collective, with לו following as a distributive, hence 'which they have made (each one) for himself' (e.g. GK §145*m*; König; Kaiser). There are several reasons for favouring the second alternative. There is no reference to craftsmen elsewhere in the passage, and indeed v. 8, which has close connections with this verse, clearly indicates that people are thought of as manufacturing their own idols. It is, furthermore, striking that v. 8 uses a comparable construction, which may have indirectly influenced the later author here. Finally, it is obvious that 31.7, another prose addition to its context, is related to the present verse, and it is possible that the same glossator is responsible. There, איש is used in the first half in the place of האדם here, but is preceded by a plural verb (ימאסון), so that it is obviously understood as a collective. In the second half (אשר עשו לכם ידיכם חטא), although the manner of expression differs from the present verse, it is again explicit that the worshipper is also the manufacturer ('your hands' as the subject of עשו, just like אצבעתיו in 2.8). It is admittedly slightly awkward that האדם governs a singular verb in the first part of the verse but a plural here, but in an addition which is heavily dependent on wording from elsewhere this would not seem to be an impossibility. Nevertheless, this awkwardness has led some scholars to favour one of two possible alternatives. LXX and V have a singular verb, so that it is proposed to read עשה (e.g. Marti; Gray; Procksch).[35] Caution is needed before adopting this simple expedient, however, since it is just as likely that they were easing a perceived difficulty; it may be noted that T and P resolve the difficulty the other way, by rendering with a plural throughout the verse. A further disadvantage is the loss of comparability with v. 8 and 31.7. Alternatively, some have appealed to 1QIsaᵃ: its damaged אשר [...] בעותיו is doubtless to be restored as אשר עשו לו אצבעותיו, and Wiklander, 59–60, and Cohen, 'Philological Reevaluation', 49 especially (but cf. Wildberger), maintain that this (or without לו, which is not represented in LXX) is the original reading. Wiklander explains the loss of אצבעתיו as a haplography following אשרעשו, and claims that this would be even more likely in Palaeo-Hebrew script. The result, of course, is to make the phrase identical with the last part of v. 8 (and cf. 17.8). This last point is the very one which should give us pause, however, since we have already seen that the scroll sometimes accommodates the reading of one passage to that of another similar one (cf. 1.15 for an irrefutable example, strangely enough again involving אצבעות; Kutscher, 545, van der Kooij, 98, and Pulikottil, 56–62, list many other examples). In view of this tendency in the scroll, it seems more likely that its reading is secondary at this point.

לחפר פרות: 'to dig wells(?)'. The latter word is unknown, but may be vocalized by association with בְּארות, which (as either singular or plural) occurs nine times as the object of חפר. The consonantal text could, of course, be פָּרוֹת, 'cows', but this makes even less sense. Saadia translated 'fruits',[36] but, though the plural of פְּרִי is not attested, it would not

---

[35] Lagarde's suggestion, adopted by Duhm, that עשו is itself a singular, with retention of the original third radical (i.e. עָשׂוֹ; cf. GK §75; the same is proposed for ישתחוו in v. 8, and cf. Gen. 20.13), does not seem plausible.

[36] See also C. Alonso Fontela, 'Una breve nota marginal de Alfonso de Zamora sobre *laḥpor perôṯ*', *Sefarad* 52 (1992), 29–32.

be expected to lose the *yôd*. It is universally agreed that a single word has here been divided into two; this is usually thought to be a simple error,[37] though Marx, 'Esaïe ii 20', suggests that it may have been an intentional scribal device to introduce a reference to the study of the law (for the image, see the Damascus Document 3.16; 6.3), for which he postulates several possible reasons. To balance this possibility, it may be noted that MT 61.1 also mistakenly divides a reduplicated form (פקחקוח; see too Jer. 46.20), so that an early scribe of Isaiah may have had difficulty in recognizing such forms for some reason. The matter remains unresolved. Either way, the evidence for treating this as a single word is overwhelming. Apart from the general question of sense, the ancient versions all took it as a single word, even if they did not always understand it correctly (and it was treated so as well by the later rabbinic commentators, even though by then the present form of the text had been established). Several thought it was a word for idols (LXX ματαίοις; P *sryqwt*, 'vanity'; T משותא), while V rendered *talpas*, 'moles'. In his commentary on this, Jerome implies that the Three also treated it as one word, though in two cases this is not certain; he will have assumed that they read the same text as he did, but there is a possibility that their renderings are based on two words. θ, at least, is clear, as it simply transliterated: *pharpharoth*. For α, Jerome reports ὀρυκτά, but without any further context it is difficult to judge whether this takes the whole as a single word or is based on חפר alone. Similarly, for σ he gives *infructuosa* (ἄκαρπους?), which might be a way of referring to idols, but which seems more likely to be related to the tradition later found in Saadia, with פרות treated as a separate word (Tur-Sinai and HUBP thus suggest חפר פרות). Finally, 1QIsaᵃ is clear, though curiously it uses the masculine form, rather than the feminine of MT: חפרפרים. The word is a reduplicated (*qᵉtaltal*) form (cf. GK §84ᵇn), hence חֲפַרְפָּרוֹת, 'diggers'. Since moles as we know them are apparently not found in Palestine, 'mole-rats' is a preferable rendering.[38] It is difficult to choose between MT's feminine and 1QIsaᵃ's masculine form; Kutscher, 389, may be right in his suggestion that the scroll has been secondarily attracted to the following עטלפים.

21. לבוא: it is unclear who is the subject of this infinitive. Most commentators treat it as האדם, and so imply that people will throw away their idols 'in order to enter' the caves, presumably more speedily because unencumbered. However, once it is realized that vv. 20-21 are an explanation for the curious (corrupt) text in 18-19, it becomes clear that it is the idols who are the subject, picking up on ובאו in 19 (so correctly Marti). It is thus almost the equivalent of 'So that is how they will enter…'.

The first line can certainly be analysed poetically (with parallelism and 3 + 2 rhythm). However, since it directly continues the prose explanation of v. 20, it seems preferable to see the same form of writing continuing here. The last line, of course, simply repeats 19*b* in a resumptive manner, and so derives its poetic form from there.

---

[37] Cf. F. Delitzsch, *Die Lese- und Schreibfehler im Alten Testament* (Berlin and Leipzig, 1920), 4.

[38] Tur-Sinai claims that V's *talpas* is simply a transcription of עטלף, and that there is therefore no evidence for חפרפר = 'mole(-rat)'. He thinks it is another form of bat. This, however, ignores all earlier Latin evidence to the contrary, and also overlooks the obvious etymological connection with חפר; cf. 'בעקבות הלשון והספר', *Leš* 23 (1958–59), 1–34 (4–5), and 'בעקבות הלשון והספר', *Leš* 26 (1961–61), 77–92 (77); see too S. Lieberman, 'לחפר פרות והספר הלשון ולעטלפים', *Leš* 29 (1964–65), 132–35, and Borowski, *Agriculture*, 156. For NEB's 'dung-beetles', see G. R. Driver, '"Another Little Drink"—Isaiah 28: 1-22', in P. R. Ackroyd and B. Lindars (eds), *Words and Meanings: Essays Presented to David Winton Thomas* (Cambridge, 1968), 47–67 (66–67). He acutely compares Egyptian *ḥprr* (see earlier Popper, 'Parallelism', 327). This would also give excellent sense, though it is not immediately clear why the Hebrew should then take this reduplicated form. In addition, without discussing our verse, M. Lubetski has argued at length that Egyptian *ḥprr* (dung beetle) = Hebrew צלצל (Deut. 28.42; Isa. 18.1), in which case חפרפר* presumably means something else; 'Beetlemania of Bygone Times', *JSOT* 91 (2000), 3–26. Clearly, at such a distance in time there can be no certainty over such details.

22. The force of חדל מן, 'cease/withdraw from',[39] often has to be inferred from the context; thus, for instance, 1 Sam. 9.5, פֶּן־יֶחְדַּל אָבִי מִן־הָאֲתֹנוֹת, 'lest my father stop *worrying* about the donkeys'; 2 Chron. 35.21, חֲדַל־לְךָ מֵאֱלֹהִים, 'Cease *opposing* God'. The problem in the present instance is that we are not directly told who is being addressed by the plural imperative. In the light of the comments below, *relying on* is the most probable (though not the only possible) implication.

במה: for the vocalization, cf. GK §102*k*. This is usually explained as an example of the ב *pretii*; cf. GK §119*p*. Wildberger observes that at 5.28 and 29.16 חשב is followed by ב, which he further thinks may lie behind the renderings in P and T. Such a slight change is possible, but by no means necessary, even though חשב is not followed by ב elsewhere in the Old Testament (though it is in the Dead Sea Scrolls; Wiklander, 75, cites 1QS 5.17-18; 1QH 8.10-11; CD 19.3).

Jerome spells out with great care that his Hebrew text reads *bama* (though it is disputed whether he was already aware of a vocalized form of the Hebrew text).[40] He is aware that the same consonants could be vocalized differently (i.e. as in MT) and so be translated *in quo* (as, he reports, by Aquila), but he ascribes this to a deliberate 'Jewish' attempt to avoid the christological implications of what he deems to be the correct reading. His rendering is therefore *quia excelsus reputatus est ipse* ('because he himself has been thought to be most high'). There is, in fact, evidence for this same reading from impeccable 'Jewish' sources, and Jerome is likely dependent upon this same tradition.[41] It is probable that behind it lies the fact that *excelsus* occurs frequently in the earlier part of the chapter and that Jerome has rationalized the different reading traditions in accordance with his prevailing polemic.

While no one follows this reading in the form represented by Jerome, several have recently been attracted to it on the understanding that בָּמָה may be an alternative spelling of בְּהֵמָה: hence 'but who must be considered a (mere) beast'.[42] In support of this it is noted that במות יער at Mic. 3.12/Jer. 26.18 is probably the equivalent of (rather than a corruption of) בהמות יער, an expression which itself occurs in Mic. 5.7. The comparison of man with animals is frequent in the wisdom literature, and the line in Isaiah 2 reads more smoothly on this understanding than with the traditional vocalization. Attractive as this rendering may seem, it rests on too great a combination of uncertainties to be adopted. Ugaritic *bmt*, from which Dahood started out, means 'back', not 'beast';[43] it is by no means certain that Mic. 3.12/Jer. 26.18 refers to animals, and whether even if it does the text is sound (the comparison with 5.7 makes the case for emendation more, not less, probable), and the current vocalization of Isa. 2.22, which is attested as far back as our evidence reaches, still has to be explained.

[39] See D. Winton Thomas, 'Some Observations on the Hebrew Root חדל', *Volume du Congrès, Strasbourg 1956* (VTSup 4; Leiden, 1957), 8–16, for a full etymological discussion with attention to the renderings in the ancient versions; E. Jenni, 'Lexikalisch-semantische Strukturunterschiede: hebräisch *hdl*—deutsch "aufhören/unterlassen"', *ZAH* 7 (1994), 124–32.

[40] Against S. Talmon, 'Aspects of the Textual Transmission of the Bible in the Light of the Qumran Manuscripts', *Textus* 4 (1964), 95–132 (127), who suggested that במה was a mistake for רמה, on the basis of the latter's frequent occurrence earlier in the chapter, see Kedar-Kopfstein, 'Divergent Hebrew Readings', 183, and Barr (above, n. 25), 118.

[41] Cf. *B. Zeraim* 14a; *Sotah* 4b, cited by Talmon, and D. R. Ap-Thomas, 'Two Notes on Isaiah', in E. C. B. Maclaurin (ed.), *Essays in Honour of Griffithes Wheeler Thatcher (1863–1950)* (Sydney, 1967), 45–61.

[42] So independently Ap-Thomas (see previous note), and M. Dahood, 'Hebrew–Ugaritic Lexicography 1', *Biblica* 44 (1963), 289–303 (302) (with an acknowledgment to Albright); more recently, P. A. Vaughan, *The Meaning of 'bāmâ' in the Old Testament: A Study of Etymological, Textual and Archaeological Evidence* (SOTSMS 3; Cambridge, 1974), 20–22; Wiklander, 75–76.

[43] Cf. J. A. Emerton, 'The Biblical High Place in the Light of Recent Study', *PEQ* 129 (1997), 116–32.

נחשב: for the gerundive force of the niph'al participle, cf. GK §116*e*; WO, 387 and 620; Gibson, 133 (who adds the observation that in such cases the participle often precedes the subject, as here, against the usual word order with the participle).

The verse as a whole is not represented in the LXX, a fact which is compatible with, but does not of itself prove, the view that it is a very late addition to the text (cf. Ulrich, 'Developmental Composition', 292–93). 56.12 is the only other verse in Isaiah to be completely absent from LXX, but substantial omissions also occur at 22.10; 40.7-8; 51.9-10 (and 47.9 in the B text); cf. Ziegler, 47–48, for a discussion of possible reasons. See further below.

Whatever the literary history of the passage, 2.6-22 now presents itself as a single whole. It is criss-crossed by words, phrases and even whole lines which require that it be treated as a single unit in the exegesis of the book.

It relates more by way of contrast than continuity with the previous passage. There, the theme of height is used to portray a day when God's order will be properly acknowledged by all peoples. Once the mountain of the Lord is established as 'loftier than the hills' (v. 2, contrast 14), the nations will come to recognize his authority and learn of him. Here, by contrast, height is used rather to refer to mankind's pride which needs to be brought low. Although the universal outlook is maintained to some extent, as we shall see, it seems that we are being asked to take a step back to see what needs to be done before the vision of 2.2-4 can possibly be realized.[44] The link in vv. 5-6 further specifies that this must begin with the house of Jacob, and that seems to remain the focus through the next few verses. Already with v. 9, however, this gives way to a more general application ('humanity' and 'mankind') which is sustained through to the end of the chapter. It is thus with ch. 3, focusing on Jerusalem and Judah (cf. 3.1), that the real narrowing down comes. Within its broader setting, therefore, our passage may be seen to introduce certain fundamental themes which establish the basis on which the more specific indictments of 3.1–4.1 (to go no further) are advanced. It may be said to supply a clear statement of some of the most characteristic aspects of Isaiah's underlying theology (see especially the connections with 6.1) and of his understanding of the moral order which flows from it. In this connection, attention may appropriately be drawn to the important article by Barton, 'Ethics', where he sets out a clear and persuasive analysis of the basis of Isaiah's ethical thought.

Poetic analysis of the passage is relatively straightforward (note that vv. 20-21 are in prose). The predominantly 3 + 3 pattern is interrupted in a few places, which are therefore noteworthy. In the present form of the text, 8 and 17*b*-18 are examples of a tricolon. Both concern the folly of idol worship, and this theme gains a certain prominence thereby. The urgency of the imperatives in v. 10 is underlined by the shorter 2 + 2 rhythm.[45] This is lengthened somewhat when it is repeated in v. 19, and

---

[44] See too Jensen, 'Weal and Woe' (though based on different critical conclusions).

[45] For some further analysis of this second part of the passage, see Barré, 'Isaiah 2.12-17'. He finds evidence for a carefully constructed chiastic pattern in vv. 12-17, but overlooks some of the wider correspondences to be described below which seem to me to have a more important structuring role in the passage as we now have it.

the further lengthening of the second line of that verse by the addition of
an extra clause is appropriate at the end of a poetic unit, as has already
been noted more than once in ch. 1. The use of repeated formulae in 7-8
and 12-16 may be partly intended to suggest comprehensiveness, while
the patterns established by the refrain-like elements throughout the
passage will be discussed more fully below.

Scholars have disagreed radically in their analysis of the composition
history of the passage.[46] Three starting points for these discussions may be
distinguished. First, there are those who conceive of it as fundamentally a
unity, and who then answer objections and difficulties which have been
levelled against such a possibility. Their success in this confirms their
initial assumption.[47] Secondly, the repetitions within the chapter have
persuaded some that it represents a now heavily damaged or corrupted
version of an originally regular refrain poem, which they then seek to
reconstruct.[48] While the ingenuity of these reconstructions cannot be
denied, they involve such radical treatments of the text (including frequent
dislocations of material, the postulation of loss of text and the rewriting of
other parts) that they invite suspicion. Not surprisingly, as confidence in
the general shape of the Hebrew text has grown in the light of the discovery of much earlier manuscripts among the Dead Sea Scrolls than were
previously available, this approach has dwindled in popularity. Thirdly,
the majority of modern commentators start from what they believe to be
the minimal core of 'authentic' Isaianic material and seek to trace the
process by which this was developed into the present text. While there is
much disagreement over details, most begin with (10,) 12-17, to which
others add (parts of) 7-8. (Wildberger in fact finds four originally separate
units.)[49]

---

[46] For the following, see my essay 'Formation'. So far as I can see, form criticism
gives us no help in the analysis of the passage. The literary units are isolated on completely separate grounds, such as repetition, and to put labels on them hardly takes us
further forward. If there are no *formal* parallels to either the parts or the whole, then we
cannot use this approach in an attempt to disentangle what may be earlier or later.

[47] See, for instance, Napier, 'Isaiah and the Isaian'; Ollenburger, *Zion*, 110–12; and
Auvray. I have already considered above the view of Roberts and others that 2-22 should
be regarded as a single, complete unit.

[48] E.g. Marti; Gray; Fullerton, 'Original Form'. The issues are further complicated by
the similar language to part of the refrain element in 5.15-16 and to a lesser extent in
10.33-34. Consequently, this material is also brought in sometimes to aid in the process of
reconstruction. However, in the case of 5.15-16 in particular, it is likely that we are
dealing with later redactional activity, which may therefore have borrowed directly from
our passage (and the easier grammatical concord there strengthens this impression). The
matters will be discussed *ad loc.*, and should not be introduced as a further complicating
factor in the analysis of ch. 2. The most that need be said here is that 5.15-16 seems to
know a version of ch. 2 which already included vv. 9a and 11; as will be seen, this is
perfectly feasible. It does not, however, demonstrate that 9b and 10 were not also present,
despite the coincidence that these lines are missing in 1QIsaᵃ; see the textual comments
above.

[49] There seems little point in describing all the different analyses which have resulted
from this basic approach; the main ones down to the time when he wrote (1974) are
tabulated in Hoffmann, 107–8, and others are added by Kaiser, 74 n. 33 = ET, 64 n. 33.

Each of these views sets out from an *a priori* assumption which effectively predetermines the final outcome. In my view, it is preferable to start from an internal literary analysis of the text, the diachronic conclusions of which may then be aligned with 'external' points of reference (such as what Isaiah himself could or could not have written) as only a secondary step.

In the first place, vv. 20-21 and 22 may be confidently regarded as additions to the passage by commentators who already knew the rest of the passage in its present form. The reasons for this are given in full in the textual and exegetical discussion of these verses and are accepted by the overwhelming majority of commentators.[50]

Within the remainder, the use of repeated formulae in series in vv. 7-8 (ותמלא ארצו) and 12-16 (ועל כל) indicates that there are two main sections for initial consideration. As the text now stands, the first seems to be bounded by the use of second person verbs at the start of v. 6 (נטשתה) and at the end of v. 9 (תשא), as has been stressed in particular by Sweeney. God is addressed, therefore, in the first section, whereas he is referred to in the third person in the second (starting already with v. 10).

Although many have eliminated parts of 10-19 at an early stage in their analysis, there are indications that it has been assembled with greater care than is generally realized. The central core of 12-16 is surrounded by a two-layered 'envelope'.[51] First, vv. 17 and 11 are almost identical, and secondly so are vv. 19 and 10, the whole passage thus reflecting an 'ABCBA' pattern.[52] It seems most unlikely that this is coincidental or the result of scribal confusion. At some stage, yet to be determined, vv. 10-19 have been put together according to a clear and intelligible plan.

Most commentators accept that v. 17 belonged with 12-16 from the start as either continuation, consequence or application, and many have also argued that v. 10 was the original beginning of 12-16/17.[53] Rather fewer have allowed the possibility that 19 may have been part of 12-17,[54] while occasionally it has been maintained that 11 belonged as some kind of a heading to 12-17.[55] I mention this here not to suggest that one or other of these is right or wrong, but rather to highlight how difficult it is to arrive at

---

[50] Contrast Neveu, 'Isaïe 2,6-22'. His attempt to defend v. 20 as part of the original poem takes no account of the main arguments to the contrary, and it skews his analysis from the outset.

[51] It is a shame that Barré, 'Isaiah 2:12-17', begins his detailed rhetorical-critical analysis from the assumption that vv. 12-17 are a complete poem without regard for the possibility of a wider artfully arranged structure.

[52] This has been recognized by Berges, 77 (followed by Beuken). His attempt to add 6-8 and 20 as a yet further layer in this structure should be rejected, however. Whereas the verses included above are virtually identical with one another, 6-8 and 20 are not; they have only certain elements in common, and even these are not related to one another in the same way in the two passages. Whatever the connection between them, it is clearly of a completely different nature from that which unites 12-19.

[53] E.g. Barth, 222–23; Clements; Höffken.

[54] E.g. Seybold, 'Die anthropologischen Beiträge'.

[55] E.g. Duhm; Procksch. Høgenhaven, 192–94, finds the original nucleus to comprise 10–17.

a decision if one starts out from an attempt to move outwards from what is initially determined as an 'Isaianic' core. The text as we have it has its own literary integrity which needs first to be reckoned with, and suggestions that, say, v. 11 is a misplaced variant or the like are wide of the mark.

So far, then, we have determined that the passage is made up of two clearly marked sections, vv. 6-9 and 10-19. The next question has to be whether they were related from the start or whether their juxtaposition is in some sense redactional. Here again, the choice of starting point for analysis may predetermine the outcome.

The best attempt to indicate a connection between the parts on critical grounds has been advanced by Blenkinsopp, 'Fragments'. He suggests that an original Isaianic poem can be extracted from the passage, comprising vv. 6-8a as the indictment, 10 as a 'link verse', and 12-16 as the verdict. It will be noted that by this selection he has neatly eliminated every reference to 'humanity' and 'mankind' which otherwise seems to dominate the second section. The whole can then be read as directed to Israel/Judah alone. The bulk of his discussion is devoted to demonstrating how and why all the rest of the material was added. Apart from inherent plausibility, his only real argument for the shape of the original poem is the fact that the parallels in the comparable passage Mic. 5.9-13 are all with material included in his original nucleus.[56]

While Blenkinsopp's argument is attractive, it is not above criticism. Since subsequent scholarship has surprisingly not interacted with his proposal, two comments may be permitted here. First, the parallel with Micah does not, in fact, support his case. One of the closest parallels is between Isa. 2.8b and Mic. 5.12b, but according to Blenkinsopp's analysis, Isa. 2.8b is part of the material which he argues has been added later to the original Isaianic nucleus. In addition, all the close parallels are with Isa. 2.6-8, so that they cannot help determine whether 12-16 was also part of the original poem. It is true that he tabulates מבצריך in Mic. 5.10 with חומה בצורה in Isa. 2.15, but this is too remote and isolated to be convincing, and in any case it cannot help settle the question whether, as most scholars believe, v. 17 was joined with 12-16 from the very start. Secondly, the poem as Blenkinsopp reconstructs it does not supply an adequate trigger for the universalist expansion of its second part. He seeks to justify his case with the following words: 'If our reading of v. 12 and 13 is correct, the way has already been prepared in the original poem for its eschatological reinterpretation, since ושפל points to a reversal of fortune and status, a central theme of apocalyptic' (p. 57). However, in his reconstruction of the original poem at this point (p. 56), he explicitly (and in my view rightly) emends ושפל: 'a word like גבוה probably stood here originally'. However much the nucleus of the second part of the poem may have been

---

[56] For reasons already noted, Blenkinsopp should not be faulted for failing to provide form-critical justification for the shape of his original poem. So far as the relationship with Micah is concerned, his conclusions are certainly more palatable than those of Vermeylen, who speculatively seeks to reconstruct an original poem by combining the two passages and suggests that this was then divided between the two books; on this, see Deck, 115–16.

expanded secondarily, it must have had something like v. 17 from the start to justify its concentration on humanity in general.

If serious difficulties thus confront an approach to arguing for a connection between the two parts of the passage if the starting point is the isolation of a hypothetical Isaianic original, can we make better progress by working back from our analysis of the present text? I believe we can. As has already been seen, the first section is clearly brought to a close by the use of the second person verb in the second half of v. 9. But now to this must be added the observation that the first half of this verse equally clearly points forward to the second section. First, rather than referring specifically to God's people, more general terminology is introduced (אדם, אִישׁ); cf. vv. 11, 17. Secondly, although there is no precise parallel for the formulation, the language is closely comparable with the refrain-like elements of these same two verses.[57] Verse 9, therefore, serves to link the two major parts of the passage together, and in particular to suggest that in its final form the more general language of 10-19 should be interpreted with particular reference to God's own people. This conscious interweaving of the two main sections of the passage points clearly, in my opinion, to the redactional nature of v. 9, and by extension, therefore, to the fact that the two parts have been artificially joined subsequent to their separate composition.

The conclusion that we are dealing with two previously separate poems is reinforced by the differences between them, to which others have also drawn attention.[58] (i) The universalistic outlook of vv. 10-19 contrasts sharply with the application in 6-8 to a single nation (see the repeated 'his land'). In line with this, ארץ in 7-8 refers to a single country, but in v. 19 to the whole world. (ii) Verses 6-9 are couched in the past tense: they seem to look back to justify the fact that God has abandoned his people, so that the humbling in v. 9 has already taken place. Verses 10-19 look to the future, however: the day of the Lord is yet to come, and the humbling is more of an eschatological expectation. (iii) As already noted, the first poem (as presently formulated) is addressed to God, whereas in the second he is referred to in the third person. I conclude, therefore, that the content of the two parts of the passage reinforces the conclusion that two originally separate pieces have been joined at a secondary stage. It should be emphasized, however, that this conclusion rests primarily on the literary analysis given above, and not on these considerations of content alone (each of which might be overcome with the exercise of only a minimum of ingenuity[59]).

---

[57] Cf. Seybold, 'Die anthropologischen Beiträge', 402: '2,9a kann wohl nur als von 2,11.17; 5,15f abhängige Kurzformulierung aufgefaßt werden'.

[58] See especially Becker, *Jesaja*, 169–75.

[59] Only so can I understand why Hoffmann, 106–24, who is aware of these differences, can nevertheless conclude that the original poem comprised 7, 8a, 9a, 12-17(? + 19). He has worked from an initial determination of what could have been original to Isaiah (a further illustration of the problems that adopting this direction of analysis poses), and justifies the connection only with the questionable observation that the two parts 'thematisch gut zusammenpassen' (p. 109).

Having reached the conclusion that a redactor has been responsible for joining the two sections, it is natural to ask whether there is evidence for any further activity on his part. Attention here focuses first on v. 18 for two reasons. On the one hand, it represents the only element in 17-19 which does not have a parallel in the careful ring composition already described. Secondly, a reference to the idols has no analogy elsewhere in 10-19,[60] but they do, of course, feature in v. 8, part of the material with which the redactor was working. Thus, although a reference to them here is fully intelligible in the context of the passage as a whole, it seems on two counts unlikely that it stood in 10-19 before it was joined with 6-9. By turning 17b into a tricolon, it has been satisfactorily integrated into its context and it contrasts well with the reference to the Lord alone being exalted just before (Hoffmann's judgment, 'schwerfällig hinter v. 17 nach-hinkend' is thus too harsh). But that cannot overcome the problem that it depends on the joining of 6-9 with 10-19 for its effectiveness.[61]

If the redactor has drawn particular attention in this way to the worth-lessness of idols, it is natural that we should ask whether he has not done precisely the same thing in v. 8b. There too the reference to אלילים has been given prominence at the end of a section by being made the subject of a tricolon, and although on its own this verse might not arouse suspicion, the close parallel with the force of the addition of v. 18 makes it highly likely that this line too is part of the same redactor's work.[62] It is clear, therefore, that part of his concern in undertaking his redaction was to draw particular attention to the folly of idol-worship.[63]

Next, we need to consider the opening of the passage. Verse 6 is often regarded as wholly redactional or else as an isolated fragment which has been added at this transitional point in the chapter. There are two reasons why it is more probable that it includes, at least, material which the redactor inherited. First, we have already noted that he has marked the limits of the first section of the passage by the second person address in v. 9 and also that v. 9 is itself a redactional construction. In view of the awkwardness of this form of address, it is likely that he was acting under some kind of constraint, and this can be provided only by the second person verb in v. 6. Secondly, this same point applies in considering the connection with v. 5. If, as is almost universally acknowledged, that verse was framed to effect the transition from 2-4 to what follows, it is inconceivable that the same writer should have continued with this awkward switch from third person ('the light of the Lord') to second if had been writing the whole passage from scratch.

---

[60] The reference to idols in 20-21 is, of course, part of a much later addition, as already noted; it presupposes the inclusion (and corruption) of v. 18 in its present position, and so has no bearing on the present analysis.

[61] While I agree with Barton, 'Ethics', that a reference to idols is appropriate to Isaiah's fundamental outlook, I cannot agree that this alone justifies attributing this particular verse (still less v. 20) to Isaiah (p. 9). His point stands regardless, of course, on the assumption that 8a is early.

[62] Whether at the same time he suppressed an original ...ואין קצה ל clause, parallel with those in v. 7, is beyond our evidence to determine.

[63] The redactional nature of the material related to idols is also recognized by Seybold.

It is sometimes claimed that v. 6 must be distinguished from 7-8 both because it uses a different construction from the stereotyped listing of those verses and because there is an awkward switch from referring to the people in the plural in v. 6 but as a collective singular in 7-8. These arguments have weight so far as an 'original composition' is concerned, but may nevertheless not force the conclusion that the verse is to be ascribed to our passage's main redactor. There are many well-known examples of the use of the catchword principle in the assemblage of parts of Isaiah's early sayings, and this could be another example of the same. In other words, while it may be accepted that 6-8a were not all a single saying in the earliest form of the book, it could still well be that they were connected already in the form of the book which the redactor inherited. Obviously, to go beyond this conclusion to a discussion of earlier forms and settings would be unjustifiably speculative. We have to be content with the conclusion that they are early from the point of view of a redaction-critical analysis. The introductory 'For' makes good sense from the redactor's point of view, as we shall see shortly, though, if he did not add it himself, it obviously connected with something else at an earlier stage; what that something was we simply have no way of knowing. Only for the phrase 'the house of Jacob' can a case be made for introduction at the redactional stage (cf. Sweeney). It seems probable that it was added to make clear the association with (the redactionally composed) v. 5. As a way of referring to the nation, it fits more comfortably with a period later than that of Isaiah himself (see on v. 5), though even that is only an argument from probability.

Finally, the same limitations of the availability of evidence have to be accepted in regard to such verses as 10, 11 and 19. These are all elements of the ring-composition in 10-19, some or all of which different scholars have regarded as either secondary or redactional. Once v. 18 and the short gloss in v. 13 are removed, however, I can see no evidence on which to base a decision about this either way, granted, as I have argued, that this is the shape in which the redactor inherited this section of the passage. It is, of course, possible that during an earlier stage in the transmission of the book the material was worked up into a ring-composition by the addition of one or more elements at either the beginning or the end. However, I know of no compelling evidence to suggest that this was the case; it is equally possible that it had this shape from the very start.

To summarize this history of the passage's composition, based on an internal literary analysis, it has been argued that the first stage (which may already reflect some undetectable reworking) is represented by (parts of) two separate poems now found in vv. 6*-8a and 10-19 (without 18). These were combined by a redactor in v. 9, and it was probably he who also added vv. 8b and 18, as well as 'house of Jacob' in v. 6. Finally, vv. 20-21 and 22 were added separately at a later date.

It remains to establish, if possible, a date for the two main layers in the text. So far as the redactor is concerned, several converging lines of evidence point to the late exilic period. (i) Verse 5 has already been ascribed to this period (see above), and the redaction of our passage is integrally related to this. Verse 5 urges the readers to 'walk in the light of the Lord' as a consequence (and hence as a first stage in realizing the vision) of vv. 2-4. Verse 6 then gives as a reason or motivation for this that God has abandoned his people. In this context (which is to be distinguished from that of its original composition; see below), this is most naturally to be understood as a reference to the fall of Jerusalem and the subsequent exile, from which the redactor is urging the kind of response which will lead to restoration. As currently formulated, vv. 6 and 9 clearly look back to a major catastrophe as having already taken place, but there is no indication that restoration has yet followed. (ii) The redactor's particular concern to direct the passage in a polemical manner against idolatry also fits this period best. It is, of course, the case that this matter was a concern to some writers throughout much of Israel's history, before, during and after the exile.[64] Nevertheless, the greatest concentration comes around the exilic period, and certainly within the book of Isaiah itself it is with Deutero-Isaiah that this motif is most strikingly associated.[65] (iii) The same conclusion follows from the language used with respect to idols. While the word אלילים itself is earlier, the phraseology of v. 8*b* is suggestive. Hoffmann, 110–11 (cf. Werner, *Plan*, 45), for instance, has listed the many passages where 'the work of [someone's] hands' is found as a way of referring to idols. With the exception of Hos. 14.4, they are all in Deuteronomistic passages, Jeremiah or later. This is not conclusive evidence that Isaiah (say) could not have penned these words, but it fits more comfortably with other evidence pointing to a later date.[66] (iv) Finally, it goes without saying that a redactor must be working later than his inherited text. Once that fact is accepted, and we take the whole composition of the book into account, it may be argued that the late exilic period (i.e. the period associated with the work of Deutero-Isaiah) is the one which provides the most likely setting for the kind of activity and interests represented by this redactor. The actual identity of this redactor (my own suggestion has been that the most plausible hypothesis is that he was Deutero-Isaiah himself) is less significant than the stage in the growth of the book as a whole to which this level belongs.

This brings us finally to the date of the two original elements which lie behind the passage. Most commentators have concluded that they (or 12-17) derive from Isaiah himself (though contrast Bosshard-Nepustil, 139–42), and in view of the close fit with his outlook as known from

[64] See most recently (with extensive bibliography) A. Berlejung, *Die Theologie der Bilder: Herstellung und Einweihung von Kultbildern in Mesopotamien und die alttestamentliche Bilderpolemik* (OBO 162; Freiburg and Göttingen, 1998), esp. 284–413.

[65] Cf. Ruppert, 'Kritik', though I cannot agree with all his diachronic conclusions.

[66] This argument would be strengthened if M. S. Smith is right that the language here consciously contrasts with that of the Babylonian *mīs pî* ceremony (mouth washing of a cult statue); cf. *The Origins of Biblical Monotheism: Israel's Polytheistic Background and the Ugaritic Texts* (Oxford, 2001), 186–87. He cites the claim of the artisans on the second day of the ceremony in which they deny their involvement in the manufacture of the statue. So far as I can see, however, different terminology is used, so that the parallel is too remote to carry conviction.

elsewhere,[67] this seems the most plausible suggestion. Although a universal judgment on the day of the Lord will have been congenial to later apocalyptic writers, there is no evidence known to me to indicate that they must, therefore, have written these verses (*contra* Kaiser, and Becker, 171). In particular, it may be noted that the judgment appears to be indiscriminating, unlike the later use of these motifs within a context of the separation of the righteous from the wicked. In addition to the argument that this material must pre-date the redactor, there is nothing here which does not fit Isaiah's time and personal outlook extremely well. The early Psalm 29, to go no further, gives a close parallel for many of the supposedly apocalyptic elements which are found here, and they have been used in 12-17 to serve Isaiah's own distinctive viewpoint, based on insights such as those found in 6.1 and elsewhere.

The question of when within his ministry these poems might best be set is less easily answered. Most scholars argue for an early date, prior to the Syro-Ephraimite war. It was then, they think, that Judah was at the height of its material prosperity, reflected in v. 7, and a reference to idols fits better then than during the reign of the reforming Hezekiah. These arguments relate to only the first section of the passage, and even then there are some who find a reference to the period during which Hezekiah was planning his revolt against the Assyrians (705–701 BCE) to be more appropriate.[68] While an early date seems marginally more probable for 6-8a, nothing in 10-19 allows us to determine its original setting more precisely. The later redactional concern to set this passage appropriately at the head of Isaiah's indictment has overshadowed whatever earlier specific historical situation may have occasioned it.

6. Many of the issues relevant to the interpretation of this verse are related to textual uncertainties and the verse's redactional function. These have been fully discussed above, with attention to a variety of alternative possibilities, and the conclusions drawn there are necessarily presupposed here.

For God to *abandon* his people implies to withdraw his protective care of them (there is nothing inherently 'covenantal' about the word). Since the following verses indicate that they have placed reliance on various forms of human strength, such as military might, and on alternative forms of man-made religion, God has simply left them to their own devices, with the implication that they must suffer the consequences. In Isaiah's day, this would seem most likely, therefore, to be part of a passage justifying in the nature of a theodicy why some (probably military) disaster is overtaking the people. While a setting related to Hezekiah's revolt against Assyria would be appropriate (so Sweeney), earlier possibilities are not ruled out. In the late exilic setting which is suggested above as the period most likely for the redactional assemblage of this chapter as a whole, however, an

---

[67] Cf. Napier, 'Isaiah and the Isaian'.

[68] E.g. Dietrich, 195; Sweeney. For the possible economic background, see A. G. Vaughn, *Theology, History, and Archaeology in the Chronicler's Account of Hezekiah* (Atlanta, 1999).

application to the Babylonian defeat and exile of Judah would naturally have been the uppermost thought. It is because (*for*) they have suffered so disastrously that they are now urged to change their ways (v. 5)

As was seen above already at v. 3 (and cf. v. 5), the designation of the people as *the house of Jacob* draws attention to God's past protection as it was celebrated in particular in the cult associated with the ark centred upon the Jerusalem temple. Its use here, therefore, underlines by way of strong contrast what might have been their true source of strength. The folly of their actions which have led to God having to abandon them is thus all the more apparent. To refer the phrase exclusively to the northern kingdom, as is sometimes suggested, is clearly unjustified in the context of the chapter as a whole. Whether the words were first included by Isaiah or, as seems more likely, whether they were added in the course of assembling the various elements of the chapter into their present shape, their reference is not primarily political but rather religio-historical: those who claim descent from the people who had earlier enjoyed God's particular blessing, provision and protection are the very ones who have forfeited those privileges. The phrase may thus be allowed a broad application, both geographically and chronologically.

From the second half of v. 6 through to v. 8, various matters are listed which explain more fully why God has abandoned his people. The parallel with Mic. 5.10-15 is particularly striking. The same background is clearly presupposed, and literary influence one way or the other is not impossible. Insofar as they can be distinguished, religious matters come first and last (6 and 8), enclosing the more secular concerns of v. 7.

Verse 6*b* is very problematic both textually and linguistically (see above), so that the details should not be pressed. It is agreed by all, however, that the main point concerns various forms of magical and divinatory practice. Then as now, such practices have their technical terminology which is used in very specialized ways by initiates (though they may differ among themselves in the use of any given term), while those on the outside tend to confuse one term with another. It is thus unlikely that Isaiah intended anything very specific by his choice of vocabulary here; if he had, it could lead to the absurd conclusion that similar practices not mentioned explicitly were therefore less blameworthy. The difficulties of the verse are therefore not as serious for interpretation as might otherwise be the case. It is precisely the general impression which is the most significant point. There is little to be gained in the present context, therefore, by any attempt on the basis of etymology or usage elsewhere to define more closely the meaning of *divination, soothsayers* and *sorcerers* (or any other terms which are similarly introduced by emendation).[69]

There was clearly an ambivalent attitude to such practices in ancient Israel, and this is reflected to some extent in the Hebrew Bible.[70] In 3.2, to

[69] For those who, independently of exegesis of this verse, wish to pursue such matters, there are recent and careful presentations in G. André, *ThWAT* iv. 375–81 = *TDOT* vii. 360–66, and particularly Jeffers, *Magic and Divination*, esp. 65–70, 78–81, 96–98.
[70] Cf. Jeffers, *Magic and Divination*; F. Cryer, *Divination in Ancient Israel and its Near Eastern Environment: A Socio-Historical Investigation* (JSOTSup 142; Sheffield,

go no further, for instance, we find the 'diviner' listed along with other leading members of society without any trace of criticism. Elsewhere, they and others are closely associated with prophets (e.g. Jer. 27.9; 29.8; Mic. 3.6-7), and if they are the subject of criticism it is because they gave a false message rather than because of the means by which they got it. Similarly, lot-casting as a means of divination seems to have been practised at least in early times without any hint of criticism, indeed, rather, the reverse (e.g. Prov. 16.33). On the other hand, there is explicit prohibition of such practices in some of the legal corpora (e.g. Lev. 19.26, 31; 20.27; Deut. 18.9-14), and they are cited as part of the cause for the loss of both the northern (2 Kgs 17.17) and by implication the southern (2 Kgs 21.6) kingdoms.

It is probable that in this matter, as in so many others, attitudes changed over the course of time as what we think of as normative orthodoxy gradually became prevalent, and this may have been the redactor's situation. So far as Isaiah himself was concerned, he no doubt had primarily in mind that any such practice was liable to detract from the immediacy and sole supremacy of God and the need to rely directly upon him in all walks of life. Like several of the other matters mentioned in this passage, such as silver and gold, they might not be evil in themselves, but they became the object of criticism as soon as people began to elevate them alongside God himself. This would particularly be the case if practitioners thought that they could manipulate God by such means.

The children of foreigners: the precise allusion here is obscure, even assuming that the text and translation defended above are correct. A reference to the post-exilic concern with insulation from foreigners *per se* (e.g. Ezra 10; Neh. 13; cf. Kaiser; Clements) seems less likely than an indication that some of these mantic practices were regarded as distinctly non-Israelite and so particularly pernicious. But why there should be a reference to children in this regard (and, as noted above, the word must mean children here; unlike בני it cannot serve to introduce a class) has never been satisfactorily explained.

7. Wealth[71] and military might are obvious resources which might lead the people away from reliance upon God (cf. Deut. 17.16-17), and the latter is the object of Isaiah's condemnation elsewhere for this very reason (31.1). In closely related circles, Hezekiah is also said to have been condemned by Isaiah for showing the Babylonian envoys 'his treasure house, the silver, the gold, the spices, the precious oil, his whole armory, all that was found in his storehouses' (39.2; cf. Nah. 2.10 for a contrasting

---

1994), and A. Laato, *History and Ideology in the Old Testament Prophetic Literature: A Semiotic Approach to the Reconstruction of the Proclamation of the Historical Prophets* (ConB, Old Testament Series 41; Stockholm, 1996), 198–203.

[71] R. Kessler, 'Silber und Gold, Gold und Silber: Zur Wertschätzung der Edelmetalle im Alten Israel', *BN* 31 (1986), 57–69, claims that the order silver–gold is earlier than the reverse. If he is right, this would be a further small pointer to the pre-exilic origin of this passage. We should then have to assume that v. 20 and the other passages which are dependent upon it were influenced by the present verse (which seems likely in any case on other grounds).

parallel). While Isaiah himself was probably referring to some particular circumstances at the time when he first formulated these words, the exilic redactor may well have had a more general assessment of the monarchic period in view. Solomon's reign is one to which these words could be most aptly applied, and if he took this together with the Deuteronomic injunction just noted, he may well have seen it as paradigmatic of the failure of the Davidic monarchy.[72]

Horses and *chariots* should be taken closely together; there is no evidence for a separate cavalry at this time. Chariot forces are frequently mentioned both in the Bible and elsewhere as expressive of the height of military power and by extension their listing in accounts of spoil symbolizes the extent of the victory (see the extensive list of references in Wildberger). Mention of them here does not by any means indicate that the northern kingdom alone must be in view, as has been suggested. Although chariots are more often referred to in connection with the north, their use in the south is securely attested at this period both by the reliefs from Nineveh depicting the siege of Lachish and, indeed, by the discoveries of excavations at the site itself.[73] Although the hill country was unsuitable for their deployment, this would not have applied to the low-lying Shephelah.

8. This short catalogue ends with a reference to *idols*. The fact that it is treated separately from the mantic practices in v. 6 suggests that we should see a close connection with the references to wealth and military power in the previous verse. Whether through trade or military alliances, agreements between states in the ancient world generally included recognition of other deities. There is a sense of closure and of emphasis in that the previous 'there is no end to...' element is here replaced by two further clauses, so that the verse as a whole becomes a tricolon. A similar device is used at 17*b*-18, again to emphasize the worthlessness (and on that occurrence the end) of idols.

While the etymology of אֱלִילִים, *idols*, is disputed,[74] there can be little doubt that it was chosen (and, indeed, Preuss suggests coined directly) here and elsewhere in order to effect a disparaging pun on אֵל and אֱלֹהִים (something like 'godling'), perhaps also combined with אֱלִיל, 'worthlessness'. Its use in Pss. 96.5 (= 1 Chron. 16.26) and 97.7 suggests to Wildberger that

---

[72] I cannot accept the assertion of Gitay, 50–51, that the third person references in vv. 7-8 are to Assyria rather than to Judah. The antecedent is 'the house of Jacob' in v. 6.

[73] Cf. D. Ussishkin, *The Conquest of Lachish by Sennacherib* (Tel Aviv, 1982), e.g., 105.

[74] For surveys of the possibilities, see Wildberger; H. D. Preuss, *ThWAT* i. 305–8 = *TDOT* i. 285–86, and *idem*, *Verspottung fremder Religionen im Alten Testament* (BWANT 92; Stuttgart, 1971), 136–37; B. Podolsky, 'Notes on Hebrew Etymology', *IOS* 18 (1998), 199–205 (203). The matter is complicated by the fact that there is a singular form אֱלִיל which (if the texts in each case are sound) is mostly used as a qualifying abstract after a noun in the construct state with some such meaning as 'worthlessness, weakness' (cf. Job 13.4; Jer. 14.14; Zech. 11.17), and for these occurrences the cognates which are usually compared (e.g. Akkadian *ulālu*, 'powerless'; Syriac *ʾallîl*, 'weak', etc.) are appropriate. There appears not to be a strict parallel for אֱלִילִים, however. This may be significant or may be due to no more than the fact that we do not expect to find ridicule of idols outside Israel.

Isaiah may have known the word from the Jerusalem cult tradition, but the uncertain date of the psalms and Isaiah's facility at word-play elsewhere (e.g. 5.7) means that the possibility cannot be ruled out that he in fact first deliberately coined the word. It occurs ten times in the first part of the book, and apart from the two psalms passages all the other few occurrences are certainly later; cf. Lev. 19.4; 26.1; Ezek. 30.13; Hab. 2.18.

The essential folly of idol worship is perceived to be that honour is given to something which must by definition be inferior, since it is manufactured by the devotee himself.[75] A true idol-worshipper, of course, would have responded that he distinguished between the idol and the god whom it represented, but it is precisely by such distortions that satire and caricature achieve their goal. From Isaiah's point of view, his words were justified by the fact that in any case any rival to the Holy One of Israel was *ipso facto* inferior.

The use of such satire is generally associated with the later period, especially because of its development in Deutero-Isaiah (e.g. 40.19-20; 41.6-7; 44.9-20); however, there are earlier antecedents which are well attested (e.g. Hos. 13.2; Mic. 5.12 [13]), and the idea seems to have been picked up by later editors of the Isaianic tradition (e.g. v. 20 below; 17.8; 31.7). It thus looks as though, as with many other motifs, this was a line of thought which was present in Isaiah, was developed by his later tradents and was then taken up in a strikingly creative fashion by Deutero-Isaiah.[76] The redactional expansion of this verse, as claimed above, may reflect this.

9. The redactional nature of this verse has already been fully discussed. The connection with what precedes was, from the redactor's point of view, quite straightforwardly that people were *humbled* and *brought low* by God because of the proud and independent spirit displayed in 6b-8. There is thus a close correspondence with the fact that he has abandoned them (6a), and the point may be underlined by the close sound association between יִשַּׁח, *is humbled*, and יִשְׁתַּחֲווּ, *they worship*, in v. 8. At the same time, the vocabulary links forward to the following section: the past experience of judgment is but a foretaste of what is to come if the people do not respond appropriately (cf. v. 17, where the same verbs are used with reference to the future). This half of the verse, therefore, almost has the status of a text on which vv. 10-17 are an extended commentary; the

---

[75] Cf. M. Tsevat, 'The Prohibition of Divine Images According to the Old Testament', in M. Augustin and K.-D. Schunck (eds), *"Wünschet Jerusalem Frieden": Collected Communications to the XIIth Congress of the International Organization for the Study of the Old Testament, Jerusalem 1986* (Frankfurt am Main, 1988), 211–20. Barton, 'Ethics', 9, and 'Begründungsversuche der prophetischen Unheilsankündigung im Alten Testament', *EvTh* 47 (1987), 427–35, finds a link with the dominant thought of the passage as a whole in seeing 'both pride and idolatry as examples of the effect of failing to observe order in the world', a theme which he rightly explains as the basis (to be distinguished from the source) of Isaiah's ethical norms. The problems of defining precisely what the biblical writers meant by idolatry and why they objected to it are well outlined by F. E. Greenspahn, 'Syncretism and Idolatry in the Bible', *VT* 54 (2004), 480–94; see too J. Milgrom, 'The Nature and Extent of Idolatry in Eighth–Seventh Century Judah', *HUCA* 69 (1998), 1–13.

[76] Somewhat differently Ruppert, 'Kritik'.

use of the present tense in the translation is intended to capture this two-way orientation.

Wildberger claims that Isaiah is here quoting a wisdom saying (it is immaterial for this discussion whether we ascribe the words to Isaiah or, as I believe, to the redactor). In support, he observes (i) the use of language for humanity in general rather than the people of Israel, (ii) that the verbs are not commonly used in the prophets, and (iii) that the outlook of the proud being humbled is more akin to wisdom thinking (e.g. Prov. 14.19; 25.7; 29.23) than to the complaints of the lament psalms, where being bowed down is a situation to be regretted as undeserved. While there is truth in these observations, the consequence does not necessarily follow. The following verses will demonstrate clearly that the theology here being given expression is at the very heart of Isaiah's own thinking, namely that in view of God's exaltation anything or anyone who sets up as a rival to him must inevitably be put down. Rather than direct dependence on wisdom traditions, therefore, it seems far more likely that this is another example where Isaiah and those who followed him shared some of their underlying outlook but developed it in their own way because of the distinctive theological emphases of Isaiah himself and of the book as a whole.

The prayer *do not forgive them* initially sounds harsh (though no more so than Hos. 9.14), but it needs to be understood in its redactional context. The use of נשא for forgiveness occurs at an important juncture in the book, namely at 33.24, which I have argued elsewhere led straight into ch. 40 in the exilic form of the book (cf. *Book*, 221–39). From both passages, it is clear that this holds out the promise of forgiveness to those alive at that time. Furthermore, Isaiah himself had experienced forgiveness, according to 6.5-7. Once the nature of vv. 6-9 in our passage as explained above is appreciated, it becomes clear that this prayer concerns specifically the generation of those whose sin had led to the fall of Jerusalem and the exile, and does not imply a blanket request to withhold forgiveness generally. There may be no forgiveness for them, but it remains an open possibility for the next generation.

However we may react to this sentiment, it at least safeguards the view that humanity's fate is not impersonal or automatic. God's sovereignty, which on the one hand means that human hubris will be punished, also includes the notion of his freedom to exercise mercy in forgiveness, as Isaiah himself experienced. The prayer at this point does not negate that truth, but indicates rather an alignment with the divine verdict that such unrepentant pride as had been seen among Isaiah's contemporaries was incompatible with a true and lasting relationship with God. It arises from an understanding of both divine freedom and genuine human responsibility for one's actions. Though seemingly harsh when considered in isolation, the likelihood should be considered that it represents a reflection on Isaiah's repeated attempts to urge his people to change their ways, attempts which had fallen on deaf ears; it may therefore indicate a reluctant acquiescence in the force of the 'hardening' saying in ch. 6.

10. On the view defended above, this verse marks the start of the major section of the passage (10-19), to which 6-9 have been redactionally prefaced. The heart of the section is the description of the day of the Lord of

Hosts (12-16). The present verse introduces the section by indicating what should be unrepentant humanity's only possible, but nevertheless desperate, response, namely to hide oneself away. The almost mocking tone of the commands to *enter into the rock* and to *hide yourself in the dust* indicates that the day will include, at least, a theophany.

Descriptions of theophanies in the Hebrew Bible take many forms, and they differ over such fundamental matters as to whether the appearance of God is for blessing or for judgment. Consequently, scholars differ in their reconstructions of the traditio-historical background and the development of this material.[77] With their characteristic desire to categorize such matters, commentators have applied some of these different approaches to the present passage. The danger of such approaches is to exceed the evidence at our disposal, for the text here is reticent about detail. It does not seem necessary to observe any more than that storm and probably earthquake[78] are involved when God appears to bring down all that is proud in society and nature. God's appearance in the storm is the commonest representation of his advent in judgment, being not only found in older and more recent poetic descriptions of all kinds, but also with deep roots in earlier Canaanite, and indeed generally in other Semitic, texts. The only other hints in the present text are that the title 'Lord of Hosts' in v. 12 may imply that he comes as a divine warrior, something which is again closely associated with the storm theophany,[79] and that there are royal overtones to some of the language later in this verse and elsewhere, suggestive of the divine king; cf. Psalm 29, to go no further, for this combination. Whether Isaiah derived such notions directly from the Jerusalem cult[80] or whether they were simply part of the common understanding at his time which he shared is neither clear nor important for exegesis. As will be seen later, his own experience of God as recorded in ch. 6 clearly had a profound effect on his presentation, and the passage gives evidence of the way in which his adoption of a general and standard approach to theophany was radically reworked to express some of his most fundamental convictions about the nature and activity of God. It may also be noted that the focus of attention remains firmly limited to the world. There is no hint of the kind of cosmic convulsions with which this circle of ideas became associated in later, apocalyptic writings (perhaps themselves a revival of much earlier, pre-Israelite notions in this regard).

In mountainous terrain caves in the *rock* (cf. v. 19) have always been a place of refuge in times of attack (e.g. Judg. 6.2; 1 Sam. 13.6).[81] *Dust* is

---

[77] For contrasting examples, with further bibliography, see, for instance, Jeremias, *Theophanie*, and T. Hiebert, 'Theophany in the Old Testament', *ABD* vi. 505–11.

[78] See especially Milgrom, 'Did Isaiah Prophesy?', 178–82.

[79] Cf. P. D. Miller, *The Divine Warrior in Early Israel* (HSM 5; Cambridge, Mass., 1973).

[80] And so by extension whether he associated this circle of ideas in particular with the enthronement of the divine king, as suggested in particular by J. Gray, *The Biblical Doctrine of the Reign of God* (Edinburgh, 1979), 141–42, and K. J. Cathcart, 'Kingship and the "Day of YHWH" in Isaiah 2:6–22', *Hermathena* 125 (1978), 48–59.

[81] Cf. S. B. Parker, 'Graves, Caves, and Refugees: An Essay in Microhistory', *JSOT* 27.3 (2003), 259–88.

amplified in v. 19 to 'holes in the dust/ground', and this is no doubt its sense here. Of course, this is not serious advice about how to escape the judgment that is coming, but uses irony to highlight that in fact there will be no escape; cf. Hos. 10.8; Amos 9.2-4.

Royal language is taken up in the second line to express something of God's character. The *terror of the Lord* is the terror which he inspires, much in the manner of a conquering king; see, for an example which may have been nearly contemporaneous, the words of Sennacherib with reference to Hezekiah, who 'was overwhelmed by the awesome splendor of my lordship' (*COS* ii. 303B). *Majesty* (הדר) is another word which is used on occasions for the human king and then transferred by extension to apply to God, particularly with overtones of (military) strength, as Brettler has emphasized.[82] The more or less synonymous word with which it is associated, גאון, can strikingly be used with a range of meanings stretching from the majesty of God through the justified pride of man to arrogant pride or hubris.[83] Since it appears not to be used of the human king, it is possible that it was recognized that in such a context it was God's prerogative alone. There is thus a certain suitability about its use here, for it draws out the fact that God's *glorious majesty* brooks no human rival; contrast the related word גאה, 'proud', in v. 12, which is condemned.

11. *Haughty eyes* occurs as a concept, if sometimes with the use of different vocabulary, a number of times as a particular example of *pride*; cf. Isa. 5.15 (עיני גבהים); 10.12 (תפארת רום עיניו); Ps. 101.5 (גבה עינים); Ps. 18.28 and Prov. 6.17 (עינים רמות); Ps. 131.1 (לא־רמו עיני); Prov. 21.4 (רום עינים); 30.13 (מה־רמו עיניו). It is a transparent notion, and such arrogance is universally condemned, especially in the wisdom literature. However, in line with what we have already seen, Isaiah does more than just adopt a commonplace; Wildberger comments appropriately: 'Isaiah sounds one of the chief notes of wisdom, but then completely transforms it by transplanting it into the conceptual framework of the Day of Yahweh. Isaiah does not speak, as wisdom does, about what is good or better, but rather about what Yahweh Sebaoth opposes with his whole being, because of his claim to be the only one who is "high," the only one who is lord and king.'[84]

The second half of the verse gives expression to the very core of this outlook—God's exclusive exaltation, which Isaiah had come to appreciate through his vision in the temple (ch. 6), and which one day would be universally acknowledged. *Exalted* derives from a verb which seems to be used of things which are inaccessibly high (like a city which is too high to be captured; cf. Deut. 2.36; Isa 26.5; or the city walls; cf. Isa. 30.13; Prov. 18.11) and hence unattainable (like the knowledge of God; cf. Ps.

---

[82] Brettler, *God is King*, 60–61, 66. For a slightly different, but perhaps complementary, emphasis, see G. Warmuth, *ThWAT* ii. 357–63 = *TDOT* iii. 335–41.

[83] For full details, see D. Kellermann, *ThWAT* i. 878–84 = *TDOT* ii. 344–50.

[84] For an emphasis on the political aspect of such vocabulary throughout this passage, see K. van Duin, 'Orgueil ou souveraineté, psychologie ou politique?', in J.W. Dyk *et al.* (eds), *Unless Some One Guide Me... Festschrift for Karel Deurloo* (ACEBT SS 2; Maastricht, 2001), 149–56.

139.6).[85] It is thus the very word to be used to give expression to Isaiah's conception of God himself (see too v. 17; 12.4; 33.5; cf. Ps. 148.13), and again it is appropriate that it should never be used of the human king.[86] The addition of *alone* reinforces the point. 'With this utterly theocentric focus, the reader finds the central pulse beat of Isaianic theology' (Childs).

That day will be further explained in the next verse. By using the ring structure described above, vv. 10-11 build up towards the climax in v. 12, as its introductory *For* makes clear, just as the reverse order in vv. 17-19 moves away from it in what we might consider to be the more logical sequence. The view that these two verses are garbled and scribally misplaced fragmentary repetitions of what comes later shows little imaginative or poetic appreciation.

12. With the announcement that *the Lord of Hosts has a day*, we reach the very heart of the passage. When this is coupled with the previous verse, the prophet is clear that his proclamation of the Lord's exaltation and human pride's abasement is not just a pious hope or aspiration, but a firm expectation. In such a context, of course, *day* need not refer to a 24-hour period, but, as frequently elsewhere, to a 'time' or 'period'.[87]

The 'day of the Lord' and some closely related expressions occur a number of times in the prophetic writings. Although on the basis of what these passages say scholars have drawn into its ambit a varying range of other texts both in the prophets and elsewhere, it seems safest to work in the first instance from those where the reference is explicit.[88]

It has occasionally been suggested that the term was first coined by Amos (cf. Amos 5.18),[89] but the way in which the prophet refers to it indicates that he is more probably interacting with something which he shares in common with his readers. Although in Amos and our passage in Isaiah the day will bring judgment on Israel, the rhetoric of the passages indicates that this is unexpected.[90] Since the phrase also occurs a number of times in some of the oracles against the nations (e.g. Isa. 13.6, 9; 34.8; 63.4; Jer. 46.10; Ezek. 30.3),[91] it is clear that the popular view of this day was that it would be one on which God intervened decisively to overthrow the nation's enemies and establish Israel's supremacy, as he had in the

---

[85] Against Wildberger, the notion of being solid and impenetrable seems more likely to be derived from this idea of height rather than its 'basic meaning'.

[86] Cf. Brettler, *God is King*, 72. Brettler also draws attention (p. 181) to the personal name אלשגב on a (seventh-century?) seal; cf. *AHI*, 128; *DCH* i. 300.

[87] Cf. E. Jenni, *THAT* i. 707–26 = *TLOT* ii. 526–39; M. Weinfeld, 'The Day of the Lord: Aspirations for the Kingdom of God in the Bible and Jewish Liturgy', in S. Japhet (ed.), *Studies in Bible* (*ScrH* 31; Jerusalem, 1986), 341–72 (343–46).

[88] Cf. Y. Hoffmann, 'The Day of the Lord as a Concept and a Term in the Prophetic Literature', *ZAW* 93 (1981), 37–50; for some possible extra-biblical parallels, see D. Stuart, 'The Sovereign's Day of Conquest', *BASOR* 221 (1976), 159–64.

[89] E.g. M. Weiss, 'The Origin of the "Day of the Lord"—Reconsidered', *HUCA* 37 (1966), 29–60.

[90] The possibility of direct literary dependence by Isaiah on Amos is, however, denied by Fey, 77–83.

[91] This is the starting point for H.-P. Müller's analysis in *Ursprünge und Strukturen alttestamentlicher Eschatologie* (BZAW 109; Berlin, 1969), 72–85.

past (cf. Isa. 9.3; Ezek. 30.9). In characteristic fashion, these two prophets, and several others after them, turn this notion on its head: because of their sin and rebellion against God, Israel and Judah have reached the position where they themselves are God's enemies so that God's action will be turned against them rather than on their behalf.

Scholarly attention has focussed primarily on the background and setting of this expression,[92] and only the major proposals which have continuing support need be mentioned here. Though he was not the first to do so, Mowinckel proposed in a manner which attracted considerable support that the phrase originated in the (hypothetical) annual cultic festival of the Lord's enthronement. From a present celebration of God's victory, this came over the course of time to be projected into the future, and, not least because of the use of the idea by the prophets, it was also detached from its cultic origins to become a more general eschatological expectation.[93]

In contrast, von Rad took note of the frequent association of the phrase with military language to argue that the day of the Lord was associated originally with the whole complex of material which he and others labelled the 'holy war'. It was the day on which God would march forth to conquer his (and hence Israel's) enemies. In origin, therefore, the concept went back to Israel's earliest days.[94] Although there had been some earlier adumbrations of this suggestion, and although it has attracted some significant criticism since, it is von Rad's view which has probably gained the widest following.[95]

Beside these two major views, note may also be taken of Weiss's observations that the day is most closely associated with biblical descriptions of a theophany,[96] of a small group of scholars who have attempted to relate the concept primarily with the covenant traditions, and in particular the execution of the treaty curses,[97] and of Barstad, who finds its setting in the public laments, thus positing a situation which combines a cultic milieu and a context of war.[98]

[92] For surveys of research, see M. Saebø, *ThWAT* iii. 582–86 = *TDOT* vi. 28–31; R. H. Hiers and K. J. Cathcart, *ABD* ii. 82–85; and especially Barstad, *Religious Polemics*, 89–110.

[93] Cf. S. Mowinckel, *Psalmenstudien*, II (Kristiania, 1922); 'Jahves dag', *NTT* 59 (1958), 1–56, 209–29; *He That Cometh: The Messiah Concept in the Old Testament and Later Judaism* (Oxford, 1959), esp. 126–33, 143–49. Mowinckel was particularly concerned to counter the view of H. Gressmann and others that there was a pre-prophetic eschatology in ancient Israel.

[94] Cf. G. von Rad, 'The Origin of the Concept of the Day of Yahweh', *JSS* 4 (1959), 97–108.

[95] For details, see Barstad, *Religious Polemics*, 91–93; B. Becking, 'Expectations about the End of Time in the Hebrew Bible: Do they Exist?', in C. Rowland and J. Barton (eds), *Apocalyptic in History and Tradition* (JSPSup 43; Sheffield, 2002), 44–59.

[96] Weiss, 'Origin' (above, n. 89); cf. Jeremias, *Theophanie*, 97–100; Weinfeld, 'The Day of the Lord' (above, n. 87), 358–66.

[97] Cf. F. J. Hélewa, 'L'origine du concept prophétique du "Jour de Yahvé"', *Ephemerides Carmeliticae* 15 (1964), 3–36; W. van Leeuwen, 'The Prophecy of the YÔM YHWH in Amos v 18-20', *OTS* 19 (1974), 113–34.

[98] Barstad, *Religious Polemics*, 103–8. Barstad earlier criticized Mowinckel both because his theory of an annual enthronement festival remains hypothetical and because

In my opinion, these disagreements stem from a problem noted several times already of seeking to move from a single expression to a rigid and exclusive form-critical (and hence situational) categorization. As others have observed,[99] there are elements of truth in several of these theories, and it seems inherently unlikely that so natural an expression should be limited to just one. Even if it was first coined in one setting rather than another, the evidence for knowing which is beyond our recall. By the time to which our extant sources bear witness it is likely that the various matters discussed had become intermingled, at least in most people's thinking, and it is at this, rather than some narrowly technical, level that the prophets engage.[100] The outward demonstration of the Lord's sovereignty or kingship would inevitably be accompanied by judgment on his enemies and by implication with victory for Israel, and this could only be described in the language of war. His advent in power to effect this was bound to be described in material drawn from the theophanic tradition, and we need not doubt (as the Psalms suggest) that it was prayed for and proleptically celebrated in public ceremonies at the sanctuary. This general hope is applied somewhat variously in the prophets, according to their different historical and social situations, and it is questionable whether any nearer definition is a helpful guide for interpretation.[101] As already noted, the title *Lord of Hosts* in the present verse hints at the military aspect of Isaiah's appreciation (see above on 1.9), and there are several connections with the description of theophanies elsewhere. But, like Amos before him, he turns it against his readers' expectations. All forms of human pride will be brought low. Although this is expressed in universal form, it is likely to have been directed primarily towards the house of Jacob.

there is no textual evidence to support his understanding of the reference of 'day' developing from a cultic feast to an eschatological idea where God destroys his enemies in battle (pp. 98–102). Similarly, he cites the influential article of M. Weippert, ' "Heiliger Krieg" in Israel und Assyrien', *ZAW* 84 (1972), 460–93, in opposition to von Rad's view: all war in the ancient world was effectively 'holy war', inasmuch as the gods were involved, and the manner in which the biblical texts describe this is by no means peculiar to Israel. In fact, it is now generally recognized that it is a mistake to talk of 'holy war' as a formal institution; the material cited by von Rad relates rather to a literary convention for the description of warfare in which the protagonists believe that their God is fighting on their side.

[99] See especially F. M. Cross, *Canaanite Myth and Hebrew Epic: Essays in the History of the Religion of Israel* (Cambridge, Mass., 1973), 91–111; Weinfeld, 'The Day of the Lord'. This approach should not be confused, however, with that of Everson, who implausibly claims that the prophets referred to 'a sequence of historical days of Yahweh'; cf. A. J. Everson, 'The Days of Yahweh', *JBL* 93 (1974), 329–37.

[100] Note the interesting inscription from Kuntillet 'Ajrud, which seems to combine elements of theophany and war: [מה]מלח[ם] בים ...[...] הרם וימסן אל [...] ובזרח, 'When God shines forth...mountains will be dissolved...on the day of wa[r]'; cf. *AHI*, 82.

[101] For the importance of a literary approach at this level, see R. Rendtorff, 'Alas for the Day! The "Day of the Lord" in the Book of the Twelve', in T. Linafelt and T. K. Beal (eds), *God in the Fray: A Tribute to Walter Brueggemann* (Minneapolis, 1998), 186–97, but this should be read also in the light of J. Barton's perceptive analysis, 'The Day of Yahweh in the Minor Prophets', in C. McCarthy and J. F. Healey (eds), *Biblical and Near Eastern Studies: Studies in Honour of Kevin J. Cathcart* (JSOTSup 375; London, 2004), 68–79.

It would be a mistake to try to distinguish too sharply between the four words in the second half of the verse which describe this pride; the whole point is that the accumulation of near-synonyms produces its own rhetorical effect. It should be carefully noted, however, that the inner pair, *high* and *lifted up* (רם and נשא), also occur at 6.1, where they find their theological (and possibly also chronological) basis. Not surprisingly, they are repeated in v. 14 (as well as in the gloss in v. 13). Similarly, *lofty* (assuming גבה is the right emendation) recurs in v. 15 (and see the related forms in 11 and 17). For *proud*, see the final comment on v. 10 above.

13. There now follows a list of eight examples of this pride (vv. 13-16). The glossator who added *high and lifted up* was thus quite correct in indicating at the start of this list that the items are linked with v. 12; the point was already clear in the original text, however, by the repetition of *against all/every*.

It is possible that the list is arranged geographically in a north to south direction, from *Lebanon* and *Bashan* through the central hill country with its fortified settlements (vv. 14-15) to Ezion-geber on the Gulf of Aqaba, where ships of Tarshish are sometimes mentioned (see on v. 16). This is not certain, however, for the ships could equally well be associated with the Phoenician coast, and there is nothing very specific geographically about vv. 14-15. If the suggestion is nevertheless correct, however (see Wildberger), it would be of interest, in that it runs counter to the dominant tradition that God appeared in theophanies from the south (e.g. Deut. 33.2; Judg. 5.4; Ps. 68.9, 18). There is one parallel, however, namely the theophany in the thunderstorm of Psalm 29. There are several similarities between this Psalm and our passage, including the emphasis on the majesty of God (vv. 1-2) and the references to the cedars of Lebanon (5) and the oaks (9, text uncertain). In this psalm too, the direction is from north (Lebanon, 5-6) to south (Kadesh, 8). It is widely recognized that Psalm 29 has many conceptual and linguistic parallels with the Ugaritic texts, and indeed many go so far as to think that it is an Israelite adaptation of an earlier hymn to Baal.[102] It is possible, therefore, that there is a reflection here of the Canaanite view of the home of the gods being in the north, a notion which may have been recalled (if at one remove) in the Jerusalem cult (cf. Ps. 48.3). If so, this would again point up Isaiah's dependence on this tradition rather than that of the Exodus and Sinai. An alternative possibility should also be considered, however, namely that he wished to indicate God's advance as being from the north because there was a tacit identification of his arrival in Judah in judgment with the Assyrians (cf. Kaiser). Both theories (and indeed the geographical basis on which they rest) remain uncertain, however.

---

[102] For extensive bibliography, see J. F. Diehl, A. A. Diesel and A. Wagner, 'Von der Grammatik zum Kerygma: Neue grammatische Erkenntnisse und ihre Bedeutung für das Verständnis der Form und Gehalts von Psalm xxix', *VT* 49 (1999), 462–86. Even so, they have regrettably overlooked the relevant discussions of P. C. Craigie, 'Psalm xxix in the Hebrew Poetic Tradition', *VT* 22 (1972), 143–51, and J. Day, 'Echoes of Baal's Seven Thunders and Lightnings in Psalm xxix and Habakkuk iii 9 and the Identity of the Seraphim in Isaiah vi', *VT* 29 (1979), 143–51.

Although there are occasions when *cedar* on its own may be used without modern botanical exactitude (e.g. Lev. 14.4; Num. 19.6), there need be little doubt that *the cedars of Lebanon* are the well known *cedrus libani*, a tree which can attain great age and grow as tall as thirty metres.[103] It was valued throughout the ancient Near East for major building work. Thus both its height and use make its inclusion at this point fully comprehensible. If the usual emendation of Ps. 37.35 is correct, it is mentioned there too as a symbol of human pride.

Oaks (אלון, to be distinguished from the אלה, 'terebinth' of 1.29-30), while not quite so magnificent as the cedar, share many of the same qualities. There are, in fact, more than one botanical species of oak known in Palestine, to any or all of which the Hebrew word may refer, and there is evidence that (unlike the cedar) they grew in many places in the land in antiquity.[104] *Bashan* refers to the extensive plateau, some 2000 feet above sea level, to the east of Galilee. It is a fertile region, making it suitable for agriculture and pasturage (Mic. 7.14), and its cattle were proverbial (Deut. 32.14; Amos 4.1; Ps. 22.13). Oaks, mentioned in the same region also at Ezek. 27.6 and Zech. 11.2, are likely to have grown in the western part of the plateau (the Golan Heights). Where *Lebanon* and *Bashan* occur together, it seems that the thought of this economically valuable fertility is uppermost (Isa. 33.9; Ezek. 27.5-6; Nah. 1.4; Zech. 11.1-2).

While the references may thus be taken straightforwardly as examples of tall trees in which people take pride when they are used in construction and from which they derive wealth and prestige, the further question arises whether they should also be read as in some way symbolic of people. The frequent metaphorical use of trees in Isaiah suggests that this is not impossible, although at this point, since there is no direct contextual steer, interpretation passes (perhaps deliberately) to the reader: 'if the cap fits, wear it'. The most obvious allusion, in the light of other uses in Isaiah, would be to leaders (even kings) in society; see, for instance, 10.33-34, a passage with obvious connections with the present verse, and with possible application to either or both Judean and Assyrian kings.[105] This interpretation is found already in T. Beyond this, Nielsen, 177–79, has made the point that the present passage has clearly been redacted, at least, to give idol worship a particular prominence. It is possible, therefore, that at one level there could also be a hidden allusion here to the pride in idols made from the finest wood available (cf. Isa. 40.20; 44.14), or directly to the widespread veneration of trees themselves (cf. 1.29-31).

14. *Mountains* and *hills* hardly require comment in themselves, but the explicit qualification *high* and *lifted up* ties them in closely to the underlying theology of the passage (see on v. 12) and of Isaiah generally (cf. 6.1). Whereas in 40.4 they are levelled out ('made low'; the same verb is used

---

[103] Cf. Zohary, *Plants*, 104–5.
[104] Cf. Zohary, *Plants*, 108–9.
[105] Slightly differently, Wiklander, 120, suggests a reference to foreign nations/ peoples, based on the analysis of the use of Lebanon in Isaiah by S. Virgulin, 'Il Libano nel libro di Isaia', *RivB* 7 (1958), 343–55.

in our passage at vv. 9, 11 and 17, and there are other verbal connections too, so that an allusion to this chapter in ch. 40 is not impossible) before the Lord as he appears in glory in order to create a smooth highway, here the point is rather that they must be brought low because of their inherent height, understood as indicative of pride. Again, the question of a possible metaphorical application may be raised. As well as being places of security and refuge, in which people might place their faith, mountains and hills are also commonly associated with holy places. It is at any rate noteworthy that a passage such as Isaiah 57 combines trees (v. 5) and the 'high and lifted up mountain' (7) as the sites of illicit worship.

15. From two couplets based on natural phenomena, the passage turns to two couplets relating to man-made features. Although physical height remains as an element in this verse, it is moving in a direction which is fully reached in the next verse of pride, and hence also faith, in human achievement. In Isaiah's view, that is misplaced, for it should be reserved for God alone.

Although a *tower* could be used for a variety of purposes, the parallelism indicates that it is its defensive capabilities which are uppermost here. Such towers could either be free-standing (e.g. 2 Chron. 26.10) or part of a city's fortifications (e.g. 2 Chron. 26.9, 15),[106] or even, apparently, some kind of fortress within a city (cf. Judg. 9.46-52).[107] The story of the Tower of Babel (Gen. 11.1-9) is, of course, a classic example of God's overthrow of human hubris. Although the same word for tower is used there, there is no evidence of direct allusion, however, and indeed it is probable that a quite different sort of tower (more like a ziggurat) is envisaged.

Most major Iron Age towns of any size were protected by a *fortified* (inaccessible, and hence impregnable; cf. Jer. 15.20) *wall*, as literary references and archaeological discoveries illustrate in abundance. They could vary considerably in style and design.[108] Although from the perspective of the Israelites the walls of the Canaanite city states could appear to be of enormous height (cf. Deut. 9.1, 'great cities, fortified to the heavens'; 3.5, 'fortified towns with high walls', etc.), that aspect is here giving way to the notion of pride in man-made security, as at Deut. 28.52, 'your high and fortified walls, in which you trusted'.

16. By and large, the Israelites were not a nautical people, and indeed they seem to have been deeply suspicious of most things to do with the sea. *Ships*, especially those designed for long-distance voyages (which is the force of *Tarshish* in this connection; see the textual notes above[109]) will

---

[106] For some examples from archaeological research, see Z. Herzog, 'Settlement and Fortification Planning in the Iron Age', in A. Kempinski and R. Reich (eds), *The Architecture of Ancient Israel: From the Prehistoric to the Persian Periods* (Jerusalem, 1992), 231–74 (271).

[107] This seems to be clear in the case of Thebez (v. 51), though the possibility has been raised that the tower of Shechem (46–49) may have been separately located; cf. J. A. Soggin, *Judges: A Commentary* (OTL; 2nd edn; London, 1987), 192–93.

[108] Cf. Herzog (above, n. 106), 269–71.

[109] The geographical location of Tarshish, which has been much discussed, and for which at least ten different identifications have been advanced, is therefore irrelevant in

have likely filled them with awe. But even with so wonderful a craft God is not impressed. The *beautiful boats* (if this is the correct rendering of an uncertain phrase) cannot be further identified. The older interpretation (see above; e.g. LXX, 'display of fine ships'), which may be reflected in the Masoretic vocalization, is probably not far off the mark.

17. This verse is almost identical with v. 11 (the comments on which may be consulted for the details), and so its repetition here serves as a frame around the central passage in 12-16. Apart from the omission of 'eyes', the only difference is that the verbs in the first line appear in the opposite order, and with the first one placed at the start of its clause rather than at the end. These variations come well within what one might expect in terms of 'distant parallelism',[110] but would be less easily explained if one or other verse (usually v. 11 is considered) were simply a corrupt and erroneous scribal repetition which did not feature in the original poem.

18. Appropriately to the context of the passage as a whole, the repeated element represented by v. 17 has been expanded by this additional clause (so effectively making a tricolon of 17*b*). Among all that will be brought low on 'that day', *the idols* (see on v. 8) are specially singled out in this way, rather as they were in v. 8. The further development of the theme in 20-21 indicates that they are the primary target of the final redactor.

The choice of the verb *vanish away* (חלף) contributes slightly to the polemical tone, for, when it has this general sense, it is usually used elsewhere of ephemeral things like grass (Ps. 90.5, 6), days (Job 9.26) and rain (Ct. 2.11). In other words, the idols are things of no lasting worth or substance.

19. In the text as it stands, *they will enter* clearly refers to the idols, and it is this which has triggered the addition of vv. 20-21. As explained in the textual notes, however, it seems certain that at an earlier stage the word was an imperative, *enter!*, so aligning the verse with 10 and extending the ring structure of the passage.

By comparison with v. 10, two expansions may be noted. First, 'rock' and 'dust' have been expanded to *the caves of the rocks* and *the holes in the ground* (lit., 'dust'). As noted already in the comments on v. 10, this is simply a spelling out of what is implied there.

---

the present context. The identification with Tartessos, a Phoenician colony in Spain at the mouth of the Guadalquiver, has been the most common view, but recently there has been strong support for the view of Josephus that it should be identified with the town (and region) of Tarsus in Asia Minor (Cilicia); in particular, this seems to fit best both the biblical passages where Tarshish is listed in association with other places in that region rather than in the far west (cf. Gen. 10.4; Isa. 66.19; Ezek. 27.12-14) and the contextual implications of the reference to *Tarsisi* in an inscription of Esarhaddon (*ANET*, 290); for a full survey of opinions with abundant bibliography, see A. Lemaire, 'Tarshish-*Tarsisi*: problème de topographie historique biblique et assyrienne', in G. Galil and M. Weinfeld (eds), *Studies in Historical Geography and Biblical Historiography Presented to Zecharia Kallai* (VTSup 81; Leiden, 2000), 44–62, and also van der Kooij, *The Oracle of Tyre* (above, n. 26), 40–47.

[110] Cf. D. Pardee, *Ugaritic and Hebrew Poetic Parallelism: A Trial Cut ('nt I and Proverbs 2)* (VTSup 39; Leiden, 1988), 189–91.

Secondly, the next line has been expanded by the addition of the words *when he arises to terrify the earth*. The verb ערץ is unusual in that it can be used both intransitively, 'be in dread, tremble', and transitively, 'strike with awe, terrify'. The intransitive use is found most commonly in Deuteronomic injunctions to Israel's warriors not to fear the enemy (cf. Deut. 1.29; 7.21; 20.3; 31.6; Josh. 1.9). There may be a hint here that it is the appearance of God in warrior guise to execute judgment on the proud that instils terror (see too on v. 12),[111] and this could be strengthened by the use of קום, 'arise'. That verb is, of course, extremely common, so that caution is needed, but in view of the wider context it is attractive, with Wildberger, to associate its use here with the appeals to God to aid Israel in her wars (cf. Num. 10.35) and with the pleas of the innocent that he should vindicate their cause (cf. Pss. 74.22; 82.8, etc.). The striking point about this is that, while *the earth* continues the universalistic orientation of the whole passage, no special privilege is extended to Israel. God is not restricted to fighting against Israel's enemies, but against challenges to his exclusive sovereignty wherever they may be found. It marks a suitable climax to the passage in one stage of its development.

One may note at this point an interesting association and contrast between this passage and Isa. 33.10-16. There, in an address directed more specifically to Zion, God proclaims that now he will arise (as above), lift himself up and be exalted (רום and נשא, as frequently in the previous passage). This too will inaugurate judgment, but now it is more selective, affecting only 'the sinners in Zion' (33.14), whereas the righteous will be spared and 'live on the heights; their refuge will be the fortresses of the rocks' (33.16; contrast vv. 10 and 19 above).[112] As in other respects, ch. 33 borrows extensively from the first part of the book, but marks a transition towards the more developed outlook of the second.

20-21. Apart from the concluding line, which repeats *verbatim* the last line of v. 19, this passage is in prose (note, for instance, the use of the prose particles את and אשר, the prosaic repetition of את־אלילי, and the lack of parallelism except where there is a close adherence to the structure of material borrowed from the preceding). Much of the language is drawn from elsewhere in 6-19, which was therefore probably already in more or less its present form by the time these verses were appended. This will have included the slight textual corruption at the start of v. 19, which evidently led an early commentator to wonder how it would come about that the idols of v. 18 should come to enter the caves. As the start of v. 21 makes clear, it is this question to which he here supplies an answer. Isaiah 30.22 and 31.7 are clearly related passages, and may come from the same hand.[113]

---

[111] Skinner finds here 'an undoubted allusion to an earthquake', though this seems less obvious to me, in spite of the fact that Isaiah had probably experienced the earthquake in Uzziah's time which made such a lasting impression (cf. Amos 1.1; Zech. 14.5).

[112] The continuation of 33.16, 'their bread will be supplied, their water assured', may indicate that the writer already knew the present order of chs 2 and 3; cf. 3.1 (see below).

[113] See further my essay 'A Productive Textual Error'.

20. The time frame is established as being the same as the previous theophany, *on that day*; cf. vv. 11, 12 and 17. The commentator's basic answer to the problem posed is that, in his haste to escape God's judgment, *a man* (cf. 9, 11, 17) *will throw away* his idols. Naturally, the same word is used for these as in 8 and 18, but they are here qualified as being made of *silver* and *gold*. While this was common enough in itself (e.g. Isa. 40.19; 41.7; Jer. 10.4), it may well be that it was mentioned here specifically to make a connection with v. 7. The polemical note *which they have made, each one for himself to worship* is based on a conflation of the last two clauses in v. 8. The introduction of a reference to *the mole-rats* (if that is the correct translation; see the textual notes for a survey of the possibilities) and *the bats* obviously takes its starting point from the fact that these are creatures which typically live in caves and crevices. It is also, however, polemical, if not satirical. The point is not only that they were unclean but even more that, when confronted with the majesty of the Lord, people will come to realize how utterly valueless are the most precious idols in which they have previously trusted in vain. It is an indication of utter contempt.

21. With somewhat different vocabulary from vv. 10 and 19, but with precisely the same connotations, the commentator makes clear the purpose of his addition. For good measure, he has allowed his dependence on 19 to run on with an exact citation of the second half of the verse as well.

22. This verse is occasionally construed with the following chapter,[114] but this is questionable. Its concern with *humanity* (האדם) links it clearly with the more universalistic outlook of the preceding (cf. vv. 9, 11, 17, 20), whereas ch. 3 is concerned explicitly with the narrower circle of Jerusalem and Judah. It therefore seems preferable to regard the verse as a comment inspired by ch. 2, in which case, since it follows the already additional vv. 20-21, it is likely to be the latest element of all. There is no indication of a more precise date; as indicated in the textual notes, there is more than one way of explaining its omission from the LXX, and even if it was absent from the translator's *Vorlage*, it is possible that it had already been added considerably earlier in a different textual tradition from that to which he had access.

The imperative *stop* is plural, and cannot, therefore, be addressed to God. Although at this late period a reference to other supernatural beings is not entirely impossible, it is far more probable that it is a scribal address to the readers of the scroll, urging them to learn the lessons of the preceding passage. Precisely what they are to stop doing has to be supplied according to the context, and *relying on* seems most likely; however, 'taking pride in' or something of the sort would also be possible, though in this context the meaning is not very different. Since humanity and all its works are going to be shown up as inferior on the day of the Lord, the positive implication of the exhortation is to turn away towards complete trust and glorying in God (cf. positively, Ps. 118.8; negatively, Jer. 17.5; Ps. 146.3-4).

---

[114] E.g. Dillmann; Feldmann; Kissane; Sweeney.

The exhortation is reinforced first by the statement that there is *breath* in his *nostril*. This is almost universally taken to mean 'only breath', a negative idea stressing the frailty of human life. It is recognized, however, that this gives the word an unusual, if not unique nuance,[115] so that an alternative possibility should be considered. There seems to be a clear allusion here to the creation of man in Gen. 2.7, where הָאָדָם, אַף and נשמה also occur. There (as often elsewhere, e.g., Isa. 42.5; 57.16; Job 27.3; 32.8; 33.4; 34.14), the *breath* of life was something given by God, making a living being of the clay creature which he had fashioned.[116] Read in the light of this, our verse seems not so much to be stressing the transitoriness of human life as its complete dependence upon God, who gave *breath*, and who can therefore also take it away. In view of this dependence upon God for life in the first place, it is illogical to place one's trust in anyone or anything else. Isaiah 31.3 makes a similar point (though with רוח instead of נשמה).

The second motivation, which is more explicitly marked as such by the introductory *for*, refers to mankind's worthlessness by comparison with God. In earlier parlance, this kind of consideration was sometimes urged upon God himself in requests that he should cease (חדל) from troubling people; cf. Amos 7.5, 'for he is so small'; Job 7.16, 'for my days are a breath'; 10.20, 'are not my days but few?' (the sentiment is, of course, common elsewhere, even when the verb itself is not used). Here, the rhetoric is turned in a different, though related direction: in view of humanity's insignificance, it is pointless to trust in people.

Although the general sentiment and some of the vocabulary are commonly found in the wisdom literature, none is exclusively so. If the verse is as late as has been suggested, it becomes in any case rather pointless to try to isolate the wisdom tradition as continuing in social isolation. The scribe has drawn generally on his knowledge of biblical thought and vocabulary to add what he considered to be an appropriate exhortation following the substance of ch. 2. There is nothing here to suggest a particular association with Isaiah himself because of his supposed membership of the class of the wise.[117]

---

[115] Cf. Wildberger; H. Lamberty-Zielinski, *ThWAT* v. 671 = *TDOT* x. 67–68.

[116] Indeed, T. C. Mitchell goes so far as to claim that it 'may be used in the Old Testament to describe the breath of God, which, when imparted to man, made him unique among the animals'; 'The Old Testament Usage of *nešāmâ*', *VT* 11 (1961), 177–87.

[117] *Contra* Fichtner, 'Jesaja unter den Weisen', 78 = 'Isaiah Among the Wise', 434; Paas, *Creation and Judgement*, 388–91.

ANARCHY IN JUDAH
(3.1-9)

[3.1]For now, the Sovereign, the Lord of Hosts,
is on the point of removing from Jerusalem and Judah
staff and stay,
the whole staff of bread and the whole staff of water,
[2]warrior and man of war,
judge and prophet
and diviner and elder;
[3]captain of fifty and man of repute,
and counsellor and one skilled in magic practices,
and the expert in charms.
[4]And I will make youths their leaders,
and they will rule over them in a childish manner,
[5]and the people will be oppressed by one another,
each person by his neighbour;
the youth will act arrogantly towards the elder,
and the base person towards the honourable.
[6]For a man will seize hold of his relative
in his father's house:
'You have a cloak; you shall be our leader,
and this heap of ruins shall be under your authority'.
[7]On that day he will cry out, saying,
'I will not be a healer,
while in my house there is neither bread nor a cloak;
you shall not make me leader of the people'.
[8]For Jerusalem has stumbled
and Judah has fallen,
because their tongue and their deeds were against the Lord
in rebelling against the eyes of his glory.
[9]Their partiality has testified against them,
and they proclaimed their sin like Sodom, without hiding it.
Woe to them, for they have brought disaster upon themselves.

1. כי הנה: LXX ἰδοὺ δέ. It is not clear whether כי was in the translator's *Vorlage* or not. As Gray points out, the same equivalent appears elsewhere for הנה alone (22.17), while the latter is also rendered by ἰδοὺ γάρ at 10.33; 13.9; 62.11. However, alongside this should be set the fact that כי הנה is also rendered by ἰδοὺ γάρ at 26.21; 66.15 and by ἰδοὺ alone at 60.2. To this lack of consistency should be added the observation that later in this verse the translator has reversed the order of 'Jerusalem and Judah' (so aligning it with 1.1 and 2.1) and has failed to supply an equivalent for the repeated כל. Clearly, the question whether כי is original or a late redactional addition should be settled without recourse to such questionable evidence, *contra* Budde (see below).

הנה + participle to express the imminent and certain future; cf. GK §116p; Driver, *Tenses* §135 (3);[1] *contra* WO, 675, who use a small selection of examples to urge that the

---

[1] Among a number of other studies, note especially P. Humbert, 'La formule hébraïque en *hineni* suivi d'un participe', in *Opuscules d'un Hébraïsant* (Neuchâtel, 1958), 54–59.

sense is immediately present (i.e. 'is now removing'). However, there are too many other passages where the context clearly refers to the future for this to be convincing.

הָאָדוֹן יהוה צְבָאוֹת: see on 1.9 and 24.

מֵסִיר: 1QIsaᵃ מהסיר; see too the 'correction' of a supralinear ה with מֵנִיף at 19.16. This seems to be a clear example of Aramaic influence. Kutscher, 72–73, observes that this form was characteristic of Official Aramaic but disappeared in later dialects, a small pointer to the likelihood that the scroll belongs to the pre-Christian era at least.

מִשְׁעֵן וּמַשְׁעֵנָה: this feminine form is not attested elsewhere (usually מִשְׁעֶנֶת), nor the spelling with ṣere of the masculine. It is therefore probable that the forms have been deliberately coined (or rare forms chosen) for the sake of closer alliteration. *Staff and stay* is an attempt to capture this in English; otherwise, 'support'. It is not quite accurate to call this a hendiadys (Gibson, 17; WO, 106); it is rather an example of the use of the two genders together to express entirety; cf. GK §122v.[2]

2. גִּבּוֹר: LXX gives two equivalents, γίγαντα καὶ ἰσχύοντα. Since there is no evidence for any Hebrew *Vorlage* other than that represented by MT, this may be taken as another example of the translator's freedom in the rendering of lists (see on 1.11, and v. 3 below). On the basis of usage elsewhere, it is likely that the second word is the free addition,[3] influenced no doubt by the repeated use of related words in the previous verse.

3. שַׂר־חֲמִשִּׁים: as at 2 Kgs 1.9, 10, 11, 13, and cf. Akk. *rab-ḫamšā* (*CDA*, 104); this is also the reading presupposed by all the versions (unless P read ראשׁ). There is therefore nothing to be said for the proposed alternative vocalization, חֲמֻשִּׁים (e.g. Procksch and Tur-Sinai, 160; cf. Exod. 13.18; Josh. 1.14; 4.12; Judg. 7.11, but never combined with שַׂר), which has conventionally been thought to mean 'armed men', though that in itself is not certain.[4]

וּנְשׂוּא פָנִים וְיוֹעֵץ: LXX καὶ θαυμαστὸν σύμβουλον. This rendering has been thought to pass over either וְיוֹעֵץ (Gray) or וּנְשׂוּא פָנִים (Marti). However, in view of, for instance, the translation of נְשׂוּא פָנִים by τεθαυμασμένος προσώπῳ at 2 Kgs 5.1 and by τοὺς τὰ πρόσωπα θαυμάζοντας at Isa. 9.14, on the one hand, and the almost invariable rendering of words from the root יעץ by forms of (συμ)βουλ-, on the other hand,[5] the most natural solution would seem to be that the translator has simply conflated the two terms of MT into one,[6] with his characteristic freedom in the rendering of lists (see v. 2 above).

חֲרָשִׁים: LXX, P[7] and V all take this as a reference to skilled builders or craftsmen, which would normally be vocalized חָרָשִׁים. Delitzsch (and see too Kissane and Auvray) defends this sense even for the Masoretic pointing by appeal to 1 Chron. 4.14 and Neh. 11.35, but in each case this occurs in a place name (and the further use in 1 Chron. 4.14 is clearly dependent upon this), which is not, perhaps, sufficient to establish this as a standard alternative. Nor does Delitzsch's further argument that such skilled artisans were included among the leading citizens who were taken into exile in Babylon (2 Kgs 24; Jer. 24.1; 29.1) demonstrate that they would have been included in a list of those who were regarded

---

[2] See too Berlin, *Dynamics*, 41–42, in contrast with Cassuto, *Studies*, 68, who argued that there is a chiastic reference back to Jerusalem (feminine) and Judah (masculine) in the previous line (cf. v. 8).

[3] Cf. Ziegler, 61; for a different route to the same conclusion, see Seeligmann, 33.

[4] Cf. J. L. Ska, *Le passage de la mer: étude de la construction, du style et de la symbolique d'Ex 14,1-31* (AnBib 109; Rome, 1986), 14–17.

[5] Cf. T. Muraoka, *Hebrew/Aramaic Index to the Septuagint* (Grand Rapids, 1998), 63.

[6] So correctly Ziegler, 137 (though his reference to 9.5 [6] needs modification in the light of his own critical edition of the text at that point). Seeligmann, 23, observes that at 9.5 (6) α actually reads καὶ θαυμαστὸς σύμβουλος, and so suggests that in our verse 'an earlier translation of נְשׂוּא פָנִים has been ousted by a quotation harking back to Aquila'. While this is, of course, possible, it seems unnecessary, since the relationship of LXX with MT can be explained on the basis of the translator's regular practice.

[7] Note further that P also avoids a magical association for נְבוֹן לַחַשׁ following by rendering 'one who understands counsel'.

by the Judean society itself as having some kind of authority. Rather, in view of the parallel with the following phrase, there is much to be said for the widely accepted alternative opinion which sees here a *hapax legomenon*, חֶרֶשׁ, 'magic, sorcery'. This has cognates in several Semitic languages, including Ugaritic[8] and some Aramaic dialects.[9] There is room for discussion about whether ultimately this is etymologically a separate root or a particular extension from the sense of craftsmanship,[10] but for practical purposes it clearly functioned as a separate verb and noun by the time from which we have textual evidence.

4. For the use of two accusatives after נתן, see JM §125*w*.

תעלולים: meaning and syntax are both uncertain, and the only other occurrence of the word (at 66.4) does not offer much help. The form of the noun together with its occurrence in the plural strongly suggests that it is an abstract (cf. GK §85*r*). Usually it is associated with the verb listed as עלל I in both BDB and *HAL*, which in the hithpa'el is thought to mean 'deal wantonly, ruthlessly; make a fool of', and in the po'el 'act severely'.[11] Derived nouns usually have the force of evil deeds, though clearly not always, since occasionally they refer to the work of God (indeed, these contrasting senses occur in vv. 8 and 10 immediately below). It is thus not at all clear how we can get from this to the usual English rendering of our word as 'caprice' (cf. NEB: 'as the fancy takes them'); 'wantonness' would seem to be more appropriate, and this may indeed be the meaning at 66.4. This cannot be ruled out as the meaning here (e.g. Skinner, 'outrage'; Oswalt: 'tyrants'), but it does not seem particularly suitable as an extension of the first half of the verse (though cf. Neh. 5.15 for a possible parallel). There is thus something to be said for associating the noun rather with עולל, 'child' (so Gesenius; it is not clear whether this is from a separate root עלל, or whether it derives ultimately from an extended meaning of עלל I), from which in our very passage there is a denominative verbal form מעולל (v. 12; when taken together with vv. 8 and 10, it seems clear that there is deliberate word-play on עלל in this passage, and in this Isaiah will not have been troubled by modern philological considerations). 'Childishness' (which may include, but is not limited to, caprice) is a suitable characterization of the nature of rule by inexperienced נערים.

There are three ways in which the syntax of this clause may be construed. (i) The versions all take the word as the personal subject of the verb, which we should have to explain as an abstract for concrete (cf. GK §83*c*). Despite this strong ancient tradition, it is unlikely to be correct. The variety of renderings in the versions shows that there was no agreed understanding of its meaning, and they seem merely to have made intelligent guesses: LXX and θ have ἐμπαῖκται, 'mockers' (influenced, perhaps, by Num. 22.29), and P is similar; V has *effeminati*, which Jerome indicates was chosen on account of Judg. 19.25; and T has חלשׁיא, 'weak ones', which could have arisen by association with children. α, ἐναλλάκται, and σ, ἐπηρεάσται, perhaps come closest to supporting the traditional rendering of 'caprice'. Given this uncertainty, it is not surprising that they should have thought that there was a reference to people, based on the parallel with נערים. Had that been the original intention, however, we should have expected something like מעוללים (cf. v. 12), not an abstract form. (ii) As Delitzsch points out, משׁל can be governed by an impersonal subject (cf. Pss. 19.14; 103.19), so that, whether it means 'caprice' or

[8] *DUL*, 371. It is on this basis that Jeffers, *Magic and Divination*, 49–51, suggests the more specific rendering 'medicine men'.

[9] Cf. *HAL* i. 344; Schmitt, *Magie*, 114. Speculatively, one might also consider a link with Akkadian *ḫarāšu* II, 'to bind (on)' (*CDA*, 107), though there is no obvious development within Akkadian itself in the direction of magic.

[10] Cf., for instance, H.-P. Müller, 'Magisch-mantische Weisheit und die Gestalt Daniels', *UF* 1 (1969), 79–94, contrasted with V. Hamp, *ThWAT* iii. 236–37 = *TDOT* v. 222–23; see too the related discussion in S. E. Loewenstamm, 'The Hebrew Root חרשׁ in the Light of the Ugaritic Texts', *JJS* 10 (1959), 63–65.

[11] For fuller analyses, see W. Roth, *ThWAT* vi. 151–60 = *TDOT* xi. 139–46; E. Carpenter, *NIDOTTE* iii. 423–25; B. Kedar-Kopfstein, 'Glossen zur traditionellen biblischen Philologie (2)', *ZAH* 3 (1990), 207–11.

'childishness', תעלולים could be the subject; that this should be the result of God's making youths into leaders would be an obvious inference. (iii) Alternatively, we may construe the word as an adverbial accusative, with נערים as the subject of the verb. While there is little difference in meaning between (ii) and (iii), the latter is marginally preferable as giving a tighter poetic structure.

5. ונגש: the niph'al here is often said to be used with reciprocal force (cf. GK §51*d*; JM §51*c*); so, for instance, Dillmann, Delitzsch, Gray, Young, and BDB, 'shall tyrannise over (ב) each other'. While possible, this is not necessary: the ב can equally well introduce the personal agent of a passive verb (cf. GK §121*f*). It would be unwise to cite the versions in this case, since they may simply have read as a qal; their translations are somewhat various, but not obviously based on any alternative reading. Similarly, parallelism with the next line need not be pressed so far as to insist that we should revocalize as qal or pi'el (*contra* Tur-Sinai, 160, following Ehrlich).

6. כי could theoretically be translated 'when', introducing a protasis whose apodosis follows in v. 7, and support for this might be claimed from the lack of the conjunction on ישא (e.g. Delitzsch; Gray; Oswalt). Although the eventual meaning is the same, this seems to introduce an implausibly lengthy and complex sentence into a poetic context which is characterized rather by terse, agitated clauses, appropriate to the content. כי can simply be a loose connective; it introduces an example of the kind of situation envisaged in the previous verses, without any necessary stress on the causal association; cf. Gibson, 159 (with reference to v. 8, but applicable also here).

בית אביו: adverbial accusative (GK §118*g*; JM § 126*h*), as frequently in definitions of place; cf. Gibson, 143 (who, however, on 108, objects to the use of 'accusative').[12] The versions have slightly misconstrued by taking the phrase to refer to the family rather than the building, so necessitating slight paraphrase in order to make the words fit, for example, LXX ἢ τοῦ οἰκείου τοῦ πατρὸς αὐτοῦ. That some of the versions add a word to introduce the direct speech following (LXX λέγων; T למימר; P wn'mr lh) is merely interpretive clarification, and does not constitute strong evidence that לאמר should be added here.

שמלה לכה: the Masoretic punctuation clearly takes these two words together, so that לכה = לך with *plene* spelling, as occasionally elsewhere (cf. GK §103*g*).[13] It has some-times been proposed, however, that שמלה should be joined to the preceding clause ('in whose father's house is a cloak'), and לכה construed as an imperative with the following ('Come, …'); cf. Marti, Gray, Kissane. This is thought to lead more naturally to the state-ment in v. 7 that 'in my house…there is no cloak'. That the resulting clause is awkward, however, is tacitly conceded by Marti and Kissane, in that they further conjecturally emend אבי to אביך, so that the clause can be taken as the first part of the (unmarked) speech: 'there is a cloak in your father's house'. This is not convincing, however. The reprise in v. 7 is not exact ('my house' for 'father's house'; addition of 'there is no food'), so that precise alignment is not required. The Masoretes' breathless string of two stressed clauses seems more appropriate to the context than the more measured lengths of the proposed reordering.

המכשלה הזאת: LXX τὸ βρῶμα τὸ ἐμόν. It is not agreed how this should be explained. (i) Ottley agrees with those who have suggested inner-Greek corruption of πτῶμα ('calam-ity'), though this still leaves τὸ ἐμόν in place of הזאת unexplained. (ii) It is possible that

---

[12] Weil, 'Exégèse', redivides the consonants as בית אבי ושמלה to give 'Let my family and a garment be yours! Be judge over us.' This is an important element in his exegesis of the passage as a whole in terms of the law of loans, where a garment serves as a pledge according to Exod. 22.24-26 and Deut. 24.10-13. The reading is wholly conjectural, however, and the unqualified use of שמלה following בית אבי is awkward. It is also question-able whether, in the circumstances envisaged, both the family and the garment would be surrendered to the creditor in the same way, as this simple co-ordination suggests.

[13] Tur-Sinai's proposal, משלה לכה, 'rule thou (over us)', is hardly an improvement on MT.

the translator's *Vorlage* read something like מאכלתי (Gray) or המבשלה, with 'my' as a free rendering.[14] (iii) Ziegler, 136, thinks that there may have been influence from לחם in v. 7 and the not dissimilar 4.1, so that this would be another example of the translator's 'leveling' tendency, already noted. Against this, however, it should be noted that he uses a different word to render לחם in v. 7 and 4.1. It may also be observed that T rendered with מגביתא הדא, 'this tribute', which suggests that some had difficulty with this rare word. No solution is self-evidently correct.

ידך: 1QIsaᵃ ידיך. The singular is usual in this sort of context, and should certainly be preferred. The plural is not impossible, however; cf. Gen. 16.9.

7. ישא: it was noted at 2.9 that there is often an ellipsis of the object of this verb. In this case, it is clear from the context that קול has to be understood, as at 42.2, 11; cf. Num. 14.1; GK §117g; Gibson, 110. 1QIsaᵃ has וישא. While this may have been acceptable as a simple conjunctive by the time the scroll was being copied (note that LXX and P also add a conjunction, though without, of course, rendering the verb in the past tense), it cannot be original; cf. Kutscher, 350–58 with 423–24.

חבש: LXX ἀρχηγός, the same word as is used to translate קצין both in the previous verse and later in this one. The 'leveling' in rendering between these three clauses is further evidenced by the addition of σου here to balance the ἡμῶν of v. 6 and by the rendering of לא תשׂימני later in this verse by οὐκ ἔσομαι, exactly as לא־אהיה is rendered here. Cheyne's proposal, *Book*, 81, to read נגש does not seem to be an improvement.

ובביתי: with GK §156b, this is best taken as introducing a circumstantial clause.

8. כי: see on v. 6, and contrast the second occurrence in this verse (so V *enim...quia*, against LXX ὅτι...καὶ; T and P, of course, are able simply to imitate the Hebrew usage: ארי...ארי and *mṭwl d...mṭwl d* respectively).

נפל: grammatically, it is usually explained that the masculine indicates that the people of Judah rather than the country (feminine) are in view (GK §122i; JM §134g); or similarly that it is in agreement with an implied 'head noun' בית (WO, 104); cf. Hos. 5.5 for a closely comparable example. Although this usage is attested with the names of some other countries as well, there are even more examples where the feminine nevertheless occurs with reference to the inhabitants, so that either gender is possible. Clearly, therefore, the poet's choice has been determined by more than the demands of grammar alone, and Berlin attractively suggests that this was in order to achieve 'morphologic parallelism': 'the two genders appear to balance each other, and may even create a merismus. The presence of this alternation in gender heightens the effect of the parallelism'.[15] Developing this insight, Berlin continues, 'The pair *Jerusalem//Judah* also creates a merismus by employing a part and its whole. The effect of totality is emphasized by the chiastic word order... I would go on to see an even more dramatic picture of totality in Isaiah's words: Jerusalem's stumbling will lead to Judah's fall. Thus the grammatical and the lexical parallelisms work toward the same end' (p. 145 n. 14). If Berlin is right, then clearly the scribe who copied 1QIsaᵃ (נפלה) and those who have followed him must be judged poetically insensitive.

אל: on the assumption that this line is syntactically self-contained, this must be the equivalent of על, which is, in fact, the reading of 1QIsaᵃ here. The two prepositions are not infrequently interchanged in manuscripts or within MT in parallel passages (see on 2.2 above) or in constructions where it might be expected that the same preposition would be used (for the evidence from the Qumran scroll, to go no further, see Kutscher, 404–5, 408–10, and for inner-MT examples, see BDB, 41A, *Note* 2), and since this is not consistently in a single direction, it is unlikely that it is to be explained exclusively on the basis of influence from Aramaic. For אל = 'against', see BDB, 40A (4), including 2.4 above. The evidence clearly does not allow us to determine which of the two forms was 'original'

---

[14] N. Herz, 'The Exaggeration of Errors in the Massoretic', *JTS* 15 (1913–14), 258–64 (261); Fischer, 19.

[15] Berlin, *Dynamics*, 44; see too Watson, *Classical Hebrew Poetry*, 123–28, who also suggests that merismus may be one of the functions of gender-matched parallelism.

(the scroll's reading עַל on the one hand is balanced by the probability that LXX's πρòς presupposes אֶל). Alternatively, it has occasionally been proposed that the two lines should be run together: 'their tongue and their deeds are in relation to the Lord of such a kind that they must provoke...' (cf. Dillmann; Koenig, 107), and this is thought to indicate that אל is correct. Apart from the fact that it would not be impossible to construe the line so even with עַל, the construction seems most unlikely in poetry.

לִמְרוֹת: the Masoretic vocalization indicates a hiph'il infinitive construct with syncopation of the ה (i.e. for לְהַמְרוֹת), a form which is found in a number of passages (cf. GK §53q), not least with this same verb at Ps. 78.17. Although this form is well attested in the Dead Sea Scrolls and thereafter,[16] it is questionable whether it had entered the language as early as the biblical period. It is more probable that an original qal infinitive (לִמְרוֹת) has been vocalized on the basis of what had become common in Post-Biblical Hebrew.[17] The meanings of the qal and the hiph'il of this verb overlap to a considerable extent, and both may be followed by the accusative. The infinitive with ל can often be used loosely to express attendant circumstances (cf. GK §114o, without explicit reference to this verse), and that seems appropriate here; it is unlikely that the people had the provocation of God as their express purpose.

עֵנִי: an unparalleled defective spelling (GK §9i), for which 1QIsaᵃ not surprisingly reads עיני. In itself, this might not arouse undue suspicion, and a simple, early (cf. LXX) scribal error would seem a more plausible explanation than Gray's appeal to the spelling in Phoenician (cf. DNWSI, 839). On this occasion, however, the unusual spelling coincides with questionable sense; some find 'eyes' a curious object for לִמְרוֹת, while others consider 'his glorious eyes' to be equally problematic. Not surprisingly, therefore, resort has been had to emendation, though in my opinion most of the proposals are not convincing; they either raise further problems of their own or do not completely escape the unease which has been felt with MT. For instance (i) Lowth took his cue from P and suggested עֲנַן, 'cloud' (he might have compared 4.5 for a suggestive parallel), but while עֲנַן כבודו seems plausible in itself, it is as difficult as MT as an object of לִמְרוֹת. (ii) Others (e.g. Procksch; BHS) simply delete עני, which is no solution at all. T might be cited in support (מרגזין קדם יקריה), but it is more likely that the Targumist was interpreting עני as an indicator of the presence of God, rather like לעיני. (iii) More popular is the emendation פני (e.g. Cheyne; Clements; NRSV), which is orthographically close but which seems to raise all the same problems as the MT. (iv) Wiklander, 77–78, taking note of the LXX, suggests vocalizing as עֲנִי. He cites the construction described in GK §117ll (and cf. JM §126g: 'accusative of limitation'), in which a 'second accusative sometimes more closely determines the nearer object by indicating the part or member specially affected by the action'. He thus translates, 'they distress the humble regarding his glory' (a reversal of v. 5b). The problems with this proposal are that, irrespective of the wider context, the parallelism within the line certainly leads us to expect a reference to an offence against God and that elsewhere the object of the hiph'il of מרה is invariably God, and so too of the qal with only one exception (Deut. 21.18, 20). (v) Kissane and Wildberger (independently?) suggest עמו, and Kissane correctly observes that this preposition follows hiph'il forms of מרה at Deut. 9.7, 24; 31.27 in place of the commoner ב. Such a scribal error is conceivable; there are well attested examples of the confusion of נ and ם, probably caused by the use of ligatures,[18] so that a similar confusion for יּ is plausible. The proposed reading makes sense and appears to be free of difficulty. If sense cannot be made of MT, this emendation should therefore be preferred; see the comments below.

The versions do not support any alternative consonantal text. While they mostly render reasonably closely, LXX is more complex, but does not seem to have had any

---

[16] Cf. E. Qimron, The Hebrew of the Dead Sea Scrolls (HSS 29; Atlanta, 1986), 48.

[17] For other examples of this phenomenon, see J. Hughes, 'Post-Biblical Features of Biblical Hebrew Vocalization', in S. E. Ballentine and J. Barton (eds), Language, Theology, and the Bible: Essays in Honour of James Barr (Oxford, 1994), 67–80.

[18] Cf. R. Weiss, 'On Ligatures in the Hebrew Bible (נו = ם)', JBL 82 (1963), 188–94.

significantly different *Vorlage*. It is clear that the translator took למרות (ἀπειθοῦντες) with the first half of the line.[19] Then he rendered the final two words of the verse as διότι νῦν ἐταπεινώθη ἡ δόξα αὐτῶν. Perhaps deterred from following the approach which seems most natural to us on account of the anthropomorphism involved,[20] he understood כבוד to refer to the people rather than God (hence the rendering of the suffix as a plural) and either understood or exploited the possibility of associating עני with the root ענה. But in my opinion the decisive factor behind the precise form of his rendering will have been an association with the major theme of ch. 2, where the same verb appears repeatedly to describe the humbling of every form of pride (see similarly Ziegler, 137). It is another example of the feature of his rendering which we have already noted several times whereby he brings one passage into line with another, and which, for want of a better term, I have called 'leveling'.

9. הכרת: this *hapax legomenon* looks like a rare, but not unparalleled, noun formation from the hiph'il of נכר.[21] The other examples of this nominal form in Biblical Hebrew are late, and may reflect influence from the Aramaic infinitive haph'el form, הַקְטָלָה; this is taken even further in 1QIsaᵃ, הכרית (cf. Kutscher, 200). This does not necessarily demand, but would certainly fit well with, the suggestion that this is part of a later addition to an original Isaianic saying. While הכיר generally means 'regard, recognize', the idiom הכיר פנים occurs several times with the meaning 'show partiality' (cf. Deut. 1.17; 16.19; Prov. 24.23; 28.21), so that the present phrase would mean 'their partiality'; so P, T (אשתמודעתהון בדינא אפיהון, 'their respecting of persons in judgment'), and cf. Ibn Ezra; Hitzig; Duhm; Marti; Gray; Kissane; Procksch; Auvray; Schoors; Wildberger.

The objection has been raised to this approach that it is contextually unsuitable: the people as a whole, not just the judges, are here being addressed.[22] Two alternative solutions[23] have therefore sometimes been proposed: (i) with the same derivation as above, understand rather as 'the look on their faces' (e.g. AV; Gesenius; Knobel; Delitzsch; Condamin; Feldmann; Young; Høgenhaven, 209; Oswalt). This seems to be the understanding of V *agnitio vultus eorum*, though Jerome's commentary indicates uncertainty. His gloss on the phrase is that 'they have admitted their own sin' (implying a look of shame), but he also accepts that the interpretation in the LXX (see below) is possible. The difficulty for this view is that the phrase הכיר פנים seems to be firmly attested as a fixed idiom, so that to suggest that it means something else here is improbable. Proverbs 28.21 indicates that the phrase need not be defined exclusively with regard to judges but may be extended to giving testimony more broadly. Furthermore, as either part or an extension of the earlier part of this chapter, the phrase may have been chosen as illustrative of the general corruption in society. (ii) Among several possibilities, Kimhi reports that his father interpreted this word in the light of Job 19.3b, לא־תבשו תהכרו־לי, and on the basis of Arabic *hakara* he took this to mean 'impudence (עזות)'; see too Rashi, and more recently Vitringa (*impudentia*) and Dillmann (*Unverschämtheit, Frechheit*).[24] The association with בוש in this passage may have influenced the LXX of our verse, αἰσχύνη, though the possibility of a free rendering of an obscure word remains. It may be readily accepted that this would be highly

---

[19] Note that, interestingly, P seems to have treated למרות as a 'two-way pivot'.

[20] Attention may be drawn at this point to the extensive discussion of LXX's rendering of this verse by Koenig, 107–17. This includes many valuable observations (such as the likelihood that LXX associated מעלל in the first half of the line with מעל), but is also driven into some unnecessarily complex explanations because of the author's convictions about the translator's sophisticated hermeneutical presuppositions.

[21] Cf. GK §85c; JM §88Lb; Y. Hocherman, 'Etymological Studies in Biblical Language', *BethM* 32 (1986–87), 235–43 (242) (Hebrew).

[22] See Duhm for a somewhat scornful dismissal of this objection.

[23] Ehrlich, Budde and Tur-Sinai proposed emending פניהם to פיהם, but this seems unnecessary.

[24] Similarly, F. Zimmermann, 'Notes on Some Difficult Old Testament Passages', *JBL* 55 (1936), 301–8, appealed to Arabic to support the meaning 'deceit'.

appropriate here because it furnishes such an excellent parallel with the second half of the line. On the other hand, both the reading and the meaning at Job 19.3 are very uncertain, and most modern commentators in fact favour those manuscripts which read a ה in place of the ה,[25] so that it would be unwise to build upon it. Additionally, the force of the argument from the well-attested phrase הכיר פנים applies here too. Somewhat reluctantly, therefore, we should therefore probably not follow this otherwise attractive proposal.

וחטאתם: there is no need to follow P and T in vocalizing as a plural; as Wildberger points out, חטאת is regularly singular in Isaiah (6.7; 27.9; 30.1). This also tells against Ginsberg's proposal, 'Emendations', 52, to take the word as the subject of the verb, 'And their sins have told everything'. It may be noted in addition that the following לא כחדו also requires the people to be the subject and their sin the object.

לא כחדו (1QIsaᵃ ולוא): I have followed GK §156g in construing as a circumstantial clause.

להם: reflexive; cf. GK §135i; JM §146k; literally, 'they have dealt to themselves evil'. Driver's suggestion[26] that this is an unrecognized Tiq. Soph. for לאלהים, is neither necessary nor appropriate. It was not adopted by NEB.

There is a general consensus in modern scholarship that chs 2–4 form a single section within the final form of the book of Isaiah and equally that this section is constructed redactionally by the assemblage of previously separate units of diverse origin and date. Among the considerations which lead to the first conclusion may be noted the facts that 2.2-4 and 4.2-6 form a balanced pair concerning the future state and role of the ideal Zion/ Jerusalem, that the various major units within the section are joined syntactically (see especially the use of כי at 2.6 and 3.1), and that there is thematic coherence generally by the focus on Jerusalem and specifically by the references back to the day of the Lord, first introduced at 2.12, by use of the formula 'on that day' at 2.20; 3.7, 18; 4.1, 2. As Sweeney, 95, summarizes, 'the structure and contents of chs 2–4 demonstrate that its intention is to explain why the projected ideal of world peace and the nations' recognition of YHWH at Zion in 2.2-4 have not yet been realized and how the suffering of Israel will lead to this goal'. In this, the section may be said to mirror in microcosm the shape of the book of Isaiah as a whole.[27] In view of the late date of 4.2-6 (see the commentary *ad loc.*), it is not impossible that this broad structure is indeed to be associated, either in formation or by way of reflection, with the final stage of the book's composition.

While it is similarly agreed by all that the section as we have it is made up of smaller units (note, for instance, the changes of speaker and addressee, the use of different forms or genres, and the shifting emphases in subject matter), the consensus breaks down when it comes to identifying the extent and original setting of these units. This issue has already

[25] See most recently, with a listing of others who take the same view, D. J. A. Clines, *Job 1–20* (WBC 17; Dallas, 1989), 428.

[26] G. R. Driver, 'Abbreviations in the Massoretic Text', *Textus* 1 (1960), 112–31 (120).

[27] For fuller discussions of the coherence of chs 2–4 as a whole, see, for instance, Vermeylen; Sweeney, *Isaiah 1–4; idem*, 'Structure and Redaction' (as well, of course, as his commentary); Wiklander; Magonet, 'Isaiah 2:1–4:6'; Berges, 76–87. For chs 3–4 alone, see Watts, 'Jerusalem'. Needless to say, these studies differ considerably from one another in terms of method.

been encountered to a limited degree in ch. 2, but it is with ch. 3 that the problem is at its most acute. Sweeney[28] helpfully sets out in tabular form the differing analyses of about ten commentators in this regard, and no purpose would be served by repeating them here (or, indeed, of adding the further proposals which have been added since he wrote). Rather, the approach to be adopted here will be similar to that defended with regard to the composition of ch. 1. It was suggested there that units of diverse origin had been assembled redactionally to make up a coherent literary section. The focus of the commentary was therefore primarily on this final form of the text, but the attempt was also made (and in the nature of the case this often took up more space) to isolate and discuss the earlier units from the work of this redactor as he joined them together and added material of his own. Similarly here, therefore, the text will be divided into its smallest component parts without thereby intending to overlook the broader thematic coherence which they now combine to serve.

So far as it is possible to judge, the association of chs 2–4 with the finished book of Isaiah has been achieved solely by the addition of 4.2-6. Apart from minor additions (such as 2.22) and glosses, nothing else need necessarily be dated so late in terms of original composition. We have already seen that the major redactional work which can be recovered in ch. 2 points to the late exilic form of the book as its major centre of gravity (see especially the discussion of the date of 2.2-4, the addition of v. 5 and the major redaction of 6-22 with regard to vv. 8-9 and 18 in particular). Earlier material by Isaiah himself (and perhaps others too) was apparently worked over and given its essential shape at that time, and it was also suggested that the heading in 2.1 belonged to that phase of the composition. In view of the connections already briefly noted between chs 2 and 3, there must, therefore, be an *a priori* assumption that the same conclusion will hold here. As we shall see, 3.1–4.1 can indeed be satisfactorily described as a collection of Isaianic material now presented in the light of the judgment which had befallen Jerusalem and Judah at the hand of the Babylonians. In this form of the book, 3.1–4.1 will have been continued by ch. 5, which shares a similar general outlook, so that the whole of 2.6–5.30 will at that stage have been concerned with description of and justification for this major act of judgment on Judah.

Although many commentators treat vv. 1-15 as the first unit of ch. 3, it seems clear that in terms of the method adopted here this should be revised. Redactionally, the major section for analysis stretches further, as we have seen. In terms of original units, several seem already to be combined within 1-15. Nevertheless, there is a significant shift of focus in 3.16–4.1 because of its concentration on women, the use of וַיֹּאמֶר at the start of v. 16 indicates some sort of a new beginning, and the similarly elaborated form of the divine name at the end of v. 15 and the beginning of v. 1 is often thought to be suggestive of an *inclusio*. The case is thus closely comparable with ch. 1, where it was recognized on similar grounds that vv. 2-20 were marked out as a significant section within the wider

---

[28] Sweeney, *Isaiah 1–4*, 147–48; see too Porath, 20–23.

composition. Neither there nor here, however, should that conclusion be confused with the distinction between original units and final redaction.

Within 3.1-15, a form-critical break coincides with a syntactical one at the start of v. 10. There are also some unevennesses within 1-9, such as the introduction of first person speech at v. 4 and the shift in tense at v. 8. In both cases, however, there is a smooth syntactical join (by the use of the conjunction at v. 4 and of כי at v. 8; note that although there is no such marker at the start of v. 7, it is clearly linked by content with v. 6). It is therefore probable that we should treat vv. 1-9 as the first unit within this section.

Form-critically, the shape of the passage appears at first sight to be an elaborated announcement of judgment (vv. 1-7) followed by the reason for the judgment (vv. 8-9a), together with a concluding and summarizing woe-oracle (9b).[29] The announcement is expressed by הנה + divine name + participle, continued as far as v. 7 by the imperfect (or *waw* + perfect). The reason, by contrast, uniformly uses the perfect tense. On these grounds, it has been thought possible to defend the unity of this paragraph as a whole (minor additions apart); see, for instance, Wildberger and Sweeney.

This conclusion may be questioned, however. First, the reason is itself divided into two parts. Verse 8a states that Jerusalem and Judah have stumbled and fallen, and this is then explained (note the second occurrence of כי) as a consequence of the people's rebellion and sin (8b-9a); thus 8a does not serve satisfactorily as part of the reason for the judgment of vv. 1-7, but seems to comprise some alternative form of announcement. Secondly, the verbs כשל and especially נפל in 8a go beyond an explanation for judgment; they imply, rather, that judgment has already occurred (see, for instance, the use of 'fallen' in Amos 5.2). Thirdly, it is unusual in eighth-century prophecy to find this order of announcement followed by reason; the standard form of judgment oracle is precisely the reverse (see, for instance, on 1.21-26). This admittedly would not on its own be a strong enough reason to challenge the usual view, but in the present case it is noteworthy that the closest analogy within Isaiah for the form introduced by v. 1 is at 10.33-34 (הנה + האדון יהוה צבאות + participle), and there it is used absolutely, without a reason either preceding or following. In the light of these considerations, and taking into account the introductory remarks above about the likely redactional history of this passage as a whole, I am attracted to the view that 8-9 is an exilic redactional addition which looks back to the eventual fall of Jerusalem as a fulfilment of Isaiah's prophecy of judgment included in vv. 1-7. As further slight support for this conclusion may be mentioned the linguistic form of הכרת (see the textual notes) and the use of כבוד in a manner which reflects later developments within the book of Isaiah as a whole.[30]

Questions have also been raised about the original integrity of vv. 1-7. First, in the light of the continuation of the passage, the 'staff and stay' of

---

[29] Cf. Westermann, *Grundformen*, 127 = *Basic Forms*, 176–77.

[30] Without reference to this particular verse, see the second half of my essay 'From One Degree of Glory to Another'.

v. 1 seems to refer to the leaders of society. The alternative interpretation given in the closing words of v. 1 has therefore long been regarded as a much later explanatory gloss, and this seems to be right (see further the commentary below).

Secondly, Gray and Porath, 36–37, also consider that the list of leaders in vv. 2-3 is a later elaboration of 'staff and stay', but this is much less certain. The inclusion of קסם and נבון לחש among the leaders without any apparent qualms certainly points to a date for this list well within the pre-exilic period (see on 2.6),[31] and since it interprets v. 1 in line with the following elaboration in 4-7, it is difficult not to retain it as part of the original written form of the oracle.

Thirdly, the abrupt introduction of divine speech in v. 4 has been considered too harsh by some, and vv. 4-7 considered to be secondary in consequence.[32] It is noted in support that the situation depicted in these verses fits well with the situation after the fall of Jerusalem; for instance, compare v. 5 with Lam. 4.16, and the use of מכשלה in v. 6. While this latter point is helpful in suggesting how the passage could have been understood in the exilic period, it is not strong as an argument for composition at that time. Against Deck's position, for instance, the reference to the 'heap of ruins' is not to emphasize destruction in itself, so contrasting with the reference to deportation in v. 1, but rather it is simply part of the background to the offer of leadership to anyone willing to accept it precisely because the previous leadership has been removed (see further in the commentary below). So far as the introduction of first person speech by God is concerned, it is admittedly somewhat abrupt (though in itself perfectly intelligible), but it would be even more surprising for a later glossator to use such a form if the context did not already justify it. The solution to all such problems by way of an appeal to later additions is too simple, and in this case raises more difficulties than it solves. It is possible that a more complicated literary history than we can now reconstruct lies behind this passage, but if so it was at the time of the earliest assemblage of Isaianic material; more than that we cannot say.

Finally, one may question whether v. 9*b* belonged with 8-9*a* from the start or whether it has been added subsequently (e.g. Wildberger). Two points at least seem clear. First, it must have been in place before the addition of vv. 10-11 since, as will be seen in the commentary on these verses below, they presuppose its presence along with the material which precedes it while at the same time they offer a somewhat different interpretation of it.[33] Secondly, the suffix on אוי לנפשם, 'woe to them', indicates that the line was composed for its present setting, and cannot be interpreted as

---

[31] Cf. Deck, 150–51. To assume that the original metre of this passage was the *qinah*, then to delete just these words from the list on that account, and finally to declare the list to be late (so Kaiser, followed by Becker, 164) is too convenient by half! The later it is thought that such people were added to a list of the leaders of society, the more implausible the proposal becomes.

[32] E.g. Vermeylen, 145–46; Deck, 149. Becker, 163–64, argues that v. 4 alone has been added.

[33] Cf. Sweeney, *Isaiah 1–4*, 177–78; Koenen, *Heil den Gerechten*, 184–89.

a free standing saying which has been added from elsewhere by the redactor. In view of the fact that (unlike הוי) אוי is not necessarily an introductory particle (see, for instance, Jer. 13.27; Hos. 7.13; 9.12), there is no particular reason why 8-9 should not always have been rounded off with this final line. Furthermore, once it is recognized that 8-9 are themselves a redactional expansion of 1-7, the case against 9b on its own looks distinctly weaker. It could, of course, be a secondary expansion, but there is no direct evidence to support the case, and even if it were true, it would have to have been relatively early (before the addition of 10-11). It therefore seems best to treat is as an integral part of 8-9.

I conclude that our passage is made up of two main sections, to which only minor later glosses have been added: 1-7, a pre-exilic and probably Isaianic proclamation of judgment, supplemented by an exilic addition in 8-9, pointing out how this had been fulfilled in the fall of Judah and explaining it in generalized theological terms. While the date of the Isaianic material cannot be determined with certainty, it would fit most appropriately around the time of Sennacherib's 701 BCE invasion (cf. Dietrich, 53; Sweeney; Blenkinsopp); the Assyrian policy of deportation would have been well known by then, and in his historical setting Isaiah envisages something close to what in fact transpired at that time. Whatever its original setting in Isaiah's ministry, however, it serves now to amplify the major theme of ch. 2 (see the connective כי) by illustrating how the socially 'high and lofty' will be removed, along with everything else which challenges God's unique supremacy, on the coming day of the Lord.

Wildberger has helpfully analysed the rhythms and line lengths of these verses and concluded that they correspond well with the content of each part. Verses 1-3, which include the expansive introduction and the list of leaders, hardly lend themselves to more detailed analysis. The list of leaders is divided into pairs for the most part, though (*contra* Wildberger) this is extended to a longer triplet at the end (v. 3b), appropriate to a conclusion. The repeated 3 + 2 of vv. 4-6a is interrupted by a string of four two-stressed phrases in 6b, which suits the agitated speech there reported. As an introductory speech formula, 7a is probably to be construed in anacrusis. By eliminating ואין שמלה as a gloss, Wildberger then recovers a five-stress colon followed by a four-stress colon for the remainder of v. 7, which he thinks suitable at the end of a section. This is less certain in both respects, however. We may agree that the regular rhythms of the preceding have broken down, and then simply propose that the verse is a tricolon. This latter observation seems to be the most important point, since it marks (in my opinion, not shared by Wildberger) the end not just of a section, but of the unit as a whole. In view of the uncertainties of how to 'count' such words as לא and אין, however, it is wise not to be dogmatic about the precise rhythm at this point.

The redactional addition in 8-9 is far less strict from a formal point of view. 8a may be taken as a 3 + 2, which is certainly suitable, but 8b-9a are more akin to rhythmic prose. Thus, to eliminate כסדם solely on the ground that it disturbs the metre is misguided. Although this approach cannot be used as an argument for the later, redactional origin of these verses, it certainly fits well with such a conclusion reached on other grounds. 9*b* might be taken as a 2 + 3 to balance the 3 + 2 of 8*a*, but this could be just a coincidence; it more probably continues the irregular pattern of 8*b*-9*a*.

1. As noted already above, it is likely that the initial *for* is redactional, consciously joining this passage with the judgment in ch. 2 in order to narrow its focus down to *Jerusalem and Judah*. Form-critically, we should normally expect such an announcement of judgment to be preceded by a reason, joined by לכן, 'therefore' (cf. 1.24), but whether such a reason ever preceded this passage in the preaching of Isaiah we have no means of telling.

The parallel with 1.24 in fact goes considerably further. The divine title, *the Sovereign, the Lord of Hosts,* is identical, in both cases the announcement is introduced by הנה (lit., 'behold'), and in both the nature of the judgment is that God *is removing* (cf. 1.25) the corrupt leadership. Interestingly, it was argued at 1.21-26 that the original Isaianic saying stopped at that point, without the positive deduction which was later made by the addition of v. 26. The present passage does the same, concentrating as it does upon the dire consequences which will follow such a removal. The rhetorical force of the passage shows rather clearly, therefore, that *staff and stay* is a reference to the leaders of society (cf. vv. 2-3) who in normal circumstances would be expected to maintain social cohesion and order.

The interpretation given at the end of the verse, *the whole staff of bread and the whole staff of water*, therefore seems to be a later addition. It probably refers to a time of siege or to the period of dire distress following some major catastrophe, and may thus be most probably associated with a reflection on the fall of Jerusalem to the Babylonians.[34] While the reference to *bread* in v. 7 may have helped to trigger the addition, it is developed in a different direction by the inclusion of *water* as opposed to the cloak of v. 7: the emphasis here is on deprivation rather than on (mock) status. Whether it was added by the same redactor as vv. 8-9 or is an isolated later comment cannot be decided with certainty. It is possible that 33.16 is a conscious reversal of the judgment implied here ('their bread will be supplied, their water assured'), in which case the former possibility would be the more attractive (assuming ch. 33 to be late exilic), but in view of the understandable frequency with which bread and water are paralleled,[35] this cannot be regarded as certain.

2. The list of leaders is probably intended to be representative rather than comprehensive, as the absence of priests, for instance, suggests (contrast 28.7).[36] Initially more surprising is the failure to mention the king, especially in view of his general role, upheld elsewhere by Isaiah, in the

[34] Cf. Jones, 'Traditio', 242, with reference to Lam. 2.12.

[35] W. A. M. Beuken lists 23 examples, from a wide variety of biblical sources; cf. *Isaiah II/2: Isaiah Chapters 28–39* (Leuven, 2000), 270. One might note especially the (exilic) Ezek. 4.16-17 as a close parallel to the thought expressed by the gloss.

[36] It has occasionally been suggested that the absence of the king from the list points to its post-exilic origin. In that case, however, the absence of the priests would be even more remarkable. The explanation advanced above therefore seems preferable.

maintenance of a just but hierarchically ordered society. The explanation cannot be that he was above criticism; rather, it may be suggested that he was single and unique, not one of a class to which any of the people might in principle aspire. He was thus in a different category from those listed here. A consequence of this is that the description of the following verses is to be understood at the local rather than state level. Although the passage has been put in that wider context by the *relecture* in vv. 8-9, Isaiah himself seems to have had in mind the effects on social life as experienced in more limited localities, whether urban or rural.

In view of the facts that, for instance, vv. 2 and 3 both start with a reference to the military and that 'religious' experts similarly appear in both verses, it is unlikely that the order of the list is of particular design or significance. The absence of the conjunction before the third type of official, *judge*, inclines the reader to group the titles in pairs (even though in most cases it clearly does not follow that the two members of each pair are specifically related to each other), and this is sustained by the similar lack of a conjunction at the start of v. 3. If that is correct, then the list ends with a triplet, which seems suitable as an indication of the conclusion.

Used on its own, גבור can refer to anyone who is outstanding in his class (whether good or bad), and so is applied to many different types of people.[37] By far its commonest use, however, is in connection with military exploits, hence *warrior*, and this seems clearly to be intended here by its association with the *man of war*. The two terms also come together at Ezek. 39.20; Joel 2.7; 4.9. It is not possible, without a wider context, to determine whether these are members of the standing army or distinguished members of the conscript army.[38] Either could have an honoured or influential position in society.

The *judge* was, of course, concerned with the administration of justice in all its many spheres. While we read elsewhere of elders, priests and the king all acting as judges in particular circumstances,[39] there is no evidence for what today might be called full-time or professional judges. Even if, as I believe, sound historical tradition underlies the account of Jehoshaphat's judicial reform (2 Chron. 19.4-11),[40] this will have led only to a greater sophistication in the work of the courts and the judges, not necessarily to a change in the nature of the people who acted as judges.[41] In other words, the reference here is likely to be to leading members of society acting in this particular role, and so in principle it could overlap with other classes included in the list. This further reinforces the point made above that the list is general and representative of leadership, not a prescription for the precise contours of pre-exilic Judean society.

[37] Cf. H. Kosmala, *ThWAT* i. 909–13 = *TDOT* ii. 373–77.

[38] It is only by selective citation that Porath, 73, among others, is able to suggest such a distinction.

[39] Cf. Bovati, *Re-Establishing Justice*, 172–84, with full reference to earlier literature.

[40] H. G. M. Williamson, *1 and 2 Chronicles* (NCB; London and Grand Rapids, 1982), 287–91.

[41] Note, for instance, that in 1.23 it seems to be the שרים who act as judges, as in Jer. 26.10-16, and similarly the ראשים in Mic. 3.11.

The inclusion of the *prophet* in the list indicates that we are here dealing with a publicly recognized and valued class, not the isolated and romanticized figure of later theological image-makers. Grabbe (who also stresses that from a sociological perspective it is not possible to distinguish between the authors of the prophetic books and others bearing the same title) offers the definition 'a mediator claiming to have messages direct from a divinity, by various means, and communicating these messages to recipients'.[42] They occur frequently as a class throughout the Hebrew Bible, as well as elsewhere in the ancient Near East.[43] While it is generally agreed that there were official 'cultic prophets',[44] who could well be included here, they by no means encompass the full range of those who seem to have been included within the term.

Although the *diviner* stands next to the prophet (and is joined by the conjunction),[45] he does not come paired with him.[46] The difficulties of defining such a term were outlined at 2.6 above (with further literature), and they will recur again at the end of v. 3. The chief distinction from the prophet seems to relate to the mode of reception of the divine will, the diviner relying more on 'mechanical' means, and possibly also to the fact that they sought divine guidance to order (and doubtless often for a fee) rather than being independent spokesmen. As seen already, this came generally to be disparaged in the later periods (though surviving in such particular instances as the use of Urim and Thummim), but the evidence of the present passage indicates that this was not the case in the pre-exilic period;[47] against Grabbe (p. 125), it is misleading to term the reference here 'negative'.[48] Isaiah's contemporaries may indeed be condemned by implication, but that is because they were bad practitioners of their role in society, not because there was anything inherently wrong with being a

[42] L. L. Grabbe, *Priests, Prophets, Diviners, Sages: A Socio-Historical Study of Religious Specialists in Ancient Israel* (Valley Forge, Pa., 1995), 116.

[43] Cf. Grabbe, 66–118, for a survey with references; see too H.-P. Müller, *ThWAT* v. 140–63 = *TDOT* ix. 129–50, with further literature. There has been a long-running debate as to whether etymologically נביא should be understood as active or passive in meaning; for clear statements of the contrasting points of view, with further literature, see respectively D. E. Fleming, 'The Etymological Origins of the Hebrew *nābî*', *CBQ* 55 (1993), 217–24, and J. Huehnergard, 'On the Etymology and Meaning of Hebrew *Nābî*', *EI* 26 (1999), 88*–93*.

[44] A. R. Johnson, *The Cultic Prophet in Ancient Israel* (2nd edn; Cardiff, 1962), remains fundamental.

[45] Prophets and diviners are closely associated elsewhere as well, for example, Jer. 27.9; 29.8; at Mic. 3.11, the prophets are condemned for 'divining' for money.

[46] Note, however, the view of J. van der Ploeg, 'Les anciens dans l'Ancien Testament', in H. Groß and F. Mußner (eds), *Lex Tua Veritas: Festschrift für Hubert Junker* (Trier, 1961), 175–91, that the four terms are arranged chiastically, so that prophet and diviner, and judge and elder, are then linked.

[47] For an apparently 'positive' usage, see Prov. 16.10; cf. R. N. Whybray, *Proverbs* (NCB; London and Grand Rapids, 1994), 243.

[48] The same applies to Stansell, 88–90. Insofar as Porath, 75–76, relies on this same point to argue that this passage reflects a different outlook from that attested elsewhere in Isaiah's writing, and that vv. 2-3 cannot therefore be from him, this also undermines his argument.

diviner as such, any more than was the case with the judge or the elder, for example.

Elder was a general term for a senior member of society to whom respect was due, but he probably occurs here more in his official role. There is no passage which explicitly defines this role, but it can be deduced that the elders functioned in a wide-ranging leadership capacity in the more traditional sectors of Judean society (perhaps especially, though not exclusively,[49] rural): within this sphere, judging and arbitration will have been prominent, but not to the exclusion of the general advisory and decision-making role which is necessary for the well-being of any community.[50]

3. The *captain of fifty* is generally understood as a relatively low-ranking military officer, since elsewhere there are frequent references to a captain of the army (e.g. 1 Sam. 17.55), of a thousand (e.g. 1 Sam. 17.18), and of a hundred (e.g. Exod. 18.21, which also mentions captains of fifties and of tens).[51] On the basis of Exod. 18.21, 25 and 2 Kgs 1.9ff., Kaiser follows Knierim[52] in suggesting that they also exercised a judicial role, though that would not seem specifically to distinguish them from other military officers, nor is it necessary to account for their presence here. It may obviously be assumed that they were the largest single group of military officers, and were therefore the most natural choice to represent that class as a whole. It may also be noted that the suggestion has occasionally been advanced that their presence here indicates that v. 3 lists minor officials by comparison with v. 2, and has therefore been added subsequently. This argument does not stand up, however. Apart from the reason given above for their inclusion here, the counsellor (see below) was certainly not regarded as a minor official (see, e.g., 1.26, where it stands in parallel with judge).

Unlike most of the others listed, a *man of repute* (lit., 'he whose face is lifted up') does not seem to refer to an official role, but rather to any distinguished member of society. At 9.14 he is mentioned beside the elder to illustrate who comprises the 'head' of Israel. At 2 Kgs 5.1 the same words are used to describe the Syrian general Naaman; his official title is given first, 'commander of the army', and then we are told additionally that he was 'great' and a 'man of repute' because of his success. Job 22.8 further makes clear that the phrase does not necessarily refer to one of whom a prophet like Isaiah might inevitably approve on moral grounds, but rather someone who was held in high esteem by his contemporaries for whatever

[49] Note, for instance, 2 Kgs 10.1, 5; Lam 2.9-10, where they appear among the highest dignitaries, including royal, of major cities; cf. V. Wagner, 'Beobachtungen am Amt der Ältesten im alttestamentlichen Israel', *ZAW* 114 (2002), 391–411 and 560–76.

[50] Cf. J. Conrad, *ThWAT* ii. 639–50 = *TDOT* iv. 122–32; H. Reviv, *The Elders in Ancient Israel* (Jerusalem, 1989), with bibliography. Curiously, and surely mistakenly, Reviv asserts on p. 7 that in our verse 'elder' refers simply to an old man and not to the elder as leader.

[51] For further references and statistics, see BDB, 978.

[52] R. Knierim, 'Exodus 18 und die Neuordnung der mosaischen Gerichtsbarkeit', *ZAW* 73 (1961), 146–71 (170), though he does not in fact refer to this particular verse.

reason: 'The powerful possess the land, and the favoured (נשׂוא פנים) live in it'.

The situation regarding the *counsellor* is somewhat different. On the one hand, we read a number of times of a single individual who held this title as a royal adviser at the highest political level (e.g. 2 Sam. 15.12, and cf. 16.23; 1 Chron. 27.32; 2 Chron. 25.16), but on the other hand, and more frequently, they are referred to as a plurality, a sort of privy council from whom the king sought advice and guidance.[53] Even this does not exhaust the matter, however, for there are also occasional references to counsellors in contexts quite separate from the court (e.g. Prov. 15.22). In the present context, the second sense is probably uppermost, though not, perhaps, to the exclusion of the third.

The last two members of the list are described with two words each, and the first word in each pair (חכם and נבון, *skilled* and *expert in*) are closely parallel; there can therefore be no justification for taking חכם on its own as a separate title, 'the wise' (*contra* Vermeylen, 145; Wildberger toys with, but then rightly rejects, this possibility). What precisely is involved in *magic practices* and *charms* is again uncertain (see on 2.6), all the more so in that חרשים is a *hapax legomenon*. The distinction between them may be that between acts, such as sympathetic magic, and words (spells and the like). The second term, לחשׁ, derives from a verb meaning 'to whisper'.[54] It is true that in some contexts this has the developed sense of snake-charming (cf. Jer. 8.17; Ps. 58.6; Eccl. 10.11), but that is always made explicit by the context; it is not the case that such a meaning inheres in the word itself. There is therefore no justification for reading that sense into it in a passage such as the present one (*contra* Porath, 78). As with 'diviner' (see on v. 2 above), the inclusion of such practitioners in this list is noteworthy and strongly suggestive of a pre-exilic date. That such practices were not regarded as inherently malicious may be supported by the use of לחשׁ in proper names (assuming that the same root is in question): לחשׁ occurs on a pre-exilic seal (cf. *AHI*, 153) and הלוחשׁ at Neh. 3.12 and 10.25.

4. God's judgment is not limited to the removal of the leaders of society, but is made worse by the installation of those not suited to replace them.[55] (On the sudden use of the divine first person at this point, see the introductory remarks above.) It is not that there are not present some who would be more suitable for this role: v. 5 makes clear that there are still

---

[53] Cf. P. A. H. de Boer, 'The Counsellor', in M. Noth and D. W. Thomas (eds), *Wisdom in Israel and in the Ancient Near East* (VTSup 3; Leiden, 1955), 42–71; McKane, *Prophets*; R. N. Whybray, *The Heavenly Counsellor in Isaiah xl 13-14: A Study of the Sources of the Theology of Deutero-Isaiah* (SOTSMS 1; Cambridge, 1971), 27–33; L. Ruppert, *ThWAT* iii. 723–26 = *TDOT* vi. 161–63.

[54] For cognates, see, for instance, Akkadian *laḫāšu(m)* (*CDA*, 175), Ugaritic *lḫšt* (*DUL*, 497), Aramaic and Phoenician *lḥšh* (*DNWSI*, 573). See too Jeffers, *Magic and Divination*, 70–74; Schmitt, *Magie*, 110–12.

[55] Against the attempt by Weil, 'Exégèse', to read this passage in a positive sense, see correctly Porath, 37–38. Among other things, he draws attention to the several parallels with the description of the aftermath of a disaster in Lam. 5.8-16.

some elders and honourable people left, while v. 6 implies the presence of at least heads of households. Moreover, the people are represented in that verse as choosing these inappropriate leaders for themselves. It is implied, therefore, that God will work through the means of dulling their senses to the point where they act in a totally irrational manner, something which Isaiah envisages elsewhere as well; cf. 6.10; 9.15; 28.7-10; 29.9-10, 14, etc. The contrast with 1.21-26 is noteworthy, for there the removal of the corrupt leaders is followed by the restoration of the earlier idyllic situation, with fully legitimate judges and counsellors. This contrast may serve to reinforce the conclusion reached there that 1.26 is a later addition to Isaiah's own words.[56]

Their leaders (שריהם, a general term, as at 1.23 above, and so suitable as a summary term for a number of those listed in vv. 2-3) will now be *youths*, נערים. The precise meaning of this word has been much discussed,[57] and in view of its frequent occurrence in a wide variety of contexts, a full survey is out of the question here. The usual rendering 'young man', with its focus on a specific age, is somewhat misleading, since the three-month-old baby Moses could be called a נער (Exod. 2.6, and cf. Isa. 7.16 and 8.4 for uses with reference to what is evidently a very young child) as could those of various ages (as determined by the context in each narrative) in many passages right through to Solomon at (apparently) age 40 (1 Kgs 3.7). It may be suggested that the word refers primarily to status rather than age: in family contexts, the נער is one who is still living in the family home, and is therefore dependent in some measure upon his father as the *paterfamilias*; he graduates from this status only when (usually after marriage) he becomes the head of his own household. He will therefore usually in fact be young, but that is not the point that is primarily in focus. It is in this way that the frequent use of נער as either a military retainer or a senior family servant in a more wealthy household may also be understood, for they are all dependent in one way or another upon their superior, even while, in some cases, they may themselves be of quite high social status in other respects. The frequent contrast with זקן, which itself combines ideas of both age and status, is thus fully intelligible.

It follows from this that the נער is inexperienced in matters of significant responsibility; he has never yet been in a position where he has to act fully independently and without reference to a more experienced senior. This, indeed, is the point of a number of passages in the wisdom literature

---

[56] Dietrich, 51–54, sees this difference between the passages clearly, but because he accepts the authenticity of 1.26 he is then obliged to date the two passages at the opposite extremes of Isaiah's ministry in order to accommodate them both; but if 1.26 is a later addition, the two passages run parallel, and Dietrich's problem does not arise.

[57] For discussion with further bibliography, see, for instance, H.-P. Stähli, *Knabe-Jüngling-Knecht: Untersuchungen zum Begriff* נער *im Alten Testament* (BEvTh 7; Frankfurt am Main, 1978); H. F. Fuhs, *ThWAT* v. 507–18 = *TDOT* ix. 474–85; Y. Avishur and M. Heltzer, *Studies on the Royal Administration in Ancient Israel in the Light of Epigraphic Sources* (Tel Aviv, 2000), 107–14; C. S. Leeb, *Away from the Father's House: The Social Location of na'ar and na'arah in Ancient Israel* (JSOTSup 301; Sheffield, 2000).

which emphasize the immaturity and dependence of the נַעַר (e.g. Prov. 7.7;
22.6; Eccl. 10.16), and it no doubt also lies behind Jeremiah's objection to
God's calling him to be a prophet (Jer. 1.6); it is inexperience rather than
youthfulness as such which is his main problem.

If this brief analysis is broadly on the right lines, then the force of the
present verse becomes clearer. The point is not just that people who are
young will become leaders, but rather those who, by definition, lack the
experience which such a position requires. Never having even 'ruled' in
their own household, they are singularly inappropriate to assume the much
wider responsibilities which authority in society entails. They will
rule...in a childish manner, able to indulge their own immature fancies
without the wisdom and consideration which only experience can bring. It
is clearly a recipe for disaster,[58] as the next verse goes on to elaborate.

5. Two consequences follow, 'political and moral anarchy' (Gray). In
the first category comes oppression. Elsewhere in Isaiah, נגשׂ can be used
for the oppression of the people by foreign conquerors (9.3; 14.2, 4, and
cf. 53.7), but the tragedy here is that it will be practised by close fellow
citizens, *by one another...by his neighbour*. The point will be repeated in
v. 12. There is no indication as to the precise forms which this oppression
might take, and so we are free to exercise our imagination in filling in the
details.

Secondly, there will be a breakdown of the accepted moral norms of
society. Needless to say, *the elder* and *the honourable* were expected to be
held in high esteem and respect by their juniors and inferiors; Kaiser
appropriately cites Lev. 19.32; Prov. 16.31; 20.29 as examples, though
they could be multiplied. Isaiah's strong sense elsewhere of morality being
expressed partly in terms of respect for such hierarchies suggests that he
would have regarded this as a particularly repugnant form of behaviour,
indicative of the severity of the coming judgment. Micah 7.6 and especially Lam. 4.16 and 5.12 reflect a closely comparable point of view. The
obvious contrast between *the youth* (נער again) and *the elder* is equally
apparent in the Hebrew for *the base person* (הנקלה, from the root 'to be
light') and *the honourable* (הנכבד, from the root 'to be heavy'). Behind
will act arrogantly towards (ירהבו), Wildberger sees a possible allusion to
the outbreak of the powers of chaos which God had subdued in creation.
This may be going too far, but the verb is certainly a strong one to use,
implying far more aggression than a simple forgetting of manners.

6. The people's desperation in this situation is illustrated (see the textual notes on כי) by the vignette in vv. 6-7. Within the context of the
extended family, the basic unit of society whose structure endures so long
as there is life, someone will *seize*, grab hold of, anyone who seems to
have even a minimal qualification and seek to compel him to assume
responsibility.

Although the expression *father's house* is often used as a technical term
for the family (extended or nuclear) as dwelling in a single locality, it can

---

[58] For some of the social norms which are presupposed here, see A. C. Hagedorn,
'Guarding the Parents' Honour—Deuteronomy 21.18-21', *JSOT* 88 (2000), 1–21.

also refer more concretely to the building itself,[59] and the clear implication of v. 7 is that this is the sense here too.

The 'minimal qualification' is that the man has a *cloak*, a garment which, as the laws of Exod. 22.25-27 and Deut. 24.12-13[60] indicate,[61] is in a context such as this almost the equivalent of the English idiom 'the shirt off one's back'. The point is, of course, deeply ironic: he has managed to preserve at least something through the crisis, and this singles him out from the others. Marti's suggestion that it refers to an official garment, passed down within the family as a symbol of their authority, is thus misguided, and has rightly not been adopted. While there are occasions in which garments play a ceremonial role and so have symbolic significance, that is always something determined by the context, not something inherent in the word itself; the context here, in fact, points in exactly the opposite direction.

For *leader*, קצין, see on 1.10 above, where the point was made that the word should not be defined too narrowly. The closest verbal parallel for the present passage is Judg. 11.6, where the elders of Gilead invite Jephthah to 'come and be our leader' (לכה והייתה לנו לקצין).[62] The continuation there ('so that we may fight with the Ammonites') shows that military leadership is intended. While that need not be ruled out here, it is clear that civic authority is nevertheless primarily in view.

The ironic tone is continued in the last line of the verse: while the man is indeed offered *authority* (the sense is usually of oppressive rule—cf. Gen. 16.9; Exod. 18.10; Judg. 3.30; 2 Kgs 8.20; Ps. 106.42—but not invariably so; cf. Gen. 41.35), it will be over only a *heap of ruins*. It is probable that this is to be taken metaphorically.[63] There has been no indication that Jerusalem and Judah have been physically destroyed, and indeed the present verse itself indicates that the houses are still standing. The reference, therefore, must be to the ruined nature of the society. That

[59] This point has been stressed in particular by G. Cowling, 'The Biblical Household', in M. Augustin and K.-D. Schunck (eds), *"Wünschet Jerusalem Frieden": Collected Communications to the XIIth Congress of the International Organization for the Study of the Old Testament, Jerusalem 1986* (Frankfurt am Main, 1988), 179–92; he cites Gen. 24.23 as a clear example; see too my essay 'The Family in Persian Period Judah: Some Textual Reflections', in W. G. Dever and S. Gitin (eds), *Symbiosis, Symbolism, and the Power of the Past: Canaan, Ancient Israel and their Neighbors from the Late Bronze Age through Roman Palaestina* (Winona Lake, Ind., 2003), 469–85 (including bibliography on the topic of the 'father's house' as a whole).

[60] Although the situations are not exactly parallel, since here a relative is in view whereas in Deut. 24 it is merely a fellow-Israelite who is making the loan on pledge, there is nevertheless an interesting contrast. Deuteronomy 24.10-11 states that the lender 'shall not go into the house to take the pledge. You shall wait outside'; here, however, the relative explicitly seizes the man *in his father's house*. As Gray observes, 'in this evil time men keep at home and need to be dragged into public (cp. Am 5^{13})'.

[61] See too the inscription from Yavneh Yam; cf. *SSI* i. 26–30; *CoS* 3, 77–78.

[62] Cf. Porath, 41–42. He notes further contrasts between the two passages, including the fact that in Judges the threat is from outside but here from within the community.

[63] Magonet, 'Isaiah 2:1–4:6', comparing 22.21 (and cf. the device used in 5.7), suggests that there may be a satirical word-play on ממשלה: 'To capture the pun in English one might replace the word "reign" with "ruin"' (p. 72).

it should later have been reinterpreted more literally in the light of the destruction of Jerusalem by the Babylonians (cf. v. 8) is nevertheless not surprising (cf. Jones, 'Traditio', 242).

7. Although *on that day* is simply a temporal note, embedded within the short 'narrative' of vv. 6-7,[64] it also serves within the wider redactional context of chs 2–4 to help link this passage with ch. 2 and its focus on the day of the Lord (2.12, 20).

In response to the pressure to assume authority, the man shouts his rejection in equal desperation. The underlying point is, of course, to emphasize the gravity of the situation; it is so bad that no right-thinking person would wish to become involved, specifically to become a *healer*. With the literal sense of 'to bind up' (of wounds), this verb was used at 1.6 in a similar context: the nation was described there too under the image of a sick and badly beaten man. (In a non-Isaianic passage, 30.26, the Lord is likewise described as one who 'binds up the injuries of his people'.) There is thus no need to look further than the use of a characteristic and vivid image by Isaiah for an explanation of its meaning here. Specifically, the fact that Ezek. 34.4, 16 uses the word in the description of the work of a shepherd gives us no ground whatever for thinking that behind Isaiah's use there lies the idea of the leader as the shepherd of his people (Wildberger), nor does the use of the word with 'turban' as its object at Exod. 29.9 and Lev. 8.13 mean that this sense can be read into the verb when the object is not expressed (Kaiser, 1st edition), nor does the fact that Neh. 4.1 (7) and 2 Chron. 24.13 use ארוכה, 'healing', as a metaphor for the restoration of the walls of Jerusalem or its temple imply that physical repair is implied here. It is possible that the verb is used with the extended meaning of 'rule' at Job 34.17, but the text there has been doubted by some, and even if it is correct there is no need to see it as more than a metaphorical extension of the sense which it carries here.[65]

In elaboration and reinforcement of his rejection, the man denies that he has even the 'minimal qualifications' to assume authority. In saying that he has *neither bread nor a cloak*, he not only disputes the contention of the speaker in v. 6 (and it is, of course, idle and unnecessary to speculate whether he is telling the truth in this or lying in order to avoid becoming involved) but also implies that he does not have the wherewithal to feed and clothe his people, the basic responsibility of any leader.

You shall not make me: לא + imperfect, a strong prohibition, thus emphatically rejecting the equally strong urging of 'you shall be our leader' in v. 6. The judgment expressed in v. 1 thus remains unalleviated.

8. As argued above, this and the following verse are probably to be taken as an exilic addition to the Isaianic material in 1-7, so applying (very appropriately) Isaiah's announcement of judgment to the fall of Jerusalem to the Babylonians, which is already depicted as lying in the past (so correctly Porath, 43–47). There is certainly a shift of emphasis from the

---

[64] Cf. DeVries, *From Old Revelation to New*, 39.
[65] See the judicious note in S. R. Driver and G. B. Gray, *A Critical and Exegetical Commentary on the Book of Job* (ICC; Edinburgh, 1921), Part II, 256.

disintegration of society in 1-7 to the fall of the nation here. *For* may therefore be taken as a loose connective (see the textual notes), not unlike its similarly redactional use in v. 1.

As is common in such cases, the redactor has picked up some of the vocabulary from the preceding material and taken it forward. Thus *Jerusalem...and Judah* echoes v. 1, and *has stumbled* (כשלה) picks up in verbal form the root used in the noun 'heap of ruins' (מכשלה) in v. 6 (though influence from Hos. 5.5 is also likely; see below). The parallel *has fallen* may perhaps imply that the judgment once pronounced upon the northern kingdom of Israel (Amos 5.2, itself already applied to the Davidic house in 9.11) has now also overtaken her southern neighbour. For the manner in which this line expresses the totality of the disaster, see the textual notes.

The reason (כי here = *because*) follows, expressed first in general and then (v. 9*a*) in more specific terms. The general indictment is that their speech (*tongue*) and *their deeds were against the Lord*. This does not, of course, necessarily mean that they were consciously defying God; rather, the general way in which they went about their daily lives was contrary to the redactor's understanding of the revealed divine will. Any theodicy which followed the fall of Jerusalem was more or less bound with the advantage of hindsight to come to this conclusion, and it is a standard theme in the Hebrew Bible's explanation of the disaster.

Indeed, the same point is made even more forcefully by the development of the last phrase with the words *in rebelling against the eyes of his glory*. As noted at 1.20 above, Isaiah himself does not use the verb 'to rebel', though he does once refer to the people as 'rebellious' (30.9). It is common, however, in Deuteronomy and related literature, and it is likely that the redactor here is therefore simply making use of what had become a widely accepted way of explaining the judgment that had fallen. As discussed in the textual notes, *the eyes of his glory* is a difficult phrase, and emendation to 'against his glory' is not impossible (עם instead of עני). Nevertheless, sense can perhaps be made of the present text when it is recognized that a redactor is responsible for this passage and that he will have been working within the wider context established by the second half of ch. 2. In the comments on v. 11 of that chapter, it was observed that 'haughty eyes' is a common idiomatic way of referring to inappropriate human pride, and indeed it comes in two other redactional passages in the first part of Isaiah (5.15; 10.12). Here, therefore, we may have a reference to its converse: only God may legitimately be said to have 'eyes of glory'. If the allusion is deliberate, the redactor will be pointing out that the judgment predicted in ch. 2 on account of human pride has been fulfilled in the events surrounding the fall of Jerusalem. Any such pride is automatically construed as rebellion because it challenges God's uniquely exalted status, and it is eventually bound to be brought down: 'The Lord alone will be exalted on that day' (2.11, 17).

Porath, 45–46, draws attention to an interesting parallel for this passage in Hos. 5.5: 'Israel's pride (גאון) testifies against him (ענה...בפניו); Israel and Ephraim stumble (יכשלו) in their guilt; Judah also stumbles (כשל) with them'. The use of 'stumble' and of 'testify against' are common to both passages; furthermore, 'Israel's pride' as a cause for judgment is also present if the interpretation of the *eyes of his glory* suggested above is correct.[66] In Isaiah 2, גאון was ascribed exclusively to God (cf. vv. 10, 19 and 21), so that the word itself could not be used negatively of Judah here: nonetheless, the culpability of human pride is clearly reflected. It is generally agreed that the last clause of Hos. 5.5 is a later addition by a Judean redactor who wished to point out that the fate of the northern kingdom had later also befallen the southern kingdom.[67] It is therefore significant that our redactor, working in the same context, uses identical phraseology; influence, if not identity of authorship, seems probable.

9. Both *partiality* and *testified against* are suggestive of technical legal terminology.[68] There seems here, therefore, to be a more specific indictment than in the previous verse, namely that of unjustly manipulating the courts and the legal system for personal advantage. In God's court, however, justice is even-handed, so that such behaviour itself constitutes testimony for the prosecution. The accusation is common in the pre-exilic prophets (as well as elsewhere, of course), not least Isaiah (e.g. 5.7, 23; 10.1-2; 29.21), so that its being singled out for mention here is not surprising. As mentioned in the textual notes above, Prov. 28.21 indicates that it need not be restricted to judges alone, but applies in principle to all citizens.

The nature of the sin of *Sodom* is variously described both in the Hebrew Bible and in later Jewish and Christian literature,[69] and judicial injustice is sometimes included. That, however, is not the point here. The emphasis rather is on the blatant nature of the sin, that it is *proclaimed* without any apparent shame, *without hiding it*.[70] This seems an entirely reasonable point to deduce from the story of Sodom's fate as known to us from Genesis 18–19. Within Isaiah comparison with Sodom is made at 1.9-10 and 13.19, while Lam. 4.6 indicates that the fall of Jerusalem was being compared with the overthrow of Sodom in the exilic period.[71] Similarly, *their sin* can hardly be precisely defined. It is likely that the

---

[66] Porath himself finds this echoed in הכרת פניהם in v. 9. As explained in the textual notes, however, this is unlikely to be correct, even though it has frequently been advocated. But in view of the interpretation of v. 8*b* offered above, nothing is lost in terms of the parallel with Hos. 5.5.

[67] See, for instance, G. I. Emmerson, *Hosea: An Israelite Prophet in Judean Perspective* (JSOTSup 28; Sheffield, 1984), 65–67; G. I. Davies, *Hosea* (NCB; London and Grand Rapids, 1992), 143.

[68] Cf. Bovati, *Re-Establishing Justice*, 74 and 188–89.

[69] For a survey, see J. A. Loader, *A Tale of Two Cities: Sodom and Gomorrah in the Old Testament, Early Jewish and Early Christian Traditions* (Kampen, 1990).

[70] Cf. S. E. Balentine, 'A Description of the Semantic Field of Hebrew Words for "Hide"', *VT* 30 (1980), 137–53. Bovati, *Re-Establishing Justice*, 101, finds here an ironic play on the sense of *proclaim* (הגיד) in a legal context of acknowledging or confessing one's guilt.

[71] It is true that כסדם, *like Sodom*, is often deleted as a gloss on the ground that the line is too long from a metrical point of view. This seems an unnecessary conclusion to draw, however, once it is recognized that the redactor in vv. 8-9 has written throughout more in a form of rhythmic prose than of strict poetry; see the introductory section above.

word is being used in the broadest and most general sense, parallel with
the third line of v. 8. The word itself, חטאת, is used very frequently and in
many different contexts. Perhaps all that can be said in the present passage
is that it indicates how much of human conduct can be regarded as guilt
when viewed from the divine perspective, and that this must inevitably
lead to judgment if atonement has not first been made (6.5-7).[72]

It was argued in the introduction above that the last line of the verse is
not an independent saying, but a conclusion to the redactional material in
vv. 8-9 as a whole. In the light of the preceding indictment, the *disaster*,
though effected at one level by the Babylonians, cannot be blamed on
anyone other than the people of Judah and Jerusalem themselves. They
must face up to their responsibilities if there is to be any hope for the
future.

Such an acknowledgment will be painful, and this is recognized by the
use of *woe*. In contrast with 1.4, אוי is used here rather than הוי. Despite
some obvious similarities, the two particles may be distinguished in terms
both of their characteristic syntax and of their meaning.[73] Although there
are a few exceptions, אוי is nearly always followed by a dative ל and a
reason, introduced by כי (as here), whereas הוי is either used in a freestand-
ing manner or followed by a substantive or participle. It was seen at 1.4
that הוי arises from funerary laments, and that in the prophetic literature it
therefore serves as an expression of threat or judgment. אוי, however, is
more a cry of anguish or despair in the face of some painful situation
(hence the opposite of אשרי; see on v. 10). The people as a whole have
suffered judgment and the redactor (without apparently involving himself
personally) gives voice to the pain which has resulted.

[72] Cf. K. Koch, *ThWAT* ii. 857–70 = *TDOT* iv. 309–19, with literature.
[73] Cf. H.-J. Zobel, *ThWAT* ii. 382–88 = *TDOT* iii. 359–64; Hardmeier, *Texttheorie*, 188–202.

A DIDACTIC REFLECTION
(3.10-11)

[10]Happy is the righteous one, for it is well (with him),
    because they will eat the fruit of their deeds;
[11]Woe to the wicked one, (for) it will go disastrously (with him),
    because what he has done will in turn be done to him.

10. אמרו צדיק כי־טוב: the text is apparently presupposed by nearly all the ancient witnesses (on the LXX, see further below),[1] and it is therefore proper that every effort should be made to understand it without emendation. Several approaches have been proposed.

(i) The scribe who corrected 1QIsaᵃ by the addition of a supralinear ל before צדיק, σ (εἴπατε τῷ δικαίω ὅτι κάλως), T (אמרו לצדיקא טוביכון), V (*dicite iusto quoniam bene*) and P, together with several of the rabbinic commentators, take צדיק as an indirect object: 'say to the righteous that it is well (with him)'. It is not clear, however, that this is grammatically acceptable (so far as I am aware, no parallels have been suggested), and the 'correction' in the scroll is tacit acceptance of this difficulty (not evidence for an alternative text).[2]

(ii) In his commentary, Jerome (with other unnamed interpreters) paraphrased *laudate iustitiam Dei*, and Ibn Ezra also refers to some (with whom he disagrees) who thought that אמרו = שַׁבְּחוּ. This approach has been followed more recently by Vitringa (*celebrare, praedicare, laudare*) and Gesenius ('Preiset den Gerechten'), with reference to Pss. 40.11 and 145.6, 11. This is rightly rejected by Delitzsch, however, who observes that even in these verses in the Psalms the sense is 'to declare'; on its own, אמר never means 'praise'.

(iii) By their more 'literal' rendering (εἴπατε δικαίος ὅτι ἄγαθον) α and θ apparently adopt what has become the usual way to explain the MT (see, for instance, Hitzig, Knobel, Dillmann, Delitzsch, Orelli, König, Oswalt, Barthélemy, Watts), namely to construe צדיק as either an adverbial accusative or a *casus pendens*, to give 'Say concerning the righteous that it is well (with him)'. Alternatively, צדיק is construed as a direct accusative after אמר (cf. Ps. 40.11), and an analogy is drawn with the construction following verbs of seeing or knowing, such as 'God saw the light, that it was good (כי טוב)' (Gen. 1.4) = 'God saw that the light was good', and 'You know David my father, that he was not able to build...' (1 Kgs 5.17 [3]) = 'You know that my father David was not able to build...'. Here, therefore, a literal rendering might be 'Declare the righteous, that it is well' = 'Declare that it is well with the righteous'. The analogy is not exact, however, both because אמר + direct object = 'declare' (itself very rare) really means 'tell of', and so

---

[1] The spelling אמרו in 1QIsaᵃ has many parallels elsewhere in the scroll for 2nd fem. sg. and 3rd pl. imperatives (see Kutscher, 193, for examples). There is no agreement as to how this should be explained, however. Kutscher discusses three possibilities on pp. 194–97—that it reflects the more primitive *qutulu* form, that it reflects Aramaic influence (since this is the form of the imperative in most types of Aramaic of the period), or that penultimate stress had spread more widely from pausal forms. He himself favours the Aramaic explanation.

[2] Bartelt, 213, suggests that the ל of v. 11 'is taken as serving double duty back to line 10a', but it is unlikely that the double duty construction can work in reverse in this way. C. L. Miller, 'Patterns of Verbal Ellipsis in Ugaritic Poetry', *UF* 31 (1999), 333–72, notes that 'backwards gapping' is rare and mostly confined to climactic ('staircase') parallelism (pp. 353–55).

is used in a slightly different way from 'declare' = 'pronounce', and because an exact application of the analogy would demand that the object of the first verb becomes the subject of the subordinate clause, which in this case would not furnish the desired sense. This alternative approach to the conventional rendering therefore seems to be more problematic than its proponents recognize. The first approach is perhaps just possible, and in my view is the best explanation of the text as it stands, but it is obviously awkward.

(iv) Several attempts, differing slightly among themselves, have been made to avoid these problems by proposing that טוב and רע (v. 11) should be interpreted as technical legal terms, 'innocent' and 'guilty' respectively.[3] Consequently, Wiklander, for instance, renders 'Say that the righteous is innocent, that they will eat the fruit of their doings'. This involves taking both occurrences of כי as introducing indirect speech after אמרו. While this is theoretically possible in v. 10, it does not work in the closely parallel v. 11. Since אוי is not a verb of speech, כי there must mean 'because' (see the precise parallel in 9b), but the result is then nonsense: '...guilty because what he has done will in turn be done to him'.[4] רע, therefore, cannot mean 'guilty', and the parallelism between 10 and 11 (and, indeed, 9b) suggests that this approach is not probable for 10 either.[5]

The upshot of this discussion of the MT is that only the first of the approaches grouped under (iii) above is remotely possible. For some, that will be sufficient, in view of the strong support for this form of the text. Others, however, will think that the awkwardness with regard to the syntax of צדיק is too high a price to pay and will thus be open to the possibility that there has been an early error in transmission, prior to the time of our extant witnesses.

In the latter case, by far the most attractive conjecture is that which stretches back at least as far as Lowth and has been adopted since by many commentators, namely to read אשרי in place of אמרו.[6] In paleo-Hebrew (which is probably the relevant consideration) the forms are much closer orthographically than in the square script (the addition of a right-hand down stroke is all that is needed to turn a ש into a מ), so that scribal misreading is plausible. Contextually, of course, the result is excellent, giving a precise contrast with אוי ל in v. 11 (and 9b); cf. Eccl. 10.16-17.

The rendering in the LXX has sometimes been thought to lend some support to this emendation: εἰπόντες Δήσωμεν τὸν δίκαιον ὅτι δύσχρητος ἡμῖν ἐστι ('saying, let us bind the just, for he is inconvenient to us'). It is suggested that 'bind' may have arisen

---

[3] See, for instance, S. Bahbout, 'Sull' interpretazione dei vv. 10-11 del cap. 3 di Isaia', *Annuario di Studi Ebraici* 1 (1963–64), 23–26; Wiklander, 78; Porath, 48–49.

[4] The same difficulty arises, *mutatis mutandis*, with the approach adopted by Holladay, 'Isa. iii 10-11'. He brings various lines of argument together to defend a rendering of the MT as 'Notice how good the righteous man is' (and he accepts the likelihood that טוב carries the overtones of 'innocent'). However, it is difficult to see how the following כי-clause can make sense after this.

[5] Wiklander does not address this point in his comments, and in his 'survey of the utterance units' on p. 67, where for his purposes he consistently omits connectives in his rendering, he avoids it by not translating כי in v. 11 at all. Porath adopts a slightly different approach to v. 10. He suggests that אמרו is addressed to the wicked of v. 9, urging them to confess that they have been in error, and that the speech they should make is limited to צדיק כי־טוב (which he renders 'Es stimmt, ja es ist recht!'); 10b is then a separate comment on the wicked, which has the advantage that מעלליהם can have its commoner meaning of 'evil deeds' (as in v. 8). However, apart from the fact that טוב cannot mean 'recht' (even with reference to Gen. 1.4, to which Porath appeals), this approach completely cuts across the clear parallel structure between vv. 10 and 11.

[6] Tur-Sinai, 161–62, suggested simply revocalizing as אָמְרוּ (rather surprisingly followed by HUPB), parallel with הגידו in v. 9, but this runs into difficulties with the following words, which he then has to render as mocking words of the people: 'Is it only the righteous who are well off...?'. But I do not see how this could possibly be justified as a rendering of צדיק כי טוב, and he offers no explanation for it.

as a misunderstanding of אשר with the sibilant construed as a שׂ = ס (cf. אסר, 'to bind'). While this possibility cannot be ruled out, two other considerations should also be borne in mind. First, the inclusion of εἰπόντες suggests that אמרו was in the translator's *Vorlage*,[7] so that the evidence is ambiguous as regards the 'original' text. Lowth, indeed, suggested as one alternative that אשרי might have been lost by haplography after אמרו, though it is more probable that the LXX has offered a double reading.[8] This seems to indicate either that there were already variant readings known to the translator which he has then sought to conflate or that the LXX text has itself been the object of an early revision. Secondly, the continuation of the translation has an exact parallel in Wisdom of Solomon 2.12: ἐνεδρεύσωμεν τὸν δίκαιον ὅτι δύσχρητος ἡμῖν ἐστι (and note that δύσχρητος occurs nowhere else in the LXX apart from these two passages). Since the LXX of Isaiah departs so markedly from the Hebrew text at this point, the possibility of influence from the Wisdom of Solomon (rather than that the latter is citing LXX Isaiah, as urged by Ottley) should be considered, especially if we are dealing with an early revision of the translation. In that case, there can be no certainty that Δήσωμεν has not entered the text from the same source. The conclusion is that the LXX may reflect knowledge of an earlier form of the Hebrew text which included אשרי, but that there are sufficient uncertainties to make it unwise to adduce the LXX as direct evidence to that effect.[9]

כי טוב: Holladay, 'Isaiah iii 10-11', has argued strongly that in this construction טוב is never verbal, but always adjectival; the verb would require the addition of לו. Some, indeed, have suggested that we should add לו (e.g. Duhm and Marti). Against both, however, it may be held that in a gnomic, poetic saying such as this, abbreviation in the form of an ellipse is acceptable (cf. Gibson, 110; see further on v. 11).

כי־פרי: Procksch (only partially, and therefore misleadingly, followed by *BHS*) conjectured that כי טוב should be construed as introducing the second half of the verse (against the Masoretic accents), and כי־פרי conflated as כפרי; hence 'for he will eat what is good according to the fruit of his works'. Weighty objections can be raised against this proposal, however: it requires several further consequential emendations, not only of the plural יאכלו to the singular (which Procksch indeed suggests), but also of the suffix on מעלליהם (which he does not), and also of כי־גמול to כנמול in v. 11 together with insertion of כי before רע, all to regain the parallelism between the two verses which the original emendation has destroyed. Such a string of conjectures is unwarranted, besides which Wildberger objects that the result makes no sense: 'one can enjoy good things in proportion to one's deeds or could even enjoy the fruit of one's deeds, but not good things according to the fruit of one's deeds'.

יאכלו: against proposals to delete the final ו, so making the verb singular, the suffix on the previous word seems, as already noted, to secure the plural reading of MT,[10] and this despite the equally securely attested singular of the parallel in v. 11. צדיק is therefore clearly being taken as collective, which in itself causes no difficulty; cf. GK §145b-g; JM §135; Gibson, 22. It is likely that there was influence in this direction from the plural forms in vv. 8-9 immediately preceding (see especially מעלליהם in v. 8).

---

[7] It was noted at v. 6 above that the translator probably added λέγων without textual warrant as an interpretive clarification (see too T and P); the same might have happened here, therefore, with εἰπόντες (cf. Ziegler, 61). The coincidence of this happening at precisely the point where MT was, *ex hypothesi*, later corrupted to אמרו rather tells against this alternative explanation, however.

[8] On this phenomenon, see Seeligmann, 31–38.

[9] For confusion about the LXX and its relation to the Hebrew text already in the patristic period, see M. J. Hollerich, *Eusebius of Caesarea's Commentary on Isaiah: Christian Exegesis in the Age of Constantine* (Oxford, 1999), 44–45.

[10] The versions also generally support MT here, which is strong evidence in view of the fact that it is the harder reading. Against support of the singular from V, see van der Kooij, 309. In his commentary, Jerome cites the verb in the plural.

11. רע: many commentators conjecture that כי should be added before this word, both to gain the required sense and to tighten the parallelism with v. 10. While this gives the required meaning, emendation is not necessary to achieve it, since in poetry the כי of v. 10 may be held to do double duty in a parallel line.[11]

כי־גמול: against the proposal to read כגמול, see above. The solitary support of the LXX for the emendation in this case is weak, since its rendering is merely a consequence of its having taken רע with the second half of the line.

יעשה: 1QIsaᵃ ישוב, which Wildberger prefers because elsewhere גמול is commonly used with a form of שוב, but only once with עשה (cf. Judg. 9.16, overlooked by Wildberger; note too the use of יעשה in a parallel clause with גמול ישוב in Obad. 15b); see Prov. 12.14 for an especially close parallel. However, since the two words are sufficiently distinct to rule out the possibility of a copyist's slip, it is far more plausible to assume that a common form of expression has been substituted for a rare one than the reverse.[12] Among the versions, only T agrees with the scroll (יהתב), doubtless for the same reason.

These two verses are obviously closely connected by verbal repetition with what precedes; cf. מעלליהם in vv. 8 and 10; אוי ל followed by כי in 9 and 11; רע/רעה and גמול/גמלו also in 9 and 11. Moreover, the form of the two parallel lines is modelled on 9b.

Despite this, a fundamental difference of outlook is also apparent. Both in vv. 1-7 and in its exilic extension in 8-9, the inhabitants of Jerusalem and Judah are treated as a single community, and it is on this community as a whole that the judgment falls. In our verses, by contrast, a distinction is introduced between the righteous and the wicked, whereby it is only the latter who suffer judgment. This distinction comes to its sharpest expression in the contrasting applications of אוי in vv. 9 and 11: in 9, it is applied to 'them' without exception, whereas v. 11 modifies this to indicate that it refers only to the wicked. Attempts to defend authorial unity on the basis of Isaiah's doctrine of the remnant therefore miss the point, since they fail to do justice to the distinction between the contrasting emphases on the society as such as the object of condemnation in vv. 1-9 and on individuals in 10-11. Furthermore, such divisions within society as might be deduced from 1-9, and which become explicit in 12-15, concern the leaders and the ordinary people, subsequently identified as the rich and the poor, whereas there is no indication in 10 and 11 that the righteous and the wicked are divided according to social class. The widely adopted conclusion that these two verses have been added to an earlier form of 3.1–4.1 therefore seems to be correct.

Within the book of Isaiah as a whole, the kind of distinctions which these verses introduce is most closely paralleled in the closing chapters, especially 65–66. There too, the previous address to the community as a whole is modified in the direction of individuals within it, and this is often reasonably explained as part of the writer's response to the apparent non-fulfilment of some aspects of the earlier promises to the restored

---

[11] Cf. Holladay, 'Isaiah iii 10-11'. He may be right to argue that this construction is archaic in origin, but the fact that he finds examples in Jeremiah to support the case indicates that its use here cannot be used as evidence that our verses were therefore composed at a very early date in the form of a wisdom saying which Isaiah could have cited.

[12] Cf. Kutscher, 290; Høgenhaven, 'The First Isaiah Scroll', 21–22.

community.[13] The theme is introduced elsewhere in the book by way of anticipation, however, and we have already seen its influence in a marked form in the closing verses of ch. 1.

In the present passage, however, this is, if possible, taken even further by the use of a manner of speech which finds its closest analogies in the wisdom literature. In summarizing the various arguments which lead to this conclusion, Wildberger notes the following: the use of אשרי, with which אוי is then associated in antithetical parallelism;[14] the outlook of the verses in terms of the direct association of deeds and their consequences, as though this was related to the order which God has established in the world rather than being the result of direct retribution initiated by divine intervention; the similarities between v. 10 and Prov. 16.20 and 28.14 (and cf. Ps. 128.2) and especially between v. 11 and Prov. 12.14; and finally the characteristic contrast in the wisdom literature between the 'righteous' and the 'wicked'.[15]

These considerations make it likely that these verses were penned explicitly for their present setting (cf. the verbal connections with vv. 8-9) at a late stage in the formation of the book of Isaiah with a view to loosening the sayings of the surrounding passages from their historically bound context so as to derive more universally applicable teaching from them (for which wisdom forms are appropriate).[16] The total condemnation of the pre-exilic society of Judah in vv. 1-9 is applicable still to the wicked of all ages, but, in the light of the book as a whole, it may fairly be concluded that there is also blessing available for the righteous; the thought is comparable with the manner in which 1.26-31 develops the Isaianic 1.21-25. In addition, as Koenen also observes, the present setting of these verses in advance of 13-15 leads to a reading of those verses which will identify the oppressors and the poor there with the wicked and the righteous here, a familiar line of thought in early Judaism.

10. *Happy* (assuming the emendation defended above to be correct): this expression occurs overwhelmingly in wisdom literature and late psalms.[17] It should be distinguished from the more solemn, liturgical 'blessed' (ברוך), its use implying that it refers to a state of well-being consequent upon certain types of action and lifestyle. It introduces Psalm 1, which,

[13] I have summarized some of these arguments in Chapter 5 of *Variations on a Theme*; see especially pp. 191–95.

[14] Cf. H. W. Wolff, *Amos the Prophet: The Man and his Background* (Philadelphia, 1973), 25–30 = *Amos' geistige Heimat* (WMANT 18; Neukirchen–Vluyn, 1964), 18–20. This argument does not necessarily entail the view that אוי 'originated' in wisdom circles, of course.

[15] Cf. U. Skladny, *Die ältesten Spruchsammlungen in Israel* (Göttingen, 1962), 7–13; J. van Oorschot, 'Die Gerechte und die Frevler im Buch der Sprüche: Ein Beitrag zur Theologie und Religionsgeschichte des frühen Judentums', *BZ* NF 42 (1998), 225–39.

[16] Cf. Koenen, *Heil den Gerechten*, 184–89.

[17] Cf. H. Cazelles, *ThWAT* i. 481–85 = *TDOT* i. 445–48; W. Janzen, ''Ašrê in the Old Testament', *HTR* 58 (1965), 215–26; H.-J. Kraus, *Psalmen*, 1 (BKAT 15/1; Neukirchen–Vluyn, 1960), 3–4 = *Psalms 1–59* (Minneapolis, 1988), 115.

with its contrast between the *righteous* (צַדִּיק) and the *wicked* (רָשָׁע), serves as a usefully extended comment on these two verses in Isaiah.[18] Since the Psalm probably comes from circles very similar to these verses, its fuller explanation of the nature and actions of the righteous is probably applicable here too.

Eat: from 1.19 to 65.13, this is a standard image throughout the book (as well as elsewhere) for the enjoyment of the blessings attendant upon a life of obedience.

Their deeds (מַעַלְלֵיהֶם): cf. v. 8, where, in common with the vast majority of cases in the Hebrew Bible, it means 'evil deeds'. In a few cases, however, this nuance is clearly reversed, since it can also be used with reference to God's deeds (cf. Mic. 2.7; Pss. 77.12 [11]; 78.7). It is therefore not necessary to insist that evil deeds must be in view here (so leading to a completely different translation; see the comments on Porath in the textual notes above); rather, the writer has exploited the possibilities of this minority usage for the sake of word association.

11. *Woe* (אוֹי): see on v. 9. *What he has done* is a free translation of a more literal 'the dealing of his hands' (cf. Judg. 9.16; Prov. 12.14). A similar thought occurs at the end of Obadiah 15, and there it is preceded by the even clearer saying, 'as you have done, it shall be done to you'. As already noted, the kind of retributive theology here expressed is especially common in the wisdom literature of Proverbs.

---

[18] See too U. Nõmmik, 'Die Gerechtigkeitsbearbeitungen in den Psalmen', *UF* 31 (1999), 443–35.

THE PEOPLE'S PLIGHT
(3.12)

[12]O my people, oppressors deal harshly (with them),
and creditors hold sway over them;
O my people, your guides lead (you) astray,
and confuse the way of your paths.

12. עמי: despite the change of person between the two lines of this verse, parallelism strongly suggests that this first word of each line should be construed in the same way syntactically. Since in the second line it is clearly a *casus pendens*, the same may be assumed for the first, so that it cannot serve from a formal point of view as the direct object of מעולל (cf. Gibson, 181).

נגשיו מעולל: this phrase raises difficulties of both grammar and meaning. On the one hand it appears that a plural subject is followed by a singular participle, and on the other the meaning of מעולל is disputed. Several attempts have been made to explain the grammar: (i) נגשיו might be a 'plural of majesty' (GK §124*k*; Hitzig), although sense and the parallel נשים tell against this: nothing leads us to expect a singular oppressor; rather, it seems that we are dealing with a group of people here.[1] (ii) More commonly, therefore, appeal has been had to the so-called 'distributive plural', whereby 'the plural of persons... is sometimes construed with the singular of the predicate, when instead of the whole class of individuals, each severally is to be represented as affected by the statement' (GK §145*l*); see especially Delitzsch. (iii) Barthélemy, 24–25, and Porath, 25, appeal to 60.17, where נגשיך is parallel with the abstract singular פקדתך and has a singular predicate, צדקה, to suggest that נגשיו in our verse has a virtually abstract meaning, 'administration'. This is unlikely, however; since the singular predicate צדקה is abstract, the analogy with our verse is not exact. Of these proposals, therefore, only (ii) is possible, but even it seems forced, given that the parallel half of the line does not follow suit (unlike the parade example of Gen. 27.29; the other examples cited by GK are either textually suspect or alternative explanations are available). If that is correct, then resort should be had to emendation. The ancient versions are unlikely to lend firm support to any proposal, since they were bound to render in a grammatically coherent way, regardless of their *Vorlage*. 1QIsaᵃ, however, may be adduced in partial support, for it spells the first word נוגשו; although there are other examples in the scroll of this spelling of the third masculine singular suffix on a plural noun, it points to the possibility that an original נגשים was wrongly divided,[2] and that the resultant נגשי was then almost inevitably read as a suffix form with final ו. Similarly, once the ם had been attached to the following word, it was equally inevitable that a final ו should be dropped (and haplography with the ו on the following word will have made this all the easier), since it obviously could not stand as the ending on a participle. The two changes necessary to arrive at the reading נגשים עוללו are thus closely related and easily intelligible. The resultant text finds further support in that it is then more closely parallel with the construction in the second half of the line. Although the meaning is not greatly affected, it seems preferable to follow this widely adopted conjecture.

---

[1] This rules out a reference to Ahab and his harem (Gesenius; Knobel; Dillmann; Wade; Motyer).

[2] This is no more hypothetical than the suggestion that the ם is an enclitic (so Hummel, 'Enclitic *Mem*', followed by Oswalt), a suggestion which in itself does not deal with the problem of lack of grammatical agreement; cf. Emerton, 'Enclitic *mem*', 334.

The rendering of עוללי (or מעולל) has largely to be determined in association with the decision taken with regard to נשים in the second half of the line.[3] If the latter is 'women', as in the MT, then we should probably associate the word either with עלל II or (the related?) עול and see here a reference to children (see the discussion at v. 4 above); e.g. RV, NRSV 'children are their oppressors'. It is striking, however, that none of the ancient versions took the word this way, and while the noun עולל, 'child', is common, there is no other example of a ע"ע verb derived from this word or of a po'lel form from עול. The suggestion seems to be no earlier than Kimhi. The versions mostly associate the word with עלל = 'glean', for which the English equivalent 'fleece' would be appropriate if the 'oppressors' are specifically creditors. Alternatively, and perhaps more suitably in the first half of a parallel line and with the general word נגשים as subject, this may simply be the usual po'el of עלל I, which can mean 'to deal harshly with'.[4] Although the po'el of עלל is elsewhere always followed by ל, the hithpa'el is always followed by ב; the possibility may therefore be considered that בו at the end of the line serves in a 'double-duty' capacity to qualify עוללי as well as משלו. (Alternatively, Kissane proposed עוללי־לו.)

נשים: the vocalization in MT, 'women', is supported by σ, V and P; not surprisingly, the major rabbinic commentators followed suit. All the other versions, however, read as נֹשִׁים, 'creditors' (from נשה), and this seems contextually more appropriate, as is now acknowledged by most commentators,[5] especially if the verse was originally written for a different context. The MT may have arisen under the influence of the surrounding context, in particular the later part of the chapter.

ארחתיך: for the vocalization, see on 2.3.

בלעו: There has been considerable discussion whether the uses of בלע should be linked with one, two or even three different roots.[6] There seems to be little difficulty in supposing that the sense of 'destroy' could develop directly from 'swallow', and in a context such as the present one, the sense of 'confuse, confound' is not far removed; cf. Isa. 19.3; Pss. 55.10; 107.27. Either way, emendation to בללו (Lowth) is unwarranted.

This verse is superficially linked with the preceding part of the chapter by a number of verbal associations: עם (5, 7, and cf. 13-15 following), נגש (5), √עלל (4, 8, 10) and ב משל (4). Together with the general theme of the failure of the leaders of the people to exercise their role aright, this shows that the verse continues to provide reasons for the judgment described in vv. 1-7. It also helps to effect the transition from a focus on the corruption of the leaders in 1-9 to their oppression of the people in vv. 13-15. From a redactional point of view, therefore, its present setting and purpose are clear and satisfying.

---

[3] For a full survey of opinions, see Barthélemy, 23–25.

[4] An alternative possibility is to postulate a second root עול, with an Arabic cognate, = 'deviate from justice' and hence 'exact more than is just'; cf. Driver, 'Linguistic and Textual Problems', 38; HAL, 753.

[5] Troxel, 'Economic Plunder', 375–81, has made a strong case for the LXX translator working in vv. 12-15 on the basis of an application of the whole passage to the circumstances of his own day in which the rulers of the people were fleecing their subjects through taxation. In this way he seeks to account for a number of unusual equivalences throughout these verses. While the case overall seems plausible (e.g. the unparalleled choice of πράκτορες to render נשיו), it is weakened at this particular point by his assumption that MT נשים means 'women' and that מעולל refers to children. In my opinion, LXX is closer to its *Vorlage* here than Troxel realizes.

[6] Cf. J. Schüpphaus, *ThWAT* i. 658–61 = *TDOT* ii. 136–39, and *DCH* ii. 609, for literature.

At the same time, however, it seems impossible to justify any suggestion that it was originally written as an integral part of the foregoing. It has been argued above that there are seams in the passage following vv. 7, 9 and 11, but v. 12 does not join smoothly with any one of these as a direct literary continuation. Wildberger may therefore be correct in his conclusion that the verse is a fragment which has been placed here redactionally because of its suitability in terms of both theme and vocabulary.

Discussion of original date and setting are further complicated by the fact that the verse itself is disjointed, the first line referring to the people in the third person, and the second in the second person.[7] Furthermore, while there is a close parallel for the second line at 9.15, that verse is itself often considered to be secondary (e.g. Gray), and it is noteworthy that 9.14 also reflects influence from our chapter (cf. vv. 2-3). While in a general way the thoughts expressed are fully compatible with Isaiah's outlook as known from elsewhere, no more specific suggestion about its historical context can responsibly be advanced. Indeed, even the proposal that it is a redactional composition (rather than an original fragment), designed to link 1-9 (or 11) with 13-15 (so intuitively Dillmann) cannot be excluded (cf. Sweeney, who suggests that Isaiah may himself have been responsible for effecting the join in this way, and Blenkinsopp, who dates it much later).[8]

12. *My people*: it is generally assumed that God is the speaker, though if this is a repositioned Isaianic fragment, the possibility that it is the prophet cannot be excluded. It is clear from the context that the ordinary people rather than the nation as a whole are in view, and the word order indicates that, as a lament, the words are spoken more in sorrow than in anger.

Oppressors: for נגש, see on v. 5 above. It seems likely that the word should be construed broadly here as well, with greater specificity coming in the parallel half of the line. It is true that many have followed the lead of the LXX in seeing here a reference narrowly to creditors (cf. NEB: 'money-lenders strip my people bare'), but if this verse is transitional between 1-9 and 13-15 it is more appropriate that the general sense of oppression in the first paragraph should first be resumed before being interpreted by way of the specific form of oppression in the continuation. In that case, *deal harshly* will most naturally be derived from the primary root עלל rather than the denominative verb 'glean' (i.e. 'fleece').

The practice of loans as such was not forbidden in ancient Israel; indeed, the law presupposes its necessity (cf. Exod. 22.24; Deut. 15.2; 23.19-20; 24.11). What is universally condemned, however, is the *creditor*

---

[7] This in itself is sufficient to rule out radical emendation of the first line, in order to draw its meaning closer to that of the second line, *contra* Tur-Sinai, 162.

[8] I find less convincing, however, the suggestion of Porath, 49–58 and 81–82 (and cf. Beuken), that vv. 12-13 have the Babylonians in view as the oppressors in v. 12, and so as the object of judgment in v. 13 (following the MT 'peoples' as it stands); see especially the textual notes on ריב and דין in v. 13 below. So far as v. 12 is concerned, I can see no direct evidence for interpreting נגש differently from in v. 5, where relationships internal to the community are clearly in view. This is not to rule out the possibility that the verse might later have been understood in the way that Porath suggests.

enriching himself at the expense of the borrower, since this could often lead to exploitation and finally destitution. Thus Exod. 22.24 explicitly states that 'If you lend money to my people, to the poor among you, you shall not deal with them as a creditor (כנשה)'.[9] As vv. 13-15 will spell out, this is precisely what had been happening, however, with the result that the lenders drew power into their own hands and so came to *hold sway* over the poor. The heart of the matter in this line, therefore, is the abuse of leadership: those whose position should have made them most suitable to build up the community were in fact exploiting their advantage for their own further gain.

Though clearly related, the second line approaches the issue differently, focusing rather on moral than on economic leadership. *Guides* (מאשריך, those who should lead aright; see on 1.17) is a word most frequently found in the wisdom or instruction literature, and this is implied too by *the way of your paths* (cf. Vermeylen, 148). Far from giving sound advice, they lead the people in a direction which will end up in confusion, if not destruction. The vocabulary (תעה and בלע) is paralleled also in 28.7, where it is the result of drinking too much alcohol; there, the effects are on the leaders themselves, but here matters are even worse, for they pass the effects on to those for whom they should be responsible.

---

[9] Cf. de Vaux, *Ancient Israel*, 170–71; E. Neufeld, 'The Prohibition against Loans at Interest in Ancient Hebrew Laws', *HUCA* 26 (1955), 355–412; H. Gamoran, 'The Biblical Law against Loans on Interest', *JNES* 30 (1971), 127–34.

THE LORD IN JUDGMENT
(3.13-15)

[13]The Lord is taking his stand to plead,
and is standing to exercise judgment on behalf of his people.
[14]The Lord will enter into judgment
with the elders of his people and their leaders:
You, yes you, have destroyed the vineyard;
what you have robbed from the poor is in your houses.
[15]What do you mean by crushing my people
and grinding the face of the poor?
—a saying of the Lord God of Hosts.

13. עמים: 'peoples'; so 1QIsaᵃ, supported by V and T. The suggestion that this refers to the tribes of Israel (Gesenius, Hitzig, Knobel, Duhm) is most unlikely (cf. Wildberger). If MT is to be retained, it must be on the basis that, as in the opening chapters of Amos, God's anticipated judgment of the foreign nations is turned against his own people in the following verses.[1] This does not, however, take adequate account of the uses of ריב and דין in the eighth-century Isaiah, where, as sometimes elsewhere, of course,[2] they seem consistently to have the sense of 'plead/judge on behalf of' some group (in the accusative); see 1.17, 23; 10.2 (and cf. 19.20: 34.8). If that is so here, then the people must be the common people of Judah, who the following verses make clear are oppressed by their leaders (זקני עמו). Although it is true that עם usually refers to the people as a whole (i.e. including the leaders),[3] that is not an invariable rule, and the more restricted meaning is warranted sometimes by the context (cf. Høgenhaven, 23–34). The problem then, however, is the occurrence in the plural. LXX and P translate as 'his people'.[4] This may, of course, represent no more than an intelligent rendering of MT in the light of its wider context,[5] but equally it may support the reading עמו, which has been widely conjectured since Lowth (e.g. Marti, Gray, Budde, Condamin, Procksch, Kissane, Wildberger, Kaiser) and which certainly seems contextually more satisfying.[6] How MT arose is uncertain. The suggestion

---

[1] See, for instance (though with differences in suggested setting), F. Hesse, 'Wurzelt die prophetische Gerichtsrede im israelitischen Kult?', *ZAW* 65 (1953), 45–53 (48–49); M. Schwantes, *Das Recht der Armen* (BEvTh 4; Frankfurt am Main, 1977), 108; Auvray; Barthélemy.

[2] Cf. Bovati, *Re-Establishing Justice*, 43 and 211.

[3] A point pressed in favour of MT especially by Porath, 26–27.

[4] For some exegetical moves within the LXX's translation here, see Baer, 'It's All About Us!', 203–5.

[5] It may be noted that LXX forges a closer connection between vv. 12 and 13 by the addition of ἀλλὰ νῦν. Since the translator frequently made such connections, however, there is no need to postulate the loss from MT of ועתה (Budde); indeed, to add it would destroy the otherwise completely regular 3 + 3 rhythm of vv. 13-15a. The translator had reasons of his own to want to join vv. 12 and 13-15, as explained by Troxel, 'Economic Plunder', 375–81.

[6] Alternatively, Tur-Sinai, 162, suggests עמם, 'with them', presumably the oppressors of v. 12. However, this both assumes that 'judge' is here used in a negative sense and that 13-15 were preceded by v. 12 at the time of original composition (rather than redactionally), neither of which is likely. R. Althann, 'Consonantal *ym*: Ending or Noun in Isa 3,13; Jer 17,16; 1 Sam 6,19', *Biblica* 63 (1982), 560–65, conjectures that ים should be separated

of enclitic *mem* is unlikely (see on v. 12);[7] if it is not simply a copyist's error, it is possible that 'a scribe wrote the plural under the influence of Pss. 7.9; 96.10; Job 36.31, where the verb דין has עמים as its object' (Emerton), or that it is a deliberate later universalizing reading (Marti, Gray, and especially Becker, 48–49).

14. בערתם: there is an unresolved dispute about how many roots בער should be distinguished in Classical Hebrew and how the occurrences of the word(s) should be distributed between them. Here, as elsewhere, the versions render variously, though within the range of meanings which have also been proposed more recently, so that there is little guidance to be had from that direction. There is certainly a common verb meaning 'to kindle, burn', and hence by extension 'to consume, destroy'. In other passages, such as the present one (and cf. 5.5; Exod. 22.4), the context has been thought to indicate that the meaning must be 'graze'; the question then is whether this is a further development from בער I (burn > consume > graze) or whether there is a separate root (with which some occurrences of the first root which indicate destruction might then also be associated). In recent times, the tendency of lexicographers has been in favour of separate roots.[8] In the absence of firm evidence to settle this etymological dispute (and it may be noted that there is little help from Arabic, which might otherwise have enabled us to distinguish roots on the basis of two separate *ayins*, no longer represented graphically in Hebrew), we should focus on usage in context, and here the important point to observe is that even in passages where 'graze' is a possible rendering, the emphasis is always on the resulting destruction; it is never a simple synonym of רעה. (It is this observation which enables Gray, xxi–xxii, to speculate that בער = 'be brutish'; בעיר, 'beast', may also have developed from this.) Since this passage is conceptually close to 5.5, we should probably envisage the destruction of the vineyard under the image of the trampling of cattle, and certainly not draw the conclusion that what has been robbed from the poor in the second half of the line is, so to speak, the beneficial result of the leaders' 'grazing'.

גזלת העני is obviously an objective genitive, like שלל איביך in Deut. 20.14, 'the spoil taken from your enemies'; cf. GK §128h. For the uncharacteristic LXX rendering here, see Troxel, 'Economic Plunder', 379.

15. מלכם = מה + לכם (cf. Q), 'what is it to you that + imperfect'; cf. GK §37c; JM § 37c.

נאם: see on 1.24. The whole of this final line is absent from the LXX. This has sometimes been taken to indicate that it did not stand in the translator's *Vorlage*, and some commentators have gone on to propose that it should be deleted as a late addition (Marti; Procksch; cf. *BHS*). Caution is needed before drawing either consequence, however. It will be noted that the next verse also begins with a divine speech formula (ויאמר יהוה). A very similar situation obtains at 22.14-15, and there too the LXX represents only one formula, again at the start of the second verse, as here. The possibility that there has been a conflation (so HUBP) will be strengthened by the further observation that the LXX seems sometimes to have construed the נאם formula as an introduction to what follows it rather than as a conclusion to what precedes it; see, for instance, the ending of 14.23, which appears as τάδε λέγει κύριος σαβαωθ at the start of v. 24 (further examples at 17.3-4, 6-7; 30.1). If that understanding was followed in our verse as well, it would hardly be surprising that the double formula which resulted was represented only once. It is thus unwise to appeal to the LXX in support of omitting the line.

from עם and joined with the following verse, to read 'The Day of Yahweh comes with judgment'. However, we should normally expect a personal subject with בא במשפט.

[7] In the present verse, Emerton, 'Enclitic *mem*', 225, notes as an additional difficulty that in pre-exilic Hebrew עמו would probably have been written עמה, and that the theory of enclitic *mem* does not account for the loss of the *h*.

[8] See, for instance, *HAL* i. 139–40; H. Ringgren, *ThWAT* i. 727–31 = *TDOT* ii. 201–5; *DCH* ii. 242–43. For discussion, see H. Cazelles, 'Les sens du verbe bʿr en hébreu', *Semitica* 23 (1973), 5–10; F. C. Fensham, 'The Root bʿr in Ugaritic and in Isaiah in the Meaning "To Pillage"', *JNSL* 9 (1981), 67–69. There is also a valuable discussion which has been frequently overlooked in an additional note by Gray, xxi–xxii.

אדוני: in 1QIsaᵃ this has been added supralinearly, and Wildberger accordingly deletes it here (so too Clements; Kaiser). This case is more difficult to judge; against Wildberger, it may be observed that it is satisfying to have the fuller form to echo its occurrence at the start of this whole section (3.1) and also that it occurs with נאם at 1.24, where Wildberger argues in favour of retaining it (see too 10.16, 33 and 19.4, where he deletes it). Admittedly, these other examples all have האדון rather than אדני, but since Isaiah uses the latter very frequently (see v. 17 following, for instance, and especially 6.1, 8, 11), this does not seem to be an insuperable objection. I conclude that even if it were an addition to whatever Isaiah originally wrote it would be sufficiently early to have been included by the redactor of vv. 1-15 as a whole and should therefore be retained. An accidental omission by the first scribe at Qumran is hardly a surprise.

On the assumption made above that God was the speaker in v. 12, there is a clear change of person as the prophet himself here resumes the speech in God's name (15b). The change in form and substance from a lament to the picture of a law court further strengthens the view that this is a separate fragment (cf. Sweeney).[9] While its focus on the social and economic corruption of the leaders differs from the emphasis of the first part of the chapter (cf. Clements), it is broadly suitable in its wider context, and the transition has, as noted above, been well prepared by the inclusion of v. 12. Finally, the elaborated divine speech formula at the end forms an *inclusio* with the introduction in v. 1, so marking 1-15 as a major redactional unit within the larger section comprising chs 2–4 (*contra* Sweeney, who argues for the major division following v. 11, with 12-15 taken closely with the following). Whether it was therefore added by the redactor in either place, or whether it is the result of a careful arrangement of inherited material, cannot now be determined.

While the passage's present literary setting is thus clear and intelligible, the search for an original historical setting, justified by the approach to the composition of this whole passage adopted here, is, as so often, far more speculative. Most discussions of this issue start, understandably enough, with the observation that there is a close connection with the vineyard passage in 5.1-7. The metaphorical use of כרם, 'vineyard', to refer to the people of Israel is common to both, as is the rare use of the pi'el of בער to describe its destruction (3.14; 5.5). Moreover both passages are concerned with judgment of some kind (3.14; 5.3). These observations have been very variously interpreted, however.

At the one extreme, Sheppard, 'Anti-Assyrian Redaction', has argued that they originally belonged together as a single piece, and specifically that 3.13-15 has been moved for redactional reasons from its setting between 5.2 and 3; he finds that the reconstructed passage is form-critically complete, whereas each passage taken independently, as in the present form of the text, is incomplete and so indicative of textual disturbance. While there need be no objection to this approach to the literary problem in principle (my discussion of parts of ch. 1 follows the same method), it is nevertheless questionable whether this particular proposal can be

---

[9] Vermeylen, 149, is able to hold the two units together only by deleting 12b and 13 as later additions. This can hardly be right, however, as then the ואתם of 14 would refer to the 'people' of v. 12!

accepted. On the one hand, it completely empties 5.1-7 of its rhetorical force, because it provides the 'clue' to the identification of the vineyard there in advance of the climactic v. 7; Sheppard is therefore obliged to reclassify v. 7 as a summary appraisal, which is weak, and to assume that the audience pronounces its judgment following v. 2, whereas they are invited to do so only in vv. 3-4 (which Sheppard includes as part of the indictment). On the other hand, it is far from certain that the same audience is in view in the two passages. In 3.13-15, the 'people' are clearly identified with the poor and oppressed (see especially v. 15), whereas in 5.1-7 they refer to the population as a whole (cf. Porath, 60 n. 174). In addition, whereas 5.1-7 is referred to both kingdoms of Israel and Judah, there is no hint in 3.13-15 that the northern kingdom is included, and certainly the passage as it now stands is specifically related to Jerusalem and Judah (v. 1). Thus, while the connection between the two passages is accepted, it is unlikely that they ever formed a single composition. It looks rather as though 3.13-15 are some kind of later reapplication to Judah alone; the fact that the 'vineyard' in v. 14 does not require any explanation strongly supports this conclusion.

At the other extreme, 'later' has in some recent writing been taken to mean as late as the post-exilic period.[10] Becker, for instance, who has already argued that ch. 5 is later than Isaiah, then maintains that the earliest core of chs 3–4 is found in 3.1-7* and 14-15. Since this would have stood immediately in front of ch. 5 at one stage, he suggests that it was added redactionally to prepare the way for what follows (in other words, it never had a separate existence), both by making clearer the grounds for the indictment in the Song of the Vineyard and by correcting the impression which it gives that all the people were at fault: it shows rather that there was a divide between the rulers and the poor, and only the former were to blame. Given his previous argument about the later date of ch. 5, the earliest elements in ch. 3 must be even later, and he suggests the beginning of the fifth century, when such religious divisions among the people (cf. especially עני and עניים) are known to have existed. Berges adds in similar fashion the suggestion that 3.14 ('the Lord will enter into judgment') points forward to 4.4 ('a spirit of judgment'). (Curiously, he follows Becker in seeing בער in 3.14 as an anticipation of 5.5 without adding 4.4—ברוח בער—to it.) Finally, Becker suggests that 3.1 (without the initial כי and with a heading which has since been lost or moved, perhaps to 1.1) was at one time the original opening of the book.

A response to these proposals has to take two forms. First, there are large presuppositions at work here about the inauthenticity of a good deal of material which is held to be Isaianic in the present commentary. It has been argued above, for instance, that there is certainly eighth-century material included in 3.1-7*, and the same will hold later for 5.1-7. If that is the case, then naturally it becomes impossible to agree with a major part of Becker's case. But secondly, even taken on its own terms, questions

---

[10] Cf. Kaiser, and especially Becker, 162–69, with whom Berges, 79–82, is in broad agreement.

arise. If, for instance, the point of 3.14-15 was to 'correct' the 'misleading' impression given by 5.1-7 that the people as a whole were to blame, it
was surely a clumsy move to identify the righteous poor with 'my people'
(3.15); although the word עם itself does not occur in 5.1-7, it would most
naturally be associated with the בית ישראל and the איש יהודה of v. 7. If a
redactor were seeking to enter the correction which Becker maintains,
why did he not use these latter terms to refer to the wicked in 14-15 but
instead confuse the situation by appearing to indicate that they were in fact
numbered among the righteous? In addition, it is not clear why a redactor
indicated his interpretation of 5.1-7 by prefacing 3.14-15 to it when it is
most often the case elsewhere that such later interpretations are added to
(and so follow) the material on which they are commenting. Finally,
against Berges' development of Becker's view, it seems far more likely
that 4.4 is drawing on (and so is later than) the wording of 3.14 than that
3.14 was written in order to 'anticipate' what follows in some unexplained
and almost unintelligible manner. On both general and specific grounds,
therefore, I find this whole approach unconvincing.

That does not of itself, of course, prove Isaianic authorship. It is certainly not impossible to read these verses in the light especially of Neh.
5.1-13, where some similar concerns come to the surface. Given my arguments above, however, in favour of finding eighth-century material supplemented by an exilic redaction in the earlier part of the chapter, I am
naturally more open than Becker to the possibility that these verses too
belong to the earlier layer. The concerns expressed are certainly widely
attested in the eighth-century prophets (see below), and the language is
consistent with Isaiah (including the characteristically colourful and otherwise unparalleled metaphorical use of טחן in v. 15; some other examples of
Isaianic style are mentioned both in the textual notes and in the exegesis).
The imagery of 5.1-7 is clearly presupposed (כרם now needs no further
explanation) but is here being reapplied to a new situation: the leaders
rather than the people as a whole are indicted and there is no reference to
the northern kingdom. It is therefore most likely that Isaiah or an early
disciple/tradent reused the earlier imagery for his new purposes. A date
during the period of Hezekiah's preparations for his revolt against Assyria
would fit the circumstances admirably (see on v. 14b below), though other
periods in the later monarchy cannot be ruled out. It could well have once
stood immediately following 5.1-7 on thematic grounds or in 28-31 on
historical grounds; clearly, we cannot tell. Along with 3.1-7 and 12, however, it was at a later (probably exilic; see the introduction to 3.1-9) stage
moved to its present position as part of the larger redactional assemblage
in 2-4*, after which all trace of its original literary setting was lost.

With the exception of the final divine speech formula, the passage is of
regular 3 + 3 rhythm throughout and uses standard forms of parallelism.
Other poetic devices are mentioned in the exegesis which follows.

13. While it is obvious that the language of the law-court is here being
used, it is equally clear that it is being used pictorially or metaphorically
from the observation that the Lord is described as acting in the character of plaintiff without any reference to a judge, witnesses, verdict or

sentence.[11] The occurrence of the word ריב should not, therefore, immediately make us think of some 'covenant-lawsuit'. Rather, this is no more than a graphic assertion of God acting on behalf of the oppressed among *his people.* If pressed, we might argue that the absence of so many elements of a normal trial is indicative of an appeal to natural justice, which requires no judge or witnesses as such. While that would certainly fit with what we have seen of Isaiah's stance elsewhere, it would miss the force of the rhetoric entirely to claim that that was his main point in this passage.

God's active involvement is underlined by the repeated stress on his *standing,* and this itself is emphasized by the fact that unusually the participle *is taking his stand* comes first, before its subject. While it is probably the case that participants in a trial stood to speak, while otherwise remaining seated,[12] it is thus likely that there is an emphasis here which goes beyond the pedantically descriptive; it answers rather to the repeated cry of the oppressed to God to 'rise up and judge' (e.g. Pss. 74.22; 82.8). The injustice to be described in vv. 14-15 has reached such a pitch that he feels compelled to intervene.

14a. This line continues the description of the narrative setting. *Judgment* here is a neutral term for a (legal) procedural action,[13] so that, within the developed metaphor of the passage, to *enter into judgment* indicates to initiate proceedings against the named party, not to presuppose its outcome. Those against whom God has a case are the *elders* and *leaders* of the people; see on vv. 2 and 4 above. While both are well known from elsewhere for their involvement in the administration of justice generally, there is perhaps an indication from the choice of terms that both local, traditional (*elders*) and centralized, state-appointed (*leaders*) officials are included in the indictment.[14] As earlier in the passage, those who should have been working for the good of the whole community have used their position for personal gain.

14b. Without further introduction, this and the following lines record God's accusation addressed directly to the leaders. The emphatic use of the second person plural pronoun at the start is preceded somewhat unusually by the conjunction. Appropriately comparing Ps. 2.6, Delitzsch explains that a tacit clause (e.g. 'I set you over my vineyard, but…') is presupposed. The effect of such an ellipse, which may be regarded as quite natural in agitated speech, is to heighten the emphasis on the directness of the pronoun: *You, yes you!*

---

[11] Cf. Davies, 51–59 (though he is hesitant about whether God is also pictured as judge here), and Hoffmann, 85–86 (who finds in the lack of a verdict evidence for his case that a final decision about Israel's future has not yet been reached; this conclusion is accepted in a modified form by Nielsen, 'Bild des Gerichts'), *contra* Skinner, Wildberger, and Nielsen, *Yahweh as Prosecutor and Judge,* 29–32 (who in my view misunderstands the force of דין at this point). To this extent, the ethical problems perceived by Davies, *Double Standards,* 128–31, may not be as stark as he presents them.

[12] Cf. Bovati, *Re-Establishing Justice,* 231–40.

[13] Cf. Bovati, *Re-Establishing Justice,* 208 and 221–22.

[14] Cf. Dietrich, 38; Schwantes, *Das Recht der Armen* (above, n. 1), 109–10; Kessler, *Staat und Gesellschaft,* 29–34; Leclerc, 52–53,

The coincidence of *destroyed* and *vineyard* occurring together here and at 5.5 suggests that they should be interpreted in the light of one another. In that case, *vineyard* must be a metaphorical reference to the people of Israel, which suits the wider context well (cf. LXX and V 'my vineyard'; T 'my people'). Although, as noted above, the precise force of בער is uncertain, its consequences are clearly destructive. The first half of the line is thus a general indictment, with the remaining line and a half spelling out the particulars.

First, the way in which the leaders have enriched themselves (*in your houses*) at the expense of *the poor* is depicted as a form of robbery. Such an accusation is in line with those found in the other eighth-century prophets, whether northern or southern (Blenkinsopp, for instance, cites Amos 2.6-8; 3.9-11; 6.4-7; 8.4-6, and Mic. 2.1-3; 3.1-4, 9-12[15]), including Isaiah (cf. 5.8; 10.1-2). This is generally associated with the development during this period of a class structure whereby wealth, and hence power, came to be increasingly concentrated in the hands of a privileged minority at the expense of small-holders and the like. The need for loans, with the consequent perils of usury (see already v. 12 above), foreclosure and ultimately debt slavery, were the means whereby this could be pursued legally but, in the opinion of the prophets, unjustly. For further discussion, see on 5.8 below.

The motives and methods whereby this came about have been variously understood, and it is probable that several factors came together rather than that a single cause can explain everything.[16] The increasing power of a centralized monarchy will have been accelerated by the international situation of developing Assyrian influence, giving rise to the need for increased taxation, whether for the payment of tribute (Ahaz) or in military preparations for revolt (Hezekiah). The sudden increase in the number of official seal impressions at this period and, under Hezekiah, the evidence of the *lmlk* jars are no doubt indications of this.[17] As part of the same development, patronage, royal land grants and the dominance of state administrators over traditional local systems of social control, which were more sensitive to the social value of safeguarding ancestral property, will have facilitated the trend. Not for the last time in history, the demands of state policy could be used as an (unconscious) excuse by those with the responsibility for carrying it out for furthering their own interests in the name of patriotic need.

---

[15] See further Fey, 62–63, and Stansell, 108–10. (For the possible influence of our passage on the later Jer. 5.27 and 12.10, see Wendel, 36–41 and 124–31.)

[16] See Dearman, *Property Rights*. He includes a useful survey and critique of the major earlier studies. In particular, he finds that the classic and influential study of A. Alt, 'Der Anteil des Königtums an der sozialen Entwicklung in den Reichen Israel und Juda', *Kleine Schriften zur Geschichte des Volkes Israel, 3* (Munich, 1959), 348–72, needs modification in its sharp contrast between supposed 'Canaanite' and 'Israelite' values and practices.

[17] A. G. Vaughn, *Theology, History, and Archaeology in the Chronicler's Account of Hezekiah* (Atlanta, 1999), 81–167.

While straightforward corruption of the courts and administration need
not be ruled out (cf. 1.23), it is unlikely that this alone would have been
sufficient to call for the kind of invective which we find in the eighth-
century prophets. When confronted with such evidence, it may be hoped
that it would have been widely condemned. Rather, the kind of criticism
that we find in the present passage and others like it goes further, star-
tlingly (for their contemporaries) proposing that it was the system as a
whole which was corrupt.[18] The demands fell unequally and so were inherently unjust. The consequences were thus symptoms of a deeper corruption in the body politic. In the absence of any channel of redress—of the
checks and balances that should characterize a society organized for the
benefit of its members as a whole—the prophets claimed that God himself
would intervene to uphold the cause of those who had no other voice. The
claim that *you have robbed* the poor[19] is designed to shock by bringing a
new perspective to bear on what had come to be accepted as an inevitability.

15. The second part of the accusation spells out the consequences
which follow from the first: once the poor have been dispossessed of their
property, the inevitable destitution which follows is like being crushed and
ground down. דכא, to *crush* (and cf. דכה, דכך, דוך), is nearly always used
metaphorically, as here, for the crushing of enemies or the oppression of
the poor.[20] (Classical Hebrew seems to have exploited the similarity with
דקק to keep a separate word for literal crushing, pulverizing.) By contrast,
טחן, to *grind* (as of flour), occurs only here with the transferred sense of
oppression, so that whereas the first half of the line would have been readily understood (if unwelcome), the second adds force to it by a bold
literary innovation which would have had a significant rhetorical impact,
and which is further reinforced by the striking addition of *face*.[21] Being, in
addition, placed last in its clause, it thus brings God's indictment to a
stinging climax.[22]

With regard to this accusation as a whole, it is worth noting that while
there are many legal texts which refer to the kinds of abuse which have
been noted above,[23] the closest parallel for the phraseology and outlook of
these verses comes at Prov. 22.22-23: 'Do not rob (גזל) the poor because

[18] On the implications of this, see N. K. Gottwald, 'Social Class as an Analytic and
Hermeneutical Category in Biblical Studies', *JBL* 112 (1993), 3–22 (15–16).

[19] So also in 10.2, and cf. Mic. 2.2; 3.2. For its use in the prophets with particular
reference to economic exploitation, see B. S. Jackson, *Theft in Early Jewish Law* (Oxford,
1972), 4–5, 109; see too J. Schüpphaus, *ThWAT* i. 999–1001 = *TDOT* ii. 456–58.

[20] Cf. H. F. Fuhs, *ThWAT* ii. 207–21 = *TDOT* iii. 195–208.

[21] Schreiber, 'Bemerkungen', 455, suggests that there is a deliberate play on נשא פנים.
Schwantes, *Das Recht der Armen* (above, n. 1), 112, goes much further in speculating that
face signifies '—pars pro toto—den Menschen von jener "wendbaren Fläche"…her, deren
Organe den Menschen in seiner Kommunikationsfähigkeit charakterisieren und durch die
des Menschen Menschsein—sein Personsein—in besonderer Weise zum Ausdruck
kommt'!

[22] So much so that the LXX actually felt the need to soften the phraseology; cf. Ziegler,
81.

[23] See the helpful table in Dearman, *Property Rights*, 58–59.

they are poor, or crush (דכא) the afflicted (עני) at the gate; for the Lord pleads their cause (ריב), and despoils of life those who despoil them'. As was emphasized in ch. 1 (e.g. vv. 2-3), it would probably be a mistake to argue in a case like this whether Isaiah was influenced more by the legal or by the wisdom tradition. Once again, rather, it is likely that these similarities reflect something of the commonly accepted standards of ancient Israelite society (cf. Dietrich, 16–18) and that Isaiah's particular contribution (and that of the other prophets) was to apply them forcefully in changed circumstances where their relevance had not previously been fully appreciated.

For the concluding speech formula and the divine titles, see on 1.9, 24 and 3.1.

THE PRIDE OF THE DAUGHTERS OF ZION
(3.16-24)

[16]And the Lord said:
  because the daughters of Zion are haughty,
walking with outstretched necks,
  and ogling with their eyes,
taking mincing steps as they go along,
  and jingling with their feet,
[17]the Lord will make bald the crown of the heads of the daughters of
  Zion,
  and the Lord will lay bare their foreheads.
[18]On that day the Lord will remove the finery of the anklets and the sun
disks and the crescents; [19]the earrings and the bracelets and the veils;
[20]the headdresses and the armlets and the ribbons and the amulets and
the charms; [21]the seal-rings and the nose rings; [22]the festal robes and
the mantles and the shawls and the wraps, [23]and the coats and the fine
linen tunics and the turbans and the flowing veils.
[24]And it shall come to pass that instead of perfume there will be the
  stench of rottenness,
  and instead of a girdle—a rope,
and instead of a well-set hair-do—baldness,
  and instead of a mantle—a loincloth of sacking,
    branding instead of beauty.

16. יען כי: the commoner form יען אשר does not occur in Isaiah, though יען alone does,
primarily in later parts of the book. Of the seven occurrences of יען כי, four are in Isaiah
(3.16; 7.5; 8.6; 29.13; see further Num. 11.20; 1 Kgs 13.21; 21.29). As here, it usually
introduces the protasis followed by the apodosis ('because...therefore') rather than
following and giving the reason for some statement; see further at 7.5 below (vol. 2).

ותלכנה: the *waw*-consecutive + imperfect follows the stative perfect גבה, and so is to
be construed as a present; cf. GK §111*r*; JM §118*p*; WO, 555–56; Gibson, 63 and 102.
There is thus no need to revocalize as a simple *waw*, *contra* Porath, 19.

נטוות: the retention of the 'original' *waw* in the inflection of a ל"ה verb is rare, but
occasionally attested elsewhere; cf. GK §75*v*. Q has the more usual נטויה, but 1QIsaᵃ
follows K (*contra* HUBP; 4QIsaᵇ is damaged for all except the last letter of the word),
which presumably reflects the earlier form. The word may be either construct (for the
construction in that case, see on 1.4; cf. König), or absolute, with גרון as an apposition
of nearer definition (cf. Feldmann).

ומשקרות: this *hapax legomenon* has been explained in two ways, both claiming
support from later Hebrew and Aramaic (cf. *HAL* iv, 1258–59, for details). Although
the sense of T (מסרבקן עיניך) is disputed, the other versions clearly favour a type of look
made with the eye, hence ogling or winking, followed by an adverbial accusative. The
alternative approach sees here a reference to eye make-up (for references, see Delitzsch
and Gray), but given that סיקרא was some kind of a red colour, this seems less likely.[1]
The reading with שׂ instead of שׁ in some manuscripts, which lies behind the marginal

---

[1] Cf. Brenner, *Colour Terms*, 151–52, in dispute with R. Gradwohl, *Die Farben im
Alten Testament* (BZAW 83; Berlin, 1963), 84.

reading in AV ('deceiving with their eyes'), is inferior, despite Lowth's long attempt to relate it to the minority approach by glossing a literal 'falsifying their eyes' with 'falsely setting off their eyes with paint'.

הלוך וטפף תלכנה: while this construction is common enough (GK §113*u*; JM §123*m*; Gibson, 125; WO, 589–90), it is rare to find the infinitives preceding the finite verb, though Ps. 126.6 provides a partial parallel. I suggest that the effect in the present context (in which תלכנה additionally is repeated resumptively from the previous line) is to make this line virtually the equivalent of a circumstantial clause.

Sweeney, *Isaiah 1–4*, 155–56, has proposed a completely different understanding of this line. In order to overcome the difficulty that a speech by God in v. 16 appears to include a reference to God in the third person in v. 17, he proposes that v. 16 be construed as a complete sentence in itself, with this third line comprising the apodosis, describing God's judgment on the women. To support this, he first observes that the first two lines of the verse are dependent on a perfect verb (ובהו) whereas the third line moves to the imperfect. He then notes that in later Hebrew טפף can mean 'join, add' and that its Arabic cognate means 'to reverse, tie backwards, to hopple (of camel)'. Similarly, עכס (from a noun meaning 'chain') 'can imply restriction'. Both words, therefore, 'convey a sense of confinement, as in chaining together'. Finally, he sees here a play on words—a form of punishment which fits the crime. Despite the ingenuity of Sweeney's proposal, it is improbable. The derived meanings of the two verbs seem forced in the present context (note the עכסים at the very start of the list of finery in v. 18, both suggesting that the line was understood in the traditional sense in early times and indicating that עכס is an ornamental chain, not a form of fetter) and they are by no means so transparent as an expression of punishment as the language of v. 17. In addition, it might have been expected that the apodosis would be clearly marked as such if so subtle a play on words were to be appreciated. The problem of the identity of the speaker in these verses must therefore be solved differently (see below).

וברגליהם: the use of the masculine form of the suffix instead of the expected feminine (especially in the case of plural suffixes) is not uncommon, even in relatively early texts; cf. GK §135*o*. 1QIsaᵃ in fact has וברגליהנה, which Cohen, 'Philological Reevaluation', 49, prefers; whether this is a correction of what was considered to be an anomalous form, or whether MT is a scribal assimilation to what later became the normal common-gender form of this suffix, cannot now be determined.

תעכסנה: for the vocalization, see GK §52*n*; JM §52*c*; the second *pathaḥ* (for expected *ṣere*) is found occasionally elsewhere (e.g. 13.18), always in pause, though not consistently. The verb, which occurs nowhere else, is generally explained as a piʿel denominative from עכס, 'anklet, ornamental chain', and so is thought to mean 'shake anklets' so as to produce a jingling sound when walking. The inevitable uncertainty about this (see on v. 18 below) was exploited by Driver to propose an alternative. He observed that the versions generally refer at this point to the manner of the women's gait, that the parallelism suggests a reference to gait rather than to ornaments, and that the Arabic cognate means 'to make jerky movements in walking'. He therefore suggested 'and they hobble on their feet'.[2] We may add that in the Qumran *Apostrophe to Zion*, line 5 (DJD iv. 86), the word appears in a context that also suits a reference to gait, and that its occurrence there in parallel with ינק might suggest a connection with children, hence 'toddle'. Certainty is clearly beyond reach, but it may be noted that the LXX, at least, is unreliable as evidence here, given that it clearly misunderstood the previous clause,[3] and that ברגליהם does not fit Driver's proposal so well. It may be

[2] Driver, 'Hebrew Notes', 241; see too Tur-Sinai, 162: 'walk with mincing steps'. Wildberger is attracted to Driver's suggestion without committing himself to it.

[3] The translator clearly did not recognize טפף. His usage of σύρειν elsewhere suggests that he either associated it with, or, less probably, read it as, a form of שטף, and so arrived at the idea of sweeping skirts. (V's *plaudebant* is not much better.) The repetition ἅμα...ἅμα indicates that he then allowed this interpretation to influence his rendering of the final clause as well.

significant that NEB itself reverted to 'jingling feet'. If it is right to take this closely with the preceding clause (see the comments below), it is in any case related to gait, so that Driver's starting point is itself invalid.

17. ושפח: *waw*-apodosis (JM §176e) + perfect (GK §112n). The medieval Jewish commentators agree in associating this *hapax legomenon* with the noun מספחת/ספחת, which occurs a number of times in Leviticus 13–14 to refer to a scab connected with 'leprosy' (better: fungal infection); it may be either malignant or benign. This gives rise to the traditional rendering 'afflict with a scab', still favoured by, for instance, *HAL* iv. 1256–57. While the interchange of the sibilants שׂ and ס is acceptable (though it gives pause, at least), it is noteworthy that (i) this meaning appears not to have been recognized by any of the ancient versions, (ii) the presence of this kind of a scab is not in itself harmful (and in some cases, at least, is to be understood as indicative of a stage in the healing process),[4] and (iii) the punishment in the second half of the line (and in v. 24, if this was once the immediate continuation of the present verse) is suggestive of something inflicted by other people rather than a divine visitation (so already Knobel). There are therefore good grounds for seeking a better explanation. LXX ταπεινώσει seems to be merely another example of 'levelling', for it is the same verb that was used repeatedly in ch. 2 (cf. vv. 9, 11, 12, 17) to indicate the humbling of human pride, which is certainly the main point at issue here.[5] This will then have had as a further consequence the figurative rendering of קדקד by ἀρχούσας. While the translator might have read either שפל (so Lowth) or שחח (each of which differs by only one letter from שפח), that is not a necessary conclusion to draw. T and P are, so far as I can tell, only further extensions of this line of interpretation. V, however, renders independently: *decalvabit Dominus verticem filiarum Sion*, and Saʿadia's נרד ('made bare') may also testify to this tradition. It has been taken up in more recent times by Driver, 'Hebrew Notes', 241–42 (followed, *inter alia*, by Wildberger, Kaiser, Schoors, Hoffmann, 10), with an appeal to Akkadian and Arabic. For the former, Driver cited *s/šuppuḫu* = 'to loosen, undo', though the more recent lexicons give as *sapāḫu(m)* = 'scatter, disperse' (*CDA*, 316), which does not fit quite so well from a semantic point of view. This may be balanced, however, by Arabic *ʿasfaḫu*, 'bald on the front of the head', for if this is related etymologically, then it indicates how the word's use may have developed. Given that this is contextually so superior a rendering, and with support also in antiquity, I have adopted it here despite the element of philological uncertainty.

אדני: so too 4QIsa^b (though the divine name or title in the second half of the line is lost). 1QIsa^a has placed elimination dots under this word and written יהוה above it as a correction; on the other hand, it reads אדני in the second half of the line, where MT has יהוה. Given some similar variations in later manuscripts at this point, it would be pointless to speculate about the earliest form of the text. If the scroll's *Vorlage* was similar to MT (which is pure surmise, though supported by 4QIsa^b as far as it goes), it is not impossible that the scribe could have erroneously written אדני twice instead of in the first half of the line only, and that the later hand then mistakenly corrected the first instead of the second occurrence.

פתהן: the vocalization of the suffix is unique (GK §91f) and unexplained; it may, therefore, simply be an early error. The noun has been variously interpreted. (i) Mostly, it has been associated with פתות in 1 Kgs 7.50, and on the assumption that the latter means (door) sockets, it has been understood as a reference to *pudenda* (though N. Wyatt, 'The Liturgical Context of Psalm 19', *UF* 27 [1995], 559–96 [589], suggests 'eye-sockets'). LXX (σχῆμα), P (ʾskmhyn) and T (יקרהון) might then reflect euphemistic renderings.[6] This is doubtful, however, since the meaning at 1 Kgs 7.50 is itself questionable, not least because gold would be an inappropriate metal to use for door sockets,

---

[4] Cf. J. Milgrom, *Leviticus 1–16* (AB 3; New York, 1991), 774.

[5] Cf. Ziegler, 137; Baer, 'It's All About Us!', 210–11.

[6] See recently Blenkinsopp; Landy, 'Torah and Anti-Torah', 329; Baer, 'It's All About Us!', 211.

and indeed, the meaning there is sometimes explained by reference to our passage—a clearly circular argument. More recent commentaries on Kings tend to suggest alternative renderings. (ii) Noting V's reference to hair, Stade and others[7] have proposed that פתהן = פאתהן, 'their temples' (cf. GK §23f for examples of the loss of א, though not for this particular word, so far as is known). There is no evidence that פאה on its own could have this sense, however; it means 'corner, side', and on the occasions where it refers to the head, the point is spelt out explicitly, for example פאת פניו (Lev. 13.41), פאת ראשכם (Lev. 19.27), etc., as would be expected. (iii) Among emendations, the most popular has been to run יהוה (which might indeed be considered redundant) and פתהן together to give חרפתהן, 'their shame' (cf. 47.3);[8] but this should not be considered if the consonantal text can be adequately defended. (iv) Nearly all commentators now follow Driver[9] in comparing Akkadian *pūtu(m)*, which is securely attested as 'forehead'. This adequately accounts for V *crinem earum nudabit* (for the possibility that ערה might have the extended meaning of 'shave', cf. תער, 'razor'; so Condamin), and it is possible, in the light of 1 Cor. 11.15, that T's יקרהון is based on a similar understanding. The suggestion gives good sense in the context (see the comments below) and can also account for 1 Kgs 7.50.[10]

18. אדני: in 1QIsaᵃ, the first hand wrote יהוה, which was then corrected (by use of elimination dots and supralinear addition) to אדוני. See on v. 17 above, where the situation was the exact opposite.

The list of women's finery which follows raises a number of methodological issues that call for some brief introductory remarks. In the case of rare words, there are three main possible approaches to help determine meaning: (i) context; (ii) comparative philology; and (iii) the evidence of the ancient versions and Post-Biblical Hebrew, which may have memories of the meaning of words since lost to us. In the case of the present list:

(i) Where the words occur in other biblical contexts, this ought to carry greatest weight, and we shall see examples where it is clear and helpful. However, many of the other terms are *hapax legomena*, so that it can only take us so far. The other main contextual steer comes from a consideration whether the list is grouped in a coherent way. Some suggestions are mentioned in the introduction and commentary below, and the conclusion is generally negative. There is a general move from jewelry to clothing to be observed but (unless our understanding is seriously at fault) it does not seem to be wholly consistent, so that this approach is of only limited help. A point which has not generally been noted, however, is that the items seem often to be in pairs (the two items in v. 21 are an obvious example). I have given this fact some weight in evaluating rival proposals, though I accept that it is far from watertight. (The presence or lack of the conjunction, reflected in the translation above and to a large extent by the verse divisions, is an uncertain factor in this. Sometimes it is intelligible, but sometimes not, and it is the sort of textual feature which is most easily corrupted in transmission; cf. 1QIsaᵃ! I have therefore not afforded it particular weight.)

(ii) Comparative philology is also important, but again not totally secure. On the one hand, perusal of the dictionaries of the cognate languages shows that the meaning of some of the words is not fully secure there either, and on the other it is entirely

---

[7] Cf. B. Stade, 'Zu Jes. 3, 1. 17. 24...', *ZAW* 26 (1906), 129–41 (130–33); Eitan, 'Contribution', 56–57; Tur-Sinai, 163.

[8] Cf. J. Bachman, 'Zur Textkritik des Propheten Zephania', *Theologische Studien und Kritiken* 67 (1894), 641–55 (650 n. 1), followed by Cheyne, *Book*, 82, Marti and Gray.

[9] Driver, 'Linguistic and Textual Problems', 38, and 'Hebrew Notes', 241–42, followed by, for instance, Wildberger, Kaiser, Clements, Schoors, and Høgenhaven, 178. Blenkinsopp rejects the proposal only by way of a misguided return to the uncertainties of 1 Kgs 7.50.

[10] See, for instance, the commentaries of J. Gray and G. H. Jones.

possible that from a common root words may have developed in different, though related, directions over the centuries in the different languages and cultures.[11] Caution is therefore required. An additional factor is that the more obscure the word, the more important it is to have a deep acquaintance with the cognate language (Arabic, Akkadian, etc.) in order to make sure that the word there is being understood accurately. I do not pretend to have such expertise, and for much of this evidence I am therefore dependent on the expertise of others.

(iii) Of the ancient versions, pride of place is usually quite rightly given to the LXX. In the present case, however, there are major problems. It does not even have the same number of items overall, and on the basis of some items whose meaning is reasonably secure the equivalents do not always come in the expected place. Ziegler's pioneering study of this list (pp. 203–11) concluded that the translator was not only influenced by the linguistic usage of his time and place (as attested by the Egyptian Greek papyri) but also by similar listings elsewhere. More recently, van der Kooij, 'Interpretation', 221–24, has developed these insights to propose that in the LXX the translation is intended to represent a list of objects which made up a bride's dowry, divided more rigidly than in MT into two sections, jewelry first and clothing second (he finds this also reflected in the expanded opening of the list in LXX). It follows that we should be cautious about using the LXX for the identification of individual items.

In fact, we may extend this point to the other principal versions to assert that we can really only be sure of equivalences when we already know on other grounds what the particular item is. In other words, there is not really any instance where we can rely on the versions as our sole source of knowledge; it is more a case of checking to see how accurate or not they are (by our lights) on alternative grounds. The same applies to the rabbinic commentators, who rarely give proper reasons for their glosses. I have therefore seen no point in citing all this material systematically, but have limited myself to the occasional examples of interest or importance. This can be extended to older English (or other) renderings as well. Not surprisingly, they are likely to tell us as much about the fashion of the translator's day as about the meaning of the Hebrew (e.g. AV's wimples and crisping pins!). No doubt my own attempt will be similarly judged in the future.[12]

עכסים (1QIsaᵃ עכיסים): otherwise only at Prov. 7.22, but that is generally thought to be corrupt. Thus older attempts to use its occurrence there to refine the sense derived from Arabic (see immediately below) are irrelevant. For the related verb, see on v. 16 above. Although the translation 'anklets' is widely adopted (cf. Kimhi), it is, in fact, poorly supported etymologically; the only obvious cognate is in Arabic, where it refers to a rope from a camel's neck or nose to the forelegs. Nor are the versions very supportive: the first word in their lists refers either to clothing (LXX) or footwear (T and V; cf. Rashi; Ibn Ezra). However, as already mentioned, it is questionable how much weight we should put on the evidence from the versions in this list. The upshot is that there is very little evidence by which to decide what the word might mean. The link of the verb with רגל gives the best contextual steer.

שביסים: a *hapax legomenon*. Traditionally, lexicographers have followed the lead of Post-Biblical Hebrew in finding here some kind of ornamental head/hair-band or net (שבץ, 'weave, plait'; see the survey in Gesenius). The third word in LXX's list is ἐμπλόκια, 'braidings', which may reflect this (it is apparently lacking in V, while T's Aramaic is simply borrowed from the Hebrew, and so has no independent force). An

[11] The same caveat applies to the occurrence of these words in Post-Biblical Hebrew, a source especially favoured by Cohen, 'Studies'.

[12] I regret that I have been unable to consult the 1957 Zurich dissertation of H. W. Hönig, *Die Bekleidung des Hebräers*; earlier major studies include N. W. Schroeder, *Commentarius philologico-criticus de vestitu mulierum Hebraearum, ad Jesai. III. vs. 16-24* (1745), and A. T. Hartmann, *Die Hebräerin am Putztische und als Braut* (Amsterdam, 1809); more recently van den Branden, 'I gioielli'.

alternative approach has often been favoured since Schroeder (1745), however (cf. GK
§186g n. 1; this view was known already to Lowth, who resisted it, however, with a
long citation from a private letter of Dr Hunt; but in view of more recent evidence, this
is now of antiquarian interest only): in view of the next word, it has been thought to
represent a diminutive form of 'sun' (so 'sun-disk' or similar). 'Sun' is usually שמש,
but Ugaritic špš (*DUL*, 836) strengthens the possibility of a ב/מ interchange, while the
final sibilant has parallels in South Semitic (and cf. 1QIsaᵃ שביש ם; 4QIsaᵇ שבשים). What
would therefore effectively be a foreign loan word would not be surprising for such an
ornament (presumably some type of pendant); cf. especially Wildberger (followed by
Schmitt, *Magie*, 185: 'Sonnenanhänger'). Platt 'Jewelry', 194–98, draws attention to
the second-millennium Mesopotamian Dilbat necklace, which has a crescent moon,
two sun-symbol rosettes and a star disk. This may illustrate this and the next two items
in the list. She also lists a number of other finds which parallel the items individually.

שהרנים: there is reasonable certainty about this word. The root is attested in a number of Semitic languages in connection with the moon or as a name for the moon-god
(cf. *HAL*, 1222; Schmitt, *Magie*, 184; the ending in ן- may, but does not invariably,
indicate a diminutive: GK §86g; note that again this is not a regular Hebrew word,
however, but is more likely a foreign loan), some of the versions also seem to have
recognized it (cf. LXX μηνίσκους, V *lunulas*; so too Kimhi and Ibn Ezra, against T
and Rashi 'nets'), and the word occurs at Judg. 8.21 and 26 for an ornament worn
round the necks of camels as well as by the Midianite kings. While the word may have
originally referred to some kind of amulet,[13] this meaning could soon have been
forgotten, as with many modern types of jewelry.

19. נטיפות (1QIsaᵃ נטפות): this word also follows שהרנים at Judg. 8.26 (apparently
overlooked by Ibn Ezra). נטף is a well-attested word meaning 'to drip' (of water,
myrrh, honey, wine, etc.),[14] so that this noun presumably means some sort of drop-like
ornament. Because of the equivalent word in Arabic, this has often been thought to
refer to earrings (see still *HAL*, 656), but a general word for pendant would seem at
first to be equally plausible, and is often now preferred because of the association with
other items that might be strung on necklaces (and cf. LXX κάθεμα, 'necklace', Rashi
and Kimhi). Bead-like pendants made of semi-precious stones are well-attested
archaeologically. A potential problem for this approach is that, if the word goes so
closely with the two previous ones as part of necklace ornamentation, why is it separated off from them by the absence of the conjunction? (1QIsaᵃ includes the conjunction here, however, as it does before every item in this list, against MT, so that this is
just another example of our uncertainties about this list.) Perhaps it is a mistake to try
to associate too many words with a single item of jewelry and we should rather seek a
maximum number of separate items. In that case, a reference to earrings might certainly be expected, and this is the only viable candidate for that. Similar considerations
will apply to the next item.

שירות: another *hapax*, though again quite well represented among the cognate languages (cf. *HAL*, 1522).[15] BDB, 1057, lists the more frequently attested שרשרות as
coming from the same root. It refers to chains of varying kinds, including ornamental
in the context of the high priest's ephod at Exod. 28.14, 22; 39.15: 'chains of pure
gold, twisted like cords'; a reduplicated form would seem appropriate in such a context. Based on the cognates, the usual rendering here has been 'bracelet', though other
forms of ornamental chain do not seem impossible; note that Akkadian *šawirum*,
še/iwerum is defined more broadly as 'torque' (*CDA*, 364). Platt has therefore extended

---

[13] For fine illustrations of sacred crescents above altars (on seals), see R. Deutsch
and A. Lemaire, *Biblical Period Personal Seals in the Shlomo Moussaieff Collection*
(Tel Aviv, 2000), nos. 41 and 84.
[14] Cf. H. Madl, *ThWAT* v. 424–32 = *TDOT* ix. 395–402.
[15] For further discussion of the relationship with Akkadian in particular, see
Mankowski, *Akkadian Loanwords*, 146.

the sequence she already found in the previous words to suggest 'necklace cords', on which the previous items listed will have been hung. As noted just above, however, this may sacrifice the variety of items listed in favour of too great a concentration on one single item of jewelry, so that the more usual rendering should perhaps be preferred.

רעלות: this further *hapax legomenon* is usually compared with Arabic *raʿl*, an elaborate kind of veil (so already Kimhi, and similarly Rashi; NRSV 'scarfs' is anachronistic). Since the next item seems also to refer to some kind of headdress, this is suitable, and it has been claimed that it may be associated either with what was once thought to be the only root רעל in Classical Hebrew, 'quiver, shake' (this describing the movement of a veil), or now with the postulated second root רעל, 'cover' (as a veil covers the face); cf. *HAL*, 1181; P. Jenson, *NIDOTTE*, iii. 1150. There have been other suggestions, however: an old one is small bells (as shaken), while more recently Platt thinks that she can move from 'quiver, shake, reel' to 'dangle' to 'beads'; however, the shift to 'dangle' is not supported in Hebrew, and she is perhaps too strongly influenced here by her interest in jewelry.

20. פארים: the general sense is secure from usage elsewhere. It is worn by a bridegroom (61.10) and is a joyful replacement for the ashes of those who mourn (61.3). Similarly, wearing one is contrasted with mourning in Ezek. 24.17, 23. Note that in the latter reference it is said specifically to be worn 'on your heads'. It is also used for a priest's headdress; Exod. 39.28; Ezek. 44.18 (again, 'on their heads'). It therefore appears to be some kind of bright or festal headdress or turban (but distinguished somehow from צניף in v. 23). Platt, 'Jewelry', 75, again tries to move in the direction of jewelry, this time suggesting that 'the object may be a "frontlet" made of a strip of metal foil with holes for ties to place it across the forehead and then knotted in the back', but in this she is certainly mistaken as the item is twice stated explicitly to be made of different types of linen (Exod. 39.28 and Ezek. 44.18).

צעדות: there are two conflicting lines of evidence to help identify this item, and it is almost impossible to choose between them. On the one hand, the root צעד is well known with the sense 'to step, march', and there is a derived noun צעדה, which means 'marching' (2 Sam. 5.24; 1 Chron. 14.15). If our word is linked with this, then it presumably refers to some kind of ankle or leg ornamentation, perhaps in the form of chains which joined the ankles, so making the women take small, tripping steps. Difficulties for this view include the possible overlap with עכסים in v. 18 (though we saw that the meaning of that word is not certain), the awkwardness of having two nouns צעדה from the same root with such different meanings (though *HAL*, 974, implies that they may be distinguished by the one only ever being singular and the other plural) and the lack of secure evidence for this use of ankle chains in ancient Israel (see the comments on v. 16 below). The alternative approach is to compare אצעדה (i.e. the same word with prosthetic *aleph*) at Num. 31.50 and 2 Sam. 1.10, in the latter of which it is explicit that it was worn on the arm (אשר על־זרעו), hence 'armlet'. It seems unlikely that we should postulate a separate root for this (*contra* BDB, 857B; they are unable to list any comparative evidence),[16] but we may see here rather that in relation to ornamentation the word could develop away from the sense that a strict etymological derivation might initially suggest. This second approach is attractive in many ways (there would then be a clear distinction from עכסים), but in that case why does the word appear here without initial *aleph*? Was this a means of distinguishing male from female wearers? Or is it just an anomalous plural?

---

[16] See D. Kellermann, *ThWAT* vi. 1080–83 = *TDOT* xii. 421–24; Kellermann also dismisses as unnecessary the suggestion of L. Kopf, 'Arabische Etymologien und Parallelen zum Bibelwörterbuch', *VT* 8 (1958), 161–215 (198), to compare Arabic *ʿaḍud*, '(upper) arm', and *ʿiḍād*, 'bracelet'. Kellermann himself favours 'anklet' in our verse and 'armlet' for אצעדה; without giving reasons, he appears to rely solely on the derivation from צעד.

קשׁרים: the verb קשׁר means 'to bind', and at Jer. 2.32 (the only other occurrence of our word) the reference is to some item prized by a bride. Sashes, ribbons and stomachers have all been suggested, though the latter seems least likely (*pace* LXX and V Jer, *HAL*, 1077, and Wildberger here), as a bride would presumably wear only one! The same argument perhaps marginally favours ribbons (cf. Rashi and Kimhi, followed by Ehrlich and Budde) over sashes.

בתי הנפשׁ: apparently 'houses of life/soul'. While LXX offers no obvious equivalent and α has the rather uninformative οἴκους τῆς ψύχης, σ and V (σκεύη τῆς ἐμπνοίας and *olfactoriola*) agree on relating this in some way with perfume. In more recent times Akkadian *nipšu*, 'breathing, scent' (*CDA*, 254) has been compared,[17] hence 'boxes of perfume' (*DCH* v. 734), 'perfume bottles' (*HAL*, 120), or something of the sort. It is suggested that these might have been carried in the sashes (if that is what the previous item refers to), and Gray compares Ct. 1.13 for a parallel. However, an otherwise unattested homonym for so common a word as נפשׁ seems unlikely (and the versions which suggest this might equally have guessed via the meaning of breath, inhalation). Wildberger also observes that such perfume bottles as have been found in excavations are not of the sort that could be carried around thus. An alternative approach,[18] which has the great advantage of fitting very well with the following item, is to work intuitively from a straightforward rendering of the words[19] to arrive at some kind of amulet (Blenkinsopp: 'talismans'; Schmitt, *Magie*, 185–86; NEB's 'lockets'[20] does not quite catch the required nuance). The precise form is uncertain. Platt, 'Jewelry', 198–200, compares Egyptian examples of small decorated cylinders which could be worn round the neck and which might contain charms written on papyrus; later Jewish *tephillin* are another, though more remote, parallel.

לחשׁים: see on v. 3 above. We may compare the tiny rolled-up silver plaques (assumed to be worn round the neck) with a version of the priestly blessing engraved on them found in a sixth-century tomb at Ketef Hinnom, near Jerusalem; cf. *AHI*, 72–73.

21. טבעות: a common word (about fifty occurrences), particularly of rings on the staves of the ark. It appears to be an early loanword into Semitic from Egyptian.[21] It is clear from the explicit language of Gen. 41.42 and Esth. 3.12 that in a context such as the present this refers to a signet- or seal-ring, worn on the hand.

נזמי האף: the meaning is obvious, and there are a number of other supportive occurrences, such as Gen. 24.47. It makes a good pair with the preceding.

22. מחלצות: this word used to be explained principally with reference to חלץ, 'strip off', the thought being that they were the type of clothes that one would strip off before resuming ordinary life, hence 'state-gowns' or the like (cf. BDB, 323A; Gesenius; Gray). Following Thomas's study of the word at its only other occurrence (Zech. 3.4),[22] where the emphasis is on the contrast with the filthy clothes which Joshua the high priest had been wearing previously, it is now usual to compare Arabic *ḫalaṣa*, 'become pure, clean, white' (and perhaps Akkadian *ḫalāṣu*, though this seems less certain[23]), to give 'new/pure/clean clothes'. This fits the context in Zechariah extremely

---

[17] There appears to be no justification for occasionally made claims of an Ugaritic cognate; cf. *DUL*, 636–37.

[18] Eitan's proposal, 'collar' ('Contribution', 57), fails to do justice to בתי.

[19] Cf. H. W. F. Saggs, '"External Souls" in the Old Testament', *JSS* 19 (1974), 1–12.

[20] This appears to follow G. R. Driver, 'Suggestions and Objections', *ZAW* 55 (1937), 68–71, where he abandons his previous favouring of נפשׁ = 'scent'.

[21] Cf. Muchiki, *Loanwords*, 247.

[22] D. W. Thomas, 'A Note on מחלצות in Zechariah iii 4', *JTS* 33 (1932), 279–80; cf. C. L. and E. M. Meyers, *Haggai, Zechariah 1–8* (AB 25B; Garden City, 1987), 190.

[23] *CDA*, 101, gives the meaning as 'comb out, filter', to which *CAD* vi. 40, adds 'press, squeeze out' (to extract oil from sesame seeds). This will be cognate with the

well (especially as the word does not appear to be a standard term for priestly garments). In our context, it might just mean 'white garments' or it could, of course, have developed to mean something like 'festal robes' (NRSV), so not unlike the traditional rendering, though differently derived.

מעטפות: the noun occurs nowhere else, but עטף means 'wrap, envelop oneself', so that some all-enveloping garment must be meant; hence, 'mantle', 'outer cloak', or similar;[24] it clearly has to be distinguished from the following item.

מטפחות (omitted by 1QIsaᵃ): this is the item of clothing in which Ruth carried the barley given to her by Boaz, so that it needs to be an item worn by both rich and destitute. 'Shawl' therefore seems preferable to 'cloak' (as often rendered here).

חריטים: once again there are two possibilities between which it is difficult to choose. On the one hand, Arabic ḥarītat means '(leather) bag, purse', and at first glance this would fit well with the other attested use of the word in Hebrew, namely 2 Kgs 5.23, where Naaman 'tied up two talents of silver in two bags' (so Kimhi).[25] So in the present passage we might have the ancient equivalent of a handbag as a fashion accessory. On the other hand, the word would clearly have to serve for bags of very different sizes,[26] and it is not obvious that the sense goes too well with the verb צור, 'bind, tie up'. Naaman might as easily have tied his silver in some pieces of cloth or leather, and the Arabic usage could be an intelligible refinement of this over time without its precise nature being determinative for Hebrew. In that case, the present reference would presumably be to some piece of cloth or leather worn as an item of clothing, such as some further type of wrap or shawl (so more or less Ibn Ezra). This would obviously follow on well from the preceding item. Much will depend on the extent to which we think that every item in this list must have been worn (as opposed to carried) by women,[27] an issue that recurs with the next item.

23. גלינים: again there is more than one reasonable possibility, as debated at length already by Gesenius; see too Cohen, 'Studies', 167–68. With acknowledgment of the difficulties of being sure about equivalences in this passage, LXX probably intends its τὰ διαφανῆ Λακωνικὰ, 'the Spartan transparent (dresses?)', to render this word. This apparently links the word with גלה, 'uncover, reveal', so that from this such deductions have been made as 'diaphanous/lace/thin garments, gauze veils'. Alternatively, following the lead of V and T, others favour 'mirrors' (based on the same root). If the previous item already shows that not everything in this list has to be worn (as ornament or clothing), then this too would be reasonable, and it has the advantage of possibly being able to fit with the use of what could be the same word at 8.1, where it refers to some kind of a hard surface that could have writing engraved on it. Given that mirrors in

noun ḥlṣ which is thought to occur once in Imperial Aramaic with the meaning 'something squeezed out (i.e. a certain type of oil)' (*DNWSI*, 378). This could be related, since it seems to imply a reference to the process of production resulting in 'pure' oil, but it is by no means obviously close.

[24] See too L. Kopf, 'Arabische Etymologien und Parallelen zum Bibelwörterbuch', *VT* 9 (1959), 247–87 (269), who appeals to Arabic to support the meaning 'Mantel, Hülle'.

[25] Curiously, the same form of wording occurs at Exod. 32.4. There, by exploiting homonyms for both the verb and the noun, the clause is usually rendered 'and he fashioned it with a graving tool' (ויצר אתו בחרט), though on the basis of 2 Kgs 5.23 'he tied it in a bag' has occasionally been proposed for that as well; cf. S. Schroer, *In Israel gab es Bilder: Nachrichten von darstellender Kunst im Alten Testament* (OBO 74; Freiburg and Göttingen, 1987), 85–87.

[26] This point is reasonably made by Driver, 'Isaiah i–xxxix', 37, and he also thinks that the context indicates a reference to an item of clothing. But his suggested translation 'flounced skirt' (followed by NEB), based on a different Arabic word, does not sound convincing.

[27] Cf. F. E. Peiser, 'Miscellen', *ZAW* 17 (1897), 347–51 (348).

antiquity were made of polished metal, this is plausible. Thirdly, a link may be made with Akkadian *gulēnu/gulīnu/gulānu*, 'over-garment' of some kind (*CDA*, 96; cf. *BHS*). Wildberger objects that this is to be compared rather with גלום, 'wrapping garment',[28] but it is not clear why this should rule out an alternative (and nearer) cognate in Hebrew. It has not, apparently, been previously noted that there is a curious coincidence in that not only does this word also occur at 8.1, but it does so in close proximity to חרט, 'stylus', which might well have been associated in some minds with the previous item in this list. I wonder whether this was noted by the Masoretes and that it influenced their vocalization at this point. גְּלִינִים would not be impossible, parallel with חריטים just before. With no great confidence, I marginally favour this third solution. I realize that 'coats' is anachronistic, but find myself rapidly running out of suitable synonyms!

סדינים: Judg. 14.12–13 indicates that these were highly valued garments and Prov. 31.24 suggests that they were the result of skilled work and so costly; both indications are highly suitable in the present context, of course. The spelling of the Akkadian cognate *saddinnu* suggests to Mankowski, *Akkadian Loanwords*, 109–10, that it was a foreign loan into Semitic 'whose phonetic imitation varied according to the receptor dialect'.[29] If its origin was still remembered, this too would have added a certain exotic quality to the item. It seems also to have been borrowed into Greek, σινδών (medial -νδ- would fit with the -*dd* in Akkadian), a word known already to Herodotus who defines it as made from linen (βυσσίνη). The LXX uses the former equivalent in Judges and (apparently)[30] the latter here. Whether the Greek evidence is sufficient to conclude that it referred to linen also in Hebrew is uncertain, but it fits, and no better suggestion is available. What type of garment these were remains completely unknown; 'tunic' is just a guess.

צניפות: clearly related to מצנפת, the high priest's turban, and both derived from צנף, 'wrap around'. In what way they differ from each other is uncertain, since in Zech. 3.5 Joshua the high priest has a צניף put on his head. In Isa. 62.3 it seems also to be associated with royalty (but then so too is מצנפת at Ezek. 21.31 [26]), which suggests that it was of splendid quality; this does not, however, justify 'crown' as a translation.[31]

רדידים: the only real clue we have about this word is that at Ct. 5.7 it is an item that the 'watchmen of Jerusalem' removed from the girl after beating her up. It must therefore be some outer garment, and perhaps one whose removal would leave her shamed. This fits veil better than mantle (which is often proposed here; alternatively, Cohen, 'Studies', 180, proposes 'wide wrapper'), though quite how it differs from the last word in v. 19 is not clear. I have followed NEB.

24. והיה...יהיה: 1QIsaᵃ has והיו at the start of the verse, and then naturally omits יהיה later. Either is possible, but MT may be more original; assuming that v. 24 was once the direct continuation of v. 17 (see below), והיה will be in sequence with ושפח, whereas the scroll's sequence may be that of a simple *waw* in sequence with יסיר (v. 18; cf. Kutscher, 357), which would be linguistically later and redactionally secondary.

נקפה: LXX σχοινίῳ ζώσῃ and V *funiculus*; hence the usual rendering 'rope', explained as being something which 'encircles' (נקף II) the waist, either as the simplest substitute for a richer form of girdle or as a restraint for a captive. Zeron[32] has

---

[28] See further Cohen, *Biblical Hapax Legomena*, 93 n. 253.

[29] *Sadinnu* is attested in the (western) dialect of the Amarna letters, for instance; cf. A. Rainey, 'El-ʿAmarna Notes', *UF* 6 (1974), 295–312 (308).

[30] Less plausibly, M. Ellenbogen assumes that the LXX equivalent is ὑακίνθινος, 'blue stuff', but he presumably reaches that conclusion by an inappropriate mechanical attempt to align each word and its Greek equivalent by numerical order; cf. *Foreign Words in the Old Testament: Their Origin and Etymology* (London, 1962), 121.

[31] *Contra* D. L. Petersen, *Haggai and Zechariah 1–8: A Commentary* (OTL; London, 1984), 186, 196–99.

[32] Zeron, 'Das Wort *niqpā*', followed by Wiklander, 80, and Beuken.

objected, however, that this leads to repetition, and possibly softening, in the second half of the following line. He therefore follows an indication from T, which has רושמין דמחא, together with much later Jewish tradition, which also refers to wounds, to suggest that the word refers to an 'encircling' skin disease: 'shingles'. This may be related to נקב (and to נקף I?), 'to pierce'. While there is an inevitable uncertainty about any *hapax legomenon*, this proposal nevertheless raises problems: the shift from wound to disease at this point is not attested in antiquity and is speculative, there seems to be some confusion between the two separate roots נקף, and in the wider context a reference to disease is not expected; as at v. 17 above, it is humanly induced forms of humiliation that are primarily in view. The parallelism with the end of the next line, which in any case is not exact, is not *per se* a problem.

מעשה מקשה: apposition (GK §131b; WO, 230). Though rendered by a single word in P, that alone is insufficient evidence to delete the first word. It is, of course, possible that מעשה is a corrupt dittograph (e.g. Duhm; Gray), and from this it has been conjectured that מחגרת later in the line might also be an addition. In view of the lack of textual evidence, however, it may be more plausibly argued on the basis of line balance that the two words are mutually supporting. Vocalized thus, מקשה is another *hapax*, though מִקְשָׁה occurs quite frequently in the priestly writing for some kind of (often gold) metal work in connection with, for instance, the cherubim, the lampstand and trumpets. In view especially of the latter (Num. 10.2),[33] it is unlikely to mean 'twisted', from which some have sought to derive the sense of plaited or braided hair for our word, but rather hammered work. If it is linked etymologically with קשה = 'be hard, firm' (which is far from certain), then 'well-set' may be the sense. While this may certainly have *included* braiding and plaiting, the emphasis is rather on the fact that 'not a hair is out of place'. What appears as an explanatory addition at the end of this clause in LXX, διὰ τὰ ἔργα σου, may represent no more than 'remnants of an older translation' of תחת מעשה מקשה, later replaced by the more accurate rendering which now precedes it (Seeligmann, 36).

פתיגיל: older commentators sought various Hebrew derivations for this further *hapax* (see, for instance, Gesenius and Delitzsch), but lexicographers are now generally agreed that the word is of unknown foreign origin,[34] so that we can only guess its meaning, as the ancient versions also apparently did. Some sort of rich clothing is indicated by the context;[35] for want of anything better, I have followed NEB. So too with מחגרת, which is some item of clothing that is 'girded' on, but apparently to be distinguished from חגורה earlier in the verse. Tur-Sinai's proposal to read חֲפֵי גִיל, 'drums of rejoicing', from which he goes on to suggest other changes earlier in the verse as well as a reinterpretation of its general sense, is unnecessary, inappropriate and wildly speculative.[36]

כי תחת יפי: in approaching this crux, it should first be noted that *BHS* and others who state that this line is lacking from LXX and V are misleading; both versions clearly read יפי, at least, but construed it with the following verse: καὶ ὁ υἱός σου ὁ κάλλιστος ὃν ἀγαπᾷς... (κάλλος is sometimes used elsewhere to render words from the root יפה) and *pulcherrimi quoque viri tui...* It is thus more probable that they simply glossed over the (to them) puzzling תחת than that they had a text in which just this word was lacking (*contra* Tur-Sinai, 164). P also clearly presupposes the MT (construing תחת as part of the verb חתת), while T includes a double rendering of יפי, one

---

[33] 'The shape of this instrument is known from its representation on Jewish coins and on the arch of Titus, where it appears as a long, straight, slender metal tube, flared at one end'; E. W. Davies, *Numbers* (NCB; London and Grand Rapids, 1995), 87.

[34] B. Gregor, 'פְּתִיגִיל in Jes 3,24', *BN* 61 (1992), 15–16, attempts a derivation from Old Persian *pati-gīr* to render 'Meister-Geraffe', though not without an element of special pleading.

[35] E. Ullendorff, 'The Bawdy Bible', *BSOAS* 42 (1979), 425–56 (430), however, conjectures some kind of chastity garment.

[36] Tur Sinai, 163–64; see earlier 'Unverstandene Bibelworte', *VT* 1 (1951), 307–9.

in each verse. The case is similar in σ (though less periphrastic than T), and he also joins the phrase to the following verse (ἀντὶ δὲ κάλλους οἱ καλοὶ τοῦ ἀριθμοῦ σου...), while α also joins the two verses, but without the double rendering of יפי: ὅτι ἀντὶ κάλλους ἄνδρες σου... None of the versions can therefore be cited in support of a text which differs materially from MT, though there is a strong tradition which construes the phrase with the following verse.

This tradition has been adopted in recent times by Wiklander, 80–81, and by Sweeney, *Isaiah 1–4*, 154, followed by Berges, 82–83.[37] They suggest that in place of the expected word following 'for instead of beauty', we in fact find the whole saying of v. 25: 'for instead of beauty, your men shall fall by the sword...'. While initially attractive as a means of conserving the MT without an appeal to unusual meanings for familiar words, this cannot be correct in terms of the 'original' meaning. The switch to second feminine singular in v. 25 (somewhat hidden in English renderings) is sufficient to demonstrate that v. 25 is not part of the address to the 'daughters of Zion' in 16-24. Furthermore, the sense obtained is not particularly good (wherein lies a contrast between female beauty and men being killed?), the connection (כי) between this and the rest of v. 24 is not obvious, and no explanation is offered for the breakdown in the otherwise well-regulated poetic rhythm. Finally, as we have already seen (see on 1.21-26), it is likely that other material once stood between vv. 24 and 25, so precluding an original connection between 24 and 25 in their present form.

As Lowth observed long ago, the form of the preceding clauses leads one to suspect that a word may have dropped out after יפי, so it is not surprising that many commentators have been attracted to the reading in 1QIsaᵃ, which in fact adds בשת, 'Truly (emphatic כי) instead of beauty—shame'.[38] This certainly makes good sense, but it has been questioned for that very reason:[39] it has the appearance of secondarily supplying what was felt to be lacking, and had it been original we might have expected it to show up in some other textual witness.[40] It is, of course, possible that there has been textual loss at this point (and this might have something to do with the evidently early redactional activity at this point [see on 3.25 below]), but if so it is beyond recall.

Since the evidence thus suggests that MT as it stands should be construed as a self-contained clause, we are driven back to what was the majority interpretation before the discovery of the Dead Sea Scrolls, namely to understand כי not as the regular conjunction but rather as a noun formed from the root כוה, 'burn' (Isa. 43.2; [Jer. 23.29?;] Prov. 6.28), hence 'brand'.[41] Other attested nouns from this root are כויה, 'burn' (Exod. 21.25), and מכוה, 'burn(-scar)' (Lev. 13.24-28). That a different form of noun should be used for the different type of burn, i.e. 'brand', is not surprising, and to derive such a form of noun from this root is unexceptional (cf. GK §§24b and 93y for several other examples). Three principal objections have been raised against this explanation. First, it is objected that the word is a *hapax*; but in the present passage (16-24), above all others, that is scarcely compelling, and anyway the root is well attested, as we have seen. Secondly, the order in the clause is different from that of the four preceding clauses: 'x instead of y', against the regular 'instead of y–x' earlier in the verse. This is

---

[37] Loretz, '*Kj*', seems to favour this construal while simultaneously taking the line as a '*kj*-Glosse'.

[38] See, for instance, Nötscher, 'Entbehrliche Hapaxlegomena', 300; Wildberger, Kaiser, Oswalt, Blenkinsopp, Porath, 20, NRSV.

[39] Cf. G. R. Driver, 'Hebrew Scrolls', *JTS* NS 2 (1951), 17–30 (25); Hoffmann, 9; Auvray; Høgenhaven, 178.

[40] It is intriguing that in his lemma to v. 17 Jerome adds (against V, and without textual comment) *et pro ornatu erit ignominia*. Could this reflect knowledge of the scroll's form of the text, but in a different position? If so, it would serve only to show that the textual damage in this passage runs deeper than we can now reconstruct, while at the same time making even clearer the original connection between vv. 17 and 24.

[41] A. Schoors, 'The Particle כי', *OTS* 21 (1981), 240–76 (240), also compares Arabic *kâ*, 'cauterisation'.

also not a strong argument; such a variation at the end of a poetic unit (which is additionally marked by the clause producing a tricolon) is stylistically forceful, and it brings a strong sense of closure to the unit. Thirdly, it is noted that this word was not recognized by the versions and that the sense was recognized first only in the rather later Jewish tradition of the Talmud, followed by some of the rabbinic commentators. That may be true, but it is true of other words in the Hebrew Bible as well, so that it is hardly a compelling objection; if the meaning of the word had been obvious from the start, there would have been no difficulty in the first place. I conclude that (with omission of the *maqqeph*[42]) this approach does most justice to the best attested form of the text. Whether it has itself arisen as the result of substantial textual disturbance during the period before our evidence begins cannot now be determined.

It was suggested in the introduction to 3.1-9 that, within the unit 3.1–4.1 (itself a part of the larger section made up of chs 2–4), there is something of a break following 3.15. The various elements which have been combined to form vv. 1-15 are held together by a number of verbal connections as well as by the *inclusio* at the start of 3.1 and the end of 3.15. Verse 16 begins with a new divine speech formula and the material following concentrates on the women of Jerusalem. The structural break thus coincides with a change in subject matter (though fitting well within the theme of the chapter as a whole).

As was the case in 3.1-15, however, it is apparent that 3.16–4.1 is not all of a piece.[43] There is a clear change in addressee at 3.25 (as again at 26 and 4.1; see below), so that the first element for consideration cannot extend beyond v. 24. Even here, however, it is generally agreed nowadays that vv. 18-23 have been inserted secondarily, so interrupting what was probably an original connection between 16-17 and 24.[44] Verse 24 follows smoothly on v. 17 both in subject matter and in form (והיה picks up ושפח). While it cannot be proved that it is not simply an unattached fragment (like those in the three verses which follow it), the most economical hypothesis is that it once belonged with 16-17. By contrast, v. 18 introduces a prose list; note the use of the prose particle את in 18 and the use of the definite article before each item in the list. It is, of course, possible to group the items in such a way that lines of balanced length emerge, but that does not make poetry out of this material. 'If Budde thinks that such a catalog is rhythmically completely accurate, that shows, more than anything else, only that one can designate every list Hebrew poetry, if one does not impose any more narrow definition on poetry than that it has alternating accented and unaccented syllables' (Wildberger; similar comments could be made about Peters, 'Two Fragments'). The introductory ביום ההוא is also widely regarded as indicative of a later addition.[45]

---

[42] For manuscript evidence which suggests that the Masoretic evidence is not united on this point, see Barthélemy, 28.

[43] The fact that there are satirical elements throughout is hardly sufficient ground for treating the whole passage as a unity, *contra* D. Fishelov, 'The Prophet as Satirist', *Prooftexts* 9 (1989), 195–211.

[44] For a different opinion, see Kissane, and Gitay, 74.

[45] See especially DeVries, *From Old Revelation to New*, Chapter 3 (esp. 47–48), with further literature.

Verses 16-17 + 24 comprise mainly the standard prophetic form of reason for judgment (16) followed by threat (17 + 24). (Against Sweeney's alternative analysis, see the textual notes on v. 16 above.) The transition between the two parts is marked only by a *waw*-apodosis, rather than the stronger לכן, which often occurs at this point (cf. 1.24). Such a form can be presented either as first person speech by God (cf. 29.13-14 for an example also introduced by יען כי) or as a third person report by the prophet. At first sight, these two seem here to be confused: v. 16*a* introduces God as the speaker, but he is referred to in the third person in 17. Consequently, many commentators delete or bracket ויאמר יהוה at the start of 16 as a mistaken redactional addition. This conclusion is only half right, in my opinion. It may be agreed that in its earliest form the oracle lacked these words, or that there was originally an indication that the prophet was speaking here. But the addition is far from mistaken. Precisely the same apparent confusion occurs at 8.5-7, again with יען כי, but nobody would assume there that v. 5 was added mistakenly; it is part of the major structural framework for that whole section of the book. Similarly here, on a smaller scale, ויאמר יהוה is part of the work of the redactor of this section as a whole, marking the transition between 3.1-15 and 3.16–4.1. Evidently, as 8.5-7 (and many other comparable examples) shows, editors in antiquity were less concerned for absolute consistency in this regard than their modern commentators. The words should certainly be retained as an integral part of the text which has been assembled from many smaller units into the larger redactional whole. It is also possible (though there can be no certainty) that the use of אדני...יהוה in v. 17 is due to the work of the same redactor, under the influence of these same two divine titles in the same order in vv. 1 and 15, where they play an important structuring role. But if so, what they may have replaced (if anything) is beyond recall.

There have been various attempts to find some coherent order behind the list in vv. 18-23. In some cases, such as the observation that the first three items in v. 20 follow the order of the Hebrew alphabet,[46] this relates to only part of the list. At the other extreme, Bartelt, 219, has proposed that 'structural features are quite apparent'. Following the introductory first item, he finds eight single terms in 18*c*-20*a* balancing the same number at the end in 22-23. In between, the four items in 20*b*-21 are chiastically arranged, and so on. More usually, scholars who see any design here at all restrict it to the more general observation that there seems to be a progression from jewelry items at the start to sumptuous clothing at the end (e.g. Wildberger). This, of course, depends in part upon the identification of a number of the items which are of uncertain meaning, and even then produces some unexpected elements (see, for instance, Gray's comment on Condamin). Unless there is a

---

[46] So Tur-Sinai, 163; he had already raised this possibility in 'Anmerkungen zum Hebräischen und zur Bibel', *ZDMG* 66 (1912), 389–409 (406).

great deal more here than we are now in a position to appreciate,[47] it seems that we should not venture beyond such a general appreciation.

Authorship and date are impossible to determine with certainty. With regard to 16-17 + 24, the familiar line of argument that 'there is no reason to doubt' authorship by Isaiah is certainly true as far as it goes, though it inevitably falls short of establishing the case positively. There is nothing here to imply that exile has already been experienced (the forms of humiliation are traditional, and could certainly have been anticipated in the eighth century), and on *a priori* grounds, based on my understanding of the growth of the book of Isaiah in general, and of ch. 3 in particular (see above), I assume with nearly all other commentators that these verses derive from an authentic oracle of the prophet (contrast Kaiser and Becker). Their theology certainly coincides closely with his (see v. 16), but I find little to indicate a particular date within the course of his ministry. One possibility is that they reflect the period of prosperity and optimism prior to the Assyrian invasion of 701 and that Isaiah was anticipating a very different outcome to the revolt from that expected by the court of Hezekiah.[48] (See on 3.25–4.1 below for the redactional association of this with the later exile.)

Isaianic authorship of vv. 18-23 is still occasionally defended, but mostly in terms of rejecting the alternative rather than on the basis of positive evidence. Sweeney, *Isaiah 1–4*, 178, for instance, observes that the 'catalogue technique' occurs at 3.1-3 and 2.12-16, and that international trade could account for the foreign influence in the vocabulary. If it is the case, however, as argued above, that this material has been inserted secondarily into its present setting, one would have to assume that it once had an independent existence as a separate saying, if it really came from Isaiah, and as such it is most unconvincing. The introduction to the list looks as though it has been written specifically for its present setting (see comments below), which is suggestive of the work of a redactor, and one can hardly imagine Isaiah writing a list of finery without any kind of context. Whether the redactor drew on a pre-existing list or penned it himself from scratch is impossible to say. Nor does any putative date commend itself over another. In view of the redactional history of this passage as a whole, a post-exilic date seems most likely, especially if יָסִיר (18) reflects knowledge of v. 1 and so is indicative of the redactor working in the light of (or is perhaps to be identified with) the redactor of the chapter as a whole.

There is little of significance to be noted about vv. 16-17 + 24 in terms of poetic analysis. Determination of line length is rendered uncertain, both because some think that occasional words have been added (e.g. in 24*b*) and because of the possibility that the redactor has himself

---

[47] We might note, for instance, the suggestion of Daiches, 'Schmuck', that the list closely follows the description of Ishtar in her descent to the underworld—superficially an unlikely parallel. Curiously, he also thinks that this justifies Isaianic authorship.

[48] Cf. Høgenhaven, 179; but contrast Wildberger, who thinks in terms of the early period of Isaiah's ministry (though on very weak grounds).

introduced small changes (e.g. in 17; see above). Wildberger satisfactorily describes the text as it now stands. The one noteworthy feature is
the presence of the tricolon in 24*b* to mark the end of the unit. This
device has already been noted several times (e.g. v. 7 earlier in this
same chapter) with the same purpose.

16. For the introductory speech formula, see above. The *daughters of
Zion* is a reference to (some of) the women of the city, perhaps in particular those who inhabited the citadel area, in view of the use of Zion
rather than Jerusalem. The phrase also occurs in v. 17 and 4.4 (and cf.
Ct. 3.11). בנות + GN (including Jerusalem) is not uncommon with this
sense (cf. *DCH* ii. 285), so that the relative rarity of our particular
phrase occasions no difficulty or surprise. It is true that the 'daughters'
of a city can also be a way of referring to its dependent villages, but in
that case the word order seems always to be 'GN + and her daughters'
(cf. *DCH* ii. 288). The suggestion that it is the hilltop settlements of
Judah which are here in view[49] is thus most unlikely, and the phrase
was certainly not understood so by the redactor who added vv. 18-23.

Are haughty (גבהו): this leading verb of the passage ties it in integrally with Isaiah's basic theology; see the use of גבהות in 2.11 and 17
and of גבה in 2.12* and 15, to go no further. Isaiah's condemnation of
the women is thus not a case of misogyny, nor of antagonism to enjoyment of the good things of life in general, nor of a hidden suggestion
that these luxuries have been obtained by social oppression (despite vv.
14-15 above); to this extent there is a different tone from Amos's criticisms of the women of Samaria in Amos 4.1 (cf. Fey, 79). Rather, as
with many other examples through this passage (beginning at 2.6), so
too now the women come under the condemnation that they have sought
to usurp that position which is God's alone. Unusual as it may seem to
us, the description in the following two lines must therefore, in Isaiah's
view, be illustrative of this basic attitude; they are all things whereby
the women sought to draw attention to themselves, which nobody who
was conscious of the majesty of God would want to do. It is probable
that the items which he singles out for mention are ones which he could
easily satirize because they were obvious to all. This is not psychological profiling, but a simple rhetorical device which he would expect his
(mainly male) audience to appreciate: 'look, you can see how stuck up
and ridiculous they look!'.

Outstretched necks, probably artificially so by the style of clothing or
ornamentation, will have been considered a sign of aristocratic grace,
but to Isaiah it suggested the idea of elevating oneself unnaturally;
Young notes idioms in other Semitic languages where a stretched-out
neck is indicative of haughtiness. Assuming *ogling* is the right translation (see the notes above), its purpose is, of course, to attract attention
in a manner that makes oneself appear available. *Taking mincing steps*
is a paraphrase for טפף. Though the word does not occur elsewhere, it

---

[49] Cf. Halpern, 'Jerusalem and the Lineages', 43.

seems to be related to מַף, 'a toddler', and may be onomatopoeic (Gray compares 'the like sounding Aryan *tap*'). It is unnatural for adults to walk thus, but the next clause probably explains it, and so should be construed closely with it: the point of walking like this was to make the anklets (bangles?) jingle, again so as to attract attention. It is sometimes stated that the anklets were chains which tied the two ankles together, so that it was possible to take only tiny steps, but I am not aware of any positive evidence in support of this.

17. The point of the judgment in vv. 17 and 24 is, as v. 24 makes especially clear, to reverse the pretensions to which the haughty attitude of v. 16 bears witness. This consideration of 'poetic justice'[50] has already had some influence on the choice of translation in what is philologically an obscure verse (see the notes above). The point of cutting off the woman's hair is not just to humiliate her (though of course that is also part of the effect), but to mark her out as a prisoner of war, whose fate was generally slavery (so already Knobel, who cites classical parallels).[51] This exchange of status expresses the humiliation of pride, as in ch. 2 (and see further, for instance, 47.1-3).

18-23. There are several indications that this list has been introduced into its present setting by the final redactor of the passage as a whole. *On that day* occurs more than once to link commentary with the fundamental statement of 2.12; cf. 2.20 and 4.2. The idea that *the Lord will remove* what is offensive came already at 3.1 (and cf. 1.24), suggesting a reader who had the wider passage in view rather than being just a late annotator who worked atomistically. The title for *the Lord* (אדני) has been seen to play an important part in the structure of the passage (3.1, 15, 17), and the very first item in the list, *anklets*, links with the verb of the same root (עכס) in v. 16. Finally *finery* (תפארת) is only one of a number of terms and phrases from 3.1–4.1 which are picked up in the development of 4.2-6, itself part of the major redactional work in chs 2–4 as a whole. The purpose of all this, then, is to indicate that on the day when the Lord acts against everything that is proud and lifted up (2.12), the finery which renders the women liable to judgment will also be removed, so opening the way for final restoration. As we saw at 1.21-26, for Isaiah himself removal was a negative concept, but it was also one which could legitimately be exploited by later writers in the more positive direction of concentrating on what was left behind, now that all impurity had been taken away. It seems that it is this thought which controls the usage at this point, once it is taken together with 4.2-6.

Finery (תפארת) governs the whole of the following list. It is a relatively common word, which is used elsewhere in terms of beauty, glory or renown with reference to such diverse matters as monarchy, rank, a country or its capital as well as clothing and jewelry, and more besides.

---

[50] See on this the classic study by Barton, 'Natural Law'.

[51] Cf. E. Szlechter, 'Essai d'explication des clauses: *muttatam gullubu, abbuttam šakânu* et *abbuttam gullubu*', *ArOr* 17 (1949), 391–418; M. A. Dandamaev, *Slavery in Babylonia: From Nabopolassar to Alexander the Great (626–331 B C)* (DeKalb, Ill., 1984), 233–34; Kaiser; Vermeylen, 150.

And that is just the point here: it is not concentrating on any particular feature of the following list in order to slant its interpretation, as it might be in the direction of religion or authority. It is, rather, a general term to sum up the fine display (judged by human standards) of all that follows.

The identity of the individual items has been discussed, so far as it is possible within so much that is obscure, in the notes above, and the general shape (or lack of shape) in the list has been touched on in the introduction to this section. Attention need here only be drawn in addition to the careful two-part article by Platt, 'Jewelry', whose main object is to demonstrate that many of the items (on whose identification she makes many helpful comments) were 'worn by both men and women as signs of high office'. She deduces from this that the list is not out to condemn the wearing of beautiful apparel as such, but is focused on the abuse of the authority of the office for which the apparel stands. As with other 'global' explanations of this list already mentioned, this one too seems to fall by the fact that it does not convincingly cover every item, and so cannot be the guiding principle in the compilation. Most of the items occur but rarely (if at all) elsewhere, and given their nature it is not surprising that it is only in contexts which speak of leaders or other prominent people that they are mentioned at all. That does not, however, mean that they are inherently indicative of office: 'all dogs are animals, but not all animals are dogs'. The list is so bizarre that the simplest explanation remains the best: it is merely a heaping up of every relevant term that the compiler could think of in order to convey the impression of comprehensiveness.

24. This verse continues the theme of 'poetic justice' which was interrupted following v. 17. It reaches its climax in the final clause, for which I have defended the translation *branding instead of beauty* (with a feeble attempt to reflect the alliteration of the original[52]). This indicates that the end result of the judgment is slavery (the branding of slaves, 'usually with the name of the slave's owner on his hand with a red-hot iron',[53] was common in the ancient Near East), and so it is probably best to follow this line in regard to the preceding clauses as well (as it was already in v. 17). In most cases, the imagery is obvious, and requires no further comment; indeed, in one case (*instead of a well-set hair-do—baldness*) it even repeats the substance of v. 17. Neither in this case, nor in the case of the reference to *sacking*, is it therefore necessary to see a covert reference to mourning, though it is of interest to note that in the reversal of the general sentiment of this verse at 61.3, the element of mourning predominates.

Only in the first clause is the connection less obvious. *Perfume* is בשׂם, an extract from the balsam tree, which was used as an ingredient in the anointing oil, as a healing agent and as 'an ingredient of perfume, for which the pungent resin was squeezed into an oil or paste' (cf.

---

[52] For Duhm, the 'rhyme' was sufficient to characterize the words as 'ein volks-thümliches Reimwort' which was added by a later reader. The logic here escapes me.
[53] M. A. Dandmayev, *ABD* vi. 60.

Zohary, *Plants*, 198–99). Its occurrence in contexts of royal gifts and the like (e.g. 1 Kgs 10.10; 2 Kgs 20.13) indicates that it was costly and highly prized. In the present verse, the contrast with *the stench of rottenness* (מק) might indicate that it refers primarily to its healing qualities (balm), but for this בשם is never explicitly used, but rather צרי. On the assumption that the verse is relatively consistent in its point of reference, therefore, we must assume that the emphasis is on the woman's conditions in her new slave status (and that will include, though need not be restricted to, her body). Whereas previously the stench of decay and rottenness could be masked by exotic perfume, now that would no longer be possible. (Note that in the only other place where Isaiah uses מק, it refers in a simile to the decay of a rotting plant root, 5.24; it need not, therefore, be limited to the festering of wounds.)

IN THE AFTERMATH OF DEFEAT
(3.25–4.1)

[25]Your men shall fall by the sword,
and your warriors in battle.
[26]And her gates shall lament and mourn,
and she shall be emptied, while she sits on the ground.
[4.1]And seven women shall take hold
of a single man (on that day),
saying, We will eat our own bread,
and we will wear our own garment;
just let your name be pronounced over us;
remove our disgrace.

25. For the versions which join this verse to the preceding, see the notes on v. 24. The LXX has three significant transformations of its *Vorlage* in its rendering, which are fully discussed by Baer, 'It's All About Us!', 213–19. He finds influence from Gen. 22.2 here, which might be added to the many examples of such 'analogical interpretations' traced by Koenig.

וגבורתך...מתיך: there is solid textual support for this second person singular suffix; the only exception is that the LXX renders the second example as plural (though it retains the singular in the first half of the line). There is thus no justification whatsoever for the conjecture of *BHS* to emend to third person feminine suffixes.[1] The awkward changes in person through this passage must be explained differently (see below).

בחרב, 'by the sword': this use of the preposition is well attested; cf. *DCH* iii. 309. The fact that לפי is also common before חרב[2] might lead one to speculate that the difficult phrase at the end of v. 24 could just conceivably have originally been a misreading (under the influence of the preceding clauses) of a marginal note ב' תחת לפי (i.e. ב' instead of לפי). But since בחרב is common, and there is no particular reason why this example should have been singled out for such a note, it would be better not to develop this playful speculation.

וגבורתך: abstract for concrete—גבוריך. The latter is, in fact, the reading of the first hand in 1QIsaᵃ, but this has been corrected by the addition of a supralinear ות (i.e. the plural of the Masoretic form). Kutscher, 370, prefers MT as the more difficult reading, but thinks that σ may agree with the scroll (οἱ δυνάτοι σοῦ against LXX οἱ ἰσχύοντες ὑμῶν).

26. ואנו ואבלו: the two verbs are more or less synonymous. LXX renders only once (καὶ πενθήσουσιν), which might be another example of the translator's carelessness in such matters. Alternatively and more probably, however, it may be noted that there is a plus at the end of the previous verse—καὶ ταπεινωθήσονται—which could well be intended as an equivalent for ואנו. The word is rare, so that he may not have fully understood it. In that case, we may have yet another example of 'levelling' (note how frequently this same verb has occurred already in ch. 2 and at 3.8 and 17), either as a guess or by an association of אנה with ענה (see the notes on ענו at 3.8 above).

---

[1] REB adds a vocative 'Zion' at the start of the verse, which may be the right interpretation, but can hardly be justified as a translation.

[2] According to O. Kaiser, *ThWAT* iii. 167–69 = *TDOT* v. 157, this use is linguistically earlier than that with ב, though the passages cited in each case do not obviously support this conclusion.

וּנִקְתָה: minor pausal form (cf. Delitzsch), not inappropriately before the following; see next note. LXX καὶ καταλειφθήσῃ μόνη can hardly have arisen as a direct translation. It looks as though it reflects knowledge of 49.21 (Seeligmann, 71), where the same phrase occurs with greater justification. Its use here is thus interpretive (and in Wildberger's opinion, it would in fact be a correct interpretation; see below).

לָאָרֶץ תֵּשֵׁב: an asyndetic construction with the imperfect, which functions as a circumstantial clause (cf. Driver, *Tenses* §163); 29.4 is a close parallel. The use of אָרֶץ + לְ after ישׁב is idiomatic for 'to sit on (i.e. to sit down on to, and therefore to be on) the ground'; cf. BDB, 511B (top); *DCH* i. 396.

4.1. וְהֶחֱזִיקוּ: the 'corrected' form in 1QIsaᵃ is והחזיקה, a third feminine plural. Although I believe that there are a few examples of this form elsewhere in Biblical Hebrew (see on 1.6), Kutscher, 191–92, is probably right to argue, in the light of other comparable examples, that in the scroll it reflects Aramaic influence rather than testifying to the survival of the use of the alternative Hebrew form at this point.

בַּיּוֹם הַהוּא: LXX has no equivalent for this phrase, and it disturbs the otherwise regular 3 + 2 rhythm of this verse. Most commentators therefore delete it as a late gloss.[3] In view of the regular use of this phrase as a connective throughout chs 2–4, it could have been consciously added by the passage's redactor at the time of initial compilation, and the evidence from LXX is not especially strong, given the translator's free approach to translation already noted (did he regard it as redundant in view of the start of v. 2 immediately following?). The evidence is thus more finely balanced than some have acknowledged. If, as is possible, the redactor was himself responsible for composing this verse (see below), then the case for deletion on rhythmic grounds is strengthened, but the matter remains uncertain.

לַחְמֵנוּ...וְשִׂמְלָתֵנוּ: the word order, with the object preceding the verb, suggests emphasis; hence, 'our own'.

These three somewhat disjointed verses are united in the fact that they all anticipate in one way or another the effects of a major defeat and that they do so from the perspective of those who will be left behind at the place of defeat rather than from the standpoint of exile.[4] Many soldiers will be killed (25), the city itself will go into mourning (26), and the womenfolk who are left behind will be desperate to be taken in by the few men who remain (4.1). While the feminine focus relates the passage closely to vv. 16-24 immediately preceding, the situation envisaged thus serves also to round out the whole of 3.1–4.1; we seem to be in the same situation as that in vv. 8-9, which I argued above was added to 1-7 in order to reflect on the fulfilment of Isaiah's words in the events surrounding the fall of Jerusalem to the Babylonians. Within the wider unit of chs 2–4 as a whole, we are thus at the point of judgment which has been so often anticipated in the previous sections, and so are finally prepared for the description of the restoration which will follow (4.2-6), thus realizing (in part, at least) the vision which was set out in 2.2-4.

Although 4.2-6 cannot have been composed until the post-exilic period, we have found very little evidence for setting the origin of most of the rest of the unit so late (see 3.10-11 for a significant exception). Rather, throughout most of chs 2 and 3 we have found material of Isaianic origin being combined with reflections from the exilic period.

---

[3] See too DeVries, *From Old Revelation to New*, 40.

[4] Schmitt, 'City as Woman', 99, offers what might be labeled a 'stream of consciousness' unified reading.

That same viewpoint seems best to account for the work of the redactor who assembled the present material here as well.

This at once raises the question, of course, concerning the extent to which he assembled pre-existing material and how much, if anything, he may have added on his own account. That he was not responsible for all three verses seems certain from the abrupt changes in person. 3.25 is addressed to a second person feminine singular subject (thus distinguishing it from 3.24), and in the context Jerusalem (or less probably Judah) must be intended. Verse 26 refers to a third person feminine singular subject, and here Jerusalem is certainly in view, as the reference to 'her gates' and to her state of mourning makes clear by comparison with many other passages both within Isaiah and beyond (see below). 4.1 then moves to a third person account relating to the women who remain. 3.25 and 26 must in origin, therefore, be separate fragments, while 4.1 could (from the point of view of strict logic) follow either of these or something else, such as 3.24 (so Duhm and Marti), or be an independent fragment or addition.

There are one or two clues to help us sort through this confusing situation. First, and most importantly, I argued at 1.21-26 that 3.25 was the original conclusion to the Isaianic oracle included now in 1.21-25 and that the whole oracle in fact once stood at this point in ch. 3 until it was moved to its present position late in the process of the formation of the book of Isaiah as a whole. The fragmentary nature of this verse, therefore, is readily explicable.

Secondly, there is an interesting parallel between 4.1 and 3.6, the latter referring to the desperation of the men-folk and the former to the desperation of the women, each thus fitting well into its prevailing context. 3.6 being an integral part of the longer composition in 3.1-7, it is thus tempting to conjecture that 4.1 might be a balancing redactional composition to give a sense of closure to the unit as a whole. Its return to a third person form would fit well with this conjecture. I cannot see that it really follows satisfactorily from the point of view of content from 3.24, as has sometimes been proposed; so correctly Wildberger, who notes that rhythmically the additional half line at the end of 24 is indicative of a conclusion. We might add that vv. 17 and 24 refer to prisoners of war, whereas 4.1 speaks of those who are left behind.

If these speculations are correct, it leaves only 3.26 as a truly unexplained fragment, distinguished from its context both by its switch to the third person feminine singular and by its 3 + 3 rhythm against the more appropriate 3 + 2 of 3.25 and 4.1. I can only assume that the redactor drew it from some other context and added it here because it suited his overall purpose so well, but where he took it from I cannot tell. There does not seem to be an obvious original setting elsewhere in the first part of Isaiah, so that it may be we should think of some other origin altogether, such as one of the exilic laments like those in Lamentations, with which it has a number of obvious similarities.

I conclude, therefore, that 3.25 is Isaianic (see on 1.21-26), that 3.26 is a fragment of unknown origin, and that 4.1 was penned by the redactor for its present setting. The important conclusion overall, however, is that the present compilation is part of the work of the exilic redactor who gave shape to so much of the material in chs 2–3.[5] Its apparently future orientation was determined, of course, by the fact that 3.25 was part of the predicted judgment by Isaiah, and the redactor continued on from this. It cannot disguise the fact, however, that he was working from the point of view of one who had experienced its fulfilment.[6]

25. Since the oracle in 1.21-25 once preceded this verse, it is clear that the reference is to Zion/Jerusalem, as befits the wider context of chs 2–3 (cf. 2.1; 3.1, 8). Wildberger finds in this threat a characteristic prophetic reversal of the holy war tradition, though in truth the language is sufficiently general and obvious as a description of a military defeat not to require any such explanation. More interestingly, there seems to be a conscious contrast at 22.2. The latter reflects the aftermath of Sennacherib's invasion in 701 BCE, and it suggests that Isaiah himself was pointing out that the judgment which he had here predicted was not fulfilled at that time. By retaining the verse at this point even when 1.21-25 was moved to its present setting, the redactor clearly implies that it was eventually fulfilled in 587.

Your men (מְתַיִךְ): the cognates of this comparatively rare word mean primarily 'man, husband' and secondly 'warrior'. Of its Old Testament occurrences, two may provide particular background for its use here. First, at Deut. 2.34 and 3.6 it occurs as part of 'an idiom [עִיר מְתִם] that may refer to a city together with its population fit for military service'[7] in connection with the ban (חרם). Secondly, מְתֵי מִסְפָּר appears several times with reference to those few people who have escaped God's judgment (cf. Deut. 4.27; 28.62). The fact that both uses are idiomatic suggests that the language is not specifically Deuteronomic, and indeed the second phrase occurs in a considerable number of non-Deuteronomistic passages. The implications for the present context may therefore be on both counts to underline the devastating nature of the defeat.

26. *Her gates*: פְּתָחֶיהָ, literally 'her entrances', rather than the usual שַׁעַר for city gate (the two also occur several times in a construct relationship: 'the entrance of the gate'). While this use is by no means unprecedented, it may be significant that the large majority of the occurrences of פתח are in the priestly source and Ezekiel, with reference to the shrine.

Lament and mourn: וְאָנוּ וְאָבְלוּ. The first of these verbs is rare, but its meaning is secure. In its only other occurrence (19.8) it is also parallel with the familiar אבל, and the derived nouns אֲנִיָּה and תַּאֲנִיָּה (which occur together at 29.2 and Lam. 2.5; אֲנִיָּה alone is probably to be restored by emendation at Isa. 43.14) support this. It is not uncommon for inanimate

---

[5] Cf. Jones, 'Traditio', 242–44; Becker, 49.

[6] Dobbs-Allsopp, *Weep, O Daughter of Zion*, 147–48, finds reflections here of the city-lament mode.

[7] K.-M. Beyse, *ThWAT* v. 109 = *TDOT* ix. 99; note that women and children are mentioned separately in each case.

objects to 'mourn' in the poetic parts of the Hebrew Bible, especially if Clines is right (as I believe he is) in his contention that there is only one Hebrew root אבל = 'to mourn', and not a second = 'to be dry'.[8] Especially close to our passage in this regard are Lam. 1.4, where the roads to Zion are mourners, and 2.8, where God makes the rampart and wall of Zion to mourn (see too Jer. 14.2). In the present context, it would seem to be the absence of people (because of defeat) who normally thronged the gates which made them mourn.

Emptied: the meaning of this verb is disputed. Wildberger, noting the paraphrase in the LXX (see above), cites several passages such as Lam. 1.1 and 2.10 to support the suggestion that Zion is here being described under the figure of a childless widow in mourning who is therefore *vereinsamt* (alone, isolated). This, however, would be unparalleled as a rendering of נקה, which, as Wildberger states, revolves round the sense of 'be bare, clean, pure'. On the usual view, Zion is alone because, as the verb implies, she has been cleaned out, emptied of her population (rather than plundered, as others have suggested). Wildberger has confused the referent with the denotation, but in doing so (as with the LXX before him) he has pointed to the right interpretation of the word.

Sits on the ground: lying on the ground (e.g. 2 Sam. 12.16; 13.31; 1 Kgs 21.27; Esth. 4.3) and sitting (e.g. Lam. 1.1; 2.10; Ezek. 26.16; Job 2.13) are both referred to elsewhere in contexts of mourning. In the present verse, the parallel with Lam. 1.1 is especially striking, since Zion is again the subject.

The comments above thus provide ample evidence for the closeness of this verse to the wording and outlook of Lamentations, and it was noted in the introduction to this passage that this may provide a clue as to the type of material from which the redactor drew this otherwise unrelated fragment. It is then further of interest that this is one of the themes which is clearly reversed in Deutero-Isaiah: to the parallel with the second half of ch. 49, to which the LXX already drew attention, one may also add especially the opening of ch. 54. The reversal of many themes from Lamentations in Deutero-Isaiah is well-known, so that it is particularly satisfying that this verse should have been included by the exilic redactor, since it gives a point of contact within the book of Isaiah itself for one of the major themes of the second part.

4.1. By the addition of this verse, the redactor links the theme of widowhood, which has been introduced metaphorically with reference to the city, to that of the women themselves, who were the focus of attention in 3.16-24. This satisfying conclusion is noteworthy, however, in that there is a shift towards a focus on the women left behind in the aftermath of the defeat. Once again, the emphasis is on the reversal of their former privileged status: here, it is summarized as *disgrace*, whereas in the earlier case it was slavery.

[8] D. J. A. Clines, 'Was there an *ʾbl* II "be dry" in Classical Hebrew?', *VT* 42 (1992), 1–10.

Seven women: the number is not so much to be taken literally as evocatively. It recalls the sequence of curses in the Sefire treaty (which are no doubt typical of a much more widespread genre), where similar cameos are listed: '...and should seven nurses anoi[nt their breasts] and suckle a child, may he not be satisfied; and should seven mares suckle a colt, may it not be satis[fied; and should seven] cows suckle a calf, may it not be satisfied; and should seven ewes suckle a lamb, [may it not be satis]fied; and should his seven daughters bake bread in an oven, may they not fill [it]'.[9] The last of these is telling, in that it has parallels elsewhere, but with a different number of women: 100 in the Tel Fekheriye inscription,[10] and 10 in Lev. 26.26. It seems probable to me that an early reader of our verse would at once recognize the similarity between the cameo presented here and that of the treaty curses,[11] and appreciate that the description is of a situation following punitive judgment.

Take hold of: attention is sometimes drawn to the parallel in Zech. 8.23 ('Ten men...shall take hold of a Jew, grasping his garment and saying...'). Though of course the situations envisaged are far from identical, 'yet, that verse does show how those who were looking for help would attempt to gain some security for themselves by being attached to men of importance and power' (Wildberger).

A single man: single in the sense of 'one' (אחד), of course, not necessarily in the sense of being still unmarried. The legality of polygyny is here apparently presupposed.[12]

Our own bread...our own garment: according to Exod. 21.10, if a man took a second wife, he was not to 'diminish the food, clothing, or marital rights of the first wife'. In a time of acute shortage, there was thus a strong economic disadvantage in taking additional wives, even

[9] The standard edition is that of J. A. Fitzmyer, *The Aramaic Inscriptions of Sefire* (BibOr 19; Rome, 1967); *CoS* ii. 213–17. The last of these curses has been the subject of considerable debate, on which see especially S. A. Kaufman, 'Reflections on the Assyrian–Aramaic Bilingual from Tell Fakhariyeh', *Maarav* 3 (1982), 137–75 (170–72), B. Zuckerman, 'On Being "Damned Certain": The Story of a Curse in the Sefire Inscription and its Interpretation', in A. B. Beck *et al.*, *Fortunate the Eyes that See: Essays in Honor of David Noel Freedman in Celebration of his Seventieth Birthday* (Grand Rapids, 1995), 422–35, and V. Brugnatelli, 'The "Chickens" of Sefire', *Henoch* 17 (1995), 259–66.

[10] Cf. A. Abou Assaf *et al.*, *La Statue de Tell Fekherye et son inscription bilingue assyro-araméenne* (Paris, 1982); *CoS* ii. 154.

[11] For a general survey of this type of material, see D. Hillers, *Treaty-Curses and the Old Testament Prophets* (BibOr 16; Rome, 1964).

[12] For an extensive discussion of polygyny in Israel, with reference also to the rest of the ancient Near East, see G. P. Hugenberger, *Marriage as a Covenant: A Study of Biblical Law and Ethics Governing Marriage Developed from the Perspective of Malachi* (VTSup 52; Leiden, 1994), 106–22 (with full coverage also of the secondary literature). If he is right in his conclusion that it was legally valid, but not regarded as ideal, it will only strengthen the emphasis on the desperate situation of the women in this verse. Similarly, his suggestion that it was largely restricted in practice to the highest social classes would fit with the view that the women here are those of high standing whose position has been dramatically reversed.

though the loss of many eligible men in battle might have made this demographically desirable. There is no direct reference to this law here (the vocabulary is different in each case[13]), but it serves well to illustrate the desperation to which these women have been reduced. Their concern is not for the material protection which marriage normally brought (though how they would be able to support themselves is not stated; we must assume that they were members of the upper economic stratum), but purely for their social status. They could not face the *disgrace* of being single. In return for what they regarded as the honour of marriage, they were therefore offering the man something for nothing (note that there is no reference to foregoing the 'marital rights' of Exod. 21.10). The reversal of v. 16 is obvious: there, their wealth and position put them in the driving seat, but here they are reduced to something little short of cheap prostitution.

Let your name be pronounced over us: this has nothing to do with the wife taking the husband's name, as in much Western culture; the wife's name as such did not change upon marriage in ancient Israel, and surnames in the sense that we have them were not used. Rather, from the not infrequent occurrence of this idiom elsewhere, it is clear that it relates primarily to ownership, with the attendant responsibility of protection (see, for instance, 2 Sam. 12.28; other passages, most of which are metaphorical for divine ownership, are listed at BDB, 896A).[14] It is generally held that it was a legal formula used in the transfer of property and that the proclamation of the husband's name over the bride concluded the marriage ceremony.[15] Since this is an inference from passages such as the present one (I am not aware of any external evidence), the danger of circular argumentation is obvious, however attractive it may be. The more important consequence is that by passing into her new husband's ownership the woman is no longer independent, but has attendant legal rights in society, a secured position in the order of things.

Disgrace (חרפה), whether justified or not (so that 'reproach' is often considered to be a better equivalent), could be the result of many situations, so that the context has in each case to determine its cause.[16] The obvious factors here will be widowhood and childlessness, both of which are characterized as a disgrace elsewhere; see Isa. 54.4 for the former, and Gen. 30.23 (with אסף, as here) for the latter; although the word itself does not occur there, the opening of 1 Samuel 1 is a classic example of the latter, with Hannah suffering what to our way of thinking was totally unjustified abuse. Yet the pressure of societal norms and

---

[13] The same vocabulary as our verse appears in Deut. 10.18, with reference to general provision for 'the stranger'.

[14] Cf. C. J. Labuschagne, *THAT* ii. 671 = *TLOT* iii. 1162; F. L. Hossfeld and H. Lamberty-Zielinski, *ThWAT* vii. 142–43 = *TDOT* xiii. 131–32. As so often, S. R. Driver already said more or less all that needs to be said; cf. *A Critical and Exegetical Commentary on Deuteronomy* (ICC; 3rd edn; Edinburgh 1902), 306.

[15] Cf. Boecker, *Redeformen des Rechtslebens*, 167–68; slightly differently K. Galling, 'Die Ausrufung des Namens als Rechtsakt in Israel', *TLZ* 81 (1956), 65–70.

[16] Cf. E. Kutsch, *ThWAT* iii. 227–28 = *TDOT* v. 213–14.

expectations is so strong, as anthropological studies of honour and of 'shame cultures' have demonstrated, that we can well understand how humiliated these women felt[17]—exactly the reverse, therefore, of their superior pride in 3.16.[18] As already noted, Deutero-Isaiah makes a good deal of elements of both widowhood and childlessness in his picture of the restoration of Zion (he does not refer to the situation of individual women), and the renaming of the city and its community is a frequent element in Trito-Isaiah. The paragraph which follows here, however, takes a different approach to restoration, though it is also one which has echoes in the later part of the book.

[17] Cf. Stiebert, *Construction of Shame*, 90, who allows that this passage may be the sole exception to her otherwise well-taken critique of the application of this anthropological model to Isaiah.

[18] There is an interesting comparison of this last line to be made with Jer. 15.16 and 20.8. In the first passage, Jeremiah recalls what delight he once took in God's word, and part of this was because God's name had been proclaimed over him. In the second passage, however, he complains that he is being persecuted, 'for the word of the Lord has become for me a reproach (חרפה) and derision'. This reinforces the opposition between the two elements. For further suggestive reflections, see W. L. Holladay, *Jeremiah 1* (Philadelphia, 1986), 458–59.

ZION'S FINAL GLORY
(4.2-6)

[2]On that day the vegetation of the Lord shall be beautiful and glorious,
    and the fruit of the land shall be the pride and finery for those of Israel
    who have escaped.
[3]And it shall come to pass that whoever is left in Zion and remains in
Jerusalem will be called holy, everyone who has been written down for life
in Jerusalem. [4]When the Lord has washed away the filth of the daughters
of Zion and has rinsed away the blood shed in Jerusalem from its midst by
a spirit of judgment and a spirit of destruction, [5]then the Lord will create
over the whole site of Mount Zion and over its assemblies a cloud by day
and smoke and the brightness of a flaming fire by night; for over everything Glory will be a canopy [6]and a booth. And it will serve as a shade by
day from the heat and as a refuge and shelter from the storm and rain.

2. צמח: the common translation 'branch' is certainly mistaken, as has been most recently
demonstrated by the full and thorough analysis of Rose.[1] As was correctly noted by
several scholars before him, צמח grows directly out of the ground, not from some other
plant or tree (see, for instance Isa. 61.11 and Gen. 19.25).

פליטה is strictly an abstract noun, 'escape', but here as frequently elsewhere it is used
with reference to those who have escaped.

ישראל: 1QIsaᵃ adds ויהודה, making for a combination which appears nowhere else in the
book of Isaiah. It is not attested in any of the other ancient witnesses and is doubtless an
explanatory addition in the light of the following verse (and more remotely 2.1 and 3.1).[2]

The LXX goes its own way in the rendering of this verse: τῇ δὲ ἡμέρᾳ ἐκείνῃ
ἐπιλάμψει ὁ θεὸς ἐν βουλῇ μετὰ δόξης ἐπὶ τῆς γῆς τοῦ ὑψῶσαι καὶ δοξάσαι τὸ
καταλειφθὲν τοῦ Ισραηλ. We note first that, against MT, the verse is joined to the
preceding by the use of δέ; this is probably related to the lack of a rendering of ביום ההוא
there (see the notes on 4.1 above). Turning then to the more significant deviations, it is, of
course, *possible* that in place of צמח in the translator's *Vorlage* there was some form of
חצח (presumably יצח), since צחו is rendered by ἔλαμψαν at Lam. 4.7 (cf. Ottley; Gray),
and that this then necessitated a free rendering later in the verse. More likely, however, he
had the same consonantal text as MT, and, given the rather odd expression צמה יהוה, he
took צמה יהיה as an auxiliary verb with participle, the latter being understood on the basis
of one of its meanings in Aramaic, 'to shine' (for the latter point, see Ziegler, 107;
HUBP). יהוה was then naturally construed as the subject. Such a 'theophanic' rendering
will have seemed appropriate in view of vv. 5-6 following, and, as Ziegler, 108, observes,
μετὰ δόξης (here, slightly freely for ולכבוד) also occurs in the context of theophanies at
30.27 and 33.17.[3] Whether by this stage the translator was simply obliged to render ופרי
הארץ with ἐπὶ τῆς γῆς in order to make sense (so HUBP) or whether he (mis)read the
words as הארץ פני (על) (so Ziegler) is impossible to tell. This leaves only the rendering of

---

[1] W. H. Rose, *Zemah and Zerubbabel: Messianic Expectations in the Early Postexilic
Period* (JSOTSup 304; Sheffield, 2000), 91–106. He includes a full survey of previous
discussions.
[2] Rubinstein, 'Theological Aspect', 188, further draws attention to parallels in 5.7 and
37.31.
[3] See too Brockington, 'Greek Translator', 28–29.

לצבי by ἐν βουλῇ to be accounted for. Here, two points need to be noted. First, the translator may have been influenced to see a reference to God's plan or counsel by his firm belief that the advent of God is 'the eventual realization of a Plan which has been in existence since time immemorial';[4] see, for instance, the renderings at 14.25-27; 25.1, 7; 37.26. Secondly, this favourite theme of his will have been suggested by the similarity with Aramaic צבא (rendered with ἠβούλετο at Dan. 5.19, as noted by Ziegler[5]). In sum, although LXX departs significantly from MT, it can all be explained on the basis that the translator was working within the parameters of the language as he understood it at the time and that he was making intelligent use of the immediate context of the verse within the overarching framework of his presupposed theological outlook as known from elsewhere. There is no point at which we are obliged to postulate a different *Vorlage*.

3. יאמר...והיה: for the sequence, see GK §112*y* (and cf. 2.2; 3.24 above), and cf. Driver, *Tenses* §121, Obs. 1. 1QIsaᵃ's ויהיה is a clear example of the linguistically later use of the *waw*-conjunctive + imperfect (so not apocopated, of course);[6] for the many other examples of this phenomenon in the scroll, see Kutscher, 357.

4. אם: since the condition is regarded as certain, it is best rendered 'when'; cf. BDB, 50; JM §167*p*; König and others compare 6.11; 28.25 etc., and German 'wenn'. While it is true that the protasis occasionally follows its apodosis (for examples, see GK §159*n*, n. 1), so that some commentators have proposed that this verse should be regarded as the direct continuation of v. 3 (e.g. Hitzig, Alexander, Dillmann, Marti, Beuken; so already LXX ὅτι; cf. RV, NRSV), to construe it so here would be awkward following the ביום ההוא of v. 2 (pleonasm; so König). Feldmann adds the observation that the subject of v. 3 already implies its own condition. According to Sweeney, *Isaiah 1–4*, 159 n. 143, 'temporal or conditional clauses introduced by *ʾim* are always used as protases... When a temporal clause follows a statement, it generally uses *ᵃšaer* or *bᵉ* plus infinitive construct.'

רחץ: for this as an equivalent of the future perfect, see GK §106*o*; Gibson, 67.

בנות: in view of the extent to which this passage draws expressly on the language of the preceding paragraphs (see below, and for this phrase cf. 3.16 and 17), there is no need to emend to בת (*contra* Feldmann, Procksch, Fohrer). Nor is it advisable to try to find some kind of rhythmic pattern in these verses and so to delete the word altogether (so Marti and Gray). LXX expands to τῶν υἱῶν καὶ τῶν θυγατέρων, probably an interpretation by the translator in the light of such passages as 43.6; 49.22; 56.5; 60.4, all of which look forward, as does our verse, to the time of restoration. Similarly, at 45.11 he expanded על־בני to περὶ τῶν υἱῶν μου καὶ περὶ τῶν θυγατέρων μου.

דמי: see on 1.15 for the force of the plural of דם.

ירושלם is not represented in the LXX, no doubt because it was considered redundant following 'Zion'. Ziegler, 51–52, lists a large number of passages where similarly a synonymous word in parallel is not translated. As a consequence, מקרבה had to be rendered ἐκ μέσου αὐτῶν.

ידיח: though this precisely matches רחץ syntactically, it is noteworthy that it has slipped over into the imperfect, which can itself occasionally serve as an equivalent for the future perfect (cf. Gibson, 77). As noted by GK §107*l*, exactly the same thing happens at 6.11.

ברוח משפט: Tur-Sinai's proposed emendation (164) to בדוח משטף, 'by a purge of ablution', is neither necessary nor textually justified.

בער: for this use of the infinitive, see GK §113*e*. Most of the versions and English translations render 'burning', which is admittedly the commonest meaning of this root. It makes poor sense here, however, after רחץ, 'wash away', and הדיח, 'rinse away'. In any

---

[4] Seeligmann, 110, and p. 116 for the connection with 4.2; see too van der Kooij, 43.

[5] The occurrence of ἐν βουλῇ (as a rendering of בסוד) in a theophanic context at Ps. 88 (89).7 (Ziegler, 108, followed by HUBP) is interesting, but seems too remote.

[6] For a different explanation (which embraces differences in the 'tenses' elsewhere in this chapter as well), see Lipiński, 'De la réforme d'Esdras'. His theory as a whole is questionable, however (see below), and in this particular case does not seem to be superior to the usual explanation offered above.

case, since this is clearly another example of our passage drawing on the preceding material, it is preferable to give it the same meaning as at 3.14; see the note there for further discussion. T's גמירא may be a move in this direction. 1QIsaᵃ reads סער. Kutscher, 269, and Wildberger both think that the copyist may have found בער difficult, and so was influenced by the stereotypical phrase רוח סערה (Ezek. 1.4; 13.11, 13; Pss. 107.25; 148.8). The possibility of mechanical scribal error should not be ruled out, however.

5. ובָרָא יהוה: for the first word, 1QIsaᵃ has ויברא; see on v. 3 above. MT's sequence is unexceptional; cf. GK §112gg. LXX renders these two words καὶ ἥξει καὶ ἔσται, which might represent ובא והיה. Wildberger is right to point out that if only the first word of this reading is adopted (following Duhm and Condamin[7]) we should expect the preposition ב before עשן, עגן and נגה later in the verse ('He will come with…'), but this does not apply if both words are emended, and this was therefore favoured by Marti explicitly in order to overcome the difficulty which Duhm's proposal engendered (so too BHS). If either reading is therefore possible, it is necessary to ask which is more likely to have arisen secondarily, and here the finger of suspicion must point towards LXX. On the one hand, MT is unusual, in that there is no precise parallel for the use of ברא with such objects, even though it is perfectly intelligible in itself; it may therefore be regarded as the harder reading. On the other hand, there is good reason to suppose that the LXX might have been motivated to introduce its slight change: Ziegler, 108, reminds us that already in v. 2 the translator moved strongly in the direction of introducing theophanic language into his rendering (see the discussion above), and the present rendering is in line with this.[8] On both counts, therefore, it is easier to see how LXX might have developed from a *Vorlage* similar to MT than the reverse.

ועל־מקראה: while it is possible that כל has been lost by haplography following על, one should hesitate before citing LXX in support: καὶ πάντα τὰ περικύκλῳ αὐτῆς. Following the recasting of the opening words of the verse,[9] the translator was obliged to omit על, and this may have led him to misread or to interpret it as כל. There is no other textual evidence to favour the change. For the defective spelling of the plural of the noun, see GK §91k (not surprisingly, some mss read מקראיה). Whether the singular was originally intended is impossible now to tell; if it was, it might have carried the sense 'place of assembly', parallel with מכון.

יומם: 1QIsaᵃ moves straight to מחרב in v. 6. Since this immediately follows another occurrence of יומם, this is most probably to be explained as a straightforward case of the scribe's eye jumping from one יומם to the other. (4QIsaᵃ attests the missing material.) In the face of such an obvious explanation, Lipiński's suggestion, 'De la réforme d'Esdras', that it was deliberately omitted due to a belief that there will be no night in the eschatological Jerusalem seems perverse, and in any case does not account for the full extent of the omission: why was the text not resumed after לילה?

לילה: 4QIsaᵃ is damaged at this point. The first ל is clear (see Plate I, fragment 4), and the editors state that 'the second letter is a virtually certain *zayin*'. The remainder being lost, they suggest perhaps restoring לזהר on the basis of Ezek. 8.2. The possibility of following MT's לילה is ruled out on the ground that the top of the second ל would be visible; but given that they also state that 'some of the surface has flaked off the top of the third and the fourth letters', it is clear that one cannot be certain. On the Plate this flaking is presumably what shows up as a lighter patch. While admittedly this does not extend quite as high as the tops of the other לs in this line, it may be sufficient to conclude that we should reserve judgment.

---

[7] See too Cheyne, *Book*, 82; Wade; H. W. Hertzberg, *Beiträge zur Traditionsgeschichte und Theologie des Alten Testaments* (Göttingen, 1962), 76; Clements.

[8] For 'coming' as the first element in descriptions of theophanies, see F. Schnutenhaus, 'Das Kommen und Erscheinen Gottes im Alten Testament', ZAW 76 (1964), 1–22, and Jeremias, *Theophanie*, 7–10, 56–66.

[9] Note also the addition of σκιάσει following, which Koenig, 53–55, traces to influence from the Greek text of Exod. 40.29 (Heb. 40.35). Goshen-Gottstein, 'Theory and Practice', 141–43, also finds influence on the rendering of מקרא from Ps. 97.2.

5b-6. This passage is uncertain. MT appears to state 'for over all [the] glory [there will be] a canopy; it [feminine, so perhaps Zion] will serve as a booth for shade by day…'. This should be explained on the basis of Exod. 40.34, where the glory of the Lord filled the tabernacle (here Zion) and where the cloud overshadowed the tabernacle. This is a possible rendering, and has been supported with only minor variations by, for instance, Dillmann, Delitzsch, Duhm, Feldmann, Auvray, and Beuken. There are, however, a number of small difficulties in this approach, none decisive in itself, but sufficient cumulatively to raise doubt as to whether this can have been the original meaning. (i) חפה and סכה are close in meaning, come next to each other in the text (which leads to slightly awkward word order at the start of v. 6), and have only a single equivalent in the LXX (which it renders as a passive [pual?] verb, σκεπασθήσεται[10]); there is thus a possibility that they should be taken together as a pair, against the current verse division, and even that one may have originated as an explanatory gloss on the other. (ii) The absolute use of כבוד is striking (contrast Exod. 40.34, כבוד יהוה); if it refers to the state of restored Zion, a feminine suffix would certainly be expected, and if it refers to God himself, as in the Exodus parallel, it could hardly be qualified by כל־. There are two interesting parallels, both in late material included in the first part of Isaiah (11.10; 24.23), which might support the view that this occurrence too should be taken absolutely (i.e. separately from כל־) as a reference to the visible manifestation of God.[11] (iii) In the light of the development of the theme of the glory of God elsewhere in the book of Isaiah, the notion that it should be overshadowed seems improbable. Rather, we expect it to be highly visible, with nothing 'higher' than it (e.g. 40.5; 60.2 [וכבודו עליך יראה]; 62.2; 66.18). While there is thus a clear allusion to the imagery of Exodus 40, we should allow that there may also be an element of development from it as well. For such reasons it has long been proposed[12] that כל should be read as a noun in the absolute state (as frequently elsewhere; cf. BDB, 482B–83A), and the passage rendered 'for over everything Glory will be a canopy (and a booth)'. It then becomes necessary to read והיה in place of תהיה, with the support of LXX καὶ ἔσται; the error would presumably have arisen once וסכה had been separated from what precedes (so Marti and Gray). Neither interpretation of this passage is self-authenticating, and the issue remains finely balanced; it may even be that there is some more deep-rooted disturbance here than our evidence allows us to detect (so Wildberger). I have hesitantly followed the second approach.

יומם is not translated by the LXX and has no corresponding לילה as it does in v. 5; many therefore delete. It must, at least, have entered the text sufficiently early to give rise to the lacuna in 1QIsaᵃ. If the passage grew incrementally through the work of various editors, rather than having been composed as a unity from the start (see below), then the use of such a resumptive catchword would not be unexpected.

---

[10] It may be noted that in an apparent reference to this verse (though in a very different context) Ben Sira also construed the word as a verb: ms B, וכן כל כבוד חפתה; Masada Scroll, חפתה […]כ כל ועל; cf. Beentjes, *Ben Sira*, 160. It is difficult to know how much weight to put upon this for text-critical purposes. The suggestion that חפה is a verb (so Gesenius and Knobel) has generally been dismissed, though it has been unexpectedly favoured again in more recent times by Barthélemy; see too Barth, 40 n. 136. The consequence that כבוד is here used in a 'profane' sense ('wealth') seems highly improbable in the context.

[11] See the discussion in my essay 'From One Degree of Glory to Another', 189–94. This use of the word as a substitute for the divine name is attested as early as Ben Sira, whose date may not be so far removed from that of these late additions in Isaiah; cf. J. K. Aitken, 'The Semantics of "Glory" in Ben Sira—Traces of a Development in Post-Biblical Hebrew?', in T. Muraoka and J. F. Elwolde (eds), *Sirach, Scrolls, and Sages: Proceedings of a Second International Symposium on the Hebrew of the Dead Sea Scrolls, Ben Sira, and the Mishnah* (STDJ 33; Leiden, 1999), 1–24.

[12] Since Clericus (1731), according to Barthélemy; see too Houbigant, Lowth, Marti, Gray, Wade.

This passage functions effectively as a climactic conclusion to the whole section comprising Isaiah 2–4.[13] In the commentary following, examples will be given where the thought and in particular the language indicate that it was written consciously to fulfil this aim. The heading to the whole indicated that the focus is on Judah and Jerusalem, and this was repeated at 3.1. In the vision of 2.2-4, the prospect was held out that Zion, the mountain of the Lord, would in a future day be the centre for God's universal purposes of peace and well-being among the nations. What followed indicated, however, that she was not in any condition to undertake this role, and indeed would have to pass through judgment as a consequence. At an earlier stage in the redactional process, this was interpreted in terms of the fall of Jerusalem, but the present paragraph looks beyond that to the time of restoration. The introductory 'On that day' connects with the repeated use of the same phrase earlier, but indicates that judgment is only a preparatory stage. For the remnant who survive, there will still be a need for cleansing, but after that the Lord's protection will be extended over Zion, and his glory will be openly seen there. When that day comes, we are obviously intended to infer, the vision of 2.2-4 will be ready for realization.

This synchronic reading does not necessarily entail the consequence that 4.2-6 was all written at the same time by the same author. Provided it is accepted that any who added to it did so in consciousness of what precedes, then a proposal that the passage grew in incremental stages remains as feasible an option as the suggestion that it was a unity from the start.[14] The case has to be determined on internal grounds and on its own merits. The opinion that it did, in fact, develop over time has been held by many commentators, despite the fact that they differ over details.[15]

In the first place, v. 2 is often regarded as an isolated fragment, separate from what follows. In support of this view, it should be noted that it can certainly be construed as poetic, whereas the following verses are definitely prose (so Wildberger, *contra* Procksch), that it has a rather different subject matter from the remainder, which concentrates on purification, and

[13] Magonet, 'Isaiah 2:1–4:6', finds 'a concentric pattern that has been used editorially to relate the different passages in this section to one another and thus create a unified whole' (p. 84). Less specifically, many commentators recognize that our passage functions as a 'bookend' with 2.2-4 around the judgment sayings which come in between.

[14] In addition to conservative scholars, who ascribe the whole to Isaiah himself, see, for instance, Duhm (who dates it in the second century); Marti; König; Feldmann; Fohrer; Berges, 84; Gosse, 'Isaïe 4,2-6'. Reference should also be made at this point to the study of Cazelles, 'Quelques questions'. Unlike most critical commentators, who so to speak divide the passage horizontally, he attempts to find an Isaianic core throughout these verses, based on what he takes to be elements which fit with royal ideology as attested at various periods during Isaiah's ministry, and then finds post-exilic elements spliced vertically throughout the chapter. It is not clear to me, however, that this is an appropriate way to approach the passage. Its thought and language throughout seem to belong firmly in the post-exilic period, as the commentary will show.

[15] Little seems to be gained by the occasional suggestion of an older generation of commentators (e.g. B. Stade, 'Miscellen', *ZAW* 4 [1884], 149–59; Budde) to transpose the order of some of the verses.

that it refers to 'those of Israel who have escaped' rather than Zion and Jerusalem.[16] The verse could have had an independent existence in some wider context elsewhere, and then been moved secondarily to its present position; we have seen examples, not least in the immediately preceding verses, of just this sort of process in the development of the book. More likely, in my opinion, is the view that it was written for its present setting in the early post-exilic period when the restoration was more focused on national rather than the later cultic concerns. It was thus a relatively early move towards the kind of interpretation of this section of the book as a whole outlined above, and it not unnaturally gave rise to later expansion in the following verses to take account of the way in which the post-exilic community developed its sense of identity and self-awareness.

It is less easy to decide whether v. 3 then followed as an isolated addition (Vermeylen) or whether vv. 3-5a belonged together from the start (Wildberger). The subject matter and focus of attention certainly differ, though not necessarily in a way which suggests that they could not have been penned by a single author. The issue is thus best left undecided. If v. 3 is closest in thought to Trito-Isaiah (see the commentary below), whose date is contested, then 4-5a seem closer in outlook to the strong emphasis on purity which developed in the middle of the Persian period with the reforms of Ezra and Nehemiah. This does not, of course, preclude them from being dated later.

Verses 5b-6a and 6b certainly have the appearance of being two short later expansions, developing and explaining aspects of the immediately preceding imagery (so even such cautious commentators as Dillmann and Condamin). The use of 6b in 25.4-5, however, indicates that they cannot have been added too long after the previous verses.

2. The introductory *on that day* has run through the preceding chapters ever since its forceful introduction at 2.12, and thus far has accordingly referred to the day of God's judgment (most recently at 4.1). Now suddenly it is turned to announce the coming of the day of salvation with its reversal of the previous state of loss. It is clearly not used in a strictly chronological sense, therefore, for the days in question do not coincide but rather follow in sequence. The same is true of its use at 28.5-6, with which our passage has a number of close parallels (see below). It refers simply to the indefinite future when God will intervene in the affairs of his people's history, and its specific place in the scenario envisaged has to be inferred from the wider context.

The vegetation of the Lord is an admittedly inelegant rendering, designed to ensure that consequences are not illegitimately drawn from reflections on the significance of the usual English rendering 'branch'. In my view, this skews Nielsen's interpretation of this passage throughout (pp. 180–87), such as when she associates the image with the references to trees in 2.13 or other tree imagery elsewhere in Isaiah (e.g. 6.13; 11.1). While there is legitimate ground for debate about the word's significance

[16] So Hausmann, *Israels Rest*, 142; Sweeney.

in the present context, that debate should not be coloured by the fact that elsewhere trees are sometimes used with reference to leaders or kings.

The word צמח is clearly used with royal or messianic implications at Jer. 23.5; 33.15; Zech. 3.8; 6.12. It is thus not surprising that the Targum should have seen a reference to the messiah in our verse (cf. Chilton, 'Two in One', 550–51). In this it was followed by Kimhi and by many commentators since, down to the present day.[17] Following on from this, *the fruit of the land* was interpreted as a reference to those who keep the law; Rashi and Ibn Ezra, by contrast, thought that צמח itself referred to the righteous remnant (see too Mauchline), and Goldingay points to the comparable imagery at 37.31 ('take root downward and bear fruit upward') in defence of a similar view: 'the people will flourish once more'. That either phrase should refer to the remnant seems to be excluded by the last words of the verse, however, where the vegetation and fruit will serve as pride and finery *for* those of Israel who have escaped.[18] In order to avoid this problem while still adhering to a messianic interpretation for צמח, it has therefore occasionally been pointed out that times of godly kingship are depicted as being accompanied by natural fruitfulness (e.g. Ps. 72).[19] Thus our verse is thought to anticipate the period of the messiah (צמח) which will be accompanied by prosperity (פרי).

The alternative, and nowadays much more common, approach interprets the phrase as a reference to what God will make to grow in the natural realm.[20] It is pointed out in particular that this is on any showing the easiest way to understand 'the fruit of the land', and that our phrase is in parallel with it and so should be understood similarly; it would be harsh to switch from a metaphorical to a literal meaning of two similar words in parallel. This, of course, is the usual meaning of צמח (e.g. Gen. 19.25; Ezek. 16.7), and is attested within the book of Isaiah itself (61.11).[21] Given

[17] Prominent examples include Vitringa; Lowth; Delitzsch; Young (with reference to 2 Sam. 23.5); J. G. Baldwin, 'Ṣemaḥ as a Technical Term in the Prophets', *VT* 14 (1964), 93–97; Wiklander, 192–94; Motyer. Against the Targum's interpretation of 'the fruit of the land', many of these commentators argue that this too refers to the messiah, suggesting, for instance, that the two phrases refer respectively to his divine and human ancestry.

[18] Contrast Vermeylen, 154, who writes 'Sans doute faut-il lire dans le même sense la première partie du même v. 2'. Roberts, 'The Meaning of "צמח ה'"', makes a brave attempt to circumvent this difficulty, though I remain unpersuaded. Gesenius and Knobel limit this final phrase to 'the fruit of the land', so that צמח יהוה can still refer to the revival of the people, but this seems quite unjustified in the light of the close parallelism between the two halves of the verse, in this case particularly לנאן ולתפארת and לצבי ולכבוד. What qualifies one pair must also qualify the other; see further Dillmann.

[19] Cf. Nielsen, 184–85; Laato, *About Zion*, 76.

[20] E.g. Calvin; Hitzig; Dillmann; Duhm; Marti; Gray; Wade; Procksch; Kissane; Rehm, *Der königliche Messias*, 253–56; Wildberger; Kaiser; Schoors; Auvray; Clements; Höffken; Tucker. König broadly supports this approach, but in the light of the contextual demand that this passage reverses the preceding judgment he interprets it as 'alles…was der Gott der speziellen Heilsgeschichte sprossen läßt, um die von ihm abirrende Menschheit zu sich zurückzuführen'; similarly von Orelli; Feldmann.

[21] Cf. H. Ringgren, *ThWAT* vi. 1068–72 = *TDOT* xii. 409–13; Rose, *Zemah* (above, n. 1), 91–120.

the absence of a clear indicator of a metaphorical application (such as 'for David' in Jer. 23.5; 33.15), one should naturally assume that this is its meaning here too.

Those who favour a messianic interpretation point to a number of special features of the present passage which, they think, makes a natural interpretation less likely. In fact, while they are correct in their initial observations, closer consideration of them can in my view help us to a better understanding of the passage even without an appeal to the presence of the messiah. Two points deserve attention in this regard.

First, it has been claimed that a reference to natural growth is unsuitable in the wider context which goes on to speak of the purification of the inhabitants of Jerusalem and of the glory of God's presence there; something less banal than a reference to fertility is required. This objection fails to take into account either the preceding context or the wider depiction of the age of salvation in the prophets generally. On the one hand, as part of a passage which is deliberately reversing the previous description of judgment, fertility may be regarded as very much to the point (*contra* Roberts, 'The Meaning of "צמח ה"'). The scenes of deprivation in 3.1–4.1 conjure up a picture of the land being completely devastated and deprived of labourers (see especially 3.6-7; 3.25–4.1). In such circumstances, an abundance of provision is the expected converse and it signifies God's blessing in a clear manner. Calvin (who interestingly claims to have pondered and then rejected the messianic interpretation) comments aptly that this growth signifies 'an unusual and abundant supply of grace, which will relieve the hungry; for he speaks as if the earth, barren and exhausted after the desolation, would hold out no promise of future produce, in order that the sudden fertility might render the kindness of God the more desirable; as if the parched and barren fields would yield unexpected herbage'.[22] On the other hand, the fertility of the land is a standard element in prophetic depictions of the coming era of salvation. The closing verses of the book of Amos are only the best known example of this, and many more examples could be added; Wildberger, for instance, cites Isa. 30.23ff.; 41.17-20; Jer. 31.12; Ezek. 34.29; Zech. 9.16-17; Mal. 3.11. One could further add Hos. 2.23-24; Joel 2.18-27; 4.18, and so on, as well as the observation that fertility features prominently as a sign of the blessings of obedience to the covenant in Lev. 26.3-13 and Deut. 28.1-14. Bearing in mind the possibility that vv. 3-6 may have been added subsequently to the composition of v. 2 (see above), v. 2 taken on its own seems in this light to be an entirely satisfactory response to and reversal of all that precedes.

Secondly, the particular combination צמח יהוה is not attested elsewhere and is sometimes thought to be unsuitable as a designation for natural growth. Indeed, at the closely comparable 28.5, it is the Lord himself who will be 'a garland of glory, and a diadem of beauty, to the remnant of his people'. We therefore expect a personal rather than a material point of reference in the present context. In response, it may be suggested that this

---

[22] Professor G. I. Davies has suggested to me that the emphasis might be rather on 'a "rural theology" antithesis to the urban elite's focus on luxury goods'.

points us to an important aspect of what is being said, and that the unique turn of phrase indeed leads us to expect something out of the ordinary. But this is not to point us to some other figure, the messiah, but rather to the direct and personal involvement of the Lord himself in the anticipated blessing of provision. Of course, there is a sense in which all growth is due ultimately to God's providence (see especially Gen. 2.9; Pss. 104.14; 147.8; Job 38.27, each of which uses the hiph'il of the verb צמח with God as subject), but here the point seems to be even stronger: God will personally attend to the tangible blessings of the restored remnant.

The fruit of the land is to be understood as closely parallel. The phrase itself is common (cf. Num. 13.26; Deut. 1.25, etc.), and will here have been preferred over the similarly common פרי האדמה, 'fruit of the ground', in order to emphasize that this will be an element of the national restoration. Wildberger is right to point to the comparable טוב הארץ in 1.19.

The effects of this bounty on the restored remnant are described by four terms. Though they are distributed in two pairs over the parallel cola, they should not be separated from each other; they each refer equally to both the *vegetation* and the *fruit*, even as the latter two terms present two expressions for a single entity. The first two terms (lit., 'for beauty and for glory') may be taken in a general sense, before greater specificity is added with the second pair by way of their allusion to the preceding material. While צבי can be used straightforwardly of decoration (e.g. 28.1, 4), it is in fact more commonly used metaphorically with reference to countries or cities as that which brings respect and prestige among the nations (e.g. positively of Israel in Jer. 3.19; Ezek. 20.6; negatively of Babylon in Isa. 13.19; of Tyre in 23.9; of the cities of Moab in Ezek. 25.9). Its meaning therefore moves in the direction of 'honour, renown' (see especially 24.16), and that is no doubt the case here too in view of its collocation with כבוד, 'glory'. The point, then, is that from a situation of devastation and shame, the land will once again assume a position of universal recognition and honour. Although there is no direct verbal link,[23] it is reasonable, in view of the position of this passage in its wider context, to see this as a move towards the situation envisaged for Zion in 2.2-4; it establishes the necessary conditions which will attract the nations in the first place.

The second pair of words draws our verse more directly into the world of the previous passage. *Pride* was one of the major terms by which the unassailable sovereignty of the Lord was emphasized in ch. 2 (cf. vv. 10, 19, 21, there as part of the phrase translated 'glorious majesty'). In view of the fact that in ch. 2 all human pride (hubris) was to be brought low, it is clear that here it indicates that the restored community will share in or reflect the majesty of God himself. By contrast, *finery*, which comes at the climax of this list, was the term used in 3.17 as the summarizing introductory word in the list of women's ornamentation. Such human efforts at

---

[23] The 'glory' of Jerusalem becomes, of course, a prominent feature of the hopes expressed in the final part of the book of Isaiah as a whole, and our verse is sufficiently late to allow for conscious anticipation of that theme here; see my essay 'From One Degree of Glory to Another'.

making oneself the object of attention will be removed in order now to be replaced by an adornment which can come only from God himself. The reversal of the previous judgment is thus unmistakable. While it is noteworthy that several of these four words come together in other passages, so that an element of stereotyping may be accepted (e.g. 13.19; 28.1-6), the context in which they are used here invests them with more than conventional significance.

All this is said to be for the benefit of *those of Israel who have escaped*.[24] Rather like with שריד at 1.9, the verb 'to escape' and nouns derived from it[25] can refer to escape from any kind of disaster (e.g. Gen. 45.7; Exod. 10.5; Joel 2.3), military defeat being not surprisingly the most frequently attested (for the noun used in the present verse, see for instance Gen. 32.9; Judg. 21.17; 2 Sam. 15.14; Jer. 50.29). Since God's judgment has previously been presented in terms of military defeat (3.25), it might be supposed that this is sufficient to explain the choice of word here. It is clear, however, that by the post-exilic period the word had also come to acquire the kind of overtones which we tend to associate with the theological notion of a 'remnant'. Even though the Judean community had not itself experienced defeat, they regarded themselves not just as the descendants of those who had but as those who in a very real sense were still suffering the consequences.[26] According to circumstances, one might then either make reference to the situation with gratitude for the fact of survival or with a tone of regret over the fact that things were still in a parlous condition (see, for instance, variously Ezra 9.8, 13-15 and Neh. 1.2). Needless to say, the former sentiment is uppermost here. Finally, beyond even this connection with escape from battle, at Joel 3.5 (where the word is in fact parallel with שריד) and Obad. 17 it refers to those who escape an entirely eschatological judgment of God without reference to human agents. In such contexts the idea of 'escape' is concentrated on the saving grace of God towards his favoured community. Our verse (and cf. 10.20) is often linked with these other passages. Although we have already noted that the preceding context does not require this fully developed sense, it can also be seen how it could well have been so understood once v. 3 had been added to it. The use of *Israel* in this setting, which both before and after concentrates rather on Judah and Jerusalem, further strengthens this conclusion. While it may have focused more on political concerns if v. 2 indeed originally stood alone, it clearly came to be understood as fully ideological or religious once it was read in combination with v. 3.[27]

3. It is clear that *whoever is left* (הנשאר)...*and remains* (הנותר) refers to the remnant in a fully developed theological sense (contrast 1.8-9). They

[24] Hausmann, *Israels Rest*, 142, notes that there is a closely parallel pairing of fruitfulness and remnant at Zech. 8.12.

[25] Cf. G. Hasel, *ThWAT* vi. 589–606 = *TDOT* xi. 551–67; E. Ruprecht, *THAT* ii. 420–27 = *TLOT* ii. 986–90.

[26] Cf. M. A. Knibb, 'The Exile in the Literature of the Intertestamental Period', *Heythrop Journal* 17 (1976), 253–72.

[27] Contrast Cazelles, 'Quelques questions', who seeks an original form of this chapter in the period following the fall of the northern kingdom.

are not just those who have survived some military or other natural disaster, but are those who have been singled out for survival and restoration by the grace of God.[28] This emphasis is indicated in a minor way by the references to *Zion* and *Jerusalem*, inasmuch as this suggests a concentration on the (post-exilic) temple-based community rather than the political entity which would have included the designation 'Judah', as in 2.1 and 3.1. This therefore continues the thought of the previous verse, even though expressed with the use of alternative terms.

The technical sense of remnant is made even clearer, however, by the added explanation at the end of the verse: *everyone who has been written down for life in Jerusalem*. The notion that God has a record or book regarding people and their deeds is frequently attested in the ancient Near East, the Hebrew Bible and later Jewish and Christian writings.[29] Since metaphorical language about God generally derives from some human counterpart, the notion is most probably to be related to registers of citizens on the one hand and to royal memorial records of deeds on the other. Given that both aspects can be found in their divine counterparts, it seems unnecessary to try to find a single point of origin to cover every type of reference. Limiting ourselves to the Hebrew Bible, the royal 'book of remembrance' of Esth. 6.1 has its counterpart in Mal. 3.16, where the loyalty of God's servants is recorded (see too Isa. 65.6; Pss. 56.9; 87.6; Dan. 7.10), while the listing of citizens or the like in Ezra 2; Neh. 7; 11; 12.22-23, for instance, seems to give a closer parallel for the idea that God has a list of his people, as in Exod. 32.32-33 (see too Isa. 34.16-17; Ps. 69.29; Dan. 12.1).[30] The usage in our verse seems to fall into this latter category, and so points to election of individuals by grace alone, rather than on the basis of desert. *Life* in this context refers to living in the enjoyment of God's blessing in this world (*in Jerusalem*), of course, although in later writers it was frequently applied to life after death.

Those who make up this remnant *will be called holy*. As was stressed at 1.26 above, the renaming of the eschatological Zion and its inhabitants is a characteristic of the last part of the book of Isaiah, and indeed the name to be given here has an exact parallel at 62.12: 'They shall be called "The Holy People, the Redeemed of the Lord"'. As Wildberger observes, people are never called holy in the sayings of the eighth-century prophet, that title being reserved exclusively for God himself, 'the Holy One of Israel'. As in v. 2, therefore, a characteristic which is previously considered to have been God's exclusive prerogative is now shared with the eschatological community (cf. the Holiness Code's 'You shall be holy, for I the Lord your God am holy', Lev. 19.2). Of course, there is a hint that purification will need first to be effected, and this is developed further in

---

[28] For discussion, see Hasel, *The Remnant*, 257–70; Hausmann, *Israels Rest*, 141–44; Pfaff, *Restgedankens*, 48–53; Werner, *Eschatologische Texte*, 91–100.

[29] In addition to the commentaries, see the surveys in S. M. Paul, 'Heavenly Tablets and the Book of Life', *JANES* 5 (1973), 345–53; W. Herrmann, 'Das Buch des Lebens', *Das Altertum* 20 (1974), 3–10, both with further literature.

[30] Other references, which cannot be so easily categorized, include Jer. 22.30; Ezek. 13.9; Ps. 139.16; Dan 10.21.

the next verse, but the positive emphasis should not be overlooked: they are to be a community wholly set apart for the Lord, with all that that entails in terms of what formerly was narrowly priestly service. Only then will the saying of Exod. 19.6 be fully realized: 'You shall be for me a priestly kingdom and a holy nation'. This theme is also close to the world of Trito-Isaiah: 'You shall be called the priests of the Lord, you shall be named ministers of our God' (Isa. 61.6).

4. This verse describes the purification which is necessary before the final manifestation of God's glory in the restored community in v. 5. We have already noted some indications of a particularly priestly outlook in the previous verse, and that is developed further here.

Filth (צאה) refers to human excrement generally (including vomit, according to 28.8); see Q at 36.12. By an intelligible development, it can then also refer to moral guilt (Prov. 30.12). The parallel with *blood (shed)* might favour that same sense here, though the wider context perhaps suggests that ritual defilement is also included. The reference to *the daughters of Zion* is undoubtedly inspired in particular by 3.16-17 (and note that it is parallel with *Jerusalem*, which by synecdoche refers to all the inhabitants of the city), so that there is no necessarily restricted reference to menstrual blood, as has sometimes been supposed, even though, as something which renders unclean (Lev. 15.19-30), that may also be included. Similarly, *blood* may be taken in a general sense covering both ethical (so usually) and ritual (Lev. 17.4) failure (Wildberger); see especially Ezek. 22.2-4. A specific reference to the bloodshed which caused the exile (Gray, with reference to 2 Kgs 21.16; 24.3-4, etc.) again seems unnecessarily restricted.

The use of the verb רחץ, *wash away*, for the removal of such defilement arises naturally from the choice of the word *filth* (so also at Prov. 30.12; note how this same consideration also accounted for its use at 1.16), and it is hardly surprising that it is also characteristic of much priestly ritual. The parallel verb דוח, *rinse away*, is far less common, occurring elsewhere in connection with the rinsing of sacrificial animals (Ezek. 40.38; 2 Chron. 4.6).

The language of the verse thus far, when taken altogether, suggests that the writer has drawn on language which is influenced by cultic usage (and this may reflect his own background) though in ways which imply a wider application. The means by which God will effect this purification certainly supports this wider view.

The precise force of the repeated word *spirit* is disputed. While there have always been some who have seen here a direct reference to the personal Spirit of God (e.g. Dillmann; Delitzsch; Gray; Skinner; Young; Wildberger; Kaiser; Motyer), others favour a reference to the wind (e.g. von Orelli; Wade; Auvray; Clements; Blenkinsopp, who suggestively draws attention especially to the combination of wind and fire in 66.15-16) or to God's impersonal power.[31] Oswalt takes this latter line to its extreme, and with justification, by referring to a number of other passages in Isaiah

---

[31] See especially Ma, *Until the Spirit Comes*, 138–39: 'The reference here is entirely impersonal, and the spirit is viewed as a divine force to execute Yahweh's purifying will'.

which have a similar construction: 'a spirit of confusion' (19.14), 'a spirit of judgment' (28.6), 'a spirit of deep sleep' (29.10), and 'a spirit in him, so that he shall hear a rumour' (37.7). Of these, particular attention should be paid to 28.5-6, since we have already noted several connections between that passage and ours and 28.6 uses the identical phrase to the first of the pair here. The parallels in 28.5-6 are instructive: God will be 'a garland of glory…a diadem of beauty…a spirit of justice…and strength'. In this context, רוח can hardly be either the personal Spirit of God or the wind. Oswalt may be slightly reductionist in his claim that on this basis 'it would be appropriate to translate "through the process of burning and judgment"', but his main point seems compelling.

Judgment (משפט) and *destruction* (בער) both occur in 3.14, and it seems likely that their use here is a further indication of how 4.2-6 reflects a conscious development and reversal of the preceding material. The first term indicates continuity with what is stated there, and may be understood in a general way,[32] whereas the second indicates reversal, a typical feature of the prophetic understanding of judgment.[33] Just as some sections of the population had 'destroyed the vineyard', so they, or at least their evil, would now in turn be subject to destruction (for this sense, cf. Deut 13.6). It is clear from the wider context, of course, that this is not the total judgment and destruction which was characteristic of eighth-century prophecy, but rather the purging or refining of a community which had already been chosen by God (the remnant), something which became the dominant understanding of how he would deal with his people in the post-exilic period. It thus becomes possible to see how, within chs 2–4, Isaiah's prophecy of judgment was reinterpreted first by an exilic redactor in terms of the events of 587 BCE and later by a post-exilic writer in terms of purifying refinement.

5a. Once this purification has taken place, Zion will be in a fit state to enjoy the benefit of protection by the overshadowing presence of God himself.

The description of God's protection as *a cloud by day and smoke and the brightness of a flaming fire by night* derives from the period of the wilderness wanderings. In Exod. 13.21-22 and 14.19-20 these phenomena appear in the form of a pillar (עמוד, not attested in the present passage) to guide the Israelites forward and to protect them from the pursuing Egyptians. This material, probably to be ascribed to J, was already familiar to Deutero-Isaiah (e.g. 52.12) as he developed the theme of the return from exile as a second exodus. In the Priestly material, however, the notion is extended to refer also to the visible presence of God, resting on the desert sanctuary, the tabernacle (see especially Exod. 40.34-38; Num. 17.7, also

---

[32] Lipiński, 'De la réforme d'Esdras', refers this process to Ezra's settlement of the issue of mixed marriages in Ezra 9–10, but there is no obvious connection between the two passages. His suggestion that אדני in our verse is a reference to Ezra himself, on the basis of Ezra 10.3, is fanciful. Vermeylen, 154, adds the consideration that the final part of the verse can scarcely be applied to Ezra.

[33] Cf. P. D. Miller, *Sin and Judgment in the Prophets: A Stylistic and Theological Analysis* (SBLMS 27; Chico, Calif., 1982).

without mention of the עמוד). In this material, God's presence is also described as his 'glory', which of course indicates that we are moving in circles close to those represented in Ezekiel's understanding of the Jerusalem temple, both past and future (e.g. Ezek. 9.3; 10.4, 18; 11.23; 43.2, 4). This development of the basic theme was certainly known to Trito-Isaiah, who exploits it at 58.8 in his explicit interpretation of 52.12 while at the same time extending the covering of God's glory to Jerusalem as a whole rather than exclusively to the sanctuary (60.1-2; 62.2; 66.18-20). The present verse stands at or after this final development of the theme.[34] Zion as a whole will stand under God's protection, now making explicit reference to the cloud and fire in this connection for the first time (though Lowth compares Zech. 2.5), and what started out as a temporary measure for the duration of the wilderness wanderings has now become a permanent feature of the eschatological community; see especially Vollmer, 176–77.

The use of the verb *create* (ברא) to describe the inauguration of this protection is striking.[35] Its application to the coming era of salvation is at its most prominent in Deutero-Isaiah, which probably inspired our author. It is of importance especially in indicating that the cloud and fire are not to be identified with God himself. In the translation tentatively supported above, he appears later and separately as an overarching presence.

The locus of this protection is described unusually as *the whole site* (מכון) *of Mount Zion*. Although, as Blenkinsopp points out, this word can be used for 'the dwelling of the deity either in the sky (1 Kgs 8:39-49; Ps. 33:14) or in the sanctuary (Exod. 15:17; 1 Kgs 8:18;[36] Ezra 2:68)', it has probably been chosen here as a deliberate echo of 2.2, where 'the *mountain* of the Lord will be *established* (נכון)'. If so, it reinforces the conclusion that 4.2-6 presages the fulfilment of the opening vision in 2.2-4. It is, in addition, difficult to be certain whether מקראה should be rendered 'its place of assembly' (which would be an easier parallel with 'site') or *its assemblies* (which corresponds more closely with the usual meaning of the word; cf. 1.13). Either way, the point is made that Zion is being regarded as a religious centre, and once again it fits suitably with the vision in 2.2-4, even though the precise word is not found there.

5b-6a. The text of this sentence is difficult, and no interpretation can therefore be more than tentative. Following the translation defended above, *Glory* overshadows even the protective shield of cloud and fire. This may best be understood as a reference to God himself, a notion that seems to find a parallel in 11.10 and 24.23. The possibility that all three passages

---

[34] Wildberger argues that descriptions of theophanies based on the Sinai event have also been integrated. The more elaborate description of 'smoke and the brightness of a flaming fire' may justify this, though it seems to bear more on the language of the passage than its underlying thought. It would be appropriate at the conclusion of chs 2–4 as a whole, given the link with 2.2-4 in particular.

[35] For a suggestion that its focus is on God's 'sovereign power and control', see S. Lee, 'Power not Novelty: The Connotations of ברא in the Hebrew Bible', in A. G. Auld (ed.), *Understanding Poets and Prophets: Essays in Honour of George Wishart Anderson* (JSOTSup 152; Sheffield, 1993), 199–212.

[36] *Sic*; the reference should be 8.13. One might also add Dan. 8.11.

(which it is agreed are of late origin) are thus redactional additions to their contexts cannot be ruled out. If this approach is correct, our verse marks a culmination of the theme of glory which can be traced throughout the book of Isaiah.[37]

The shelter is described as a *canopy* (חפה) *and a booth* (סכה). While the former is used elsewhere with reference to the chamber of a bridegroom (Ps. 19.6) or bride (Joel 2.16), it seems doubtful whether any such allusion is present here. Indeed, there is a possibility that the word originally stood here alone, and that as it developed the more specific meaning, the commoner word *booth* (see on 1.8) was added to guard against misunderstanding. At any rate, it is difficult to see any significant difference between the sense of the two words in the present context.

6b. At first sight, the last sentence of the chapter seems to pick up the imagery which precedes and to apply it in a very literalistic fashion to protection from inclement weather. That the sentence has been added later is probable, given the repetition, in a manner familiar from such later additions, of the word *by day* (יומם) from v. 5. That it is meant to be taken literalistically is less certain, however. The language is stereotypical, and occurs relatively frequently elsewhere in the Hebrew Bible (e.g. in the Psalms), not least in Isaiah. The use of bad weather as a metaphor for threat occurs, for instance, at 28.2, 17 and 30.30. More significantly, the imagery of shelter from such storms, with some of the same vocabulary, occurs in 32.2, where it refers to human rulers. If there is a conscious allusion, then the point being made here is that God himself will henceforth guard his people, and one may suppose he will do so more effectively than Israel's former leaders. Furthermore, our verse seems in turn to have inspired 25.4-5, where the same language is again used, but this time to speak of God's defence of the poor and needy.[38] It thus looks as though the metaphorical interpretation was understood from early times.

---

[37] See my essay 'From One Degree of Glory to Another' for fuller details.

[38] Cf. M. A. Sweeney, 'Textual Citations in Isaiah 24–27: Toward an Understanding of the Redactional Function of Chapters 24–27 in the Book of Isaiah', *JBL* 107 (1988), 39–52 (45–46), where he finds a universalistic interpretation, the poor and needy belonging to all peoples, not just Zion; D. Rudman, 'Midrash in the Isaiah Apocalypse', *ZAW* 112 (2000), 404–8.

THE SONG OF THE VINEYARD
(5.1-7)

[5.1]I will sing for my dear friend a song about my intimate friend
concerning his vineyard:
> My dear friend had a vineyard
>> on a very fertile ridge.

[2]He dug it thoroughly and cleared it of stones
>> and planted it with choice vines;
> he built a tower in the middle of it
>> and also hewed out a winepress in it;
> he expected it to yield grapes,
>> but it yielded diseased grapes.

[3]And now, inhabitants of Jerusalem
> and men of Judah,
please judge between me
> and my vineyard.

[4]What more should have been done for my vineyard
> that I did not do in it?
Why, when I expected it to yield grapes,
> did it yield diseased grapes?

[5]Well, now I will tell you
> what I am about to do to my vineyard:
I shall remove its hedge so that it will be destroyed,
>> I shall break down its wall so that it will be trampled down,
>>> [6]with the result that I shall make an end of it.
It will not be pruned or hoed any more,
> but it will be overgrown with briers and thorns;
and I shall command the clouds
> not to let any rain fall upon it.

[7]For the vineyard of the Lord of Hosts
> is the house of Israel,
and the people of Judah
> are the planting in which he took delight.
He expected justice,
> but found only bloodshed,
righteousness,
> but heard only a cry of distress.

1. אשׁירה נא: for the use of the cohortative with נא (for the daghesh, see GK §20*c*; the word
is lacking in 1QIsa^a) to express a statement of determination, see GK §108*b*; Gibson, 82
(where this verse would be better included under the first category—where 'the speaker is
free' and expresses intention or resolve—than the second—where 'he is dependent on
others' and so expresses a wish or entreaty, as Gibson supposes).[1] JM §114*d* categorizes
as 'resolution' (which is acceptable) but renders 'I want to sing' (which is not); see too
אודיעה־נא in v. 5.

---

[1] See too E. Jenni, 'Untersuchungen zum hebräischen Kohortativ', *ZAH* 15/16 (2002–
2003), 19–67 (50).

לידידי: the force of the preposition is ambiguous and, within certain limits, must be contextually determined. Despite the versions, Jerome and Luther, it is unlikely to mean 'to', because in v. 2 the friend is referred to in the third person.[2] 'For' = 'on behalf of' and 'about, concerning' are both possible. If לכרמו at the end of the line means 'concerning his vineyard', as seems probable,[3] then 'for' is more natural here.[4] This is the rendering emphatically preferred by Rashi (תחת ידידי ובמקומו ובשליחותו), who compares Exod. 14.14, and by Ibn Ezra (בעבור), who compares Gen. 20.13.

שירת דודי: although there is no textual evidence for any change, this phrase has elicited much discussion. Assuming that דוד can mean (intimate) friend without any necessary sexual element (although that is admittedly present in some passages; see below), as argued most recently and fully by Emerton, 'Translation', then there is no problem about seeing the word as an alternative (and presumably a stylistic variant) to ידידי; P in fact renders with the same word, and LXX uses a close synonym. In the following lines, what seems to be the song itself is recorded with reference to the friend in the third person, and this is clearly awkward if 'my intimate friend's song' means that he is its author. Emerton rejects attempts to solve this problem by emendation or repointing,[5] such as דודים, 'song of loves' (abstract plural, i.e. love-song: Lowth, who compares שיר ידידת at Ps. 45.1; Cheyne, Book, 83),[6] דודיו (Houbigant, with similar sense), דּוֹדִי, 'my love-song',[7] or דּוֹדִי (construct in prepositional phrase, Condamin), to say nothing of more radical proposals such as Gunkel's ריבו, 'his legal suit'.[8] Instead, he follows Hitzig and Knobel in reading as an objective genitive: 'a song about my friend' (see too Fohrer and Childs, though without comment; he has been explicitly followed by Irsigler, 'Speech Acts', and Weren, 'Use'). His case may in fact be strengthened by the observation that in the only other two places where שירה occurs in the construct it also clearly has the meaning 'song(s) about', not 'by'; cf. Isa. 23.15; Amos 8.3. Virtually the same applies to the commoner masculine form שיר: where it occurs in the construct, the following noun is nearly always objective in some sense, such as 'the Lord's song', 'a song for the dedication of the temple' and so on (cf. Ezek. 33.22 [if the text is sound]; Ps. 30.1; the headings to Pss. 120–34; 137.3, 4; Neh. 12.46; 1 Chron. 6.16; 2 Chron. 29.27); Ps. 45.1 and Ct. 1.1 are uncertain, but certainly do not denote authorship; Neh. 12.36, 1 Chron. 16.42 and 2 Chron. 7.6 refer to musical instruments; thus only Eccl. 7.5 is subjective. Blenkinsopp's objection to Emerton that his proposal 'is syntactically anomalous' is thus wide of the mark. Bjørndalen, Untersuchungen, 250–55, follows Kissane in dismissing this possibility on the ground that we should have expected שירת דודי וכרמו, but this is to introduce a slightly different sense. The focus of the song, as its continuation in the first person in vv. 3-6 makes clear, is the friend in relation to his vineyard, not the friend and the vineyard equally, as Kissane's

---

[2] Contra B. Stade, 'Zu Jes. 3, 1.17.24…', ZAW 26 (1906), 129–41 (134–35), who then has conjecturally to emend לידידי to לדודי in the next line in order to make his interpretation work.

[3] Pace Bartelmus, 'Beobachtungen', 62, who argues that following אשירה the preposition should mean 'to' (though he does not explain why this applies to לכרמו but not to לידידי). He admits that there is an awkwardness here, however: 'selbst wenn er zunächst nicht persönlich, sondern nur neutral in der 3. Pers. angesprochen wird'. For a good parallel to counter-balance Bartelmus's examples, see 27.2 (as noted already by Gesenius).

[4] See Willis, 'Genre'. The alternative is favoured by P. A. H. de Boer, 'Cantate Domino: An Erroneous Dative?', OTS 21 (1981), 55–67 (61–62).

[5] Detailed objections to such emendations are also entered by König and Bjørndalen, Untersuchungen, 250–55; see too Bathélemy, 30–31.

[6] Blenkinsopp ('my love song'), Brueggemann ('my love-song') and by implication Sweeney ('he will sing of his friend's love for a vineyard', p. 123) seem to suggest that דוד can itself have this abstract meaning, but they do not justify the implication, and I know of no evidence to support it, pace RSV, NRSV, etc.; see earlier Bentzen, 'Erläuterung'.

[7] Cersoy, 'L'apologue', followed by Marti, Budde, 54, and NEB (cf. Brockington, 176).

[8] H. Gunkel, Das Märchen im Alten Testament (Tübingen, 1917), 26–28 (repr., Frankfurt am Main, 1987, 38).

objection implies. Bjørndalen makes a fair point about the integral connection between vv. 1*b*-2 and 3-6 (where the friend indeed takes up the speech in the first person),[9] but that still does not overcome the disjunction between the two lines of v. 1 if the genitive is subjective, as even he is forced eventually to concede ('Man muß anerkennen, daß die Einleitung nich *ganz* genau auf den poetischen Text abgestimmt ist', 255; see too Tromp, 'Un démasquage graduel'). Nor is there any evidence to suggest that vv. 1*b*-2 are the singer's own rewording of what he had first heard the friend sing (Dillmann).[10]

לכרמו: LXX τῷ ἀμπελῶνί μου. The use of the first person here is isolated among the textual witnesses but sustained in the verbs of the following verse in the LXX. (T also uses first person verbs in v. 2, but follows MT at this point in v. 1.) It is not clear whether this is due to the translator's sensitivity to the awkwardness discussed in the preceding note, but if so he has not carried it through consistently (thereby showing that it is a secondary interpretation rather than a witness to an earlier Hebrew text), since he retained the first clause of the next line ('My beloved had a vineyard') which hardly fits with the use of 'my vineyard' in v. 1*a*. Gray toys with going even further and overcoming this difficulty by conjecturally emending לידידי in 1*b* to לי (he thinks that MT might have arisen by corruption 'under the influence of the same word in the previous line'—and we may note that we have come across this type of error elsewhere in Isaiah; cf. 1.7 etc.), but in the end even he holds back. He is right to do so: not only is the textual evidence slim in the extreme, but to introduce the speaker as the owner of the vineyard from the start would ruin part of the passage's major rhetorical effect (see also Willis, 'Genre', 340–41).

קרן, 'horn', does not occur elsewhere with the topographical sense which it apparently must have here. LXX and V both render with what were ultimately Indo-European cognates of the Semitic form,[11] namely κέρατι and *cornu* (though LXX then shows it understands correctly by continuing ἐν τόπῳ πίονι), while P simply uses the Syriac cognate, qrn². T stands at the head of the usual exegetical tradition with בטור רם, 'in a lofty mountain', followed by Kimhi and Ibn Ezra. Something of that sort is clearly meant, though the precise nuance escapes us. Budde, 55, has attracted some support (e.g. Wildberger) for his opinion that vineyards are not usually on a hilltop, so that 'spur', 'ridge' is better than 'hill', whereas Kedar-Kopfstein (see n. 11) thinks 'favoured corner, nook' is preferable. Comparable metaphorical uses in related languages such as Arabic (Gesenius; Gray) and others (Kedar-Kopfstein) are likely independently reached and so cannot give certain guidance. Its use here may have been determined by the desire for alliterative effect with כרם (similar alliteration is used to brilliant effect in v. 7, of course, as well as elsewhere; cf. Lys, 'La vigne', and Korpel, 'Literary Genre'); were there sexual overtones to the vineyard image, as usually thought, there could also be an intention to maintain an element of *double entendre*, but this whole approach will be questioned below.

בן־שמן: for the construction (ב denoting a particular characteristic), see GK §128*v*; BDB, 121B.

2. עזק is a *hapax legomenon*, but known from Post-Biblical Hebrew[12] and Arabic,[13] and cf. P, 'dig, cultivate'. LXX φραγμὸν and V *sepivit* (Jerome *sepsit*), followed by Ibn

---

[9] Willis's position, 'Genre', 343, is similar.

[10] Similarly, Schottroff, 'Das Weinberglied', toys with the idea that 1*b*-2 is the narrator's own exposition of the situation so that the audience will understand what they need to know when the 'song of the friend' is taken up for the first time in v. 3. Going even further, the suggestion of D. L. Petersen and K. H. Richards, *Interpreting Hebrew Poetry* (Minneapolis, 1992), 82–83, that the song begins only at v. 3 (with 1*b*-2 as part of the introduction), is unlikely. Whereas v. 1*b* is a suitable opening, 3*a* is clearly dependent upon what precedes (ותתה).

[11] Cf. B. Kedar-Koppfstein, *ThWAT* vii. 181–89 = *TDOT* xiii. 167–74.

[12] To references long known may now be added the occurrence at 1QH 8.22, where it has פלגים, 'ditches, channels', as its object, so that 'dig' is likely.

[13] Cf. F. E. Greenspahn, *Hapax Legomena in Biblical Hebrew: A Study of the Phenomenon and its Treatment Since Antiquity with Special Reference to Verbal Forms*

Ezra (who claims Arabic support), Luther and AV, 'he fenced it', evidently did not recognize the word and deduced from v. 5 what they thought it must mean (cf. Ziegler, 137–38). Though paraphrasing, T's וקדישׁתנון, 'and I sanctified them', may well reflect a similar understanding (by way of separation). Borowski, *Agriculture*, 104, objects to 'dig' that it cannot precede the removal of stones; he therefore suggests that it refers to the removal of the ʿajjaq-bush (which commonly grows in the Judean mountains). This seems less secure etymologically, however, and in any case may rest on a misunderstanding: digging would be necessary in order to get at some of the stones that were to be removed, while in practice digging and removing stones were probably undertaken together rather than sequentially.

ויסקלהו: a presumed denominative privative pi'el (GK §52*h*; WO, 412 n. 47); see especially 62.10, where the addition of מאבן puts the meaning beyond doubt. LXX translated correctly there, but curiously here either did not recognize the word without the accompanying אבן or was further influenced by v. 5 (which speaks of both a hedge and a wall) in rendering ἐχαράκωσα, 'and I fenced it'. Both here and with the previous verb Ziegler, 179, finds that in addition to v. 5 the translator will have been influenced by his knowledge of current viticultural terminology, as revealed in contemporary papyri.

ויטעהו שׁרק: in traditional parlance the verb governs a double accusative; cf. GK §117*ee*; WO, 175; to the same effect, Gibson, 144, explains it more satisfactorily as an adverbial use of the noun. שׁרק occurs elsewhere only at Jer. 2.21, though related terms are found also at Gen. 49.11 and Isa. 16.8. In every case a type of vine seems to be intended. At Zech. 1.8 שׂרקים is a colour term, and on the basis especially of Gen. 49.11 it seems to be some kind of red; for this there is further etymological support (cf. Brenner, *Colour Terms*, 114–15). It seems unlikely, however, that colour is particularly significant here, since all wine prior to the Hellenistic period in Israel was red.[14] There is also a place name, נחל שׁרק, Judg. 16.4, and one may speculate that originally the word denoted a species of vine which originated there or was characteristic of the region; that would seem to have been the understanding of LXX, ἄμπελον σωρηχ (*contra* Seeligmann, 33 and 59, who thinks rather that ἄμπελον has been added secondarily). However, there seems to have been a tendency for such place names to develop a superlative sense for the best in its class (e.g. gold of Ophir, cows of Bashan) and such may have been the case here too. In that case, the rendering 'choice vine' might be justified. It would find further support from the context both here and in Jeremiah, in both of which it seems to be contrasted with something of lesser quality.

 וגם־יקב: Budde's proposed emendation (p. 55) to וגם ויקב is rightly rejected by Wildberger. On the LXX rendering here, see Ziegler, 179.

ויקו לעשׂות: despite Driver's protestations[15] it remains easiest to assume that there is a change of subject between the finite verb and the infinitive following: 'he expected *it* to yield...'; cf. GK §114*m*; changes of subject with the infinitive in somewhat similar semantic contexts may be found, for instance, at Ps. 101.6 and especially 104.27. There is then no need to seek an alternative root עשׂה either here or in v. 4; for עשׂה = 'yield', see the many examples at BDB, 794B (2). Still less is there any ground for detecting scribal expansion (Haupt, 'Parable', 198)!

באשׁים: LXX ἀκάνθας, 'thorns', is wide of the mark and seems once again to come from consideration of the consequences later in the passage, this time in v. 6. P חרובא, 'carob pods' (see on 1.20), seems likewise to assert that the vine simply produced the wrong sort of fruit. Usually the word is rendered 'wild grapes', following V *labruscas*, but here Driver is probably right to object that 'a cultivated plant cannot produce wild fruit' (p. 53

(SBLDS 74; Chico, Calif., 1984), 89 (on p. 146 he notes C. Rabin, *Ancient West-Arabian* [London, 1951], 28, as 'the sole dissenter', comparing the Himyaritic dialect [Yemen] ʿazīqa, 'plain', to give something like 'he levelled it').

[14] See Walsh, *Fruit*, 106–10, *contra* Borowski, *Agriculture*, 104.

[15] Driver, 'Difficult Words', 53–55; but cf. D. W. Thomas, 'Translating the Hebrew ʿāsāh', *The Bible Translator* 17 (1966), 190–93.

n. 6),[16] while Walsh, *Fruit*, 89, adds that if these were wild grapes the owner would have planted the wrong vines: 'Much, if not all, the prophetic sting is lost if Yahweh planted one kind of vines and then expected them to yield some other kind of grape. He becomes an ignorant or sadistic vintner, an unlikely subtheme to Isaiah's Yahwistic theology.' Rather, from the root באש, 'have a bad smell, stink', we may derive the idea of diseased (and hence rotting) grapes (Walsh suggests 'fetid fruit'); following the careful study of Byington,[17] Driver notes α's rendering σαπρίας, 'rottenness', in support; Blenkinsopp compares 1QH 8.25, but the context there (עצי באושים) is insufficiently specific to help here.

3. יושב: 1QIsaᵃ has וישבי (and cf. LXX), which is equally possible, and an error either way before the *yōd* of ירושלם would be understandable. The singular is not infrequently used as a collective (e.g. Gen. 4.20; 34.30; 50.11), but it remains marginally the harder reading while being stylistically attractive with the parallel collective איש and should therefore be preferred.[18] For both this and the following variant, Bjørndalen, *Untersuchungen*, 248, suspects influence on the Greek translator from Jer. 4.4; while that is possible, it does not account for the agreement on this point but not the following one with 1QIsaᵃ.

יושב ירושלם ואיש יהודה: LXX inverts the order of these two phrases: ἄνθρωπος τοῦ Ιουδα καὶ οἱ ἐνοικοῦντες ἐν Ιερουσαλημ; see also P (in which this order is standard, however; note that P also makes both elements plural). Unless this is the result of mechanical error,[19] the translator has assimilated to later preference in this matter (see the discussion at 1.1), which is a small pointer to the pre-exilic origin of the formulation in MT.

4. מה־לעשות: for the construction, see GK §114*k*, and for the gerundive use of the infinitive construct, see Gibson, 131–32. The expression is deliberately impersonal in this first half of the line in order to emphasize that the owner had done everything possible (what more could anyone have done that I did not do?), *contra* WO, 609–10.

לכרמי...בו: there is uncertainty about the prepositions here. 1QIsaᵃ achieves consistency by reading the first as בכרמי, whereas the versions translate the second as though it were ל, and some Hebrew manuscripts actually have לו. Wildberger favours this latter on the ground that a copyist made the error because he did not realize that the vineyard is a metaphor for wife, but that is misguided: whatever the interpretation of the vineyard, at this point we are still living in the world of the imagery, and in v. 2 the owner undertook his work for the vineyard 'in' it (בתוכו and בו). It is likely that the versions have rendered under the influence of the parallel לכרמי, so that we cannot be sure which preposition stood in their *Vorlage*. Textual assimilation to the nearer לכרמי by the mss which read לו rather than to the more distant v. 2 by MT is also a more likely source of scribal error. Conversely, were 1QIsaᵃ correct in its reading, it would be difficult to understand where or why the ל had entered the textual tradition at all. בכרמי remains a textually isolated reading, and Pulikottil, 50–51, may be right in including it with other cases of harmonization in the scroll: he finds influence from v. 2 here as well. One may note in further support of MT that לכרמי also follows עשה in the next verse.

מדוע: when an interrogative governs two co-ordinate clauses, the first is subordinate and the second is, properly speaking, the one to which the interrogative applies; cf. GK §150*m*; JM §161*k*.

קויתי לעשות: see on v. 2 above.

---

[16] Note the difference with Jer. 2.21, where a genuine vine (זרע אמת) was planted, but a wild vine (גפן נכריה) grew instead.

[17] S. T. Byington, 'Hebrew Marginalia III', *JBL* 64 (1945), 339–55 (341–43).

[18] Chaney, 'Whose Sour Grapes?', argues to the contrary that these singulars refer to the king, or at any rate the ruling elite. He accepts that the collective interpretation is grammatically possible, however, so that his interpretation depends upon prior agreement with his wider theory about the passage, which is not convincing; see the exegesis of v. 7.

[19] There is some inner-Greek confusion on this matter, the B text, for instance, following the same order as MT. It is not wholly clear whether this reflects later correction towards MT; the Old Latin witnesses seem to follow the majority LXX reading; cf. Haelewyck, 'La cantique de la vigne'.

ויעש: 1QIsaᵃ וישה. Wildberger suggests that the scroll may represent וישא, since at Ezek. 17.8 (and cf. 36.8 and Ps. 72.3) נשא פרי means 'bear fruit' (in view of v. 2 this would still not be a superior reading, of course). But in fact it is far more likely to be an alternative spelling of ויעש. In v. 2, the scroll spelling was ויעשה,[20] which accounts for the final letter, and elsewhere we find that ע is frequently weakened to א (see ואתה for ועתה in the next verse!) or even dropped altogether (cf. Kutscher, 57 and 505–10). Indeed, the very spelling וישה recurs at 48.14 (for MT יעשה) in a context where נשא is inconceivable.

5. עשה: the participle is often used to describe imminent action; cf. Driver, *Tenses* §135 (3); GK §116*p*; JM §121*e*.

הסר: 1QIsaᵃ אסיר. The *yōd* suggests that this is a first person singular imperfect hiph'il rather than a simple orthographic variant, despite the fact that the weakening of ה to א is otherwise common (Kutscher, 506). Given the decline in use of the infinitive absolute in the post-biblical period, it is probable that the scribe simply wrote *ad sensum*.[21]

פרץ...הסר: the use of the infinitive absolute for the finite verb is well attested, but its precise function here is most likely dependent upon אני עשה just preceding, almost as an object, either directly (so GK §113*d*; Marti) or as an apposition to the object introduced by את (so König, *Syntax* §400*d*).

משוכתו: the Masoretes clearly thought that the root was שכך, as the daghesh shows; cf. GK §9*o* for other examples of the use of *waw* in this position. However, it remains unusual, so that others prefer the spelling without daghesh, hence from the root שוך (as at Prov. 15.19; Mic. 7.4 has מסוכה, and given the interchange of ס and שׂ in the case of both roots, this is likely the same word). Both derivations give rise to the sense of hedge, either as brushwood woven together or as something which encloses and shuts in.

והיה: 'the *wəqataltí* construction can represent a situation consequent to that envisioned by the infinitive absolute... These sentences could also be classified as apodoses because the leading situation usually implies the condition for the subsequent situation' (WO, 538); hence 'so that it will...'.

לבער: for discussion of this word, see on 3.14. There too it has vineyard as its object, so the meaning is likely to be the same in each passage; the popular rendering here, 'devour, graze', is thus improbable, and while 'burn' would not be impossible (governing 'hedge'; cf. Bartelt, 127), it would be less suitable there, and should probably not be adopted here either; the parallelism in fact strongly suggests that we should mentally supply vineyard as the object, so that 'destroy' is the only realistic rendering. LXX has εἰς διαρπαγήν, 'for plunder', and the other versions are similar: V *in direptionem*, P *lbwz* and T לבז (1QIsaᵃ = MT, though without the ל). Our initial thought would be that this is strong evidence for a variant reading (not necessarily superior, of course), presumably לבז. Troxel, 'Economic Plunder', 387–90, argues differently, however. He first shows that LXX Isaiah never renders בז in this way, despite its relatively frequent occurrence in the book. He then suggests that the renderings in the other versions can all be independently explained (V may derive from LXX via the Old Latin; T and P both have exegetical reasons in their own contexts for their rendering, e.g. T has already abandoned the vineyard imagery and resumed talking about God's people, so that a literal rendering of בער would not be appropriate. We may add that for some reason P has reordered some items in this passage, so that the fence appears in v. 2 and the tower here—and there are limits to what one can do to a tower). Against Ziegler, 180, he then aligns the rendering in LXX here with others he has examined where the translator has shown a particular interest in the plunder

---

[20] It is well known that the scroll frequently differs from MT over the use of the *waw*-consecutive with both *qatal* and *yiqtol* forms and with regard to the so-called 'shortened imperfect'. These features are fully in evidence in the present passage; in addition to vv. 2 and 4, see also v. 5 (ויהיה for והיה, twice); in addition to Kutscher, 328 and 350–58, cf. A. Schüle, 'Deutung und Neugestaltung: Althebräische Grammatik in alttestamentlichen Texten', *ZDPV* 116 (2000), 14–25, with particular attention to Isa. 5.1-7 on 17–18.

[21] See too Høgenhaven, 'First Isaiah Scroll', 22, who speaks of 'syntactical simplification'. Bartelt, 127, inexplicably treats אסיר as if it were the scroll's reading for נדרו.

of the people through taxation, which he believes to have been a matter of concern in the translator's own Seleucid days. This theme is clearest in the rendering of 3.12-15, and in that context 'pillage' (ἁρπαγή) occurs as a rendering of גזלה immediately after what Troxel takes to be a reference to burning the vineyard which, as we have seen, is the same fate as in our verse. The translator has therefore introduced the idea of plunder here too 'under the influence of the theme of economic plunder and under the impress of 3,14 in particular' (p. 389). Troxel's arguments against LXX attesting a *Vorlage* including לבו are convincing, though it remains hard to believe that all the versions have arrived at the same rendering independently. While that is possible for T, for the reasons given, it seems more probable that not only V, but also P, has been influenced by LXX.[22]

והיה למרמס :4QpIsa[b] has ויהי, and 1QIsa[a] has ויהיה both here and earlier in the line, where the *pesher* text is lost. While the Isaiah scroll reading is probably just one of the many instances where the distinctive *waw*-consecutive form of MT is lost in the direction of later linguistic convention (cf. Kutscher, 357), this hardly seems possible as an explanation of the *pesher* text. Perhaps it has historicized this prediction of future judgment; unfortunately what is preserved of the passage is too fragmentary to be sure.[23]

6. ואשיתהו בתה: the simple *waw* with imperfect indicates purpose or result; this is only one of the factors which indicates that this first clause really belongs with what precedes as a climax (see further below). The general sense of the *hapax legomenon* בתה, evident from the context, has never been seriously in doubt, though there is no agreement about its etymology or whether emendation is required. LXX ἀνήσω τὸν ἀμπελῶνά μου, 'I will abandon/leave untilled my vineyard', is clearly a contextual rendering, combining deductions from the following clause with consideration of the preceding verse which indicates that the vineyard will become a place for animals; cf. Ziegler, 179–80. There is no basis here for emendation (*pace* Budde, 57, who proposes ואשבית כרמי). T ואשוינון רטישין, 'and I will make them (to be) banished', is also influenced by the context, since as we have already seen in T's paraphrase the imagery of the vineyard has long since been referred explicitly to the people. V *desertam* and P *nḥrb* are closer to the mark, and the main medieval commentators follow suit, all glossing the word with שממה, 'desolation', and referring to בתות in 7.19. This latter point has then become the basis for much traditional lexicography. The vocalization בָּתּוֹת indicates the root בתת, which on the basis of Arabic means 'to cut off'. 7.19 may then mean 'cut-off places', i.e. 'precipices', while here it would signify rather 'something cut off', i.e. 'end, destruction'. Some then favour vocalizing בָּתָּה in consequence (most recently Grätz[24] and Beuken), though others such as Hitzig and Dillmann (see too BDB, 144B) think that the Masoretes have vocalized by analogy with the similar כָּלָה (cf. כלה עשה, 'to make an end', in 10.23; alternatively, one might consider that the Masoretes wanted to distinguish the two different meanings of the same word, or that they had an ע"וי form—בות—in mind; cf. König, *Lehrgebäude* §80). As the climax of a string of 2-beat cola (see below) this seems to give good sense.[25] (The alternative etymology proposed by Driver, who here renders 'ruin', founders on the fact that according to the recent Akkadian Lexica there is no such word as *batū*, 'destroy'.[26] If he

[22] For examples of this elsewhere, see van der Kooij, 287–89. For an authoritative discussion of the relation of P and LXX, see M. P. Weitzman, *The Syriac Version of the Old Testament: An Introduction* (UCOP 56; Cambridge, 1999), 68–86.

[23] Note that in the next verse Allegro, *Cave 4*, 15, read יעלה, but Horgan, *Pesharim*, 90, maintains that this would be better read as יעלה, with MT.

[24] S. Grätz, *Der strafende Wettergott: Erwägungen zur Traditionsgeschichte des Adad-Fluchs im Alten Orient und im Alten Testament* (BBB 114; Bodenheim, 1998), 177–79.

[25] *Contra* Gray, who argues rather that the phrase should be interpreted in the light of the following clauses. They, however, clearly have their parallel in the clause which follows them; note too that the conjunction joins the first clause of the verse with what precedes, whereas the lack of it at the start of the next clause (*pace* 1QIsa[a]) indicates a break.

[26] Driver, 'Linguistic and Textual Problems', 38, followed by, for instance, Wildberger, Clements, Watts and Oswalt. Blenkinsopp also comments that the medieval commentators were aware of this word (though we have seen that this is not how they

meant *abātu* [*CDA*, 2], he offered no explanation for the loss of the initial consonant, and in Akkadian, at least, the verb appears not to have given rise to a noun.) Those who remain unconvinced by this line of reasoning resort to emendation. An old proposal of Perles, followed by, for instance, *BHS*, is to read ואשביתהו, 'and I will make an end of it'. More recently, a suggestion of Berger, 'Unerklärtes Wort', has found some support,[27] namely to read as בְּתָה, '(put in) desolation', i.e. 'allow it to become desolate, waste'. He cites Ps. 12.6, שית בישע, 'place in safety', as a parallel for the use of שית ב. Cohen, 'Philological Reevaluation', 50–52, adds a further point in support, namely that 1QIsaᵃ reads the next word as ולוא (MT לֹא); he suggests that the *waw* of תהו was wrongly added to the following word. He explains the ב as a *beth essentiae*, 'and I shall put it into a state of being a wasteland', i.e. I shall turn it into a wasteland'. This seems the best of the alternative proposals, and yet the preposition ב following שית remains problematic. Berger's analogy is inappropriate, since in Ps. 12.6 שית means 'put or place' followed by locative 'in', which is completely different from the supposed use in our verse, while Cohen's appeal to the *beth essentiae* is desperate: שית in the sense required here may be followed by the so-called double accusative (GK §117*ii*; JM §125*w*; Gibson, 113–14), or by ל, or occasionally כ (Hos. 2.5 is an example that is close in sense to the present verse, and see too Isa. 40.23), but never ב. Cohen's alternative explanation is no better: he records an unpublished proposal of M. Held to take this as an example of שית ב = 'set among' (e.g. Jer. 3.19; 2 Sam. 19.29). Elsewhere, as sense demands, this is always followed by a plural. to which he responds that תהו has no plural, but this is no answer at all. Furthermore, the proposed translation 'I will set it among wastelands' is hardly convincing. Without great confidence I come to the negative conclusion that association with בתה faces fewest difficulties.

ועלה: the subject is the vineyard, with שמיר ושית as adverbials ('it shall grow up with...', i.e. 'be overgrown with'); see Prov. 24.31, where עלה is followed by כלו as a singular subject and then a plural adverbial noun, so putting the construction beyond doubt, and Isa. 34.13 (Orelli); cf. GK §117*z*; JM §125*o* (differently Korpel, 'Genre', 137–38).

מהמטיר: for the use of מן to negate the infinitive construct, see GK §119*y*; Gibson, 132. It is followed by the cognate accusative, which cannot be rendered elegantly into English.

7. כי is not always strictly causal ('because') but may rather supply the explanation for what precedes (Gibson, 159; A. Schoors, 'The Particle כי', *OTS* 21 [1981], 240–76 [265]). Becker's claim (p. 128) that v. 7 is not properly integrated is thus exaggerated. Nor is it necessary to maintain that this must be an emphatic כי (Kaiser).

Common sense dictates which elements are subject and predicate in the first two lines; the chiastic structure of the lines means that the word order is different in each case; cf. Gibson, 53.

ויקן: LXX (ἔμεινα), V (*expectavi*), P and T (אמרית) all render as first person singular, presumably under the influence of v. 4 (and as noted above LXX and T rendered vv. 2-3 as first person singular as well); it is doubtful whether they had a variant *Vorlage*. It is clear from the first line of the verse that the prophet is speaking here, so that a third person reference to God is expected.

I have not tried to imitate in translation the obvious word-play between משפט and משפח, צדקה and צעקה. Attempts to do so seem rather jejune to me, e.g. 'He looked for rule and behold misrule; for redress but behold distress' (Wade), 'He looked for order, what he saw was murder; he looked for right, what he heard was the cry of fright',[28] 'Il espérait l'éthique, et voici la clique; le droit, et voici le cri d'effroi' (Lys, 'La vigne', 2), or the Zurich Bible (as cited by Blenkinsopp): 'Er hoffte auf Guttat, und siehe da Bluttat, auf Rechtsspruch, und siehe da Rechtsbruch'.[29]

---

explained it) and that it occurs in Post-Biblical Hebrew (which may be explained entirely as influence from the presumed sense in this very passage).

[27] E.g. Schoors; Korpel, 'Genre', 137; Bjørndalen, *Untersuchungen*, 249; Fechter, 'Enttäuschte Erwartungen', 69.

[28] Barr, *Comparative Philology*, 48.

[29] Several earlier attempts are listed by Haupt, 'Isaiah's Parable', 201 and 202.

משׂפה: the word-play has here been elevated to the visual level by the substitution of שׂ for the regular ס. 1QIsaᵃ goes further by repeating ל before it, but this is surely in error. Delitzsch's attempt to relate the word to ספה I, 'join, sweep towards', hence 'grasping', 'forcible appropriation of another man's property',[30] is most unconvincing. ספה II, 'pour out', gives a satisfactory explanation. Though not used elsewhere in Hebrew with blood as object (contrast Arabic), it is intelligible, and will have been chosen, of course, even if unusual, for the sake of the word-play (so most moderns since at least Gesenius). It is not, perhaps, surprising that the versions did not recognize the word but rendered *ad sensum* with general words for wickedness or evil. The medieval commentators generally associated the word with ספה III, hence 'disease', and this was still favoured by Vitringa, even though he knew well of the possibility of 'bloodshed'. Korpel, 'Genre', 141, also adopts this derivation, translating 'scab', with a reference to the apparent use of the denominative verb at 3.17. However, quite apart from the doubts expressed at 3.17 above, the attested nominal forms in Hebrew are מספחת/ספחת, and the association with ספה II seems contextually much superior.

והנה (twice): though frequently rendered as if related to visual perception (e.g. 'behold'), הנה is simply a presentative particle (WO, 675–78), so that one should be free to supply whatever is the most suitable form of perception in the context.

לצדקה: LXX misunderstood the nature of the parallelism here, and so rendered the ל as if it were the negative לא: οὐ δικαιοσύνην (cf. HUBP).

It is universally accepted that a new section of the book of Isaiah begins at 5.1; indeed, Becker, Chapter 4, argues that it was once the start of an earlier form of the book itself. We have seen that 4.2-6 was shaped (perhaps in stages) to conclude the more extensive section in chs 2–4. Conversely, as will be seen more fully in the comments on the remainder of Isaiah 5, 5.1-7 has connections mainly with the series of woes following, so that although it is clearly to some extent a self-contained unit, its introductory role is also apparent.

It is less certain how far the unit introduced by 5.1-7 extends. Because of the appearance of a woe saying at the start of ch. 10 and because the so-called refrain poem of 9.7-20 (and cf. 10.4) seems to have one of its sections in 5.25-29, scholars have developed a large number of theories concerning either accidental misplacement or redactional reordering of material to explain how these two types of material now find themselves distributed around the so-called Isaiah Memoir in 6.1–9.6. In recent work there have been some particularly strong and attractive proposals which suggest that we should speak of 5.1–10.4 (or 12.6, according to Sweeney) as the next major section in the book.[31]

At this point we run up against the problem that the relationship between diachronic and synchronic readings is not always entirely smooth. As we shall see later, and as I have sought to argue in detail elsewhere (*Book*, 125–43), there has at some point in the growth of the book been a major redactional concern to parallel the closing paragraph of ch. 5 with the closing paragraph of ch. 11, this to be followed by what is obviously some sort of conclusion in the hymnic material in ch. 12. This will explain how it came about that what we now find in 5.25-29 came to be in its

---

[30] Still apparently favoured by Weinfeld, *Social Justice*, 218.

[31] See, for instance, L'Heureux, 'Redactional History'; Anderson, ' "God with Us" '; Bartelt, 96–139; Berges, 87–91.

present position (so any suggestion that this was the result of some textual accident should be discounted). Probably at the same time and by the same redactor, 5.30 was added by way of *Fortschreibung*. It seems that this redactor was consciously rounding off a major section of the book which he took to be primarily a word of judgment, whereas the way in which he shaped the end of ch. 11 and ch. 12 points to his view that that section was more promissory. Since on any showing 6.1 marks some kind of fresh start in the book, it seems clear, therefore, that he was working with the overarching concept that the first half of chs 2–12 was to be contrasted with the second. And the fact that no other material intervenes between 5.30 and 6.1 and that 11.11–12.6 too does not appear to have been subsequently worked over means that this remains as a legitimate approach to one kind of a final-form reading, one which develops in a satisfying manner out of a diachronic analysis. While the links between chs 5 and 9–10 need not be denied, they have been overridden by this later redactional shaping.[32]

Unfortunately, that is not the end of the story, however, for we have also seen that there has been an even later layer of material which has disrupted part of this scheme. In the first part of the book, this latest layer is represented most clearly by 4.2-6 (it is likely that some verses in the middle of ch. 11 also belong). This late insertion overrides the otherwise entirely judgmental material in 2.6–5.30 and has made for a new section comprising chs 2–4. But the fact that this has not been carried on through the following chapters with any consistency means that we are left with two competing patterns of final form which cannot really be held together in a single fully neat and tidy structure.[33] Because I find that the first of these two redactional structures explains the overall shape of chs 1–12 more comprehensively than the second, I conclude that it is best to see the section introduced by 5.1-7 as stretching only as far as the end of the chapter.

There have been many attempts at a detailed analysis of the poetic structure of the passage, and many differ in essence only as to whether they count stresses, syllables or letters.[34] Some, however, affirm that only

[32] In her study of the canonical form of Isaiah through its use of the term Torah, Fischer, *Tora*, 37–42, followed by Berges, 90 (and cf. Kustár, 65–71), also finds that 5.24-30 has many links with ch. 1 which she thinks points to the paragraph's function as a conclusion to chs 1–5 as a whole.

[33] Blum has sought to overcome this by way of the elaborate concentric structure which he proposes for 1.21–11.5 (though even then he excepts a certain amount of material of later origin). Apart from problems with his general theory which we have already noted, however, it is striking that 5.1-7 is not really integrated into his scheme. He takes it as part of 5.1-14a, which he parallels with 10.1-4 under the general rubric of *Sozialkritik*. However, it is the woe sayings which he explicitly mentions as linking these two sections; there is nothing specific to 5.1-7 to associate it with 10 (quite apart from the obvious imbalance in length between the two proposed parallels).

[34] In addition to the commentaries, see, for example, H. Kosmala, 'Form and Structure in Ancient Hebrew Poetry', *VT* 16 (1966), 152–80 (167–68); Loretz, 'Weinberglied', and 'Zitat'; Prinsloo, 'Isaiah 5:1-7'; Folmer, 'Literary Analysis'; Korpel, 'Literary Genre'; G. Fecht, *Metrik des Hebräischen und Phönizischen* (Ägypten und Altes Testament 19;

1b-2 (the song proper) is poetic (e.g. Cersoy, 'L'Apologue'), which they use as an additional argument for claiming that the passage was not written as a unity from the first (see below). This seems to imply an unnecessarily rigid approach to the question.

In line with our previous procedure, which seeks to explain what we have in front of us while doing so in a somewhat pragmatic fashion because of all the uncertainties which confront this type of analysis, we may note that the first line is a 3 + 3 and so slightly longer than what is to follow. It is thus set slightly apart, appropriate for an introductory rubric.

The song itself then follows in what may certainly be read as 3 + 2. The suggestion that this *qinah* rhythm already hints at the denouement is, of course, absurd; such a rhythm is by no means restricted to laments.[35]

Despite the change in person (see below), v. 3 continues in the same way, but in order to maintain the rhythm in the shorter second line, the reading has to be slowed (the second half of the line is merely ובין כרמי), which seems entirely suitable at this point where the audience is first asked for some reaction.

The first line of v. 5 is long, and includes prosaic particles (את, אתכם and אשר). Once again, however, the line functions, as did 1a, as a form of introductory rubric, and so is set apart somewhat from the remainder.

What follows is, in my opinion, a most effective change of rhythm. Announcing what he is going to do, the owner gives us a series of two pairs of two words (2 + 2), followed by an extra pair at the beginning of v. 6. This is reminiscent of the pairs in 1.16-17, where the prophet was urging action upon his audience. And the first two words of v. 6, having no partner, act rather in the manner of a tricolon, drawing a certain emphasis to itself.[36] This seems wholly appropriate to their summative meaning ('with the result that I shall make an end of it').[37] We then resume with a further pair (2 + 2) balanced by a three-stress consequence, and then the verse (and the 'story' as a whole) is rounded off with a regular 3 + 3 (but without parallelism).

Finally, in the climactic v. 7, where the prophet openly takes up the speech in his own persona, the effect is achieved more by chiasmus in the first two lines and by word-play (with gapping) in the third than by rhythm or strict parallelism, though it can certainly be read as more elevated language than standard prose. Examples of assonance and the like earlier in the passage are noted elsewhere in the commentary.

Wiesbaden, 1990), 148–52; Petersen and Richards, *Interpreting Hebrew Poetry* (above, n. 10), 81–89; Yeo, 'Isaiah 5:2-7'; Bartelt, 124–29; Seybold, 'Das Weinberglied'.

[35] Cf. R. de Hoop, 'Lamentations: The Qinah-Metre Questioned', in M. C. A. Korpel and J. M. Oesch (eds), *Delimitation Criticism: A New Tool in Biblical Scholarship* (Assen, 2000), 80–104.

[36] For the effect, see Watson, *Classical Hebrew Poetry*, 177–85, though without reference to the present passage. It should be said that only one other analysis that I have seen (Folmer, 'Literary Analysis') takes the words in the way I am proposing; they are mostly joined with what follows (see the survey of proposals in Loretz, 'Zitat', 501–4).

[37] One can therefore only regret attempts to delete the clause as a later addition; cf. Fohrer; Vollmer, 151; Hoffmann, 88.

I conclude that, despite uncertainties, the passage is susceptible to a very reasonable poetic analysis in which form and content are well suited. The form or genre of the passage has been even more fiercely disputed. Already in 1977 Willis, 'Genre', surveyed no less than twelve possible definitions of genre, and although it is possible to be critical of aspects of his analysis (cf. Bartelmus, 'Beobachtungen'), it nevertheless served the valuable purpose of categorizing a great many suggestions (which need not, therefore, be repeated here) and of eliminating at least some of the more outlandish proposals from the first part of the twentieth century from further consideration. Willis's own preferred solution was 'a parabolic song of a disappointed husbandman' (which of course is neither a form-nor a genre-definition as such).

Things have not stood still since Willis's article, however, and there have been noteworthy contributions in the meantime by (among others) Graffy, Prinsloo, Yee, Sheppard, Evans, Niehr, Bjørndalen, Korpel, Niel-sen, Irsigler, Bartelmus and Fechter.[38] It is difficult to escape the impres-sion that, even though some of those listed were seeking to build on or otherwise to refine the suggestions of those who preceded them, there must be some fundamental problem with the method, or at least its application, that can produce such diverse results (see too Yeo, 'Isaiah 5:2-7', 82–86). The following factors need to be kept in mind.

Form and genre are not the same thing, though they are all too fre-quently confused. Form should apply to the shape, structure or outline of a passage which may be laid alongside and compared with others that are similar. They need not be identical, but they should at least have a suffi-cient number of elements in common to allow one to speak of a 'form' at all. Genre, on the other hand, concerns the literary type of the passage. Secondly, there will obviously be differences of definition according to how much text is under analysis: in principle it is possible to discuss the genre of a whole book (e.g. 'prophetic book') all the way down to a brief passage within it. And finally, it is rather clear that even within the present short passage there are different elements to which justice needs to be done if the analysis is to be faithful to the text.

In my opinion, we may first agree without difficulty that there are two small genres included within the passage (this is not to be confused with the question of the genre of the passage as a whole), namely a song (in narrative form, which seems acceptable[39]) in vv. 1*b*-2, as clearly stated in 1*a*, and a lawsuit in vv. 3-6.[40] These elements are clearly contributing to a more extensive whole, however, so that it would be foolish to divide the text up on this basis alone. Secondly, so far as the *form* of the passage is concerned, the closest parallels are those tabulated by Graffy, Yee and

---

[38] Graffy, 'Genre'; Prinsloo, 'Isaiah 5:1-7'; Yee, 'Form-Critical Study'; G. T. Shep-pard, 'More on Isaiah 5:1-7'; Evans, 'Vineyard Parables'; Niehr, 'Gattung'; Bjørndalen, *Untersuchungen*, 293–343; Korpel, 'Genre'; Nielsen, 90–100; Irsigler, 'Speech Acts', 56–57; Bartelmus, 'Beobachtungen'; Fechter, 'Enttäuschte Erwartungen'.

[39] Cf. R. Alter, *The Art of Biblical Poetry* (New York, 1985), 27–61.

[40] Cf. Boecker, *Redeformen*, 81–83; Nielsen, 92–94, and 'Bild des Gerichts', 317–19; Bovati, 'Le langage juridique', 191–94.

Niehr (*pace* Höffken, 'Probleme'), namely 2 Sam. 12.1-7a; 14.1-20; and 1 Kgs 20.35-42 (Graffy adds Jer. 3.1-5),[41] and on this basis the term 'juridical parable' (or 'anklagende Gerichtsparabel') has become popular as a designation.[42]

Finally, so far as genre properly speaking is concerned, the main discussion has been whether parable is appropriate or whether the passage should be classified rather as an allegory (so especially Bjørndalen, who has been followed by Korpel and Sweeney). The principal objection to the designation as parable has been the view that a parable should have only one moral, whereas the present passage is open to more than one application and its goal or intention is not a moral. This conclusion may be overly restrictive, however, and seems to be based upon an understanding of New Testament parables which nowadays would not be so rigidly applied. Conversely, in an allegory each element of the story represents something in the real world, but there is no suggestion that each of the vineyard owner's actions in 1*b*-2 is meant to be interpreted as descriptive of Israel's past history (so correctly Vollmer, 149–55, who points to the similar situation in 1.2-3).[43]

Arguably more important than a concern for genre[44] is an appreciation of the rhetoric of the passage, characterized as 'frustrated expectations' by Williams and 'discourse-level paradox' by Clark.[45] While some of the examples Williams suggests may be considered over-subtle, his general point holds good that as the passage unfolds it turns out more than once that all is not as it at first appears, and it is this, indeed, which makes the whole so effective. The most obvious example, of course, comes with the last verse, where the identity of the vineyard (and by implication its owner) is revealed, very much to the audience's discomfiture. This is what aligns the passage so obviously with passages like 2 Sam. 12.1-7, with its equally devastating 'you are the man!'. A first consequence to draw from this is the realization that vv. 1-6 as a whole have to be taken as belonging to the fictitious world of the parable (so rightly Bentzen, 'Erläuterung'); to

---

[41] The differences in the order of the constituent elements, as well as some omissions, may be explained as contextual adaptations; they do not justify Sheppard's conjectures ('More on Isaiah 5:1-7') about material misplaced from 3.13-15, concerning which we have already noted that there are considerable difficulties on other grounds as well.

[42] Here the influence of Simon's study should be acknowledged, even though he was not dealing with our particular passage: U. Simon, 'The Poor Man's Ewe-Lamb: An Example of a Juridical Parable', *Biblica* 48 (1967), 207–42.

[43] The Targum moves in that direction, but interestingly not in the way that one would expect of an historical allegory (e.g. applying the removal of stones to the expulsion of the Canaanites); its concern rather is with the temple and its altar; cf. de Moor, 'Targumic Background'. That line of interpretation seems to be extremely early, being apparently attested already in the fragmentary 4Q500; cf. Brooke, '4Q500 1'.

[44] Nielsen, 99, expresses a certain frustration with the discussion of genre, for if the matter is open to such prolonged discussion the question must to some extent be an open one. She therefore prefers the more neutral term 'metaphorical narrative', so leaving it open to multiple interpretations. That is acceptable in many respects, though I should differ from her when she argues that what she calls 'the erotic code' is dominant.

[45] Williams, 'Frustrated Expectations'; Clark, 'Song'; see too Gitay, 90–100.

suggest that the cat is gradually let out of the bag as the parable proceeds, as many commentators do, is to empty the rhetoric of its force.

I suggest that similar considerations allow us to appreciate the force of the change of person at v. 3. Following the introduction in 1*a*, we naturally expect that the song will be by the singer about his friend and his friend's vineyard; and so it is in 1*b*-2. In v. 3, however, there is a sudden summons to the audience, ועתה, and as their attention is thus focused it is suddenly revealed that, against initial expectations, the singer and the owner are one and the same (so, for instance, Wendel, 17); it is a simple ruse that has been used, and certainly no reason for literary-critical surgery.[46] It serves to heighten the tension as we move from one part of the parable to the next.

Finally, given the lack of evidence that vineyard imagery had ever been applied to Israel before Isaiah's time (see on v. 7 below) and the equal lack of any evidence, despite the contrary assertion of most scholars, that vineyard imagery was used of women in Israel or the ancient Near East at this time, I see no reason why the audience should have had any clues towards the application of what at face value is a bizarre notion. The vineyard is clearly being personified in some sense, and the owner might be thought to be acting unreasonably in some respects; most husbandmen would try to solve the problem of the production of diseased grapes before moving to destroy the whole vineyard. Thus, just as the second main section captures attention by the change in person in v. 3, so the third does in v. 5 (again with ועתה) by its announcement of the owner's peculiar procedure. This heightening of puzzled interest[47] thus leads up effectively to the denouement in v. 7.

The aim or purpose of the passage within Isaiah's overall agenda is best understood against the background of this same rhetoric. He is clearly trying to persuade his audience of something—to bring them to acknowledge some point of view that they evidently would not have done had he addressed them directly about the matter. Put like that, it seems obvious that he wishes them to agree with the Lord's verdict that they are guilty of far-reaching social injustice, and that their destruction is a fair punishment or consequence.[48] Deck, 200, correctly observes that it is precisely the 'reaction' element in the form-critical parallels (2 Sam. 12.13; 14.18-21; 1 Kgs 20.43) which is completely missing in our passage, so that it would be a mistake to think too quickly that Isaiah is appealing for repentance. She suggests that the final word of the passage, צעקה, 'cry', points the readers in the direction of accepting the need to seek God in the distress which their history has led them to; but this is surely muted at best. That repentance may follow from such an acknowledgment need not be denied

---

[46] *Contra* Loretz, 'Weinberglied'; Höffken, 'Probleme'; Niehr, 'Gattung'; Becker, 127–34. Their view is critically examined by Fechter, 'Enttäuschte Erwartungen'.

[47] Clark, 'Song', even goes so far as to wonder whether this is not an example of 'slapstick comedy' ('I'll tell you what I'll do...'), which would have a similar effect.

[48] We may note here Nielsen's discussion, 100–4, of the performative as well as the 'informative' function of the passage.

(see 2 Sam. 12.13!), but that does not make 'repentance' a proper expression of the prophet's purpose *per se*.[49]

The need to gain his audience's agreement in general terms in this striking manner also accounts for the passage's present literary position, for only then are their ears open to hear the more specific charges in the woe sayings which follow, for they serve merely to amplify the nature of the charge. It is not possible to relate all this simply to the oral stage of Isaiah's ministry, about which we have little knowledge.[50] From the perspective of the reader, the whole serves as justification not just for the imminent Assyrian incursions (5.25-29) but also for the longer-term and even more devastating Babylonian judgment (adumbrated in 5.30) which dominates so much of the book as a whole.

The Isaianic authorship of the passage was universally assumed until it was first challenged by Vermeylen, 159–68, principally on the grounds that the closest comparable passages (2 Sam. 12.1-12; 1 Kgs 20.35-43) show Deuteronomic influence, some of its features (such as vine symbolism in relation to Israel) are not generally earlier than Jeremiah, and the vocabulary is not characteristically Isaianic. Vermeylen has been followed by Kaiser, and on rather different grounds by Becker, 130–34. In replying specifically to Vermeylen, Bjørndalen[51] maintains first that the significant material in 2 Samuel 12 is probably pre-Deuteronomic, that the vineyard imagery has a parallel in 3.14-15, at least, which Vermeylen regards as Isaianic, and that the argument from vocabulary proves nothing: some occurs in texts prior to Isaiah, two of the words are *hapax legomena*, some others are too rare to enable conclusions to be drawn, and so on. We may agree with Bjørndalen that Vermeylen has not succeeded in establishing his case for an exilic date, but that negative argument does not, of course, prove Isaianic authorship either.

There are, in fact, very few clues that would enable one positively to establish that Isaiah was the author. The usual arguments—that there is nothing to prevent it, that the fine style and use of word-play is characteristic, and that the concern for social justice is appropriate—are all true, but not finally conclusive. The only tiny scraps of additional evidence I suggest are (i) that the alliterative שמיר ושית in v. 6 is of a piece stylistically with the rest of the poem and yet becomes a trope in Isaianic material from early days on, so suggesting that this occurrence must be very early (see below), (ii) that the order 'Jerusalem–Judah' in v. 3 is pre-exilic (see the notes above), (iii) that in all probability 3.13-15 (*q.v.*), which is itself early, is dependent on this passage, and (iv) that the use of Israel in v. 7,

---

[49] *Contra* Hoffmann, 86–90; more cautiously, Vollmer, 154; for a survey of these various possibilities with a valuable fresh analysis, see Irsigler, 'Speech Acts'.

[50] This is not, of course, to deny the possible oral origin of the material, on which see L. Boadt, 'The Poetry of Prophetic Persuasion: Preserving the Prophet's Persona', *CBQ* 59 (1997), 1–21 (12–16); but it comes to us now very clearly as literature.

[51] Bjørndalen, 'Zur Frage der Echtheit'; see too Deck, 195–98, for a similarly detailed refutation. We may further note that Wendel, 11–35, argues specifically for the literary dependence of Jer.2.21, 6.9 and 8.13 on Isa. 5.1-7, so supporting an earlier date for the latter (similarly Porath, 181–82). He also deals with the argument from language on p. 14.

though not referring exclusively to the northern kingdom, appears to include it (see the exegesis below), so that a date in the first part of Isaiah's ministry would be most natural.

1a. Within the world of this text (whether a physical reality lies behind it is beyond our recall), the prophet in the first person announces in this introduction that he is about to *sing*.[52] Since the audience is referred to in v. 3 as the 'inhabitants of Jerusalem and men of Judah', it is evident that we must imagine some public occasion when people were gathered not just from the city but also from the countryside; a major festival seems therefore to be presupposed (it is immaterial for exegesis to seek to identify which it might be). As Bartelmus, 'Beobachtungen', 58–62, has correctly observed (apparently for the first time), the use of the precative particle נא with the cohortative of אשׁיר (which occurs ten times elsewhere) is unparalleled. Against his speculative explanation, however, we may observe that this is also the only occurrence of this form in a secular context, which reminds us how little evidence we have for much everyday speech in Classical Hebrew; given the envisaged setting, it may be explained as part of the device whereby a singer sought to attract the attention of an open-air audience; a different, though also unusual, usage occurs at 55.1 in a comparable setting (הוי as an attention-grabbing exclamation without any negative overtones,[53] together with a considerable element of repetition following).

It is in line with this general approach that, as Williams observes ('Frustrated Expectations'), this introduction (see the use elsewhere of שׁיר followed by ל) initially leads us to expect 'a joyful song in praise of the poet's good friend'. This is just the first of several examples that he finds of 'frustrated expectations' in reading this passage, the sequel revealing that the song is not in praise of the friend at all, nor is its outcome joyful. This latter point may also be explained by the introductory nature of this line: at the surface level a public singer would hardly be likely to attract a crowd if he had indicated at the start how this particular song was to turn out; at the literary level, of course, the whole rhetoric of the passage is founded upon such deliberately induced misprision.

The rendering of ידידי as *my dear friend* seems unassailable. The noun occurs eight times in the Old Testament, in addition to which there are some personal names and an abstract noun formed from the same root. The verb occurs in a number of Semitic languages (though not as such in Hebrew), and its general association with love is not in doubt.[54] It is true that (as with the English word 'love') there can sometimes be explicit sexual overtones in some of these languages, but this is not always the case, so that it would be a mistake to assume that such a meaning must

---

[52] The use of the first person at 28.23 is comparable, introducing, as it does, what is often called the 'parable of the farmer'.

[53] Otherwise only at Zech. 2.10 and 11.

[54] For full details, see H.-J. Zobel, *ThWAT* iii. 474–79 = *TDOT* v. 444–48; see too G. Toloni, 'L'interpretazione greca di yādîd nei profeti', *BeO* 38 (1996), 3–40.

always be present. In Hebrew, it most often occurs in relation to God's love, whether for the tribe of Benjamin (Deut. 33.12), the people of Israel (Jer. 11.15; 12.7; Pss. 60.7; 108.7), or an individual (Ps. 127.2), but even so not quite exclusively; at Ps. 84.2 it is applied to an inanimate object (though it is not clear whether God's dwelling places there are loved by God himself or by the Psalmist). The relative infrequency with which the word occurs means that it would be foolish to deny that it could be used in a secular context, and it has been suggested that some uses of the root in proper names are also secular: a child beloved or 'the darling' of its parents, in which connection it might be significant that both the names ידידה, 'beloved', and ידידיה, 'beloved of Yah', are attested. It is clear that the context has to be the decisive factor in defining the precise nature of the relationship and the nature of the love involved. In the present passage, given that one party to the relationship is the singer, who is merely a cipher for the prophet, and therefore may be assumed to be male (but see further on דודי below), and that it is clear already by the end of this line ('his vineyard'), to go no further, that the 'beloved' is also male, one must deduce that the relationship is that of close friendship. No sexual content need be presupposed; it is well known (e.g. from 2 Sam. 1.23 and especially 26) that the language of love could be used for close friendship between males without embarrassment, and there is no reason why the same should not be true here.

Wildberger, Vollmer, 152, and Clements have followed Junker, 'Literarische Art', in arguing that the relationship is more specifically that known from John 3.29 as 'the friend of the bridegroom', one whose duties in connection with a marriage ceremony are further defined in several rabbinic texts. This, however, seems inverted; if that were the role that the singer adopts here, he should be the ידיד, not the bridegroom (and it is not clear how between his discussion of 'form' and his verse-by-verse exegesis Wildberger seems to be able to shift from ידיד as the friend of the bridegroom to the bridegroom himself).

It is sometimes objected that it would be inappropriate for Isaiah to refer to the Lord as ידיד (see Gray, for instance, for a forceful expression of this; also Scott),[55] but that is an objection which rests on a misunderstanding. It is true that by the end of the passage we come to learn that the relationship of the ידיד for his vineyard is that of God for Israel, but that is not at issue here. At this point we are entirely within the world of the story and it is completely inappropriate to apply to the language of the story descriptions which derive from the theological realm of which the story may be an illustration or parable.[56]

[55] This seems to have been felt as early as T, which applies ידיד and דוד to Israel, not God; cf. J. C. de Moor, 'The Love of God in the Targum to the Prophets', *JSJ* 24 (1993), 257–65 (260–61).

[56] So too correctly Bjørndalen, *Untersuchungen*, 283–84. This same point seems also to raise a difficulty for the suggestion of Olivier, 'Benevolent Patron'. He proposes that ידיד means 'friend in the sense of patron', and even that 'it should be rendered as "patron"'. In addition, it is difficult to see how such a rendering could fit with the parallel דוד, and it also suggests that the prophet was the client of the ידיד, whereas in fact in the

The rendering of דּוֹדִי as *my intimate friend* is more controversial, even if, as maintained above, textual emendation is not justified. Nevertheless, two older suggestions may be quickly eliminated. (i) It is certain that in the Pentateuch and some narrative texts דּוֹד means (paternal) uncle.[57] How this relates semantically to the other main uses of the word (see below) is not certain, though there is no reason to doubt that it is indeed the same word.[58] Jerome, noting that Aquila rendered πατράδελφον, adopted a slightly different meaning *patruelis*, 'cousin' (though this is not linguistically paralleled), which he justified christologically. He was followed explicitly by Luther. In modern times, Ehrlich has adopted this approach as a possibility. He thinks that an uncle's song is a moralizing address, and he compares the English idiom 'to talk like a Dutch uncle'. Ehrlich has not attracted any support for this bizarre notion.[59] (ii) It has been suggested in the past that 'Dod' is the name of a deity, and that the passage should therefore be interpreted as a satirical polemic against the fertility cult supposedly associated with that deity. The most sustained representation of this position was advanced by Graham,[60] who thought that the prophet's intention was to give 'his version of the Dod-song' (p. 169). This could presumably best be represented by a rendering such as 'Let me sing…*my* Dod-song'. This view has now also been more or less uniformly abandoned and no modern commentary on Isaiah follows it. For one thing, it is hardly conceivable that a proper name would have a suffix attached. More tellingly, there is no firm evidence that such a god ever existed, and most scholars who have studied the matter in recent years have denied it. Barstad,[61] for instance, observes that the popularity of the view was predicated on the assumption that such a deity was well-known in surrounding cultures, but that this is itself now highly problematic, and is certainly flatly denied in the case of Northwest Semitic by Sanmartín-Ascaso (the significance of אראל דודה in line 12 of the Moabite Stone is so uncertain that it should not be adduced as evidence); at best the word 'beloved' may serve as an appellative, not a name, in some personal names. So far as the Hebrew Bible is concerned, Barstad affirms with most modern interpreters that דוד in the Song of Songs simply refers to the 'darling lover *par excellence*' in the context of secular, erotic poetry and has no reference to any deity whatsoever. The finding of a deity Dod in Amos 8.14 is based upon conjectural emendation (and in any case even if it were to be accepted it would be better interpreted as a divine title rather than a name, as the

sequel it becomes clear that they are one and the same; this seems possible under the guise of 'friend' but more difficult if at the start the two partners are of unequal standing.

[57] D. R. Ap-Thomas, 'Saul's "Uncle"', *VT* 11 (1961), 241–45, argued that in 1 Sam. 10.13-16 the word meant rather 'deputy ruler, governor'. This is itself highly speculative, and despite Ap-Thomas's hesitant suggestion it does not shed any helpful light on our verse.

[58] See J. Sanmartín-Ascaso, *ThWAT* ii. 152–67 = *TDOT* iii. 143–56.

[59] See further Willis, 'Genre', 337–38.

[60] Graham, 'Notes'; others who follow this general approach are documented in full by Bjørndalen, *Untersuchungen*, 257–66.

[61] H.M. Barstad, 'Dod', in *DDD*, 259–62.

suffix would again suggest). Barstad concludes that 'there is little evidence to support the existence of a deity Dod' and none at all in the Bible; indeed, it is not even certain that the word was used as a divine appellative or title at all.[62]

Turning now to a more positive approach, parallelism would most naturally suggest that our word is to be put on a par with 'my dear friend' in the first half of the line. The objection to this has sometimes been advanced that elsewhere the word always has erotic overtones. This, however, is uncertain in itself, and is in any case most probably the result of the very uneven distribution of the word (when it does not mean uncle): the overwhelming majority of its occurrences are found in the Song of Songs, where it is used by the girl of her male lover (it is never, apparently, used by him of her). In such a context, erotic overtones are clear, but that does not mean that they must always be so. Emerton ('Translation', 19–22) has argued strongly against Sanmartín-Ascaso, for instance, that the more neutral meaning of 'friend' is attested earlier than Middle Hebrew, namely in Ben Sira 40.20. In fact there may well be a biblical example in Ct. 5.1 itself, for there דודים is parallel with רעים, 'friends, companions' (and note that the same two words occur in the singular at 5.16, where דוד must, therefore, have a personal, not an abstract, meaning). It is true that it is often taken as an abstract adverbial noun ('be drunk with love'), but there is at least a case to be made for the alternative: 'Eat, O friends; drink, yea drink abundantly, O beloved ones' (cf. LXX, V and P, followed by AV, RV, RSV, NIV). Similarly, the use of this word in personal names is unlikely to be erotic, and the fact that the same word could develop the sense of 'uncle' points in the same direction. As was the case with ידיד, therefore, there seems to be no good reason why דוד should not refer to a close friend without necessary sexual overtones if the context so demands (see too Bjørndalen, Untersuchungen, 280–83).

It has occasionally been thought that, since elsewhere דוד is usually used by a female of a male, the singer is here adopting the guise of the woman in the relationship, singing of her lover's vineyard.[63] Such an interpretation cannot be sustained for long in reading, as already by the end of the next verse, to go no further, it is clear that the vineyard has proved a disappointment, and it is hardly to be supposed that the woman would sing of herself in those terms.[64] Nevertheless, the possibility may be entertained that this is another deliberate example of 'exegetical frustra-

---

[62] Similar conclusions have been reached by, for instance, Sanmartín-Ascaso; Bjørndalen, Untersuchungen, 257–66; Willis, 'Genre', 338–40; Nielsen, 90–91. The suggestion that the Aramaic stele from Tel Dan might refer to this deity (cf. ביתדוד) is most unlikely; cf. H. M. Barstad and B. Becking, 'Does the Stele from Tel-Dan Refer to a Deity Dôd?', BN 77 (1995), 5–12; more polemically, K. A. Kitchen, 'A Possible Mention of David in the Late Tenth Century BCE, and Deity *Dod as Dead as the Dodo?', JSOT 76 (1997), 29–44.

[63] See, for instance, Budde, 53; Fohrer; Lys, 'La vigne', 8–9; Loretz, 'Weinberglied', 574; in 'Zitat', Loretz still maintains that a woman is the 'original' singer, though he argues that דודי itself is a later addition.

[64] Cf. Junker, 'Literarische Art', 261; Schottroff, 'Weinberglied', 78–79.

tion' (Williams, 'Frustrated Expectations', 460), presumably with the purpose of catching and keeping an audience's attention.

Finally, it is curious to observe that the two words for friend in this line could be associated with David (דוד) and Solomon (who at 2 Sam. 12.25 is called ידידיה), even though they here occur in the 'wrong' order. This has occasionally been noted by others,[65] but no one seems to have made anything of it exegetically, and indeed it is difficult to see what significance it might have. If it is not coincidence, it must just be noted as an oddity.

Vineyard: in view of what follows, this is clearly to be taken at face value. As Bjørndalen points out (*Untersuchungen*, 285–86; cf. Matthews, 'Treading the Winepress'), the tasks of vineyard cultivation which are listed in the following lines are never—in Israel or elsewhere—associated with vineyard as a topic in love poetry; there, it is always the enjoyment of the fruit and other pleasures that are referred to. Nevertheless, the use of vineyard in love poetry has led many to suppose that similar overtones are present here; Müller, for example, states that 'when Isa. 5.1 calls Yahweh *yādîd* and *dôd*, and both "with respect to his vineyard" (*lᵉkarmô*), we are dealing with a mythological transfer of erotic language to Yahweh'.[66] This seems to be going too far, as we have no certain evidence that such imagery was widespread; within the Hebrew Bible, it seems to be confined to the Song of Songs, and so may not have been a convention as early as Isaiah. Furthermore, despite the frequent assertions of commentators, there seems to be no solid evidence that this was a literary convention outside Israel either. Those who give detailed lists of texts in support of their position generally fail to note that nearly all refer to fields, not vineyards.[67] Ploughing a field is a far more obvious sexual metaphor, and is indeed quite widespread. But vineyards were not ploughed, so far as we know, and it is pure supposition that the thought of one would automatically involve the other. Even the one text from Ugarit which seems clear (*KTU* 1.24.23) is not fully agreed (Müller). Consequently, there is no evidence that would allow us to say that it is specifically a love-song that is here introduced;[68] that could only be based on unnecessary emendations (see above). Any such suggestion illegitimately elevates possible allusions to the level of primary intention.

1b. *My dear friend had a vineyard* (כרם היה לידידי): this form of wording is found twice elsewhere, at 1 Kgs 21.1 to introduce the story of Naboth's vineyard (כרם היה לנבות, 'Naboth had a vineyard'), and at Ct. 8.11 (כרם היה לשלמה, 'Solomon had a vineyard').[69] The fact that this occurs

---

[65] Peters, 'Two Fragments'; Lys, 'La vigne', 7 and 9; Hayes and Irvine.

[66] H.-P. Müller, *ThWAT* iv. 334–40 = *TDOT* vii. 319–25 (324).

[67] For those who appeal to fields as supporting a sexual sense for vineyard, see, for instance, Wildberger; Willis, 'Genre', 345–46; Sanmartín-Ascaso; M. H. Pope, *Song of Songs* (AB 7C; Garden City, N.Y., 1977), 323–25.

[68] Among those who have comprehensively rejected the love-song theory are Schottroff, 'Weinberglied', 74–84; Høgenhaven, 58–63; Bjørndalen, *Untersuchungen*, 280–90.

[69] Clark, 'Song', 134, draws attention to the comparable שני אנשים היו at 2 Sam. 12.1, which is of interest in view of the form-critical similarities between the two passages.

in three such different literary genres raises the question, as I have suggested elsewhere,[70] whether this is a stereotyped idiom, comparable with English 'once upon a time'.[71] In each case (including the Naboth story, in my opinion) the form introduces a tale of sorts rather than a piece of historical reporting. Bartelmus, 'Beobachtungen', finds a disjuncture here with the introduction, which suggests that a song should follow. He is correct to observe that vv. 1*b*-2 take the form of narrative (note especially the *waw*-consecutive verb forms, which do not recur in the following verses), but wrong, apparently, to deny that this can at the same time be poetic; the parallel in Song of Songs is sufficient indication. And if our speculation about the precise form of narrative is correct, then there is no reason why such a tale should not be told poetically or in song as much as in narrative prose (see the analysis above).

Ridge (קֶרֶן, literally 'horn'): there is no parallel for this usage, so that the precise signification has to be a matter of intelligent guesswork; see the notes above for a survey of possibilities. In addition to such *realia*, we may note the obvious use of word-play with כרם, as elsewhere in this passage. Those who read this passage according to an 'erotic code' have surprisingly not generally commented on this phrase. We might have expected them to point to the obvious possibilities of depicting a 'vine-yard' on an 'oily horn', but no doubt that would be too lewd even for them to contemplate. Such reticence only serves to underline that that whole line of interpretation is unsustainable.

Very fertile: for oil as indicative of fertility, see 28.1 and 4 (and cf. Num. 13.20; Ezek. 34.14; Neh. 9.25; 1 Chron. 4.40). With analogies in Ugaritic as well the biblical passages just mentioned, Zobel[72] maintains that oil metaphorically signifies the rain which makes the ground fertile. While the latter point is obvious, the suggestion as a whole seems a little unimaginative.

2. The work of preparing the ground to make a vineyard is described in a straightforward manner. Note that vv. 5-6 refer to other aspects of this work which are not directly mentioned here. It is hyper-critical to suggest that this is the consequence of different stages in composition or even to suggest that a different vineyard is there in view (so, for instance, Höffken, 'Probleme', 400); enough is said here to make clear that the owner took pains to prepare his vineyard carefully, and enough elements are mentioned there to serve the purpose of expressing the severity of the judgment on the vineyard. Those who first heard or read this material will have been familiar with all these elements and would not have needed them to be pedantically spelt out twice. Broadly speaking, the present verse speaks of the initial preparation of the vineyard and vv. 5-6 of what would have been necessary for its ongoing care (maintenance of the hedge; pruning

---

[70] H. G. M. Williamson, 'Jezreel in the Biblical Texts', *TA* 18 (1991), 72–92.

[71] Korpel, 'Genre', 125, therefore seems to me to be mistaken when she uses the parallel with Ct. 8.11 alone to argue that this clause is indicative of a love song.

[72] H.-J. Zobel, 'Der bildliche Gebrauch von *šmn* im Ugaritischen und Hebräischen', *ZAW* 82 (1970), 209–16.

and hoeing) but which hardly had time to come into effect. Against any attempt to apply each element in this verse allegorically, see above.

In order to *dig* in most parts of the hill-country of Judah and Samaria it would have been necessary first to *clear* the ground *of stones*, and the stones may well have been used in turn for both terracing and construction of the *tower* and surrounding wall (v. 5). The ground was then ready to be *planted...with choice vines*. As noted above, these will have been vines either of the 'Sorek' variety or more probably, by extension of the significance of that expression, of the finest quality. Erotic overtones have again sometimes been detected here; 'dig', 'clear stones' and 'plant' have all been mentioned in this regard, but Blenkinsopp is rightly dismissive of the suggestion.

The interval between planting and harvest (several years in the case of newly planted vines[73]) allowed ample time for the considerable effort required (i) to build the (watch)*tower* to help guard the vineyard, to keep necessary tools and equipment, and perhaps also to store wine during the initial period of fermentation[74] (commentators regularly contrast this with the more temporary 'hut' of 1.8, though its purpose is actually completely different), and (ii) to *hew out a winepress*. This latter word seems to be used in slightly different ways. There is another common Hebrew word that is also often thought to mean winepress, namely נת. The winepress was usually in two main parts (there is considerable variety in detail), an upper basin or surface for treading or otherwise squeezing the grapes and a lower basin (joined by a shallow trough) into which the juice could flow and then settle.[75] It may be guessed, on the basis of contextual indications from the commonest uses of each word, that strictly speaking נת referred to the upper part and יקב to the lower (perhaps as at Joel 4.13). In some contexts (16.10; Job 24.11), however, יקב is the place where the grapes are trodden out. It thus seems that either term could serve, *pars pro toto*, for the whole complex. Additionally, however, there are passages which indicate that the יקב was a place where wine was stored, and the presumption must be that this was for a longer period than it would remain in the settling basin (e.g. Hag. 2.16; Prov. 3.10). We now know, from a site such as El Jib, that large holes with narrow openings could be dug into the rock

---

[73] Cf. Walsh, *Fruit*, 20; Borowski, *Agriculture*, 110.

[74] Walsh, *Fruit*, 128–42, provides a full discussion of the use of such towers based upon literary sources, archaeological remains and observation from current practice in the West Bank. She notes that the only other Old Testament reference to such towers is at 2 Chron. 26.10 (where interestingly it is related to King Uzziah, during or soon after whose reign this passage was written). She maintains that the building of such a tower was not exceptional at this period. Her survey need be supplemented only by Chaney, 'Whose Sour Grapes?', 108, who reports on some features of towers in the West Samaria region as pointing to their use for fermentation and storage: 'only wine's need for darkness and moderately low, constant temperatures...can explain the unique features of these "towers," whose construction required an enormous expenditure of labor'.

[75] For a full discussion of the archaeological evidence, see Walsh, *Fruit*, 148–57, and especially R. Frankel, *Wine and Oil Production in Antiquity in Israel and Other Mediterranean Countries* (JSOT/ASOR Monograph Series 10; Sheffield, 1999).

where wine in jars could be stored,[76] and it could well be that these too were referred to as יֶקֶב; clearly, the verb *hew out* would be suitable for all these uses and so cannot help settle the issue. While it is not clear in which sense the word is being used here, it would be attractive to suppose that it is used for the whole winepress complex; as Young says, 'there would be no point in merely mentioning the digging out of one part'.

Not unnaturally, the owner of the vineyard *expected it to yield grapes*. This verb always means to wait hopefully or expectantly for something (e.g. 8.17),[77] so that its use here is entirely suitable, but the owner's expectations were frustrated (the point which Williams finds to be mirrored also in the literary style of the passage). Though the vineyard yielded grapes, they turned out to be *diseased* (see the notes above) and so useless. Borowski, *Agriculture*, 161, seeks to identify the disease in question specifically as 'black rot', not only because it is common and virulent, but also because it develops late in the growing season, a fact that would have added to the owner's disappointment.

3. *And now*: as usually in many forms of discourse, וְעַתָּה marks the shift from setting out the circumstances of a situation or other introductory or subsidiary material to the essence of the case; it is so used especially in letters.[78] Here, it marks appropriately the shift from tale to request for some sort of judgment, and it will be echoed by the 'and now' of v. 5, where the owner in turn responds to the assumed verdict of his audience (i.e. what do you think?… Well now, I will tell you what I think). It is beside the point to ask why the owner did not undertake measures first to remedy the situation, as any normal farmer would (contrast Luke 13.6-9). The tale was told for the sake of the judgment to follow, and so the singer hurries on to that with the minimum delay.

Inhabitants of Jerusalem and men of Judah: see on v. 1a. In principle, the whole nation of Judah is addressed.[79] This should not determine in an exclusive way whom the passage is about (see on v. 7). The supposed listeners are certainly included, but that does not prohibit the later third person reference from including an even wider circle.

Judge between… is a frequently used judicial term.[80] The courts often had to rule not just in the case of whether an individual was innocent or guilty of a crime but also in disputes between two parties, one of whom would eventually be declared to be in the right (צַדִּיק, literally 'righteous')

---

[76] Cf. J. B. Pritchard, *Winery, Defenses, and Soundings at Gibeon* (Philadelphia, 1964); Walsh, *Fruit*, 158–62; D. C. Hopkins, *The Highlands of Canaan: Agricultural Life in the Early Iron Age* (The Social World of Biblical Antiquity 3; Sheffield, 1985), 229–30. It should be noted, however, that unusually most of the winepresses at Gibeon do not have a collecting vat, so that these two unusual features should probably be connected.

[77] Cf. G. Waschke, *ThWAT* vi. 1225–34 = *TDOT* xii. 564–73.

[78] H. A. Brongers, 'Bemerkungen zum Gebrauch des Adverbialen *weʿattāh* in Alten Testament', *VT* 15 (1965), 289–99 (though on p. 295 he in fact ascribes a cohortative function to the use in our verse, unlike in v. 5: *Auf!*); E. Jenni, 'Zur Verwendung von *ʿattā* "jetzt" im Alten Testament', *TZ* 28 (1972), 5–12.

[79] Porath, 175–79, examines the terminology used here to underline that these terms refer to the whole population, not just to one element (such as the elite) within it.

[80] Cf. Bovati, *Re-Establishing Justice*, 185–86.

and the other in the wrong (רשע, literally 'wicked'). Such judgments were generally made by groups of respected senior members of society, such as 'elders', but here, unusually, the population at large is invited to play that role. That 'play' is an appropriate term is evident from the fact that by now it has become clear that the foregoing was no ordinary song. It is absurd literally to judge between a person and a vineyard. It is at this point, therefore, that the listeners are finally obliged to take on board, if they have not already done so, the fact that the vineyard has been coded language. They might well think at this point of a man and his wife, but I cannot see that this is an inevitability; as we have noted, it is only in the later Song of Songs that vineyard as wife or female lover comes to the fore, so it might not have featured in the conceptual world of Isaiah's audience. But that at least some sort of personal relationship is involved will have become obvious at this point, though again without any clear indication of how this will eventually be applied in v. 7.

At this same point, there is another unexpected twist, namely that whereas up to now we have lived with the fiction that the singer was speaking on behalf of his friend, now suddenly it emerges that he and his friend are one and the same: *me...my vineyard*. At the level of first reading (or hearing), this is supportable; without any sense of threat to the audience, but perhaps, they might suppose, out of personal embarrassment, the singer has so far kept his true identity veiled but now he comes out into the open. It seems unlikely to be a coincidence that both these shifts in perception fall at the same point; it is part of the passage's deliberate rhetorical strategy. The listener is moved from hearing about a third party with his vineyard to hearing about the speaker himself and some other character, such as his wife. The level of involved engagement is immediately heightened, although of course there will be the further step yet to come of moving from an engagement of interest to that of personal involvement (v. 7).

4. This verse acts as a pause. It adds nothing significantly new, but draws out the implications of what has gone before. It therefore serves to allow time for the audience to reflect on their response to the request to judge, and it prompts them in the direction their decision should go. In the light of v. 2, there is only one answer to the question *What?* (see too the textual comments above), while conversely there is no convincing answer to be given to the question *Why?* There is therefore no need to postulate that after this verse 'a pause may be assumed' in which the audience silently allows that the owner had done everything he could and that the vineyard had no excuse (Gray; Budde, 56). The verse itself functions in precisely that manner.

5a. *Well, now* (ועתה) is the same as 'And now' in v. 3. There, it marked the shift from tale to request for response; here, it indicates the movement from verdict (as presupposed in v. 4) to sentence. The implication of the first line of v. 4 is that the owner had 'done' (twice) everything that could be reasonably expected for his vineyard. What had the vineyard 'done' in return? It had not 'yielded' (which is the same verb as 'done' in Hebrew) good grapes but diseased. So now the owner announces what he will 'do' next for his vineyard. This sevenfold use of the same verb in the space of four verses is unlikely to be accidental. Similarly, we may observe that *I will tell you* gives us a third use of the particle נא in this passage (cf. vv. 1 and 3).

5b-6a. The first part of the sentence is a threefold positive statement of action, the third (v. 6a) being climactic and summative. The protective *hedge*, probably made of thorn,[81] will not just not be maintained but positively removed, so that *it* (i.e. the vineyard, not the hedge) will be destroyed. The same verb is used here of the vineyard as was used in a similar context in 3.14. There is an important difference, however: there, the leaders of the people are accused of destroying the 'vineyard' (understood as a reference to the people); here, the 'vineyard' (not yet identified, but soon to be said again to refer to the people at large, presumably including the leaders) will be destroyed because of its own failings. Although we are not specifically told so, the implication is that the destruction will be brought about by others entering the vineyard from outside, a point which would have made the process of *relecture* straightforward in the exilic period. As was noted in the textual notes to 3.14, some scholars find here a different verb, meaning to graze. Even if that were so, it should be noted that the result would be the same, as the next line will make clear.

In close parallel with the first line of the sentence, the owner announces his intention to *break down* or breach the *wall* which also provided protection for the vineyard from marauding wild or even domestic animals. If they are then free to roam in and *trample down* the vineyard, the inevitable result will be total destruction—*an end of it*. This is not the common word for city wall but one used more generally, including for a vine(yard?) symbolizing the people at Ps. 80.13; indeed, the same verb, פרץ, is used there too, suggesting the possibility of some form of citation,[82] and Ps. 89.41 is similar (though without reference to a vineyard; see too Eccl. 10.8). The most frequent object of פרץ is, in fact, a city wall (חומה),[83] so that although it does not occur in descriptions of the fall of Jerusalem to the Babylonians, one may again see how it could have been so re-interpreted at a later date.

6b-c. A more negative side to the sentence comes next; the owner will not care in any way for the vineyard as no doubt he had been planning to. Without pruning, the vine soon grows more than allows for the efficient yield of grapes (Walsh, *Fruit*, 119–22; cf. Lev. 25.3-4; Isa. 18.5, on which see especially Wildberger's comments), and without hoeing[84] the whole soon becomes *overgrown with briers and thorns*, so smothering the vines.

---

[81] See Borowski, *Agriculture*, 105, according to whom the cactus, currently used for hedges in Palestine and often referred to by commentators on this passage, was imported from the New World only in the nineteenth century.

[82] See H. P. Nasuti, *Tradition History and the Psalms of Asaph* (SBLDS 88; Atlanta, 1988), 99.

[83] See J. Conrad, *ThWAT* vi. 763–70 = *TDOT* xii. 104–10.

[84] For the *realia* of hoeing, see Walsh, *Fruit*, 97–98; there are pictures of excavated hoes at Borowski, *Agriculture*, 107–8.

Although there are two roots זמר in Hebrew, this is the one that means 'prune', as the immediate collocation with 'hoeing' makes clear;[85] the suggestion that there is a reference to some form of cultic music[86] (perhaps in connection with a fertility cult) is wholly unjustified.

Briers and thorns might have been rendered 'thorns and thistles' in order to indicate that there is here another clear case of alliteration (שמיר ושׁית). The collocation is relatively frequent in Isaiah, mostly in redactional material, though 9.17 is usually considered to come from the prophet himself (see further 7.23, 24, 25; 10.17; 27.4). Not surprisingly, the phrase always has negative connotations (like the comparable קוץ ודרדר at Gen. 3.18), though whether that justifies us in concluding that 'a political code lies behind the use in all cases', as Nielsen, 104–6, argues, seems less certain. If the phrase was coined more for the sake of alliteration than out of any specific botanical consideration (for a survey of attempts at identification, see Wildberger), then it is attractive to suppose that Isaiah used it here first, in view of the several other examples of this device that we have already seen in this passage. In that case, given that 9.17 precedes the fall of Samaria, it would serve as a further small pointer to the setting of this passage very early in his ministry.

Just as the positive series of punishments built to a climax, so these more negatively expressed ones do too with the owner commanding *the clouds not to let any rain fall upon it*. The lack of rainfall is arguably the worst problem that the hill-country farmer can face, because unlike most other problems there is nothing he can do about it. Not surprisingly, therefore, it stands at the end of the list of curses based upon the natural order in Deut. 28.23-24; cf. Lev. 26.19; 1 Kgs 8.35; Amos 4.7-8; for extrabiblical parallels, see, for instance, Amherst Papyrus 17.5-13 (*CoS* i. 323); the vassal treaty of Esarhaddon, lines 530–33 (*ANET*, 539). It features not only in curses, however, but also in other expressions of extreme situations, such as 2 Sam. 1.21, 'You mountains of Gilboa, let there be no dew or rain upon you'. Of course in an ultimate sense Isaiah's audience would have confessed that only God can *command* that there be no rain, for which reason most commentators have concluded that by this point, if not sooner, the true identity of the owner has been made clear. This is unimaginative, however. Bentzen was surely justified in holding on the basis of 2 Sam. 1.21 that the present saying could be put into the mouth of a human being at the end of his tether,[87] and he might have added the observation that in the Elijah story the prophet effectively commands the cessation of

---

[85] It has occasionally been suggested that זמר in the Gezer Calendar, line 6, means (or includes) grape harvesting; see, for instance, A. Lemaire, '*Zāmīr* dans la tablette de Gezer et le Cantique des Cantiques', *VT* 25 (1975), 15–26, and Borowski, *Agriculture*, 26. Even if this were the case (which is far from certain), it would clearly not provide a contextually suitable rendering here.

[86] So Graham, 'Notes', 170, following a suggestion of T. J. Meek about זמיר in Ct. 2.12 ('The Song of Songs and the Fertility Cult', in W. H. Schoff [ed.], *The Song of Songs: A Symposium* [Philadelphia, 1924], 48–69).

[87] Bentzen, 'Erläuterung' (his point stands regardless of whether we follow him in identifying the passage as a love song), *pace* Hoffmann, 89.

rainfall for several years (1 Kgs 17.1). Within the fiction that has been maintained up to this point, it is the final outburst of the owner of the vineyard.

7. Whether or not the audience had already guessed where things were heading, with this final verse of the passage the target of the rhetoric becomes explicit: *the vineyard of the Lord of Hosts is the house of Israel.*[88] (Was it out of a sense of propriety that Isaiah did not explicitly state that God was the 'dear, intimate friend', the owner of the vineyard, of v. 1? Höffken, 'Probleme', 397, emphasizes that this identification would in any case not be the main point of the passage.) The parallel with *the people of Judah* gives rise to the theoretical possibility of three referents for 'house of Israel'. (i) The two terms could be synonymous, so that Israel is just another way of referring to Judah; (ii) the two terms could be quite distinct (the term antithetical is hardly appropriate, but that is how this usage would conventionally be characterized), so that Israel refers to the northern kingdom and Judah to the southern; or (iii) this could be a case where the first line of the couplet is further specified by the second, i.e. Israel refers to the people of God as a whole, further defined more specifically as the people of Judah.

Despite the fact that Isaiah certainly could refer on occasions to the northern kingdom as Israel (e.g. 9.7),[89] so that the second possibility has been quite popular,[90] it seems the least likely here. The vineyard and the *planting in which he took delight* are clearly not two wholly separate elements but at the least overlap in some measure, and it would be very strange if Judah were not also included within the referent of the vineyard. Similarly, to make the two terms completely synonymous, as in the first possibility,[91] also seems unlikely. If this passage dates from early in the prophet's ministry, when the northern kingdom still existed, such usage would at the least be confusing, and while there is no doubt that the name Israel was eventually adopted as an alternative designation for Judah alone, there is no strong evidence that Isaiah ever used it so. The third possibility, by contrast, has much to commend it.[92] It fits best the form of

---

[88] Some scholars imply that 'house of Israel' has, so to speak, replaced 'inhabitants of Jerusalem' by comparison with v. 3. This is a mistaken approach, however. Verse 3 addresses the audience directly, in the vocative, and although they are clearly included in the application here (see 'the people of Judah' in the next line), there is no reason why the application should not refer to a wider circle than just the immediate addressees of the story. To make this the basis for literary-critical surgery (Porath, 174–86; Becker, 127–30) is unjustified.

[89] For a discussion of all possible such references in Isaiah, see Høgenhaven, 8–10; for examples of the same usage elsewhere, see Wildberger. It should be noted that when Isaiah needs to emphasize that he is speaking of the northern kingdom in contrast with Judah as a separate political entity, he tends to use 'Ephraim'.

[90] E.g. Clements; Yee, 'Study', 37–38; Porath, 183–84; Seybold, 'Weinberglied', 117.

[91] So Wildberger; Schottroff, 'Weinberglied', 89; Nielsen, 108–14 (though she allows that it may have been reapplied to the northern kingdom in a later reinterpretation).

[92] Cf. Bjørndalen, *Untersuchungen*, 316–18, who lists many earlier commentators who adopted this view; add Muntingh, 'The Name "Israel"'; Irsigler, 'Speech Acts', 64; Beuken.

parallelism here (nearer definition), and it also reflects Isaiah's most common use of Israel, namely the people of God as a whole, as, for instance, in such divine titles as 'the Holy One of Israel', and elsewhere (e.g. 1.3; 8.18 etc.). The use of the title *the Lord of Hosts* also fits well with this interpretation (see on 1.9). At 8.14 Isaiah speaks of 'the two houses of Israel', which implies that he regards the totality of Israel as made up of two parts. Here, Wildberger may be right to suggest that by choosing to use the name Israel 'the religious aspect is highlighted', and of course the nearer definition of the second line makes clear that Judah is the primary target of the polemic, but it is in their capacity as part of the people of God that they come in for judgment.

In line with this interpretation, we may note that the *vineyard* is, pedantically speaking, more extensive than just the area that was planted (see the references to wall, hedge and tower, for instance). By further specifying the people of Judah as the *planting in which he took delight*,[93] therefore, Isaiah implies that they were an especially favoured or privileged section within the wider group. The word שעשעים may be used of a parent's delight in a child (Jer. 31.20; note too the use of the cognate verb at Isa. 66.12), while in Prov. 8.30-31 it qualifies both God's delight in Wisdom and her delight in human beings. There is a tender intimacy here[94] which serves only to heighten the sense of disappointment experienced by God. To that extent the nature of the relationship seems not to have deteriorated to the same extent as in the harsher 1.2-3, with which there are otherwise some points of comparability.

We saw at v. 1 above that there is no evidence for the use as early as Isaiah of *vineyard* as a metaphor for a (female) lover. Nor, we may now add, is there evidence that it had ever previously been referred to Israel (cf. Bjørndalen, *Untersuchungen*, 294). It seems to come in Isaianic material later than and dependent upon the present passage, first in 3.13-15 (see the discussion in the commentary *ad loc.*) and then in the Isaiah Apocalypse (27.2-5), which reverses the present judgment. Beyond that, we move forward to Jeremiah. It may well be, therefore, that our present passage is the first to use this metaphor, and if so, we can appreciate all the more how unexpected the outcome in this verse would have been to the original audience: they could have had no way of guessing what was to come.

This is not to deny that the way had been prepared for Isaiah's new coinage. Israel is compared to a vine (גפן) in Hos. 10.1 and Ps. 80.9-15 and the image of her as God's *planting* in the land occurs for instance in Exod. 15.17; 2 Sam. 7.10; Pss. 44.3; 80.9 and 16, some of which at least probably predate Isaiah. It was thus a natural development to make, but that is not the same at all as saying that his audience would have immediately recognized it because it already had wide currency.

---

[93] Against some older misguided attempts to find here a reference to the gardens of the Adonis cult (contrast 17.10-11), see Bjørndalen, *Untersuchungen*, 275–76. In addition, he points out on p. 288 that שעשעים never has erotic connotations in the Hebrew Bible.

[94] Note the LXX rendering ἠγαπημένον, and cf. Toloni, ''Ἀγαπάω'.

That God *expected justice* and *righteousness* is in line with Isaiah's understanding of the ideal society elsewhere, as outlined fully at 1.21. A primary reason behind the choice of the specific words *bloodshed* and *cry of distress* to indicate the opposite[95] was, of course, paronomasia (see the notes above). Nevertheless, they are not inappropriate. Bloodshed was effectively seen as the climax of the indictments in 1.15 and is seen as the most heinous of crimes in many societies. The cry of distress, by contrast, may be occasioned by any form of injustice and oppression, so that it avoids limiting the application of the judgment by over-specifying.[96] It might be inferred that such oppression makes the leading classes guilty while the oppressed themselves are innocent, which would enable us to align this passage more closely with 3.13-15, where the vineyard image is used explicitly as part of an indictment of the leaders of society.[97] In fact, neither murder nor oppression are necessarily the preserve of the rich, nor are the poor always the victims of such crimes. At this point the whole passage seems to refer to the people without distinction, though this may admittedly be refined in the woes that follow.

---

[95] It is noteworthy that this contrast is slightly strengthened by a small difference here from the form used in vv. 2 and 5, namely the introduction of the form ויקו ל...והנה, for which see 59.9; Jer. 8.15 (and Hag. 1.9 is comparable), and Höffken, 'Probleme', 397.

[96] The occurrence at Exod. 3.7 may illustrate the serious nature of this cry, but scarcely indicates Isaiah's familiarity with the text, *contra* Deck, 'Kein Exodus bei Jesaja?', 43–45.

[97] So explicitly, for instance, Kessler, *Staat und Gesellschaft*, 34–35; Chaney, 'Whose Sour Grapes?' Chaney maintains that in the eighth century 'the peasant majorities were the victims of viticultural injury', so that the vineyard would have been interpreted as a symbol of oppression. The passage is therefore targeted only at the elite. The difficulty with this view, however, is that in this passage the vineyard owner is clearly identified as the Lord of Hosts. It is difficult to see how this can be squared with Chaney's interpretation. This is not for one moment to deny that in what follows the woes will interpret the judgment as being of particular relevance to the elite, but that does not mean that we should read this into the present verse without clear evidence; cf. Weinfeld, *Social Justice*, 218–19.

A SERIES OF WOE-ORACLES
(5.8-24)

Following the Song of the Vineyard we have a series of six woe-oracles
(5.8-24) concluded by what looks like a prediction of final judgment
(5.25-30; see the commentary there for discussion of that section's origins
and role in the present form of the book). It is generally agreed that the
woe-oracles have a separate origin and that they have been deliberately
placed here to amplify the nature of the indictment in v. 7 concerning the
lack of justice and righteousness and so further to justify the pronouncement of judgment that is threatened.

Many commentators have taken the view that there were originally
seven woes in this series. Very occasionally it has been suggested that an
additional woe should be restored in the present text, at v. 23, for instance
(see the commentary below), but more usually it has been thought that the
seventh woe was moved from the present chapter to the start of ch. 10;
indeed, some commentaries and even translations seek to restore what
they think was the original order. This needs to be taken together with the
similar approach that the same scholars adopt towards the closing verses
of the present chapter, which they believe should be returned to their
original location in ch. 9 (a position that I reject in the commentary on
vv. 25-30 below). In my opinion, this is mistaken. 10.1-4 has a further
oddity, in that it also concludes with a form of the 'refrain' which characterizes the poem in 9.7-20. It is likely that this poem originally had five
stanzas (see again on 5.25-30 below), so that the repetition in 10.4 is
unexpected. This combination of a woe and the refrain in a single passage
following the two longer extended series seems more likely to be the
result of later redactional imitation, drawing the varied material to a unified close, than to be the result of accidents in transmission. Besides, there
is another woe in 10.5, so that there is no reason to think that 10.1 is out of
place where it now stands.

It will be recalled that I argued that the woe saying in 1.4 could well
have been moved to its present position from an original setting between
5.7 and 8. The arguments were set out there and need not be repeated here.
If that is correct, however, then clearly the problem of the 'missing' seventh woe-oracle is resolved. I note further that 1.4 would have helped to
ease the transition from an address to the people as a whole in 5.1-7 to the
series of woes directed at particular sections of society in vv. 8-24.

So far as I can see, the order of the woe-oracles is determined on the
rather mechanical basis of catch-words and the like (an observation which
tells against occasionally suggested schemes to rearrange the order). The
evidence is set out separately in the introduction to each woe in the
commentary below. In addition, a few pointers are discovered to the fact
that the ordering of the woes occasionally reflects a slightly different
interpretation from their likely original purport when read in isolation (see

especially on vv. 20 and 21). This suggests that the series was arranged by an early (pre-exilic) editor or collector of Isaiah's sayings rather than by the prophet himself. This is the first piece of firm evidence we have found that is relevant to the difficult topic of recreating the earliest form of the book subsequent to Isaiah's own individual sayings.

Most commentators date the individual sayings to the early part of Isaiah's ministry. In some cases, there is simply no evidence to determine the date of a saying either way, but on those occasions where there is evidence, it seems to me to point rather to a later date—to Hezekiah's rather than Ahaz's reign. In this the sayings differ from the Song of the Vineyard, and this may help to explain further why the audience is slightly different between the two main parts of the chapter. That some of the woes (mainly the first few in the series) have been further expanded later is hardly in doubt, and the evidence is presented in each separate case below.

FIRST WOE-ORACLE: PROPERTY SPECULATORS (5.8-10)

[8]Woe to those of you who add house to house,
    who join field to field,
until there is no more room,
    and you are made to dwell alone in the midst of the land.
[9]The Lord of Hosts has revealed himself in my hearing:
Surely many houses shall become desolate,
    large and good ones, without any inhabitant.
[10]For ten 'yoke' of a vineyard will produce a single bath,
    and a homer of seed will produce only an ephah.

8. For the syntax of woe sayings, see especially the analysis by Hillers, '*Hôy* and *Hôy*-Oracles'. As was noted at 1.4, it is not unusual for such sayings, which appear to start as third person address, to switch, as here, to the second person (see too GK §144*p*). Hillers (for whom this verse is a parade example) has argued that in fact the whole saying should therefore effectively be construed as vocative continued by direct address; just as a vocative may be followed by third person as well as by second person elements referring back to it (see, for instance, 22.16-17), so here following the woe construed as introducing direct address we find the participle followed by a second person finite verb (הושבתם).[1] The words 'of you' have therefore been supplied in English to clarify the situation.

בית בבית: 1QIsaᵃ omits the preposition, which looks like a simple case of haplography. The attempt of Pulikottil, 21–22, to argue that this judgment is too quickly biased in favour of MT overlooks the fact that it is reinforced by the correct occurrence of שדה בשדה immediately following, so that his own explanation (the scroll could be an example of 'local determination') itself looks like special pleading. Besides, Pulikottil fails to produce any example of the lack of a preposition in anything comparable to the present construction; the situation in 37.38, which he cites, is different and represents a regular sort of adverbial accusative.

יקריבו: for the participle continued by an (unmodified) imperfect, 'before which the English construction requires us to supply the relative pronoun implied in the participle', see GK §116*x*. Gibson, 137, draws attention to the use of apposition with chiasmus in this line to explain further the poetic construction.

עד אפס מקום (a 'frozen construct', according to Gibson, 142): for this negative, 'carrying the notion of non-existence, but usually with the added nuance of *still more*' (hence:

---

[1] GK §147*d* is oddly equivocal: 'the object of *commiseration* (after הוי) follows mostly in the vocative, or rather in the accusative of exclamation...*ah! they that*'.

'until there is no more place/room'), see JM §160n. LXX reads ἵνα τοῦ πλησίον ἀφέλωνταί τι ('that they may take away something of their neighbour's'). Ottley suspects misreading by the translator of יאספו, 'they take away', for יאספ and either רע for עד or alternatively paraphrase of מקום. HUBP thinks that this is impossible, since אסף is scarcely ever rendered by ἀφαιρεῖν (cf. HR, 180), and so suspects a simple alternative lexicographical understanding of אסף. However, this rendering does occur at 4.1, so that we cannot be so sure that it was not part of our translator's understanding. T's reading עד דנחסין, 'until we possess' (and cf. P), strengthens the possibility that there was a textual tradition in which אפס and אסף were somehow confused, and to that extent tells against Gray's alternative conjecture that this may be 'a paraphrastic rendering of perhaps the same words as now stand in 𝔊'. Even if that were so, however, MT may be judged to be textually superior.

והושבתם: for the sequence here (waw + perfect following עד־), see GK §112w. The hoph'al of ישב occurs only twice, here and at 44.26. Against the sensitivities of older commentators such as Marti and Gray, however, we have seen that there is no cause for suspicion in the use of the second person plural; nor, we may now add, is there any particular reason to doubt its meaning, literally 'you will be caused to dwell'. This is admittedly slightly different from 44.26 ('she shall be inhabited'), but not so as to cause difficulty,[2] and, as we shall see in the exegesis below, there may have been particular reasons for this slightly odd choice of expression. The major textual witnesses are mixed, but equally do not support any change. 1QIsa^a has וישמתם, which would presumably have to come from an otherwise unknown ישׂים* (the suggestion, which has been made [e.g. in *The Dead Sea Scrolls Bible*, 278], that it is from the imperfect of שׂיח, 'to put, place', is morphologically impossible, of course); it must be an error for וישבתם (i.e. qal for hoph'al: 'and you will dwell'),[3] and this would align the reading with the scroll's treatment of 44.26, where again it prefers qal (ושב), which, however, is more or less impossible to construe (*The Dead Sea Scrolls Bible*, 343, here simply follows MT without even a note); cf. Kutscher, 364. P and T (slightly more paraphrastic) also seem to construe as a qal, which may be regarded as *lectio facilior*. On the other hand, LXX μὴ οἰκήσετε and V *numquid habitabitis* both render as a question, presumably reading as הֲיֻשַׁבְתֶּם, and this is most easily explained as a slight misreading of MT (*pace* HUBP), which these versions therefore indirectly support.

9. באזני יהוה צבאות: this first line lacks a verb: 'In my ears the Lord of Hosts', and not surprisingly it has traditionally been supposed that an appropriate verb merely needed to be understood.[4] This has the appearance of making the best of a bad job, however, and most commentators have agreed that a verb should in fact be supplied, even though there is no obvious reason why it should have been lost (none of the proposals can be explained as a loss by any form of haplography, for instance).[5] Because of the אם־לא following, the

---

[2] Cf. J. H. Kroeze, 'The Hof'al in Biblical Hebrew: Simple Passives, Single Passives and Double Passives—and Reflexives?', *JNSL* 28/1 (2002), 39–55 (47).

[3] Cohen, 'Philological Reevaluation', 52–53, thinks that this (restored) scroll reading must be original, but without fresh argumentation. Of course good sense can be made of the qal reading, but MT is not as impossible as he seems to suppose.

[4] So, for instance, the rabbinic commentators; König, *Syntax* §391m; Delitzsch, who suggests that 'in the pointing, בְּאָזְנָי is written with *tiphchah* as a pausal form, to indicate to the reader that the boldness of expression is to be softened down by the assumption of an ellipsis'; Oswalt; Barthélemy, 32; Gitay, 101–2.

[5] For that reason, one should at least note the conjecture of Ehrlich, 20, to emend באזני to באדני, the whole phrase ('By the Lord Yahweh of Hosts') then being seen as an oath formula. Ehrlich might have further noted in support of this conjectural but in some respects attractive emendation that at 1.24 and 3.1 we have precisely the same divine name and title (האדון יהוה צבאות). Budde rejects the proposal on the ground that the אם־לא oath following is to be understood as sworn by God, not the prophet, as Ehrlich's suggestion implies.

almost universal view nowadays is that we should supply נשבע (לכן), '(Therefore) the Lord of Hosts has sworn in my hearing'. Some versional support is claimed for this: LXX ἠκούσθη γὰρ might indicate כי נשמע, which is thought to be a corruption of the expected כי נשבע[6] (though Duhm favours simply restoring נשמע כי כה without further ado). T is again more expansive ('The prophet said, With my ears I heard [הוריתי שמע] when this was decreed by (lit. from before) the Lord of Hosts') but might go back to a comparable original. Wildberger also cites P ʾštmʿ in support. On the other hand, 1QIsaᵃ agrees with MT at this point, and this was also clearly the text presupposed by V. It is noteworthy. however, that none of the versions actually refers to 'swearing', and it would be strange if they all had the same corrupt text with שמע; it is much more likely that they are merely translating *ad sensum*. That is not to say that the proposed emendation is impossible, only that it is technically unsupported. In these circumstances, it seems to me preferable to return to an alternative proposal which has occasionally been advanced in the past (e.g. Lowth; Cheyne, *Book*, 83; Budde; recently Porath, 105[7]) but which seems to have been lost from sight in more recent times. At 22.14, we find the following: נגלה באזני יהוה צבאות אם...‏. Since this is identical with our verse apart from the provision of the missing verb, it seems an obvious emendation to adopt. LXX and P admittedly use a different verb in translation there from here, but that is to be expected if the text was already corrupted in early times, and at any rate before the LXX, as seems to have been the case. Conversely it is noteworthy that T translates identically in both places, indicating either that it recognized the similarity or even possibly that the original text had somehow been preserved in its tradition.

באזני: a further point to notice from the LXX is that this is taken as a construct, not a noun with suffix: ἠκούσθη γὰρ εἰς τὰ ὦτα κυρίου σαβαωθ ταῦτα, and this has occasionally been favoured as the correct reading (even by a number of Masoretic manuscripts); though Rashi indicates that these are the ears of the prophet, Kimhi unequivocally refers them to God and Ibn Ezra mentions both possibilities. By using the verb עלה in his comments, Kimhi may be alluding to 37.29, where God is represented as saying that news of the Assyrian king's arrogance 'has come to my ears' (עלה באזני). Luther followed this approach (these matters 'touch my ears through the cry of the poor, and because of this cry my ears are constantly ringing'), and so did Calvin ('the Lord sits as judge, and as taking cognizance of those things'). LXX took the same line at 22.14 where, *pace* Ibn Ezra, such an approach seems less easy to sustain. Furthermore, we should have expected such a statement to be followed by כי rather than אם־לא. The Masoretic vocalization should therefore be retained, though whether *qāmeṣ* is used in preference to the expected *pataḥ* precisely to avoid any possible confusion in sound with the construct form with *ṣērê* (so Dillmann and Budde) cannot be determined.

אם־לא: for the use of this conjunction in oaths (whether formally expressed or not) see JM §165; Gibson, 187.

מאין: 'Two negatives in the same sentence do not neutralize each other...but make the negation the more emphatic'; GK §152y. The same expression occurs at 6.11 and frequently in Jeremiah, whereas Jer. 2.15 and 9.10 favour מבלי ישב.

10. צמד: the daghesh is unexpected, being 'contrary to the rule'; other examples of the same exceptional usage (though without explanation) are listed at GK §93m; JM §96Ad (where it is rightly noted that it is not covered by Nöldeke's suggestion that such forms are due to influence of an immediately preceding sibilant[8]). The translation 'yoke' is retained simply because we cannot be certain what size of land unit is involved; see further below.

בת אחת is masculine at Ezek. 45.14 (twice), so that 1QIsaᵃ's אחד may well be right (cf. Cohen, 'Philological Reevaluation', 53); Kutscher, 517, looks like special pleading when

---

[6] It seems that Marti was the first to advance this suggestion.

[7] Vitringa, Gesenius, Knobel and Orelli all think that this verb should be understood here, though without apparently suggesting that it should actually be restored, and Dillmann is explicit that no such restoration is required.

[8] Th. Nöldeke, 'Zur semitischen Pluralendung', *ZA* 18 (1904–5), 68–72 (72).

he suggests that we do not have enough examples to determine its gender, though see too König, *Syntax* §349a, for an attempt to explain the Ezekiel usage as anomalous. Unless the word is of mixed gender, I can only suggest that in the Masoretic tradition either a scribe was at some stage unconsciously influenced by the ת at the end of בת which it follows and qualifies or that he unthinkingly had בת = 'daughter' in mind.

זרע: this is most easily taken as a *casus pendens*: 'and as for seed, a homer will yield…'. There is no evidence that it can refer to a unit of land that required a homer of seed for sowing (*contra* Beuken, following *ABD* vi. 901).

The LXX has clearly gone for 'dynamic equivalence' in the second line: 'he that sows six ἀρτάβας [some sort of Persian measure = 1 medimnus, six of which Ottley reckons to be a fair equivalent of a homer] shall get three μέτρα [three of which are also used as the equivalent of an ephah at Exod. 16.36]'.[9] This is obviously an attempt to give intelligible equivalents for what will have been unfamiliar measures to Greek speakers (cf. Ziegler, 193), and so is no evidence for an alternative text. The question then arises, however, whether the same may be said for the first half of the verse: οὖ γὰρ ἐργῶνται δέκα ζεύγη βοῶν ποιήσει κεράμιον ἕν, 'for where ten yoke of oxen plough, it shall yield one jar'. 'Jar' for 'bath' is the same sort of equivalence as in the second line, but 'where ten yoke of oxen plough' is rather different. Although HUBP dismisses the possibility on the ground that 'yoke of oxen' is a familiar phrase from elsewhere, it remains striking that there is no equivalent for 'vineyard' and the similarity of כרם and פרים leaves open the possibility either that the translator had a different *Vorlage* or that he misread his text to assimilate it to a familiar phrase (Ziegler, 108, is also undecided). The other versions certainly presuppose MT, though P uses equivalents (Kor and Seah) rather than the same measures in the second line.

As the text stands, this first in the series of woe-oracles seems to effect a good transition from the Song of the Vineyard. Verse 10 in particular may be thought to operate on the catchword principle with its references both to 'vineyard' and to 'produce' (עשׂה) as the relevant verb repeated seven times in vv. 1-7, while Beuken points to the general theme of devastation as a consequence of injustice as a further thematic point of contact.

There is a significant shift in focus, however, in that while 1-7 concerns the nation as a whole, the present saying (as indeed those that follow) is obviously directed at only one portion of the population. To that extent, it is closely comparable in outlook with 3.13-15, where we saw similarly that some wording that was very close to that in 1-7 was being reapplied to the wealthy oppressors alone.

It has been suggested above that at an earlier stage the transition in this regard was eased by the inclusion of 1.4 between 5.7 and 8, for there we have a woe-oracle which is directed to the nation as a whole. To that extent, therefore, it shares characteristics with both what precedes and what follows and so would have functioned well from a redactional point of view; see 2.5 for a similar, though briefer, example.

The basic structure of the saying is typical of one form of the woe-oracle (see the notes on v. 8 above). Slightly unusually it has been expanded in v. 10 with an explanatory clause. This is not unparalleled, however (see several examples in the series in Hab. 2, but note that the כי in v. 24 at the end of the present series functions differently). Although some have

---

[9] See too H. St J. Thackeray, 'The Greek Translators of the Prophetical Books', *JTS* 4 (1903), 578–85 (583).

occasionally regarded v. 10 as a later expansion,[10] I do not find the evidence compelling. There is no evidence to suggest that all woe sayings must be of identical length, and, especially if it originally followed directly on from v. 8, its thought seems to fit perfectly with its context.

The situation with regard to v. 9 is rather different, however. From a formal point of view (the introduction of a divine oath) it is certainly unparalleled in woe sayings, and in the exegesis below arguments will be advanced both to suggest that it is in substantive contradiction with vv. 8 and 10 and that there is a fully intelligible reason (based on similarities with 6.11) why it might have been added as a piece of later exegesis of v. 8. With some reserve (since these arguments do not appear to have struck previous commentators), therefore, I am inclined to think that it did not form part of the original saying.

The date of this saying, as with the other woes, is not easily determined.[11] The usual view seems to be that they derive from the first part of Isaiah's ministry (e.g. Wildberger and Clements). A case can be made for the alternative, however (cf. Dietrich, 47–48; Høgenhaven, 169–71 and 176), namely to see the focus on the misdeeds of the wealthy as reflecting something of a development in Isaiah's thinking, which started in 5.1-7 and 6.1-11 (to go no further) as directed to the people as a whole but which gradually narrowed in focus to settle on the elite, perhaps in particular because of the role that they played in the preparations for Hezekiah's revolt against Assyria, to which Isaiah was so bitterly opposed. The comments on v. 8 below develop this thought, and 3.14 may again be compared.[12]

The poetry of this passage does not appear to be of especially noteworthy quality. There is effective use of parallelism throughout with chiasmus (8a) and ellipsis (9b), but the rhythm seems to be somewhat irregular. Korpel, 'Structural Analysis', argues that this paragraph comprises a canticle of three strophes which differs from the regular two-strophe canticles of the remainder of 5 + 10.1-6 (minus a few later additions) which she finds according to the analytical method of the so-called Kampen school. On this basis she argues that the passage (which may represent an authentic word of Isaiah) has been inserted into its present position from elsewhere because of its close word associations with the Song of the

---

[10] E.g. Beuken. I do not, therefore, agree with Kaiser and Kilian either, when they argue that vv. 9 and 10 are both later expansions; see too Porath, 126–29. Becker, 136–38, agrees that vv. 9-10 probably reflect late, exilic ideas as well as literary dependences (Amos 5.11; Mic. 2.1-2; Isa. 6.11) which he thinks rule out Isaianic authorship, but he sees no good reason to separate v. 8 from them, so that he saves the unity of the passage by dating the whole of it late.

[11] The case for an eighth-century date in general terms has recently been carefully and fully set out in response to various alternative minority positions by Houston, 'Social Crisis', and so does not need to be repeated here; the overwhelming majority of commentators takes it as axiomatic that the basic saying is Isaianic and that its major concern is reflected in a number of other eighth-century prophetic passages, as we shall see below.

[12] Similar conclusions are reached on rather different grounds by W. Zwickel, 'Die Wirtschaftsreform des Hiskia und die Sozialkritik der Propheten des 8. Jahrhunderts', *EvTh* 59 (1999), 356–77.

Vineyard. The problem with this approach seems to me to be that it uses a severely synchronic form of reading, based upon the late Masoretic divisions and accents, in order to arrive at a conclusion concerning what may have been diachronically 'original'; but the Masoretes had no access to this latter point, and were clearly working on the basis of the inherited text. If, as suggested here, a diachronic analysis based on conventional critical methods suggests that v. 9 may represent a later expansion, then the remaining vv. 8 + 10 would, in fact, produce the two strophes that Korpel reckons to be original. (All this is without regard to questions that will arise later about her judgment concerning what may or may not be 'original' further on in the chapter.)

8. *Woe*: see on 1.4.
Those of you who add house to house, who join field to field: while it is clear that there is a reference here to the inappropriate accumulation of landed wealth by a privileged minority,[13] the detail of what is involved and its social or political background are less certain. Among the possibilities which have been advanced are (i) that the reference here is to the growth of latifundia (large estates, in which the former small land-owners are reduced to slavery or at the least become estate workers) through foreclosure on mortgages,[14] with the consequence that *house* can include land, *room* (lit. 'place') means small landholding,[15] *many houses* (v. 9) means large landholdings, and *dwell* includes the idea of the ownership of land; (ii) that a more modest form of land acquisition is in view (again through the manipulation of mortgages) in which the small farmers remained on their holdings but were obliged to pay over much of their produce to the new owner;[16] (iii) that transfer of ownership is not at issue, but rather the wealthy were holding the property as a pledge against a loan and were able to enjoy its usufruct in the interim (cf. Hab. 2.6; Davies, 65–69); and finally (iv) that we should not be thinking of injustice on such a large scale, but rather of inequalities within the village or extended family unit (the בית אב or 'father's house'), where more powerful members exploited the weaker.[17]
The fact is that, rather as at 3.14, we do not have sufficient evidence to argue decisively in favour of one or other of these possibilities. Nevertheless, the two extreme positions seem least likely. There is no evidence for latifundialization in its full sense being practised on a wide scale. Had

---

[13] That such avarice was not limited to ancient Israel is well illustrated by the almost identical wording reached apparently independently by Seneca (*Epistula* 90, 38–39), as noted by van der Horst (following F. Buhl), 'A Classical Parallel'.

[14] See Dietrich, 15, Dobberahn, 'Jesaja verklagt', and especially Premnath, 'Latifundialization'.

[15] Premnath appeals here especially to W. Johnstone, 'Old Testament Expressions in Property Holding', *Ugaritica* 6 (1969), 308–17.

[16] Cf. Dearman, *Property Rights*, 39–42; Porath, 121–26; Kessler, *Staat und Gesellschaft*, 35–37.

[17] See S. Bendor, *The Social Structure of Ancient Israel: The Institution of the Family* (beit 'ab) *from the Settlement to the End of the Monarchy* (Jerusalem Biblical Studies 7; Jerusalem, 1996), esp. 252–53.

small landowners being reduced to slavery in the service of large estates been a common occurrence, we should certainly have expected references to it to surface more explicitly among the many prophetic diatribes against the sorts of practice condemned here.[18] The evidence from archaeology, which has sometimes been adduced in favour of either extreme, is also not particularly clear, and a recent careful survey and evaluation of the evidence concludes that though there is some evidence for latifundia in some areas, it tends to be restricted to marginal areas (so far as Judah was concerned), possibly reflecting the development of royal estates in the Shephelah and the fringes of the Judean wilderness and so probably not affecting the bulk of the population in the Judean heartland.[19] At the other extreme, Houston also shows that Bendor is able to maintain his minimal position only by ignoring some of the evidence which tells against him and in particular by a questionable series of deductions drawn from his consideration of 2 Kgs 15.19-20. On the assumption that v. 10 points to a punishment that is meant to be suitable for the crime, the probability must be that it was from the produce of the land that the wealthy aimed further to enrich themselves, not that property owning for its own sake is the main concern. On the whole, therefore, it would seem most prudent to opt for either the second or third option outlined above, or indeed a combination of the two: it seems entirely reasonable to suppose that conditions may have varied from one area or landowner to another.

It has been common in the past to explain the development of this situation in terms of a combination of the steady rise in the economic prosperity of the region during the eighth century with the influence of the increased centralizing tendencies of the monarchy leading to a situation where the egalitarian ideals of the past gave way to the opening for capitalist speculators. Additional contributing factors are sometimes said to include the growth in population, leading to pressure on the traditional small holdings and their ability adequately to provide for the whole extended family,[20] and the development of a monetary economy, in which buying and selling of land became easier; and this latter point has been combined with the suggestion that the reference here is to a rather specific situation caused by an influx of wealthy refugees from the north following the fall of Samaria who wanted to acquire property in Judah.[21]

---

[18] See, for instance, the extensive list of passages treated by Dearman, *Property Rights*, including especially Mic. 2.1-5, whose comparability with our passage is explored by Stansell, 127–31.

[19] Houston, 'Social Crisis'; he interacts in particular with W. Zwickel, 'Wirtschaftliche Grundlagen in Zentraljuda gegen Ende des 8. Jh.s aus archäologischer Sicht', *UF* 26 (1994), 557–92, and J. S. Holladay, 'The Kingdoms of Israel and Judah: Political and Economic Centralization in the Iron IIA-B (ca. 1000–750 BCE)', in T. E. Levy (ed.), *The Archaeology of Society in the Holy Land* (London, 1998), 368–98; see previously C. H. J. de Geus, 'Die Gesellschaftskritik der Propheten und die Archäologie', *ZDPV* 98 (1982), 50–57.

[20] See especially G. Fleischer, *Von Menschenverkäufern, Baschankühen, und Rechtsverkehrern* (BBB 74; Frankfurt, 1989), 370–83.

[21] Bardtke, 'Die Latifundien'. This particular suggestion has attracted much criticism, however, and no support that I am aware of.

The evidence for an economic boom in the eighth century is not as strong as popularly supposed, however (see Houston, 'Social Crisis'), so that other possibilities should also be considered. First, Davies, 65–89, has made a strong case for the possibility that 'the prophet was referring to the royal officials who were attempting to expand the crown-land which had been granted to them by the king. These officials were in a position to promulgate new decrees which had the effect of legalising the royal claim to property'. Secondly, Holladay ('The Kingdoms', 383–86 [above, n. 19]), has suggested that the rise of Assyrian control of the Levant generally led to the loss of state income from travel tolls. At the same time, the need to raise tribute would have put additional pressure on the main remaining source of revenue, namely tax on agricultural produce, so leading many into debt. Third, allied with this, Hezekiah's preparations for revolt against Assyria would have probably included not only conscription but also the need for massive additional resources at state level (see too on 3.14, and cf. 22.10). Given Isaiah's well-known opposition to this policy and the likelihood already noted that this passage comes from the later period of his ministry, it is attractive to see the vehemence of this woe saying arising from his perception of the social injustices which he saw as flowing from this wrong-headed policy.

It is noteworthy that there is no hint in this saying that the wealthy or ruling elite were acting illegally in the strict sense, and the probability that they were not is strengthened by the explicit condemnation later in 5.23. It is agreed by most commentators that the situation here envisaged could easily arise in the normal legal course of events, so that the prophet's condemnation has to be based on some other considerations. As we have seen before, the probability is that this was simply a sense of basic human justice in a society lived under God (see on 1.2-3), an appreciation which was shared by the wisdom writers as well without the need to argue for any specific direct influence from that direction.[22] For this reason, the way he describes the judgment here and in v. 10 is to press the logic of their actions to an extreme, in order to show how counterproductive they are (v. 8b). Only later has an editor moved on to a more direct form of divine intervention in judgment in v. 9.

Until there is no more room: in the light of the previous comments, it is not necessary to find any technical language here. The point is simply that if they carry on as they are, the few will eventually own all the available land. Yet this will not benefit them, because they will have come to the point where they *dwell alone in the midst of the land*, a fate that, apart from its obvious injustice, is also counter-productive in that there will be no one else left to work the farms, with effects spelt out in v. 10.[23] The

---

[22] Against Whedbee, 93–98 (and cf. Porath, 122–23); see in more detail Davies, 83–86. Both Whedbee and Davies also argue against Fey's proposal, 59–61, that Isaiah was specifically influenced by such passages as Amos 5.11-12. Again, shared cultural values seem more probable.

[23] This is not to deny, of course, that there may well be an element of satirical exaggeration here; see generally Z. Weisman, *Political Satire in the Bible* (SBLSS 32; Atlanta, 1998), esp. 83–100.

somewhat unusual use of the hoph'al here, *you are made to dwell*, may reflect an appreciation of the fact that ultimately the land was God's gift to his people and that no one 'dwelt' there except by his grace.[24] Even behind the cause and effect continuum that is uppermost in this expression of judgment there is to be detected the overruling hand of God with his concern for all his people, including the dispossessed.

9. *The Lord of Hosts has revealed himself in my hearing*: given that this is based in part upon a conjectural restoration we should obviously be cautious about building too much upon it,[25] but even in the text as it stands the impression of some personal and private communication from the deity is apparent. The notion that the prophets stood in God's court is not peculiar to Isaiah, of course (cf. Jer. 15.1, 19; 23.18, 22; Amos 3.7), but the only occasion on which we explicitly learn of him having such an audience is in ch. 6, where v. 11 is so similar to our verse (see below) that some sort of connection seems very probable. Likewise, the substance of 22.14, which has the same form of introduction as restored here (and even without that it remains very close to it), also seems to reflect ch. 6, on that occasion v. 7, where the atonement granted to Isaiah is denied to the faithless in Jerusalem. Since ch. 22 comes from the later period of Isaiah's ministry, it suggests that application of his early vision at a later date was not exceptional.

The substance of God's oath is that the *many houses* which have been expropriated will become *desolate* and deserted (*without inhabitant*); cf. 6.11, 'Until cities are left *without inhabitant*, and *houses* without people, and the land is utterly *desolate*'. This looks very much like some form of catastrophe taking place in the land,[26] and on the face of things it is difficult to harmonize with the previous verse (note that *inhabitant* comes from the same verb as 'dwell', so that the two statements are saying exactly the opposite). Beuken comments with regard to the tension between this verse and the following one[27] that poetic speech operates according to other rules than pure logic. While it would thus be possible to say that the poet has simply anticipated judgment to come without presenting a fully consistent picture of what will happen, the facts that v. 9 is out of step not only with v. 10 but also v. 8, together with its clear dependence upon 6.11, tips the

---

[24] For this theological use of ישׁב, 'dwell', see M. Görg, *ThWAT* iii. 1012–32 = *TDOT* vi. 428–29. I find no evidence for the view that is sometimes expressed that 'dwell' refers only to enjoyment of full citizenship rights and status.

[25] For this reason I shall in particular not comment here on נגלה, 'revealed himself'. For basic orientation with bibliography, see H.-J. Zobel, *ThWAT* i. 1018–31 = *TDOT* ii. 476–88.

[26] We may note that, in line with the general development in this paragraph from people as a whole (5.1-7; 6.1-11) to one section of society only, so the universal 'houses' of 6.11 have been limited appropriately here to the 'many houses...large and good ones' that we must assume are the property of the wealthy.

[27] He refers to the contradiction between a deserted land in v. 9 and the evidence for harvesting continuing (albeit on a reduced scale!) in v. 10. In addition, however, we may note a further and more serious point of tension: v. 9 comes in the form of a directly interventionist judgment by God, whereas v. 10 deals more in terms of the cause and effect continuum that is characteristic of the wisdom outlook.

balance of probability in favour of it being a later updating of an earlier saying. The probable trigger for this will have been the observation that the final words of v. 8, 'in the midst of the land', are identical with a phrase also found in 6.12; our verse thus becomes exegetical of the end of v. 8 by aligning it with the use of the same phrase in 6.12.[28]

It has sometimes been suggested that the reference to the lack of inhabitants points to the punishment being that of exile, coupled with the further point that this would be an appropriate form of punishment since the Assyrians and later the Babylonians tended to exile only the upper echelons of society.[29] Attractive as this might seem, it appears in the light of 6.11 to be far removed from the expression of judgment by exile; in ch. 6 that comes only with the added vv. 12-13, where we are told explicitly that 'the Lord will send everyone far away'. No such language is found in the present passage.

10. The general drift of this verse is clear: the crops from which the wealthy no doubt expected to benefit will in fact be so poor as to yield even less than the original outlay.

In the second half of the line, this is easily understood. According to Ezek. 45.11, there were 10 *ephahs* to a *homer*,[30] so that seed will yield only 10% of what was sown. (A *homer* is usually explained as deriving originally from the load that a donkey, חמור, could carry, but what this is precisely in terms of modern equivalents is not known, and may even have varied through time; cf. *ABD* vi. 903–4, which suggests an upper limit of 200 litres; this would seem to fit with my comments on *bath* below.)

The first part of the verse is not quite so easy to understand in detail, though again the main point is clear and obvious. According to Ezek. 45.11 again, the liquid measure *bath* and the dry measure *ephah* had the same capacity. Given the ratios already established, this would suggest that a *bath* should approximate 20 litres. Interestingly, Ussishkin has independently calculated on the basis of a storage jar discovered at Lachish that a *bath* measured 21 litres or less,[31] which seems to fit very well.

Needless to say, however, such precision was far from the mind of the prophet; he was concerned hyperbolically to stress the poor yield to the wealthy landowners on their 'investment'. But on the basis of how large a vineyard was he making his point? *Ten 'yoke' of a vineyard* is usually thought to comprise the area that ten yoke of oxen could plough in a day,

---

[28] See also F. Hartenstein, *Die Unzugänglichkeit Gottes im Heiligtum: Jesaja 6 und der Wohnort JHWHs in der Jerusalemer Kulttradition* (WMANT 75; Neukirchen–Vluyn, 1997), 174–75.

[29] Cf. Dietrich, 47. Dietrich is surely correct in maintaining that the passage does not speak of natural, but rather of military disaster and its consequences. His further suggestion, however, that vv. 9 and 10 reflect the judgment relating to the first and second halves of the first line of v. 8 respectively founders on the fact that v. 10 explicitly does not refer to 'fields'. It is more naturally understood as a consequence of the second line of v. 8, to which it may originally have been immediately joined.

[30] The English translation of Wildberger's commentary is muddled at this point, and does not accurately represent Wildberger's perfectly correct original.

[31] D. Ussishkin, 'Excavations at Tel Lachish, 1973–1977', *TA* 5 (1978), 1–97 (87).

and this is variously put at five acres (NEB), ten acres (the majority view) or ten hectares (about 25 acres; Blenkinsopp). While these figures are guesses, the use of 'yoke' in 1 Sam. 14.14 suggests that the basic approach is correct (and even if 1 Sam. 14.14 is corrupt, as many believe, we may assume that the scribe who wrote it incorrectly understood it so, which is sufficient for our purposes). On the basis of the Roman equivalent measure (the *iugerum*) a 'yoke' has been calculated at about half an acre (hence NEB's five acres in total), but we have no means of telling whether in fact the Judean measure is the same (for further discussion, see *ABD* vi. 901–2). But the whole notion is somewhat strange, as vineyards are not usually ploughed, for which reason other scholars prefer to think of the *yoke* as referring to the espaliers on which the vines may have been trained (in which case we should be even further from being able to calculate the area involved), while Walsh, *Fruit*, 111–12, suggests that the reference may be to the use of a plough for spacing between rows of vines (she estimates that the vineyard is about 40 dunams and so considerably larger than the average, which, of course, is the whole point). Fortunately, the prophet's main meaning is not affected by these uncertainties concerning the *realia* with which his readers were no doubt perfectly familiar.

Wildberger points out that crop failure is included in the so-called covenant threats at Lev. 26.20 and Deut. 28.38. That in itself is hardly surprising, for the idea is something of a commonplace. In no way does it justify treating the present passage as though Isaiah were explicitly drawing attention to covenant violations. Rather, as the introductory יִּכ, *For*, makes clear (especially if it once joined directly to v. 8), he regards these consequences as the inevitable outworking of the avaricious greed of the landowners to whom the woe saying as a whole is directed.

SECOND WOE-ORACLE: HEEDLESS DRUNKARDS (5.11-17)

[11]Woe to those who get up early in the morning
     merely in order to pursue strong drink,
who tarry late into the evening
     while wine inflames them.
[12]And there are lyre and lute,
     drum and pipe
          and wine at their feasts,
but they do not regard the activity of the Lord,
     nor do they see the work of his hands.
[13]Therefore my people go into exile
     for lack of knowledge;
their nobility are famished,
     and their multitude are parched with thirst.
[14]Therefore Sheol has stretched wide its throat,
     and opened wide its mouth without measure;
her nobles and her multitude go down,
     together with her raucous revellers—even those who exult in her.
[15]So humanity is humbled and mankind is brought low,
     and the eyes of the haughty will be brought low,

[16]but the Lord of Hosts is exalted in justice,
    and the Holy God shows himself holy in righteousness.
[17]And lambs will graze as in their pasture,
    and fatlings [strangers] will feed upon the ruins.

11-14 are preserved in their entirety in 4QpIsa[b] II, lines 2-6 (Allegro, *Cave 4*, 15). The text is generally very close to MT, and most of the few variations are orthographic (see Horgan, *Pesharim*, 91–92). One or two other issues are noted below.

11. משכימי בבקר and בנשף מאחרי: according to GK §130a, the use of a preposition following the construct is especially frequent in the case of participles; see too JM §129m-n; WO, 155; Gibson, 34.

ירדפו and ידליקם: the first verb is an example of an imperfect without co-ordination following a participle with the same subject, which generally expresses purpose (GK §120c, *contra* JM §159c). In the second case, however, although initially the construction looks similar, there is in fact the important difference that יין is the subject of the imperfect (whereas in the first line שכר is the object). While it would not be impossible for this also to express purpose, it is preferable to recognize the distinction by construing the second line as a standard circumstantial clause (GK §156d; Driver, *Tenses* §163). Procksch's suggestion that a הוי has been lost from the start of the second line is unnecessary.

מאחרי: 1QIsa[a] מאחזי. Kutscher, 217 and 313, ascribes this to a simple mechanical error on the part of the scribe, but Pulikottil, 192–93,[32] suggests that the scribe may have been influenced by ידליקם following, given that (he claims) אחז can have the meaning 'kindle a flame' in Rabbinical Hebrew. Koenig, 297–305, is severely critical of this suggestion (which was first advanced by Kutscher in his attempt to explain why the scroll's scribe was misled), questioning both the linguistic evidence and the presuppositions about likely scribal practice. Instead, he suggests that the reading is that of a passive (probably pu'al) participle, 'seized (*sc.* by drunkenness)'. This is possible, and would give a certain moralistic turn to the saying as well as introducing judgment by reversal: those who pursue strong drink will in turn be overtaken by it. Far more speculatively he also wonders whether the reading may not have arisen initially by a ר/ד confusion (מאחרי) which was then 'translated' back from what the scribe took to be an Aramaic form to Hebrew אחז. This seems most improbable. He is also inclined to find some support for his interpretation in T, which agrees with MT on the word in question, but which then adds למפטר, 'to depart', but which can have the sense of 'untie/let go'; he suggests that the Targumist thereby reflects awareness of the alternative reading. Whichever is the correct explanation of the scroll reading, it is agreed by all that MT reflects the original on this occasion, being uniformly attested by the other versions and contextually superior.

ידליקם: as noted above, this word functions in a syntactically different manner from ירדפו despite the otherwise almost exact parallelism of the two lines. For this reason, a few commentators have been tempted to find here rather the alternative sense of דלק, namely 'hotly pursue', 'chase after'. This requires slight emendation, either to ידלקו(ן) (qal)[33] or ידליקון (hiph'il; Kissane), which would result either way in 'that they may pursue wine'.

---

[32] Pulikottil also states that this is 'the only point where 4QpIsa[b] shares a reading with 1QIsa[a]'. Here, he is wrong on both counts. According to both Allegro, *Cave 4*, 15, and Horgan, *Pesharim*, 92, the *pesher* text agrees with MT at this point, and Pulikottil offers no justification for a different reading; indeed, it is difficult to see how he could, given that Allegro's Plate VI is perfectly clear on this matter. Equally, the *pesher* and the scroll agree against MT elsewhere (see on ביום below).

[33] Ehrlich, 21; Ginsberg, 'Emendations', 52. Note that, although 4QpIsa[b] ידלקם might be a qal (though a defectively spelt hiph'il is equally possible; see Horgan, *Pesharim*, 91), it cannot be cited in support of this emendation because the pronominal suffix shows that the word is understood in the same way as in MT. Alternatively, Cohen, 'Enclitic-*mem*', 248–51, has suggested that the final *mem* is enclitic, so that the line can be rendered 'and pursue wine until late in the evening' without the need for emendation.

Though he does not appear to favour the emendation, Roberts ('Double Entendre', 41–43) suggests that there is a deliberate play on the ambiguity of דלק. Because of the parallelism, by the time the reader reaches this last word of the verse s/he is bound to be thinking that there will be some form of synonymous parallelism with ירדפו, and the use of דלק at first suggests this. Then, however, the reading has to be reconstructed in order to accommodate the different syntactical construction here. 'By playing on this meaning of *dlq*, Isaiah suggests a surprising reversal of roles. It is not just that the alcohol that the wealthy pursue inflames them. The issue is expressed more sharply as a matter of control. The alcoholic is no longer in charge; the wine one began by pursuing ends up as the chaser.' It is hard to adjudicate the strength of such a proposal, since it falls somewhat into the realm of reader response.

12. The syntax of the first line may be understood in one of two ways. Usually, it is explained as an example of the extension of the appositional construction to nominal clauses, i.e. their feasts are lyre…etc.; there are many examples of this construction listed at GK §141*d*; Driver, *Tenses* §188 (2); Gibson, 42. Explanatory paraphrases are sometimes used, such as 'whose feast is wont to be (made merry with) lute and harp' (Gray), or 'whose feasts are (replete with) harp and lyre' (Gibson). Alternatively, it would be possible to construe משתיהם as an adverbial accusative: 'and there are…*at* their feasts' (so that it does not seem necessary to emend by adding the preposition ב, *contra* Blenkinsopp). There is no effective difference in meaning (cf. WO, 228); I suspect that the first possibility is more likely in keeping with Hebrew idiom, though English idiom prefers a rendering as if it were the second. I have adopted this in the translation above primarily because it allows a closer visual representation of the line divisions of the MT, not because I favour the adverbial accusative as a solution. LXX paraphrases: μετὰ γὰρ κιθάρας… τὸν οἶνον πίνουσι. It is not clear whether this represents a misunderstanding of the Hebrew syntax or merely a free translation (the lack of a formal equivalent of והיה is unexceptional, of course); it certainly does not warrant Budde's unnecessary emendation to וייום הם שתים, 'while they drink their wine'.

והיה…משתיהם: if the syntactical analysis just given is correct, משתיהם is the subject. Despite appearances it could be singular (cf. GK §93*ss*), and is often said to be so. But a plural seems more natural in terms of sense, and of course there is no problem about a plural subject following a singular verb, especially in poetry (cf. GK §145*o* and especially *q*).

ויין: the four previous nouns in this list are clearly grouped into two pairs by the use of the conjunction.[34] Here, the fifth noun is unpaired, and so, while it is closely joined to the list (note the conjunction with pre-tonic *qameṣ*) it gains a certain emphasis, which seems suitable: 'and of course, especially wine'. The attempts either to delete it altogether[35] or to emend to בְּיִן משתיהם,[36] or to emend to בין with temporal force ('during their feasts')[37] are thus misguided (beside the consideration that a temporal sense of בין is uncertain[38]).

משתיהם: suggested emendations to משעתם or משעתיהם or משעיתם, all = 'their interests' (Ginsberg, 'Emendations', 52), or מזמתם, 'their scheming' (Fohrer), are unsupported and seem unnecessary.

יביטו…ראו: both perfect and imperfect can have present effect, so that their use in parallel in a way which is almost indistinguishable in English usage is not uncommon; cf.

---

[34] 4QpIsa[b] differs from MT in the occurrence of the conjunction in this series: it is included before תוף but not before יין. Although this necessitates a slightly different rendering, the effect is still to separate יין somewhat from the previous nouns.

[35] See, for instance, Feldmann; Procksch; Eichrodt; Fohrer; Ginsberg, 'Emendations', 52.

[36] Porath, 106; he compares the use of 'the wine of/at a feast' several times in Dan. 1, which is fine, but it does not explain the supposed loss of the preposition here.

[37] Caspari, 'Hebräisch בין temporal', followed by, for instance, Wildberger and Jacob.

[38] The case is based principally on the difficult text in Neh. 5.18, where it is likely that בין should be understood substantivally; cf. L. Köhler, 'Hebräische Vokabeln III', *ZAW* 58 (1940–41), 228–34 (229).

GK §106*l*; Driver, *Tenses* §35.[39] Gibson, who seeks to press the aspectual understanding of the Hebrew verbal system to its limit, conjectures that in such a case the imperfect may represent a surviving instance of the short *yiqtol* form and that it does so here throughout vv. 11-12 (cf. p. 75). But we have already seen that the imperfects in v. 11 are to be differently explained, so that it is the perfect ראו which is the more unexpected element here; contrast the use of two imperfects in an otherwise comparable setting in 1.23 (last line). The possibility may be considered that the flexibility afforded by parallelism has here been exploited in order to pave the way for the 'prophetic perfect' גלה in the next line. The consistent use of the perfect in 1QIsaᵃ and 4QpIsaᵇ (and cf. T) at this point (הבישו for יבישו)[40] is thus likely to reflect the view that this word of judgment has already been fulfilled in the past from the scribe's point of view (cf. Pulikottil, 134–35).

13. גלה: however it is to be explained ('prophetic perfect' is the traditional terminology[41]), this is clearly an announcement of future judgment, following לכן; cf. לכן...יגלו at Amos 6.7. Driver, 'Isaiah i-xxxix', 37–38, objects that the threat of exile in more than a century's time would not be an appropriate deterrent, and so he proposes the rendering 'disappear, are swept away in death'. The meanings are, of course, very closely related, so that the difference is less than Driver implies.[42] Since exile would have already been well known as a tool of international politics by Isaiah's time, it is not clear why it would have been any less effective as a threat. Other conjectural emendations which have occasionally been proposed seem similarly unnecessary (e.g. כלה,[43] or חלה [Ehrlich]), and MT is now further supported by a tiny fragment of 4QIsaᶠ as well as 4QpIsaᵇ (and probably 1QIsaᵃ, though the scroll is somewhat damaged at this point).

מבלי־דעת: it is not certain whether מבלי is causative ('because of lack of knowledge'; so the versions; Knobel) or privative ('without knowledge', i.e. unawares; so Gesenius; BDB, 115B). Delitzsch, for example, argues strongly for the latter on the ground that this is always the meaning of the word elsewhere, while Young supports him on the ground that in Isaiah's theology the people were punished for sin, not want of knowledge. On the other hand, Delitzsch's argument seems misguided in the light of Deut. 9.28 and especially Hos. 4.6, where it is again used with דעת, but this time explicitly the knowledge of God, while 1.3 (to go no further) is an adequate response to Young's argument. Since either rendering is thus possible (so Gray), the context has to be the decisive factor; see below.

---

[39] For further discussion, where the case is made on the basis of the need for stylistic variation because of the use of the same verb in parallel, see Cassuto, *Studies*, 57–58; M. Held, 'The *YQTL–QTL* (*QTL–YQTL*) Sequence of Identical Verbs in Biblical Hebrew and in Ugaritic', in M. Ben-Horin *et al.* (eds), *Studies and Essays in Honor of Abraham A. Neuman* (Leiden, 1962), 281–90; Watson, *Classical Hebrew Poetry*, 279–80; Berlin, *Dynamics*, 35–36. Examples in the Psalms of *yqtl–qtl* of (mostly) different verbs referring to the present are listed at M. J. Dahood, *Psalms III: 101–150* (AB 17A; Garden City, N.Y., 1970), 423.

[40] Strictly speaking this represents an assumption on my part, as damage to the scroll means that ראו is not actually attested; but the assumption seems reasonably secure. ראו is the reading in 4QIsaᵇ, and for later rabbinical citations which follow suit, see HUBP. Kutscher, 352, lists this verse with other passages where the scribe has harmonized the tenses; this may well be a factor, but it does not explain why the tense of the second verb was chosen rather than, as might have been expected, the contextually prevailing imperfect form as represented in the first verb.

[41] For a survey and discussion, see G. L. Klein, 'The "Prophetic Perfect"', *JNSL* 16 (1990), 45–60; the most recent discussion of this phenomenon is M. Rogland, *Alleged Non-Past Uses of* Qatal *in Classical Hebrew* (SSN 44; Assen, 2003).

[42] Cf. F. A. Gosling, 'An Open Question Relating to the Hebrew Root *glh*', *ZAH* 11 (1998), 125–32. Even if he is correct to distinguish two roots, he still sees 'go into captivity' as only a developed sense of his *glh* II, 'depart, disappear'.

[43] Marti reports this as the opinion of Duhm, though it does not occur in either the first or the fourth edition of his commentary.

מתי רעב: 'men of hunger'; there are enough examples of this use of מתי to suggest that this is a perfectly regular and acceptable idiom (cf. a very insistent Kimhi; Gesenius; BDB, 607A; GK §128s). 1QIsaᵃ and 4QpIsaᵇ are identical at this point (we might have expected מיתי if they understood the word in the same way as the versions). With such recent commentators as Blenkinsopp and Beuken, I find no difficulty with this reading. The versions, however (and see too Rashi), all link with the root מות, either reading as a construct plural noun מֵתֵי (dead because of hunger; so LXX[44] and P; cf. 22.2) or as a plural verb מֵתוּ (have died of hunger; so V and T).[45] The former has sometimes been adopted, as it is thought to give better sense than MT and to require only a change of vocalization (cf. NRSV, 'are dying of hunger'; NEB 'are starving to death').[46] Objections to this emendation have included the observation that it leads to a less satisfactory parallelism, since those in the second half of the line are not dead, and the suggestion that it does not fit the wider context of people being led into exile (they may be hungry, but presumably not dead). It is a matter of opinion whether these objections are found convincing or whether they are thought to press the meaning of a word too literalistically. Either way, it has led other scholars to conjecture the alternative emendation מְזֵי (or מְזֵה), 'wasted with famine', as at Deut. 32.24.[47]

14. שְׁאוֹל: the initial daghesh is unexpected; GK §20f is not explanatory but descriptive (and pretty tortuous at that).

נפשה: despite the persistence of a translation such as 'appetite' (NRSV), there is now no doubt that נפש can also have the concrete sense of 'throat, gullet', as in Ugaritic npš (DUL, 636–37) and Akkadian napištu(m) (CDA, 239); cf. HAL, 672; H. Seebass, ThWAT v. 531–55 = TDOT ix. 497–519; and for further bibliography, DCH v. 911–12. This is obviously a contextually superior rendering here.

ופערה....וירד: this sequence of w + qatal forms following the free-standing qatal הרחיבה is noteworthy; the first is clearly copulative, as at 1.2; the second might be as well, but is perhaps better construed as 'epexegetical', which, according to WO, 533 (though without reference to this verse) may signify a (future) consequence; they cite Driver, Tenses §108, in support.

הדרה והמונה ושאונה: so-called abstracts for concrete. There is no proximate antecedent for the feminine suffixes,[48] for which reason it has occasionally been suggested that they

---

[44] This much at least seems clear from what is otherwise an especially free translation by the LXX in the second part of this verse: ...διὰ τὸ μὴ εἰδέναι αὐτοὺς τὸν κύριον καὶ πλῆθος ἐγενήθη νεκρῶν διὰ λιμὸν καὶ δίψαν ὕδατος. The translator has clearly overridden the parallelism by combining the references to hunger and thirst. In that case, he may have also conflated כבוד and המון in πλῆθος (differently Ottley), as its position in the sentence aligns it with כבוד but its meaning with המון (Ziegler, 51, categorizes המון with examples of a LXX minus in cases where there is a synonymous word in the parallel; I am not sure that this is correct). Alternatively, it is tempting to think that he may have taken כבוד as a reference to God (pace HUBP) and construed it with the first line, where MT has no equivalent of his τὸν κύριον, so leaving him with only המון to serve as the subject of the second line.

[45] The uncertain evidence of one or two Masoretic manuscripts and of some of the minor versions is surveyed by Barthélemy, 33–34. He also shows that the diversity of opinion continued from antiquity through the middle ages.

[46] E.g. Gray; Procksch; Kissane; Porath, 106; McLaughlin, The marzeaḥ, 156–57.

[47] E.g. Hitzig; Dillmann; Orelli; Duhm; Cheyne, Book, 83; Marti; Condamin; Feldmann; Budde; Fohrer; Kaiser; Wildberger; Watts; Werner, Plan, 21; even Oswalt considers this 'an attractive option'.

[48] Blenkinsopp refers them to Sheol, but even if this were possible to start with (though הדרה in particular seems unlikely to me), it cannot be sustained in the closing words of the verse, which he is thus obliged to treat as a 'syntactically inappropriate gloss'. Independently, the suffixes are also referred to Sheol by Moberly, 'Whose Justice?', 65; he retains the final phrase and suggests that the problem which it raises for his view 'could perhaps be resolved by the clear...reference to certain scoffers' misplaced

should be vocalized as or emended to the masculine, so aligning them with the comparable כבודו and המונו of the previous verse (cf. *BHS*). Claims that the versions support this
change are misguided, however: LXX, V and P offer no support, while T has masculine
plural suffixes, which does not really help either.[49] 1QIsaᵃ also agrees with MT at this
point. It is more likely that the explanation is literary-critical; see below.

ועלז בה:[50] traditionally 'and he who rejoices/exults in/on account of her'. As it stands,
it is undoubtedly awkward, however. The previous nouns are naturally construed as collectives, and so have a plural significance, whereas עלז is singular. Emerton, 'Problems',
137, finds a further difficulty in that 'it is very awkward to have a personal adjective after
three abstract nouns which are thus not *eiusdem generis*'. While not all commentators
have felt the force of these difficulties, those who have have adopted one of several
solutions. Ehrlich, for instance, argued that a verbal adjective עָלֵז could not possibly be
derived from a verb which regularly has an imperfect in 'o' and so he proposed emending
to וְעֶלְיָהָ, 'and her exultant ones', which gets over the problem of number but leaves the ב
unexplained. Driver, 'Notes', 42–43, compared Arabic *ʿaliza*, 'was jubilant, was restless,
had colic', and so initially proposed 'and suffer pangs therein' (and he thought that LXX οἱ
λοιμοὶ αὐτῆς, 'her plagues', perhaps retained a memory of that meaning); later, however,
he revised his opinion in favour of 'and shall be restless therein', though this does not fit
with the usual portrayal of Sheol (cf. Job 3.13-18).[51] Emerton, 'Problems', conjectured
that two letters had been accidentally transposed in the course of transmission and so
proposed the reading וְעֹז לִבָּהּ, 'and her stubbornness/courage'. It would be another example of abstract for concrete which could also be construed collectively ('and her stubborn/
courageous ones'), so aligning it nicely with the previous sequence of nouns. Though the
exact phrase is not attested in the Old Testament, there are sufficient parallels for the use
of such idioms with לב and for the semantic field of 'strength' to make it plausible. More
recently, this latter point has been vindicated by the occurrence of the very phrase עז לב in
a Phoenician papyrus from a tomb in Malta, where in context the meaning 'courage' is
appropriate. Emerton concludes his more recent study by affirming that 'a phrase which I
had conjectured in Isa. 5.14 is made more plausible by the existence of a similar phrase in

confidence in some kind of agreement with Sheol (Isa. xxviii 16)'. This suggestion was in
fact advanced long ago by Hitzig (followed by Alexander), who also referred to 28.15 to
justify the idea that the reference was simply to those who scoff at the threat of Sheol, but
this is not an appropriate rendering of עלז; there is no hint of scoffing, for instance, in the
survey of the word's semantics by G. Vanoni, *ThWAT* vi. 126–31 = *TDOT* xi. 115–20
(though in fairness one might point to the later evidence of 4QpIsaᵇ II, 6–7; see n. 50
below). Knobel also objected to Hitzig's interpretation that Sheol is a place of stillness
and sadness, so that it would be inappropriate to link this string of nouns with it in any
way. As we shall see in the course of the discussion of this phrase, עלז is commonly used
with reference to cities, and that seems to be a more natural interpretation here as well.

[49] See the careful survey in Emerton, 'Problems'.

[50] 4QpIsaᵇ has עליו בא. Horgan, *Pesharim*, 92, appeals to Kutscher, 163–64, to justify
the explanation that בא is simply an orthographic variant of MT בה. But Kutscher does not
cite any examples of this with a preposition, as it would be here, and it seems doubtful.
Coupled with the lack of the conjunction on עליו, I wonder if a better explanation could be
that these two words have been understood as a separate clause, 'the exultant one has
come'. At Isa. 14.9 it is said of the tyrant that 'Sheol beneath is stirred up to meet you
when you come (בואך)', and twice in the following verses there is talk of him being
'brought down' (hophʻal of ירד) to Sheol (14.11, 15). The author of the *pesher*, who
interprets our line as referring to אנשי הלצון אשר בירושלים, 'the Scoffers who are in
Jerusalem', could well have seen a parallel here (note וירד at the start of the line).

[51] Driver's revised opinion was not published, so far as I know (though it presumably
lies behind NEB's 'noisy bustling mob', with the marginal variant 'noisy mob, and are
restless there'); it was reported only orally to Emerton, who also raises objections to it; cf.
'Problems', 138–39.

Phoenician'.[52] Emerton's proposal has not been widely followed, despite the difficulties in the present form of the text to which he reasonably draws attention. It is considered too conjectural (see, for instance, Wildberger), and indeed, there is no versional evidence to support such an emendation, as Emerton's own full analysis accepts.[53] I should wish also to draw attention to the fact that at 22.2 we find a rather comparable description: 'you that are full of shoutings (תשאות, which may be related to שאון), tumultuous city (הומיה, which is tantalizingly reminiscent of המון!), exultant town (קריה עליזה)', which suggests the appropriateness of עלז in such a context; indeed, the commonest use of עליז is in connection with a city (cf. Isa. 23.7; 32.13; Zeph. 2.15; 3.11,[54] while at Isa. 24.8 it occurs in combination with שאון). Emerton's point about עלז being unexpectedly singular is well taken, though his argument that we expect a further example of abstract for concrete seems less compelling (indeed, Hitzig seems almost to make a virtue of it). Given Ehrlich's comments on the unexpected form of the verbal adjective עלז (which as such is a *hapax legomenon*) and the use of the commoner עליז elsewhere, I propose reading וְעֹלְזֵי בָהּ. For the construction, see on v. 11 above; the suggestion has the advantage of supplying the expected plural, and this difference from the previous collectives is sufficient to empty Emerton's other perceived difficulty of its force (this would be even more so if the *waw* be construed as explicative); unlike Ehrlich's proposal, however, it retains the ב of the MT (note that the verb עלז governs the preposition ב on five occasions, e.g. Hab. 3.18); it may be conjectured that the earliest consonantal form of the text (prior to the use of *matres lectionis*) was identical with MT and that for some reason it was never provided with the expected fuller orthography.

15. The first line is identical with 2.9a, the comments on which may be compared for discussion. Given the likely redactional activity here (see below), the verbal sequence is probably derivative, so that we should be cautious about drawing conclusions from it, still more changing it (*contra* Duhm). 1QIsaᵃ has simply ישח for the first word, but since, like MT, it continues with וישפל, it seems probable that this is secondary; perhaps, as Moberly, 'Whose Justice?', 55, wonders, it has been somehow attracted to תשפלנה later in the verse.

The second line is similar to 2.11a, but without the awkwardness that we observed there.

16. וינבה: for the anomalous spelling in L, see on 2.15.

נקדש: Wildberger favours the slightly less well attested pointing as a perfect (נִקְדָּשׁ) because he thinks that it follows the *waw*-consecutive of the first line better. But the shift from *waw*-consecutive to imperfect in the previous closely related verse gives one pause. We have repeatedly seen (most recently at v. 12) that other factors than simple 'sequence' can affect the tenses in poetry. Moberly, 'Whose Justice?', 55, in fact prefers the participial form because it 'better expresses a general truth about YHWH than the perfect pointing'. He notes that the LXX renders all the verbs in these two verses consistently as future, but maintains that 'the MT, with its apparent inconsistencies, may still convey much the same sense' without the need for changes to the pointing in either verse.

17. כבשים: 1QIsaᵃ has כבושים,[55] and this seems also to be the text presupposed by LXX, οἱ διηρπασμένοι, 'those who were spoiled, plundered' (as a paraphrase for 'subdued, trodden down').[56] The other versions support MT (σ and α: ἀμνοί; P: ʾmrʾ; V: *agni*) with

---

[52] Emerton, 'Phrase'. It may further be noted that לב occurs with the verb עוז in CD 20.33; cf. H.-P. Müller, 'Ein phönizischer Totenpapyrus aus Malta', *JSS* 46 (2001), 251–65 (257).

[53] He rightly makes a virtue of the LXX's freedom of translation method in Isaiah to dismiss the suggestion of Ottley that its *Vorlage* may have had עריציה in place of ועלז בה; see too Seeligmann, 104.

[54] This point of comparability does not, however, justify Ginsberg's more radical speculations about the relationship between the two passages; 'Emendations', 53.

[55] This is not spotted by *The Dead Sea Scrolls Bible*, 278, which renders 'lambs', as in MT.

[56] As Kutscher, 247 and 473–74, rightly observes, this LXX evidence tells heavily against R. Meyer's alternative suggestion that this is part of a regular *ā* > *ō* shift that he

the one reservation that T paraphrases by introducing 'the righteous' here as part of a righteous/wicked interpretation of the verse as a whole (see below). Gray thought that LXX might be an example of what he called this 'early allegorising interpretation', but this now seems unlikely in view of the scroll reading (which Gray could not have known, of course). Similarly, Troxel, 'Economic Plunder', 382–84, is also cautious about speculating as to what might have stood in the LXX's *Vorlage*, given the unusual equivalence. He sees the greater influence coming from 'the translator's conviction that those to benefit from the Lord's judgment will be those who have suffered economically'. This may indeed have influenced the choice of translation equivalent, but the scroll reading (to which Troxel makes no reference) still seems to make it overwhelmingly probable that the LXX was working with a similar form of the text. We are therefore confronted with a genuine variant, the merits of which can be evaluated only in the light of how it fits within its wider context; see further, therefore, on the next word.

כדברם: the modern understanding of this word seems not to have been recognized in antiquity. Since Gesenius it has usually been taken to be דֹּבֶר, 'pasture' (with preposition and suffix). For the (not uncommon) use of the single preposition כ to represent what in English requires two prepositions ('as in'), see GK §118s-t; WO, 204. The noun occurs elsewhere only at Mic. 2.12 (though the text there is not certain), and possibly in the (variously spelt) place name Lo-Debar. Though not, therefore, strongly supported in Classical Hebrew, it has cognates in Ugaritic, Aramaic and Syriac, and it may be derived from דבר = 'drive' (Delitzsch; cf. Ibn Ezra, שם כאילו נהגים היו להיותם, also with a reference to Aramaic). The major alternative (and more ancient) understanding has linked this with דבר = 'word', as in T כמא דאמיר עליהון ('as was promised concerning them') or = 'manner' (see BDB, 183B [7]), as in V *iuxta ordinem suum* (similarly Rashi, Kimhi; Calvin 'in [God's] usual manner', and AV, 'after their manner') and P *bzdqhwn*, 'according to their entitlement/as is their due'.[57] (It should be noted, therefore, that, with the possible exception of P so far as the preposition is concerned, these all support the consonantal text of MT, as in this case does 1QIsaᵃ.) A minor alternative was to link the word with דבר = 'lead', giving rise to 'without restraint' (i.e. 'as their own will shall lead them'; so Lowth). LXX, by contrast, renders ὡς ταῦροι, 'like bulls', presumably (with defective spelling) כְּאַבְּרִם.[58] This retroversion is sufficiently close to MT to accept that either text could have arisen from the other by scribal error, so that as in the case of the previous word it may be that we again have a genuine variant (the whole line in LXX may therefore be rendered 'and those who were plundered shall be fed like bulls'). On the other hand, the LXX rendering is completely unsupported in this case, so that the possibility should also be allowed that the translator was led to misread a text such as 1QIsaᵃ in the way he did because of the wider context and the difficulty of understanding כדברם. On balance, it seems to me that MT as interpreted above is contextually superior (the focus is on what will become of the city rather than the fate of the former inhabitants), and it also furnishes a much more satisfactory parallel with the second line—a judgment which applies to all renderings of that line! (There is no rendering or emendation which produces a parallel to the passive כבושים.) The rare word כדברם may have misled the LXX translator here, while the introduction of גרים in the second half (see below) may have led a Hebrew scribe to read כבשים as כבושים, so giving rise to the text shared by both the scroll and LXX.

finds in the language of the scroll; cf. 'Bemerkungen zu den hebräischen Aussprache-traditionen von Chirbet Qumran', *ZAW* 70 (1958), 39–48 (41).

[57] The proposal favoured by *BHS* (following Procksch) to read the preposition as ב rather than כ is misguided. To say that lambs will graze in their pasture is to say nothing! What is meant is that they will graze on the site of the ruined city *as if* it were their pasture, a very different proposition.

[58] NEB, 'Young rams shall feed where fat bullocks once pastured, and kids shall graze broad acres where cattle grew fat', is partially influenced by this, as well as Ginsberg, 'Emendations', 53–54 כד בראם = 'pasture of the fat ones'). But apart from the severely conjectural nature of the rendering (see Brockington, 176), it completely misses the point that it is the *city* which is to be turned into pasture, not other farmland!

חרבות: as pointed, this is in the construct state, as it needs to be before מחים if any sense is to be made of MT. I shall eventually propose repointing as an absolute, חֲרָבוֹת, though that decision is based entirely on considerations relating to what follows.[59] There is no evidence whatsoever to justify emendation to רחובות, 'wide spaces'.[60]

מחים: 'fatlings', as at Ps. 66.15, where it is parallel with אילים, 'rams'. It is hardly surprising that the versions had difficulty here, an added problem for them being how to construe with the uncoordinated גרים following. V *in ubertatem*, 'in richness', construed it adverbially from the same root; T pursues its interpretive approach from the first line, but by rendering מחים גרים as נכסי רשיעא, 'the riches of the wicked', it looks as though it too has recognized the root; and P d*tbny*, 'which was (re)built', may be working etymologically from חיה, which is occasionally related to (or at least, has been thought to be related to[61]) rebuilding/restoring (so Gesenius; HUBP). LXX, as part of its major reconstrual of this verse, has τῶν ἀπειλημμένων, '(of) those who are taken away', though it has often been proposed that this should be emended to ἀπηλειμμένων, 'those wiped off'.[62] Either way, this no doubt associates the word with a passive form of מחה (Duhm in later editions. Procksch, Kissane and Driver, 'Linguistic and Textual Problems', 39, all propose מְחָים, which they adopt as the best reading), though 1QIsaᵃ supports the Masoretic tradition of vocalization of the first syllable with its plene spelling מיחים. It is difficult to suppose that LXX should be taken seriously at this point from a strictly text-critical point of view; it must reflect the continuation of influence from the passive οἱ διηρπασμένοι in the first line. If 'fatlings' is therefore the best supported reading and meaning, it is nevertheless difficult to construe in context; see further on the following word.

גרים: plural participle of גור, which Delitzsch explains as follows: 'The *gârim* themselves are men leading an unsettled, nomad, or pilgrim life; as distinguished from *gērim*, *strangers* visiting, or even settled at a place'. In order to derive sense from this and the preceding words as they currently stand, Gray offers the following amplified rendering: '*(Shepherd-)wanderers shall feed*, i.e. cause their flocks to feed, *on the ruins*, which were once the home *of the fat*, i.e. of the prosperous persons'. This seems an improbable reading, however; Gray himself objects to the explanation of גרים, and in addition, as we have seen, מחים in its only other use in the Bible refers to animals, not humans (though this may well have been the trigger for the line of interpretation attested in T and elsewhere). Finally, there is no evidence for this causative sense of the qal of אכל, while to make 'the ruins' into its direct object ('nomad shepherds eat the waste places of the fat ones', Delitzsch) would be most peculiar (Knobel); Delitzsch tries to defend this with reference to 1.7, but there the object is אדמה, which is completely different and makes for good sense. Driver, 'Linguistic and Textual Problems', 38–39, proposed גָּרִים (with Akkadian,[63] Syriac and Arabic cognates), 'young beasts, sheep', but this has not found favour. If we want a reference to animals here, there is a more convincing way of finding them, namely to note LXX ἄρνες, which usually means lambs or sheep, but which occurs occasionally elsewhere as the rendering of גדיים, 'kids' (HR, 159), a suitable parallel for lambs.[64] The

---

[59] Blenkinsopp's assertion that MT means 'swords' must rest on no more than a mistaken understanding of the vocalization. I suspect that he has derived it without realizing the mistake from the English translation of Wildberger's commentary, where (without warrant in Wildberger himself) 'swords' is added as an incorrect gloss on חרבות at the end of the notes on 17b-b (p. 192).

[60] So Ginsberg, 'Emendations', 54, followed by NEB and *BHS*.

[61] For my reservations on this, see my *Ezra, Nehemiah* (WBC 16; Waco, Tex., 1985), 127 and 214; it does appear once in Phoenician with this meaning, however; cf. *DNWSI*, 355.

[62] Cf. Ottley; Seeligmann, 11 n. 8; see too Barthélemy, 35.

[63] His Akkadian *gurū* is not supported by *CDA*, however, though they do list *gu(r)rutu* meaning 'ewe'.

[64] Others have occasionally suggested כרים, 'lambs'. Note should also be taken of Barthélemy's alternative suggestion to a similar end, but without the need for emendation,

ר/ד confusion is one of the commonest of all scribal errors, so that the mistake in MT is conceivable, and many commentators have adopted this as an emendation;[65] cf. NRSV, 'fatlings and kids shall feed among the ruins'. Nevertheless, there are still unresolved issues. גדי in fact hardly ever occurs on its own, but is nearly always used in the construct before עזים; the absolute plural occurs only once, at 1 Sam. 10.3. Secondly, as Driver observed, it is improbable that such a well-known word that fits the context (and so would be easily recognized by any scribe) would be miscopied to one that is difficult, if not impossible. Thirdly, the fact that it follows מחים, which is in the absolute, without a conjunction is difficult; NRSV's silent addition of 'and' merely highlights the problem. And finally, though not a decisive argument on its own, it could be argued that there is one word too many in this second line for regular rhythmic balance. For these sorts of reason, some commentators have therefore argued that either מחים or גדיים (emended) should be deleted as some sort of gloss: the latter might be an explanatory gloss on the rare word מחים,[66] for instance, or vice versa (so Gray). A consequence is then the need to repoint חרבות as an absolute, as indicated above. I believe that this solution is heading in the right direction, but would suggest that גרים may not need to be emended (at least in this way) and then be declared an explanatory gloss so much as left as it is (or changed slightly differently) and taken as a historicizing gloss.[67] At 1.7, in the description of the aftermath of a military defeat, we read that 'foreigners are devouring (זרים אכלים) your land'. It is plausible to suppose that the similar situation envisaged in our verse, with a link provided in particular by the word אכל, caused a historically minded commentator to gloss 'fatlings' with גרים in order to explain how this threat worked out historically following the fall of Jerusalem. Indeed, one might wonder whether in fact גרים may not originally have been זרים, exactly as at 1.7; the words are graphically very similar, and a slip once the glossator's intention was no longer understood would not be surprising. I find this final conjecture attractive, but the proposal as a whole is not dependent on adopting it.

The woe series continues with an extended passage condemning those of (apparently) the urban elite who indulge themselves so much in drinking and revelry that they are heedless of God's work in their midst. This is therefore not only bad behaviour in itself (and as such generally condemned in prophetic and wisdom literature alike—though not explicitly in the law—so suggesting that it is a shared value of traditional Israelite or Judean society), but indicative of a self-sufficient human pride, which always attracts Isaiah's severest condemnation. The fate of such people is described under two headings—exile on the one hand (v. 13) and destruction on the other (v. 14). This leads on to a wider application of the principle against human pride in general: it will come to nothing, because it

namely to compare the use of the verb גור at 11.6 of animals 'qui pâturent en transhumant'; he therefore suggests that גרים might be 'des transhumants'. This is not an attested meaning of the participle, so far as I know, however, and it would be seriously liable to misunderstanding, given that there is another animal גור, 'lion's whelp', with which it could too easily be confused. Nor will the latter serve in our verse, in parallel with lambs: the conditions of 11.6-9 (where indeed lions and lambs dwell together) are not yet envisaged as having arrived!

[65] E.g. Lowth, 'and the kids shall depasture the desolate fields of the luxurious'; Wade; Procksch; Kissane; Scott; Jacob; Oswalt.

[66] So Duhm in his first edition, but he later changed his opinion; Marti; Condamin; Fohrer; Schoors; Wildberger.

[67] So already H.-W. Hertzberg, *Beiträge zur Traditionsgeschichte und Theologie des Alten Testaments* (Göttingen, 1962), 71, followed by Vermeylen, 173, Kaiser, Werner, *Plan*, 21, and Porath, 107.

challenges God's sovereign exaltation (vv. 15-16). The territory that such people once inhabited will revert to wasteland (v. 17).

The setting of this woe saying in the series is readily intelligible. On the assumption that the sayings have been redactionally rather than authorially ordered, we can see how the opening focus on heavy drinking might be joined not just to the reference to a vineyard in v. 10, but through that to the Song of the Vineyard which was set as the introductory statement of this section of the book as a whole. Moreover, the social standing of those addressed seems to be close to that of vv. 8-10 as well.

Despite all this, there are clear signs that this section is itself the result of literary growth, and this is recognized by nearly all commentators.[68] First, the most obvious seam occurs with v. 14. The string of third person feminine singular suffixes have no antecedent (and we have seen other places, such as the end of ch. 3, where this seems to mark literary disjuncture) and to this must be added the fact that the verse's introductory 'therefore' comes awkwardly after the 'therefore' of v. 13. While Anderson, '"God with Us"', has nicely shown how this 'double therefore' phenomenon is a feature of the redaction of Isaiah, that does not mean (and Anderson explicitly does not claim it means) that it is anything other than the result of redactional compilation. (It may be noted that what looks like something of a similar mythologizing of the judgment will recur at the end of the chapter, v. 30, in what is probably a redactional *Fortschreibung*.)

Secondly, it seems very probable that vv. 15-16 have been slotted secondarily into their present setting. On the one hand, v. 17 is a far more natural continuation of v. 14 than of v. 16.[69] The theme of inhabited land reverting to waste which can be used for pasture is a frequent one (see below), but it is always used in association with cities. On the usual understanding of v. 14 (which I share), that verse describes with poetic imagery the downfall of the population of Jerusalem, so that v. 17 follows on naturally to describe the further fate of the site, whereas there is nothing in vv. 15-16 that leads in that direction. On the other hand, vv. 15-16 seem clearly to be modelled on the second part of ch. 2 and so give the impression of a later commentator providing a universal application to the specific example of v. 14. Although there are no exact catch-words, the theme of nobility going down in v. 14 could well have been sufficient to prompt what amounts to a developed cross-reference.

Sheppard, 'Anti-Assyrian Redaction', has argued that in fact these two verses once belonged in ch. 2 and that they were moved to their present location by the anti-Assyrian redactor whom, following Barth and Clements, in particular, he finds to have been influential in the shaping of this whole section of the book. He cannot eventually decide whether their original location was in front of 2.7 or following 2.21, and this indecision

---

[68] Contrast the elaborate chiastic structure which Biton finds in vv. 11-17 as a single unit: 'New Outlook'.

[69] Some have seen v. 17 as the continuation rather of v. 13 (e.g. Høgenhaven, 171, citing also among others Marti and Procksch), but this seems less likely on the ground that on the basis of parallels elsewhere we should expect v. 17 to follow a reference of some sort to the loss or destruction of a city.

is telling: there is nowhere in ch. 2 where we miss this material, unlike in cases of a similar sort of procedure which we traced in the case of several parts of ch. 1. Furthermore, there are several other difficulties for his view. In my analysis of ch. 2, I argued that the material in *6-8 and *10-19 had been joined at v. 9 by a redactor of probably exilic origin. This rules out the possibility that 5.15-16 (whose parallels are in 9 and 10-19) could have belonged before 2.7 as early as the Josianic period, and equally, given that 2.20-21 are patently a late *Fortschreibung* of the preceding verses, a position following v. 21 is also impossible. In addition, the fact that 5.15-16 are so similar in wording to parts of ch. 2 suggests the far greater likelihood that they are citations than dislocations. And finally, given that vv. 15-16 seem to interrupt what is already an addition to the chapter, the probability must be that they were added later than the time envisaged by Sheppard.

I see no reason, therefore, why vv. 15-16 should not be as late as the kind of universalizing application of earlier material that we find in the Isaiah Apocalypse (Isa. 24–27). Kaiser has argued that in fact a great deal of Isaiah 1–39 comes from this period. The fact that such concerns surface most explicitly in material which can be seen to be considerably later than its prevailing context both supports the view that this was still a significant period for the growth of the book as a whole but equally that it is a mistake to assign the bulk of the material to it; a consequence of diachronic research works both ways: if some material is late, then *ex hypothesi* other material must be earlier. Similarly, while there is little evidence on which to date vv. 14 and 17, a date in or close to the exile would seem best to fit what they are saying and the parallels in other biblical books. Once more, therefore, I find no evidence here for a Josianic redaction but rather a further pointer to the importance of an exilic redaction in the early formation of the book.

The conclusion of our discussion so far, then, seems to be that vv. 11-13 are the original woe saying, and that this has been expanded first by the addition of 14 and 17, and then later by the added comment of 15-16. This is probably the majority opinion.[70] It remains to ask about the unity of 11-13, since a few scholars have suggested that either v. 13 or v. 12 is not original. In my opinion, the case for regarding v. 13 as secondary is stronger, but ultimately not conclusive.

In favour of the unity of the passage are the observations that form-critically it comprises a woe saying (11-12, which seems to be a reasonable length; cf. 8 + 10 or 18-19), to which a consequence, introduced by 'therefore', has been added, as sometimes elsewhere,[71] and in particular that it has a close parallel in Amos 6.1, 3-7. This is, indeed, a parade example of dependence for Fey, and with good reason.[72] Form (a developed woe saying) and theme (excessive drinking with accompanying

---

[70] In addition to many commentaries, see, for instance, Vermeylen, 172–74; Barth, 192; Stansell, 61.

[71] Cf. Westermann, *Grundformen*, 138–39 ('die Ankündiging') = *Basic Forms*, 192 ('the announcement'); Hardmeier, *Texttheorie*, 249; Sweeney, 124–25.

[72] Fey, 10–22, recently defended anew by McLaughlin, *The* marzeaḥ, 159–61.

music) are the same down to the level of some detail, and there is also some shared vocabulary; on this occasion, therefore, the objections to Fey's argument by Whedbee and Davies do not seem so forceful.[73] A further small pointer towards unity may be the observation that the judgment by reversal in v. 13*b* binds the whole together and that it makes for a further parallel with the general pattern of 8 + 10.

To my mind, the biggest potential objection to this conclusion is the threat of exile in v. 13, and this is sharpened by the observation that the 'lack of knowledge' which is said to cause the exile is close to (and perhaps influenced by) Hos. 4.6, but that there the punishment is destruction, which would be far closer to Isaiah's usual understanding of judgment. Exile is certainly not characteristic of Isaiah himself. There is no other reference to it in his own sayings, though at 20.4 the exile of Egypt and Ethiopia is predicted in a third person passage reporting what Isaiah had said. There is sound historical memory behind Isaiah 20, but it is probable that it was written up some time after Isaiah's life; it would therefore be hazardous to argue from it that exile was a characteristic threat of his, and in any case it is not related to Judah. Isaiah's usual anticipation of judgment, as we have seen already several times, is of defeat and destruction within the land (in view of the close association between this passage and ch. 22, one may compare in particular 22.4, 'the destruction of the daughter of my people' and 22.14, 'until you die'). We might, therefore, have expected him to express himself more in the style of Hos. 4.6 at this point. A further argument against the originality of v. 13 has been noted by Deck, 240–41 (following Kilian), who thinks that the shift from revellers in vv. 11-12 to 'my people' in v. 13 is indicative of a later 'actualization'.[74]

While the possibility that this verse is therefore to be ascribed to a later redactor should be seriously considered, consistency of thought on a matter such as this is insecure ground for a decision on its own. The constraint of Amos 6.7 (לכן יגלו בראש גלים), a passage on which we have agreed that Isaiah is drawing extensively in these verses, is sufficient to account for this uncharacteristic usage. The notion of exile in itself would not have been unknown to him, and if this passage is indeed to be dated late in his ministry (see below), he would have already witnessed it in regard to Israel. Needless to say, this usage would have had particular resonance later on in the exilic period when, we believe, significant redactional work was undertaken on the book. Once again, however, we must be careful not to conclude too quickly from this that the passage must have been written

---

[73] Whedbee, 100–1; Davies, 37–38. The trouble with both rejoinders is that they take each element of the argument in turn and show that it may have been common in other contexts, and so on, but they do not consider the remarkable accumulation of parallels distinctively in these two passages to which Fey has drawn attention.

[74] The position of Porath, 113–16, that v. 13 is a later addition that separated the original woe saying in 11-12 + 14 and 17 seems to me most unlikely. It is based primarily on the verbal 'tenses' in this passage (especially the perfect גלה in v. 13), which is an uncertain ground for argument, and it fails to deal with some of the contrary evidence outlined above: his handling of the third person feminine singular suffixes in v. 14, for instance, is most unsatisfactory.

then. And so far as Deck's argument is concerned, though it undoubtedly has weight, we should recall on the one hand that Isaiah is not entirely consistent in his use of 'my people' (e.g. contrast 1.3 with 3.15; see further Høgenhaven, 31–34) and on the other that in his view the sin of the leaders often has serious consequences for the people at large.

The argument that v. 12 is a later addition is far weaker, in my opinion. It has been urged in particular by Werner,[75] but on unsatisfactory grounds: he dislikes the style ('das nachklappende משתחם [*sic*] וייך'), but that proves nothing. Similarly, he maintains that the vocabulary about God's activity and work comes only in later texts, but again one must question what that proves; in particular there is a danger of circular argumentation (see v. 19, for instance).[76] Once again, I am more impressed by the observation that this verse too is one element of a larger series of points of connection with Amos 6.

I argued above that a case could be made for dating vv. 8 + 10 to the late period of Isaiah's ministry. In the case of 11-13 that case seems to be stronger. In particular, there are a number of points of close connection of both vocabulary and theme with 22.1-14 (generally agreed to be one of his last sayings; see especially Dietrich, 181–82), and these are noted throughout the notes and commentary (see especially on vv. 12-13 below). At such a time, knowledge of Amos's words and the reality of the threat of exile are easily accommodated.

The poetry of both the original woe saying and its later expansions is not especially noteworthy. There is an interesting (though stylistically not very impressive) further example of the use of a tri-colon for emphasis at v. 12, but beyond that the rhythm of the passage is somewhat erratic and the use of parallelism may be characterized as no more than standard.

11. While ancient Israelite society may not have been averse to heavy drinking in certain contexts,[77] the pursuit of drink as an end in itself is regularly condemned on account of its attendant dangers in both the prophets (e.g. in addition to the present verse 5.22; 22.13; 28.1, 7; 56.11-12; Hos. 4.11; Amos 4.1; 6.6; Mic. 2.11) and the wisdom literature (e.g. Prov. 20.1; 21.17; 23.20-21, 29-35; 31.4-5; Eccl. 10.16-17); there are also a number of stories in narrative texts which scarcely veil their criticism. It is thus improbable that we should associate the condemnation with any specific sociological group, such as the wise (so Whedbee, 98–101); it is more likely that all these passages reflect something of the shared values of ancient Israelite society. Here, the point is that this has become an all-consuming pursuit (see below), to the exclusion of more important matters (12*b*); hence the hyperbole of starting *early in the morning* (often, השכים is

---

[75] Werner, *Plan*, 23; see too Kaiser, but apparently only on the ground that he expects woe sayings to be consistently short.

[76] The possibility that some of the elements to which Werner takes exception may be attested in the eighth-century plaster inscription from Deir 'Alla has been raised by Dijkstra, 'Balaam', 57–58, but it is hard to know how much weight to put on this.

[77] See C. E. Walsh, 'Under the Influence: Trust and Risk in Biblical Family Drinking', *JSOT* 90 (2000), 13–29.

used in an auxiliary sense for 'to do X early', but its independent use here, parallel with 'tarry late', indicates that it must refer to the time of getting up) and continuing till *late in the evening* (that cooler part of the day when the evening wind, the רוח היום of Gen. 3.8, starts to blow, נשף, and when activity resumes after the heat of the day—whether for good or ill; cf. 21.4; Job 24.15; Prov. 7.9). The close parallel with Ps. 127.2 suggests that this is effectively a merismus for 'all the time'. This leads Korpel to the nice observation of the contrast between this passage and Ps. 92.2-5: 'Whereas the psalmist rises early in the morning (בקר) to praise his God and plays the כנור and נבל to sing about his פעל and his מעשי יד, the drunken leaders forget the work of Yahweh' ('Structural Analysis', 58). For *tarry late* in connection with drinking, see also Prov. 23.30. Although not explicitly stated, it would seem probable that only the relatively affluent would have been in a position to indulge to this extent (cf. Davies, *Double Standards*, 51–52), so that an element of Isaiah's familiar polemic against the upper classes is included—not because of their social position as such, but more because they abused that position rather than using its privileges for the benefit of society as a whole.

To *pursue* is used metaphorically, as here, with such positive objects as knowledge of the Lord (Hos. 6.3), righteousness (Deut. 16.20; Isa. 51.1; Prov. 21.21), peace (Ps. 34.15) and goodness (Ps. 38.21). Its converse here is thus suggestive of something which one makes the whole object of life. The precise identification of *strong drink* is uncertain. Its effects everywhere (as well as its derivation from שכר, 'be/ become drunk') justify the qualifying adjective 'strong', and suggest that identifications with beer are unlikely. With only one exception (Num. 28.7) it is used in association with *wine*, which is certainly a product of the grape. Based on this, one suggestion has been that originally שכר simply meant any alcoholic drink but that when the Israelites adopted יין for grape wine, שכר came to do duty for every kind of fermented drink (e.g. from dates, honey, raisins, etc.) except wine. More narrowly, Walsh, *Fruit*, 200–2, argues for 'date palm wine'. It is known that such wine was made in Palestine in antiquity, and she draws attention to an ostracon from Ashkelon with the words יין אדם, 'red wine'. Since all wine at this time was red (see on 5.2), this must be grape wine and is therefore used to distinguish it from date palm wine, which was brown. It is not clear, however, why her argument limits the alternative to date palm wine; the ostracon would seem to allow the conclusion only that it referred to grape wine in distinction from any other, of whatever sort.

12. As we move from a general word about drinking to that associated in particular with *feasts*, so we find the addition of other forms of entertainment, in this case music, to add to the distractions from what Isaiah regards as more important priorities. That music accompanied feasts is known from elsewhere in the Bible (e.g. Gen. 31.27 [by implication]; Amos 6.4-6) and indeed it is an almost universal custom. While there can be no certainty about the precise nature of the instruments listed (and note that they occur together also at 1 Sam. 10.5), it seems likely that the first two were stringed instruments. They occur frequently in parallel, often accompanied singing, and could be played with the fingers (1 Sam. 16.16 and probably Amos 6.5[78]). If the second, נבל, is linked somehow to the shape of a skin-bottle, then *lute* seems most appropriate. Whether it differs from the *lyre* in terms of size, design or the number of strings (or any combination of these) cannot be certain; pictorial and archaeological evidence suggests that any might be appropriate. *Drum* (תף) could probably be any sort of instrument that is played by striking (cf. Nah. 2.8) on a stretched membrane or skin; I render drum as the most neutral term, but in principle tambourine (Wildberger) and timbrel would also be possible, though the evidence suggests that at this relatively early period the simple drum might not yet have developed so far. Finally, חליל suggests an instrument into which holes have been bored or pierced, though others suggest that it refers to the buzzing sound of a reed instrument; hence, perhaps, *pipe*, as a general term; 'flute' or 'oboe' gives too modern an impression.[79]

This entertainment may be added to *wine*, which was the principal subject of the previous verse, as constitutively present at *their feasts*. Given the close parallel between this passage and Amos 6.1, 3-7 (see above), the question arises whether this should also be taken as a reference to a *marzeaḥ* feast. The matter has recently been carefully studied by McLaughlin, *The* marzeaḥ, 155–62. He maintains that although as in other references to the *marzeaḥ* there is clear evidence for upper-class participation and the consumption of large amounts of alcohol, the third component that he considers constitutive of such a gathering, namely the religious context, is lacking. It is therefore significant that, whereas in Amos 6.7 the word מרזח occurs, here this is precisely altered to the general term משתיהם, *their feasts*.

So caught up are Isaiah's addressees in their pursuit of such pleasures that they have no time or inclination to contemplate *the activity of the Lord* or *the work of his hands*. Within the book of Isaiah as a whole, this kind of language is common (see Beuken!), so that at the literary level of the book as a whole one should not seek to interpret it too narrowly: creation of Israel (e.g. 45.11; 60.21; 64.7) or of Assyria (19.25), past blessing (5.4), present threat (5.19; 10.12, 23) and future promise (e.g. 29.23; 43.13; 62.11) may all be included. Going further afield, there is even justification for seeing here an allusion to creation itself.[80] But if we seek to restrict our exegesis to the likely reference of an eighth-century

---

[78] See P. J. King, *Amos, Hosea, Micah—An Archaeological Commentary* (Philadelphia, 1988), 154.

[79] For all the above, see T. C. Mitchell, 'The Music of the Old Testament Reconsidered', *PEQ* 124 (1992), 124–43; J. Braun, *Music in Ancient Israel/Palestine: Archaeological, Written, and Comparative Sources* (Grand Rapids and Cambridge, 2002) (this is a revised and updated edition of the German original: *Die Musikkultur Israels/Palästinas: Studien zu archäologischen und vergleichenden Quellen* [OBO 164; Freiburg and Göttingen, 1999]); I. H. Jones, *ABD* iv. 934–39; and D. A. Foxvog and A. D. Kilmer, *ISBE* iii. 436–49. Mitchell and Braun (especially) give detailed attention to archaeological and iconographic as well as textual evidence.

[80] See Paas, *Creation and Judgement*, 371–74. For a survey of all biblical uses of God's מעשה, see Werner, *Plan*, 16–18, from which again the variety of applications emerges as a clear conclusion.

Isaiah, it is probable that we shall conclude that it is God's general care for the nation in its past history that will have been uppermost in his mind.[81] We saw that this was the burden of his accusation in 1.2-3, where again rebellion against such care was seen as a failure of 'knowledge' and 'understanding'. Similarly, the exegesis of the Song of the Vineyard in 5.1-7 pointed in the same direction as the likely notion behind the owner's preparation and early tending of the vineyard (note the sevenfold use of the root עשה in that passage). Furthermore, there is a closely parallel constructed line at 22.11b: 'But you did not look (הבטתם) to him who did it (עשיה), or have regard for (ראיתם) him who fashioned it (יצרה) long ago'. Here the creation language is even stronger (see especially יצר), but such a reference is clearly out of the question in the context. Although the matter is not completely certain, the most likely reference is again to God's past care of his city and people[82]—creation language, which may well have been familiar to Isaiah from the Jerusalem cult, in view of its frequent occurrence in the Psalms, is applied by him in particular to God's work in the history of his people. Equally, one may compare from outside Isaiah Ps. 28.5, where the wicked will be destroyed on the same grounds, and there are other passages in the Psalms which point in a similar direction (see Porath, 129–30). This interpretation then leads on naturally to the application in the next verse.

13. *Therefore* the punishment of the nation is due to *lack of knowledge*. We saw in the notes above that strictly speaking this was ambiguous, but it will now be clear that the context points strongly to the causative meaning rather than the privative (i.e. 'suddenly, unawares'). Consideration of God's past goodness is linked with knowledge and understanding in 1.3, and indeed, in particular in association with seeing, it is a familiar theme in the book of Isaiah as a whole, starting at 6.9-10 (see my *Book*, 46–50). There is a close parallel also at Hos. 4.6 which points in the same direction: 'My people are destroyed for lack of knowledge (מבלי הדעת, so the only difference is the presence of the definite article), because you have rejected knowledge'. According to Wolff, this knowledge is again related to 'the basic deeds of salvation performed by Yahweh in Israel's earliest period'.[83] The understanding of what these comprised may have differed somewhat between Israel and Judah in the eighth century, but the basic similarity remains.

The major difference with Hos. 4.6 is the nature of the punishment: destruction there, but *exile* here. The reason for this, and its implications, were discussed above in the introduction to this section.

[81] It should be noted that, despite the parallelism in v. 19 following, there is no need to see here a reference to God's 'plan'. Without a reference here to עצה, such a notion should not be read into the passage, *pace* the assumption of a number of commentators and especially Ginsberg, 'Emendations', 52.

[82] The main alternative is that it refers to what God is doing in the wider international political scene, and such an application would not be impossible in 5.12 as well; cf. Høgenhaven, 171–72.

[83] H. W. Wolff, *Hosea* (Philadelphia, 1974), 79 (German original: *Dodekapropheton. I. Hosea* [BKAT 14/1; Neukirchen–Vluyn, 1961], 97); similarly G. I. Davies, *Hosea* (NCB; London and Grand Rapids, 1992), 88.

Unlike at 3.15, but very much in line with 1.3 and 5.7, *my people* seems to refer to the population at large, although this is further qualified in the following line. Historically speaking, of course, both the Assyrians and the Babylonians were selective about which members of the population they deported, and the next line, as well as Amos 6.7, seems to reflect awareness of that fact. It would therefore be rhetorically insensitive to press that point here in isolation; the line needs to be read in close conjunction with the 'nearer definition' provided by the following line.

Their nobility (lit., 'his glory') is used as a collective abstract for concrete, as at 16.14; 21.16; Mic. 1.15. While it might refer specifically to the military elite (cf. 8.7; 10.16), a more general sense seems contextually preferable. It is often thought that *their multitude* then refers to the remainder of the population, but this seems unlikely. The same word occurs again in the next verse, where it is one of several abstracts for concrete referring to the revellers who were the subject of the previous verses. המון refers basically to noise, and so by extension to a crowd, but although a crowd may often include members of the general population, there is nothing in the word which demands that; it is more easily understood here as the crowd of revellers, which we saw will have been mainly comprised of the upper classes.

While defeat and exile will almost inevitably have been accompanied by being *famished* and *parched with thirst*, the particular point here, of course, is that the punishment is a reversal of the feasting and drinking of the previous two verses. Although differently expressed, 22.12-14 is again not dissimilar.

14. A different form of judgment (and one that in some respects might be considered more in keeping with Isaiah's usual outlook) is here added (together with v. 17), namely the destruction of the Jerusalemite revellers, leading to the site's desolation. Here again, it is probable that we are to think of the Jerusalemite population being regarded as predominantly upper-class (the so-called urban elite), in contrast with the bulk of the population who will have been rural. Naturally there is an element of over-simplification and stereotyping here, but that is not uncharacteristic of prophetic speech.

To depict this judgment, the colourful image of *Sheol* as a voracious monster is effectively deployed.[84] The image is far from unique to Isaiah. Habakkuk 2.5 makes use of similar language (*has stretched wide its throat* is the same in both) in its comparison of Babylon with the voracious Sheol, and comparable ideas appear also in the wisdom literature; cf. Prov. 1.12; 27.20; 30.15-16 (see less exactly, but still within the same broad circle of ideas Isa. 14.9, 11; 38.18; Hos. 13.14; Ps. 49.15; see too the reversal of the image at Isa. 25.8). In the Ugaritic texts, Mot (Death) is also depicted as having a voracious appetite, with some similar language being used, and many scholars therefore think that this mythological portrayal lies behind the biblical depictions of Sheol (note that in a passage such as

---

[84] For recent discussions of Sheol with further literature, see H. M. Barstad, *DDD*, 768–70; L. Wächter, *ThWAT* vii. 901–10; P. S. Johnston, *Shades of Sheol: Death and Afterlife in the Old Testament* (Leicester and Downers Grove, 2002).

Hab. 2.5 Sheol is parallel with מוח, which is also personified).[85] This latter opinion is not universally shared, however, so that the matter remains one of current dispute. Barstad, for instance, has argued trenchantly that the biblical personification of Sheol should not be related to Mot in any way; he finds nothing more than a metaphorical way of referring to the universal awareness of the greediness of death, and that it demands no more mythological background than do the other insatiable things listed in Prov. 30.15-16 (leech, barren womb, earth and fire). Perhaps the linguistic comparisons with Mot at Ugarit are no more than the standard idiom for the description of such voracity.[86] Either way, this verse is as extreme an expression of the image as any (*without measure* has no parallel elsewhere, though 'and is never satisfied' at Hab. 2.5 comes close).

The language of swallowing does not occur here as it does in several of the other Sheol passages mentioned. Instead, those destined for judgment *go down*. Of course, these are really only two sides of the same coin, as their use in combination at Num. 16.32-33 makes clear. But the different emphasis seems appropriate: in their hubris, it is almost as though they make their own way consciously to their destination. It is even stronger than 14.11 and 15, where it is the passive of the causative of ירד that is used, indicating an element of compulsion.

In the second half of the verse there is repeated use of the third person feminine singular suffix, and I have argued in the notes above that these lack a stated antecedent. We encountered a similar situation at 3.26, where the reference to gates indicated that a city (obviously Jerusalem) was in mind. The same is widely agreed to be the case here too. Interestingly, we also concluded that the unattached suffixes at 3.26 were the result of redactional movement (rather than *Fortschreibung*), and it seems probable that this accounts for our verse as well.

The characterizations of those going down to Sheol are (i) *nobles* (הדר, hence not the same as the word rendered 'nobility' in v. 13). This word occurred and was discussed at 2.10, where it is used with reference to God. It therefore implies those who are perceived as distinguished, but at the same time its use here for the revellers points in the direction of hubris. It may be that its use in ch. 2 was the trigger for the addition here of the next two verses, which are closely comparable with the same passage; (ii) *multitude*; see on v. 13; (iii) *her raucous revellers* (שאונה); like the previous word, the idea of noise is predominant, but is if anything stronger (e.g. the roar of waters, the din of battle, the crashing of ruins). This seems to be its only use as an abstract for concrete; and (iv) *those who exult in her*. This is conjectural (see the notes above), so that we should not base too much upon it. The word's semantics were briefly sketched there, and from that it emerges that it refers to those who take an

---

[85] See R. T. O'Callaghan, 'Echoes of Canaanite Literature in the Psalms', *VT* 4 (1954), 164–76 (169), and J. Day, *Yahweh and the Gods and Goddesses of Canaan* (JSOTSup 265; Sheffield, 2000), 185–86.

[86] This may not, however, account for the less usual point of comparison in Ps. 49.15 and *KTU* 1.6.II.21-23, as noted by Day, and the parallel personification of Mot at Hab. 2.5 remains suggestive.

unjustified, bragging self-assurance in Jerusalem. Such an attitude was roundly condemned by Isaiah (not least again in ch. 22), because it reflected a misplaced faith if it was not associated with a modest and dependent attitude towards God. These four characterizations are thus closely related to one another.

15-16. These two verses are obviously inspired by the second half of ch. 2, and following what we have just seen in v. 14 we can understand why an editor should have wanted to include them here—in order to comment on the judgment of v. 14 in familiar Isaianic terms and to draw out the theology behind it.[87] The whole of v. 15 has parallels in 2.9 and 11, the comments on which may be compared for exegetical detail.

The start of v. 16, *the Lord of Hosts is exalted*, is also somewhat similar to 2.11 and 17 (*q.v.*), but in this new setting it is developed in a fresh manner by combination with another of Isaiah's favourite themes, that of *justice* and *righteousness*, for which see on 1.21 and 27. As in this latter verse (where the words are also preceded by the preposition ב, 'in, with, by'), there is uncertainty here whether these are meant to be attributes of God or his people. The common view is the former: as God exercises his justice and righteousness in the judgment of the haughty, so he is exalted and seen to be holy. There are some points of resemblance with aspects of 4.4 in this. Moberly, however, has entered a strong plea for the alternative interpretation.[88] His principal argument is that in v. 7 justice and righteousness are qualities that God seeks in his people, and so contextually we should expect them to mean the same in the present verse. Indeed, this is the commonest use of this word pair in Isaiah 1–12, although he admits that 1.27 and perhaps 9.6 are less certain. Given the uncertainty, however, he makes a virtue of it by allowing that

> the Isaianic text presumes a certain kind of analogy between divine and human which may be summarized: Israel is to embody those moral qualities which characterize YHWH himself—Israel is to practise justice and righteousness because this is how YHWH himself acts. Further, it is a basic prophetic axiom that YHWH acts in and through the actions of his servants... Thus YHWH's actions of justice and righteousness may be seen precisely in the actions of justice and righteousness performed by those accountable to him. (p. 63)

The following considerations may be added to those of Moberly. First, we saw at 1.27 that there was something of a similar ambiguity, but that the context there favoured the view that human justice and righteousness was the predominant thought. Secondly, although the verb there was different (פדה), there was a rather clear distinction in usage to be drawn regarding the force of the preposition according to whether God or a human being

---

[87] Moberly, 'Whose Justice?', 66, observes that the imagery of descent in v. 14 'can readily lead into the imagery of bringing low' in v. 15.

[88] Moberly, 'Whose Justice?'. He cites only the commentary of Brueggemann as anticipating his position (though without elaboration). We may note without further ado that Moberly is surely right to insist that any interpretation must consider the meaning of משפט and צדקה as a pair (if not a hendiadys), rather than seeking to build an exegesis of the passage upon the way that either term is used elsewhere in isolation (as von Rad did, and see Wildberger).

was the subject. (The situation at 1.27 itself was complicated by the fact that the verb was passive; the verbs here are niph'al as well, but not strictly passive in the same way.) If the same holds true here, then that would lead us to expect, against Moberly, that it is God's justice and righteousness that is predominant. Third (and this is an important point which Moberly does not consider, so far as I can see), if the niph'al נִקְדָּשׁ is correctly rendered *shows himself holy* (and for this it makes no difference whether we keep the Masoretic vocalization as a participle or revocalize as a perfect)—and that is certainly the usual meaning of the niph'al of this verb (cf. BDB, 873A)—then it is difficult to see how this could be done by anything other than his own justice and righteousness. This argument admittedly does not apply to the first verb in the line, *is exalted*, but in a parallelism of nearer definition the second half of the pair should have the final say, so to speak. Finally, without wishing to discount the importance of 5.7, it is not clear that it is so close to the present verse as to be contextually compelling. I accept, of course (by precisely the reverse argument of that which obtained at 1.27), that, as Moberly himself maintains, an element of both senses may be present, but I should want to put the weight the other way round from him: human justice and righteousness are not just derivative, as Moberly agrees, but also in this context distinctly subordinate. I conclude that, in this interpretive comment comprising vv. 15-16, the thought is appropriately drawn out that in the judgment executed on the revellers—a judgment which, v. 15 reminds us, will befall anyone who similarly exalts him- or herself in boastful pride—God is seen to be exalted and his holiness to be moral and ethical; for Isaiah and for those who understood his message this was always uppermost: 'the Lord alone will be exalted on that day' (2.11, 17).

The Holy God: this divine title does not occur elsewhere. It is obviously closely connected with the ascription of holiness to God in the title 'the Holy One of Israel' (on which see at 1.4, where it was seen to exert influence into the later Isaianic tradition), but I suggest that in the more universalizing context of these two verses it was considered appropriate to detach the title from any specific nationalistic connections.

17. This verse was probably originally the continuation of v. 14: after the disappearance of the inhabitants of Jerusalem, the site of the city will revert to use as pasture. In its new context, following the more universal vv. 15-16, 'the ruins of *v.* 17 may be not just of one specific place (Jerusalem?) but of a wider context of divine judgment on the earth (cf. Isa. xxiv-xxvii)' (Moberly, 66). In other words the redactional reuse of this verse fits well with the development of the theology of the book as a whole.

This idea of the fate of a destroyed city is not uncommon; Wildberger, for instance, compares 17.2; 27.10; 32.14; Zeph. 2.6, 14; similarly Mic. 3.12; Lam. 5.18. Nor is it far, of course, from the description of the fate of the vineyard in vv. 5-6, especially as that is later interpreted in 7.23-25. The aim is not to depict some idyllic pastoral scene, but to underline the completeness and irrevocability of the judgment. The glossator who added *strangers* as an interpretation of the animals was not far from the mark, though he narrowed the application to the political realm, with the presupposed loss of land and sovereignty.

THIRD WOE-ORACLE: MOCKERS OF THE DIVINE PURPOSE (5.18-19)

[18]Woe to those who drag iniquity along as with bulls-leather cords,
  and sin with a rope of heifer-leather,
[19]who say,
'Let his work hurry and make haste,
  so that we may see it;
let the counsel of the Holy One of Israel draw near and be fulfilled,
  so that we may acknowledge it.

18. העון: so too 4QIsaᵇ; in 1QIsaᵃ the ה has been added above the line as a correction. This doubt about the definite article here may well be connected with the uncertainty about the parallel חמאה at the end of the verse (see below).

בחבלי: textually, the preposition ב is strongly attested (both extant Qumran scrolls, V, T, etc.). LXX, σ and P, however, render as though they read with כ, as in the parallel וכעבות, and if השוא is to be emended (see below), this becomes attractive, though perhaps not absolutely essential, given that the line is in any case patently using a metaphor. Those who favour the slight emendation can, of course, reasonably argue that the slight corruption will have arisen in connection with the misreading of the next word, so that it predates any of our Hebrew witnesses.

בחבלי השוא: 'with cords of falsehood/vanity'. 1QIsaᵃ was at first thought to read השו, using the same spelling as it does at 59.4 in order to avoid mispronunciation (Kutscher, 174). The latest edition seems to be correct in transcribing as השי, however, and this cannot be so neatly explained (unless it is itself a scribal error). 4QIsaᵇ is damaged following the ש, but in the editor's opinion the space before the next word indicates that its text was the same as MT. The versions generally support MT, though in the case of LXX, ὡς σχοινίῳ μακρῷ, this has to assume either an inner-Greek corruption from ματαίῳ, comparable with the ὡς σχοινίῳ ματαιότητος of σ (Ottley), or a midrashic interpretation by the translator,[89] rather than a different Hebrew *Vorlage*, שרוע, 'extended' (Lowth, following Houbigant; Duhm). P renders השוא differently from his practice elsewhere; he may have been thrown by the difficulty of the text and so merely followed the LXX. The sense is difficult, however. Despite the use of חבלי with various other metaphorical senses, to which appeal is regularly made at this point (e.g. חבלי שאול, 2 Sam. 22.6/Ps. 18.6; חבלי אדם parallel with עבתות אהבה [interestingly, also with משך], Hos. 11.4; חבלי מות, Ps. 116.3; חבלי עני, Job 36.8; חבלי חמאתו, Prov. 5.22), such an approach does not make for good sense here. The context demands something strong, which is the very opposite of שוא. T paraphrases in line with standard rabbinic interpretation[90] to try to make sense of MT, 'Woe to those who begin to sin a little, drawing sins with the cords of vanity, continuing and increasing until sins are strong as cart ropes', but it is difficult to believe that this is anything other than *post factum* rationalization. Suggestions of magical significance are no better,[91] not least because of the parallel line. Two similar philological solutions have been proposed: Dahood, 'Ugaritic', compared Ugaritic *ṯat*, 'ewe' (hence שֶׂה here), while Driver, 'Isaiah i–xxxix', 38, independently added Akkadian *šuʾu* and Arabic *ṯaʾwatu* to propose a Hebrew word שׂוא, also meaning 'ewe'. A 'ewe-rope' would be used to tether a ewe while milking, for instance: 'These men set themselves to keep a hold on iniquity with as much zeal as a shepherd holds a reluctant beast where he wants it to be'. This,

---

[89] So Goshen-Gottstein, 'Theory and Practice', 139–41, *contra* Delekat, 'Septuagintatargum', 236.

[90] For a number of rabbinic parallels of varying date, see Kellermann, 'Frevelstricke', 92–93.

[91] S. Mowinckel, *Psalmenstudien*, 1: *Āwän und die individuellen Klagepsalmen* (Kristiania, 1921), 28 and 51–52; M. A. Klopfenstein, *Die Lüge nach dem Alten Testament: Ihr Begriff, ihre Bedeutung und ihre Beurteilung* (Zürich and Frankfurt, 1964), 315.

however, does not fit with the verb משׁך, and there is no evidence that ewes were ever dragged along with ropes. The same problem arises for the emendation to שׂה, 'sheep', favoured, for instance, by Clements and Blenkinsopp. There is thus much to be said for adopting the old conjectural emendation to השׁור (א and ר are more easily confused in certain forms of the old Hebrew script than the square script, suggesting that the corruption is in principle very early). Winckler, who according to Kellermann, 'Frevelstricke', was the first to advance this proposal,[92] construed the phrase as an explicative genitive: cords made of (bull's) leather, but most of those who have followed his proposal (see the representative list in Kellermann, n. 22) have taken it in the sense of the kind of cord needed to tether or lead a bull (i.e. especially strong). Either interpretation seems possible, so that the parallel must be adduced to help decide; see immediately below.

עבות העגלה, 'the rope of a cart'. Since עבות is a singular noun (as correctly stressed, for instance, by Barthélemy, 36–38), 'cart-ropes' (NRSV) and the like are inadequate renderings. Moreover, carts were not dragged along by rope, so far as we know, so that it becomes in any case necessary to seek a slightly different approach if the parallelism with the usual understanding of the emended version of the first half of the line is to be maintained; Kellermann, for instance, thinks that it refers to the rope by which the animals pulling the cart are led along. Following the emendation to השׁור in the previous phrase, many commentators have, not surprisingly, taken their cue from the LXX here (ὡς ζυγοῦ ἱμάντι δαμάλεως) to join the final ה of העגלה to the next word (hence החמאה, which makes a better parallel with העון in the first half) and to read הָעֵגֶל in consequence. (An alternative approach to a similar consequence is simply to revocalize the present consonantal text as הָעֶגְלָה, but it then becomes more difficult to understand why the Masoretes should have misunderstood the word, and in addition it does not have the advantage of the alternative proposal of 'killing two birds with one stone'.) So this too could then mean 'heifer rope', i.e. the kind of rope needed to tether or lead a heifer. It is at this point, I suggest, that parallelism comes into play in favour of Winckler's minority opinion. The usual approach seems to me to have two disadvantages: it has the effect of focusing attention on the animal rather than the rope, and in addition it lacks the 'what's more' element of parallelism that we usually expect, given that a heifer is not so strong as a bull. Despite the admitted dangers of an approach to semantics by way of etymology, I nevertheless suggest that the real point at issue here is the move from חבל to עבות. The latter appears to mean 'rope' in its proper sense, i.e. twisted, interwoven, hence made up of many strands and so much stronger than the single-corded חבל (which had therefore to be plural to gain the necessary strength). It is here that the crescendo of the line falls, not on the virtually synonymous animals in question; they are included simply to indicate that we are dealing with leather cords and ropes as opposed to any other kind of material.

19. ימהר יחישה: on its own this line could be construed in different ways, particularly with regard to the subject. For instance, God could be the unexpressed subject of the first verb, or indeed of both (cf. LXX; T; NEB).[93] The following line is closely parallel, however, and there the feminine form of the two verbs indicates that עצה is the only possible subject. Although traditional opinion is divided on the matter (see the list of commentators favouring each possibility in Delitzsch), it is therefore best to take מעשׂהו as the subject here as well. The lack of a conjunction following מהר is not a problem, of course; cf. GK §120g. There is therefore no need to follow P in restoring יהוה as the subject of (ה)יחישׁ (contra BHS, NEB; cf. Brockington, 176), nor to take its final ה as an abbreviation for the divine name.[94] The case is strengthened by the observation that in the parallel the second

---

[92] H. Winckler, *Altorientalische Forschungen* III/2 (Leipzig, 1905), 216–17.

[93] יחישׁה may be either qal or hiph'il, of course, so that מעשׂהו could be either its subject or its object; cf. G. R. Driver, 'Studies in the Vocabulary of the Old Testament. II.', *JTS* 32 (1931), 250–57 (254 n. 6).

[94] So Y. Qoller, 'Symbols, Abbreviations and Acronyms in the Bible', *BethM* 31 (1985–86), 10–16 (14–15 [Hebrew]). Such a device was completely unknown as early as biblical times.

verb is also cohortative, תבואה, both being rare but not unparalleled examples of the cohortative on a third person verb; cf. GK §48d; JM §45a. It should be noted, however, that there is considerable fluidity on this matter in the early Hebrew witnesses: 4QIsa[b] agrees with MT on יחישׁ (*pace* Blenkinsopp, who seems to have confused this with 1QIsa[a]) but then in the next line it reverses the forms to read ותקרבה ותבא, whereas 1QIsa[a] has no cohortative form in the first line (ימהר יחישׁ) but conversely makes both verbs in the second line cohortative (ותקרבה ותבואה);[95] it also has ונדע for MT ונדעה at the end of the verse. The one stable element in all this is the consistent use of the feminine in the second line, so confirming the main point about the subject of each line in parallel.

ונדעה (for 1QIsa[a] ונדע, see immediately above): a standard example of the use of simple *waw* + cohortative 'to express an intention or intended consequence' (GK §108d; cf. JM §116b), exactly parallel with למען נראה in the previous line (JM §168a, n. 2).

This third woe-oracle is the first in a series which appear not to have been expanded in the way that the first two were. In other respects, however, it continues in very much the same vein as the preceding ones, so that there is no reason to think that two earlier and separate cycles have here been joined. First, we saw that the first two were related in a somewhat mechanical manner; that is to say, there were connections in each case with what went before (primarily through the theme of vineyard and drinking), but not with any close sequence or connection of thought or argument. The same applies here. Bearing in mind that the second woe-oracle was originally limited to vv. 11-13, the connection by way of reference to the work of God in vv. 12 and 19 will have been more readily apparent originally than it is now. However, as we shall see, what is referred to as God's work differs somewhat in each verse, so that there is no smooth transition in thought from the one to the next. Secondly, on the assumption that will be justified below that it is primarily the political leaders of the nation who are in view here, it seems that the basic audience being addressed remains unchanged.

This evidence seems to point to the conclusion that the woe-oracles were collected into this sequence before the expansions in vv. 14-17 in particular, and thus go back to an early stage in the formation of the book (probably pre-exilic if I am right in suggesting that 14 + 17 might be part of the exilic redaction).

The original unity of these two verses has been assumed by virtually all commentators. Kaiser relegates v. 19 to his much later eschatological interpreter. He admits, however, that taken on its own this verse suits what might be expected of the political leaders in Isaiah's time and he therefore also honestly admits that the decision that the saying in v. 18 has been later expanded in 19 is based entirely on his prior conclusion that woe sayings were originally short and that in the case of some of the other sayings in this passage it is clear that there has been subsequent expansion. This is unnecessary, however. Whatever may have been the original form of a (funerary) woe saying, it is clear from many examples that by

---

[95] Kutscher's attempt (p. 328) to explain the scribe's reasoning in making these changes from a presumed *Vorlage* that was identical with MT is wildly speculative, and the whole process is now undermined by the evidence from 4QIsa[b] which favours the view that there was random variation on this matter.

the time they are used in prophetic and other transferred contexts they could be somewhat longer. In the absence of any supporting evidence, the unity of the passage is thus better maintained, not least because v. 19 is needed to explain the nature of the sin in v. 18.[96]

Werner, *Plan*, 14–20 and 27–32, has sought to advance just such additional supporting evidence, but without carrying conviction, in my opinion. General parallels in the Psalms (especially 28.5 and 92.6-7) do not seem to get us very far. The difficulties of knowing to what exactly the work and plan of God refer are no argument for or against any particular date, and finally the correct observation that v. 19 adds precision to the generalized indictment of v. 18 is not in itself evidence that it has been added redactionally. Indeed, as Deck has pointed out, Werner seems to be presupposing a reverse of the usual position in which eighth-century sayings tend to have concrete referents while much later writers (Werner dates v. 19 to the fourth century) tend to spiritualize: 'Der von Werner vorgeschlagene umgekehrte Weg, daß ein allgemeingültiger, genau genommen sogar inhaltsleere Weheruf...vier Jahrhunderte später konkret aktualisiert wird, wirkt von daher eher unwahrscheinlich' (Deck, 246). Provided 'plan' is not overtheologized (see the comments below), the verse has so many links with other Isaianic material that it is most easily ascribed to Isaiah.[97]

These links are more fully explored below and they point clearly to a date specifically in the later part of Isaiah's ministry. It is true that the majority dates the saying early, but without any more reason than that the saying comes in ch. 5. We have seen, however, that this is no argument at all, and with Dietrich, 168–70, and Høgenhaven, 172–73, we may conclude that this woe-oracle joins those that precede it in coming rather from the period of the crisis under Hezekiah when the political leaders of the nation were working for what Isaiah regarded as a misguided alliance with Egypt.

The poetic quality of the saying is again only modest. The rhythm is unremarkable, but the two halves of v. 18 and the two lines of v. 19 display a very tight form of parallelism, as was mentioned in the notes above. Though this may not bring particular aesthetic satisfaction, it is a great help to the exegete in adjudicating several issues that would otherwise be uncertain.

[96] I can see no evidence to support Gray's speculation that an occurrence of הוי has been lost from the start of v. 19. The difference in rhythm, which is the only consideration he advances, is certainly not a factor that should be allowed to determine such a matter.

[97] Assuming his reconstruction to be sound, Dijkstra's adduced parallel with this saying in the eighth-century Balaam inscription from Deir 'Alla is striking: it too would be a woe saying, followed by a quotation from the prophet's opponents in which they question whether he has been asked for counsel (עצה); 'Balaam', 57. However, the text is severely damaged, and Dijkstra partially relies on this text in Isaiah (and others from the biblical prophets) in his reconstruction. It would therefore be a circular argument to appeal to this as evidence for an Isaianic date for our passage.

18. *Iniquity* and *sin* were discussed at 1.4.[98] It was seen that this was a standard parallel pair, not least in Isaiah, and that they could be used elsewhere in a wide variety of contexts, including the political (see, for instance, 30.1 and 13), so that they are entirely suitable as an introduction to v. 19 and need not be limited to social sins (*contra* Kaiser). The picture conjured up by the use of *drag...along* implies that this is wilful and conscious sin; there is no possible excuse that this was in any way inadvertent. Those addressed are therefore fully responsible for the consequences that will follow (implied in the *woe*). The development of the imagery (*cords...rope*) is dependent as to its detail on text-critical issues, which have been addressed in the notes above, though the main point of the verse would not be affected were a different solution to be preferred.

19. *Who say*: the topic of how and why prophets cite others has been fully examined by Wolff.[99] He shows that the purpose, as obviously here, is to condemn them out of their own mouth. This raises problems in that the citations are often clearly fictitious, but, in view of the connections with other passages noted below, the present example probably comes rather into the category of slight paraphrase only. Blenkinsopp has observed how often Isaiah uses this technique 'as a direct witness to arrogant self-sufficiency (9.10 [9]; 10.8-11, 13-14; 14.13-14)'—which of course was the cardinal sin in Isaiah's opinion—as well as religious skepticism, as here (28.15; 29.15-16; 30.10-11). In 28.14, Isaiah refers to those who are depicted as speaking thus as 'scoffers' (אנשי לצון), which would be suitable here as well.

In v. 12, God's *work* was seen in principle to be applicable to a wide range of activities but in that context probably to refer to his past care of the nation. Here, however, it is clear that the reference is to something still future. This is evident both from the way that the scoffers urge that it be made manifest and especially from the parallel line, where again the verbs look to the future (*let the counsel of the Holy One of Israel draw near and be fulfilled*) and where the parallel noun is *counsel* or plan (עצה). While there is thus a clear verbal connection with v. 12, it would be a mistake to try to join them more closely, as though they were more or less saying the same thing.[100]

Von Rad originally thought that this work was part of God's saving work: with reference to our verse, he wrote: 'when Isaiah speaks of "purpose," he is thinking of something planned for the deliverance of Zion, that is to say, of a saving work. Isaiah sets this saving act of Jahweh in the widest possible historical context, namely that of universal history.'[101]

---

[98] Strictly speaking, 'sin' there is חטא as opposed to the very rare form חטאה here (elsewhere only at Exod. 34.7). It is impossible to draw any distinction in meaning or to see why the rare form should be preferred here.

[99] H. W. Wolff, *Das Zitat im Prophetenspruch: Eine Studie zur prophetischen Verkündigungsweise* (Munich, 1937), reprinted in *Gesammelte Studien zum Alten Testament* (TBü 22; Munich, 1964), 36–129.

[100] *Contra* J. Vollmer, *THAT* ii. 368–69 = *TLOT* ii. 950–51; H. Ringgren, *ThWAT* vi. 430 = *TDOT* xi. 401–2.

[101] G. von Rad, *Old Testament Theology*, II (Edinburgh and London, 1965), 162 = *Theologie des Alten Testaments*, II (Munich, 1960), 173. Based on the use of עשה in 9.6,

Later, however, he seems to have modified his position[102] in the direction that the majority of commentators adopt, namely that the reference is to God's work of judgment on Judah and Jerusalem. This common opinion will be much strengthened if the saying indeed comes from the later part of Isaiah's ministry. As we have seen just above, there is at this time a remarkable congruence between the vocabulary of these verses both for sin (v. 18) and for the mocking attitude of the political leaders of the nation (v. 19; cf., e.g., 29.15; 30.11) and Isaiah's opposition to the plans to forge an anti-Assyrian coalition. The sentiments expressed here by his opponents, picking up on his ideas and vocabulary, thus seem to fit this period like a glove, and so confirm that it is Isaiah's relaying of God's warnings and threats of judgment which attracts their scorn; they are confident that Zion has been promised unconditional freedom and protection (e.g. 28.15).

Counsel, or plan (עצה), has perhaps been rather over-interpreted by some commentators in connection with Isaiah. It is true that its frequent occurrence (together with that of the verb יעץ) in Isaiah, especially in theological contexts, is striking, but that does not lead to the consequence that he was responsible for coining the term or using it in some idiosyncratic way.[103] The word means 'counsel, advice', especially in the political sphere, and then in approaching half its occurrences it has the developed meaning of 'plan'. The distribution of usage does not by any means favour the view that it was a specifically 'wisdom' term. On this, Ruppert's conclusion seems judicious: '"giving counsel" was the task of political officials who had been trained in Wisdom, not of the "sages" as such, who were not directly concerned with concrete political decisions' (p. 165). The theological usage, we may assume, develops from the depiction of God as king presiding over his heavenly court (as in Isa. 6); as part of that depiction the adoption of plans on the basis of debate seems natural enough,[104] and it is not surprising that it should have been particularly congenial to Isaiah in the light of his roots in the Jerusalem theology of the divine king and court. That God's 'plan' has universal implications in

---

Høgenhaven, 172–73, also thinks that the reference is to God's promise, the speakers (in Hezekiah's time) impatiently waiting for God to implement his plan to throw off the Assyrian yoke.

[102] G. von Rad, 'Das Werk Jahwes', in W. C. van Unnik and A. S. van der Woude (eds), *Studia Biblica et Semitica Theodoro Christiano Vriezen...Dedicata* (Wageningen, 1966), 290–98; repr. *Gesammelte Studien zum Alten Testament*, II (TBü 48; Munich, 1973), 236–44. Whedbee, 129, notes that in this essay von Rad also changed his mind on another matter in that he now agrees that Isaiah's understanding of this topic was dependent upon cultic tradition.

[103] For the full statistics, together with a detailed and balanced treatment of the subject, see L. Ruppert, *ThWAT* iii. 718–51 = *TDOT* vi. 156–85. Earlier studies, which require some modification in the light of Ruppert's work, include Fichtner, 'Jahwes Plan'; McKane, *Prophets*, though his translation 'policy' (p. 66) is a clever attempt to catch both aspects of the way the word is used; Whedbee, Chapter 4; Jensen, 'Yahweh's Plan'; H.-P. Stähli, *THAT* i. 750–52 = *TLOT* ii. 557–59. Subsequently there has appeared the major study of Werner, *Plan*, though his radical literary-critical conclusions are not always acceptable.

[104] For the language of the royal court in connection with the heavenly, see Brettler, *God is King*, 100–9.

some passages will be a consequence of Isaiah's whole outlook on the relation of God, Israel/Judah and the nations, not its origin. Finally, rather as with the divine title 'the Holy One of Israel', it is obvious that the use of this term was recognized as characteristic by later tradents of Isaiah's heritage who adopted and adapted it widely in their writing as well.

For *the Holy One of Israel*, see on 1.4. As we saw there, the other most securely Isaianic uses of the title are in 30.11, 12, 15, and 31.1. It is interesting to compare these with the present verse: in 30.11 we again have Isaiah's opponents saying 'let us hear no more about the Holy One of Israel', which is closely similar in sentiment, and in the following verse Isaiah responds in the name of the same deity with a word of judgment which probably relates to the alliance policy which he condemned. Likewise in 31.1 he berates the Judeans for their trust in Egypt and draws a contrast: 'but [you] do not look to the Holy One of Israel or consult the Lord': the vocabulary is different, but the sentiment is comparable with 5.12. These references to 'the Holy One of Israel' in 30 and 31 (as well as in other oracles which have not survived, no doubt) were evidently distinctive enough to be picked up in mockery by Isaiah's opponents.

Draw near and be fulfilled (lit. 'come'): this slightly unusual expression to refer to the fulfilment of God's stated intention is not precisely paralleled in Deutero-Isaiah, but its language is familiar from the trial speeches where God invites the idol worshippers to draw near for the trial and challenges the idols to show whether they have fulfilled their predictions of 'the coming things' and so on (see, for instance, 41.1-5, 21-29; 43.8-13; 44.6-8; 45.20-25). While the allusion is probably not conscious, there is a sense in which the trial speeches serve to answer the challenge here thrown down by the scoffers.

So that we may see it…so that we may acknowledge it: this language about the perception of God and his activity is a unifying theme in the book of Isaiah as a whole; see already on 1.3. The two verbs used here occur together quite frequently elsewhere, not least in the hardening saying in 6.9: 'keep looking (seeing) but do not understand (know/ acknowledge)' (וראו ראו ואל־תדעו). Evidently it too was recognized as sufficiently Isaianic to be picked up in mockery by the scoffers. If my speculation is right that 1.2b-3 originally stood between 30.8 and 9, then of course this language will have once occurred in close connection with some of the other material reflected here (see 30.11-12).

FOURTH WOE-ORACLE: MORAL DEVIANCE (5.20)

[20]Woe to those who call evil good,
   and good evil,
replacing darkness with light,
   and light with darkness,
replacing what is bitter with what is sweet,
   and what is sweet with what is bitter.

20. שמים: there are occasional examples of the participle lacking the definite article when it follows another participle that has it (see Gibson, 135; WO, 622), but in the present instance it seems more probable that the second two lines, which both begin with שמים, are intended to be explanatory of the first, the latter, therefore, giving expression to the substance of the woe saying. The translation above is deliberately free; literally: 'making darkness into light...making bitterness into sweetness'.

The somewhat mechanical way in which the woe sayings are arranged continues here. Not only is this one included in the second group which have in common that they are briefer than the first and lack an explicit statement of judgment or threat, but its position within the group seems to be determined by the catch-word האמרים. The artificial nature of the join is clear from the fact that in v. 19 it introduces a citation, 'who say', whereas here it is part of the expression ל אמר, 'who call'. This reinforces the conclusion that these woe sayings were probably originally independent sayings, but equally the fact that care has been taken over their present literary arrangement suggests that we should also consider the effect of this wider context in exegesis (see below). It is not unreasonable to think that there may be two different levels of meaning.

The lack of a threat or judgment in this saying has led some scholars to propose that vv. 23-24a once followed it immediately as part of the same saying (cf. Wildberger). It is argued that v. 23 is unsuitable as a continuation of v. 22, that it follows on well in content from our present verse, and that v. 24a then provides the expected judgment. Alternatively, Fey, 57–59, followed by Kaiser (and cf. Deck, 183), joins v. 23 alone to v. 20; he finds a number of similarities with Amos 5.7, 10 and 12b, and as these verses also lack a threat, he thinks that this is an additional point of comparison.

While it is not impossible that v. 23 once stood with 20, the arguments adduced are not strong enough to make this probable. As we shall see, the movement of thought between 22 and 23 is not unparalleled, and there is no reason why the saying in v. 20 should be restricted to cases of legal injustice (contra Gesenius); indeed, had that been the case, we should have expected legal language (צדיק and רשע) rather than the broader terms we find here (Dillmann; Knobel). As we have had repeated cause to observe, woe sayings do not necessarily require the inclusion of a threat or judgment, since the pronouncement of a woe may already include that within itself. Fey's points of comparison with Amos 5 have been specifically challenged by Whedbee, 102–5, who observes in addition to other matters that the similar word pairs prove nothing, since they are so common. This point is reinforced by Stansell's observation, 113–14, of equally striking parallels with Micah (e.g. 3.2). By the same token, it seems unnecessarily restrictive to limit this saying to the product of wisdom circles. While we may agree with Whedbee that the wise made good use of contrasting word pairs, it is unlikely that they were the only ones to do so. Such a common form of speech is likely to have been widespread whenever the rhetorical situation demanded it, so that this is just another of the many instances where wisdom circles shared ideas and expressions with Israelite culture in general.

There is no way of dating such a brief saying within the ministry of Isaiah. As before, many assume an early date because of its presence in ch. 5, but we have already seen that this is an unsatisfactory argument. It

could equally well come later, as may the other woe sayings we have
already studied. Porath, 148, draws attention to the parallel in 28.15, which
would support that conclusion.

The poetic quality of the verse is again modest; that it achieves its
effect by the use of repetition and reversal is too obvious to call for additional comment (cf. Korpel, 'Structural Analysis', 62–63).

20. Blenkinsopp comments well that this verse is 'a denunciation of moral
sophistry expressed in what seems to be a claim on the part of those
addressed to advertise a private morality of their own in defiance of traditional norms'. By 'morality' we should not think in the rather narrow
terms in which the word is popularly used today. (Equally, it is only the
unjustified joining of this verse with v. 23 which allows Kaiser to limit the
evil to lack of justice in the courts.) *Good* and *evil*[105] may apply as much to
physical well-being or misfortune (e.g. Amos 3.6; Isa. 45.7) as to private
ethics and morality, and the remainder of the verse, which may be taken as
explanatory, bears this out: *light* and *darkness* are a frequent pair with the
widest range of uses, including (especially in Isaiah) notions of salvation
and well-being (e.g. 2.5; 9.1; 42.16; 45.7; 58.10; 59.9; 60.1-2, etc.), so that
we may assume that the same applies in the present context to the much
less common *sweet* and *bitter* (Prov. 27.7). The life of any close-knit
society depends in large measure upon the adoption of common standards
and norms in matters large and small, so that those condemned here will
have been perceived as posing a significant threat.

The placing of this saying immediately after vv. 18-19, however, suggests that at the level of the book's compilation a more specific interpretation may be in view. The mocking in v. 19 of the prophet's proclamation
of God's purposes for his people is here equated with the confusion of
moral categories. According to McKane, *Prophets*, 65, 'this reflects the
passionate ethical commitment of the prophet and his dislike of the flexibility of old wisdom' (by which he means the wisdom of the statesmen of
Judah). More specifically, it may involve 'denying the reality of the crisis
that confronts the community, saying things are going well when they are
on the way to disaster' (Goldingay).[106] This may be generally along the
right lines, but on the basis of our understanding of the compilation of this
chapter this cannot be ascribed to Isaiah himself (at least, not on the basis
of the present passage, though cf. 28.15); it needs rather to be ascribed to
those responsible for the early (pre-exilic) collection of his sayings. It is
not difficult to imagine that this is how they would have understood
Isaiah, at the least.

[105] Cf. H.-J. Stoebe, *THAT* ii. 794–803 = *TLOT*, 1249–54; C. Dohmen and D. Rick,
ThWAT vii. 582–612 = *TDOT* xiii. 560–88. The point is repeatedly made that Hebrew
does not distinguish lexically between 'bad' and 'evil', so that the context has to decide
the particular nuance of the word's use in each case.
[106] This interpretation raises difficulties of another sort, since it is hardly to be
supposed that those accused would have agreed that this was what they were doing. The
problem is more directly raised by the following verse, however, and so better addressed
there.

FIFTH WOE-ORACLE: HUBRISTIC WISDOM (5.21)

[21]Woe to those who are wise in their own eyes,
who consider themselves to have discernment.

21. Although there is no verbal connection between this saying and the previous one, there is an obvious connection in thought with the way in which it was suggested the compiler construed v. 20. Once again, therefore, the evidence points clearly to the arrangement of these woe sayings being secondary rather than from Isaiah himself. On this occasion, however, it appears that the compiler's understanding of the present saying is likely to have coincided closely with Isaiah's own. (I assume Isaianic authorship on the ground that it comes in a series of sayings for which there is good evidence that the core, at least, is from the eighth-century prophet and that there is no good reason to deny it. There is no independent evidence for this assumption, however.) We have evidence for Isaiah's clash with 'the wise' in the latter part of his ministry (e.g. 29.14, where חכם and נבון again occur in parallel; 31.2), so that this saying would also fit that period well (cf. Høgenhaven, 173–74), as has been argued above for the other woe sayings. In the case of so short a saying, however, alternative dates cannot be ruled out.

McKane, *Prophets*, 65–68, is probably right to insist that in this passage the *wise* and those with *discernment* are the king's political advisers. This is not at all to take the extreme position which was once briefly popular that all wisdom in the Bible was somehow directly related to this narrow circle, but that in the historical context of Isaiah's ministry and his usage as known from elsewhere in the book (see above) this seems by far the most plausible group to have come under his censure.

In ideal terms, the wisdom and discernment needed for political success were regarded as a gift of God's spirit (cf. Wildberger): Joseph was recognized by Pharaoh to have had precisely these gifts (נבון וחכם, Gen. 41.39), and this is ascribed in the previous verse to the fact that 'the spirit of God' was in him; similarly, the first two characteristics of the ideal and spirit-endowed ruler in Isa. 11.2 are that he will have 'a spirit of wisdom and understanding' (רוח חכמה ובינה). Similar qualities occur not infrequently in comparable contexts, e.g. Deut. 1.13, 15; 1 Sam. 16.18 following v. 13; and especially, of course, 1 Kgs 3.12.[107] The wisdom writers too recognized that these qualities were desirable in wider walks of life, e.g. Prov. 1.5 ('clearly used in a non-technical sense'[108]) 10.13; 14.6, 33; 16.21; 17.28; 18.15; and cf. Hos. 14.10, which seems to reflect a wisdom outlook.[109] With such wisdom Isaiah clearly had no quarrel.[110]

---

[107] The words appear separately for wisdom in such settings in an even wider range of contexts; cf. Beuken.

[108] R. N. Whybray, *Proverbs* (NCB; London and Grand Rapids, 1994), 33.

[109] Cf. G. T. Sheppard, *Wisdom as a Hermeneutical Construct* (BZAW 151; Berlin and New York, 1980), 129–36; C. L. Seow, 'Hosea 14.10 and the Foolish People Motif', *CBQ* 44 (1982), 212–24; A. A. Macintosh, *A Critical and Exegetical Commentary on Hosea* (ICC; Edinburgh, 1997), 582–83.

Equally clearly, however, there were those in his day who had lost sight of the fact that wisdom derives from God and so were relying entirely upon their own abilities to frame policy. In Isaiah's view they were by definition, therefore, not really wise at all, but wise only *in their own eyes* or (lit.) 'in front of their faces', i.e. *who consider themselves* to be discerning. As we have seen several times previously, any such independence from God is condemned by Isaiah because it is indicative of pride, which for him is the height of sin. In the present instance, this is well illustrated by the boast of the Assyrian king in 10.13: 'By the strength of my hand I have done it, and by my wisdom, for I have understanding (discernment)'. For Isaiah, any such assertion condemns itself out of its own mouth.

In fact, of course, the wisdom writers themselves take the same view, as Whedbee, 105–6, has amply demonstrated; he refers to Prov. 8.13b; 11.2; 16.18; 21.4 to illustrate the dangers of pride, and to 3.7*a*; 26.5, 16, 12; 28.11 to illustrate how the specific phrase 'wise in one's own eyes' is almost stereotypical. But he outstrips the evidence when he concludes that 'this exact parallel with wisdom teaching confirms the wisdom backdrop of the woe word', for he does not consider either the likelihood that this was shared by wider circles in Israel or the possibility that conversely the wisdom writers were influenced by Isaiah. All we can safely say is that it was agreed by all that self-dependent wisdom was dangerous and foolish and that Isaiah considered that the politicians of his day had fallen into that danger.

This raises a difficult epistemological question, for we can hardly suppose that the wise would have actually asserted that they were acting independently of God any more than in the prophetic realm Hananiah did when he was opposed by Jeremiah (Jer. 28). At a deeper level, therefore, this short saying reveals much about the different ways in which it was thought that one had access to a knowledge of the divine will. For our present purposes, it suffices to observe that Isaiah clearly considered that he had prophetic insight which overrode the deductive reasoning of the wise. It is possible that even this can be tied into his wider theology which takes as its starting point the nature of God as 'high and lifted up', for it will have been the political alliances which called forth his condemnation, and there is arguably 'a coherence between his condemnation of social injustice and his political oracles; for in these, too, he stresses the perversity or blindness to an obvious order of priorities manifested by those who encourage the Egyptian alliance... The trouble with human alliances is that they exalt human strength above its natural place.'[111]

---

[110] At 3.3 the two words occur in a list of the honourable members of society, but in each case as part of a construct pair which means that the use cannot be directly compared with the issue under discussion (חכם חרשים ונבון לחש, 'one skilled in magic practices and the expert in charms').

[111] Barton, 'Natural Law', 6–7, developed in 'Ethics'; see too Gonçalves, 267–69, and the last part of my essay 'Isaiah and the Wise'.

SIXTH WOE-ORACLE: SUMMARY AND CONCLUSION (5.22-24)

[22]Woe to those who are heroes at drinking wine,
    champions in the art of mixing strong drink,
[23]who acquit the guilty for a bribe,
    but who deny the innocent his acquittal.
[24]Therefore, as the tongue of fire devours the stubble,
    and chaff sinks down in flame,
so their root will become rotten,
    and their bud will go up like dust;
for they have rejected the instruction of the Lord of Hosts,
    and they have spurned the word of the Holy One of Israel.

23. שחר: 1QIsaᵃ שחור. Elsewhere in the scroll, the spellings שחד (1.23) and שחור (45.13) are also found. (There are comparable variations in the spelling of the place name סדם.) The pronunciation of *qotel* forms shows considerable variation, the familiar Tiberian tradition (which is standard also in Jerome) becoming dominant only well after the turn of the eras. Kutscher, 502–4, argues on the basis of LXX evidence that in the Hebrew of the scroll there were two current pronunciations, *qotel* and *qotol*. He suggests that the reason the latter is not more frequently represented orthographically is because of the tendency (as also in MT) not to represent both of two contiguous *o* sounds by *plene* spelling. If so, *qotol* may have been commonest.

צדיקים: this plural is awkward because ממנו following is singular and has to be in grammatical agreement. Although ממנו might be construed as a distributive (so Hitzig; Knobel; GK §145*m*, though with the express preference for emendation, as below; Gibson, 23),[112] in fact this is not the only point to be explained. The parallel word, רשע, is also singular, and in addition LXX (τὸ δίκαιον τοῦ δικαίου; σ also has a singular, though α 'corrects' to plural)[113] and V (*iustitiam iusti*) also translate צדיקם as singular. (T and P attest acknowledgment of the difficulty by rendering ממנו as plural: מינהון and *mnhwn* respectively.) HUBP cites some medieval manuscript evidence to the same effect, but the strength of this sort of evidence is uncertain. Taking all this evidence into account, the simplest solution is to emend to the singular צדיק (so already Lowth; more recently Duhm; Cheyne, *Book*, 84; Marti; Feldmann; Procksch [who unnecessarily also deletes ממנו *metri causa*]) and to explain the error as a dittograph before the following כי (rather than appeal to the hypothetical enclitic *mem*[114]).[115]

יסירו: an imperfect continuing a participle, as frequently; cf. GK §116*x*; JM §121*j*; Gibson, 137. The subject is therefore the same as for the earlier part of the woe saying, so that צדקת צדיק(ים) is a *casus pendens*: literally, 'as for the innocence of the innocent, they remove (it) from him'.

[112] Porath, 108, has recently advanced a comparable defence of MT by suggesting that צדקת צדיקים is a stereotyped expression ('ein geprägter Ausdruck'); he compares Prov. 11.3, צדקת ישרים תצילם. But there, of course, the singular verb correctly agrees with the singular צדקת, whereas in our verse the antecedent of ממנו is the plural צדיקים. The presence or otherwise of a stereotyped phrase does not affect the grammar in the way that he seems to think.

[113] For other aspects of the LXX rendering of this verse, see Olley, '*Righteousness*', 45–46, and the response by T. Muraoka, 'On Septuagint Lexicography and Patristics', *JTS* NS 35 (1984), 441–48 (443–44).

[114] Cf. Ginsberg, 'Emendations', 54; Jirku, 'Weitere Fälle'; Hummel, 'Enclitic *mem*', 94.

[115] Alternatively, Emerton, 'Enclitic *mem*', 331, suggests 'an unthinking and inappropriate assimilation to the plural verb יסירו', though he acknowledges the uncertainty of this. He does not consider the possibility of a faulty dittograph.

24. The word order in the first clause—infinitive construct followed immediately by its object and then the subject after that—is unusual, but not unparalleled; see GK §115*k* for other examples (including 20.1). So far as I can see, in nearly every other case the object is expressed pronominally (with אֵת), so that it is not surprising to find it following the verb immediately (the text at 2 Sam. 18.29 is uncertain). This is not the case in the present instance, but I suspect that the same considerations are in play, namely that the short word קַשׁ would follow lamely after the two-word phrase לְשׁוֹן אֵשׁ.

וְחָשַׁשׁ לֶהָבָה: in theory, this could be a construct: 'as flaming chaff (sinks down)' (e.g. Rashi; Ehrlich), but the parallelism suggests that it is better to take חשׁשׁ as an absolute (as at 33.11, where it also occurs in parallel with קשׁ), with לֶהָבָה as an adverbial accusative, 'in flame' (cf. Ibn Ezra). 1QIsaᵃ has לוהבת וְאשׁ (4QIsaᵇ = MT). Several of the versions attest a comparable (and therefore possibly related) interpretation. LXX took חשׁשׁ as a verb and rendered the line καὶ συγκαυθήσεται ὑπὸ φλογὸς ἀνειμένης, 'and shall be burned up by a blazing flame' (cf. Ottley); the three minor versions all have θέρμη φλογὸς at this point, V *calor flammae* (33.11: *ardorem*), and there is evidence for a comparable understanding in rabbinic literature (cf. Speier, 'Zu drei Jesajastellen', 311–12). The explanations for this common tradition vary: Ziegler, 9–10, thought that the LXX translator did not recognize חשׁשׁ either here or at 33.11 (where the scroll reads חששׁה) and was simply influenced by the preceding line (καυθήσεται) as well, perhaps, as by the similarity with אשׁ, while Jerome was merely dependent on the Three. The discovery of the scroll and the awareness of the rabbinic tradition have happened since Ziegler wrote, however, and have obviously complicated the situation. Nevertheless, Kutscher, 221–22, 240 and 375, still seeks separate explanations. For the scroll, he considered three influences to be operating simultaneously in our verse: the copyist was not familiar with the word (at 33.11 the scroll has חששׁה, which Kutscher is unable to explain fully), the pharyngeals were weak in Qumran Hebrew, resulting in the substitution of א for ח (though note that Kutscher cites no parallel for this particular substitution on pp. 506–7), and we have the word אשׁ immediately preceding חשׁשׁ (and note that אשׁ לֶהָבָה is a common combination elsewhere). He explains the readings of the other versions and the Piyyutin as deriving in a similar but independent way from consideration of the context. Koenig, 305–16, is sharply critical of Kutscher's atomistic explanation, which he thinks is driven by a presupposition about the inferior quality of the scroll. He does not deny some of the elements in Kutscher's explanation of our particular reading, but he is concerned to add that these readings (and, he thinks, the very different reading in P: *dʾḥdʾ*, 'which seizes/takes hold') can all be linked together not so much by contextual considerations as by the exploitation of the semantic possibilities of Aramaic חשׁשׁ. Whatever the precise explanation for the reading of the scroll, all agree that it must be inferior, not least because of the inelegance of its וְאשׁ.

יֵרֵפֶה: the infinitive with preposition is regularly continued by a finite verb with the force of the preposition carried over (as though it were כַּאֲשֶׁר; cf. Marti); cf. GK §114*r*; Driver, *Tenses*, §§117–18; Gibson, 131. 'Sink down' seems acceptable within the semantic range of this verb, even though there is no precise analogy. There is no support whatever for the conjectural emendations which have been proposed: שׂרֵפֶה (Ginsberg, following M. Perles;[116] see also the footnote in NJPS, 'is burned by flame'—but the qal is usually active and transitive, and is not combined with לֶהָבָה elsewhere, but rather אשׁ or occasionally שׂרֵפֶה), or יֵסֹפֶה, 'sweep away' (Tur-Sinai, 167; note, however, that he mistakenly thinks that LXX συγκαυθήσεται was an attempt to render this word rather than חשׁשׁ, as argued above).

פרח: cf. 3.24. Some of the versions had difficulties with this word, e.g. LXX χνοῦς, presumably thinking of פרץ, 'chaff' (see equivalents elsewhere, HR, 1471–72), V *favilla*

---

[116] H. L. Ginsberg, '"Roots Below and Fruit Above" and Related Matters', in D. Winton Thomas and W. D. McHardy (eds), *Hebrew and Semitic Studies Presented to Godfrey Rolles Driver* (Oxford, 1963), 72–76, rejected in this particular respect by J. Becker, 'Wurzel und Wurzelsproß: Ein Beitrag zur hebräischen Lexikographie", *BZ* NF 20 (1976), 22–44 (26).

(influence from the parallel; cf. 29.5), and P ḥP, 'chaff'. This is not evidence in favour of emending to מץ, however (*contra* Tur-Sinai and Ginsberg). MT has the support of 1QIsaᵃ and seems contextually superior, since even if שרש means 'stock (including the root)' rather then 'root' alone, as argued reasonably by Ginsberg, that still does not mean that one may envisage it becoming chaff rather than rotting. Furthermore, from the point of view of the ancients, מק may be judged the more difficult reading, both because it is rare as a noun and because of the references to stubble and chaff in the previous line and the parallel 'dust' in this line. (In addition, Ginsberg's further proposed emendation of פְּרִים for פרחם also seems unnecessary.) Beuken also observes (though without applying it text-critically) that there is a parallel 'Reimwirkung' between the first two lines of this verse: חשש/קש and אבק/מק.

יהוה צבאות׃ צבאות is lacking in 4QpIsaᵇ 2.7, though it seems to be attested by all other witnesses. Brooke, 'Pesharim', 314–15, speculates that this may have been the original form of the text, partly because of the evidence from the next verse (see below), and partly because in a case such as this there is a presumption that the shorter text is likely to be earlier. A further possible small pointer in the same direction may come from the fact that if we read the shorter text it will be even closer to the parallel in 1.4.

This last woe-oracle does not link directly with the previous one, in the manner that we have been able to trace for each of the previous ones, but it seems to have been equally deliberately given its present position because of the way in which it serves to act as a concluding and almost summarizing woe. Its two main elements link back to the first two in reverse order—excessive alcohol consumption in v. 22 answering to the main issues in the second woe-oracle (vv. 11-13), and social injustice in v. 23 corresponding with the first (though admittedly in a different sphere, vv. 8-10). In addition, as Beuken has observed, its stress on the root צדק, which occurs three times, links this concluding woe back to the conclusion of the parable of the vineyard (cf. v. 7). In both respects, it rounds off the woe series and the role of the whole series as a development of the theme of the parable. There is thus every reason to find at work in the positioning of this saying the hand of the same compiler whom we have identified as responsible for the original layer of the whole the chapter so far.

That said, there is some unevenness in the passage which calls for comment. First of all, the last line (v. 24c) is certainly no part of the original saying, but has clearly been added by the compiler/redactor. On the face of it, it explains what has called forth the judgment of 24a-b (כי), but that judgment is itself occasioned by the material in the woe-oracle preceding (לכן), and the reasons it gives are very different from those of 24c. Secondly, its repeated use of the prose particle את, combined with the considerable length of the line, shows that it is no original part of the woe saying with which it is now joined. And third, it introduces a far more 'religious' explanation than anything which has come before in the original parts of this chapter. It is therefore extremely probable that the line has been added redactionally as an interpretation and explanation of the whole. It has sometimes been called Deuteronomic (e.g. Clements, with reference to Amos 2.4; Kustár, 66), but while there are some points of similarity, there are also some sharply distinguishing elements, as correctly noted by Blen-kinsopp: 'neither the designation qĕdôš yiśrā'ēl ("the Holy One of Israel") nor the term 'imrâ ("word") belongs to the Deuteronomic vocabulary'.

Indeed, the former designation puts the language very much into the Isaianic world. The position is similar to what was seen as the redactional layer in ch. 1 (see v. 10, for instance, and especially the extended discussion in the commentary on vv. 18-20). The closest parallel by far, however, is with 1.4, as set out fully in the comments on that verse. The suggestion was further advanced there that in fact that verse was taken by the compiler of ch. 1 from its original setting between 5.7 and 8. Together with our line, 24c, we may conclude that this was once a redactional frame which the compiler of the woe series put around his compilation, both to give it a more general interpretation than the very specifically targeted woes of Isaiah himself and also (see above) to help effect the join between the woes and the parable.

Secondly, there are doubts about the integrity of the saying itself. Form-critically there is no difficulty: it is a woe-oracle with associated threat introduced by לכן, just like vv. 11-13.[117] But at the level of sense there are some awkward shifts within each of these two parts of the saying: drunkenness (22) and the perversion of legal justice (23) are not at first obviously related on the one hand, and on the other the first part of the threat, with its description of the effect of fire on stubble or chaff is not easily compatible with rottenness of a plant's stock or its blossom being blown away. Finally, as Duhm and others have observed, v. 23, at least, is metrically distinct from the remainder (4 + 4 as opposed to 3 + 3, if הוי and לכן may be taken in anacrusis, as I assume).

It is difficult to know how far to press this. Some, for instance, as already noted, think that v. 23 has been displaced from its original setting following v. 20, but we have seen reasons to doubt that. Equally, there is no evidence whatever for Orelli's suggestion that v. 23 was originally a separate, independent woe saying. Duhm, and to some extent Marti, thought that the passage represented just the rather clumsy work of the later compiler of the woe series; all the fragments are Isaianic, but they were not assembled very intelligently. The difficulty with this view is that it is virtually impossible to imagine fragments as short as a single line remaining in independent isolation but yet in circulation until the compiler's time. Again, some others (e.g. Budde) have deleted a line here or there as a later addition, but the rationale for any addition becomes impossible to explain the more one stresses the differences of substance between the lines.

On further reflection, perhaps the unevenness is not so serious as has been thought. The commentary below will point to a number of parallels to justify the transition in thought between vv. 22 and 23; it may not be the way we should write, but it seems to have been more than acceptable in antiquity, and we must allow an ancient writer to speak with his own voice. With regard to 24a-b, I cannot point to such striking parallels, but perhaps the distinction is in any case not so great: both lines make use in one way or the other of the image of the destruction of vegetation, so that the

---

[117] The Masoretes join v. 24 with what follows rather than with the preceding woe-oracle, but I am not persuaded that this should be determinative for modern exegesis; for some discussion, see Fischer, *Tora*, 37–42, and Korpel, 'Structural Analysis', 64–65.

purpose of using two different images may have simply been to stress that the judgment will be complete and total. Both images occur elsewhere with this sort of emphasis; at the conclusion of the series, and especially following some woes which do not otherwise have an explicit threat (unlike in the first part of the series), it may have been felt appropriate to give the matter some particular emphasis. The possibility may therefore be allowed that the compiler expanded upon Isaiah's original word, but if so we have no means of isolating his contribution other than the addition of 24c.

The passage offers no new clues as to date over those already noted in the earlier woe sayings. A late date within Isaiah's ministry is therefore probable (Høgenhaven, 174), but the possibility of an earlier date cannot be ruled out.

In addition to the comments above about the longer length of line in v. 23 and Beuken's observation of a paired use of rhyme mentioned at the end of the notes on v. 24, we may also draw attention to the suggestion of Delitzsch that there is an example of sound play at the start of v. 24: in its four short words with three sibilants 'we hear, as it were, the hissing of the flame'.

22. For a general comment on the condemnation of excessive drinking of *wine* and *strong drink* as well as for a discussion of these terms in particular, see on v. 11. A new element is the reference to *mixing*. It seems contextually unlikely that this should refer to the addition of water to the drink but rather the addition of spices and other such ingredients to make it stronger and more intoxicating (see on 1.22 above).[118]

A sarcastic note is introduced by the use of military language: *heroes* and *champions*. For the former, see on 3.2 (there translated 'warrior'); as with that word, so with *champions* (אַנְשֵׁי־חַיִל) the word is not used in an exclusively military sense,[119] but that is certainly its commonest meaning and the parallel use of the two terms suggests that this is how we should take it here.

23. In itself, this verse is straightforward: the language is legal,[120] and those condemned are accused of perverting the course of justice in the courts by the taking of a *bribe* (for which see on 1.23). As before in this woe series, we may deduce that it is the ruling classes who are in view: they will have occupied the honourable role of judges, and it would have been only the wealthy who could afford a bribe in the first place. It is thus not difficult to detect an element of collusion here whereby the privileged classes maintained their position at the expense of the poorer classes.

The more difficult question with regard to this verse concerns the sequence of thought from v. 22; as was mentioned above, some have found the transition to be sufficient of a *non sequitur* to conclude either that this

---

[118] Cf. O. Loretz, 'Ugaritisch-hebräisch ḥmr/ḥmr und msk(/mzg): Neu- und Mischwein in der Ägäis und in Syrien-Palästina', *UF* 25 (1993), 247–58.

[119] According to H. Eising, *ThWAT* ii. 902–11 (905) = *TDOT* iv. 348–55 (350), 17 of the 23 occurrences of אִישׁ/אַנְשֵׁי־חַיִל refer to warriors. Otherwise, wealth, rank or influence may be involved (from חַיִל = 'strength, power').

[120] Cf. Bovati, *Re-Establishing Justice*, 202–7.

verse has been misplaced from its original setting after v. 20 or that it has been added later or that it was once a separate woe-oracle.

In fact, the sequence from drunkenness to the perversion of justice is not unparalleled. At Prov. 31.4-5, for instance, the connection is made explicit: 'It is not for kings to drink wine, or for rulers to desire strong drink; or else they will drink and forget what has been decreed, and will pervert the rights of all the afflicted' (see already Hitzig); the same point is repeated differently in the following verses as well (6-9). In Amos, there are several passages from which a similar connection of thought may be deduced.[121] At 2.8, the prophet complains about those who use the (unjust?) fines they have imposed to finance drinking, at 4.1 oppression of the poor and drinking are brought into close association, and at 6.6 there is a reflection on the obscenity of drinking a lot without concern for the wider perils facing the society which, in Amos, are largely due to the lack of care in the administration of justice. Finally and closer to home, we find the same connection made directly in Isa. 28.7: 'These also reel with wine and stagger with strong drink...they err in vision, they stumble in giving judgment'.[122] It seems therefore that, not only in Isaiah's thought but also in his wider social setting, the connection between vv. 22 and 23 would not have occasioned surprise.[123]

24. Just as it was the lack of justice which explained the end of the vineyard in the parable of vv. 1-7, so here the addressees of the woe-oracle are condemned to complete destruction. To emphasize how comprehensive it will be, two agricultural images are related somewhat artificially by the 'as...so' construction.

The first treats the destruction by fire of those elements of cereal crops which remain after harvesting, *stubble* and *chaff*. (קשׁ, here rendered *stubble*, is sometimes more likely chaff, or at least that part of the stalk which has both been harvested and from which the head of grain has also been cut, i.e. straw, as blown away by the wind: e.g. Isa. 40.24; 41.2, etc. In view of the rarity of חשׁשׁ, which at its only other occurrence, 33.11, is again in parallel with קשׁ, it is not possible to be sure of the precise distinctive connotation of each lexeme.) References elsewhere to the stubble being consumed/devoured (אכל) by fire point to its comprehensive nature;

---

[121] Ironically, Fey, 57–59, sought to establish a connection with Amos 5.7, 10 and 12 by connecting our verse directly with v. 20. But quite without regard for the question of the original order of verses in Isaiah, this proposal has been sharply criticized by H. W. Wolff, *Amos' geistige Heimat* (WMANT 18; Neukirchen–Vluyn, 1964), 56–57 = *Amos the Prophet: The Man and His Background* (Philadelphia, 1973), 80–85; see too Whedbee, 101–3.

[122] This word (פליליה) is a *hapax*, and thus not the usual word for 'giving judgment'. Its precise force is uncertain. Since the saying is directed against priests and prophets, it may well be that some form of cultic decisions or judgments are in view. The sequence of thought remains the same, however.

[123] Bovati, *Re-Establishing Justice*, 180–81 n. 28, has drawn attention to a connection of a different sort between our two verses. At Exod. 18.21, אנשׁי חיל, who among other things 'hate dishonest gain', are to be installed as judges. In our passage we have the same vocabulary to describe the drinkers in v. 21 followed by the reference to bribery (different word) in v. 22; Bovati regards this as an ironic echo. It is difficult to know whether it is anything more than coincidental, however.

cf. Exod. 15.7; Isa. 47.14; Joel 2.5; Nah. 1.10. We have seen several times before that at least as far as the leaders of society were concerned this was Isaiah's own view of the coming judgment, and unlike in some other passages (e.g. 1.21-26) this has not been supplied later with any more hopeful addition.

The expression *tongue of fire* does not occur elsewhere in the Hebrew Bible (but cf. Acts 2.3), though 30.27, where God's tongue is said to 'devour like fire', is close. The image is transparent, however, and has its analogue in English in the metaphor of a fire 'licking' something. Some have objected to the use of *sink down* (רפה) *in flame*. While it is true that the verb is not used quite like this elsewhere, it may be easily associated with the simple observation of the way that burning embers of chaff float down after the heat has initially sent them up into the air.

If the comparison is with destruction of part of the crop by fire, the substance of the judgment of the leaders of the people makes use of the metaphor of *root* and *bud* (or sprout) and thus moves to the image of something far more substantial—probably a tree or at any rate a sizeable plant. The *root*, which may include also the first part of the trunk, is simply left to rot; whereas in 6.13 (and cf. Job 14.7-9) the idea of the people being like a tree which had been felled gave rise in later interpretation to the hopeful image that it might sprout again, no such possibility is envisaged here. Similarly, anything that grows fresh above that, the sprouting buds of the tree, will simply be carried off like dust; in contrast with Job 14.9 (יפרח), there is no future to be found here either (cf. 29.5).

It is likely that we should regard *root* and *bud* as a merism for the whole tree (Beuken), rather like 'root and branch' in Mal. 3.19; Job 18.16 (whence the English expression to the same effect) or 'root and fruit' in Amos 2.9 (and cf. Isa. 14.29; 37.31). The whole body politic, as we might say, is doomed.

The last line of the verse has been added by way of a summarizing reflection on the whole of the woe series. Typically of later theologizing redaction, it sees all the abuses which have been spelt out so colourfully as a flouting of God's *instruction* (תורה) and *word* (אמרה).[124] The sentiment, and some of the vocabulary, is identical with 1.4 (*q.v.*). Where there they are said to have 'abandoned' (עזב) the Lord, here we have the even stronger *rejected* (מאס; see Amos 2.4 for another probably redactional use of this verb with תורה), a word which, without particular discussion of our present verse, Levine has recently concluded retains its 'graphic, physical meanings'.[125]

For the divine titles in this verse, see on 1.9 and 4 respectively (though see also the notes above).

[124] Cf. Fischer, *Tora*, 37–42, and Sweeney, 'Prophetic Torah', 60 (though he dates the whole passage earlier than I have proposed), in the context of a study of Torah in the book as a whole, *contra* Jensen, *The Use of tôrâ*, 95–104, who argues both for the Isaianic authorship of the line and for its primary reference to wisdom instruction.

[125] B. A. Levine, 'When the God of Israel "Acts-Out" His Anger: On the Language of Divine Rejection in the Biblical Literature', in J. Kaltner and L. Stulman (eds), *Inspired Speech: Prophecy in the Ancient Near East: Essays in Honor of Herbert B. Huffmon* (JSOTSup 378; London, 2004), 111–29.

JUDGMENT IS COMING
(5.25-30)

[25]Therefore the anger of the Lord was kindled against his people
    and he stretched out his hand against them and smote them;
and the mountains quaked,
    and their corpses became like offal
        in the streets.
Yet despite all this his anger has not turned back,
    and his hand is still stretched out.
[26]And he will raise a signal to nations far away,
    and whistle for one (to come) from the ends of the earth.
And look! here it comes with all possible speed;
    [27]none is weary and not one of them stumbles,
        [none slumbers or sleeps];
not a loincloth is loose,
    not a sandal-thong is broken;
[28]their arrows are sharpened
    and all their bows are strung;
the hooves of their horses are like flint;
    their wheels are reckoned to be like the whirlwind.
[29]They roar like a lion,
    and growl like young lions;
they seize prey and carry it off,
    with none to rescue it.
[30]And they will growl over it on that day like the roaring of the sea; and
if we look to the land, behold the darkness of distress, and the light
grows dark because of its clouds.

---

25. עַל־כֵּן: 4QIsa[b] lacks כן and LXX renders merely with καὶ (and 1QIsa[a] writes as a single word). It is hard to say whether these two slightly unusual versions are related. The following note suggests that they may be.

יהוה: in 4QIsa[b] [צבאות] has been added supralinearly; LXX has σαβαὼθ; expansion under the influence of the previous verse is likely.

נבלתם: the suffix refers back to עמו (collective), of course; there is no ground here for conjecturally emending the first two words of the line to ויהרג השרים (Ehrlich; so correctly Wildberger, *contra* Steinman, 113, and *BHK*) or ורזנו החרים, 'and has utterly destroyed his rulers' (Tur-Sinai).

חוצות: conventionally, 'streets'. On the basis of his discovery of an open-air bazaar area outside the city gates of Dan, Biran has argued that חוצות refers to such a space.[1] We may perhaps simply accept that it can refer to any outdoor public area, not just to 'streets' in the anachronistic modern sense of the word.

בכל: cf. Kaddari, 'Concessive Connectors', 106.

---

[1] A. Biran, 'The *ḥûṣôt* of Dan', *EI* 26 (1999), 25–29 (Hebrew); cf. L. Stager, 'Ashkelon and the Archaeology of Destruction: Kislev 604 B.C.E.", *EI* 25 (1996), 61*–74*.

ידו נטויה: 1QIsaᵃ has ידיו both here and regularly in the same refrain in ch. 9. Although it looks plural, that is hardly possible with נטויה following. Kutscher, 51 and 447, shows that this must be a dialectal pronunciation for ô.

26. לגוים מרחוק: although the plural is awkward (see below), it is attested by all the texts and versions that have survived. Where the witnesses do not follow MT exactly in this regard (as they do in the case of 1QIsaᵃ, V and T), they make the following singulars into plural rather than the present plural into singular; so LXX[2] and P. Despite this uniform evidence, the overwhelming majority of commentators (Beuken is a rare exception among modern commentaries) has long proposed a slight emendation in order to harmonize with the singulars which follow (לו and יבוא), either to לגוי מרחוק (dittography) or to לגוי מְמֶרְחָק (wrong division of words, and cf. Jer. 5.15 for the expression).[3] I have little doubt that this, or something like it, will have been what Isaiah originally wrote. However, as we shall see, there is strong evidence for the view that this passage has been deliberately moved from its original setting by a later redactor, and I regard it as probable that at that time the original singular was deliberately changed to the present plural in order to align this verse with 11.12 and 49.22.

לו: the identical syntax at 7.18 shows that the antecedent must be the one to whom the Lord whistles; it cannot be that he whistles for someone to come to him (cf. Barthélemy, 39). If the antecedent is the plural גוים, then either the suffix must be understood distributively (GK §145*m*), or there is an awareness that the imperial army (singular), whether Assyrian or Babylonian, was made up from peoples of many nations (Knobel; Dillmann; Beuken; cf. 17.13, where there is a similar shift from plural לאמים to singular בו and ונס; 30.28), or as the nations approach they assume the form of a compact mass (Delitzsch), or 'the ruling nation among the many is singled out' (also Delitzsch), or the foreign king is singled out as representative (T introduces 'a king with his armies' into the next line), or there are many גוים but they all make up one single עם (Hitzig). None of these explanations is very convincing, of course (note, for instance, how in the following verse the singular clearly refers to the army, not its leader), but we may assume that one or more could have been the understanding of the redactor once he changed an original singular גוי to plural; in the earliest form of the text, the problem would not have arisen.

מהרה קל: a noun and an adjective both being used adverbially (speedily, quickly) but without a conjunction (obviously the adjective, which is masculine, cannot be intended to qualify the feminine noun). Attributes are sometimes repeated for emphasis (cf. Kimhi; e.g. מאד מאד and עמק עמק; for more examples, see GK §133*k*), and the same concern may account for the choice to combine feminine and masculine (the masculine adjective מהר would have meant the same, of course), but this seems to be the only instance of two lexically unrelated words functioning together in this way. The identical combination, though in reverse order, occurs also at Joel 4.4, so I assume this is strongly idiomatic, and have rendered slightly freely accordingly.

27. From this verse on, at least, it is clear that the reference is to the foreign army and that the singular suffixes refer to this collectively (and in the second line almost personified). It is necessary to paraphrase slightly in order to achieve at least intelligible English.

---

[2] We may note, however, that LXX may well have read the preposition ב instead of ל (cf. Troxel, 'Exegesis', 104), though that does not affect the point at issue. Gray is uncharacteristically mistaken in commenting here that LXX has singular 'nation', though he is closer to the mark in suggesting that the error may have arisen by 'a scribe who wished to assimilate to 11¹²'. On my view, for 'scribe' (implying late and mistaken), read 'redactor' (implying earlier and deliberate).

[3] According to Barthélemy, 38, the first suggestion was originally advanced by J. B. Koppe, the translator into German of Lowth's commentary, with additional notes (1779–81), while the second is ascribed to an undocumented comment of Roorda cited by Duhm, from whose work it has become the more popular of the two.

עֵיֵף: so too 4QIsa[b], but 1QIsa[a] has יעף; 28.12 is somewhat similar. Kutscher, 243–44, thinks that there was a distinction in some circles (as reflected in the LXX) between עיף = 'be hungry/thirsty' and יעף = 'be weary'. He therefore thinks that the scribe deliberately changed his *Vorlage* to יעף to fit this distinction. Interestingly, Ehrlich had long ago conjectured that יעף should be read. Whatever the position elsewhere, the LXX evidence is not fully clear in this verse, however. It renders the first line οὐ πεινάσουσιν οὐδὲ κοπιάσουσιν οὐδὲ νυστάξουσιν οὐδὲ κοιμηθήσονται. While the last two verbs clearly fit the last two in the Hebrew, the first two might be a double rendering of עיף with כושל omitted; note that at 40.30 and 31 the same two verbs render עיף and יגע in parallel. Alternatively, Troxel, 'Exegesis', 105, points out that כשל is rendered by κοπιᾶν at 31.3 and 63.13, so that the matter is far from certain. Given the loose way in which the LXX handles lists elsewhere (see on 1.11), it is likely that he saw several more or less synonymous verbs here and rendered accordingly. In that case, it would be hazardous to conclude which of the two alternatives he considered closer to עיף.

וב: lacking in 1QIsa[a]. LXX has no equivalent for it either, but we have seen that its evidence is unreliable at this point. While σ and θ correct LXX's κοπιάσουσιν, they do so without adding an equivalent for וב. Either reading seems reasonable, so that there is no basis on which to decide which is earlier.

נפתח...נתק: for the essentially stative use of the perfect niph'al, see WO, 385–86. Ehrlich thinks that נפתח is more active, 'will be loosened', on the ground that none of the soldiers will be going to sleep on the march, but this runs into difficulty when it comes to the parallel נתק, which could hardly be a deliberate action.

28. קֻשְׁתֹתָיו: for the vocalization with *daghesh* in the *shin*, see GK §20*h*.

דרכות: when used in connection with a bow, this verb was generally translated 'bend/draw' by the versions and this was followed by most in the medieval period as well as by many since. This meaning does not fit comfortably in all the contexts where the idiom is found, however (including the present passage if the verb refers to the use of a foot for drawing a large bow), so that 'trodden' is more probably a reference to the manner in which a bow was strung in preparation for combat. The whole history of interpretation has been exhaustively discussed and documented by Emerton, and his conclusions seem entirely convincing.[4]

צר: the meaning is not in doubt, but the vocalization is unique; elsewhere it is always צֹר, and indeed 1QIsa[a] reads צור. Commentators invariably adopt the common vocalization here, but what is gained thereby? The Masoretes must have been aware of what they were doing and had a reason for it. The fact that we no longer know what that was does not lead to the conclusion that we should undo their work if there is no need to do so. (Bartelt, 107, wonders whether they intended a pun on צר from צרר II, as in v. 30.) Of course, we may read the pre-Masoretic consonantal text however we think best, and for this the Qumran scrolls are important evidence, but that is a different matter from suggesting that the MT is faulty on its own terms. The sense is excellent (see below), so that emendation to סער (Ehrlich) or צנור (Tur-Sinai) is needless. Similar reasoning tells against Driver's proposal to find a Hebrew word צר = 'meteor' here (cf. Akkadian *ṣarāru*, 'to flash').[5]

וחשבו: as the text stands, this verb is included in the first half of the line: 'the hooves of their horses are reckoned as flint'. It is attractive to suppose, however, that it originally belonged in the second half (as rendered above). The line balance in what is otherwise a remarkably regular passage is much better, and the idea of 'reckoning' seems more appropriate as a qualification of the obviously picturesque comparison of wheels with a whirlwind than the straightforward comparison of hardened horses' hooves with flint. This requires only that we delete the *waw* on וגלגליו, a simple case of dittography (this seems a far more elegant solution than Procksch's proposal [followed

---

[4] J. A. Emerton, 'Treading the Bow', *VT* 53 (2003), 465–86.
[5] G. R. Driver, 'Uncertain Hebrew Words', *JTS* 45 (1944), 13–14, and 'Difficult Words', 55.

by Kaiser] to move חשבו to the end of the verse, though he is certainly moving in the right direction; so rightly Wildberger). It is likely that this was still the situation in the LXX *Vorlage*. Certainly, there is no rendering of 'and' before 'wheels' (surprisingly not noted by Troxel, 'Exegesis') and ἐλογίσθησαν can well be construed with what follows. Ziegler admittedly takes it with the first half by adding a comma after it, but that, of course, is a matter of editorial opinion, which we may presume was influenced by MT; for the opposite opinion, see Ottley and Gray. 1QIsaᵃ, 4QIsaᵇ and pap4QIsaᵖ all agree with MT, however, so either the error occurred soon after the LXX translation or there were variants still in circulation (which is entirely likely); neither V nor T render חשבו directly, though both include 'and' before 'wheels', as does P.

29. Gray's comment that 'the form of the text is suspicious...but the sense is clear' has been reinforced by the new evidence which has become available since he wrote. Many of the small details on which this assessment rests are interrelated and so need to be treated together. The germane facts are as follows: (i) MT itself indicates a dual reading tradition with K וְשָׁאַ and Q יִשְׁאָ. (ii) pap4QIsaᵖ is not completely certain, but the editors think it most likely that it agrees with Q, though they allow that it may agree with K; either way, it does not add any completely new evidence. (iii) 1QIsaᵃ is materially different, however: it not only agrees with Q, but it adds the conjunction to the next word and does not have it on the word following that: ...ישאג וככפירים ינהם... (iv) The LXX text is itself uncertain at the start and thereafter it does not follow MT closely: ὁρμῶσιν/ὀργιωσιν ὡς λέοντες καὶ παρέστηκαν ὡς σκύμνος λέοντος..., 'they will rush/rage like lions and stand near like a lions' whelp...'. In the following line it represents the first two verbs in reverse order and renders ויפליט most unusually by καὶ ἐκβαλεῖ.

MT must be rendered, 'His (collective singular again) roaring is like (that of) a lion, and he roars (K)/he will roar (Q) like young lions; and he will growl and seize prey and carry (it) away and there is none to deliver'. This certainly makes sense, but raises questions: the sequence of tenses with the following line is a bit awkward whether we read K or Q, and this no doubt explains the conjecture in *BHS* to read the unattested וישא. The repetition of words from the root שאג is thought to be suspicious by some. While this is a matter of opinion, of course, it is at least worth noting Watson's suggestion that we retain K (against the majority of commentators), vocalize it as a noun and take the repetition as an example of gender-matched parallelism.[6] But in any case, why has the author shifted to the awkward שאגה לו form rather than continuing to use possessive suffixes as in the previous verses?

I see no easy way to account for all this; one may either just live with the awkwardnesses or else make a bold conjecture which can be related to the evidence we have but which is not itself directly attested. I therefore suggest that we follow the lead of 1QIsaᵃ and redivide the lines accordingly as follows:

שאגה כלביא ישאג
וככפירים ינהם
ויאחז טרף ויפליט
ואין מציל

In this conjecture, the problem of the repetition of שאג is resolved by making it an example of the cognate accusative construction, which is both frequent and idiomatic. Once the לו had accidentally come into the first line, the various stages in the redivision of the lines which our witnesses attest will have followed on. The parallelism is improved (נהם is now parallel with שאג) and the line lengths seem satisfactory—twice 3 + 2, with the second demanding a slowing in the reading (ואין has to carry a full stress on its own), which seems entirely appropriate at the end of a poetic unit (as we shall see, v. 30 was added later); we had exactly the same feature at 1.31. So far as the

---

[6] W. G. E. Watson, 'Gender-Matched Synonymous Parallelism in the Old Testament', *JBL* 99 (1980), 321–41 (334 n. 63).

LXX is concerned, we may no doubt take the variant for the first word in the B text to be a correction towards MT; this seems to account for the situation better than arguing for an inner-Greek corruption in the other direction. The oddities in the remainder of the rendering used to be explained by a variety of devices: Ottley considered ὁρμῶσιν to be merely a guess, while Ziegler, 16 (followed by Wildberger), suggested that παρέστηκαν was based on a different *Vorlage*: קול וישא which LXX read as וישקול. I do not find any of this convincing. The problem seems to have been solved by Goshen-Gottstein, 'Theory and Practice', 145–48 (favoured also by Troxel, 'Exegesis', 106), who drew attention to the parallel with Num. 23.24 and so ascribed the rendering to the translator's interpretation rather than to an alternative text. Its value at this point for textual criticism is therefore significantly qualified. The oddity that it (or better, its *Vorlage*; cf. Troxel, 'Exegesis', 105) reverses the singular and plural of MT with regard to the number of lions in the first two lines reinforces this conclusion.

ויפליט: this is certainly puzzling. The hiph'il occurs only once elsewhere (Mic. 6.14), and assuming the text there is sound (many emend to the pi'el) it seems to mean 'save', which is what we should expect on the basis of the normal meaning of the other verbal themes from this root. Here, however, it must have the sense of remove to a place where the lion (not the prey) will be safe to eat undisturbed (cf. Gray). There is no obvious alternative to the conclusion that this is simply an unexpected and otherwise unattested development in the meaning of the word (cf. Hausmann, *Israels Rest*, 144–45); Ehrlich's conjecture ויבלע does not seem to me to fit the eating habits of lions.

30. The identification of the subject of וינהם and the object of עליו is a matter for exegesis; see below. My rendering ('they will growl') reflects my conclusion that the subject remains the same as in the previous verses. Interestingly, 1QIsaᵃ does not have the conjunction on this opening verb (contrast pap4QIsaᵖ, which agrees with MT), thus agreeing with its lack in the previous verse in the scroll text as well. In both the scroll and the MT, therefore, the forms in each verse are identical, suggesting that, regardless which form is more 'original', the scribes consciously read the two in parallel and not as antithetical.

ונבט: as it stands, this seems to be either niph'al (so Rashi and Ehrlich) or pi'el (Kimhi and Ibn Ezra), but elsewhere this very common verb is always hiph'il without exception. pap4QIsaᵖ in fact reads והביט, though otherwise the traditional consonantal text is well supported: for the LXX's interpretative use of the plural (likewise P), ἐμβλέψονται, see Troxel, 'Exegesis'; T is paraphrastic,[7] but in a way which suggests that it is working with the current form of the text; for V, see below. As things stand, either the subject is the same as in the previous line, or, more probably, there is an impersonal subject: 'and if one looks to the land…'. V, however, actually construes as a first person plural imperfect hiph'il, *aspiciemus*, presumably a defectively spelt וְנַבֵּ֥ט, and there is much to be said for this:[8] it takes the verb as hiph'il, as we should expect, it restores the sequence of simple *waw* + *yiqtol* of the previous lines, and it solves the problem of who is the subject by introducing a first person plural in a redactional context referring to light (and darkness), just like at 2.5 (see further below). That such a defectively spelt form should not have been universally recognized later is understandable.

והנה חשך צר ואור: the Masoretic accents indicate that we should read 'and behold darkness, distress and light', the last pair being taken closely together (some rabbinic commentators thought in terms of moon and sun [and cf. Luther], though Ibn Ezra, at least, insists that צר must refer to distress, not צר = צהר = סהר). This is defended by Delitzsch, for instance (see too Gesenius), who thinks that it indicates that there will be a period during which there is 'an alternation of anxiety and glimmerings of hope,

---

[7] Houtman, 'Doom and Promise', discusses this passage as one of a number where the Targumist tends 'to soften the harsh words of the prophet'.

[8] This has generally been ignored by the commentators. Auvray thinks it may be preferable to MT, though even he does not include it in his translation.

until at last it had become altogether dark in the cloudy sky over all the land of Judah'. This is not only improbable in itself, but it also depends upon an optimistic construal of the previous line, which will be rejected in the exegesis below. LXX cannot help us here, because it has no equivalent for וְאוֹר חָשַׁךְ; either these words were not in the translator's *Vorlage* (so Ziegler, 138) or the aim was to align the verse even more closely with 8.22 than it already is (Duhm). V and P certainly, and T probably, divide differently, making צר the end of one line and וָאוֹר the start of the next (cf. the related צרה and חשכה together also in 8.22[9]). This seems preferable (see already Kimhi and Vitringa) and has been widely adopted (though contrast Bartelt, 108).[10]

בַּעֲרִיפֶיהָ :עָרִיף is a *hapax legomenon*, but the root is well enough known (cf. עָרְפֶל, 'cloud'; Akk. *erēpu(m)*, 'cloud over, grow dark'; Ug. *ʿrp*, 'to cover, darken', etc.; it should not be linked with the other root עָרַף = 'break, destroy', *contra* Ibn Ezra; Gesenius seems to be tempted, but ultimately not persuaded), and the suffix can easily refer back to אֶרֶץ. Emendation does not seem to be required, therefore, though there have been several proposals in the past: Ziegler, 139, toys with בַּעֲרָפֶלָה, בָּאֲפֵלָה and בַּצַּר וָעֵיפָה; *BHS* בְּעֲרִיפֶיהָ, Duhm בַּעֲרִיפִים, Wade and Procksch בַּעֲרָפֶל and Kissane בְּעֵיפָה (i.e. in all cases absolute, without suffix). LXX ἐν τῇ ἀπορίᾳ αὐτῶν is again influenced by the parallel with 8.22 (Ziegler, 138–39). The equivalents there are not entirely clear, but it looks as though it may well be used to render מָעוּף, which is certainly close enough to (יה)בַּעֲרִיפ to have allowed the translator to bring them together. (Whether this hints at some earlier form of the text in which these two verses were once even closer than they are now is completely beyond our recall.) The other versions give no handle for emendation (cf. Troxel, 'Exegesis', 106).

The position of this passage within the book as we have it is relatively straightforward. The indictment of the people in the Song of the Vineyard in 5.1-7 was developed through to v. 24 by a series of woe-oracles, summed up in v. 24*b* as wilful rejection of the word of God and his instruction. Following such an extended indictment, we are not surprised to find a severe word of judgment, introduced by 'therefore'. A major military onslaught by the nations whom God has summoned is described, and it leads to a cataclysmic denouement (v. 30). It is difficult not to read the text at this level as anticipating the Babylonian defeat (Jerome reports that the Jews of his time were already interpreting the text this way), just as the salvation which will be a dominant theme of the next section through to ch. 12 has many features which will be echoed later in the parts of the book of Isaiah which look towards the end of exile and the restoration in Jerusalem.

It is when we move to the diachronic process which may have led to the text we have that disagreement arises, and indeed this passage has been at the heart of many of the different theories which have been put forward over the years to account for the shape of this whole part of the book. A full survey is clearly not possible in the present context, but a few representative major positions may be mentioned.

[9] It is therefore not necessary to emend צר to צַר with Zolli, 'Jesaja 5, 30'.

[10] Hitzig, followed by Knobel, suggested restoring a ל before אור so as to make it into a second indirect object to נבט (thus cleverly producing the upwards as well as downwards look that we miss by comparison with 8.21-22). In fact, we could even read MT that way by invoking the notion of the double-duty preposition. But we should then expect the conjunction on חשך immediately following, for which unfortunately there is no shred of evidence.

The reason for such a concentration of attention on this paragraph is because it combines several elements, each of which require some sort of explanation. The main points are: (i) It is followed immediately by what is often taken to be an account of Isaiah's call (ch. 6), with which many link the following two chapters as well as some form of Isaiah Memoir. If, as the theory holds, those chapters had a separate existence before their inclusion in the book, we need to know why they were included just here, and whether their inclusion had any affect upon the surrounding material. (ii) The first verse of this paragraph (25) ends with a line which forms a refrain in 9.7-20 (or 10.4)—just after the hypothetical Memoir, therefore. It is widely believed that at some stage part or all of this paragraph once stood somewhere in that passage. Where that was exactly, and whether the present order is the result of accident or design, is not agreed. (iii) At 10.1 we have the start of a woe saying which seems to conclude in 10.4 with the refrain just mentioned. How this woe saying relates to those in ch. 5 is again not agreed, though many think they once all belonged together.

Two main types of theory have been advanced to account for these observations.[11] (i) For a long time it has been thought by some that the present text has arisen as the result of some accidental or at best mechanical textual disturbance, and since the time of Budde this has been associated in particular with the inclusion here of the Isaiah Memoir.[12] Consequently, many commentaries and even some Bible translations (see NEB, for instance) abandon the canonical order at this point and seek to restore what they regard as the original order of the material. Naturally enough this involves putting some or all of the present paragraph in with ch. 9 and part of the opening of ch. 10 somewhere with the woes of this chapter. (ii) More recently, under the impact of concerns that more justice should be done to the final form of the text which we have inherited, a number of scholars have detected some form of chiastic or ring structures in these chapters.[13] Again, the details vary (e.g. how far does the structure extend? Just through chs 5–10, or as far as 1–11?), but the principle is the same: the present arrangement is deliberate but it is due more to literary patterning and the desire to emphasize the centrality of the Memoir than to concerns arising from a

[11] The number of those who argue for the originality from the very beginning of the present order of the material is small; in addition to the more conservative commentaries, see Kissane (though he includes 8.21-22 after 5.30); Dietrich, 185–88; Chisholm, 'Structure'; Brown, 'The So-Called Refrain'; Gitay, 87–116; Irvine, '*Denkschrift*' (with a very useful summary of the whole position on pp. 218–22); Vargon, 'Description'. Korpel, 'Structural Analysis', 64–65, suggests that v. 26 was once joined directly to 24*b*, 24*c*-25 being a post-exilic addition. Becker, 145–48, also argues that this material never stood anywhere else, but only because he sees it as a post-exilic addition, written for its present setting but drawing almost by way of citation on other material (including, of course, the refrain poem); somewhat similarly Porath, 191–97.

[12] In addition to many commentaries, see, for instance, Fey, 83–104; Donner, 66–75; Vollmer, 130–44; Høgenhaven, 44–53; Deck, 71–78 (with reservations).

[13] See, for instance, L'Heureux, 'Redactional History'; Sheppard, 'Anti-Assyrian Redaction', 195–98; Bartelt (and also Bartelt, 'Isaiah 5 and 9'); Blum; Berges, 87–91.

straightforward sequential reading of the material. (Nevertheless, some of those who hold to this view also merge with the third view below.)

In my view the data can be better accounted for by way of a third approach—one which accepts some aspects of the first in the sense that it recognizes that there has certainly been some displacement of material from its hypothetical original position but that this is not the result of scribal accident in the course of transmission but rather is the result of deliberate redactional activity.[14] Since we have seen that this also happened elsewhere in the preceding chapters, it should not surprise us to find the same happening here at this crucial juncture in the book.

We may start by agreeing with those who have argued that v. 30 is an addition to (better, *Fortschreibung* of) the preceding verses, interpreting the military attack in more global, even mythological, terms. The main reasons are given in the commentary below.

Secondly, I accept the view that 25*b* (at least)-29 was originally part of the refrain poem in 9.7-20.[15] Exactly where it belonged is disputed (Sweeney, for instance, holds that our paragraph was the original introduction, not conclusion, to the refrain poem), but what is probably the majority opinion seems plausible, namely that it formed the concluding stanza of the poem. Whereas previously the judgments that had fallen were less than final, as the refrain makes clear, now the final judgment is threatened, after which the refrain can obviously not be repeated. The 'tenses' also change following the refrain in 25*b*, suggesting that it would fit better at the end rather than somewhere in the middle of the poem as a whole. Historically, then, we need not doubt that Isaiah himself had Assyria in view,[16] and indeed, if this material originated with the refrain poem we must assume that it comes from the time of the Syro-Ephraimite invasion (and so much earlier than the woe series) and that it was originally directed against Israel rather than Judah. When the redactor moved the material to its new position following the woes of ch. 5, however, he reinterpreted it more eschatologically—of the Babylonian defeat as a first fulfilment, but potentially of the final onslaught of the nations before the inauguration of messianic rule. For this reason, and to make explicit the reversal of the theme in 11.12 and 49.22, he changed the singular 'nation' in v. 26 that Isaiah himself had written to the plural 'nations' of the present text. Since all these points are closely related and share the same outlook, it seems most economical to hypothesize that it was the same redactor who gave the material its

[14] The importance of Barth's discussion, 109–12, should be acknowledged here; see further Vermeylen, 174–76; Clements (though he still does not order his commentary according to the present text); Anderson, 'God with Us'; Barthel, *Prophetenwort*, 46–50; Kustár, 65–71.

[15] It will be remembered that the issue of the woe series and the possible association of 10.1-4 with it was discussed in the introduction to 5.8-24 above. It was concluded there that there was no case to be made for including anything from that passage in this present chapter.

[16] Differently Vargon, 'Description', who thinks that only general, traditional terms for a military threat are used, without a specific enemy in view. His positive point is acceptable without the negative consequence necessarily following.

new position, referred its threat to the nations and added v. 30 by way of explanatory extension.

The question how much of the first half of v. 25 also belonged with the refrain poem is obviously less certain, and it is not important in terms of understanding the broad outline of the textual development. In the commentary below it will be suggested that the first line may have also been penned by the redactor when he moved the material to its present position but that the second line perhaps represents a fragment of the stanza which preceded the refrain in the original poem, the rest of that stanza having been omitted (and so lost to us) at that same time.[17] If that is correct, then there will have originally been five stanzas in the poem as a whole, the first four of which were followed by the refrain— 9.7-11, 12-16, 17-20; lost material ending with 5.25b, 26-29. (Unlike Gray or Donner, 66–75, therefore, we have no need to include 10.1-4 in the poem, a situation about which Gray himself expresses grave uncertainty.) But such a suggestion can obviously be only very tentative.

It remains to observe that, once the second half of the first line of v. 27 is bracketed as a later addition (see the commentary below) and the slight textual emendations in vv. 28b and 29 accepted (see the notes above), then vv. 26-29 form a stanza of seven perfectly balanced 3 + 3 lines with the exception of the two closing lines, which change to 3 + 2, which is appropriate at the end of a poem. This fits very well with the length of the preceding stanzas (see especially Gray, 177–80). By contrast, v. 30 is elevated prose rather than poetry, so confirming that it is not part of the original poem. As already noted, the position with v. 25 is uncertain and it has likely been altered in the course of being given its new position, so that analysis is inevitably hampered.

25. *Therefore* is a different word in the Hebrew from that in v. 24, and in this it differs from the 'double therefore' at vv. 13-14; this may indicate that we should take what follows as a comment on the whole of the preceding section, perhaps as far back as the start of the chapter.

What follows is cast in the past tense (contrast vv. 26-29) and to start with comprises a somewhat stereotypical expression of completed judgment. It is difficult not to conclude that if this whole passage has been given its position by an exilic redactor, he and his readers will have had the Babylonian defeat in mind. For *the anger of the Lord* being *kindled against his people*, one may compare, for instance, Exod. 32.10-11; Num. 11.33 (also followed by *and smote them*); 25.3; 32.13; Deut. 6.15; 7.4; 11.17; 31.17; Josh. 7.1; 23.16; Judg. 2.14, 20; 3.8; 10.7; 2 Sam. 24.1; 2 Kgs 23.26; Hos. 8.5. It would thus have been a very natural way for someone to comment on the judgment that had fallen upon the nation. Interestingly, however, Beuken lists thirteen other places in the book of Isaiah which refer to the anger/wrath of God

---

[17] Barth, 112, suggests that the material was deliberately omitted by the redactor because it applied specifically to Israel, as does the rest of the refrain poem, and so was mostly unsuitable for its new 'Judean' setting.

(and this excludes the several uses in the refrain poem), but not one of them uses this particular stock idiom; in fact, this is the only place in the book where the verb חרה occurs.

The idea that God *stretched out his hand* in judgment is part of the repeated element of the refrain poem (starting already in the last line of this verse) and it occurs elsewhere in Isaiah as well (14.27; 23.11; 31.3), in addition to being reasonably common in many other parts of the Hebrew Bible.[18] Here, however, there is a contrast with the refrain of the poem (even with the last line of this verse) in that whereas there God's hand is still stretched out as an indication that despite the judgments that have fallen the people have not responded as they should, so that there remains further judgment to come, here we are given the impression that he has now moved to fulfil that threat, so that the saying is appropriately followed by the statement that he *smote them*. It should be noted, however, that within the idiom of Isaiah this does not necessarily refer to final judgment with no further future, as the use at 1.5 programmatically shows, and equally it can occur within the refrain poem itself in a way that shows that it is not necessarily final but is an act designed to elicit repentance (cf. 9.12). It can therefore in principle refer to any one of a number of potential catastrophes, such as plague or earthquake, besides military defeat. In its present redactional setting, it may be suggested that it is being used rather in the manner of 1.5 (cf. Kustár, 69–70). A severe blow has fallen upon Judah, and there is an imminent danger that one even more severe will fall: God's hand is stretched out still! There is thus combined an interpretation of the past disasters that have befallen the nation (whether at the hand of the Assyrians or the Babylonians) with an implied appeal for response.

This raises an interesting point with regard to the next line. On the one hand, the expression *the mountains quaked* could be linked with theophanic language elsewhere (e.g. Nah. 1.5; Ps. 18.8, with closely comparable expressions in many other passages; cf. Jeremias, *Theophanie*, 10–16). In that sense, it suggests an exilic reading of the Babylonian disaster that is moving away from the purely historical, a feature which will recur in v. 30 (and see already v. 14). On the other hand, it is perfectly possible to take it at the more literal level as a reference to an earthquake which could have been interpreted by Isaiah as an expression of God's non-final judgment in the sequence of such events which we find in the rest of the refrain poem. It is known that there was a significant earthquake during the reign of Uzziah, and so shortly before the start of Isaiah's ministry; cf. Amos 1.1; Zech. 14.5.[19] A reference to it at this point (i.e. as the last in the sequence of the original poem; see the analysis above) would be entirely appropriate. It is therefore a good illustration of how material which had been evoked by one

---

[18] Cf. S. Kreuzer, 'Die Mächtigkeitsformel im Deuteronomium: Gestaltung, Vorgeschichte und Entwicklung', *ZAW* 109 (1997), 188–207 (193–95).

[19] Cf. W. G. Dever, 'A Case-Study in Biblical Archaeology: The Earthquake of *Ca.* 760 BCE', *EI* 23 (1992), 27*–35*.

historical situation could be reused to apply to a later situation during the long course of the book's formation.

The same may apply to the following words: *their corpses became like offal in the streets*. This was no doubt the consequence of many natural as well as human-made disasters (Kaiser is somewhat pedantic in objecting that this could not apply to the aftermath of an earthquake, because then the corpses would be buried under the ruins), but it is mentioned again with particular poignancy in the wake of the fall of Jerusalem; cf. Lam. 2.21; Isa. 51.20; Jer. 14.16; 16.4; Ezek. 11.6. In the present setting, the pronominal adjective (suffix) *their* refers back to *his people* in the previous line, but the fact that some commentators have difficulty with this (see the textual notes above) suggests that this may not be original; the slight awkwardness is a further small pointer to the redactional nature of the first line; whatever originally stood in front of this line has now been lost, apparently. *Offal* (סחה) is a *hapax legomenon* which caused earlier commentators a good deal of difficulty (many thought that the comparative particle כ was part of the root), but such disagreements are now consigned to history (cf. סחה, 'to scrape off'; סחי, 'offscouring', Lam. 3.45);[20] the idea expressed in our verse has a close parallel in Jer. 25.33, where the much commoner word דמן, 'dung', is used.

The last line of the verse, which is an example of the refrain repeated several times in ch. 9, indicates that in the past God has acted punitively in order to encourage some sort of response from his people. But this has not happened, apparently, and he is therefore still poised to act again in judgment. As we shall see, the implication of what follows is that this time it will be final.

26. *Signal*: some form of standard, such as was in common use in the ancient Near East as a rallying point for troops by being raised in some prominent place.[21] It is quite a common trope in Isaiah, sometimes with a more or less literal application (13.2; 31.9; and as a point of comparison in 30.17), but more often, as here, as a metaphorical expression of God's summoning of the nations to do his bidding for or against his people (11.10, 12; 18.3; 49.22; 62.10). In this latter sense, the word occurs in sufficiently similar clauses to suggest that there is an element of literary dependence, so that it has played an important role in recent discussions about the unity of the book as a whole.[22] Our verse is especially close to 11.12 and 49.22, in that in each case the wording is very similar, if not identical, and equally in all three passages a reference to God's hand comes just before. The difference, of course, is that whereas here the action is threatening, in the other two passages it is indicative of restoration, so that they are reversing Isaiah's own use

---

[20] Differently G. A. Rendsburg, '*Lāśûah* in Genesis xxiv 63', *VT* 45 (1995), 558–60, who links our word with שׂיח/שׂוח, 'urinate, defecate'.

[21] See further B. Couroyer, 'Le *NĒS* biblique, signal ou enseigne?', *RB* 91 (1984), 5–29.

[22] Cf. Clements, 'Beyond Tradition-History', 108–9; Davies, 'Destiny', 115; Williamson, *Book*, 63–67.

of the image. For possible consequences for the redactional history of the book, see above. Whereas Isaiah himself is likely to have referred to only one nation (see the textual notes), the redactor has purposely made the reference plural (in line with 11.12 and 49.22) as part of his tendency to dehistoricize (and hence make more timelessly applicable) the original time-bound sayings of Isaiah himself.

The next part of the line uses a different image, also found elsewhere in Isaiah (7.18; cf. Zech. 10.8), which derives from the world of bee control: it was apparently the practice to *whistle* as the means to attract a swarm. Gray, in his comment on 7.18, cites Vergil, *Georgics*, iv. 64, as a parallel (as do a number of commentators), even though Vergil does not refer directly to whistling but rather the sounding of cymbals. More telling, therefore, is the comment of Cyril on our verse: 'Beekeepers are accustomed to whistle to the bees, and so entice them out of their hives to the flowers and herbs, or to get them in from the fields and make them stop at home'. There is no direct evidence for bee-keeping in Palestine earlier than the Hellenistic period (though it was practised earlier elsewhere, such as Egypt and Mesopotamia),[23] but wild honey was certainly used from much earlier times (e.g. Deut. 32.13; Judg. 14.8-9; 1 Sam. 14.24-30; Ps. 81.17, to say nothing of the description of the land as 'flowing with milk and honey'), and presumably it was necessary to attract the swarm away from the comb in order to get access to it.

Far away...from the ends of the earth: this is stereotypical language in connection with God's summoning of foreigners to exercise his judgment; see, for instance, Deut. 28.49 for the use of exactly the same language (also probably with Assyria originally in mind); Isa. 10.3; 30.27, etc. It also gets taken up in descriptions which anticipate the reversal of judgment by speaking of foreign nations bringing the people back to their land (cf. 11.12). It is naturally of no specific geographical significance; rather, it contributes to the frightening (because unfamiliar) and so threatening nature of the description, and this is further heightened by the description of their advance as being *with all possible speed*. The judgment will come suddenly and so apparently be unstoppable (cf. Machinist, 'Assyria and its Image', 722).

27. The meaning of the first line is transparent[24] and reinforces the impression of a relentless advance to which resistance would be futile. The soldiers are in excellent physical condition; to *stumble* when engaged in combat could be fatal (Lev. 26.37; Jer. 46.6), and elsewhere this is associated with being *weary* (40.30), but it does not apply here.

The only uncertain issue is whether the second half of the line, *none slumbers or sleeps*, is integral to the original composition or a later addition. Those who think it is an addition point out that the identical words appear in Ps. 121.4, and on this basis Duhm (followed by

[23] Cf. E. Neufeld, 'Apiculture in Ancient Palestine (Early and Middle Iron Age) within the Framework of the Ancient Near East', *UF* 10 (1978), 220–47.

[24] For an analysis of the whole semantic field of sleep, see T. H. McAlpine, *Sleep, Divine and Human, in the Old Testament* (JSOTSup 38; Sheffield, 1987).

Procksch) went so far as to say that it could therefore only be used of God. This last point is of no value, of course, because then it becomes impossible to explain why a later scribe should have added it here. Those who think that the words should be retained (e.g. Kissane; Young) argue that they are necessary as the parallel to the first part of the verse, but in fact a stronger argument of the same sort might be made for holding the first part of the verse to be the parallel to the final clause of the preceding verse (see the arrangement in the translation above), making our present half line redundant. (This would be even better rhythmically if בו were indeed secondary; see the textual notes.) The case is finely balanced, but in view of the general regularity of the refrain poem as a whole (see Gray, 177–79; Wildberger), the case for seeing these words as a later addition is marginally the stronger.

The preparedness of the oncoming army for combat is emphasized next. The *loincloth* would be loosened when resting or at ease, but here it is girded so that the soldier is ready for immediate and unencumbered action. Despite their long approach march, their footwear is in perfect repair so that speed and security of movement will not be impaired.

28. Similarly their weapons are in good order (*their arrows are sharpened*) and ready for immediate use; this is the point about the *bows*. Normally, when not in use the bow was left unstrung so that the tension would not be lost; before combat, the string was inserted, and in many cases this would have involved putting one's foot on one end of the bow and then bending it from the other end by hand because the tension could be considerable. Hence the expression 'treading the bow', which is here rendered *strung* (see the discussion in Emerton, above n. 4).

Finally, we learn of the superiority of their cavalry and chariot forces. In antiquity, *horses* were not shod, so that for their *hooves* to be *like flint* would have been a great advantage: they were not injured or rendered unfit during the long march, and they would be able to operate securely on any surface. Thus the *wheels*—of their chariots, obviously —were *reckoned to be like the whirlwind*, fast and agile. The end of the description of the army thus echoes the emphasis with which it began in v. 26, namely its devastating speed.

29. The original poem ends with a pictorial summary of the moment of attack. Hebrew has several different words for *lion*, the precise distinctions between some of which escape us.[25] They were clearly not uncommon in the land in antiquity, so that writers would have been familiar with their habits and were well able to exploit them in imagery, as here for warriors. Indeed, such a comparison is common enough to be called a cliché by Machinist, 'Assyria and its Image', 728–29 (with

[25] Wildberger reports several different attempts. A major study has recently appeared: B. A. Strawn, *What is Stronger than a Lion? Leonine Image and Metaphor in the Hebrew Bible and the Ancient Near East* (OBO 212; Freiburg and Göttingen, 2005). Appendix I (pp. 293–326) surveys all Hebrew words for lion in great detail; my renderings above are in line with his conclusions.

whom? A considerable number of commentators assume that the purpose of the verse is to reverse the judgment of the previous paragraph: either God or some other unnamed subject is now going to growl over Assyria (= *over it*), so that eventually there will be unrelieved darkness for the former oppressor of Israel. This sort of reversal would not be untypical of eschatological expectations, as we see from Deutero-Isaiah, to go no further.[30]

The alternative position is to observe that there is an exact repetition of *and they* (lit. he) *will growl* from the previous verse without any indication of a change of subject, so that it is more natural to suppose that the same subject is in view; the editor picked it up with the intention of developing its meaning. Those who think that there is a change of subject are embarrassed by the failure to mention it and have to justify the view either that God is implied or that there is an impersonal subject, neither of which is the most obvious reading. In my view, the conclusion that this verse is a development of the preceding rather than a reversal of it is the more convincing.[31]

If that is the case, then an exilic date for this addition commends itself as the most probable (so too Clements). It would have been then that a statement strengthening the seriousness of the judgment would have been most appropriate, whereas a reversal might have been expected to come slightly later.

The roaring (lit. growling) *of the sea* is a deliberate application of the language about lions from the previous verse and the start of this one to a more cosmic level. (It may not be coincidental that 'sea' does not have the article: there could therefore be an allusion to the god Yam.) The sea is well known throughout much of the Hebrew Bible not just as the symbol but as the very embodiment of the forces of chaos which threaten to overturn the good order which God has established.[32] Not only does it underlie some of the descriptions of creation (and its reversal in the flood), but God's control of the seas is a constant theme of faith and praise in the Psalms. Sometimes this could be taken up (not least in association with Zion) and applied politically to the threat of the nations that might come against Jerusalem (e.g. Ps. 46). Previously, the psalmists had praised God for his control of them as much as of the sea in creation, but now that has been overturned; the Babylonians have 'flooded in' and carried away all before them.

This theme of the return to primeval chaos as a depiction of the disaster of the fall of Jerusalem is continued in the next line with its emphasis on *darkness*, and then that even such *light* as may remain *grows dark because of its clouds*. 'Darkness on the face of the deep' characterized the state of the universe before God brought order to it

[30] For this kind of approach, see, for instance, Duhm, Marti, J. Becker, *Isaias*, 50–51, Kaiser, Barth, 193, Vermeylen, 185, and Blenkinsopp.

[31] So too Delitzsch, Eichrodt, Wildberger, and Beuken.

[32] Beuken gives numerous references. The whole theme is fully discussed in J. Day, *God's Conflict with the Dragon and the Sea: Echoes of a Canaanite Myth in the Old Testament* (UCOP 35; Cambridge, 1985).

according to Gen. 1.2, to go no further. But light and darkness also constitute a profoundly 'Isaianic' theme.[33] We met it first in 2.5 where the
same redactor (in my opinion) used the notion of light as a means of
referring to the way of life according to God's instruction which was
the theme of the opening vision of his work in 2.2-4. The use of the first
person plural there may be reflected here as well, if my vocalization of
the first word of the line is correct (*if we look to the land*). At this first
major section break in the exilic form of the book of Isaiah, it is shown
that the people have failed to live up to that exhortation; in the second
part, however (which runs to the end of ch. 12), the mood changes as
judgment is set in a predominant context of salvation. We saw at v. 26
above how that difference is partly reflected in the reversal of the
'signal' motif in 11.12. Somewhat similarly, in the case of the present
verse there is a clear verbal parallel at 8.22 (noticed from antiquity on;
see the notes on the LXX above), in which the darkness that is seen at
present gives way to the light of the promise in 8.23–9.6 ('the people
that walked in darkness have seen a great light…').

---

[33] For the theme of light further on in Isaiah, see Clements, 'Light to the Nations',
and 'Arise, Shine'.

further references). Whether military divisions might also be named after them is speculative and hardly to the point here.[26] Equally, we should not press the imagery too far by asking, for instance, whether the reference to *prey* being carried off is an allusion to the exile. The main point of the picture is clear and sufficient: the lion's *roar* is frightening, as elsewhere (e.g. especially Amos 3.8; also Jer. 2.15; 25.30; 51.38; Ezek. 22.25; Ps. 22.14; cf. Judg. 14.5), and once he has seized his prey there is no possible escape. The finality of *with none to rescue it* brings the poem to a forceful conclusion. This time, God's judgment is complete, and the refrain, which previously had hinted at the possibility of continuation, even if only under God's wrath, cannot be repeated.

There is a precise reversal of this judgment in Nah. 2.12-14—so precise, in fact, that it is difficult not to believe that it is a direct literary allusion (cf. Machinist, 'Assyria and its Image', 735–36). If so, it would reinforce the position that the original form of this judgment speech goes back to Isaiah's time, regardless of its later redactional re-use.

30. This verse is usually, and rightly, regarded as an addition to the preceding passage.[27] Moreover, it bears all the hallmarks of an example of *Fortschreibung*, a short passage which is deliberately added to another in order to draw out its significance for later, or at any rate other, circumstances. The main verb *growl*, of course, is picked up from the previous verse and so taken forward. It is going to be developed, however, by reference now not to lions, but to the *roaring* (lit., growling) *of the sea*, which immediately conjures up the image of primeval chaos. The military defeat of v. 29 is now widened to encompass a more mythologically expressed universal catastrophe. The words *on that day* are often an indication of the editorial application to the future, and that seems to be their purpose here as well. We have come across its use in just this sense several times before (2.20; 3.18; 4.2).[28] The verse is probably to be construed as prose, in contrast with the preceding poetry, and finally, as we saw, v. 29 provides its own conclusion and gives no impression of expecting any continuation.[29]

The date and purpose of this addition are very much bound up with an interpretive *crux* at the start of the verse: who is growling over

[26] Cf. B. Mazar, 'The Military Élite of King David', *VT* 13 (1963), 310–20 (312).

[27] Clements limits the addition to the second line only, but does not say why; in fact, two of the main reasons for detecting an addition here in the first place come in the first line. Procksch's proposals for this verse are also unconvincing. He thinks that the verse originally belonged with v. 25a. He bases this on metrical considerations for the most part, but is able to do so only after radical surgery on our verse. Among the casualties of this operation is the phrase 'on that day', but there is no evidence to support its deletion and it is itself one of the markers of the nature of the verse as *Fortschreibung*.

[28] See DeVries, *From Old Revelation to New*, 118, where in my opinion the present example should be included with the majority of examples which are redactional expansions, not the tiny minority of uses by Isaiah himself.

[29] I see no reason to regard the second half of the verse as 'a snatch of text transposed from elsewhere' (Skehan, 'Problems', 47); it is more plausibly a continuation of the same redactor's composition, with a clear allusion to 8.22, of course.